MESOAMERICAN ARCHITECTURE AS A CULTURAL SYMBOL

Edited by JEFF KARL KOWALSKI

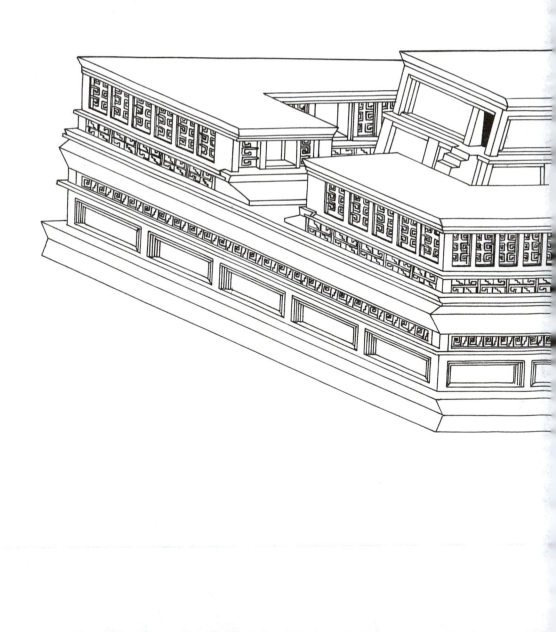

MESOAMERICAN ARCHITECTURE AS A CULTURAL SYMBOL

New York • Oxford

Oxford University Press

1999

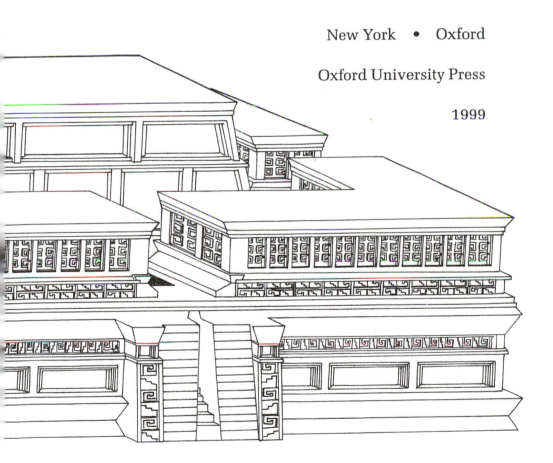

Oxford University Press

Oxford   New York
Athens Auckland Bangkok Bogotá Buenos Aires Calcutta
Cape Town Chennai Dar es Salaam Delhi Florence Hong Kong Istanbul
Karachi Kuala Lumpur Madrid Melbourne Mexico City Mumbai
Nairobi Paris São Paulo Singapore Taipei Tokyo Toronto Warsaw

and associated companies in
Berlin Ibadan

Library of Congress Cataloging-in-Publication Data
Kowalski, Jeff Karl, 1951–
Mesoamerican architecture as a cultural symbol
edited by Jeff Karl Kowalski
p. cm.
Includes bibliographical references and index.
ISBN 0-19-507961-2
1. Indian architecture—Mexico.   2. Indian architecture—Central America.
3. Architectural design—Mexico.   4. Architectural design—Central America.
5. Symbolism in architecture—Mexico.   6. Symbolism in architecture—Latin America.
7. Mexico—Antiquities.   8. Central America—Antiquities.
I. Title.
F1219.3.A6K69   1998
720'.972—dc21   97-14821

9 8 7 6 5 4 3 2 1

Printed in the United States of America
on acid-free paper

This book is dedicated to

Esther Pasztory and George Kubler,

two scholars who have opened eyes,

minds, and hearts to the study of the

art and architecture of ancient Mesoamerica

Preface

This book stems from the session "Mesoamerican Architecture as a Cultural Symbol" that I organized and chaired at the 44th Annual Meeting of the Society of Architectural Historians in Cincinnati, Ohio, April 24–28, 1991. Several of the authors of individual chapters of this volume originally presented papers on related topics at this session. These include Augusto Molina Montes, Cynthia Kristan-Graham, John Martin Deland Pohl (in a paper co-authored with Bruce E. Byland), Andrea Stone, Virgina Miller, and Merideth Paxton. After the session was completed I had discussions with the conference participants regarding the possibility of publishing the papers in a collection devoted to Mesoamerican architecture.

Although the papers presented at the Society of Architectural Historians meeting considered a diverse range of Mesoamerican architectural traditions, sites, and individual structures, I decided that for a volume to have greater scholarly integrity it would be necessary to gather several other chapters to present the diversity and richness of the Mesoamerican architectural tradition in a more comprehensive fashion. To expand the coverage, during late 1991 and 1992 I contacted a large number of Mesoamericanists with expertise in different regional architectural styles and cultural traditions and asked whether they would like to contribute an article in their area of specialization. Several scholars responded positively to the idea of assembling a related group of articles which would provide a reasonably comprehensive overview of several major Mesoamerican architectural traditions through time and space. From this group, I made a final decision regarding which sites and monuments would be included in the final volume. Unfortunately, due to space limitations, I had to omit the work of some fine scholars who submitted abstracts for potential book chapters. I hope they will accept my regrets.

In some cases my efforts to line up specialists for particular topics proved extremely daunting. This was particularly true in the case of Teotihuacan. Despite my efforts to enlist various Teotihuacan experts, others' commitments to provide papers for conferences, or chapters and catalogue entries for exhibitions of Teotihuacan art, made it difficult to fill this gap. Therefore, I decided to expand a paper on the dissemination of the Teotihuacan *talud-tablero* architectural profile which I presented at the 1986 Annual Meeting of the Society of Architectural Historians. In doing so I have presented a synthesis of several aspects of recent scholarship regarding the ideological significance of Teotihuacan's principal civic-ceremonial edifices, as well as updated my previous study of its distinctive terracing system. I am particularly indebted to Dr. George L. Cowgill and to Dr. René Millon for reading my chapter on Teotihuacan prior to publication and for providing extensive helpful critical comments. In addition, Dr. Mary Ellen Miller read this chapter and suggested several improvements. I wish to thank these scholars for sharpening my discussion and making it as factually accurate as possible, but I remain responsible for its content.

Once a final group of scholars was assembled, their abstracts and a book prospectus was submitted to several scholarly publishers. I am grateful that Oxford University Press, after submitting the prospectus and abstracts to several outside readers, agreed to publish this volume. I am particularly grateful to Joyce Berry, Senior Editor at Oxford University Press, for working with me, providing helpful advice, and for tolerating the innumerable delays that accompany the production of a book based on the contributions of so many individual scholars, many of whom have been involved in ongoing archaeological fieldwork and have had to honor other commitments while contributing to this volume. In addition, I thank Lisa Stallings, my copy editor, who provided me with a revised version of the final manuscript that eliminated some grammatical problems I had overlooked and that improved the literary quality of the text.

I greatly appreciate the technical assistance of Walt Hines, with whom I began collaborating on this project when he worked in the Design Division of the School of Art at Northern Illinois University. During the course of the project he took a new job in the private sector, but provided time, energy, and technical expertise as we transformed the text into preliminary working layouts. Special thanks are due to Joyce Berry and Lisa Stallings, who arranged for an Oxford University Press production team to produce the galleys and final layout. I also thank Manuel Hernández, Associate Professor in the Design Division of the NIU School of Art, for drafting the map of Mesoamerica that appears in the introduction. In addition, Gordon Means, Keith Lowman, Dan Grych, Barbara Watson, and various other members of NIU's Art Photo division have assisted me by producing many of the photographs, photomechanical transfers, and other artwork needed for this book.

Another word of thanks goes to E. Wyllys Andrews, V, Director of the Middle American Research Institute of Tulane University. He was kind enough to put me in touch with Francine Cronshaw, to whom I am grateful for having created the index for this volume.

I would also like to say a word about the two people to whom this book is dedicated, Esther Pasztory and George Kubler. Esther Pasztory first introduced me to the aesthetic sophistication of Pre-Columbian art and architecture, and made me aware of the intellectual challenges its study posed, when I was an undergraduate student in art history at Columbia University from 1971 to 1973. Her enthusiasm for the subject, and her long-term interests in studying Mesoamerican art and architecture in cultural context, as a semiological system, and as an ideological expression, have continued to inspire me. I was privileged to have George Kubler as my doctoral advisor when I was a graduate student at Yale University from 1973 to 1981. His continuing efforts to apply rigorous theoretical methods to the study of Pre-Columbian art and architecture of the Americas helped gain recognition that they constitute one of the great aesthetic traditions of the world. His insistence on maintaining the importance of aesthetic systems in communicating specialized perceptual/emotional states which cannot be transmitted in textual-based media, coupled with his ongoing interests in the phenomenon of style, have continued to stimulate my own thinking about artworks. Since studying with Kubler my own work has tended toward an emphasis on interpreting Mesoamerican buildings, monuments, and other artworks as visible cultural expressions of the ideologies of the various societies in which they were produced. Nevertheless, I remain indebted to Kubler's insights regarding the power of architecture and art to give a coherent shape to the viewer's experience, thus actively organizing his or her perceptions of the world within the context of a particularized art tradition, rather than simply "reflecting" life in an imitative manner.

Finally, I would like to give special thanks to my wife, Mary, and to my three children, Sarah, David, and Anna, for putting up with the long hours I have spent behind a computer screen or at the photocopy center as this book moved from concept to reality. Mary has been particularly helpful with making final adjustments to the manuscript and for generally keeping my spirits up.

Contents

Contributors

Nicholas P. Dunning, Professor, Department of Geography, University of Cinncinati, Cincinnati, Ohio

William L. Fash, Bowditch Professor of Anthropology, Peabody Museum, Harvard University, Cambridge, Massachussetts

David Freidel, Professor, Department of Anthropology, Southern Methodist University, Dallas, Texas

Jeff Karl Kowalski, Associate Professor, School of Art, Northern Illinois University, DeKalb, Illinois

Cynthia Kristan-Graham, Professor, Atlanta College of Art, Atlanta, Georgia

Joyce Marcus, Professor, The University of Michigan Museum of Anthropology, Ann Arbor, Michigan

Eduardo Matos Moctezuma, Director, Museo del Templo Mayor, Mexico, D.F.

Virginia E. Miller, Associate Professor, History of Art Department, College of Architecture, Art, and Urban Planning, The University of Illinois at Chicago, Chicago, Illinois

Augusto Molina Montes, Escuela Nacional de Conservacíon, Restauracíon y Museografía, INAH, Ex Convento de Churubusco, México, D.F.

Merideth Paxton, Visiting Scholar, Latin American Institute, University of New Mexico, Albuquerque, New Mexico

John Martin Deland Pohl, Visiting Professor, Department of Art History, University of California–Los Angeles, Los Angeles, California

F. Kent Reilly III, Assistant Professor, Department of Anthropology, Southwest Texas State University, San Marcos, Texas

David W. Sedat, Research Specialist, American Section, University of Pennsylvania Museum, Philadelphia, Pennsylvania

Robert J. Sharer, Shoemaker Professor of Anthropology, Department of Anthropology, University of Pennsylvania, and Curator of the American Section, University of Pennsylvania Museum, Philadelphia, Pennsylvania

Andrea Stone, Professor, Department of Art History, College of Letters and Science, The University of Wisconsin-Milwaukee, Milwaukee Wisconsin

Charles Suhler, Research Associate, Department of Anthropology, Southern Methodist University, Dallas, Texas

Loa P. Traxler, Research Assistant, Museum Applied Science Center for Archaeology, University of Pennsylvania Museum, Philadelphia, Pennsylvania

Philip C. Weigand, Professor de Investigaciones, Centro de Estudios Anthropológicos, El Colegio de Michoacán, Zamora, Michoacán, Mexico. 59690

S. Jeffrey K. Wilkerson, Institute for Cultural Ecology of the Tropics, 221 E. Van Buren-78550, Harlingen, Texas

Richard Williamson, Ph.D. Candidate, Department of Anthropology, Tulane University, New Orleans, Louisiana

MESOAMERICAN
ARCHITECTURE AS A
CULTURAL SYMBOL

Mesoamerican Architecture as a Cultural Symbol

An Introduction

Jeff Karl Kowalski

This volume considers the interrelationship between buildings, builders, and the culture that produced them. In other words, it is a book about architecture as a social enterprise and as a carrier of cultural meanings. The term *architecture* commonly refers to buildings that are constructed with more permanent materials, have a more monumental form, and that exhibit a particularly refined and sophisticated treatment of architectonic forms. This is still a common definition, although the term can be extended to include less permanent, imposing, and "vernacular" or "nonelite" structures as well (Kostof 1985: 14–15; Rapaport 1969; Guidoni 1975). Although it is feasible to discuss the arrangements of such building forms in primarily aesthetic terms, each of the contributors to this book has endeavored to examine and clarify the way in which architectonic-aesthetic structures are associated with wider social processes and cultural practices and beliefs within the societies that built them.

The various architectural traditions and individual edifices discussed in this book were constructed in the culture area known as Mesoamerica. Paul Kirchoff (1943, 1952) first proposed the concept of Mesoamerica, based on significant commonalities of material and ideational culture among societies that developed in a geographic region incorporating central and southeastern Mexico, Guatemala, Belize, western Honduras, and western El Salvador (see map on p. 4). Among the most distinctive of these cultural traits is the use of a common calendar based on the permutation of a 260–day sacred round cycle (composed of 20 named days and 13 numbers) and a 365–day solar year count (composed of eighteen 20–day "months" and a 5–day period of bad luck at the end of the year).

Other important features shared by many Mesoamerican societies include hieroglyphic writing systems, bark-paper or deerskin screen-fold manuscripts (often referred to as codices), extensive astronomical

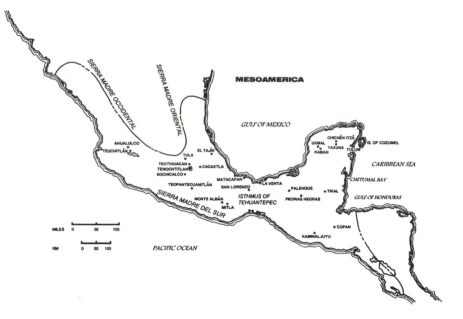

knowledge based on horizon observation, a sacred ritual game played with a rubber ball, warfare practiced to obtain sacrificial victims, organized priesthoods, self-sacrifice and penances involving fasting, sexual abstinence, and drawing blood from one's own ears, tongue, or penis, and a complex pantheon of gods and goddesses personifying natural forces and/or serving as patrons of various social classes and professions.[1]

Although the term Mesoamerica has attained common currency among anthropologists, ethnohistorians, art historians, and others who study this region, its continued validity and relevance could be challenged on the basis that it represents an effort to segregate and legitimate certain Native American societies (e.g., those of the "nuclear" regions of Mesoamerica and the Andean area) as examples of "high culture" or "advanced" civilizations, while implicily condescending toward other Pre-Columbian peoples. However, if we emphasize the concept of Mesoamerica as a "culture area" in the sense of sharing many general underlying beliefs and practices as the result of a historical evolutionary process involving relatively frequent, interregional, elite-level contacts that disseminated important beliefs or technologies, then use of the term can be justified. In particular, as Gary Gossen (1986: 1) has observed, many of these traits and practices are embodiments of a particular ideological worldview and are concerned with "noncorporeal formal entities—gods, language, cosmology, metaphors, knowledge, symbols— which, through their agency, give form and meaning to the empirical world."

In considering Mesoamerican architecture as a cultural expression or "cultural symbol," we are defining the term *culture* in its broader anthropological sense(s), rather than in the more restricted sense of the

European humanistic tradition, in which to be "cultured" refers to a specific training in and usage of refined elite manners, opinions, and tastes. Rather, we are referring to a concept that has been formulated from comparative studies of worldwide human communities, which can be applied to all human societies, and which in a fundamental way serves to define what it is that makes us human. Providing an exact definition of culture is problematic, however. As Clifford Geertz (1973: 89) has noted, "The term 'culture' has by now acquired a certain aura of ill-repute in social anthropological circles because of the multiplicity of its referents and the studied vagueness with which it has all too often been invoked."

In variants of the traditional Tylorean definition, anthropologists sometimes have defined a society's culture in fairly static terms as a "set of rules or standards that, when acted upon by the members of a society, produce behavior that falls within a range of variance the members consider proper and acceptable" (Haviland 1991: 280). This type of definition puts an emphasis on extracting lists of a society's core beliefs, practices, and elements of subsistence and technology that constitute its shared "culture." Culture interpreted in this way takes on a somewhat ideal or normative character, as though some essential set of mental guidelines stands behind and determines the individual expressions and actions of society's individual members. Culture in this sense could be likened to the "langue" of Saussure's (1959) linguistics, a kind of idealized template of the syntax, grammar, vocabulary, and pronunciation of a given language, of which individual utterances are simply partial and always somewhat changeable and idiosyncratic expressions.

Another definition is provided by Sanders and Price in *Mesoamerica: The Evolution of a Civilization* (1968: 214), in which culture is described as "the specifically human mechanism of adaptation to the environment, enabling man to compete successfully with other animals—including his fellows—with plants, and with the elements." This definition is based on cultural ecological theory, related to the theory of biological evolution, which asserts that cultural practices and beliefs are retained or "selected" to the extent that they enable human groups to effectively survive in a particular natural environment. Unlike earlier structural-functionalist interpretations of cultural practices (e.g., those of Radcliffe-Brown or Malinowski), which tended to emphasize their "timeless" unchanging nature and their "organismic" character, Sanders and Price stress the means by which culture change takes place, and by which varying forms of more complex sociopolitical organization have arisen. Thus Sanders and Price (1964: 215) assert that the "basic principles underlying cultural evolution—those of variation, adaptation, selection—are considered applicable as well to the higher analytical level" involving the superorganic concept of culture." Sanders and Price, as well as other scholars of the cultural ecology school (e.g., Mac-Neish 1964), acknowledge the role of ideology in Mesoamerican history but view it as more "epiphenomenal" or "ancillary to the growth of

Mesoamerica's vast cultural complexity" (Gossen 1986: 2). Others, such as Kent Flannery (1972, 1976) have suggested that a more balanced inter-action between material factors and cultural expressions exists, with the latter providing "information" that helps human beings in societies to manage evolutionary change effectively. In this volume, Joyce Marcus follows in this tradition in her discussion of Oaxacan architecture in chapter 3, in which she charts how architectural changes correlate closely with evolutionary transformations in social structure and politi-cal organization.

Clifford Geertz (1973: 89), with his interests in interpretive anthropol-ogy, has offered a more ideological definition of culture, viewing it as, "an historically transmitted pattern of meanings embodied in symbols, a system of inherited conceptions expressed in symbolic forms by means of which men communicate, perpetuate, and develop their knowledge and attitudes toward life."

Like Sanders and Price, Geertz believes that the development of cul-ture played an adaptive role in human evolution and helped assure human survival. In fact, he has asserted the creation of various material tools and technologies and advances in social organization and commu-nication provided an impetus for the selection of human beings who were physically and mentally more like ourselves (Geertz 1973: 67). However, Geertz views culture less as an epiphenomenon and more as an active agent in maintaining the viability of human societies, arguing that our complex central nervous system

> is incapable of directing our behavior or organizing our experience without the guidance provided by systems of significant symbols. What happened to us in the Ice Age is that we were obliged to aban-don the regularity and precision of detailed genetic control over our conduct for the flexibility and adaptability of a more general-ized, though of course no less real, genetic control over it. To sup-ply the additional information necessary to be able to act, we were forced in turn, to rely more and more heavily on cultural sources—the accumulated fund of significant symbols. Such symbols are thus not mere expressions, instrumentalities, or correlates of a bio-logical, psychological, and social existence; they are the prerequi-sites of it. Without men, no culture, certainly; but equally, and more significantly, without culture, no men. (Geertz 1973: 49)

Geertz has commented on the importance of the symbolic aspects of culture in providing the affective dimension to life, instilling a sense of social identity and motivating socially meaningful action, arguing that human beings are not concerned only with "solving problems, but with clarifying feelings," and that

> the existence of cultural resources, of an adequate system of public symbols, is just as essential to this sort of process as it is to that of directive reasoning . . . . In order to make up our minds we must

know how we feel about things; and to know how we feel about things we need the public images of sentiment that only ritual, myth, and art can provide. (Geertz 1973: 491)

In ancient Mesoamerica, architecture was one of the important "public symbols" used to express basic cultural perceptions and worldview. Spiro Kostof (1985: 7), noting that every building constitutes a "social act" involving the collaboration of groups of people, suggests that a consideration of the "total context of architecture" must involve the interconnections between architecture and the "social, economic, and technological systems of human history." He has noted that architecture is a "medium of cultural expression" rather than simply a passive backdrop or container for various daily activities and functions, and that buildings thus should be interpreted as "palpable images of the values and aspirations of the societies that produced them" (Kostof 1985: 19). Lee Anne Wilson (1993: 273) similarly has observed that

Buildings are rarely constructed solely for shelter . . . . While protection from the actual environment may be necessary for physical survival, humans do not live by shelter alone. Larger concerns about life and death, world view, cosmic images, roles of the sexes, and the relationship of the human realm to that of the supernatural also affect building size, shape, form, function, and location. Not only do individual buildings reflect these concerns but so do village layouts, often visually depicting the relations between the sexes, images of the cosmos, and human links both to the ancestors and the supernatural realm.

The chapters in this volume are concerned with the notion that architecture constitutes a "built environment" (Presiozi 1979). Presiozi (1979: 1) argues that architecture forms part of an elaborate array of material objects that form part of culturally determined "sign systems" or semiotic codes:

Like verbal language, the built environment—what will here be called an architectonic code—is a panhuman phenomenon. No human society exists without artifactually reordering its environment—without employing environmental formations (whether made or appropriated) as sign-tokens in a system of visual communication, representation and expression.[2]

The architecture created by members of particular Mesoamerican societies is closely related to social structure and community organization. Differences in building types, plans, materials, size, and "decorative" programs provide clues to the amount of hierarchical organization and differential access to wealth present in the society, the type of kinship and gender relationships, and the division of labor present (cf. Abrams 1994; McAnany 1994). As in the case of other traditional societies, the manner in which Mesoamerican peoples designed their temples, palaces, ballcourts, shrines, sweatbaths, and ordinary dwellings, and the way they were distributed in space, reflected and reinforced the behavioral codes by which the larger society was organized. In chapter 7 Cynthia Kristan-Graham interprets the architecture and architectural sculpture of Tula, Hidalgo as creating an idealized image of the "body politic" which downplayed factional divisions and reinforced the sociopolitical organization of the community.

Because it is relatively permanent, provides relatively fixed "landmarks," and determines parameters of movement and access, architecture creates a powerful sense of social identity by defining "social space" for members of a particular community. As Nabokov and Easton (1989: 30) have noted with regard to closely related architectural traditions of native North America, "Architecture . . . was a principal tool for socialization—a means by which members . . . learned rules of behaviour and a particular worldview." The notion that the creation of architectural structures and spaces creates systems of more-or-less stable social meanings is evident in the discussion of Early Classic architecture at Copan by Robert Sharer and his co-authors in chapter 10. Later modifications to the Acropolis, Main Ballcourt, and other centralized structures at that site indicate a complicated effort to simultaneously conserve a knowledge of the meaning of original ritual spaces and ancestral shrines, while enlarging and modifying structures to accord with growing economic power and sociopolitical complexity at the site.

The notion that architecture plays a role in socialization and acculturation is surely correct, emphasizing the intimate connection between architecture, social structure, and political organization in ancient Mesoamerica. The brief definition of Mesoamerica offered earlier presented an abbreviated "trait list" outlining some basic elements of material culture and ideology shared by groups throughout the region. The authors of *Ancient Mesoamerica: A Comparison of Change in Three Regions* have stressed that many of these diagnostic traits arose in the context of hierarchical societies of the chiefdom or state level of organization and were used to support a social structure of "elite prestige." They have further suggested that

> elite activities were the inter-regional contacts that made the Mesoamerican world what it was to its participants and what it is to us [twentieth-century scholars]. Elite-level communication was the principal social mechanism behind the common Mesoamerican culture beliefs and symbols and the widespread distributions of material culture items from 1000 B.C. on. (Blanton et al. 1993: 220)

Architecture provided one of the most monumental, visually impressive, and semiotically potent expressions of the authority and power of Mesoamerican elites. Most Mesoamerican societies were organized into broad classes with a large number of agricultural laborers or "commoners" governed by a small, restricted aristrocratic class of rulers, nobles, priests, and warriors drawn from high-ranking lineages. A relatively small "middle class" of artisans and merchants also existed.[3] Because basic commodities were not regularly transported long distances in ancient Mesoamerica, the principal source of wealth was land and control of the human labor needed to work it. The construction of large-scale buildings was a visible demonstration of the elite's ability to organize and manipulate such labor. As Esther Pasztory (1984: 25) observes, monumental buildings in Mesoamerica

> were not erected purely for religious or aesthetic reasons. Monument building was the most permanent form of power display these states could undertake, since it showed the full extent to which they controlled both a large population and its economic resources.

In addition to displaying the elite's power, architecture also could physically protect it. Competition among elites often turned violent in ancient Mesoamerica, leading to the development of fortifications and other defensive structures (see Armillas 1951; Webster 1976, 1993). In chapter 6, Augusto Molina and Jeff Kowalski describe such defensive systems at the hilltop site of Xochicalco, Morelos, as well as discussing the military symbolism of its best-known building, the Pyamid of the Plumed Serpent. Other walled sites discussed in this volume include Uxmal (Jeff Kowalski and Nicholas Dunning, chapter 12) and Tulum (Meredith Paxton, chapter 14).

In ancient Mesoamerican complex societies, different segments of the population had differential access to particular spaces and edifices and lived in different neighborhoods in housing ranging from relatively permanent and opulent to perishable and plain. As part of a general system of semiotic communication, architecture conveyed cultural meanings to viewers, but these meanings varied depending on one's position in society. In this respect, Dirks, Eley, and Ortner (1994: 1) recently have pointed out that

> one of the core dimensions of the concept of culture has been the notion that culture is "shared" by all members of a given society. But as anthropologists have begun to study more complex societies, in which divisions of class, race, and ethnicity are fundamentally constitutive, it has become clear that if we speak of culture as shared, we must now always ask "By whom?" and "In what ways?" —and "Under what conditions?"

Although organized by elites, large-scale architectural construction in Mesoamerica was not simply the result of coercion and despotic rule, but was promoted by ideological factors (see Cohen 1974 for a discussion of the active role symbols play in mediating power relationships in hierarchical societies). Throughout Mesoamerica religion provided a powerful motivating force for the creation of architecture, as well as providing a justifying rationale for the organization of society (Conrad and Demarest 1984; Demarest and Conrad 1992). As Michael Coe (1981: 170) has commented, "Even the very forms of cities and the reason for their location can, in part, be explained through the religious orientation of the Mesoamericans." In most communities the dominant structures were the lofty pyramid temples, which served either as sanctuaries for various deities or deified ancestors, sepulchral monuments housing the tombs and burials of high-ranking members of society, or a fusion of these two purposes (M. Coe 1956; Nicholson 1990). From descriptions of their cultic significance and associated architectural sculptures, it is clear that many ballcourts also had an important association with myths concerning astral and agricultural deities (Krickeberg 1966; Pasztory 1972; Cohodas 1978; Kowalski and Fash 1990; Gillespie 1991). Smaller shrines, sweat baths, and specialized platforms provided ancillary places where preparations were made for worship, where dances were performed to honor the gods and bind society together through communal ritual, or where sacrifices were performed and/or publicly displayed (Virginia Miller discusses the specialized Tzompantli or "skull rack" platform type in chapter 15).

Often, the specific design of such temples, the iconography of larger building groups, or the layout of more comprehensive site plans incorporates Mesoamerican beliefs concerning the quadripartite and vertically layered structure of the cosmos (Benson 1981), as well as reflecting the forces of nature and landscape forms associated with numinous power (Stone 1992; Townsend 1992). Many of the contributors to this volume discuss the religious symbolism or cosmological meanings of Mesoamerican architecture. In chapter 1 Kent Reilly discusses Preclassic Olmec architecture and site planning at La Venta, Tabasco, as efforts to create a sacred cosmogonic landscape. Associations between sacred geography (mountains and caves), astronomical time cycles, and the principal buildings at the great urban center of Teotihuacan are outlined by Jeff Kowalski in chapter 4. In chapter 9 Eduardo Matos discusses the tradition of creating walled sacred precincts in central Mexico, culminating in the sacred space of the Aztec Templo Mayor of the Mexica-Aztecs, who also conceived of the two halves of the structure as mythical mountains.

Mesoamerican structures did not simply visibly embody religious ideas, they also served as "theaters," providing settings for "ritual-architectural events," and defining spaces in which participants in recurring rituals reenacted myths and reinvigorated the cosmic and natural forces on which human beings' survival depended (Stone 1992: 111; Demarest 1992; Townsend 1992; Jones 1995). Phil Weigand, in chapter 2, suggests that the circular layouts of platforms of the Teuchitlán region of west Mexico were associated with *volador* rituals and the cult of the wind god, Ehécatl. In chapter 13, Andrea Stone interprets the possible ritualistic functions of the Temple of the Warriors at Chichén Itzá on the basis of its abundant relief sculptures and mural paintings. Although religious beliefs were certainly "shared" on some level, and often have their origins in shamanistic religious concepts (cf. Freidel, Schele, and Parker 1993), because most Mesoamerican societies were organized at the level of advanced chiefdoms, divine kingdoms, or state-level societies with divinely sanctioned administrative leadership and priesthoods, it was the elite members of society who were thought to have more direct geneaological ties with the gods, more direct contact and ability to mediate with the superatural realm, and therefore greater prestige, charisma, and political power. Thus, in chapter 12 Jeff Kowalski and Nicholas Dunning interpret the design of several of the prinicipal late structures at Uxmal as a "cosmic plan" that identified the site as a world center, correlating with Uxmal's presumed political dominance of the Puuc region of Yucatán. Likewise, in chapter 1 Kent Reilly provides evidence that Complexes A and C at La Venta together functioned as a place where Olmec rulers appeared in the guise of the maize god, and in which they were subsequently buried to undergo resurrection in the same manner as the deity.

The "ritualistic" aspects of both overtly religious and more secular buildings was an important aspect of their significance. Indeed, as John Pohl demonstrates in his discussion of the Mitla palaces in chapter 8, or as David Freidel and Charles Suhler (chapter 11) show during their comparative analysis of specialized "dance platforms" at Yaxuná, such ritualized significance often transcends conventional distinctions between "temples" and "palaces" made by archaeologists. Similarly, in chapter 14 Merideth Paxton presents evidence for the use of Structure 16 at Tulum in connection with cenote and agricultural rituals.

By structuring a "built environment" in relatively fixed and permanent forms, Mesoamerican peoples created spaces in which ritual actions occurred. Both in its more formalized, institutional modes as coordinated communal activities timed to mark important calendrical, astronomical, and/or agricultural cycles and as "rites of passage" designed to validate changes in social and political status (Van Gennep 1960; Turner 1969; Rappaport 1971), or in its more personal and domestic expressions as repeated patterns of daily behavior or habitus (Geertz 1973; Bourdieu 1977), ritual emotionally reinforces the sense either of the "sanctity" or simply the "rightness" of social interactions and social roles, demonstrating that one's position in society and unequal access to power is part of "the order of things" (Foucault 1980; for such interpretations of Mesoamerican art and ideology, see Klein 1986). As Dirks, Eley, and Ortner (1994: 5) observe

> there is a major recognition of the degree to which power itself is a cultural construct. The modes of expression of physical force and violence are culturally shaped, while force and violence in turn become cultural symbols, as powerful in their nonexecution as in their doing. And, of course, force in turn is only a tiny part of

power, so that much of the problematic of power today is a problematic of knowledge making, universe construction, and the
social production of feeling and of "reality."

The fact that the architectonic forms of various Mesoamerican societies display recognizable categories of buildings and discernable rules
governing the design of their structural and decorative components in
itself reflects the desire to create edifices that are such culturally significant systems of forms. Although the plans of sites and designs and adornments of individual buildings may refer to phenomena outside of themselves (i.e., myths, legends, historical events, astronomical events, etc.),
they are also inherently "meaningful" insofar as they serve to create a
series of visual self-images for members of that society. Differing architectural and artistic styles provide a sense of common cultural identity, as
well as establishing various types of social, political, ethnic, or gender-
based "boundary marking," or "information exchange" (cf. Wobst 1977;
Washburn 1983; Berlo 1991). Such uses of architectural and/or artistic
style in Mesoamerica have been discussed by George Kubler (1973) and
Esther Pasztory (1991, 1992), among others. Jeffrey Wilkerson addresses
various aspects of the uses of a distinctive regional style in chapter 5 on
Classic Veracruz architecture.

Each of the authors of the chapters in this book has considered the
architecture of a particular chronological period, region, or site from a
variety of the vantages discussed earlier. Although an effort has been
made to provide a wide-ranging consideration of many different architectural Mesoamerican traditions and forms, this volume is not intended
to provide a comprehensive survey of all of Mesoamerican architecture,[4]
nor is it intended to provide ultimate keys that will unlock single,
authoritative meanings of individual sites or buildings. Rather, it is our
hope that the discussions contained herein will provide the reader with
fresh critical perspectives, useful syntheses, and new interpretations
of the Mesoamerican built environment as a carrier of cultural meanings.

Notes

1. See Davies (1982), M. D. Coe (1984), Litvak King (1985), Adams
(1991), and Porter Weaver (1993) for overviews of Mesoamerican archaeology. Mesoamerican culture history is generally divided into chronological periods known as the Preclassic (also known as the Formative,
ca. 2000 B.C.–A.D. 250), the Classic (ca. A.D. 250–900), and the Postclassic
(ca. A.D. 900 to the conquest). Although still widely used, this chronology
is problematic because it is based primarily on the developmental
sequence as it was defined by earlier archaeology in the Maya region.
Thus, "Classic" referred to the time during which stone monuments
bearing Initial Series–Long Count inscriptions were being erected regularly in the Maya lowlands. The Preclassic, Classic, Postclassic nomenclature also originally carried implications of sequential developmental
stages (Willey and Phillips 1958) involving a transition from simpler

farming village societies to a largely peaceful and theocratic Classic stage of sociopolitical development, culminating in a more secular and militaristic Postclassic stage exemplified by the Mexica-Aztecs. Subsequent archaeological discoveries and iconographic interpretations have led to the realization that Mesoamerican culture history is much more complex than this early paradigm suggested. Thus, the Preclassic, Classic, Postclassic schema is now used primarily to refer to chronological periods rather than to developmental stages. Using the date A.D. 250 to define the beginning of the Classic period has become particularly problematic because many of the largest pyramid-temples at the central Mexican site of Teotihuacan were already constructed and the site grid layout had been established by that time (see Kowalski, chapter 4, this volume; for an alternative Mesoamerican chronological sequence, based on the archaeology of the Basin of Mexico, see Sanders, Parsons, and Santley 1979). Likewise, even in the Maya region archaeology has revealed that many of the traits considered to define Classic Maya civilization, such as large-scale public architecture, and the formation of a monumental art style, already existed by the Middle to Late Preclassic periods (ca. 600 B.C.–A.D. 250), with southern Maya monuments bearing early forms of hieroglyphic writing and long count dates carved during the Late Preclassic period from about 37 B.C. onward. For a comprehensive overview of Mesoamerican regional chronologies and archaeological sequences, see Taylor and Meighan (1978).

2. Presiozi's interpretive approach owes an acknowledged debt to the writings of the Czech thinker, Jan Mukarovsky (1978), whose semiological analysis of art and architecture was summarized in the book *Rethinking Art History*. Presiozi (1989: 116) notes: "For Mukarovsky every artwork was an autonomous sign composed of (1) an artifact functioning as perceivable signifier; (2) an aesthetic object registered in the consciousness of a community functioning as signification; and (3) a relationship to a thing signified—to the contextual sum of the social, political, philosophical, religious, political, and economic fabric of any given historical milieu." From this perspective, the task of the art historian or theorist is the fullest possible accounting of the nexus of relationships within which any artwork stands and from which it derives its significance.

3. See Chase and Chase (1992) for a recent discussion of Mesoamerican elites and differing viewpoints on the extent and nature of a "middle class" in Mesoamerican societies.

4. Various general surveys of Mesoamerican architecture exist, such as those of Robertson (1963), Marquina (1964), Hardoy (1964a, 1964b), and Heyden and Gendrop (1973). Architecture is covered in the broader art surveys of Kubler (1984) and M. E. Miller (1986; 2nd ed. 1994). An overview of Aztec architecture appears in Pasztory (1983). Surveys of Maya architecture include those by Spinden (1913), Totten (1926), Pollock (1965), and G. Andrews (1975). Regional surveys, individual site reports, and studies of individual buildings are too numerous to list separately, but Berlo (1985) provides an excellent bibliographic source.

1

Mountains of Creation and Underworld Portals

The Ritual Function of Olmec Architecture at La Venta, Tabasco

F. Kent Reilly, III

Mesoamerican ceremonial centers stagger the modern viewer with their vast scale and the height of their pyramids. Despite their size, they share with Navajo sand paintings and the Ojibwa midewiwin lodge a common ritual purpose. All these constructions were intended by their Native American creators to function as a sacred landscape through which supernatural power could enter the community of humankind. As such a sacred landscape, each Mesoamerican ceremonial center contained an architectural complex whose arrangement was, in effect, a three-dimensional cosmic model (Coggins 1980; Carrasco 1990: 21–23). Within such ceremonial precincts, monumental architecture served as a backdrop, a ritual stage, and a sanctified location for world renewal ceremonies and ritual reenactments of creation events. Recent archaeological, art historical, and iconographic research has repeatedly demonstrated that these ceremonies, and the architectural locations where they were performed, provided the performance mechanism through which the rulers of ancient Mesoamerica publicly validated their political power (Schele and Freidel 1990: 64–77; Ashmore 1992: 173–184).

La Venta

The earliest large-scale Mesoamerican ceremonial centers were located in the Gulf Coast heartland of the Olmec archaeological culture.[1] One of the archaeologically best known of these centers is the site of La Venta (figure 1.1a). La Venta is located in western Tabasco on a large island in a swamp some 10 kilometers from the Gulf of Mexico. At the time of its apogee (ca. 900–500 B.C.) this island location centered La Venta within a rich, low-lying, riverine and estuarine environment (Rust 1992). Excavations conducted in the 1940s and 1950s (Drucker 1952; Drucker et al.

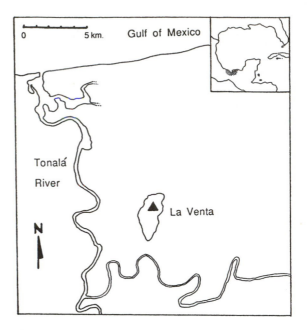

Figure 1.1a. The Olmec heartland site of La Venta is near the western border of the Mexican state of Tabasco. La Venta's location, within a rich estuarine environment some 10 kilometers from the Gulf of Mexico, provided the nutritional base to support a large, socially stratified population during the Middle Preclassic period (ca. 900–500 B.C.) (redrawn by Barbara McCloud from Rust 1992: figure 8.1).

1959) revealed that La Venta consisted of several large complexes of earthen architecture. These same excavations recovered many examples of monumental sculpture and the greenstone ceremonial deposits which have made La Venta unique in Mesoamerican prehistory.

More recent excavations and a thorough mapping project conducted by the Mexican Institute of Anthropology and History (INAH) under the direction of Rebecca González Lauck (1988, 1994) have uncovered evidence that La Venta and its environs possessed a substantial population from the Early Preclassic period (ca. 2250–1150 B.C.) until the site's abandonment sometime around 400 B.C. It can now be said with some certainty that during its apogee, La Venta's inhabitants constituted "a diverse and stratified range of groups including artisans, subsistence workers such as fishers and farmers, religious specialists, and chiefly or elite families" (Rust 1992: 124).

The architectural complex which functioned as both the residence of La Venta's elite and the ceremonial center for the site's entire population is today a series of earthen mounds positioned along a low ridge running north–south through the center of the island. These mounds are laid out on either side of an axis which runs 8° west of magnetic north (figure 1.1b). This north–south axis or center line divides the several groups of earthen architecture in a way that makes many of their components appear to be mirror images of each other.

La Venta is also separated into northern and southern zones. These two zones are positioned on either side of a large Central Plaza, which was almost certainly the focus of much of La Venta's public ritual. Many sculptural fragments have been recovered from a central mound in this

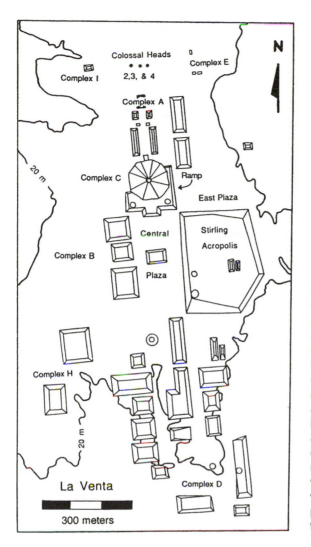

Figure 1.1b. The architecture of
La Venta consists of a series of earthen
mounds positioned on either side of a
north–south axis running 8° west of
magnetic north. At the center of these
mound complexes is a large plaza bordered on the north by Complexes A
and C, on the south by Complex D,
and on the east by the Stirling Acropolis. To the north of Complex A/C, the
architects of La Venta positioned three
colossal heads so that they all faced
north. Access to the large platform
which supported the La Venta pyramid
was restricted to a ramp within Complex C (redrawn by F. Kent Reilly, III
from González-Lauck 1994: figure 6.6).

plaza. The plaza was also augmented with such large monuments as
Colossal Head 1 and Stela 2 (Heizer et al. 1968). Public access to this Central Plaza appears to have been from the southeast, with more restricted
access along a processional way which ran through the multimound
group (Complex D) that borders the plaza to the south (Grove 1995,
1996). Access along the western edge of the plaza was blocked by the
three mounds which make up Complex B, and along the east by the
Stirling Acropolis. David Grove (1995, 1996) recently hypothesized
that Complex D served as the elite residential area of La Venta. I would
further suggest that the Stirling Acropolis, which literally overlooked the
Central Plaza and Complex D, supported the residence for the paramount
ruling lineage of the La Venta polity.[2]

Both Complex D and the Stirling Acropolis have been subjected to
only minimal archaeological investigation. By contrast, the mound group

about which we know the most archaeologically consists of Complexes A and C. These two architectural complexes border the central plaza on its north side. The designations Complex A and Complex C imply the existence of two distinct architectural assemblages, but, in reality, these two complexes form a single, unified ritual space consisting of a pyramid and an enclosed court linked by two range mounds.

Complex A/C had no access from the Central Plaza at all. Instead, Complex A/C appears to have been most accessible to the inhabitants of the Stirling Acropolis, who could have entered and exited through a narrow entrance that lay directly across a plaza (the East Plaza) that bordered the Stirling Acropolis on the north. The elite inhabitants of the Stirling Acropolis would have used this East Plaza to enter the Central Plaza as well as to gain access to the platform which supported La Venta's great pyramid.

The La Venta Pyramid

Rising some 32 meters above the rest of the site, the La Venta pyramid (Complex C) is the earliest large pyramidal structure erected in Mesoamerica (figure 1.2). The current ridged conical form of the pyramid (reminding some of an upside-down cupcake) in particular and excavations at La Venta in general have been the subject of a long and heated debate (Heizer et al. 1968: 129–130). Robert Heizer was convinced that the peculiar shape of the La Venta pyramid strongly indicated that its builders intended it to be a replica of the volcanic cones so plentiful in the region of the Tuxla Mountains northwest of La Venta itself. This interpretation is still uncertain, because the La Venta pyramid has never been investigated by archaeological means. However, since Mesoamerican pyramids were universally understood to replicate mountains (see Kowalski, chapter 4, this volume, and Matos, chapter 9, this volume), the La Venta pyramid would almost certainly have carried the same metaphorical message for its creators.

The La Venta pyramid was positioned atop a large earthen platform. The southern side of this platform was constructed in the shape of three arcs or a trefoil (shown in rectilinear form in the plan in figure 1.1b), which jutted out into the Central Plaza (Heizer et al. 1968: 138). Access to this platform was up an earthen ramp which began to the north on the east side of Complex A/C. Atop this platform, and below the pyramid, the Olmec builders of La Venta positioned, on either side of the site's center line, two throne/altars (Altars 2 and 3; Grove 1973) and a number of large stone monuments (Stelae 4 and 5), all of which faced the Central Plaza.

At some point toward the close of La Venta's occupation, these monuments were intentionally broken and buried at the base of the pyramid. When these monuments were excavated, each broken fragment was given a separate numerical designation (Drucker et al. 1959). These mon-

Figure 1.2. The La Venta Pyramid (Complex C) and its supporting platform mound as it appears today seen from the south. This photograph gives some idea of what the inhabitants of La Venta would have seen when they were assembled in the Central Plaza for ceremonial occasions (photograph by F. Kent Reilly, III).

ument numbers stood unchallenged until Rebecca González-Lauck (1988: 129) demonstrated that Monuments 25 and 26 were in fact fragments of a single monument. When Monuments 25 and 26 were reattached (and were thus renamed as La Venta Stela 4), a comparison of the incised image revealed a zoomorphic supernatural wearing a trefoil device in its headdress (figure 1.3). Another broken monument (Monument 27), excavated in the same area of the pyramidal platform, also bears an identical zoomorphic image.

When these two monuments are compared to the maize god and world tree/*axis mundi* imagery incised on various other Olmec style objects, there can be little doubt that these large, stone stelae were created to represent the Olmec Maize God in his manifestation as the source of vegetative fertility (Taube 1996) and cosmic axis (Reilly 1994a). The placement of these maize god images at the foot of the pyramid/mountain supports a hypothesis that identifies the La Venta pyramid as an Olmec version of the First True Mountain, the source of maize, potable water, and the site of the creation of human beings that would figure prominently in later Maya ideology (Freidel et al. 1993: 138–141). The fact that these maize god stelae were erected on the pyramid platform facing the largest public space at La Venta in association with the thrones of rulers suggests that this platform was the site of periodic world renewal ceremonies and ritual reenactments of creation events through which the rulers of La Venta validated their elite position.

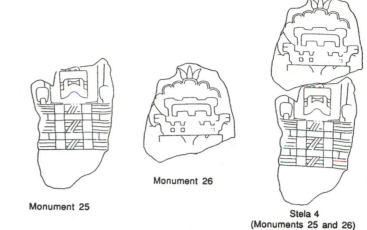

Figure 1.3. Monuments 25, 26, and Stela 4; restored from the fragments currently labeled Monuments 25 and 26. The supernatural depicted on Stela 4 can be identified as the Olmec Maize God by the trefoil emerging from its forehead (drawings by F. Kent Reilly, III based on González-Lauck 1994).

Monument 25

Monument 26

Stela 4
(Monuments 25 and 26)

Range Mounds as Liminal Space

Immediately north of the La Venta pyramid were constructed two range mounds (Mounds A-4 and A-5), which bordered an interior space 87 meters long by 40 meters wide (figure 1.4). The northern end of the space defined by these two mounds was occupied by the second of the famous La Venta mosaic pavements (Mosaic Mask 2), and a large cone-shaped mound (Mound A-3), which was erected over Tomb C. Tomb C was a stone-lined cavity that contained the burial goods of an elite personage (Drucker 1952: 65–71) (figure 1.5a). The profile drawings of La Venta's Mound A-3 excavation reveal that this earthen structure was added after the space bordered by Mounds A-4 and A-5 had ceased to function as a ritual space and had filled with at least a foot of drift sand.

Figure 1.4. A view of the two range mounds and the former site of Complex A as seen from the top of the La Venta Pyramid. To the north the remains of the runway, constructed in the 1950s and which destroyed Complex A, can also be seen (photograph by F. Kent Reilly, III).

Before Mound A-3 was constructed at the northern end of the area encompassed by the range mounds, Mosaic Mask 2 occupied the principal central location between the range mounds (figure 1.5b). When excavated, Mosaic Mask 2 (4.8 meters in length and 4.35 meters wide) was missing many of its pieces and was worn smooth in several areas (Drucker 1952: 75). Its worn condition indicates that this mask, unlike its more northerly counterparts, was not buried immediately upon its completion. The placement of this mosaic mask at the time of its construction almost in the dead center of the space defined by the range mounds almost certainly suggests that it functioned as a center marker. Throughout the long history of Mesoamerican architecture, just as pyramids normally were metaphorical mountains, range mounds accompanied by central markers functioned as ballcourts. However, unless further evidence is obtained, the enormous area defined by mounds A-4 and A-5 makes the interpretation of this space as a ballcourt seem implausible. What can be said about this clearly demarcated and restricted area is that it is a liminal space, which is further defined by the inclusion of a center marker. Perhaps this space functioned as a grand processional way, which defined ritual movement between Complex A and C (Reilly 1995).

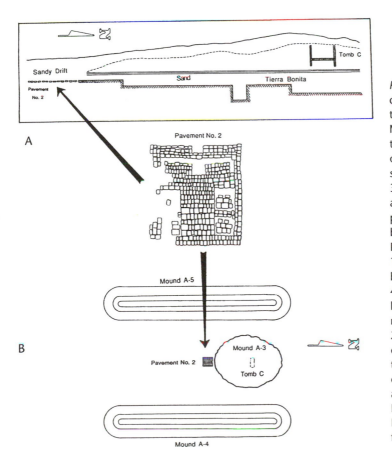

Figure 1.5a. A profile drawing of the excavations associated with Mound A-3. Note that the Mosaic Mask 2 is overlaid only by drift sand and that Mound A-3 itself is positioned atop earlier construction phases (redrawn by Barbara McCloud from Drucker 1952: figure 14). b. The liminal space bordered by Mounds A-4 and A-5. When the later Mound A-3 is removed, Mosaic Mask 2 is positioned at the center of what appears to be a processional way connecting Complex A and C (redrawn by Barabara McCloud from Drucker et al. 1959: figure 4).

La Venta Complex A: The Enclosed Court

The enclosed court in La Venta Complex A consists of a series of three mounds (Features A-1 through A-5) grouped around a plaza. Both mounds and plaza were double-bordered by a bracket-shaped wall (figure 1.6). Major excavations were conducted in Complex A during 1941–1943 and again in 1955 (Stirling 1941: 321–332; Stirling and Stirling 1942: 635–661; Drucker 1952; Drucker et al. 1959). These excavations uncovered many of the construction details of this enclosed court, revealing that it had undergone four major phases of construction and that each of these major construction phases was initiated with the deposit of a massive offering of serpentine blocks (Drucker et al. 1959: 27–29, 46). Carbon samples obtained during the 1955 excavations revealed that the enclosed court in Complex A had been in use between 1000 B.C. and 600 B.C. (Heizer et al. 1968: 14). Unfortunately, since these excavations, much of Complex A has been destroyed by an airstrip which was built through the middle of the court in the late 1950s. Because of this destruction, and because Complex A is the most thoroughly investigated of all La Venta's architectural complexes, it is worth reviewing its construction history in some detail.

La Venta Complex A: The Construction Phases

The first of these construction phases saw a massive deposit of clay which would serve as a foundation for the court. Construction phase 1 also saw the borders of the court defined by the erection of a red-clay embankment. This clay embankment was open at both its southern and northern ends. The interior of this demarcated space was paved with a series of light brown and buff floors of water-sorted sand. Within the court, on the east, west, and south sides, construction began on three platform mounds. At some point in phase 1 the Olmec builders excavated the center of the court, and a deposit of serpentine blocks was laid out as pavement, which then was covered with fill (Drucker et al. 1959: 46, illustrations 9, 10).

In phase 2, the red clay embankment was topped by a larger adobe wall which was marked by a single row of basalt facing blocks on its interior face. The brown and buff floors laid down in phase 1 were now covered with a series of white sandy floors. Interestingly, the latest discernible level in this white sandy floor series is differentiated from the others by a thin layer of crushed green serpentine. The serpentine deposits associated with phase 2 (Massive Offering No. 1 and pavements Nos. 1 and 3) are two of the most remarkable discoveries in the history of Olmec studies (figure 1.7). The southern entrance of the enclosed court was augmented by the addition of two bastionlike platform mounds (Features A-1-d and A-1-e). Located under each of these two adobe platforms

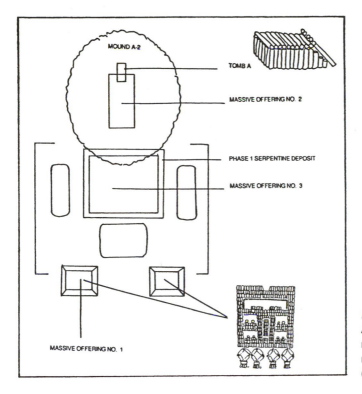

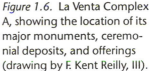

Figure 1.6. La Venta Complex A, showing the location of its major monuments, ceremonial deposits, and offerings (drawing by F. Kent Reilly, III).

was a serpentine deposit consisting of 28 courses of rough serpentine blocks weighing some 1,000 tons (Drucker et al. 1959: 97). On top of each of these enormous deposits of serpentine, a mosaic pavement was laid (Pavements No. 1 and 3). Each mosaic pavement or mask, as they have come to be called, measured some 4.8 by 4.4 meters and was constructed from some 485 squared blocks of cut serpentine. Each mask has a squared cleft in the middle of its northern border and four feathered or fringed diamonds that extend out from the southern border. The brilliance of the polished greenstone from which both masks were constructed was further enhanced by setting each mask in a deposit of multicolored clays. Deposited in the fill above the mosaic masks were cruciform-shaped caches of jade and greenstone celts and, in one instance, a hematite mirror (Wedel 1952: 55).

Construction phase 3 began with the deposit of massive red, purple, and pink clay fill throughout the court. At some later date a new series of multicolored floors (Tierra Bonita in Wedel 1952: 38; the Old Rose Floor Series in Drucker et al. 1959: 23). The buildup of the floor level within of the court led to alterations in the height of the three platform mounds and the surrounding adobe wall. The center of the court was reexcavated by the inhabitants and a massive deposit of six layers of serpentine blocks was buried some 3.9 meters under the layered floors of the enclosed court. According to the excavators, this offering (Massive Offering No. 3, measuring 18.9 by 19.8 meters) caused the removal of the ser-

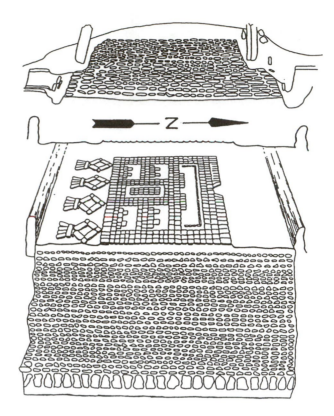

South Entrance, the enclosed court,
La Venta Complex A

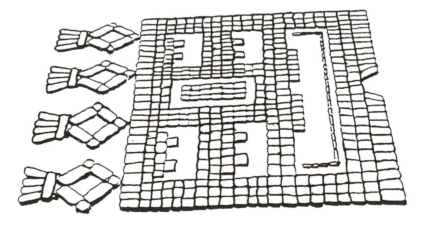

Pavement 3

Figure 1.7. La Venta Mosaic Mask 3 (Pavement 3) shown in context and as a separate detail. Laid atop 28 courses of uncut serpentine blocks weighing around 1,000 tons, this mosaic pavement and its twin, Mosaic Mask 1, is composed of 485 blocks of cut and polished serpentine. These masks depict an abstracted image of the "Olmec Dragon." The top of the mask is indicated by the cleft positioned in the middle of its northern side (drawing by F. Kent Reilly, III).

pentine block deposit associated with the phase 1 construction. The blocks from Massive Offering 1 were then deposited in a trench dug around Massive Offering No. 3, (Drucker et al. 1959: 185–186). Directly above Massive Offering No. 3 the builders deposited a cruciform-shaped cache of 38 serpentine and jade celts (Offering No. 10).

Construction phase 4 saw the continued buildup of the multicolored clay floors within the enclosed court. This buildup raised the floor level to the top of the surrounding adobe wall and necessitated a startlingly new architectural innovation—the construction of a basalt column fence atop the adobe wall. The addition of the basalt column fence would have restored a sense of secrecy and exclusiveness to the enclosed ritual activity, which over time was becoming more visible due to the buildup of the multicolored floors.

The court's northern entrance was now almost entirely blocked by a greatly enlarged, low-lying, stepped pyramid (Mound A-2). Constructed during earlier phases, Mound A-2 served to shield the interior of the court and its ritual activity from public view. At the close of phase 4, the Olmec excavated Mound A-2 to a considerable depth. At the bottom of this excavation, a layer of bright red sand was deposited, and on top of this layer was laid a solid pavement consisting of a single layer of cut and polished serpentine blocks (Massive Offering No. 2). Measuring 14.8 meters north–south by 6 meters east–west, Massive Offering No. 2 was immediately covered with earthen fill. Atop this fill, and directly above the center of Massive Offering No. 2 was placed a sandstone sarcophagus carved in the likeness of the Olmec Dragon (Olmec God I, see Joralemon 1976; see figures 1.11 and 1.13). Above, and straddling the northern edge of Massive Offering No. 2, the builders placed a tomb (Tomb A), constructed from basalt columns similar to those used in the construction of the never-completed basalt column fence (see figure 1.12).

The subsequent abandonment of the enclosed court is heralded by the deposit of a one-foot-thick red clay cap over the entire complex. This terminal construction event evidently signaled the end of ritual activity in La Venta Complex A (Drucker et al. 1959: 25). The four construction phases of Complex A were carried out over a period of some 500 years. At a psychological and behavioral level, the goal of the Olmec planners who supervised the construction of this enclosed court appears always to have been to define a ritual space with a limited accessibility for elite use. Over time the ritual deposits, many of which were laid down precisely on La Venta's center line, became more elaborate. On a conceptual level, these same builders were using these ritual deposits as a mechanism for defining Complex A as the spatial centerpiece of a cosmogonic myth. However, before the relationship between Olmec myth and architecture can be explored more fully, it will be helpful to briefly examine the architectural usages of the Classic Period Maya. Such an examination should provide analogous situations that will be helpful in any interpretation of the ritual function of La Venta Complex A/C.

Water Iconography and the Maya Otherworld

For the Classic Maya, the pyramids that contained the tombs of their dead rulers were frequently decorated with plaster masks depicting *witz* monsters to define the towering structure as a mountain (*witz* is the Maya word for mountain or hill; see Kowalski and Dunning, chapter 12, this volume). At the Maya site of Uaxactun sometime around 300 B.C., a facade mask program of this type on Structure H-X-Sub-3 specifically describes this structure as the *Yax-Hal-Witz*, the "First True Mountain" in this creation, which was the source of maize, the waters of fertility, and the location of the creation of humankind (Freidel et al. 1993: 139–140). Such pyramids were also understood by the Maya to be one of the locations of ancestral power as well as portals to the supernatural Otherworld.

The plazas, around which the Maya erected their great pyramid mountains, were designated in the hieroglyphic texts by the same term (*Nab*) used to identify the numerous lakes, swamps, and large sheets of still water that cover much of the tropical lowlands during the rainy season (Schele and Grube 1990). Such still, watery surfaces, which so often are covered with water lilies and other aquatic vegetation, also were conceived by the Maya as portals to an underwater Otherworld (Hellmuth 1987).

To determine whether this later and more specific Maya Otherworld symbol set has a Preclassic origin, it is necessary to examine the ritual deposits and the architectural setting for La Venta Complex A/C. This is because at La Venta, as at no other Olmec heartland site, it was the function of Olmec architecture, like the architecture of the Classic Maya, to serve as a three-dimensional human-made expression of Olmec cosmology (cf. Coggins 1980, for Maya architecture). This architecturally embodied cosmic model could then be manipulated to provide a ritual setting for the public enactment of the supernaturally derived political charter that justified the elite position of Formative Period Gulf Coast rulers.

The Iconography and Interpretation of the Phase 2 Mosaic Masks

I have already proposed that La Venta's great pyramid (Complex C) was intended by its builders as a replication of the First True Mountain. I now propose that for La Venta's elite lineages, Complex A functioned specifically as a royal mortuary and a location for the access to supernatural power. As such a mythic location, Complex A, standing to the north and behind the pyramid, also functioned generally for the inhabitants of La Venta as a source of ancestral power and thus a watery Otherworld location.

As previously stated, the liminal space defined by Mounds A-4 and A-5 appears to have provided a grand processional way that led from the north side of Complex C to the southern entrance of Complex A (figure 1.6). It was this southern entrance that was augmented during construction phase 2 with bastionlike projections that contained the unique, buried mosaic masks and enormous deposits of serpentine. The placement of these mosaic masks on either side of the entrance of the enclosed court shows that they function similarly to the stucco facade masks that flank the staircases leading to the tops of the platform mounds and pyramids of both Preclassic and Classic Maya sites.

Notwithstanding the fact that the mosaic masks of Complex A were buried immediately after construction, they are just as much vehicles for ideological information as facade masks displayed on later mound and pyramidal structures. The difference involves the audience for whom the message was intended. Facade masks identify the function of structures that rise above plazas and convey their ideological message to a broader public audience. La Venta's buried masks identify the function of an enclosed and restricted ritual space used primarily by a nonpublic, elite audience. Therefore, the flanking masks that carry the ritual identity of that space are themselves hidden from view.

What then is the ideological message carried by these buried masks? The answer to this question is conveyed through motifs on the masks' surface that are rendered as a positive pattern by outlining each motif with negative space, and through the green serpentine blocks from which the mask is created (figure 1.7). Recent iconographic studies have been quite successful in interpreting many of the symbolic elements on the surface of the masks. The mask itself can be identified as an animate supernatural through the cleft positioned in the middle of the upper or north edge (Guthrie 1995: 120–121). The motifs rendered on the surface of both masks consist of a double merlon symbol and a bar and four dots motif in which each of the dots is defined as a double merlon. The double merlon is used widely within the Olmec symbol system. Most probably the double merlon functions as an abstract symbol for a portal between natural and supernatural space (Reilly 1994a: 157–159; Guthrie 1995: 121).[3] The presence of a large double merlon on the La Venta mosaic pavements identifies one of the functions of the ritual space whose entrance they flank as a portal to an otherworld location.

Now that the function for the large double merlon motif on the mosaic pavement has been proposed, an identification of the bar and four dots motif will allow a symbolic identification of the mosaic pavement itself (Figure 1.7). Elizabeth Benson (1971: 29) first suggested that the bar and four dots motif was a possible place sign for the La Venta polity. However, a later identification by David Joralemon has demonstrated that the bar and four dots is a symbol that refers to his God I, the Olmec Dragon (Joralemon 1976: 47–52). As Joralemon further states, "God I's primary associations are with earth, water, and agricultural fertility." Representations that depict vegetation sprouting from the deity's body suggest that the Olmec identified God I with the earth itself and imagined this saurian creature as the ultimate source of agricultural abundance. As an abstract symbol of the Olmec Dragon, the bar and four dots motif further functions as a five-directional cosmic model (Guthrie 1995: 228–229).[4]

The green polished surface of the mosaic masks symbolically represents both water and agricultural fertility. How does a greenstone pavement symbolically become water? At first glance this is a problem, but it is generally accepted by scholars of ancient America that in Mesoamerican cultures greenstone could carry the symbolic value of water as well as that of vegetative fecundity (Thompson 1960: 44, 289). In modern Mexico, at least one group of native peoples, the Huastecs, retain this greenstone/water association in the story of the Lints'i'. According to the Huastec, the mythological Lints'i' could create a water source simply by burying a greenstone in the ground (Alcorn 1984: 60). The bar and four dots and the double merlon motifs laid out within the mosaic pavements strongly indicate that the pavement itself is symbolically the Olmec Dragon, the surface of the earth whose gaping maw is the portal to the otherworld. The greenstone from which the mosaic masks are constructed functions as the primordial ocean in which the dragon floats. In addition, metaphorically the greenstone functions as a symbolic locative, identifying the court in which they are buried as an underworld/Otherworld location or portal.

The identification of the fringed diamonds (Joralemon 1976: 16) extending out from the southern border of the mosaic pavements is more tenuous. The difficulty of providing any sort of conclusive iconographic interpretation for this specific motif is the paucity of comparable designs within the Olmec symbol system. However, Rosemary Joyce, in the symposium held before the 1987 Maya Hieroglyphic Workshop at the University of Texas at Austin, suggested that the fringed diamonds represented vegetation. This vegetation identification fits well with the function and other depictions of the Olmec Dragon (e.g., La Venta Altar 4, La Venta Monument 6; Chalcatzingo Relief 1, etc.), whose association with the mosaic pavement is more definitively signaled by the bar and four dots motif.

The Enclosed Court as an Otherworld/Ancestral Location

The placement of the bar and four dots motif along with the large double merlon on either side of the entrance into the enclosed court identifies the court as the mythic site of primordial creation. In a broad sense, La Venta's enclosed court can be understood as the Formative Period version of the Lying-down-Sky, First-Three-Stone-Place which in later Maya myth was the site of the present creation and the location where First Father, the Maize Lord, raised the world tree and animated the cosmos by establishing his North House in the celestial realm (Freidel et al. 1993:

59–122). The placement of cruciform-shaped offerings of stone celts (in one case containing a mirror) over La Venta's serpentine pavements suggests that the Olmec, like the later Classic Maya, considered the watery underworld to be not only the location of the ancestors and thus of supernatural power, but a realm pierced by the cruciform-shaped world tree as well.

This interpretation is further supported by the triadic arrangement of the mounds within the court and the enormous greenstone pavement that underlies the open area of the court itself as well the three colossal heads (Colossal Heads Nos. 2, 3, and 4) positioned some 20 meters to the north of the court (figure 1.1b). These colossal heads, aligned east to west and all facing the north, were carved early in La Venta's history and probably were moved from the Central Plaza where Colossal Head 1 is still located (Stirling 1945: 57–58). Anyone who approached the north entrance of Complex A passed among these three colossal heads. Since scholars generally agree that Olmec colossal heads were portraits of Olmec rulers,[5] the positioning of these three heads north of Complex A signaled to anyone who approached from the north that Complex A was both a "three stone place" and a source of ancestral power.

As already stated, the greenstone pavement underlying the court, with its explicit water symbolism, functions doubly as the primordial sea from which, in later Maya myth, the sky will be raised as well as the watery aspect of this Otherworld location. However, the location of this pavement also indicates the purpose of the ritual activity taking place in that plaza. Almost certainly, activity centered on rituals that initiated communication with the underwater underworld and the ancestors who dwell there. The cruciform-shaped deposit of jade and greenstone celts with their maize and vegetation associations (Joralemon, in Coe 1972: 187; Taube 1996) is metaphorically the world tree waiting to be raised. The three flanking mounds correspond to the three stones the gods set as the first act of creation itself. The assembled gods themselves (or their human impersonators) may also be present in the enclosed court, represented by the greenstone celts and the greenstone figures of Offering 4 buried within the Northeast platform mound of Complex A (figure 1.8).[6]

The question now arises as to the role played by the La Venta ruler within the enclosed court. Whatever ritual activities the ruler participated in during his lifetime, it is reasonably clear that his ultimate role was that of a corpse. Many of the so-called offerings buried within the court are almost certainly elite burials! Though these burials lack skeletal material, this absence can be accounted for by the acidity of the soil, the excavation techniques of the 1940s and 1950s, and the destructive activity of Gulf Coast fauna. Three of these "offerings" in particular contain ritual objects which strongly suggest that they were the final resting places of La Venta's highest-ranking elite individuals.

Offerings 5, 6, and 7 (Drucker et al. 1959: 162–179), located in the same Northeast Platform that contained Offering 4, all appear to be burials.

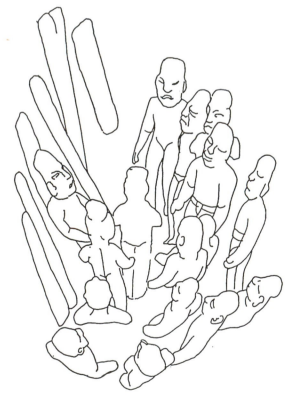

Figure 1.8a (above). La Venta Offering 4 seen from above during excavation (photograph courtesy of George Stuart and the National Geographic Society).

Figure 1.8b (at right). La Venta Offering 4 seen from above (drawing by F. Kent Reilly, III).

Jade Maskettes

Offering No. 6

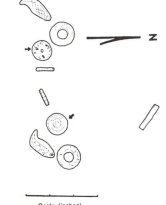

Scale (inches)

z

Figure 1.9. La Venta Offering (Burial) 6 and the plaques from the burial, which would have been sewn to a bark paper headband. This plaque assemblage and its accompanying three drilled beads functioned as an early version of the Jester God headdress for the rulers of La Venta (redrawn by Barbara McCloud from Drucker et al. 1959: figures 43, 44).

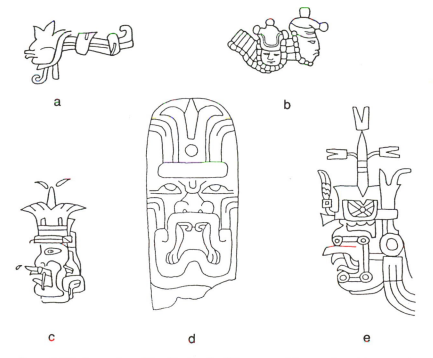

a   b

c   d   e

Figure 1.10. Examples of the "Jester God" iconographic complex: (*a*) example of a Late Preclassic Maya Jester God headband; (*b*) Classic period example of the Maya royal headdress (*a* and *b* after Schele and Freidel 1990: figure 3.14); (*c, d, e*) Preclassic depictions of the trefoil element, which is the Olmec prototype for the Maya Jester God, can be seen worn by humans and supernaturals on Olmec greenstone celts (redrawn by F. Kent Reilly, III after Joralemon 1976: figure 8f; 1971: figures 170, 172).

31

Although they lack skeletal material, an analysis of greenstone costume elements, and, in one case, ceramic vessels, indicates that these three offerings are laid out (east to west) as if these costume details had been positioned on a body. In all three instances, ear flares were placed on either side of where the skull should be. In two cases (Offerings 5 and 6), below the ear flares, approximately where the shoulders should be on a human, were positioned a string of greenstone beads on either end of which is a disk (figure 1.9). This string of beads may have functioned as the clasp for the cloaks that Olmec heartland rulers are so frequently depicted wearing. In all three offerings, above the earflares, in the position of the forehead, are plaques that are arranged in a pattern that resembles the supreme identifier of Classic Maya royalty—the Jester God headband (Schele 1974; Fields 1990; Freidel 1990).

The Classic Maya Jester God headdress consisted of a white bark headband to which was affixed a plaque that was carved in the form of a supernatural wearing a trefoil headdress (figure 1.10). Often this central trefoil supernatural was flanked by two other disks or plaques. Fields (1990) has clearly demonstrated that the Classic Maya Jester God had its origins among the Olmec and that its iconographic source was a sprouting maize plant. In all three offerings/burials, the same arrangement of three disks, each carved to represent a face, is positioned between the ear flares as if the disks had been tied around the forehead (figure 1.9). Each of these disks is drilled so that they could be sewn onto a headband. In the case of Offering/Burial 6 there was an unadorned disk, which would be used as a type of backing to support the weight of the frontal disk when sewn to the reverse side of the headband. In other words, the two disks functioned similarly to a modern lapel pin. Around these disks were scattered drilled greenstone beads which appear to have been attached to the disks themselves. Functionally, these beads would have been the points of the Jester God trefoil. Until now, artistic depictions have provided our sole evidence for a Middle Preclassic Jester God. These three offerings/burials provide dramatic archaeological proof that the Olmec Jester God is directly ancestral to its Maya counterpart. These three offerings/burials also prove that Complex A functioned as a mortuary complex for the interment of La Venta's elite dead. However, it is with the fourth construction phase and the reconstruction of Mound A-2 that Complex A was also defined by its Olmec builders as a three-dimensional cosmic model as well as an Otherworld location.

Mound A-2 and Tomb A in La Venta Complex A

Olmec tombs are quite rare, and those recovered under archaeological conditions are rarer still. In the Olmec Gulf Coast heartland, the one site where tombs have been uncovered by archaeological methods is La

Venta, and all of them have been excavated in Complex A. To date, however, only Tomb A associated with Mound A-2 was found to have contained human bones. As previously mentioned, Tomb A (the basalt column tomb) was erected when the center of Mound A-2 was excavated by the local inhabitants at the beginning of the fourth construction phase (ca. 600 B.C.). In this construction episode a trench was excavated through the top of the mound down through the underlying ground surface to a depth of some 4.8 meters. At the bottom of this pit was placed a layer of bright red sand, on top of which was deposited Massive Offering No. 2 (Drucker et al. 1959: 128; Reilly 1994b: 126–128).

Atop this filled-in pit, a large sandstone sarcophagus (Monument 6) was positioned squarely above the middle of the serpentine pavement buried below it. The sandstone sarcophagus was covered with a rectangular sandstone lid. The sarcophagus itself (2.8 meters long, 0.96 meters wide, and approximately 0.86 meters high) contained a cache of jade jewelry laid out as if it had adorned a human body. However, no skeletal material was found, presumably for the same reasons that no skeletal remains were found in Offerings/Burials 5, 6, and 7. The exterior of the sandstone sarcophagus is carved to represent a north-facing Olmec Dragon (figure 1.11). The split-stemmed plants emerging along the back of this supernatural zoomorph make its identity as the saurian earth monster certain.

When one takes into account the placement of this Olmec earth-crocodilian sarcophagus directly mid-center over the serpentine pavement of Massive Offering No. 2, within the context of the other archaeological evidence retrieved from the excavation of Mound A-2, it seems quite evident that the two features were part of the same construction episode. I propose that all the caches and other paraphernalia associated with Mound A-2 were associated with the burial of a paramount ruler of La Venta and that the placement of the sarcophagus and the accompanying caches occurred during the construction of that ruler's elaborate funerary monument. The overall iconographic program that was conveyed by the objects contained in this funerary monument was intended to associate the buried ruler with the act of cosmic creation and thus with world renewal and agricultural regeneration.

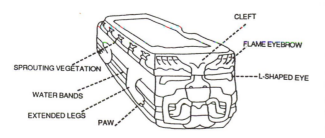

Figure 1.11. The iconography of the Olmec terrestrial dragon as depicted on the sandstone sarcophagus (Monument 6) from La Venta Complex A (drawing by F. Kent Reilly, III).

Within this proposed iconographic program, the green polished surface of Massive Offering No. 2 symbolically represents the waters of the underworld that underlie the primordial ocean on top of which floats the earth in the form of the Olmec terrestrial dragon. The placement of the dead ruler within such a sarcophagus directly associates him with regeneration and the primal forces of creation. The placement of the deceased ruler within the earth monster carries the implication that the human will be transformed into a divinity, as Pakal is transformed into the Maize God as he descends into the maw of the earth dragon on his sarcophagus lid (Freidel et al. 1993: 76–78, 276, figure 2.12). Likewise, the message of the Olmec Dragon sarcophagus undoubtedly was that the Olmec ruler would be reborn as the Maize God in a manner similar to that in which he is resurrected by his sons, Hunahpu (Hun Ahaw) and Xbalanke (Yax Balam), and emerges from the turtle earth on Classic period Maya painted ceramics (Taube 1985; see Freidel and Suhler, chapter 11, figure 11.14, this volume). As mentioned, there is considerable evidence that Olmec rulers were associated with, and perhaps were considered to be embodiments of, the Olmec Maize God.

Tomb A and Its Contents

Tomb A, positioned within the north end of Mound A-2 (approximately 3 meters long by 2 meters wide and 1.8 meters high), was entirely constructed of 44 close-fitting vertical and horizontal basalt columns (figure 1.12). These columns were so "fitted as to present a smooth and even surface on the interior, leaving the outside rough" (Stirling and Stirling 1942: 640). The entrance to this structure faced north and was closed by five inclined basalt columns. When Matthew Stirling excavated Tomb A, he found the interior tightly packed with clay. When this packing was cleared, he discovered that the southern 2.2 meters of the tomb floor was paved with eight water-worn flagstones. Tomb A was constructed so that the southern, flagstone-covered half of its floor sits directly over the fill that covers Massive Offering No. 2, while the entrance to Tomb A rests on the original ground surface under Mound A-2 (Drucker et al. 1959: 49). It was on these flagstones that bundle burials and a remarkable set of grave goods were placed before the tomb was sealed.

The basalt columns with which Tomb A is constructed are identical to those erected around the perimeter of Complex A. As previously stated, the enclosure of Complex A by the basalt column fence was never completed. It may be that the gaps in the basalt column enclosure wall were caused by removing the missing columns in order to erect Tomb A.

If an argument can be made that the Olmec Dragon/sandstone sarcophagus, located three meters to the south of Tomb A, was symbolically seen as floating in the primal ocean symbolized by Massive Offering No. 2, then it can also be hypothesized that the southern or flagstone-paved half of the floor of Tomb A and the accompanying burials were them-

Figure 1.12. The basalt column tomb (La Venta Tomb A) from Complex A in its present location in the Parque La Venta, Villahermosa, Tabasco, Mexico (photograph by F. Kent Reilly, III).

selves symbolically located in the watery Otherworld (figure 1.13). The entrance to Tomb A, however, could be considered to occupy a nonwatery Otherworld location because it does not overhang Massive Offering No. 2 and thus is located in the natural world. For the Olmec builders, the entrance of Tomb A functioned symbolically as a portal between the natural and the supernatural realms. This interpretation is supported by the objects that were chosen to accompany the dead of Tomb A into the underworld.

Directly atop the eight flagstones of Tomb A was a coating that Stirling described as a thin layer of blue clay and that Drucker called a layer of heavy olive-brown swamp muck (Stirling and Stirling 1942: 640; Drucker 1952: 23). Either of these substances can be argued to have associations with water. Atop this deposit were two large areas of red cinnabar. It was within these red stains that the remains of the bundle burials of two or perhaps three individuals were found (Stirling and Stirling 1942: 641; Drucker 1952: 23). Many of the funerary objects associated with these bundle burials had strong water connotations. Among such beautifully crafted objects as jade ear flares, jade perforators, jade figurines, and a necklace or headdress composed of a jade stingray and six stingray spines set with small squares of glittering hematite were a large shark's tooth (on which was placed a translucent blue–jade standing figure), a jade frog, and a carved jade clamshell (Stirling and Stirling 1942: 640–642). The jade clamshell was a "realistic reproduction of a fresh-water clam shell . . . perforated for use as a pendant. Inside it was a small oval mirror of brilliant crystalline hematite" (Stirling and Stirling

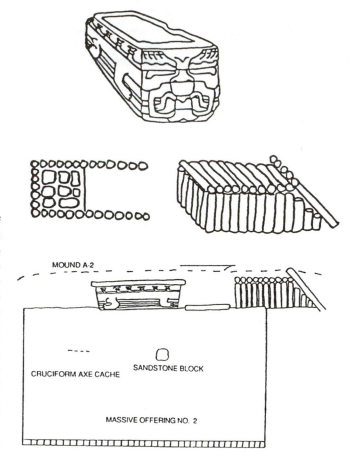

Figure 1.13. A profile view of Mound A-2 with its associated monuments, showing the relationship of these monuments to the underlying serpentine deposit identified as Massive Offering 2. As can be seen clearly, the "Olmec Dragon" sarcophagus (Monument 6) is positioned directly above the middle of Massive Offering 2, while the southern or paved half of Tomb A overhangs the northern section of this serpentine deposit (drawing by F. Kent Reilly, III).

1942: 640–641). Underneath the clamshell was one of the carved jade seated figures.

When we consider that the objects from Tomb A, many of which have watery connotations, were placed on a layer of blue clay or olive green swamp muck—which, because of either its color or source, can be interpreted as a watery surface—and when we architecturally relate the entire tomb to Massive Offering No. 2, which was constructed atop a layer of red sand, just as the waters of the underworld apparently were a mixture of blood and water (Stuart 1988), then there is unmistakable evidence that the Olmec Otherworld, like that of the Maya, was an underwater realm.

Conclusions

What then was the overall symbolic message that the rulers of La Venta conveyed by means of this architectural, sculptural, and artifactual metaphor? As I illustrated, the La Venta pyramid, the sarcophagus, the three platform mounds, and the three north-facing colossal heads were constructed and positioned in order to lay out an Otherworld location connected with a specific mythic time. The combination of architecture, monuments, and caches indicates that the sacred location the builders of La Venta were constructing was the place of creation; the primordial location that the Classic Maya would later call the First True Mountain and the Lying-down-Sky, First-Three-Stone-Place.

In order for an Olmec ritual space to be identified as a Formative Period counterpart to these Classic Maya sacred cosmogonic locations, it should have structures, caches, and an iconographic program that function to identify certain human-made architectural settings as mythic places. I have presented arguments that La Venta Complex A/C does embody such mythic places, containing symbolic representations of the primordial sea that existed before the earth was formed or the sky raised, structures that symbolize the three stones that were set by the gods as the first step in the creative act, and the First True Mountain where human beings were created. There are also ritual objects contained in Complex A that can be identified with First Father (the Maize God) and the world tree with which he raised the sky. Finally, there is a basalt column construction that could function as a representation of the North House, the celestial location of First Father, whose establishment, the Classic Maya believed, set the cosmos in motion. As I have illustrated, all these creative actions and mythic locations are fully represented in the architectural forms and iconographic details associated with the construction of Complex A in general, and specifically with Tomb A and its accompanying constructions within the previously existing Mound A-2.

Thus it can be said that the Olmec constructed the northern section of La Venta to represent a three-dimensional model of the cosmos at the time of creation. The function of this architectural grouping was at least twofold. First, Complex A/C provided an architectural platform where the rulers of La Venta performed the ritual that publicly validated their rule. Almost certainly, the specific location for these performances was the platform that supported the La Venta pyramid. Facing the main public space of the site, the Central Plaza, the platform was augmented with altar/thrones and with stelae that identified the towering pyramid as the First True Mountain. This south-facing platform, with its ideological monuments, seems a perfect site for the public reenactment of creation events. The fact that the rulers of La Venta wore the Jester God headdress indicates that they identified themselves with First Father, the Maize Lord. Thus adorned, it is likely that they appeared to their people in the costume of the maize god as they reenacted the events of creation on the south-facing platform below the pyramid.

Second, Complex A, located immediately behind and to the north of the pyramid/mountain, provided both a mortuary site and a locus of ancestral power for La Venta's rulers. Just as the sky could not be raised or the North House established without the act of First Father's rebirth, the rebirth of the occupant in the Olmec Dragon sarcophagus and the other elite occupants of graves within Complex A are also linked to originary time and ancestral power. At La Venta, Olmec rulers designed an architectural and iconographic mythic environment that provided the cosmic validation for their elevated social status and political authority, establishing a basic pattern that was modified by later Classic Maya polities.

Notes

1. Scholars of the Mesoamerican past continue to debate the temporal and cultural primacy of the Gulf Coast Olmec within the Preclassic period. Within these debates, different researchers often use the term *Olmec* in different ways. Moreover, the definition of Olmec culture and art style has changed through time as new artifacts from a limited number of archaeological excavations and art objects from unprovenienced collections have been added to the corpus. Additional ambiguity has resulted from the various emphases, biases, and viewpoints of the scholars involved in study of the Preclassic period (Coe 1965; Flannery 1968; Grove 1989; Reilly 1995). However, in the most commonly applied definition, Olmec refers both to an archaeological culture centered in a Mexican Gulf Coast heartland whose principal sites include La Venta in Tabasco, and San Lorenzo, Laguna de los Cerros, and Tres Zapotes in Veracruz, as well as to an early, geographically dispersed Mesoamerican art style that shares stylistic and iconographic features with stone monuments created by the Gulf Coast Olmec culture. Scholarly discussion centers particularly on whether and to what extent the Gulf Coast centers can be considered the principal place of origin for the Olmec art style and iconographic system, or whether the widespread dissemination of a shared Preclassic art style and symbol set represents more reciprocal exchange of ideologically significant valuables and associated symbols among various regional elites whose cultures were undergoing parallel paths of sociopolitical evolution.

2. Philip Drucker (1981) provides a thoughtful discussion of the nature of sociopolitical leadership at Olmec heartland sites. Various scholars have noted that the authority of Olmec leaders must have depended heavily on religious sanction and their participation in important rituals, as evidenced by the emphasis on sacred architectural spaces and frequent emphasis on cosmological/religious themes and specific iconographic motifs in Olmec art. Important relationships between Olmec rulers and various shamanistic beliefs and practices (e.g., human–animal transformation, ability to traverse different cosmic realms, etc.) have been pointed out by several investigators (Furst 1968; Reilly 1995).

The identification of the Stirling Acropolis as an elite residential compound is hypothetical and based on limited supporting archaeological evidence. This evidence includes the fact that the Stirling Acropolis is the largest single mound structure at La Venta, it is the location of many sculptural fragments, and it was the location of a hydraulic drain system constructed of carved basalt segments (Heizer et al. 1968). Recent excavations atop the acropolis at the Early Preclassic site of San Lorenzo have uncovered a palatial residence—the Red Palace—which was almost certainly the residence of the elite lineage at this site (Cyphers Guillén 1994). Just as on the Stirling Acropolis, the Red Palace has a complex hydraulic system constructed of basalt segments, as well as a monument workshop located within its precincts (Cyphers Guillén 1994). This monument workshop consisted of numerous sculptural fragments which were being reworked into new monuments. Current archaeological evidence suggests that a palatial residence similar to that at San Lorenzo will be uncovered by future excavations on the Stirling Acropolis.

3. The "double step," or "double merlon," as it is more commonly called, was used widely within the Olmec symbol system (Benson 1971: 16 n. 2). The double merlon appears as a motif embedded in the leafy section of the bundles of sprouts held by both human rulers and supernatural zoomorphs. It was shown surrounded by circles, contained within triangles, and was one of the motifs carved on the ground lines of tabletop altars. Most importantly, it was frequently incised across the mouth of zoomorphic supernaturals. These renderings of the double merlon demonstrate that this motif should be placed in the symbol set that includes the open mouth of the earth-crocodilian, the U and inverted U elements, and the cleft element, all of which function as symbolic entrances to the underworld/Otherworld in Olmec iconography. The cleft element also functions as a crack in the earth, an identification supported by the many depictions of vegetation sprouting from the cleft element. Although functioning similarly in Olmec iconography, the double merlon is actually a cross-sectional depiction of an enclosed court, and thus is a reference to the cleft earth opening as it is embodied in artificial architectural space. The enclosed courts of La Venta, Tabasco, Chalcatzingo, Morelos, and Teopantecuanitlán, Guerrero, all have the double merlon motif incorporated into their overall design (Reilly 1991).

4. In Olmec, as well as in other Mesoamerican art styles and iconographic systems, renderings of cosmic models could be vertical as well as horizontal. Horizontal depictions usually contained a central element that corresponded to an *axis mundi*. This *axis mundi* could take the form of a tree, maize vegetation, an up-ended saurian whose upper body branched into vegetation, or more simply, a bar or staff. Surrounding this central element were four symbolic elements. Within the cosmic model these four elements corresponded to intercardinal directions (Reilly 1994a, 1994b; Schele and Freidel 1990: 64–95). The bar and four dots and four dots/double merlon motif on La Venta's mosaic masks certainly appears to function as just such a horizontal cosmic model. In a manner similar to the association between the Olmec Dragon and the bar and four dots symbol, the Classic Maya associated one of their manifestations of the earth, a cosmic turtle, with the *k'an* cross to indicate that it formed the centerpoint (or fifth direction) of a quadripartite spatial system.

5. The most widely accepted explanation for the function of the Olmec colossal heads is that they are the "portraits" of Olmec rulers. This interpretation rests on the fact that no two heads have identical physical features (Grove 1981: 65) and on the variable nature of the badges displayed in the caps or headgear worn by these heads. These badges appear to be insignia which specifically identify or "name" the individuals who wore them (Coe 1977; Grove 1981).

6. Although the relatively standardized features of these figures and their lack of costume precludes exact identification, their placement in an assembly with a probable headman or "speaker" recalls the council of gods associated with the creation date on the Vase of the Seven Gods (Freidel et al. 1993: 67–69, figure 2.6).

2

The Architecture of the Teuchitlán Tradition of Mexico's Occidente

Philip C. Weigand

The recently discovered architectural tradition from the Formative and Classic periods of western Mexico is unique within the repertoire of Mesoamerica and, indeed, the world. Organized on the concept of concentric circles, the monumental buildings from the highland zones of Jalisco and Nayarit are impressive. In nonmonumental forms, this distinctive architectural style has been found in a much broader geographical area, which includes lowland Nayarit, Colima, Guanajuato, parts of Zacatecas, and also possibly southern Sinaloa (figure 2.1). Although exceptional in Mesoamerica, hundreds of these buildings exist in the Occidente, and around 100 have been surveyed in detail and mapped. The cultures that have this distinguishing style of architecture have been called the Teuchitlán Tradition, named after the precinct in Jalisco where some of the best preserved and most monumental structures are located.

In normative archaeological thought, western Mexico has not been considered as part of Mesoamerica until the civilizing influences from central Mexico arrived during the Epiclassic or Postclassic. Civilization thus was thought to be late and largely derivative. Except as dogma, these prejudgments and suppositions are now difficult to maintain in light of recent field work. This research has demonstrated beyond a doubt the existence of complex, highly organized societies in the Occidente which date from the Formative and Classic periods (Oliveros 1974, 1989; Weigand 1977, 1985a, 1992a; Soto de Arechavaleta 1982; Galván 1984; Michelet 1989; Boehm and Weigand 1992; Carot 1992; for an instructive parallel from another New World area, see Roosevelt 1991). To deny the place of the Occidente as another hearth (among many) of the overall Mesoamerican civilization raises more questions than it solves. However, it is not the purpose of this study to review the evidences for complexity in the Occidente, but rather to examine the possible cultural meanings of the high architectural tradition from the area. I will not examine in detail

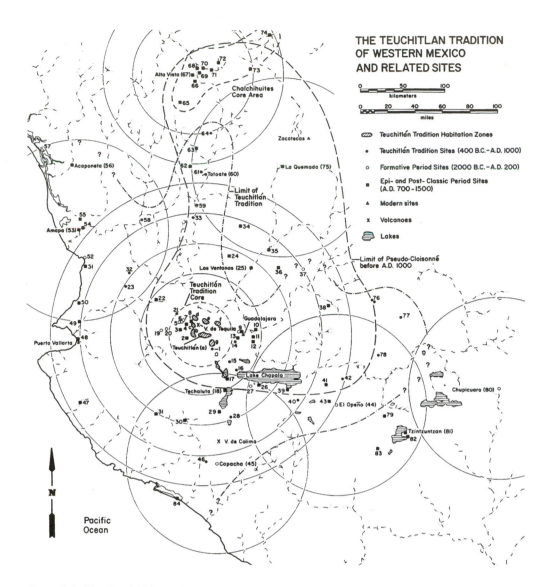

Figure 2.1. The Teuchitlán Tradition of West Mexico and related sites: a, Teuchitlan/El Refugio; b, Ahualulco; c, La Providencia; d, Huitzilapa; e, Las Pilas; f, Santa Quiteria; g, San Juan de los Arcos (a–g refer to Teuchitlán tradition core area habitation zones); 1, Santa Maria de la Navajas; 2, Santa Cruz de Barcenas; 3, Etzatlan; 4, Las Cuevas; 5, El Arenal; 6, Santa Rosalia; 7, San Pedro; 8, La Joya; 9, Tabachines/El Grillo; 10, Matatlan; 11, Coyula; 12, Tonala; 13, Ixtepete; 14, Bugambilias; 15, El Molino; 16, Jocotepec; 17, Zacoalco; 18, Techaluta; 19, Pipiole; 20, San Felipe; 21, Llano Grande; 22, Ixtlan del Rio; 23, San Pedro Lagunillas; 24, Teul; 25, Juchipila/Las Ventanas; 26, Tizapan; 27, Citala; 28, Gomez Farias; 29, Sayula; 30, Tuxcacuezco; 31, Autlan; 32, Santa Maria del Oro; 33, Cerro Cototlan; 34, Tlaltenango; 35, Jalpa; 36, Nochistlan; 37, Teocaltiche; 38, San Miguel el Alto; 39, Cojumatlan; 40, Jiquilpan; 41, Ixtlan/El Salitre; 42, Ecuandureo; 43, Jacona; 44, El Openo; 45, Capacha; 46, Comala; 47, Tomatlan; 48, Ixtapa; 49, San Juan de Abajto; 50, La Penita; 51, Santa Cruz; 52, Matanchen; 53, Amapa; 54, Ixcuintla; 55, Coamiles; 56, Acaponeta; 57, El Calon; 58, Guaynamota; 59, Las Juntas; 60, Totoate; 61, Cerro Prieto; 62, Tenzompan; 63, Huejugilla; 64, La Florida; 65, San Andres de Teul; 66, El Chapin; 67, Alta Vista; 68, Pedragoso; 69, Calichal; 70, Gualte-rio; 71, Moctezuma; 72, Cruz de la Boca; 73, Sain Alto; 74, Rio Grande; 75, La Quemada; 76, San Francisco del Rincon; 77, La Gloria; 78, El Cobre; 79, Zacapu; 80, Chupicuaro; 81, Tzintzuntzan; 82, Ihuatzio; 83, Tingambato; 84, Cuyutlan

the funerary architecture from this region, but instead stress the monumental surface architecture that dates from the Classic period.

The Setting

The highland lake districts of Jalisco and Nayarit are resource-rich areas. The region is well watered and has extremely fertile soils and an abundance of rare mineral resources. High-quality obsidian deposits (Spence, Weigand, and Soto de Arechavaleta 1980; Soto de Arechavaleta 1982; Weigand and Spence 1982), copper and quartz crystal outcrops (Weigand 1982), salt (Neal and Weigand 1990), and other minerals abound. This combination of strategic and rare resource wealth gave the area a natural endowment equal to or greater than the other early hearths of civilization within Mesoamerica. Resource deprivation does not account for the region's cultural trajectory. Indications of large scale mining activities and *chinampa* systems to maximize these resources appear early in the archaeological sequence.

The first indications of sociocultural complexity occur during the Early Formative, or El Opeño phase (ca. 1500–1000 B.C.; see table 2.1 for a regional chronology). Richly furnished shaft-tomb cemeteries have been found in Michoacán (Oliveros 1974, 1989) and in three localities in Jalisco. No surface architecture from this general time period has yet been identified from the highlands. In the lowlands, however, there is an exception. The El Calón site, located in southernmost Sinaloa, on the edges of the Marismas Nacionales, has a an 80 meter by 100 meter pyramid, which is 25 meters high (Scott 1985, 1992). This structure's many carbon-14 dates consistently fall within the early Formative period. Along with Poverty Point in Louisiana, this may be one of the earliest monumental building complexes yet documented for the North American continent. Although both the tombs of the El Opeño variety and the El Calón pyramid are indicative of complex cultures, little is known about their broader cultural contexts.

With the Middle Formative, or San Felipe phase (ca. 1000–300 B.C.), surface architecture becomes more common. Circular or oval platforms

Table 2.1. Chronology of the Teuchitlán Tradition and Region

Date	Phase Name
1500–1000 B.C.	El Opeño (Early Formative)
1000–300 B.C.	San Felipe (Middle Formative)
300 B.C.–A.D. 200	El Arenal (Late Formative)
A.D. 200–400	Ahualulco (Early Classic)
A.D. 400–700	Teuchitlán I (Middle Classic)
A.D. 700–900/1000	Teuchitlán II (Epiclassic)
A.D. 900/1000–1250	Santa Crúz de Bárcenas (Early Postclassic)
A.D. 1250–1500	Etzatlán (Late Postclassic)

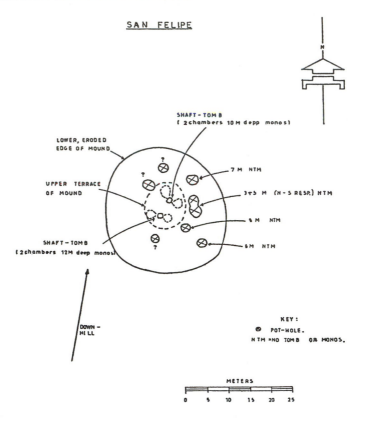

Figure 2.2.
The Middle Formative Burial Platform at San Felipe, Jalisco.

characterize the complex cemeteries from about a dozen sites in the lake districts of Jalisco. These platforms average 28–30 meters in diameter (though one is 40 meters) and 2 meters high. Each platform has a least two deep shaft-tombs, and many simple pit graves (figure 2.2). These platforms are evenly spaced along the upper shores of the lakes, and, aside from being focal points for community mortuary ceremonialism, were centers for small, seminucleated settlements. Due to heavy looting and agricultural damage, none of these centers is well preserved.

By Late Formative, or the El Arenal phase (ca. 300 B.C.–A.D. 200), apparently using the burial platforms as the nucleus, more ambitious circular ceremonial buildings were constructed. These buildings were reproduced in the architectural figurine art that characterizes this time period. The best illustrations of these complicated architectural figurines, illustrating patios, altars, and platforms, are found in von Winning (von Winning and Stendahl 1968; von Winning and Hammer 1972). These architectural figurines present detailed vignettes of life in ancient western Mexico. Their accuracy and reliabilty are demonstrated from field studies and mapping. For example, compare figure 2.3 in this chapter (a map of an El Arenal phase structure located at La Noria) with figure 16 in von Winning and Hammer (1972: 24) and plates 143 and 144 in von Winning and Stendahl (1968). At first glance, these small architectural groups appear to have a cruciform plan (with four platforms facing a circular altar), but many have indications of circular banquettes. Thus they are the forerunners of the more complex circular compounds that also date to this phase.

During the El Arenal phase, the circular compounds gradually became more complex. By the end of that phase, eight platforms commonly surrounded the patio. The five-element circles, described below (cf. Weigand 1985a, 1992b, 1993), became common, though they did not attain monumental proportions until the Early Classic, or Ahualulco phase (ca. A.D. 200–400). By this later phase, and the Middle Classic, or Teuchitlán I phase (ca. A.D. 400–700), the circular compounds are arranged in a hierarchy representing complexity at both the community and zonal settlement pattern levels. A rapid increase in population occurred during the Early Classic period, which augmented an apparent large natural increase indicated by huge habitation zones which had materialized by A.D. 400. The largest of these is located in an arc that extends from Ahualulco through Teuchitlán to San Juan de los Arcos (Jalisco). Aside from dozens of ceremonial precincts, many of them of monumental scale, there are the poorly preserved remains of more than 2,000 habitation compounds. Whether or not the Teuchitlán area was an actual city, the processes of urbanization certainly seemed firmly underway. This habitation zone had well over 20,000 inhabitants by A.D. 500, with a demographic concentration of 600–800 per square kilometer in the densest zones. In addition, there are about 30 square kilometers of proven *chinampas* in the swamp-

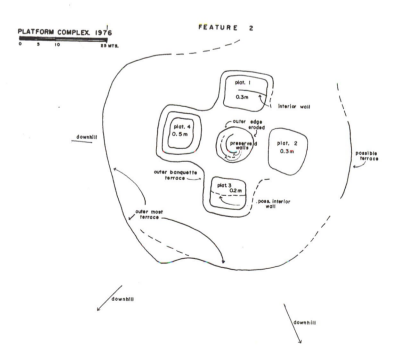

Figure 2.3.
The Late Formative
La Noria Compound,
near Teuchitlán.

lands that adjoin the denser areas of habitation, along with hundreds of square kilometers of open terraced fields (Weigand n.d.). Aside from a hierarchy represented with ceremonial precincts and their ballcourts, a hierarchy is evident with obsidian workshops as well (Soto de Arechavaleta 1982). Craft specialization is best represented by three artifact classes: obsidian blades and eccentrics, the codical-style pseudocloisonné ceramics (referred to below), and shell work.

Around A.D. 700–900 this tradition collapsed. The circles were abandoned, and square/rectangular ceremonial and administrative complexes were constructed in new localities. The new architectural influences are, without doubt, from the Bajio and the northern sections of central Mexico. The collapse was undoubtedly related to the pan-Mesoamerican sociocultural changes that occurred during the Epiclassic and Early Postclassic, and should be studied further from that perspective (Weigand 1992a).

The Grammar of the Five-Element Architectural Circles

A distinction can be made between the five-element circles that show "formal" characteristics, and those that seem to be "vernacular" (cf. Moholy-Nagy 1957; Rudofsky 1964; Stiny 1976; Chippindale 1986; Tzonis and Lefaivre 1987; Wells 1987). I have chosen this terminology, based in architectural studies from the Italian Renaissance, such as those of Alberti (1986) and Palladio (1965; see also Ackerman 1984), rather than using the public–domestic dichotomy that is more common in archaeology. I argue that, while formal architecture has a tendency to be public, the later term obscures important social criteria used in design for these structures. Classic period design is of primary interest in this study.

Formal design embodies working from abstract architectural conceptions that are then replicated rather consistently for a series of buildings located in different places. Although there are certainly differences between them, they nonetheless share the very basic features that allow them to be called a class. The organizational principles, or grammars, within formal architectural classes are *explicit* and imply a deliberate design process, though clearly derived from earlier, and hence vernacular, prototypes. Vernacular design, in contrast, displays more variability within the grammar, which is *implicit*, and the process of design is inseparable from the process of construction. In the Occidente, this distinction can be related to the hierarchies of precincts that we have documented both between habitation zones and within them. It applies to the circular buildings, as well as to the ballcourts and cemeteries.

As can be seen from figures 2.4 and 2.5, the monumental circular buildings of the Teuchitlán Tradition show a high degree of symmetry and proportionality in plan and appear to represent formal layouts. Smaller circles often have the symmetry but not the proportionality of

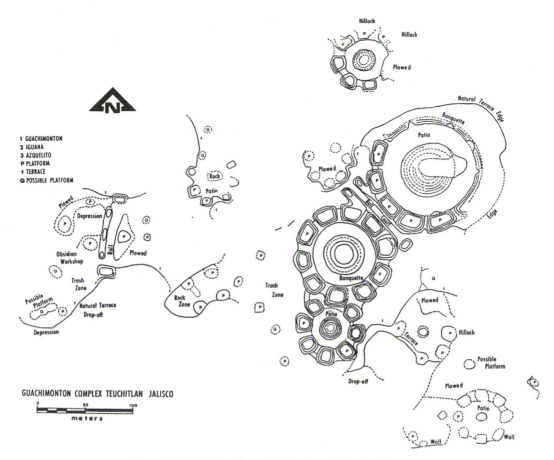

Figure 2.4. The Guachimontón Precinct at Teuchitlán, Jalisco.

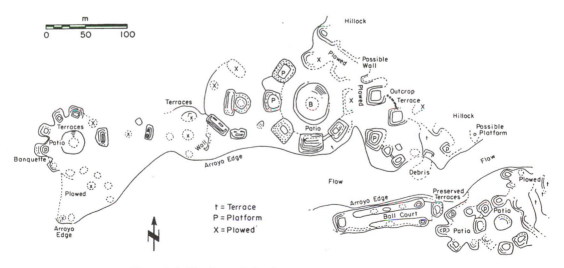

Figure 2.5. The Santa Quitería Precinct, near Arenal, Jalisco.

their greater neighbors, and hence are much more likely to represent vernacular design. The five diagnostic features, seen in an idealized profile (figure 2.6) and schematic plan (figures 2.7 and 2.8), are: (1) a terraced, truncated, conical pyramid with an occasional semisubterranean room on the top and/or the foundation courses for a circular building. There are indications of stairways into the surrounding circular patio. Most have earthen fills, consolidated by interior stone bracing walls. They were stone faced, plastered, and painted red and white. Some of the largest, such as the Guachimontón pyramid at the Guachimontón complex (figure 2.4), were constructed from stone set into adobe and caliche mortar, and hence are masonry structures; (2) Surrounding the truncated, conical pyramid is a circular, elevated patio, which is made from extremely clean, fine-grained tamped earth. Different patio floors, representing various construction levels, are visible in profiles. Most often, they are very compacted layers of the same floor fill and seldom have actually plastered surfaces; (3) Surrounding the circular patio is a circular and terraced banquette/platform, which completes the arrangement of three concentric circles (see figures 2.4–2.7). The banquette/platform top surface is always higher than the patio floor and can represent a formidable elevation when viewed from the exterior of the circle; (4) Atop the circular banquette/platform (element 3) are 8 to 12 rectangular platforms or small pyramids. These are terraced with stairways into the patio. The platforms or small pyramids served as bases for wattle and daub superstructures, which had high, gabled roofs and often multiple rooms (see the ceramic figurine house models in von Winning and Stendahl 1968; von Winning and Hammer 1972; Kan, Meighan, and Nicholson 1989). Field finds of burnt daub confirm construction details visible in these house models, including the existence of paint on the mud-plastered thatch roofs. Tule, otate, various types of grasses, oak, and pine served as the organic construction materials; (5) Beneath some of these platforms or small pyramids are reusable family crypts, with modest shafts and at least one side chamber for the burials and offerings. These shaft tombs decreased in architectural complexity as the Classic period progressed, though most continued to be richly furnished and occasionally painted with murals.

Each circular structure is a single construction, with its concentric elements laid out as a unit. These elements do not exist in isolation but are attributes of an integrated architectural entity. The truncated, conical pyramids, for example, are part of the overall concentric circular structure. In addition, many circles are linked in still larger arrangements that were also laid out during a single building project. For example, the three largest circles of the Guachimontón precinct (figure 2.4), plus the attached ballcourt, were apparently laid out as a single construction. This building precinct grew to incorporate two other circles (one to the north and the other at the western edge of the ballcourt). Upon completion, the combined group measured about 400 meters by 200 meters.

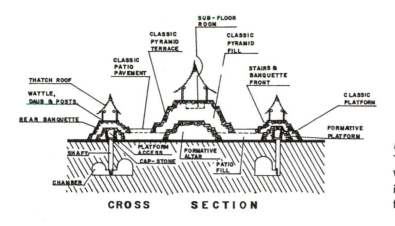

Figure 2.6.
Teuchitlan Tradition, Western Mexico. Idealized profile through a five-element circle.

Many of these structures are monumental, as mentioned. Although these circular precincts are not of enormous volume, they do represent a major investment in physical labor. However, sheer volume is not the sole criterion of monumentality. The amount of skill invested in formal design and its translation into construction has to be considered along with volume. The complexity of design is an intrinsic corollary of monumentality.

In direct association with most of these circles are open-ended, I-shaped ballcourts and rectangular compounds of platforms and patios. The ballcourts come in four sizes and closely follow the same hierarchy that the tomb types and circles do (Weigand 1991). The rectangular

TEUCHITLAN TRADITION GEOMETRY
The layout of the platforms atop the banquette: the hidden geometry

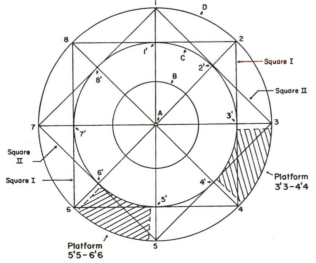

Figure 2.7.
Teuchitlán Tradition architectural geometry. Both Squares I (2–4–6–8) and II (1–3–5–7) are tangents to Circle C and secants to Circle D, with the tangents touching at 1'–3'–5'–7' and 2'–4'–6'–8', respectively.

TEUCHITLAN TRADITION GEOMETRY

The layout of the three concentric circles: the obvious geometry

Proportionality: 4 measures for banquette and patio, each twice,
and 10 measures for the central pyramid; or: 4:4:10:4:4 (1:1:2.5:1:1)

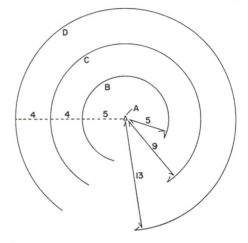

Figure 2.8. Teuchitlán Tradition architectural proportionality. Key: A = Radical center for 3 proportionally related concentric circles. B = Outer diameter of the central pyramid, and inner diameter of the elevated patio. C = Outer diameter of the elevated patio, and inner diameter of the banquette. D = Outer diameter of the banquette.

compounds appear to be elite residential features. Obsidian workshops and other specialized features adjoin the circles as well.

It must be stressed that the concentric circles (elements 1, 2, and 3) are organized as families of circles, each family being laid out from a radical center. Consistent formal rules apparently govern the proportions of the radii of the concentric elements, while still stricter rules concern the symmetrical placement of the platform/pyramids (element 4) on top of the circular banquette/platform (element 3). Concerning the former, in reading across the diameter of the entire building (see figures 2.6 and 2.8), the banquette is one module (no matter what the size of the actual feature may be), the patio is one module, the pyramid is 2.5 modules, the patio is another module, and the banquette is another module. In other words, the formula 1:1:2.5:1:1 was rather closely followed in the formal planning and design of the monumental buildings (figure 2.7). This formula often is not evident in the submonumental or small circles. In the cases where it does not fit the last phases of construction on monumental structures, profiles often reveal that rebuildings have crowded the patios to a point where the formula no longer is evident.

The geometry of both the formal or vernacular concentric circles is rather easy to observe and is immediately apparent to anyone viewing these buildings. The circles could have been laid out by two or three individuals using a rope or ropes with the appropriately measured distances marked. One individual could stand at the radical center and another could walk the circumference of each concentric element being laid out.

The planning techniques for the rectangular platform/pyramids (element 4) atop the banquette (element 3) are less obvious. This is due largely to the fact that this geometry (based on straight lines and squares/

rectangles) is partially obscured within the finished circular buildings. Two techniques may have been used for the symmetrical layout of the platforms atop the banquette (see figures 2.7 and 2.8): (1) The simplest technique requires that even measurements are made along the circumferences of Circles C and D, with each of these sets being aligned to the radical center (Point A). These even measurements are gauged to the number of platforms (8, 10, or 12, and, in one case, 16) that the circle is to contain. (2) A more complicated technique requires bisecting the 90° angles made from perpendicular lines drawn through the radical center (Point A) which extend to the outermost circumference of the building (Circle D). The bisected angles then allow one to draw another set of perpendicular lines, which thus, when their alternating end lines are connected (on the circumference of Circle D), form two overlapping sets of squares within the family of circles. Squares I and II (figure 2.7) then can be used to lay out the platforms with the requisite symmetry. Both Squares I (2-4-6-8) and II (1-3-5-7) of figure 2.7, are tangents of Circle C and secants to Circle D, with the tangents touching at 1'-3'-5'-7' and 2'-4'-6'-8', respectively. This degree of geometric correlation, coupled with the considerations given above, is unlikely to be coincidental, though it must be emphasized that most of these observations are made from unexcavated buildings. Only four circular compounds have been excavated, though many more have been tested.

Experimentally (using only ropes and sticks), neither method is more time consuming than the other, nor basically more or less accurate. Backsighting to check the accuracy in platform placement is easier with the second technique. Another major difference would be the level of decision-making required of the individual stationed at Point A, the radical center. The second technique requires much more from this individual than does the first. Large circles can be laid out in several hours using either method. The time required depends to a large degree upon the amount of backsighting performed. Our experiments, of course, did not consider the amount of ceremonial time involved in the layout of these precincts.

Regardless of which technique was used to lay out the platforms atop the banquettes, the end effect is one of balance and symmetry. These architectural layouts are unique in the Mesoamerican repertoire. This tradition was so unmistakably different from its neighbors as to offer highly visible boundaries for its distribution. In effect, it was an innovative architectural style of unusual aesthetic sophistication which served as a signature for a well-organized, hierarchical social system. The contrasts between this architectural style and that represented at Teotihuacan are reviewed in Weigand (1992b).

A Cultural Interpretation of the Architectural Circles

Whatever the ideological superstructure of the Teuchitlán Tradition, it was conveyed successfully over an extensive area and over a long time period. Without doubt, its best markers were the concentric circular architecture and the adjoining ballcourts. I have argued that the ballcourts served as the institution through which the political and economic hierarchy expressed itself, both between wards within the same settlement and between settlements within the nuclear area of this system (Weigand 1991). In a ranked hierarchy, the ritualized competition embodied within the ballgame could have served as the marker for political integration that facilitated the exchange of critically needed resources within the core zone. Disputes over irrigation rights, land, and other matters, could have been mediated through the ballgame as well.

It is important to note that the ballcourts, as monumental structures, closely parallel the hierarchy observable with the circular precincts. However, the ballcourts are not found in large numbers outside the nuclear area of the Teuchitlán Tradition. Within this area, approximately 55 ballcourts have been located, of which three, at Guachimontón, Ahualulco, and Santa Quitería, are truly monumental (more than 100 meters long and 25 meters wide). This pattern of distribution probably means that the ballcourts primarily served a purpose of political integration within the demographically dense core zone rather than between the core and its hinterlands, although that interpretation remains an alternate possibility. The circles found farthest from the nuclear area, for example at La Florida, Zacatecas (Jaramillo 1984) or El Cobre, Guanajuato (Sánchez and Marmolejo 1990), do not appear to have ballcourts. Thus, it seems likely that, in addition to the ballcourts, the themes of sociopolitical and economic integration for the participants within the Teuchitlán Tradition were expressed with another institution—the ceremonialism expressed by the circular compounds. This statement should not be taken to imply a conceptual separation between the ceremonialism of the ballcourts/games and the circles, as that was clearly not the case. However, while the circles do appear to be more widely distributed than the ballcourts, the ballgame per se probably had a still wider distribution in the Occidente.

The circles seem so specialized as buildings that only a few of the ethnographically and ethnohistorically known ceremonies might conceivably have been performed within them. If it is assumed that the form of ceremonial buildings is largely shaped by the rituals to be held within them, then the circular morphology of these buildings must reflect regional religious and/or cosmological concepts, and their ritualized enactments, in a more or less precise fashion. With the possible exception of Cuicuilco, circular ceremonial buildings in the rest of Mesoamerica were components of and were to be viewed contrastively in the context of more comprehensive rectangular/square plazas and platform arrangements. The circular structures from the Occidente, however, are fundamentally different in this respect. Square or rectangular buildings, when they exist at all, are located *outside* the main area of the precincts and were clearly minor elements within the ceremonialism featured in the circles and ballcourts.

The circles are inward-looking, focused upon activities within the patios and, most especially, on the central pyramid (element 1). The circles were not sealed, however. Patios were accessed by the walkways that exist between each of the platforms atop the banquette (except when blocked by a ballcourt or other ancillary building; see figure 2.4 for an example). Indeed, at the Guachimontón complex, a large amphitheater-type structure was constructed in the hillock to the northeast of the major circles. This possible amphitheater was steeply terraced. It still affords an excellent view into almost all of the patios of the precinct. In addition, we have noticed that words spoken in a normal tone of voice from the Guachimontón circle are audible in the amphitheater. It is possible that the terraced area northeast of the major circles was acoustically engineered to accommodate a larger audience than could fit comfortably in the circles. Whether or not the amphitheater actually existed, the great size of many circles, plus the large number of platforms surrounding the patios, meant that large numbers of observers and participants were desired. The outermost circumferences (Circle D in figure 2.7) of some of the largest circles are between 350 and 400 meters. One, the Guachimontón circle (figure 2.4), is greater than 400 meters in circumference. In addition, the earlier figurines, showing the circular compounds, display crowds of people. Thus, the great circular structures probably were designed for performance and viewing of public ceremonies.

Within Mesoamerica, circular architecture most frequently is thought to be associated with Quetzalcoatl and/or Ehécatl (see Pollock 1936; Marquina 1951; Nicholson 1971). If so, then the early and widespread distribution of complex architectural circles in the Occidente might argue for the presence of early variants of the symbol sets later identified as belonging to Quetzalcoatl/Ehécatl. To evaluate that proposition we need evidence in both architecture and iconography. In addition to the architectural figurines and the maps of the concentric circular structures, we have the codical style, pseudocloisonné ceramic vessels that date from the Teuchitlán I phase. In the rest of this section, I attempt to relate the architectural circles from the Occidente to the iconography that we have from the Teuchitlán area.

It has long been recognized that many of the architectural figurines from the Occidente show scenes associated with the *volador* ceremony (Bell 1971; von Winning and Hammer 1972; Kelley 1974). These figurines (e.g., von Winning and Stendahl 1968: plate 155; Bell 1971: figure 17-c; von Winning and Hammer 1972: plates 1, 77–86; ; Kan, Meighan, and Nicholson 1989: figure 34) represent two types of ceremonies: those which feature only the pole, the *volador(es)*, and a number of participants and/or helpers (figure 2.9), and those that have all of the attributes of the first type, but which also have far more people and the circular architectural features (elements 1–4).

A figurine from the Denver Museum of Natural History collections (figure 2.9) clearly shows the actual *volador* and his accoutrements. Over 1,000 years and hundreds of kilometers separate the ceremonial circles and figurine *voladores* of the Occidente from the ethnohistorical materials from central Mexico, so it is important to note that we are not suggesting any direct ethnographic analogies. However, the circle/*volador* complex in the Occidente must certainly be among the prototypes and/or earlier variants of the ceremonialism documented so extensively elsewhere in Mesoamerica (Dalgrén de Jordan 1954; Kurath and Marti 1964; Kurath 1967). In the areas with extant *volador* ceremonialism, the *volador* is a bird-man, and, in earlier drawings, the birds are often shown (for example, see Kurath 1967: figure 3, taken from Clavigero 1807: figure 17). This symbolism is also evident in the figurines from the Occidente. At the American Museum of Natural History a figurine shows an arrangement of birds on a pole erected from the geometric center (Point A in figure 2.7) of a circular compound (von Winning and Hammer 1972: figure 49). This piece is undergoing further analysis by Christopher Couch (personal communication, 1985). Most *volador* figurines, however, show humans (clearly males), and these individuals usually have the following attributes: (1) elaborate, swept-back feathered headdresses, or conical hats; (2) little clothing, except for a loincloth, or penis shield, supported from a waistband; (3) red, white, and black body paint in bold designs; (4) ear and nose rings/plugs; (5) conch shells or fans held in the outstretched hands.

The makers of the figurines were attempting to portray motion, with the *voladores* swaying to one side, leaning backwards at precarious angles, or soaring forward with both arms extended. Most are shown on

Figure 2.9. Formative-period volador figurine from West Mexico (photograph courtesy of Department of Anthropology, Denver Museum of Natural History).

their stomachs. Some figurines show two poles, one slightly offset from the circle's center and at a lower, bent angle from the erect one, as if to show the process of flight over the patio (von Winning and Hammer 1972: plate 1, figure 79). These figurines are dynamic representations of pole-bound *voladores*, unmistakably associated with the conch shells, feathered headdress, conical hats, and circular compounds that characterize the Occidente.

Bird-men appear in a separate symbol set in the Occidente. The codical style, pseudocloisonné ceramics have been recognized as one of the Occidente's contributions to Mesoamerican art since Noguera's (1965) baseline study of Mesoamerican ceramics. These pseudocloisonné materials have been analyzed in detail more recently by Holien (1977) and by Weigand (1992b, 1992c). The earliest of the codical pseudocloisonné pieces date from the Teuchitlán I phase (ca. A.D. 400–700), though more geometrically designed pieces are still earlier. Many of the codical pieces have glyphs. About 50 of these have been identified. To qualify as a glyph, the motif must occur on multiple occasions, in highly patterned formats, and must be comparable to motifs identified as glyphs elsewhere in Mesoamerica. The most clear-cut cases involve numbers. Others are place designators, particularlized hand gestures, the tassel headdress insignia (see C. Millon 1988 for Teotihuacan), personal names, lineage or office names and titles, and so on. It seems clear that this is an early ideographic writing system, restricted largely to place names, numbers, lists of personages, and portrayals of deities. One list of personages, which may have been kings and/or priests at Teuchitlán, where the pseudocloisonné pieces were discovered, consists of eight individuals. Several have personal names, as well as being identified by lineage or office.

A number of these pieces, mostly recovered from the Teuchitlán habitation zone, show remarkably uniform depictions of an apparent Ehécatl-like figure (keeping in mind the above qualifications concerning considerations of time and distance; figure 2.10). These individuals have many of the attributes usually associated with Ehécatl, including bent-over posture, long, pointed nose, wing and tail feathers, and bird's claws instead of feet. Figure 2.10 clearly portrays a bird-man. The conch shell beneath the wing feathers of the figure on the left is another attribute (and glyph) helping us identify the depiction as an Ehécatl and/or *volador*. The pseudocloisonné figure does not have the conical hat that is visible in some of the ceramic figurines. Instead, the headdress is a complex rendition of a fan and feathers. These feathered headdresses occur more frequently than the conical hats in the ceramic figurines.

The bird-man/sky/wind/*volador* symbol set apparently visible in the figurines and codical style pseudocloisonné ceramics is clearly related to the architectural circles. While the volador ceremonies portrayed with the ceramic figurines are fascinating enough, the poles do not seem to be much higher than 10 meters. Of course, this may represent an intrinsic limitation in ceramic modeling. Even so, using the monumental circles as

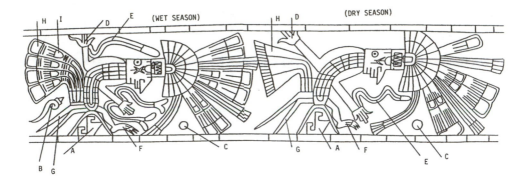

Figure 2.10.
The "Ehécatl"
Códice from
Teuchitlán,
Jalisco.

a guide for the scale of Classic period *volador* ceremonialism, the poles must have been considerably higher in order to assure that the fliers would clear the terraced sides and stairways of the central pyramid and land safely in the patios. With central pyramid elevations greater than 12 meters above the elevated patio floor and 50 meters in diameter, the poles must have been an additional 25 meters or more high to assure that landings would occur in the patios. This total elevation of the *voladores* some 35 to 40 meters above the patio surface must have made an impressive spectacle.

In addition to the *volador* ceremony proper, many ceramic figurines show circular dance forms. Ethnohistorical and ethnographic accounts of *volador* ceremonialism also mention an associated dance, the *cadena* (Kurath and Marti 1964). It is possible that circular dances around the patios of these great compounds accompanied the *volador* ceremonialism.

The presence of monumental, ceremonial buildings (which themselves are embedded in a regional hierarchy of sites and habitation zones) argues against the interpretation that features shamanism as the basic organizing principle for the Occidente's religious practices during the late Formative and Classic periods (e.g., Furst 1973). Certainly, shamanism coexisted with more formalized religious practices, as it still does today. However, the architectural tradition described in this study supports the existence of a pantheon of gods, with a priestly group performing recurrent rituals in their honor in formal circular complexes.

Conclusions

There is much that is still uncertain about the proposed interpretation. Nonetheless, I have attempted to explain some aspects of sociopolitical organization and cultural practices that might have played a role in determining the form of these monumental circular buildings. The discussion of the "grammar" of their formal design is probably better grounded than the interpretation of specific religious symbolism. A major point has been to distinguish between formal and vernacular design categories concerning the circular buildings from the Occidente. Two overall criteria seem basic in separating the formal from the vernacular: (1) how well the circles display the idealized modular proportionality across their diameters (see figures 2.6 and 2.8) and (2) how well the symmetrical placement of the platforms atop the banquette is achieved (see figure 2.7). Some buildings seem clearly formal, using monumentality as an additional criterion. Some late structures, for example those at Los Ceborucos, were laid out as huge circles but were never finished. Volumetrically, these compounds are small, but the grandiose scale of the concentric elements means that they are indeed monumental. Monumentality, as a concept, is used two ways in this study: as a purely quantitative measure of volume (i.e., the sheer mass of material brought to the construction site) and as a qualitative assessment of the aesthetic and engineering skill used in the arrangement of that mass into the complex shapes represented by the circles.

As archaeologists, we often forget Louis Kahn's observation that "architecture is the *thoughtful* making of space" (in Saslly 1962: 118; emphasis added). Both scale and proportional effects need to be considered together when discussing monumentality. When they are, the Classic period buildings of the Occidente seem all the more impressive.

The Occidente's experiment in architecture did not survive the collapse of the Teuchitlán Tradition during the Epiclassic period, except in the Bolaños valley of northernmost Jalisco. There, several highly modified circular structures lasted throughout the Postclassic, one of which is still in use by the Tepecanos of the *comunidad indígena* of San Lorenzo de Azqueltán (Weigand 1985b, 1992d; Cabrero 1989). Because circular buildings are extremely difficult to remodel for a tradition of square/rectangular ceremonial compounds, most of these ruined structures were left alone, except as quarries for building materials. The circular buildings, with their highly specialized ceremonialism, apparently were too specialized to survive the sociopolitical and cultural collapse that attended the Epiclassic period throughout Mesoamerica. This experiment in architecture was unique, without any close counterpart elsewhere in Mesoamerica.

Acknowledgments   The field research for this study was accomplished under permit from the Instituto Nacional de Antropología e Historia (INAH) de México. I thank Dr. Brigitte Boehm de Lameiras for the support that she has given this research in recent years. The field aid of Lic. Celia García de Weigand, Ing. Francisco Ron Siordia, Dr. Michael Spence, Dr. Ma. Dolores Soto de Arechavaleta, Ing. Jésus Lomelí, and many others is gratefully acknowledged. Dr. Thomas Holien, Dr. John Molloy, Dr. Christopher Chippindale, and Dr. J. Charles Kelley have been most helpful in conceptualizing the problems outlined in this research. My thanks also to Jodi Griffith of the Museum of Northern Arizona, who drafted many of the illustrations.

3

Early Architecture in the Valley of Oaxaca

1350 B.C.–A.D. 500

Joyce Marcus

In 1965, the *Handbook of Middle American Indians* presented a series of articles on what was then known about the archaeology and architecture of Oaxaca (Acosta 1965; Bernal 1965a, b; Caso 1965a, b, c; Caso and Bernal 1965). The articles were excellent, but Oaxaca prehistory at that time went back only to Period I of Monte Albán (ca. 500 B.C.). A long sequence of Formative cultures leading up to Monte Albán, each with its own distinctive architecture (Flannery and Marcus 1976a; Flannery and Marcus [eds.] 1983; Marcus and Flannery 1996) has since been revealed. In addition, we now know more about the urban layout of Monte Albán (Blanton 1978) and about settlement patterns in its hinterland (Kowalewski et al. 1989).

To understand the origins of Monte Albán's elite residential and public architecture, we must look to the sites that preceded it in the region. At San José Mogote, the largest site in the Valley of Oaxaca before Monte Albán, we can document a long evolution in wattle-and-daub, adobe, and stone masonry architecture that leads directly into the architectural forms and styles employed at Monte Albán (Acosta 1965; Bernal 1965b).

In this chapter we look first at the earliest wattle-and-daub residences and lime-plastered public buildings that emerged during the egalitarian village period, from 1350 to 1150 B.C. We will then look at the more impressive adobe residences and stone-masonry public buildings constructed between 1100 and 600 B.C., as Oaxaca society reached a chiefdom level of development. Finally, we will shift our attention to the palaces and standardized temples of the Zapotec state, at both Monte Albán and its secondary-level administrative centers (A.D. 150–500).

1350–1150 B.C.

By 1350 B.C. in the early villages of the Valley of Oaxaca, the most frequently encountered structure would have been the house. Most houses

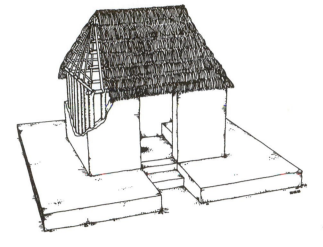

Figure 3.1. Artist's reconstruction of a typical public building of the Early Formative Tierras Largas phase in Oaxaca (1350–1150 B.C.). Oriented 8° west of true north, the structure consists of a small lime-plastered wattle-and-daub build-ing on a low platform of crushed bedrock, sand, clay, and lime (drawing by D. W. Reynolds).

were 3–4 meters wide and 5–6 meters long; their construction involved pine posts, wattle-and-daub walls, a thatched roof, and a clay floor with a surface of sand. The door was usually on one of the long sides, and it sometimes had a stone threshold; other stones could appear in the foundations of the wattle-and-daub walls. Sometimes silica exoskeletons of reed mats were found on house floors. No differences in social rank can be detected in the houses of this period.

During this early period, the Tierras Largas phase, it appears that only the largest communities in the Valley of Oaxaca had public buildings (Drennan 1983; Marcus 1989). As early as 1350 B.C., villagers at San José Mogote were building small public buildings atop crushed bedrock foundations (figure 3.1). These early public buildings differed from ordinary residences in at least seven ways. First, they were oriented roughly 8° west of true north, an orientation shared by later public buildings in Oaxaca and other regions, but not by ordinary houses.

Second, a public building contained two to three times as many posts as an ordinary house, and those posts were set within the wattle-and-daub walls. The walls themselves were weight-bearing, in contrast to some ordinary houses whose wattle-and-daub walls were set just outside the weight-bearing posts that supported the roof.

Third, the walls of public buildings were given a coating of white lime plaster (stucco) inside and out. The floor was surfaced with lime plaster, in contrast to the floors of ordinary houses, which were of stamped clay with a layer of sand. Fourth, several early public buildings had a lime-plastered storage pit built into the center of the floor, a feature not encountered in ordinary residences. Those pits were filled with powdered lime, perhaps stored for later use with some ritual plant such as tobacco or *Datura* (Flannery and Marcus 1976b; Marcus 1989).

Fifth, these early public buildings were set on rectangular platforms up to 40 centimeters high, also coated with lime plaster. The fill of the platforms contained stones, crushed volcanic tuff bedrock, sand, earth, and lime. A sixth feature of these buildings is the fact that the floor of the building was not flush with the top of the platform. Rather, the floors were recessed between 20 and 40 centimeters into the platforms. (In the case of a floor recessed 40 centimeters into a 40-centimeter platform, the floor would actually be level with the base of the platform; thus, it would be more accurate to say that the building was "surrounded" by a platform rather than "set on" a platform.) The floors of such buildings had a low step just inside the door, allowing a person to enter by stepping down from the threshold.

A seventh feature was the steps just outside the door, allowing a person to reach the doorway by stepping up. Those external steps occurred within small stairways inset in the platform, similar to other early Oaxaca stairways. While we have fragments of such outdoor stairways, no complete examples were recovered. Significantly, no ordinary houses had such stairways.

1150–850 B.C.

Several houses of this period, the San José phase, were excavated from three different residential wards at San José Mogote. The data suggest that there were status differences, but these took the form of a continuum from relatively low status to relatively high status without a true division into social strata such as occurred in later periods. One of the simplest residences was House 13, a rectangular wattle-and-daub house approximately 4 by 6 meters, with a stamped clay floor surfaced with river sand and walls constructed of pine posts 10–15 centimeters in diameter.

An example of a higher-status household in the southernmost ward of San José Mogote consists of two structures designated Houses 16 and 17. House 17 was a whitewashed wattle-and-daub residence; its floor included a scatter of stone biface manufacturing debris as well as pots imported from other regions. Below House 17 was the burial of a middle-aged woman with fine jade earspools; an even larger similar jade earspool was found on the floor of House 16, a shed or lean-to possibly attached to House 17.

House 16 had served as a workshop to produce chert bifaces; it contained a small hearth and large fire pit (Feature 61) where the chert may have been heat treated. Other activities suggested by the floor remains were basketry making and pearl oyster ornament manufacture. Broken on the floor were excised white vessels depicting the were-jaguar or "Earth" (Marcus 1989). On the same floor were items probably associated with bloodletting (stingray spines) and other rituals (pottery masks). Additional evidence for ritual activity came from a cache of four complete figurines, found buried beneath the floor of House 16 (Flannery and Marcus 1976b; Marcus 1989: 181–184).

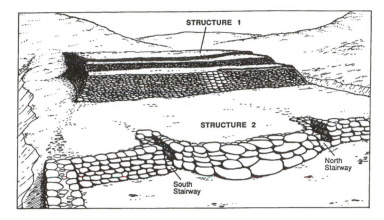

Figure 3.2. Structures 1 and 2 at San José Mogote as they might have looked at 900 B.C. Each structure was an earthen platform faced with dry-laid rough stones and boulders. Not shown are the wattle-and-daub buildings that once sat atop the platforms, but were almost obliterated by erosion after abandonment (drawing by D. W. Reynolds).

By this time period, Oaxaca society had developed hereditary inequality, and public buildings had become more monumental. "Bun-shaped" adobes (oval to circular in plan, and planoconvex in cross-section) made their first appearance toward the end of this period, as did drylaid stone masonry. Major sites began to place public buildings on large pyramidal platforms constructed of earthen fill, rising in several tiers, faced with stones, and accompanied by simple stairways. Structures 1 and 2 at San José Mogote are examples of this kind of architecture (figure 3.2). Each appeared to be the pyramidal platform for a public building. Both were contoured to a gentle slope coming down off the piedmont spur on which most of the later ceremonial architecture of San José Mogote was built. Each platform was different, a rough-and-ready structure adapted to the slope without much concern for bilateral symmetry or straightness of walls. It is likely that the public buildings atop the platforms were more carefully constructed and symmetrical, but they had been largely eroded away. All that remained were a few patches of hard-packed, almost burnished clay floor to indicate where the perishable buildings had been. Structure 2, the easternmost part of the complex, stands 1 meter high and may once have run the full 18 meter width (north–south) of the gentle slope. The structure's irregular eastern edge was faced with boulders, some of them local and some of them brought in from as far away as 5 kilometers. The facing included limestone brought from Rancho Matadamas and travertine brought from Fábrica San José (Drennan 1976); this evidence suggests that San José Mogote villagers traveled 5 kilometers or so to the west or east to procure some of the raw material to construct a public building. Two small carved stones, one depicting a feline and the other a raptorial bird, had fallen out of a nearby east–west wall (Marcus 1976a; Flannery and Marcus 1983a: figure 3.7).

The east face of Structure 2 contained the earliest stone stairways (figure 3.2). Each was so narrow (60–75 centimeters) that it could only have accommodated one person at a time. The north and south stairways were inset into the wall and consisted of three to seven stones serving as steps. Anyone ascending either stairway of Structure 2 would have reached a level platform surface with a clay-floored building on it.

Moving 9–11 meters west of the boulder-lined face of Structure 2, one reaches the base of the east wall of Structure 1 (figure 3.2). Structure 1 was a pyramidal platform faced with stones, originally at least 18 meters wide north–south, and running east–west for more than 9 meters until traces of it were lost. The lower stage of the platform had a lower tier 1.5 meters high and an upper tier 0.5 meters high. At a slightly later date, a final tier had been added; now badly destroyed, it may once have contributed another 0.5 meters to the height of Structure 1.

850–700 B.C.

The best preserved public building of this era was Structure 3 at Barrio del Rosario Huitzo, a 3-hectare village located 15 kilometers to the north of San José Mogote (figure 3.3). This platform was constructed at 850–700 B.C., and was approximately 1.3 meters high and 11 meters long east–west. The north–south width could not be determined because so much of the

Figure 3.3. Artist's reconstruction of Structure 3 at Barrio del Rosario Huitzo, a public building of Oaxaca's Middle Formative Guadalupe phase (850–700 B.C.). The structure consists of a wattle-and-daub building atop a platform of earthen fill retained by bun-shaped (planoconvex) adobes. Both the building and its platform were surfaced with puddled adobe, then with lime plaster (drawing by D. W. Reynolds).

platform had been removed by modern adobe makers. What remained was the northernmost 3.5 meters, which included a stairway 7.6 meters wide and surfaced with thick lime plaster. The entire platform was oriented 8° west of true north. Its basic plan had been executed with retaining walls of planoconvex adobes; then the areas between the walls had been filled with earth and covered with puddled adobe and lime plaster.

700–500 B.C.

During 700 to 500 B.C. San José Mogote emerged as a probable paramount chief's village with a population of 1000 people spread over 70 hectares. It served as the ceremonial center for perhaps 18–20 villages in the northern arm of the Valley of Oaxaca.

Elite residences of this era included Structure 25-26 at San José Mogote (Flannery and Marcus 1983b: figure 3.11). This was a multiroomed structure surrounding a central patio; the rooms had walls of rectangular adobes above a foundation of field stones. While some rooms were residential, others were used for storage; for example, Room 1 of Structure 26 continued for more than a meter below the floor of the building and contained five stored vessels including an incense burner. The room's cubic volume was perhaps three to four times as great as the bell-shaped pits that had been used for storage in earlier time periods (Flannery and Marcus [eds.] 1983).

While these residences were more elaborate than the wattle-and-daub houses used by lower status families, it seems clear that even the largest could have been built by the members of one family. Such residences needed no corvée labor, such as was required by the later palaces of Monte Albán (see below, in the discussion of Monte Albán archtitecture ca. A.D. 150–500).

Platforms for public buildings of this era, the Rosario phase, were built of rectangular adobes, multiton limestone blocks brought from the Matadamas quarries, and smaller travertine blocks brought from Fábrica San José, a 3-hectare village that was one of San José Mogote's satellite communities during this period (Drennan 1976). Such satellite villages presumably contributed to the construction of public buildings at San José Mogote because those structures served the whole region, not just the chiefly center, and because small communities had neither the manpower nor political power to build them (Marcus 1974).

A major construction of this era was Structure 19 at San José Mogote (figure 3.4). Its first stage of construction was Structure 19B, a rectangular drylaid stone masonry platform approximately 17 meters by 17 meters and oriented 8° west of north. On top of this stone-faced platform was Structure 28, a platform built of rectangular adobes and earthen fill with a whitewashed surface. Structure 28 supported a large wattle-and-daub public building with a ceramic offering under each corner.

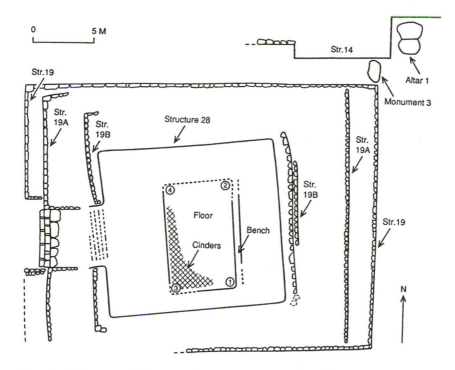

Figure 3.4. Plan view of Structure 28, a platform of earthen fill retained by rect-angular adobes and covered with lime plaster. Atop was a wattle-and-daub pub-lic building—perhaps a "temple" in the most general sense—that was ultimately burned by a fire so hot it turned the sand floor to cinders and silica slag. Under the four corners of the "temple" were offering vessels (numbered 1–4 in the drawing). Structure 28 sat on an earthen platform faced with half-ton limestone blocks brought from 5 kilometers away (Structure 19B); it was enlarged twice (Structures 19A,19). During the course of these Middle Formative Rosario phase enlargements (700–500 B.C.), the building orientation changed from 8° west of north (Structure 19B) to true north (Structure 19).

Later, the stone-faced platform (Structure 19B) was enlarged; this new platform (Structure 19A) measured 25.5 meters by 20 meters and was ori-ented true north rather than 8° west of north (figure 3.4). Its stone stair-way was on the west side (Flannery, Marcus, and Kowalewski 1981: fig-ure 3-22; Flannery and Marcus 1983b: figure 3.17a).

Still later, this same stone masonry platform was enlarged a second time, to 21.7 meters by 28.5 meters. In the construction of this final enlargement (Structure 19), huge stones were used, but the stairway from the previous stage (19A) was maintained. Two events of this period were the destruction by fire of the wattle-and-daub building atop Structure 28 and the carving of Monument 3. This stone monument depicts a sacrifi-cial victim, possibly a captive enemy, whose heart has been removed (Marcus 1976b, 1980). The co-occurrence of these events may indicate that this was a period of chiefly conflict, during which rival communities burned each other's "temples" and sacrificed prisoners taken in raids.

500–150 B.C.

San José Mogote was virtually abandoned ca. 500 B.C., at roughly the time that Monte Albán was being founded. Monte Albán's earliest architecture follows some of the traditions first developed at San José Mogote, but that architecture is deeply buried below later structures, which means that we have no complete plans for buildings of this era. For a look at the architecture of this period (called Monte Albán I), we must therefore look to Monte Negro, a site that lies more than 70 kilometers away in the mountains but had a pottery complex strongly influenced by early Monte Albán.

Like Monte Albán, Monte Negro is set atop a 400-meter mountain (Acosta n.d.). The entire site of Monte Negro is quite small; it would fit inside the Main Plaza of Monte Albán. Monte Negro's buildings were set on platforms, often composed of large stone blocks (Flannery 1983). Elite residences (figure 3.5) consist of open interior patios with a column in each corner, surrounded by three or four rooms. Columns supported the roof of each room. Walls were adobe or wattle-and-daub, set above a stone foundation two courses high. Courtyards were paved with stone, and there were drains below some of the buildings.

Public buildings, such as Temple X at Monte Negro (figure 3.6), often had a "plus-sign" shape. After ascending the steps of Temple X, one would have stood in the roofed portico and looked into a room whose four columns once supported a roof. In the back of the structure are two *tlecuiles* or offering basins. This type of one-room "temple" continues the tradition of the one-room public buildings constructed earlier at San José Mogote, but it differs in that it has columns to support the roof.

Another one-room temple of this era is known from Dainzú, a site in the eastern arm of the Valley of Oaxaca (figure 3.7). This small building,

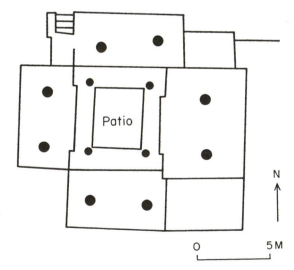

Figure 3.5. Elite residence at Monte Negro, Oaxaca, consisting of four rooms around a patio. Black circles are column bases. Probable date, 300–150 B.C. (redrawn from Acosta n.d.).

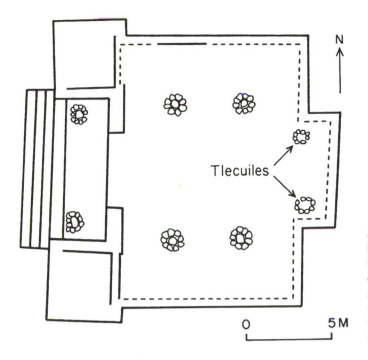

Tlecuiles

Figure 3.6. Temple X at Monte Negro, Oaxaca. Rubble columns are indicated by circular clusters of small stones. An area at the rear of the temple had two tlecuiles or offering basins (redrawn from Acosta n.d.).

0   5 M

Figure 3.7. The Yellow Temple at Dainzú, Oaxaca. This is an example of a small one-room shrine with a doorway framed by columns; the entire room is only about 3 meters by 1.5 meters. The walls and columns are of adobe encased in heavy stucco. Rather than a public temple for the whole site, this sanctuary might have been incorporated into a residential compound serving an elite family. The date is Transition Monte Albán I-II (200–150 B.C.)

called "The Yellow Temple" by Bernal and Oliveros (1988: 9) because its walls are painted with yellow ochre, is believed to date to the transition from Period I to Period II of Monte Albán (ca. 200–150 B.C.). It may be our earliest excavated example of a Zapotec temple with columns flanking the doorway.

The Yellow Temple of Dainzú, as well as the one-room temples known from Monte Negro, evidently precede the appearance of the standardized Zapotec two-room temple or *yohopee*.

150 B.C.–A.D. 150

The standardized Zapotec two-room temple seems to have appeared first during Monte Albán II (150 B.C.–A.D. 150), the period during which we believe a state level of political organization was achieved in Oaxaca (Marcus and Flannery 1994). The addition of a second room to the temple is significant in evolutionary terms because it may indicate that for the first time a staff of priests lived full-time in the inner room of the temple, while the outer room continued to serve as a slightly less restricted-access area to which the public could bring objects for sacrifice (Burgoa 1934a [1674]). Sixteenth-century Spanish documents suggest that full-time personnel ate and slept in the inner room of the temple, and were said to have "never left" (Espíndola 1580; Marcus 1978: 174,178–179; Marcus 1983b: 348–350). Nearly all Monte Albán II two-room temples face east or west, aligned to the axis of the rising and setting sun.

With the appearance of the Zapotec state during Period II, Monte Albán became a capital at the head of a four-tiered hierarchy of sites. Two-room temples with colonnaded doorways were present at the capital; at secondary centers like San José Mogote; and at tertiary centers like Tomaltepec (Marcus 1978; Flannery, Marcus, and Kowalewski 1981; Whalen 1981).

The layout of the city of Monte Albán underwent important change at this time, with the development of an overall plan for the center of the city. As part of this plan, architects leveled off an area approximately 300 meters north–south and 150 meters east–west to produce the Main Plaza roughly as we see it today, paving it with white plaster (figure 3.8). New types of buildings designed at this time—each standardized in plan and in dimensions, but differing in function—included two-room temples, stone masonry palaces, I-shaped ball courts, and other special-function structures such as arrowhead-shaped "secular" buildings (Acosta 1965: figures 10–11; Flannery and Marcus 1976a: figure 10.9). This diversity of standardized plans of functionally specific buildings is important evidence for documenting the diversification and segregation of specialized state personnel (Marcus and Flannery 1996).

As these architectural changes were made at the capital, Monte Albán was in a position to impose changes on its dependencies in the Valley of

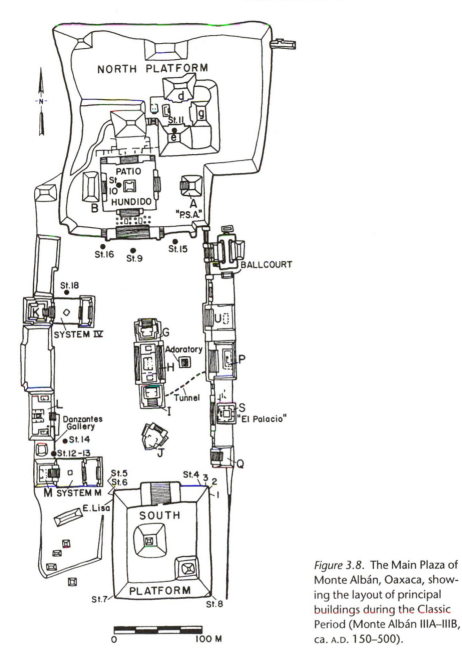

Figure 3.8. The Main Plaza of Monte Albán, Oaxaca, showing the layout of principal buildings during the Classic Period (Monte Albán IIIA–IIIB, ca. A.D. 150–500).

Oaxaca and beyond. For example, San José Mogote was reoccupied during Monte Albán II and redesigned as a secondary center with a Main Plaza laid out to replicate the one at Monte Albán. Like the North Platform at Monte Albán, the north side of the Main Plaza at San José Mogote supported administrative buildings; like the South Platform at Monte Albán, the south side of the Main Plaza at San José Mogote supported major temples. Within the Main Plaza at San José Mogote were a series of temples on elevated platforms and possible rock outcrops, analogous to Structures G, H, and I at Monte Albán (Acosta 1965). Finally, on the west side of the Main Plaza at San José Mogote was an I-shaped ball court like the one on the east side of the Main Plaza at Monte Albán. The dimensions of the two ball courts are nearly identical (Flannery and Marcus 1976a: 219, 1983c: 112–113). Thus, the specific layout of a Main Plaza, and a plan for segregating activities to be carried out there, seem to have been handed down from the capital to its secondary centers.

Some important details of Zapotec religion and ritual can be inferred from a sequence of stratigraphically superimposed temples at the south side of the Main Plaza at San José Mogote. Structure 36, the oldest in the sequence, dates early within Monte Albán II (figure 3.9). It measured 11 meters by 11 meters and was approximately T-shaped, with the inner room slightly smaller than the outer. All the supporting columns were tree trunks of bald cypress (*Taxodium* sp.), covered first with a layer of small stones and then with white stucco. Other details of Structure 36 included a niche in tle south wall of the outer room, in which priests may have stored incense burners or effigy vessels.

The floors of Structure 36 and the temple above it, Structure 35, were burned or stained gray with smoke or soot wherever incense burners had been allowed to sit for any length of time. The circular stains from this activity allowed us to see which areas had been favored locations for burning copal incense. Especially common were sooty circles in the centers of the inner and outer rooms, the back wall of the inner room, and the step separating the outer and inner rooms. The white-plastered interior walls of Structure 36 bore geometric designs in polychrome paint, like those seen on certain stuccoed ceramics of Monte Albán II (Caso, Bernal, and Acosta 1967: lám. III–IV).

Above the remains of Structures 36 and 35 lay Structure 13 (figure 3.10). This temple dated to relatively late in Monte Albán II, and was poorly preserved. It measured about 15 meters by 8 meters and was rectangular rather than T-shaped (Marcus 1978). Its columns—one to either side of the inner doorway, and two to either side of the outer doorway— were built of rubble with a core of larger stones. One of Structure 13's most distinctive features was a basin 75 centimeters in diameter and 22 centimeters deep, built into the floor near the southeast corner of the inner room. Unlike the *tlecuiles* seen in Temple X at Monte Negro (figure 3.6), there were no signs of burning in this basin. On the basis of ethnohistoric analogy, it may have served either to hold water for washing the artifacts of sacrifice or to receive blood from some type of sacrifice.

Most Zapotec temples we have excavated appear to have been swept periodically (with the debris dumped in extraordinarily large cylindrical or bottle-shaped trash pits in the talus slope behind them), but some artifacts were occasionally left behind in the smoky, windowless inner room. Artifacts left behind were usually of obsidian, such as bifacial daggers or sacrificial knives, lancets, and prismatic blades. While the

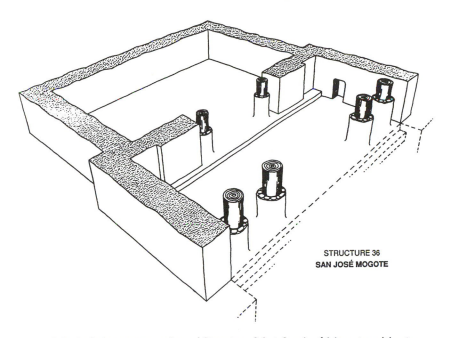

Figure 3.9. Artist's reconstruction of Structure 36 at San José Mogote, a Monte Albán II two-room temple. In this temple, built early in the phase (perhaps 150–100 B.C.), the columns to either side of the doorways were trunks of bald-cypress trees covered with small stones and stucco. The walls were of adobe over a stone foundation covered with white stucco and, in some cases, poly-chrome painting (drawing by D. W. Reynolds).

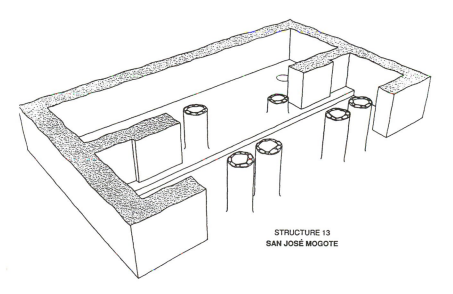

Figure 3.10. Artist's reconstruction of Structure 13 at San José Mogote, a Monte Albán II two-room temple. In this temple, built late in the phase (A.D. 100–150), the columns to either side of the doorways are of stone rubble covered with stucco. The walls were of adobe over a stone foundation, covered with white stucco (drawing by D. W. Reynolds).

lancets and prismatic blades are artifacts usually associated with ritual bloodletting by nobles and priests, the daggers are of the type shown in codex scenes of human sacrifice.

A.D. 150–500

Due to lack of preservation, we rarely have direct archaeological evidence of roof construction and roof decoration on Zapotec temples. However, stone and clay models of such temples are fairly abundant at major Valley of Oaxaca sites. Such models show that Zapotec temples had flat roofs (Acosta 1965: figure 25; Caso 1969: 39–40), and that the supernatural being, patron, or royal ancestor to whom the temple was dedicated might be depicted above the doorway or on the roof (Easby and Scott 1970: figure 165). Some temples show the head or bust of a figure above the doorway (Easby and Scott 1970: figure 165) or the sign for "sky" or "divine descent" on the roof (Caso and Bernal 1952: figure 502 bis). At least one temple model (figure 3.11) shows a feather curtain used to close off the doorway, providing privacy.

Elaborate palaces with larger inner patios also made their appearance during this era. A well-known example is Monte Albán's Building S, situated on the east side of the Main Plaza (figure 3.12). This palace measures about 25 meters on a side and includes 10 or 11 rooms surrounding its inner patio. Privacy was provided by a "curtain wall" inside the doorway. The L-shaped corner rooms are also typical features. Some of the small rooms appear to have been kitchens for cooking; others were bedrooms for sleeping.

Figure 3.11. Small stone model of a Classic Zapotec temple (probably A.D. 300–700). This model, found near Tlacolula, Oaxaca, shows a feather curtain drawn across the door for privacy (drawn by J. Klausmeyer from Caso 1969: figure 26c).

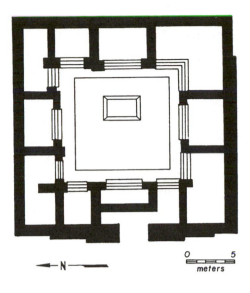

Figure 3.12. Building S on the Main Plaza at Monte Albán, an example of a Late Classic Zapotec stone masonry palace (perhaps A.D. 500–700). A "curtain wall" blocks the view of the interior for anyone passing the doorway. The lowest point in the palace is the floor of the central patio, which contains a rectangular adoratory. From the patio, steps ascend to each room of the palace; some were kitchens and others were sleeping rooms.

N

0   5
meters

Summary

The evolution of architecture in the Valley of Oaxaca reflects, at least indirectly, evolutionary changes in society. During the period when villages were small and society was egalitarian (1350–1150 B.C.), the most elaborate residence was a wattle-and-daub house. As chiefly societies emerged between 1150 and 850 B.C., houses began to display a continuum between simple mud-plastered thatched huts and well-made, whitewashed wattle-and-daub houses with ramadas or outbuildings. In the more elaborate chiefdoms of 700–500 B.C., elite families lived in adobe houses with interior courtyards, while ordinary families lived in wattle-and-daub houses.

As chiefdoms evolved to the threshold of the state, elite residences like those of Monte Negro (ca. 300–150 B.C.) had interior patios surrounded by four rooms; considerable use was made of columns both in the rooms themselves and in the patio. Finally, with the formation of the state between 150 B.C. and A.D. 150, we see the emergence of the true palace at cities like Monte Albán. Classic palaces (A.D. 300–500) were built of stone masonry by corvée labor and had 10–11 rooms arranged around an inner courtyard; privacy was ensured by a "curtain wall" that shielded the palace interior from view.

Public architecture underwent a similar evolution during that same sequence of periods. In the egalitarian villages of 1350–1150 B.C., public buildings were one-room affairs on small platforms, oriented 8° west of north and given a coating of lime plaster. We cannot argue that these small buildings were "temples" in the sense of later public buildings; rather, we suspect that they were analogous to the communal "men's houses" of ethnographically documented village societies.

As chiefly societies emerged, public buildings grew more and more elaborate, especially in regard to the platforms on which they were set. Those platforms were built of bun-shaped adobes by 900 B.C., rectanglar adobes by 700 B.C., and drylaid stone masonry between 900 and 700 B.C. Usually, however, the adobes or stones were used only for the outer walls and for a series of retaining walls that divided the interior of the platform into cells. These cells were then filled with basketloads of earth. Interestingly, the public buildings set atop them continued to be made of wattle-and-daub, either because of tradition or religious archaism. For reasons we do not know, the orientation of those buildings changed from 8° west of north to true north between 700 and 500 B.C.

We do not know exactly when the early, generic, one-room "public building" evolved into the standard two-room temple of the Classic Zapotec. The "temples" of Monte Negro are elaborate, with columns and stairways, but most still seem to be one-room structures. The Yellow Temple at Dainzú (200–150 B.C.) is a one-room temple of adobe, stone, and stucco with columns to either side of the doorway. Does it represent a stage in the evolution of the colonnaded two-room temple, or just a separate category of temple? More work is needed to answer this question.

The standard two-room temple with columns to either side of the inner and outer doorways appeared between 150 B.C. and A.D. 150, and remained the dominant type of Zapotec temple until the time of the Spanish conquest. Presumably the two-room plan evolved so that full-time priests could live in the temple. Monte Albán had dozens of such temples during the Classic period; San José Mogote, a secondary administrative center, had at least 10. Zapotec temples had variable ground plans, from rectangular to T-shaped, but shared many features: the inner room was always higher, had a narrower doorway, and was of more limited access. The temples usually faced east or west, the path of the sun.

It should be pointed out that the evolution of public buildings in Oaxeca did not occur in isolation. Many of the trends we see can be detected in other regions of Mesoamerica, such as the Maya area, suggesting an exchange of ideas between ethnic groups. The widespread trends include: (1) an increase in the size of public buildings and the volume of their platforms over time; (2) a decrease in their accessibility over time; (3) an increase in platform height, so that the structures resting on top were removed farther and farther from the ground surface on which commoners lived; (4) an increase in public messages—designed to be seen by commoners—conveyed in the iconography and sculpture displayed above the doorway or on the roof; (5) an increase in the number of private messages—restricted to elites who could enter those structures—such as the hieroglyphic messages painted on murals and carved on benches and lintels; (6) an increase in the human labor recruited for building public structures, which sometimes accompanied and paralleled growth in population, an increase in specialization, an increase in the number of levels of decision-making, and an increase in internal complexity; and

(7) a pattern whereby, once an area of the site had been "sanctified" for the construction of a temple, a sequence of several temples might be built one above another on that spot.

On a more general level, the evolution of public buildings in Oaxaca shows a long-standing interest in bilateral symmetry; an increase in the elevation of temples to decrease their accessibility and bring them closer to the clouds, lightning, and sky; an increase in privacy through the use of curtains in temples and the construction of curtain walls in palaces; and an increase in the number of temples in the main plaza at large sites, perhaps because each was used and maintained by a different segment of the population and/or dedicated to a specific royal ancestor or supernatural patron.

4

Natural Order, Social Order, Political Legitimacy, and the Sacred City

The Architecture of Teotihuacan

Jeff Karl Kowalski

Even in an age when monumental architectural projects have become commonplace, the site of Teotihuacan, dominated by the massive Pyramid of the Sun and Pyramid of the Moon and oriented along a central processional way known as the Street of the Dead, impresses viewers by the scale of its buildings and by the comprehensive order of its urban layout (figure 4.1). Archaeologists have extensively mapped and excavated significant portions of Teotihuacan, and a host of books and articles have described and interpreted the site since the beginning of the twentieth century.[1] Teotihuacan' s great size and complexity make it difficult to present a summary of the form and meaning of the site's architecture in a book of this length. Nevertheless, this chapter presents some critical aspects of our current knowledge of the cultural and religious motives and political history that determined the urban design and appearance of the principal ceremonial buildings of this ancient city. In addition, the recognized influence of Teotihuacan culture throughout Mesoamerica during the Early Classic period (ca. A.D. 300–550), accompanied by the appearance of its distinctive *talud-tablero* platform profiling at far-flung centers such as Kaminaljuyú in the Guatemalan highlands, Tikal in the Maya lowlands, or Matacapan in southern Veracruz, is outlined. The important archaistic revival of Teotihuacan *talud-tablero* forms by the Mexica-Aztecs is also discussed.

Location, Size, and Early History

Teotihuacan is located in a northeastern branch of the Basin of Mexico some 40 kilometers from the heart of Mexico City (Gamio 1922; R. Millon 1973). Unlike some of the other "lost cities" of the New World, Teotihuacan

Figure 4.1. General view of Teotihuacan, showing the Pyramid of the Moon at the northern termination of the Street of the Dead (lower center), the Pyramid of the Sun to the east of the ceremonial avenue (center left), and the Ciudadela south and east of the intersection of the Street of the Dead and the East and West Avenues (after Millon 1981: figure 7-1).

was never forgotten completely since the time of its abandonment, although even by the 1400s, when the powerful Mexica-Aztecs dominated the Valley of Mexico, the site's original name was lost and much of its history was shrouded in myth (Matos and López 1993). The name Teotihuacan, which means "the place of the gods,"[2] was supplied by the Mexica-Aztecs, who marveled at the size of the pyramids of the Sun and Moon and at the orderliness and length of the Miccaotli, or Street of the Dead, whose earth-covered boundary platforms they took to be the burial places of ancient kings (Sahagún 1950–1982, book 10, f. 142r–142v). The Mexica-Aztecs also considered Teotihuacan a hearth of civilization and a place of origin, where the gods sacrificed themselves to create the current "sun" or cosmic era.[3]

The scale of Teotihuacan's structures has always impressed visitors, but the full extent of the urban zone has been revealed only as a result of the Teotihuacan Mapping Project, which began in 1962 under the direction of René Millon. The mapping project used a combination of aerial photography and ground surveys to chart the boundaries of the city, document the density of its population, and examine the processes of its growth and decline (Millon 1970, 1973, 1981; Millon, Drewitt, and

Cowgill 1973) (figure 4.2). In addition, a series of excavations carried out by Mexican and North American archaeologists has shed light on the process of development at the site, from its beginnings before the time of Christ, its florescence during the period between A.D. 1 and 650, and its decline after A.D. 650–700 (Bernal 1963; Cabrera Castro, Rodríguez, and Morelos [eds.] 1982a, b; McClung de Tapia and Rattray [eds.] 1987).

The mapping project revealed that at its largest extent Teotihuacan spread over at least 22.5 square kilometers (8 square miles) of the San Juan River valley. Just southwest of the ancient city are year-round springs, which provided water for several thousand hectares of agricultural fields. At its height, from ca. A.D. 300 to 650, the population of the city rose to between 85,000 and 200,000 people (Millon, Drewitt, and Cowgill 1973; Millon 1981: 208), with 125,000 considered to be a reasonable estimate (Millon 1992: 344). Teotihuacan was a true preindustrial city, consisting of a central ceremonial district surrounded by some 2,000 densely clustered multiroom apartment living compounds (Millon 1993: 17). These residential quarters varied in size and quality. Although they tend to be relatively more sumptuous and palatial toward the heart of the city and graded into more shoddy construction and crowded arrangements on the outskirts, there is a mix of construction quality and apartment types throughout the site.

Teotihuacan's phenomenal growth began during the last centuries before Christ. Although the Teotihuacan valley was sparsely occupied during the Early Preclassic period (1200–900 B.C.) and was culturally marginal to great lakeside centers such as Tlatilco, by the Late Preclassic Teotihuacan had become one of two main regional centers in the Basin of Mexico. Teotihuacan was apparently already beginning to exploit the potential of the region as evidenced by salt production, use of the lake, and obsidian workshops (Millon, Drewitt, and Cowgill 1973; Sanders, Parsons, and Santley 1979; Porter Weaver 1981: 189). Teotihuacan's competitor in the southern basin was Cuicuilco (Sanders 1981: figure 6.13). Its massive circular pyramid attests to Cuicuilco's political and economic power during the period from about 500 to 200 B.C., but its career was cut short by the eruption of the Xitle volcano (in the Ajusco range at the southern rim of the basin), which left Teotihuacan the undisputed leader in the basin. It is likely that many of the inhabitants of Cuicuilco relocated to Teotihuacan (Sanders, Parsons, and Santley 1979; Evans and Berlo 1992: 7).

At about the time of Cuicuilco's demise, there was also a noticeable drop in population in Tlaxcala east of the Basin of Mexico. From 300 to 100 B.C. Tlaxcala had seen the construction of buildings using a variant of the slope-and-panel (*talud-tablero*) terracing later common at Teotihuacan, and great advances were made in agricultural technology for construction of terracing, irrigation canals, and dams. It has been suggested that many of the skilled workers of this area may have moved westward to Teotihuacan (Garcia Cook 1981; Porter Weaver 1981: 189).

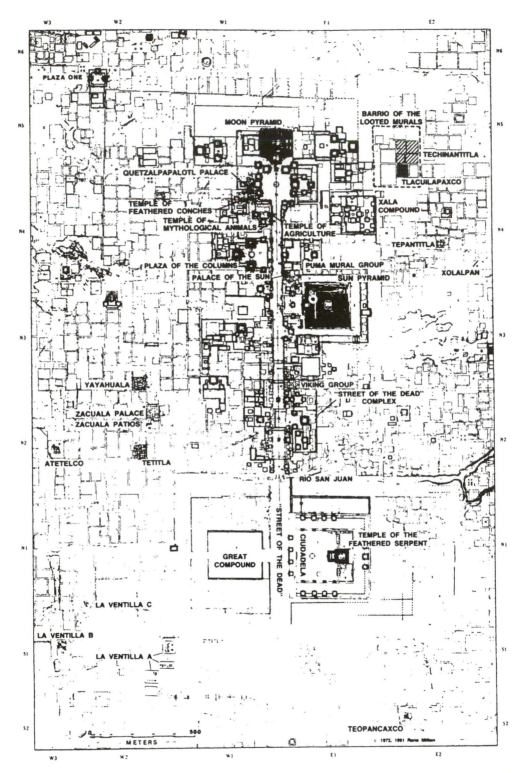

Figure 4.2. Map of the central section of Teotihuacan, showing the layout and orientation of the principal structures (after Millon 1993: figure 3).

Between 150 B.C. and A.D. 1, or what is known as the Patlachique phase, the stage was set for the tremendous growth of the city. During this time the settlement contained between 20,000 to 40,000 people and expanded to cover an area of more than 6 square kilometers, located in what would later be the northwest quadrant of the city (R. Millon 1973: 51; 1992: 351; Cowgill 1979: 55). It is likely that by this time one of the most important bases for the city's prosperity was being utilized; obsidian mining and production. A cluster of nine obsidian workshops has been discovered near the western boundary of the Patlachique phase settlement, and Millon (1981: 224) argues they had their origins during Patlachique times. The importance of obsidian is difficult for us to understand today, but we should remember that Mesoamericans used a stone-age technology. From specially prepared cores of this volcanic glass, skilled workers produced exceptionally sharp blades and points for local use and export. Indeed, Teotihuacan's control of major sources and distribution routes of obsidian has been cited as one of the reasons for the city's growth and the powerful influence it exerted elsewhere in Mesoamerica (Spence 1981, 1987; Santley 1983; but see Clark 1986 for a contrary view). Although economic specialization was probably beginning during the Patlachique phase, knowledge of architecture dating to this time is spotty. René Millon (1973: 51) suggests that a small structure found within the Pyramid of the Sun may date to this time, which could indicate that the location occupied by the Pyramid was already considered holy. It will take further excavations to determine if earlier phases of structures such as the Court of the Columns may be of Patlachique date (R. Millon 1973: 51).

Teotihuacan experienced remarkable growth during the Tzacualli phase, between about A.D. 1 and 150. During this time the city expanded enormously in area to extend over 8 square miles of the valley floor. Millon's (1973) early population estimate of 25,000–30,000 has been revised upward to the staggering level of 70,000–100,000 (Sanders, Parsons, and Santley 1979; Millon 1992: 351). It was also at this time that the great monumental building projects and comprehensive city planning were initiated. The northern stretch of the Street of the Dead, perhaps culminating at the inner Moon Pyramid, was certainly laid out at this time. In addition, many three-temple complexes were built lining both sides of this ceremonial concourse, and the bulk of the huge Pyramid of the Sun was constructed.

The next phase at Teotihuacan is known as Miccaotli and dates from ca. A.D. 150 to 200. During this time the city came to cover aproximately the area it would occupy for the subsequent 450 years. Although the total area covered continued to be about the same as during the Tzacualli phase (ca. 20 square kilometers) there was a shift to the south and east. More people continued to move to Teotihuacan, although it was during the subsequent Tlamimilolpa and Xolalpan phases (A.D. 200–650) that the population reached its greatest density. The Miccaotli phase witnessed

several new monumental architectural projects, including the penultimate phase of the Moon pyramid and the beginnings of Citadel or
Cuidadela (R. Millon 1973: 52). The construction of the Ciudadela signals
a general shift toward the south taking place at this time, also evident in
the southward extension of the Street of the Dead from the Pyramid of the
Sun to the area between the Ciudadela and the Great Compound (which
is thought to be a marketplace and lies opposite the Ciudadela on the
western side of the avenue).

The Pyramid of the Sun, Caves, and World Creation

The most impressive and ambitious architectural undertaking in Teotihuacan's history occurred during the Tzacualli phase (A.D. 1–150). This
was the construction, between A.D. 50 and 125, of the first Sun Pyramid,
which was more than 600 feet per side at the base more than 150 feet
high. According to Millon (1992: 390), "The interior of the first Sun Pyramid is primarily of earth with outer retaining walls of adobe. The outer
facing of the inner pyramid is not known." He suggests that it had two
temples at its summit, one dedicated to the Great Goddess, and the other
to the Storm God, although there is no definite evidence for this at present. Later, beginning about A.D. 225, the Pyramid of the Sun was enlarged to its present size. This massive structure is some 61 meters (210
feet) high with basal side lengths of 213 meters (about 724 feet) (Porter
Weaver 1981: 190; Millon 1992: 390). Construction was of a mixed fill of
earth and adobe faced with unshaped stones. Surface irregularities were
concealed beneath concrete and lime plaster (Millon 1992: 391). The
pyramid probably originally rose in stepped terraces, each with a
severely plain sloping profile (the additional fourth terrace of the five terraces seen today apparently is an incorrect restoration made early in the
twentieth century by Leopoldo Batres). Although some authors have suggested that the terraces used an enlarged variant of the slope-and-panel
molding found on later Teotihuacan architecture, this is unlikely given
the early date and colossal scale of the Sun Pyramid. Rather, the Sun
Pyramid's terrace profiles recall those of its predecessor, the circular
pyramid of Cuicuilco (Kubler 1984: 47, 51). The small, originally sculptured *adosada* platform was constructed in front of the larger pyramid at
this time.

The precise location of the Pyramid of the Sun (both in its earlier and
later versions) apparently was determined by the sacred topography of
the region. Almost directly beneath the center of the pyramid is a lava
tube that forms a natural cave which was roofed over with basalt slabs,
and whose walls were plastered with mud (figures 4.3a, b). The cave ter-
minates in a lobed, four-leaf clover chamber which was artificially
enlarged. It is well known that caves were generally held to be sacred
throughout Mesoamerica (Heyden 1973, 1975, 1981; Taube 1986; Bassie-

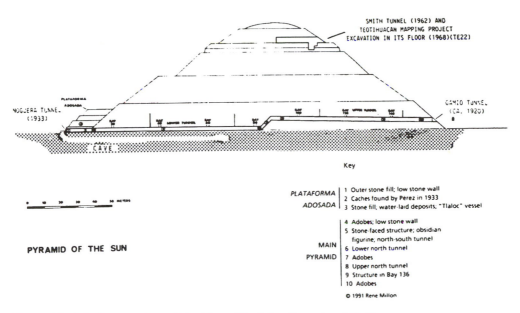

SMITH TUNNEL (1962) AND
TEOTIHUACAN MAPPING PROJECT
EXCAVATION IN ITS FLOOR (1968)(TE22)

PLATAFORMA
ADOSADA

NOGUERA TUNNEL
(1933)

GAMIO TUNNEL
(CA. 1920)

CAVE

0 10 20 30 40 50 METERS

PYRAMID OF THE SUN

Key

PLATAFORMA
ADOSADA

1 Outer stone fill; low stone wall
2 Caches found by Perez in 1933
3 Stone fill; water-laid deposits; "Tlaloc" vessel

MAIN
PYRAMID

4 Adobes; low stone wall
5 Stone-faced structure; obsidian
  figurine; north-south tunnel
6 Lower north tunnel
7 Adobes
8 Upper north tunnel
9 Structure in Bay 136
10 Adobes

© 1991 Rene Millon

Figure 4.3. (*a*) Cross-section of the Pyramid of the Sun, showing the cave located 20 feet beneath it and archaeological tunnels excavated near its base and at its summit (after Millon 1993: figure 5a).

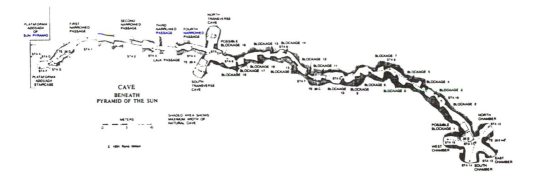

CAVE
BENEATH
PYRAMID OF THE SUN

Figure 4.3. (*b*) Plan of the artificially modified cave located underneath the Pyramid of the Sun at Teotihuacan (after Millon 1993: figure 5b).

Sweet 1991). As earth openings, they provided entrances to the under-world and were generally considered to be the domain of the chthonic spirits of water and rain. It was once thought that the cave beneath the Sun Pyramid contained a spring (Heyden 1975; Porter-Weaver 1981: 190). However, U-shaped stones forming a drainage conduit along its route are now believed to have been used to direct artificial water flow in rituals (Millon 1981: 234). Doris Heyden (1975; 1981) has compared this cave to the legendary *Chicomoztoc*, or 'Seven Caves,' which the Mexica-Aztecs regarded as their place of origin (figure 4.3c). If earlier versions of this myth date to the Classic period, then the Teotihuacanos may have revered the cave below the Sun Pyramid because of such associations.[4] Another possible interpretation of the cave's significance is that of René Millon (1981: 232–233, 235, 1993: 23), who suggests that it is connected with myths of the creation of the sun and the moon, the current cycle of time, and a new humanity. Taube (1986: 51) points out that these two interpretations need not be mutually exclusive, since "the origin of the sun and of human beings can be viewed as episodes in a single creation event." At any rate, the cave could be entered via a pit, a stairway cut into bedrock, and a long tunnel, so it was evidently an important religious locale and may well have been a natural attraction for pilgrimages to the site (Millon 1981: 235, 1973: 49). As Millon (1981: 235) puts it, "the pyra-mid must be where it is and nowhere else because the cave below it was the most sacred of sacred places . . . the rituals performed in the cave must have celebrated a system of myth and belief of transcendent importance."

Figure 4.3. (*c*) Chicomoztoc, or "Seven Caves," the Aztec place of mythical origin, with the twisted hill symbol of Colhuacan visible above the cave, from the Historia Tolteca-Chichemeca, fol. 16r (after Heyden 1981: figure 12).

The Pyramid of the Sun faces west and is oriented 15° 25' north of west. This orientation is perpendicular to that of the Street of the Dead, which has an alignment of 15° 25' east of north. Nearly every other major structure built at Teotihuacan has an alignment within about 1° of this original axis, giving the entire site a comprehensive spatial order. There is evidence that astronomical considerations governed the original layout of the site. An implied baseline has been discovered to run between a marker located about 100 meters north of the Viking Group, an apartment compound on east side of the Street of the Dead southwest of the Pyramid of the Sun, and a similar marker on the southeast slope of the Cerro Colorado, a prominent hill located about 3 kilometers west of the Street of the Dead (Millon 1973: figure 57a, b; Aveni 1975: 168, 1980: 222–226; Aveni, Hartung, and Buckingham 1978: 269–272, figure 3). The azimuth of this baseline is 15° 21' north of west, differing by just 4 minutes of arc from a perpendicular to the azimuth of the Street of the Dead, suggesting that the east–west baseline was fundamental in the original layout of the city. Dow (1967) suggested that the Pleiades constellation, which set at nearly the same azimuth (14° 40' east of north at A.D. 150) may have determined the baseline. As Aveni (1975: 170) points out:

> The Pleiades could have served the function of "announcing" the first annual passage of the sun through zenith at Teotihuacan, since their heliacal rising and the passage of the sun through zenith occurred approximately on the same day (58 days after vernal equinox).[5]

This presumed astronomical alignment governs both the Pyramid of the Sun and the Street of the Dead, and from all indications both had been layed out and large portions constructed by the end of the Tzacualli phase (ca. A.D. 150). In addition, most later edifices at Teotihuacan were laid out following the alignment. As George Kubler (1984: 54) has noted, "The orderly distribution of hundreds of smaller platforms along a roadway determined by the eastern or Sun Pyramid therefore obeys the relationship of a cosmic order, and the spatial arrangement reflects the rhythm of the universe."

The Street of the Dead, the Pyramid of the Moon, and the Sacred Mountain

In addition to the construction of the bulk of Pyramid of the Sun, at least the northern half of the Street of the Dead was also marked out during the Tzacualli phase. The Street of the Dead is a broad ceremonial avenue, some 44 meters wide and extending some five kilometers from north to south. Rising gradually in a series of enclosed plazas and courtyards, this avenue should not be considered simply a functional roadway, but a great *via sacra*, affording a strong sense of axial order to the entire site, and bordered by the city's most holy shrines and temples. Several three-temple pyramid complexes were also constructed along the east and west sides of the avenue (Millon 1992: 390). Construction of the inner Moon Pyramid was also completed at this time, so that the northern terminus of the roadway was already marked by a monumental temple-pyramid.[6] Millon (l973: 52) suspects that the East and West Avenues may also have been laid out at this time, giving the city the distinctive cruciform or quadripartite plan it possessed throughout its development.

In addition to its astronomical associations, Teotihuacan's architecture also appears to have been planned to replicate several essential natural land forms in the mountainous topography defining the San Juan valley. We have already seen that the Pyramid of the Sun contained a sacred cave (and an artificial watercourse or simulated "spring") at its base. In Mesoamerican religious thought, caves are closely associated with mountains (see Stone 1992: 117ff), and later pyramidal substructures such as the Templo Mayor are known to have been identified as artificial mountains (e.g., *Tonacatepetl* and *Coatepetl*; Broda 1987a, b; Matos 1987a, b; see Reilly, chapter 1, this volume, for an Olmec parallel; see Kowalski and Dunning, chapter 12, this volume, for a Maya parallel). The nahuatl word for city, *altepetl*, meaning "water-mountain," refers to this conceptual link between cave-springs, mountains, and human settlement (Pasztory 1983: 102), and demonstrates that the large temple-pyramids defining the heart of the city were considered artificial mountains. This pyramid-mountain equation is made explicit in the relationship between the dominant local mountain known as "Cerro Gordo" and the Pyramid of the Moon (Tobriner 1972) (figure 4.4). As Esther Pasztory (1992: 137) has noted:

> Looking north from the Ciudadela quadrangle toward the Pyramid of the Moon, along the impressive North-South Avenue, Teotihuacan is so harmoniously situated in the landscape that it appears

Figure 4.4. View of the Pyramid of the Moon from the south, looking north along the Street of the Dead. The Moon Pyramid is framed by and echoes the shape of the sacred mountain, known today as Cerro Gordo, and was called Tenan, "Mother of Stone," in the sixteenth century (after Millon 1993: figure 6).

Figure 4.5. Composite view of mural from Tlalocan Patio of the Tepantitla apartment compound at Teotihuacan, showing the Great Goddess as a source of water and fertility on the central axis of the upper panel. In the lower panel the central axis is marked by a mountain with a cave opening from which streams of water emerge to water agricultural fields (redrawn by Jeff Kowalski after Delgado Pang 1992: figure 2.5 and Pasztory 1972: figure 36).

"inevitable." Cerro Gordo frames the Pyramid of the Moon, creating a dramatic vertical endpoint for the processional avenue.

Stephen Tobriner (1972) has pointed out that the Cerro Gordo, known in the sixteenth century as Tenan, the "Mother of Stone," is an important source of springs (audible through a cavelike fissure), which provided the water for fertilizing the crops of the ancient farmers of the San Juan Valley (Nuttall 1926: 76). This connection between the mountain, the cave, and water is pictured explicitly in the so-called Tlalocan mural (Mural 3 of Patio 2) of the Tepantitla apartment compound (figure 4.5), where the lower panel of the mural features two streams of water flowing from a scalloped cave opening at the base of a pyramid-shaped hill. In the upper panel, on the same axis as the mountain-cave, is a depiction of the important Teotihuacan female deity, now known as the "Great Goddess," shown as a source of water and fertility (Pasztory 1976, 1988a: 228, 1992: 141, figure 8a, b).[7] The fact that the monumental "Water Goddess" sculpture (Kubler 1984: 60, figure 16; Pasztory 1988a: figure III.4), which probably is a variant of the "Great Goddess," was found near and probaby came from the Moon Pyramid supports the idea that the pyramid was dedicated to this deity and was conceived as an artificial mountain and source of water (Millon 1992: 359–360). Taube (1986: 51) identifies the Tepantitla mural cave as a "place of emergence—in other words, an idealized counterpart of the actual cave underlying the Pyramid of the Sun." While this seems a correct interpretation, it remains true that the Pyramids of the Sun and Moon can both be viewed as artificial mountains and represent the elite's efforts to capture and control the numinous forces of nature in the regularized ritual space of the urban community (Stone 1992: 124–125).

The Ciudadela, the Temple of Quetzalcoatl, and Rulership

The Ciudadela was apparently constructed during the Miccaotli and early Tlamimilolpa phases (ca. A.D. 150–300).[8] It has been called "one of the most impressive open-volume compositions in the entire history of architecture," (Kubler 1984: 55) and it does indeed demonstrate the Mesoamerican architects' particular gift for arranging civic-ceremonial spaces as coherent assemblies of strong masses and enclosed volumes. The Ciudadela precinct possesses an overwhelming sense of the quadrilateral "existential space" (Norberg-Schulz 1988) embodying Mesoamerican cosmography and illustrates what Eliade (1959) has termed the "non-heterogeneity" of space in religious architecture, where the skillful ordering of structures reinforces in the worshipper the sense that he or she occupies a numinous and sacred place (see Matos Moctezuma, chapter 9, this volume, for a discussion of continuities between these spatial concepts at Teotihuacan and those of the Mexica-Aztecs).

The Ciudadela contains a broad plaza at the center of which is a temple-pyramid known as the Temple of Quetzalcoatl (figure 4.6a). The immense plaza measures some 44,000 square meters, and was capable of holding 100,000 persons, probably the entire adult population of the ancient city (Cowgill 1983: 322–323; Millon 1992: 393). It is framed by a nearly square primary platform, which in turn supports 15 symmetrically distributed and rhythmically ordered smaller pyramidal platforms. Interestingly, the north–south axis of the compound conforms to the 15° 30' east of north orientation of the Street of the Dead, while the east–west axis is 17° south of east. Virtually this same alignment (16° 30' south of east) was also adopted for further development of the East Avenue stretching east from the Ciudadela. The central courtyard of the Ciudadela is divided into a larger open western area and a smaller, more private area containing a number of rooms to the east. The room arrangements have led some to suggest that the Ciudadela may have been constructed to serve as the principal administrative center and the palace of the rulers of Teotihuacan (Armillas 1964; Millon 1973: 55; Cowgill 1983). On the other hand, a similar elite residential function has been proposed for the imposing architectural assemblage known as the Calle de los

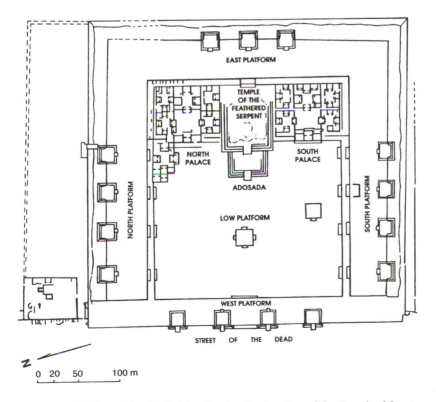

Figure 4.6. (a) Plan of the Ciudadela, showing the location of the Temple of Quetzalcoatl and of the large room complexes to the north and south (redrawn by Jeff Kowalski after Pasztory 1988a: figure III.8 and Cabrera Castro 1993: figure 1).

Muertos (CDLM) Complex, which flanks the Street of the Dead between the Ciudadela and the Pyramid of the Sun (Wallrath 1966; Cowgill 1983; Pasztory 1988: 53), and which nearly equals the Ciudadela in area (30+ acres for the CDLM Complex versus 40 acres for the Ciudadela, Millon 1992: 341). Pasztory (1988b) has pointed out that mural paintings, which are common in other elite residential compounds, are virtually absent in the Ciudadela room complexes.[9] As Cowgill (1992: 207–208) has observed, determining whether the Ciudadela, or some other room complex, served as some sort of "royal palace" is hindered by the fact that

> The office of rulership itself, or headship of the state, has proven curiously elusive at Teotihuacan, in contrast to its high visibility in Classic period Maya inscriptions and monuments. . . . Teotihuacan art—mural painting, decorated pottery, and small and large stone carvings—is notable for the absence of scenes in which some humans appear subordinated to others (R. Millon 1988 [b]; Pasztory 1988b). Humans are sometimes shown subordinated to deities, but not to one another. We also do not see scenes that center on a single person. Typically several persons are shown, often in procession, and all as similar to one another in the details of their postures, facial features, and costumes as freehand drawing allows.

With a few exceptions, such as the use of possible nominal glyphs used to identify warriors wearing the distinctive "tasseled headdress" and garbed as the Storm God in the Techinantitla murals (C. Millon 1988; R. Millon 1988b), human figures in Teotihuacan art seem so stereotyped as to preclude the identification of single individual rulers or "kings." The large number of sumptuous apartment compounds with more-or-less similar formal interior patios fronted by temples suggests that many prosperous and powerful lineages and/or craft/production units co-existed at Teotihuacan (Millon 1976, 1993: 29–30; Manzanilla 1993).[10] These larger, more permanent apartment compounds began to replace less imposing and less permanent residential buildings during the Miccaotli period, and their numbers burgeoned during the Tlamimilolpa and Xolalpan phases (ca. A.D. 250–650). It has been suggested that this change is associated with a shift from more centralized rulership to some sort of lineage-based conciliar government (Millon 1992), perhaps more like that which has been suggested to exist at the Early Postclassic site of Chichén Itzá (see Schele and Freidel 1990: chapter 9; Stone, chapter 13, this volume). In this regard, Millon (1993: 29) has suggested that "Apartment compounds served as the city's basic political units with neighborhood or barrio headquarters standing between groups of compounds and the central hierarchy."[11]

At the heart of the Ciudadela is the Temple of Quetzalcoatl (figure 4.6b), so named for its high relief architectural sculptures featuring alternating images of the feathered serpent (known as Quetzalcoatl among the later Aztecs) and a scaly reptilian figure related to other images in Teoti-

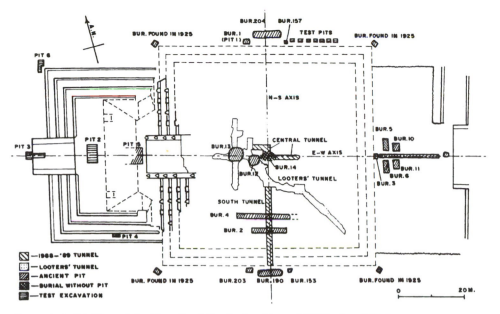

Figure 4.6. (b) Plan of the Temple of Quetzalcoatl as of 1991, showing excavated areas, locations of burials discovered to date, and looter's tunnel (after
Cabrera, Sugiyama, and Cowgill 1991: figure 1).

huacan art (figure 4.7). Only sections of four terraces and a part of the
central stairway of this temple are preserved, as a result of having been
covered by a later Tlamimilolpa phase stepped platform known as the
Adosada (Cowgill 1983). Having a basal dimension of some 65 meters per
side (about 4225 square meters), the Quetzalcoatl temple originally rose
in six or seven tiers and was completely covered with the alternating
heads seen on its front. Marquina's (1964: 88, lám. 19) calcuations of the
size of the terraces led him to estimate that the total number of heads was
originally 366, signaling a link with the solar year and suggesting that the
temple was the focus of calendrical rituals (Marquina 1964: 88; Drucker
1974; Coggins 1983a, 1993). More recent excavations by Cabrera Castro
and Sugiyama (1982), however, suggest that there may have been 399
such heads.

The sculptures of the feathered serpents on the Temple of Quetzalcoatl are among the first distinctive representations of this deity in
Mesoamerica.[12] On the lower sloping section of each terrace, low-relief
profile depictions of the serpents face the stair. Surrounding their undulating bodies are carvings of conch and bivalve shells, indicating a
watery environment. On the framed upper panel of the terrace, larger
feathered serpent bodies are joined to three-dimensional heads projecting from petaled, flowerlike collars and a feathered disk, which Taube
(1992b) interprets as a mirror. Traces of red and white paint on plaster
remain on some of the sculpture, giving a pale indication of what originally was a striking polychrome treatment.

Figure 4.7. (Top) View of the sculptured facade of the Temple of Quetzalcoatl, showing low-relief feathered serpents on the sloping *talud* and alternating projecting feathered serpent and scaly reptilian heads on the vertical framed *tablero* (photograph by Jeff Kowalski); (bottom) drawing of a section of facade of the Temple of Quetzalcoatl (redrawn by Jeff Kowalski after Coggins 1993: figure 2).

The great antiquity and popularity of feathered serpent symbolism in Mesoamerica makes it somewhat problematical to interpret. By the time of the Mexica-Aztecs, the deity known as Quetzalcoatl had become an extremely complex godhead, incorporating aspects of creator, benefactor, wind, and Venus as morning star (Nicholson 1979). In addition, the identity of the deity had become confused, and to some extent merged with the personality of Ce Acatl Topiltzín Quetzalcoatl, a king of Tula and legendary culture hero (Nicholson 1957; Pasztory 1972: 126; Gillespie 1989). At Teotihuacan, however, the image of the feathered serpent does not seem to carry the same complex cultic and historical meanings, but rather to be associated primarily with water, fertility, and divine creativity (although connections with war, sacrifice and political authority are also evident; Millon 1992: 362–363; Sugiyama 1992).[13] This is implied not only at the Temple of Quetzalcoatl, but also in other representations at the site. In the Tlalocan complex of the Tepantitla palace, the image of the feathered serpent appears as a border design in the Sowing Priest's Room. There the serpent is formed from two intertwining bands marked with trapeze-and-ray signs and has a stream of water gushing from its mouth. At Atetelco the feathered serpent is used as a border around the doorway of the east portico of the White Patio, the only one of the three porticoes clearly associated with water symbolism (Pasztory 1972: 125–126). The feathered serpent has been associated with divine generation by Coe (1981: 168), who likens the image of the snake slithering through shell-filled waters to the description in the K'iche' Maya epic, the *Popol Vuh*, of the movement of K'ukulcan, the plumed serpent who gives birth to living things from the primordial waters (Tedlock 1985: 72–73).

The other projecting heads have often been identified as representations of the Teotihuacan Storm God (e.g., Gamio 1922: 66; Armillas 1945, 1947; Carrasco 1982: 115; Delgado Pang 1992: 48), known to the later Mexica-Aztecs as Tlaloc, who is depicted in numerous contexts in art at Teotihuacan and in Teotihuacan-influenced art abroad (C. Millon 1973, 1988; Pasztory 1974; Berlo 1984; Stone 1989; Schele and Freidel 1990). This identification seemed tenable because two prominent disks are displayed on the forehead of the creature, recalling the distinctive goggled-eyes of the Teotihuacan Storm God or the later Aztec Tlaloc. However, the disks clearly do not encircle the creature's eyes, nor does the projecting and fanged upper jaw much resemble the more usual thick lip-bar of Tlaloc.[14] More likely the creature represents one of the other composite reptilian deities or "saurian creatures" depicted in Teotihuacan art (see Sarro 1991: 251). Saburo Sugiyama (1989b) suggests that these heads depict a Teotihuacan headdress of feathered serpent form, thus complementing the more naturalistic serpent sculptures on the facade. More recently, López Austin, López Luján, and Sugiyama (1991) have reidentified this head as that of the Cipactli earth crocodilian, a symbol of the calendar and the passage of time. Karl Taube (1992a) also interprets the heads as headdress forms, but, building on a suggestion by Caso (Caso and Bernal 1952: 113–116), he has plausibly identified them as the "Teotihuacan War Serpent," a forerunner of the Postclassic Xiuhcoatl (Fire Serpent). The rhythmic repetition of the two heads on the facade may be connected with the cyclical alternation of the rainy and the dry seasons at Teotihuacan (Caso and Bernal 1952: 114; Pasztory 1988: 57).[15] The later Mexica-Aztecs divided the year into such a rainy (*xopan*) and dry (*tonalco*) season, and may have used solar zenith and nadir passage to mark the division (Broda 1983, 1987a; Milbrath 1988). The already-noted connection between the pleiades and solar zenith passage suggests that similar concepts may have guided the original layout of

Teotihuacan. Perhaps the multiple human burials recently discovered in connection with the structure (discussed further later) represent a perceived need to sustain such seasonal agricultural cycles by means of human sacrifice, whether of captives taken in battle, loyal retainers of the ruler, or of "volunteers" chosen from among the city's own populace (Pasztory 1990: 187; cf. Cabrera, Sugiyama, and Cowgill 1991: 89).

Because of its centralized location and the complex iconography of its combined low- and high-relief architectural sculpture, it is clear that the Temple of Quetzalcoatl was a preeminent ceremonial structure during the Miccaotli and early Tlamimilolpa phases. Although the front of the structure was covered by the "plataforma adosada," later in the Tlamimilolpa phase, Cowgill (1983: 328) has suggested that the entire Ciudadela complex continued to function as an important religious locus throughout the subsequent Tlamimilolpa, Xolalpan, and Metepec phases, when Teotihuacan's influence throughout Mesoamerica was most pervasive and intense. Although the feathered serpent has multiple referents at Teotihuacan, it is clear that, in a broad sense, it became an important symbol of political authority throughout later Mesoamerican history (Carrasco 1982). Undoubtedly, this was one of its meanings at Teotihuacan, although this does not clarify whether the icon was used to validate the royal power of a paramount ruler who used the Ciudadela as a "palace" and administrative center, or whether the shared worship of this deity (along with that of other important communal deities such as the Great Goddess) served to integrate a polity in which power was distributed among various high-ranking lineages who convened at the Ciudadela for communal rituals.[16]

Although the exact nature of such rituals cannot be determined, recent excavations of the Temple of Quetzalcoatl have revealed evidence of large-scale, multiple burials, evidently reflecting the practice of human sacrifice (Cabrera Castro, Sugiyama, and Cowgill 1991; Sugiyama 1992). According to Cabrera Castro, Sugiyama, and Cowgill (1991: 77):

> The Feathered Serpent Pyramid (Temple ot Quetzalcoatl) was built in a single episode involving the sacrifice of around 200 individuals, in Miccaotli or Early Tlamimilolpa times. Most were males with military gear. Many had shell collars with pendants of imitation human jaws made of worked shell teeth set in stucco; rarely were real jaws used. At the center, 20 individuals (probably all males) were buried with very rich offerings including greenstone beads, earspools, nose pendants, figurines, and strange conical objects; obsidian blades and figurines; shells, and remains of wood and probable textiles. We also explored a looter's tunnel that had severely disturbed two large pits under the pyramid; in one of these an individual of exceptional importance may have been buried.

The apparent lack of other such mass sacrifices at Teotihuacan leads these authors to suggest that Teotihuacan's system of government underwent a transformation at about the time the Temple of Quetzalcoatl was built, with "an early period of autocratic rulers, followed by a shift to more emphasis on a collective, group-oriented ethos" (Cabrera Castro, Sugiyama, and Cowgill 1991: 77; cf. Millon 1992: 362–363, 394–397).

Such human sacrifices were not depicted in narrative form in Teotihuacan art, but were referred to obliquely in mural art or on painted ceramics, taking the form of warriors brandishing obsidian knives with impaled human hearts or indicated metaphorically as predatory coyotes killing a deer (Kubler 1967: figure 13; Berrin 1988: 207-221, plates 37, 38; Pasztory 1990, 1992: 143, figure 10). Pasztory (1992: 142) recently suggested that military and sacrificial imagery in Teotihuacan art

> may have been an exhortation and a demand for self-sacrifice in a more general sense for the sake of the community. The community evidently put the value of the group above that of the individual. . . . Perhaps both actual and symbolic sacrifice were believed to bring about the terrestrial paradise during rites that marked the change of time cycles or seasonal transformation.

Architecture, Ideology, and the City of Teotihuacan

Pasztory's recent observations lead to a broader consideration of the extent to which religious ideology, which is powerfully expressed in Teotihuacan's architecture and visual arts, can be seen as an active force in explaining the rise and longevity of the city. As many scholars have pointed out, Teotihuacan's location in a spring- and rain-watered arm of the Basin of Mexico, coupled with its proximity to and apparent control over several important sources of obsidian (e.g., Otumba, Cerro de las Navajas; R. Millon 1973: 45–46, 53; Spence 1981, 1987), account for the city's ability to sustain a large, nucleated population and explain why its leadership established long-distance elite trade networks with other regions of Mesoamerica. Various investigators, including William Sanders, Barbara Price, Jeffrey Parsons, Robert Santley, and David Webster, view these ecological conditions as providing the primary key to Teotihuacan's rise (and the evolution of Mesoamerican civilization generally) and interpret religion and art as "epiphenomenal" in this process (e.g., Sanders and Price 1968; Sanders, Parsons, and Santley 1979; Sanders and Santley 1983; Sanders and Webster 1988). In contrast, Conrad and Demarest (1984) have suggested that ideology (particularly religion, but also material symbol systems such as art and architecture) plays a more active and causal role in maintaining social order and in shaping culture change. In a similar manner, other scholars including René Millon, George Cowgill, Saburo Sugiyama, Doris Heyden and Esther Pasztory have stressed the critical integrative role played by religion and art, noting that the dramatic transformation of Teotihuacan from village to city at the very outset involved the construction of the two largest pyramid temples in the site's history and the establishment of a grid plan which seems to owe its origin not to "rational" town planning but to the architects' efforts to link the principal ceremonial buildings (and later, by extension, the apartment compounds) to mountains, caves, springs, and significant stations of astronomical bodies such as the sun and the Pleiades. These astronomical observations in turn were associated with change of the seasons and with agricultural fertility. Millon (1992: 382 ff.) has argued forcefully that the audacity and comprehensiveness of this early architectural vision attests to an initial period of centralized, charismatic rulership at Teotihuacan. The physical embodiment of such sacred, natural forms and forces and astronomical relationships in the entire plan of the city, and in the form and decoration of individual edifices, helps to explain how a city of such size and evident diversity of ethnic composition, statuses, and occupations remained integrated and how the rulers of the city's hierarchical political organization maintained authority. In this regard, Pasztory (1992: 136–137) has suggested that Teotihuacan's longevity may have depended on the power of its "civic myths" as much as on its actual military and economic power. She contrasts the more ahistorical art of Teotihuacan with the dynastic monuments of the Maya region, observing that

> Teotihuacan images suggest a neutral, impersonal world inhabited by largely benevolent deities and by an anonymous elite preoccupied with the proper performance of ritual. The images evoke a terrestrial paradise through the depiction of waters teeming with marine life, a land of fruit and flower-bearing plants, and mythical birds, canines, and felines. Paradoxically, in the creation of the first great urban metropolis in Mesoamerica, Teotihuacan came up with the natural world for its civic metaphor. . . . Teotihuacan's strategy was largely "integrationist": apparently, its leaders validated the new state by suggesting that the new living arrangements were more harmoniously adapted to the ways of the cosmos. This is not uncommon strategy in early states, but, while many came up with the transparent device of making the ruler a divine intermediary between gods and people, Teotihuacan, by denying politics altogether, suggested a civic order of nature.

Although René Millon (1992: 382 ff., 1993) rejects some of Pasztory's more utopian interpretations, he likewise stresses the important role that ideology, myth, ritual, architecture, and art played in the formation of the Teotihuacan urban community:

> To rationalize the reality of domination, to foster social cohesion, the city's emerging ideology would have had to stress the unity in this diversity, to promote the theme that Teotihuacan as the custodian of the place where the universe began had become a city united, favored, honored, and charged with the responsibility of keeping the cosmos in motion through the performance of common rituals on calendrically prescribed occasions in public and

domestic settings from the city center to the household. This would have been a powerful source of integration and motivation in an increasingly stratified, ethnically divided society.

Teotihuacan's art and architecture undoubtedly helped shape public perceptions and motivated publicly beneficial behavior, but ultimately they could not conceal nor counter what must have been growing divisions within Teotihuacan society, far-from-utopian actual living conditions for the majority of the city's inhabitants (Storey 1985, 1992), and pressures from competitors elsewhere in Mesoamerica. There is evidence of large-scale burning in the center of the site at around A.D. 750, after which the site was reoccupied, but as what Richard Diehl (1989) has aptly termed "a shadow of its former self." Even this final destructive act, which Millon (1988a: 156–158, 1992: 350) suggests was the result of internal dissension rather than outside invasion, demonstrates the psychological power of the site's ideology. It was the central zone of temples and civic-ceremonial architecture, rather than the suburban apartment compounds, that bore the brunt of the flames, as though it was deemed necessary to destroy the site's most sacred architecture so as to preclude a revival of its closely allied political order (Millon 1988a: 145–146, 1992: 346, 1993: 32-33).

The *Talud-Tablero* Architectural Profile

Pasztory (1993: 144–145) has suggested that Teotihuacan's geometric and abstract art style was developed and conserved because it complemented the sense of "natural" order and suggested "a cosmos of impersonal laws, outside the control and feelings of men." In architecture this abstract tendency is clearly evident in the so-called *talud-tablero*, or slope-and-panel form of Teotihuacan terrace profiling (figure 4.8). *Talud-tablero* style terraces first appeared at Teotihuacan during the Miccaotli phase, when they were used at the Temple of Quetzalcoatl. The system features a sloping lower section or talus supporting an inset vertical panel surrounded by a heavy rectangular frame. The framing members are supported by thin slabs or stone (lajas) which are tied into the rubble and adobe core of the structure (Acosta 1964: 21, figure 14; Kubler 1973; Jarquín Pacheco and Martínez Vargas 1982). Although the facade was executed in stone sculpture at the Temple of Quetzalcoatl, the usual procedure was to apply a 5–8 centimeters thick layer of gravelly concrete, followed by a finish coat of plaster, which could serve as the support for frescoed mural paintings or be left plain. This slope-and-panel style of architecture remained popular at Teotihuacan throughout its history, and virtually every structure of permanence or significance was articulated in this fashion.[17]

Talud-tablero architecture predating that of Teotihuacan occurs by 350–200 B.C. at the site of Tlalancaleca, Puebla (Garcia Cook 1981: 252,

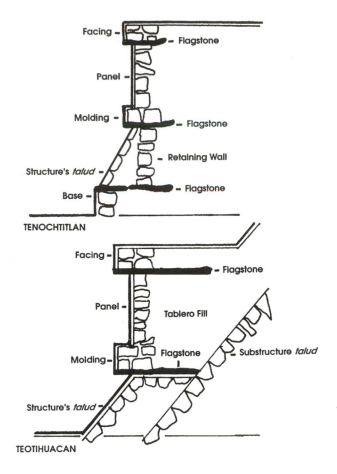

Figure 4.8. Section drawing showing the construction of a typical Teotihuacan talud-tablero platform terrace, compared to the *talud-tablero* platforms constructed by the Mexica-Aztecs north (Building C) and south (Templo Rojo) of the Templo Mayor (redrawn by Jeff Kowalski after Matos and López 1993: figure 3).

1984: 28–32), and on early stages of the Great Pyramid at Cholula (Marquina 1964: 121, lám. 36, fig. 5), causing Gendrop (1984: 8, 18, figure 17a–c) to posit the existence of a "Tlaxcaltecan-Teotihuacan" regional development of the profile. However, Teotihuacan became a focus for the Classic period development of *talud-tablero* architecture, which remained popular throughout the site's later history. The proportional relation of *tablero* to *talud* varies, with the general tendency for taller bases to be earlier and shorter bases later. Kubler (1973: 28) suggests that a ratio of 3:1 was "canonical" during the period of Teotihuacan's "urban renewal," but that other ratios could be applied in special situations. The consistent and widespread use of this distinctive architectural form gave Teotihuacan not only a visual coherence, but psychologically probably helped create a sense among the city's inhabitants that they shared a common cultural identity (Wobst 1977).

That Teotihuacan exerted a powerful influence on the Guatemalan highlands site of Kaminaljuyú during the Early Classic period (ca. A.D. 300–550) has long been known (Kidder, Jennings, and Shook 1946; Parsons 1969; W. Coe 1972; Santley 1983: 75; M. Coe 1987: 69–73;

Demarest and Foias 1993). Two structures with *talud-tablero* profiles dated at about A.D. 300 are known at Solano, Guatemala, a site located near Kaminaljuyú (Brown 1977a, b). Both Solano and the larger center of Kaminaljuyú have been interpreted as highland ports of trade with strong connections with Teotihuacan (Brown 1977a, b), although Kaminaljuyú's use of Teotihuacan *talud-tablero* architectural forms begins at about A.D. 400, roughly when Solano ceased to use such profiles.

Although several types of artifacts (e.g., cylinder tripods, candeleros) testify to Teotihuacan-Kaminaljuyú contact, its most significant expression took the form of Teotihuacan-style *talud-tablero* architecture. Teotihuacan-style platforms have been found in two zones: in the area of the Parque de Kaminaljuyú and in the area 1700 meters to the southeast where Mounds A and B are located (figure 4.9a). In the Parque de Kaminaljuyú there are two major groups: C-II-4 or the Acropolis and Mounds C-II-12 and C-II-14, known as the Palangana (Cheek 1977a; 1977b: 443). Charles Cheek interprets the architectural relationship between Kaminaljuyú and Teotihuacan as passing through three phases: a period of contact and integration between A.D. 400 and 500, during which aspects of local and Teotihuacan styles are combined; a period of strong Teotihuacan influence between A.D. 500 and 650, when a large number of *talud-tablero* structures essentially similar to those of Teotihuacan in form and technology were constructed (Cheek 1977b: 445); and a subsequent withdrawal phase from A.D. 650 to 700 when Teotihuacan architectural elements disappear. Cheek's estimate of A.D. 400 for the beginning of Teotihuacan influence at Kaminaljuyú probably should be revised, however, in light of evidence for substantial contact elsewhere in the Maya region at an earlier date (Pendergast 1971; Coggins 1975, 1983a: 51, 55–56; LaPorte 1985: 3; LaPorte and Fialko 1990).

Teotihuacan-style *talud-tablero* architecture also occurs at the large site of Matacapan, Veracruz (Santley 1983: 76). Mound 2, located west of the site's central plaza, was a two-stage, *talud-tablero* temple platform constructed in typical Teotihuacan style (Valenzuela 1945: map II; Coe 1965b: figure 23) (figure 4.9b). Excavations near two low elongated mounds east of Mound 2 unearthed a significant number of Teotihuacan artifacts, both utilitarian and ceremonial. *Talud-tablero* profiles similar to those of Teotihuacan have also bee reported at La Victoria and Cuajilotes, Veracruz (see Wilkerson, chapter 5, this volume).

Teotihuacan influences have been recognized in the Early Classic sculpture, pottery, and artifacts of Tikal, Guatemala, for some time, but only more recently have examples of Early Classic Teotihuacan style *talud-tablero* architecture been discovered (cf. Coe 1972: 265). Several later structures, including 5D-43 (in the East Plaza), 5C-53 (in the Lost World Complex), and 6E-144 (southeast of the ceremonial zone), constructed in a variant of *talud-tablero* style, were known (Coe 1967: 73–74), but all date to the Late Classic Ik (or early facet Imix) phase (ca. A.D. 550–700). Furthermore, structures such as 5D-43, which has a flaring

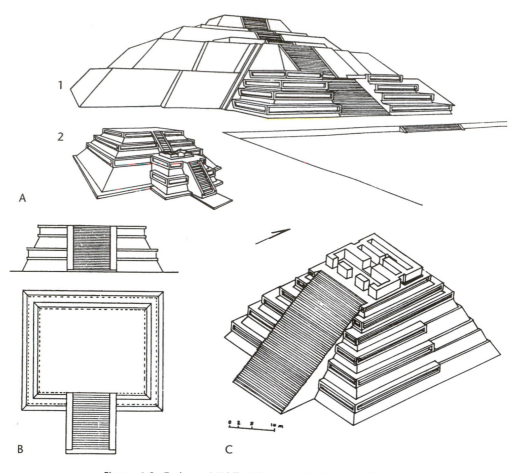

Figure 4.9. Early or Middle Classic period *talud-tablero* style architecture at Mesoamerican sites, (a) Structure B4 at Kaminaljuyú, Guatemala (2), compared with the Pyramid of the Moon at Teotihuacan (1) (redrawn by Jeff Kowalski after Kubler 1984: figure 6); (b) Mound 2 at Matacapan, Veracruz (from Coe 1965b: figure 23, after Valenzuela 1945); (c) Structure 5C-49 of the "Lost World Group" at Tikal, Guatemala, phase 4 (redrawn by Jeff Kowalski after the drawing by P. Morales in LaPorte 1985).

cornice surmounting the *tablero*, have been related to later eclectic, Teotihuacanoid architectural styles, such as those of El Tajín or Xochicalco, rather than being considered the result of direct Teotihuacan influence (Pasztory 1978: 109). Such architectural revivals seem closely related to reuse of Teotihuacan-inspired iconography in the sculptures of Ruler A's reign at Tikal and are part of a general cultural revitalization movement (Dahlin 1976: 48).

Excavations directed by Juan Pedro LaPorte in Tikal's "Lost World Complex" as well as in the residential zone to the southwest have revealed striking examples of *talud-tablero* architecture of Early Classic date. The most impressive *talud-tablero* building is Structure 5C-49, the second highest platform of the "Lost World Complex" (figure 4.9c).

Construction phase 1, probably of *Manik* 1 date (ca. A.D. 250–350), consisted of a 7-meter high pyramid composed of three sloping terraces supporting a plain, vertical *tablero* at the summit. Structures 5C-49 2-4 were built during *Manik* phases 2 and 3 (ca. A.D. 350–550) with true *talud-tablero* terracing, in which the framed panels surmounted sloping bases on the front (south) and front parts of the sides, while the rear sides and back consisted of simple sloping terraces. LaPorte (1985: 17) compares this partial *talud-tablero* treatment with that seen on the Teotihuacan-style pyramid at Tepeapulco (or Tepepulco), Hidalgo (Ribera 1984), or at the Ciudadela at Teotihuacan (Jarquín Pacheco and Martínez 1982). During these phases, only the uppermost terrace of Structure 5C-49 had a continuous *tablero*. The ratio of *talud* to *tablero* is 1:1, with little variation. During the Late Classic (early facet Ik phase, possibly contemporaneous with the construction of Platform 5C-53-2, ca. A.D. 550–600), Structure 5C-49-5 was remodeled, increasing the height of the structure by two more *talud-tablero* terraces (LaPorte 1985: 21). A residential compound from the "Lost Quadrant" (6C on the Carr and Hazard 1961 map) also features examples of *talud-tablero* platforms (LaPorte 1985; LaPorte and Fialko 1990), including one which supported a Teotihuacan-related "ballgame marker"(or "battle standard"; Freidel, Schele, and Parker 1993). That the *talud-tablero* profile carried connotations of Teotihuacan ethnic identity (and by extension, Teotihuacan's prestige) for the Maya of Tikal is most clearly documented on the cylinder tripod vessel found in Miscellaneous Deposit 50. On this vessel, figures wearing Teotihuacan-style tasseled headdresses depart from a site (likely Teotihuacan) symbolized by a *talud-tablero* platform, to arrive ultimately at another site (likely Tikal) featuring Maya terrace profiles (Freidel, Schele, and Parker 1993: 300).

In addition to Matacapan and Tikal, *talud-tablero* buildings also occur at Becan, Campeche (Structure XIV; Ball 1979b: 275), Dzibilchaltún, Yucatán (Andrews and Andrews 1980: 73–74, 325–326, 339), Tingambato (see figure 2.1, site no. 83, for location), Michoacan (Siller 1984), Teticpac el Viejo, Guerrero (Arana and Quijada 1984), and Ixtepete, Guadalajara (Schondube V. and Galvan 1978; Porter Weaver 1981: 220).[18] Monte Albán architecture features a local version of sloping lower zone and overhanging panels known as the *doble escapulario* or scapulary panel (Hartung 1970). *Talud-tablero* buildings, however, are portrayed graphically on the Estela Lisa and Stela 1, where they clearly refer to Teotihuacan, identifying it as the home of an emissary to Monte Albán named 9 Monkey (Marcus 1983a: 175, 181). There is other evidence that Teotihuacan and Monte Albán maintained some sort of "special relationship," which seems to have been peaceful and based on commercial, ambassadorial and perhaps dynastic-marriage contacts between the capitals of two large, independent political states (Millon 1973: 42; Flannery and Marcus 1983d: 165–166; Spence 1992).

In its appearances during the Early and Middle Classic periods in the architecture of Kaminaljuyú, Matacapan, Cholula, Tikal, Tepeapulco, Becan, Dzibilchaltún, and Tingambato, as well as in the art of Tikal and Monte Albán, *talud-tablero* terracing apparently attests to some commercial or political link between these centers and Teotihuacan. It is used as an unmistakable architectural reference to the powerful central Mexican city, reflecting either the efforts of enclaves of Teotihuacanos to construct temples for familiar cult practices, as seems to be the case at Kaminaljuyú and Matacapan (Kidder, Jennings, and Shook 1946; Sanders 1977; Santley 1983), and perhaps at Tikal (C. Millon 1988); attempts by local elites to emulate the architecture of a city whose formidable power, military cults, and mythic stature bolstered their own claims to authority, as at Tikal (Schele and Freidel 1990; Coggins 1983a, 1993); or as references to elite-level diplomatic contacts with the central Mexican metropolis, as at Monte Albán (Flannery and Marcus 1983d; Marcus 1983a; Millon 1988a: 129–130).

During the Epiclassic and Early Postclassic periods (ca. A.D. 700–1200), in the wake of Teotihuacán's collapse, various centers developed new variants of slope-and-panel architecture, which, although owing something to the Teotihuacan system, seem to be localized and independent architectural expressions. During the period from about A.D. 750 to 1162, the site of Teotenango in the Toluca Valley became an "imposing civic-ceremonial center with spacious plazas and temple platforms with *talud* and cornices somewhat like Teotihuacan" (Porter Weaver 1981: 376), but lacking the heavy rectangular framing members (Piña Chán 1975). At Tula, Hidalgo the terraces of Pyramid B display a talud supporting a continuous *tablero* above a series of framed panels alternating with recessed panels. Although this "scalloped" system differs from Teotihuacan originals, it may well represent a conscious reworking of the earlier Teotihuacan terracing (Kubler 1984: 81) (Figure 4.10a).[19] The Temple of the Warriors at Chichén Itzá (Morris, Charlot, and Morris 1931, 1: fig. 100; see Stone, chapter 13, this volume) also has *talud-tablero* terraces. Kubler (1984: 293) suggests that Chichén's architects may have modeled the terrace profiles directly on "highland [i.e., Teotihuacan] examples of five hundred to a thousand years earlier." However, the disproportionately high *taluds* differ from the Classic models, supporting the idea that such forms were revived not by direct imitation of Teotihuacan buildings but by way of intermediaries such as Tula and Xochicalco (see Molina and Kowalski, chapter 6, this volume).

The variants of *talud-tablero* architecture that occur at Tula, Chichén Itzá, and Teotenango, instead of being provincial imitations of a current metropolitan style, were partial and modified revivals in which aspects of older forms were invested with new meanings. The proportions and visual effects of the Epiclassic and Early Postclassic terraces differ from the Teotihuacan models. This selective borrowing from an earlier architectural vocabulary occurs at centers that replaced Teotihuacan as the primary politico-economic powers in Mesoamerica, but which had parvenu dynasties that depended for their authority both on the creation of dynamic new ideologies as well as the annexing of architectural, artistic and religious symbolism from various predecessors and competitors (Parsons 1969; Pasztory 1978; Diehl and Berlo 1989; see Molina and Kowalski, chapter 6, this volume; Kristan-Graham, chapter 7, this volume, and Stone, chapter 13, this volume).

During the Late Postclassic period, buildings displaying true Teoti-huacan-type *talud-tablero* terraces are rare. The most significant examples are four structures constructed by the Mexica-Aztecs in their capital city of Tenochtitlan (figure 4.10b). These include the two so-called "Templos Rojos" or Red Temples on the north and south sides of the Templo Mayor, and two other platforms, one west and one north of the Templo Mayor (Matos 1965, 1981b, 1982: 42, 65–66; Gussinyer 1970). All feature characteristic Teotihuacan *talud-tablero* profiles, as well as polychrome painting. The temple north of the Templo Mayor (Platform C) has what Umberger (1987: 87) terms "pseudo-Teotihuacan paintings in the form of broad vertical bands, each containing a large red-rimmed eye, on the sloping *talud*,"while such horizontal bands adorn the *alfardas* (sloping balustrades) framing the stairway. Bands containing eyes are common in Teotihuacan mural painting, where they are interpreted as symbols of brilliant, flowing liquid.[20]

The Teotihuacan-style buildings near the Templo Mayor stand out clearly from neighboring Mexica sacred, administrative, or residential architecture (Boone 1985: 179). The deliberate, archaistic use of Teotihuacan-style edifices undoubtedly had important symbolic purposes related to the Mexica's view of Teotihuacan's role in Mesoamerican myth and history. The best-known such mythic reference occurs in the Aztec accounts of the cosmogony, in which the fifth "sun" or world era is created at Teotihuacan. As Alfonso Caso (1927, 1958) has noted, a critical purpose of this myth was to identify the Mexica as "the people of the sun," whose warriors were obligated to obtain sacrificial victims necessary to repay humanity's blood debt to the gods. This religious belief system was a dynamic element in cultural transformation and helps account for the phenomenal rise of the imperialistic Mexica (Townsend 1979: 53; Conrad and Demarest 1984).

Given the central importance of Teotihuacan in the Mexica cosmogony, and given the mythic rationale for the imperialistic expansion of the Mexica state, it is not surprising to find direct references to the art and architecture of the ancient city in the sacred precinct of Tenochtitlan. It seems likely that rather than simply alluding to this myth, the Teotihuacan-style buildings represent attempts to concretize the myth by providing physical locations in which it could be reenacted. Eliade (1954), Wheatley (1971), and others have noted that one of the hallmarks of sacred architecture in traditional societies is that it conforms to a mythic paradigm and replicates a sacred cosmography. It is clear that the Mexica conceived of the Templo Mayor in this sense, that is, as an

Figure 4.10. Postclassic period reinterpretations or revivals of Teotihuacan-related talud-tablero style architecture; (*a*) Pyramid B, Tula, Hidalgo (photograph by Jeff Kowalski); (*b*) Structure C , located on the north side of the Templo Mayor at Tenochtitlan (redrawn by Jeff Kowalski after Heyden and Villaseñor 1984).

embodiment of Coatepec where Huitzilopochtli defeated and slew his sister, the Moon Goddess Coyolxauhqui (Matos 1981a, 1987b; and chapter 9, this volume). The careful imitation of Teotihuacan forms in Tenochtitlan suggests that they may have been more than an homage to the ancient city, but rather an effort to replicate the hearth of creation at the heart of the Mexica's most holy precinct (Matos and López 1993).

The archaistic architecture of the "Templos Rojos" probably also refers in a broader sense to the Mexica's claim to be the legitimate inheritors of the intellectual, cultural, and artistic achievements of their predecessors known as the Toltecs. In one sense the Mexica used the term *Toltec* to refer to the historical group that occupied the site of Tula, Hidalgo (Tollan Xicocotítlan) (Jiménez Moreno 1941). However, the words *Toltec* and *Tula* (Tollan) had several alternative meanings. The Late Postclassic Aztec peoples of the Valley of Mexico used the term *Toltecayotl* (having the qualities of the Toltecs) to refer to a complex of cultural ideals inherited from the Toltecs, who were described as surpassing artists, craftsmen, and architects (Sahagún 1950–1982, 10; Sodi 1962; Leon-Portilla 1963, 1980). Interpreted in this broad sense as a hearth of civilization, Teotihuacan, with its vast number of temples, palaces, and mural paintings, was probably considered the first Tollan or "great metropolis"(cf. Davies 1975, 1977: 44, 1984).[21]

The Mexica buildings, although not exact duplicates of any known Teotihuacan building, nevertheless display a concern for archaeological accuracy in both form and painting style. Moreover, the difference between these buildings and typical Mexica ceremonial temple architecture makes it clear that the Mexica recognized that a gulf of time separated them from the original creators of such architecture. By carefully duplicating Teotihuacan buildings, the Mexica signaled their ties with that ancient metropolitan center of art, culture, and political power. The Mexica *talud-tablero* structures may be compared with the periodic revivals or 'renascences' of antique forms during the Middle Ages, particularly with the Carolingian *renovatio* (Panofsky 1960: 42–47; Kubler 1985: 198). Like Odo of Metz, who adapted classical and Byzantine architectural forms in the Palace Chapel at Aachen to support Charlemagne's claim to rule as "Holy Roman Emperor," and to suggest that the Frankish empire was the legitimate successor to Rome, the Mexica placed replicas of *talud-tablero* buildings in their most sacred precinct to demonstrate their links with a "Toltec" past and to validate their imperial supremacy as the "people of the sun" created by divine sacrifice at Teotihuacan.

Notes

1. See Millon (1992) for a review of archaeology at and changing interpretations of Teotihuacan.
2. Variant interpretations are cited in Millon (1992: 359). Thelma D.

Sullivan, cited in Millon (1992: 359; 1993: 34) provides an alternate translation as "the place of those who have the road (or avenue) of the gods."

3. Two gods, Tecuciztecatl and Nanahuatzín, competed for the honor of becoming the sun, with Nanahuatzín courageously effecting the self-transformation by immolating himself in a divine hearth. Then a communal sacrifice of the assembled gods assured that the sun, moon, and other heavenly bodies would shine and move in their paths. The convocation of the deities and their resultant sacrifice, which assured light and life for the present humanity, are described in various conquest-period sources, including the Anales de Cuauhtitlan and the *Leyenda de los Soles* (Anales de Cuauhtitlan 1973: 5), the Historia de los mexicanos por sus pinturas (1973: 32, 36) as well as in the Florentine Codex by Bernardino de Sahagún (1950–1982, 7: 4). Caso (1958) provides a redaction of the cosmogonic myth from these sources.

4. Linda Manzanilla (1993; Manzanilla et al. 1989) notes that Teotihuacan is built over a series of such caves and discusses their significance. According to George Cowgill (personal communication, June 1996) Manzanilla now feels that these caves are artificial rather than natural. Millon (1992: 385) observes that, "The Teotihuacanos altered the form of the cave [beneath the Sun Pyramid] in various ways, made offerings of food and performed rituals in it involving fire, water, fish, and shell."

5. Millon (1993: 35) points out that the sightline in question also seems to have marked the sunset position on April 29 and August 12, which are separated from one another by day counts of 260 and 105 (52 + 1 + 52), numbers which "other Mesoamericans would have regarded as charged with meaning." The August 12 date is particularly important, because it coincides with the date (13.0.0.0.0 4 Ahaw 8 Cumku) associated with the beginning of the present world era and new creation in Maya calendrical inscriptions. Millon (1993: 35) writes

> Since the sacred cave at Teotihuacan was believed to be *where* time began, the fact that a sightline from its mouth to the western horizon commemorated *when time* began must have been seen as having extraordinary significance.
>
> Consequently, the sightline from the cave to the western horizon (15.5 degrees north of west) commemorated the birth of the cosmos at Teotihuacan, the beginning of the present era, the day that time began, and the zenith passage of the sun at Teotihuacan and in part of the Maya area, as well as two sacred counts—the 260-day ritual calendar and the 52-year calendar round.

6. According to Millon (1992: 390), "The avenue extended north for half a mile where it culminated in a surrogate sacred mountain, the first great pyramid, probably dedicated to the Great Goddess. This was the first Moon Pyramid, much simpler than the final one."

7. Berlo (1992) provides a recent overview of the "Great Goddess," and her important role in Teotihuacán religion and iconography. Pasztory (1992) has specifically proposed that a goddess was featured as the principal deity at the city in order to create a universal symbol that would integrate an urban community that was probably multiethnic and of differing ranks, statuses, and occupations.

8. However, significant amounts of Tzacualli phase ceramics have

been found in the Ciudadela, and René Millon (1973: 52) suggests that the planning and initial stages of the compound may date to this period. Sarro (1991: 251) similarly notes that

> The layout of at least the northern half of the Avenue of the Dead and the earliest phases of the pyramids of the Sun and of the Moon date from the Tzacualli phase. If the Ciudadela had been planned at this time it would have been as part of a unified urban plan that included these three great structures, with the Pyramid of the Sun near its center.

9. The CDLM Complex's principal period of occupation and construction was during the Late Tlamimilolpa and Xolalpan periods, so it is possible that there may have been a shift from the Ciudadela to the CDLM as a principal administrative center (George Cowgill, personal communication, June 1996). According to Cowgill (personal communication, June 1996), INAH excavations in 1993–94 revealed geometric mural decorations in the earliest stage of the North Palace of the Ciudadela, although there seems to be a paucity of later murals.

10. According to Millon (1993: 40), evidence suggests that the compounds housed cognatic descent units, with a preference for patrilocal residence. Many of the more prosperous apartment compounds have important and consistent formal similarities, both in their orientation, which they share with that of the Street of the Dead, and in their general layouts, although Millon (1993: 29) also points out that none of them have identical plans.

11. Millon (1993: 40) also notes that

> When the "Street of the Dead" was laid out in the first century A.D., many three-temple complexes were built on or near the "Street of the Dead" and in the city's northwest quadrant. The early political role these temple complexes appear to have played may indicate that they subsequently formed part of the city's administrative structure.

12. Earlier Olmec examples of apparent feathered or crested serpents occur in cave murals at Oxtotitlan and Juxtlahuaca, Guerrero, and on Monument 19 at La Venta, Tabasco (Bernal 1969: plate 58; Joralemon 1971: 82–83).

13. Nicholson (1979: 35) observes of Quetzalcoatl that "This god clearly expressed, above all, the fundamental fertility theme with particular emphasis on the fructifying–vivifying aspect of the wind."

14. Coe (1981: 168) interpreted these paired rings in a numerical sense, as a reference to duality. According to Sarro (1991: 251), Coe "sees the pyramid as depicting the creation of the universe through oppositions, and the power of the city's ruler through his association with this dual creator god."

15. Coggins (1983b) also views the temple as the focus of calendrical rituals, but interprets the two heads as front and rear heads of a bicephalic creature related to the Maya "cosmic monster" or "celestial dragon." Sugiyama's and Taube's identification of the saurian head as a headdress rather than as a rear head seems more plausible. Sarro (1991: 253) compares the composition to the coupling of feathered serpent images with superimposed Tlaloc faces on an altar from the Painted

Patio at Atetelco, and notes that "The representation in both is less that of a two-headed serpent, as as been suggested, than that of a feathered serpent depicted in relationship to the saurian creature."

16. The use of the feathered serpent cult to cross-cut lineage ties and to integrate a segmentary state seems to have been characteristic among the K'iche' and other Late Postclassic Maya groups in the Guatemala highlands (see Fox 1987). A similar function has been proposed for the feathered serpent cult at early Postclassic Chichén Itzá (Kubler 1982; Schele and Freidel 1990: chapter 9; see Stone, chapter 13, this volume).

17. Important previous studies of variants of *talud-tablero* architecture and related architectural profiles throughout Mesoamerica include those of Kubler (1973) and Gendrop (1984). Giddens (1995) has reexamined the topic.

18. The front and side walls of Structure 612 at Dzibilchaltun (dated to Early Period I, ca. A.D. 600–700) feature a heavily framed *tablero* atop a sharply battered *talud* (Andrews and Andrews 1980: 73–74, figures 71–75; Andrews 1981: 325, figure 11-9) whose 2:1 *tablero*-to-*talud* ratio is closer to Teotihuacan models than the 1:1 ratios at Kaminaljuyú, Matacapan, and Tikal. Unlike these other sites, however, there are no Teotihuacan-style ceramics accompanying Structure 612, making the nature of Teotihuacan's contact with Dzibilchaltún unclear. Andrews (1981: 325–326, 339) has speculated that the architectural similarities may "reflect the presence of a small elite group of foreigners who controlled the local populace in order to exploit nearby salt resources." Dzibilchaltún Structure 38 featured a variant of *talud-tablero* profiling on its lowest platform terrace. The *tablero* is open-ended and has stepped frames on two levels, unlike true Teotihuacan models. The Pure Florescent date (ca. A.D. 800–1000) of Structure 38 suggests that it incorporates influences from Epiclassic central Mexican sites such as Cholula (Andrews and Andrews 1980: 162–163). The exact nature of interaction with the West Mexican sites is also poorly understood, as is their dating, although Tingambato and Teticpac el Viejo are generally placed in the Middle to Late Classic (ca. A.D. 500–900), while Ixtepete is apparently of Early Postclassic date (Gendrop 1984: 48).

19. Giddens (1995: 69) refers to this form as a "scallop talud-tablero profile." Ellen Baird (1981: 5) has suggested that the feline, coyote, and jaguar-bird-serpent sculptures adorning the Tula terraces also may derive from Teotihuacan, and that the Toltecs "turned to the most prestigious Central Mexican culture, Teotihuacan, for such symbols of legitimacy." Diehl (1983: 94) reports a minor example of *talud-tablero* terracing on a rectangular altar against the south wall of room 6 of the Corral locality house at Tula. The El Corral round temple has terraces with *taluds* supporting simple, nonframed tableros like those at Teotenango (Diehl 1983: 64, figure 15). Variants of the "scallop" *talud-tablero* profile also occur on several smaller platforms at Chichén Itzá (e.g., Platform of the Eagles and Jaguars, Venus Platform, small platform east of the High Priest's Grave) as well. Giddens (1995: 67, figure 53) notes that an Epiclassic version of the "scalloped" *talud-tablero* also appears on Structure F at Cacaxtla, Tlaxcala (see Lombardo de Ruiz et al. 1986: lám. 28).

20. Such bands are usually small-scale border elements, but larger versions exist in the Quetzalpapalotl Palace (Miller 1973: 44, plates 6–7). A close parallel also exists between the Mexica platforms and the altar in a patio south of the Zacuala Palace at Teotihuacan (Séjourné 1959: figure 86).

21. Indeed, specific reference to Teotihuacan as a "Toltec" city is made by Ixtlilxochitl (1952, 1: 18, 84, 138), while a glyph of tules (or rushes), normally used as the name for Tollan, is used to identify Teotihuacan on the *Mapa Quinatzin* (Davies 1984: 209). The multivalent meanings of the word *Toltec* seem to be attested in Mexica artworks such as the Chacmool sculpture, which duplicates the general pose of Chacmools from Tula, Hidalgo (or Chichén Itzá) (Nicholson and Keber 1983: 32–33; Umberger 1987), but which also displays the goggle-eyed features of the Teotihuacan god Tlaloc (Pasztory 1988b).

5

Classic Veracruz Architecture

Cultural Symbolism in Time and Space

S. Jeffrey K. Wilkerson

Although the cultural patterns of the ancient high cultures of Mesoamerica sprang from common origins of great time depth, there were highly distinctive regional traditions of symbolism, particularly in architecture and art, which denote significant nuances in both time and space. Nowhere is this more apparent than along the Mexican Gulf Coast around the central portions of the present-day state of Veracruz. This environmentally diverse swath of tropical Mexico produced one of the most expressive, and eccentric, components of Mesoamerican civilization.

The lands adjoining the arching western shore of the Gulf of Mexico can be divided into several major subareas which conform to overlapping natural and culture units of great antiquity (Wilkerson 1972, 1974a, 1988). The portions that are the focus of this chapter correspond to the north-central and south-central Gulf areas (figure 5.1). These units approximate, but are not restricted to, the core of modern Veracruz. Much of this vast region slopes sharply seaward from the Sierra Madre Oriental, which soars up to 5,700 meters in height at Mount Orizaba *(Citlatepetl)*. While most of the known archaeological remains are found in the humid low-lands adjacent to the coast, there are closely related sites situated at least as high as 2,500 meters elevation in the dry, and today largely arid, plains of the central Mexican Plateau which abut the mountains on the west.

In this broad expanse of country, there existed during the Classic Period (ca. A.D. 300–900), and a local Epiclassic Period (ca. A.D. 900–1100) highly distinctive architecture characterized by niches, unique "flying cornices," and repetitive stepped frets. Contemporary in both time and space with these structures was an elegant and complex art style utilizing ornate scrolls that has also been called "Classic Veracruz" (Proskouriakoff 1954, 1971). Unemphasized in many examinations of this highly expressive art is the fact that much of the sculpture comes from an architectural context or depicts architectural locations in its

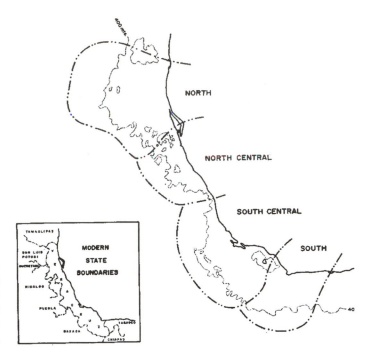

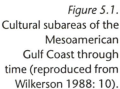

Figure 5.1.
Cultural subareas of the
Mesoamerican
Gulf Coast through
time (reproduced from
Wilkerson 1988: 10).

motifs. In reality, the cultural symbolism of both the architecture and the art was interwoven to such a degree that neither is amply intelligible without an understanding of the other.

The maximum known expression of Classic Veracruz architecture and art is the great city of El Tajín. As the metropolitan center of a major culture and the capital city of a significant pre–Hispanic state, it contains many of the more elaborate examples of both the architectural and art styles. It is here that engineering concepts of nearly modern scope evolved, resulting in massive poured-concrete roofs, as well as some innovative experimentation with shell-form ceilings. Here too, a large walled enclosure was constructed in the shape of a gigantic fret, and huge columns were completely sculpted in elaborate ritual scenes celebrating a major ruler. This densely packed site also contains one of the greatest concentrations of ballcourts known in Mesoamerica. In the narrative sculptures that are found in these courts are depictions of some of the very same buildings of the city, showing their direct relationship to this important complex of rituals. Still other structures contain murals and painted designs in the Classic Veracruz style, paralleling those found on the better known portable stone sculptures (yokes, *hachas*, and *palmas*) associated with ballgame ritualism throughout the greater Gulf Coast.

Although many examples for this study are drawn from El Tajín, also included are data from other sites throughout central Veracruz, including some newly discovered centers of considerable importance (figure 5.2).

The purpose here is to examine across time and space as much of the region as possible. Building features displayed on portable sculptures, a hitherto rarely utilized source of architectural information, are also considered. Additionally, for comparative purposes, there is some discussion of Preclassic and Postclassic architecture as well as contemporary architecture in areas contiguous to the core Classic Veracruz domain.

The Metropolitan City of El Tajín

The extensive region where Classic Veracruz architecture and art was dominant was probably never completely unified politically, culturally, or even ethnically. Nevertheless, if one had to select a "capital city" for the apogee of Classic Veracruz expression, based on current archaeological knowledge, it would have to be El Tajín (figures 5.2 and 5.3). It is not the city's large size alone that obligates this designation, but rather

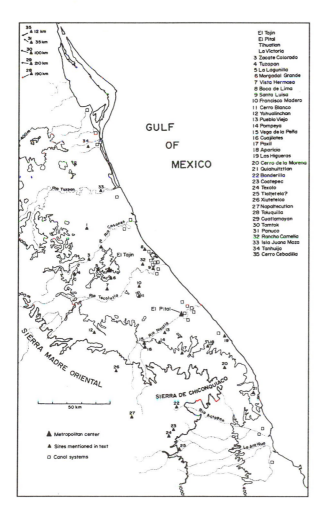

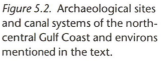

Figure 5.2. Archaeological sites and canal systems of the north-central Gulf Coast and environs mentioned in the text.

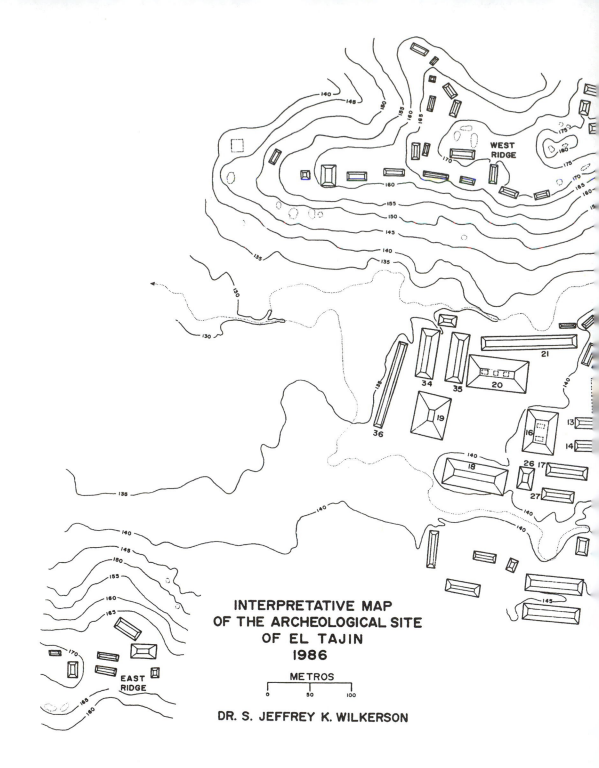

Figure 5.3. Interpretative map of El Tajín (Wilkerson 1986).

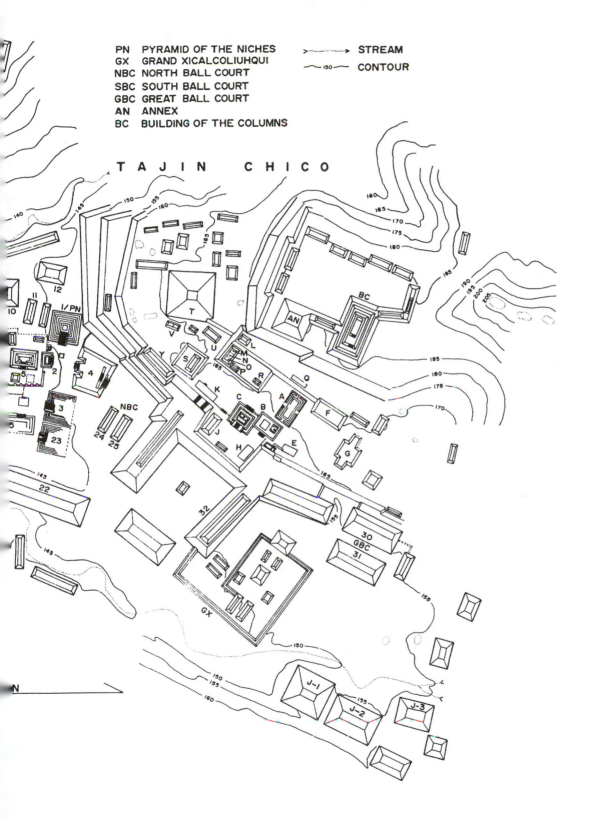

PN   PYRAMID OF THE NICHES
GX   GRAND XICALCOLIUHQUI
NBC NORTH BALL COURT
SBC SOUTH BALL COURT
GBC GREAT BALL COURT
AN   ANNEX
BC   BUILDING OF THE COLUMNS

STREAM

CONTOUR

T A J I N   C H I C O

the mature florescence of its architecture and art from the middle of the Classic period through the Epiclassic period. El Tajín was a city of ornate sophistication that rivaled virtually any of its Mesoamerican contemporaries.

The rulers glorified—even deified—in the huge sculptural corpus of the city certainly held sway over broad domains and were at the center of extensive commercial networks. They traded with polities that may have been situated well beyond their immediate central Gulf Coast homeland and probably even beyond the northeastern frontier of Mesoamerica itself (Wilkerson 1972, 1985, 1994a). At their disposal were artists, architects, and engineers of the highest caliber, perhaps even "schools" of such creative artisans and craftsmen. Their expressive works have slowly come to light in recent decades and are forceful testimonies to both ample talent and creative experimentation. In short, during the city's florescence, El Tajín was a thriving metropolitan center in the broadest cultural and artistic sense, and it is likely to have been considered as such by the ancient inhabitants of the Gulf Coast. It is here, at this major focus of expression, that we must focus the examination of the symbolism of Classic Veracruz architecture.

El Tajín fills a steep-sided valley situated in a ridge separating the Tecolutla and Cazones catchments in north-central Veracruz. The city spills out of its confining slopes around a brook that joins the Tlahuanapa Stream, an affluent of the Tecolutla River. The approximately 20-kilometer stretch of meandering waterway running eastward to the juncture with the river, where there appears to have been an important canoe port center, is marked by a series of satellite sites placed, in some instances, as close as a kilometer apart. The river itself, passing other important Tajín culture sites, winds through hills and rich alluvial plains to the Gulf of Mexico coast some 53 kilometers distant. Nearing the coast, the deltaic plain around the major site of Santa Luisa is covered with truly massive hydraulic systems for the intensive production of food, and, very likely, trade and luxury items such as cacao and cotton for cloth (Wilkerson 1975, 1976, 1983, 1990).

There was another axis of satellite sites in a northwestward direction from El Tajín, traversing the low hills toward the Cazones River, a smaller and less navigable watercourse than the Tecolutla. Some of these centers, such as La Lagunilla, had ornate palace structures similar to those of the city itself, suggesting elite compounds along a major route of access. On the Cazones itself were a number of important related sites, such as Zacate Colorado and La Victoria. Both of these were situated at ideal points to control both fluvial traffic and the rich alluvial plains of the river's middle drainage. The immediate environs of El Tajín at its apogee was a densely populated realm stretching from the Gulf of Mexico to the eastern face of the Sierra Madre Oriental with the great city at its center.

As an urban center El Tajín is, in spite of its proximity to the urbanized cultures of the central Mexican plateau, largely a lowland phenomenon.

Its builders placed a conceptual emphasis on structures designed to be individual visual units. Instances of symmetry, either in multiple building complexes, or often within a larger building itself, tend to be more apparent than real. Enclosed plazas are used to unify building groupings rather than the streets or cul-de-sac plaza alignments common in the highlands at the time. These general attributes are part of a pattern that the city shares with the greater southeastern Mesoamerican lowlands. El Tajín contrasts in this measure with cities of the much closer contemporary cultures of central Mexico, which placed a considerable emphasis on symmetry as well as visual repetitiveness of both design and layout (see Kowalski on Teotihuacan, chapter 4, this volume). This, however, does not mean that architectural attributes of highland origin are absent in the city.

Flat roofs on major masonry structures and stone merlons on the tops of temples are shared with central Mexico (see figure 5.11). It also appears that the distinctive cornice-niche-*talud* profile of many structures at El Tajín is derived from the simpler, and ultimately older, *talud-tablero* format used in central Mexico throughout the metropolis of Teotihuacan (figures 5.4 and 5.5). In intermediate areas, such as the Valley of Puebla, the use of this combination of lower sloping wall supporting a vertical upper panel encased by a border, may be earlier still (García Cook 1981). While there is no known utilization of pointed cornices of Tajín style at Teotihuacan, the ornate Temple of Agriculture has a molding capping a *talud* in a similar manner (figure 5.4). However, the extensive use of the cornice at El Tajín, where it becomes an integral part of the distinctive architectural symbolism of the city, is exceptional and culturally motivated.

The process by which earlier architectural influences reached El Tajín is still somewhat speculative. There has yet to be an intensive archaeological examination of the crucial Protoclassic (ca. A.D. 100–300) and Early Classic (ca. A.D. 300–600) periods in this portion of the Gulf Coast, the time when the highly dynamic Teotihuacan culture profoundly affected much of Mesoamerica. Toward the end of this chapter, some of the possible roots of this relationship are considered in the light of new field exploration at El Pital and interpretive analysis in the region.

The city itself appears to have been divided into several units which developed through time in response to differing factors, and not just demographic expansion (figure 5.3). The gently inclined valley base, its triangular core confined by two merging streams, contains most of the major ballcourts and many of the still visible older buildings. Here too are numerous later, and larger, multiple sanctuary structures. This area, built around a series of plazas paved with large flagstones, is known as El Tajín proper. The now seasonal waterways along its borders may have been modified at points to create dry season reservoirs or even protective barriers. Above the valley base, perched on both natural slopes and massive areas of artificial fill, is an acropolis protected by huge sloping walls

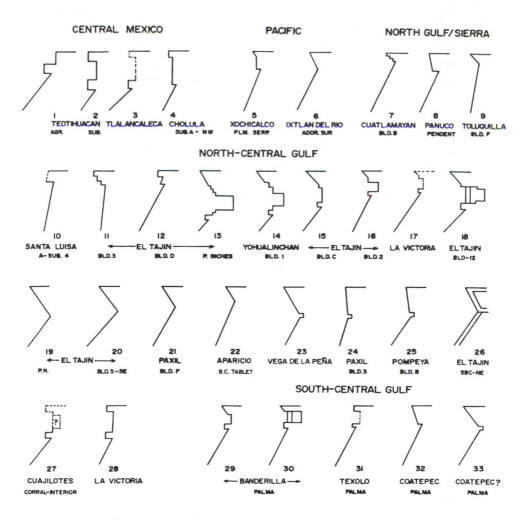

Figure 5.4. Profiles of Classic Veracruz and related building platforms. (Sources from which profiles were derived or abstracted: 1. Marquina 1964: 89; 2. Marquina 1964: 98; 3. García Cook 1981: figure 8–10; 4. Marquina 1964: 120; 5. Marquina 1964: 133; 6. Corona Nuñez 1953: figures 66–70; 7. DuSolier 1945, Marquina 1964: 408; 8. Beyer 1934: plate 1; 9. Marquina 1964: 240; 10. Wilkerson 1972: figure 215; 11. García Payon in Wilkerson 1987: 54; 12. García Payon in Wilkerson 1987: 44; 13. García Vega in Marquina 1964: 428; 14. Wilkerson field observation; 15. García Payon in Wilkerson 1987: 39; 16. García Payon in Wilkerson 1987: 33; 17 and 18. Wilkerson field observation; 19. Kampen 1972: figure 19a; 20. Tablet in Museo de Antropología, Xalapa; 21. García Payon 1947: 96; 22. Wilkerson field observation; 23. Wilkerson field observation, Wilkerson 1993: figure 18; 24. García Payon 1947: 94; 25. Wilkerson field observation, Wilkerson 1994c, d; 26. Kampen 1972: 140; 27. Wilkerson field observation; 28. García Payon 1971: 527; 29 and 30. Arrelanos and Beauregard 1981: 144, 147, 148, 157; 31. Fewkes 1907: plate 106; 32. Krickeberg 1933: grab. 8; 33 Proskouriakoff 1954: figures 6–11.)

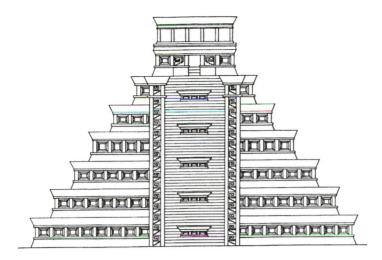

Figure 5.5.
Reconstructive rendering of the east front of the Pyramid of the Niches, El Tajín (drawing by Wilkerson, reproduced from Wilkerson 1987: 32).

for defensive purposes. In this portion, called Tajín Chico, temples are also found, but so too are most of the major palace structures. To either side of the city were densely inhabited slopes, enhanced in places by inclined defensive walls, named the East and West Ridges. Mostly smaller temples, palaces, and ballcourts are situated here. A fifth area, apparently the principal direction of access, stretches southward from the juncture of the two streams. This includes numerous stucco-floored plazas and unexplored low structures. Some of these may be of late date, as there is ceramic evidence of a terminal Postclassic village in this area. This still undefined unit, now covered with much erosional silt caused by modern deforestation, extends more than a kilometer to the present Totonac village of El Tajín.

These five areas represent the major concentrations of stone buildings. But close in and about them, as was found at Santa Luisa (Wilkerson 1972, 1974b, 1975, 1978, 1980), would have been many other perishable structures and living areas. The greater city, not just the central portion of major stone structures described above, is likely to have approximated 1100 hectares in extent according to a preliminary survey (Ponciano Ortíz, personal communication).

Niches and Cornices

One of the most distinctive aspects of the architecture at El Tajín are the ubiquitous niches. These are generally set in the vertical wall (*tablero*) arising from the sloping *talud* and are capped by a pointed cornice. These features, uniquely combined in Tajín architecture, provide a horizontal emphasis to the structures. This was sometimes highlighted by the use of color, for El Tajín was an emblazoned city. Although most of the buildings in the city were painted red, and occasionally Maya blue and yellow, some of the major structures were polychrome at different periods in their histories. At times the niches were painted with black or other dark shades, which provided a striking visual contrast with the lighter exteriors. Even later in time, when niches were replaced by stepped frets, these were recessed so as to provide the same darkened illusion of a horizontal niche line.

Much has been made, particularly in analysis of the Pyramid of the Niches (figure 5.5), about the number and significance of the niches. The total count varies, depending on whether it includes the niches buried beneath the stairway or the selected theoretical reconstruction of the now-destroyed summit of the structure. Nevertheless, interpretations have ranged from proposing each niche as an individual shrine containing its own, now lost, image, to considering the building a monumental calendar of the solar year. While the Temple of Niches may indeed be special, probably as the principal shrine of the city erected by, or in memory of, an important ancestral ruler (Wilkerson 1987, 1990), dozens of other buildings fail to correspond to such numerological propositions. It is not unusual for niche lines on buildings in the city to be asymmetrical in number about a stairway, or even to have a differing number on each side of an apparently square structure. The core symbolic meaning of the niche is certain to reside in criteria other than how they can be counted.

Caves, at least since Olmec times (more than a millennium before El Tajín), were a major Mesoamerican symbol of the entrance to the underworld, the abode of the gods, especially the rain god, and dead rulers (see Kowalski, chapter 4, and Freidel and Suhler, chapter 11, this volume). Deities and mortals of high status are often portrayed officiating from an elevated niche. There is a connotation of both extreme sacredness and rank associated with such recesses. The lingering supernatural nature of caves and fissures, particularly those with springs, is still acknowledged today by offerings of flowers and candles on the Day of the Cross (May 3). This practice, occuring at the height of the dry season but just before the first sharp storms that herald the initiation of the rains, is still common throughout much of the lowlands. At the Temple of the Niches offerings were sometimes placed in some of the lower niches as recently as the early 1960s.

At El Tajín niches may occur on any structure, but they are most common on temples, administrative buildings, and open platforms used for public rituals. They may also be placed on retaining walls, such as that which surrounds the acropolis of Tajín Chico (by Building D), and even on buttresses erected to contain slumping structures (as probably on two sides of Building A and the fronts of Buildings 16 and 23). Stairways, some on temples otherwise devoid of these features, may have sets of three or more niches placed at intervals along the center line, much like altars on the ascending stone pathways to the sanctuaries (Arroyo Group structures). The tops of balustrades, both functional (Buildings 3, 15) or simply decorative in low relief (Building A, south front), may also be capped with niches. With time there appears to be a general reduction in the size of the niche utilized. This tendency coincides with the selection of a reduced *tablero*, extended *talud*, and a general shift to fret symbolism.

The common significance of these niches, throughout their long and varied use at El Tajín, seems to be to emphasize the sacredness of the precincts and the symbolic relationship to the supernatural abode of both the gods and deified rulers. Their mode of employment at El Tajín, especially in the massive—yet visually delicate—Temple of the Niches, constitutes an achievement of elegance unique in Mesoamerican architecture.

At the present time, the use of such features in the immediate vicinity of the city is only confirmed from a few sites in the Tecolutla River valley (figure 5.6). There is some evidence from several other sites in the adjoining drainages, the Cazones and Tuxpan to the north and the Nautla to the south, suggesting that they may also have buildings with niches. Southward, but at a generally higher elevation, there is further evidence of the use of niches. In the region of Banderilla-Coatepec-Xico a number of portable ballgame sculptures, called *palmas*, have been found. These depict rituals, some sacrificial, atop small platforms with niches (figure 5.7). These structures are similar to the open platforms found near the South Ballcourt (on the basal platform of Building 5 and between Buildings 5 and 15) at El Tajín and seem to depict ritualism similar to that found on the massive columns of the local ruler 13 Rabbit at the site. Further south of Xico, between Jacomulco and Huatusco, a site (Tlaltetela?) with niches has been reported (Ponciano Ortíz, personal communication). It seems that the area of niche use was quite extensive indeed (figure 5.6).

Many structures, particularly basal platforms for other buildings, for instance the platform surrounding Building 5, have only a cornice and *talud* and no *tablero* or niche at all. While such basal platforms are markers of an architectural horizon in the El Tajín heartland, the nicheless profile with a prominent cornice is also common throughout the greater region at sites such as Vega de la Peña, Pompeya, and Paxil. It occurs even at points of probable El Tajín influence at considerable distances to the northwest, as at Cuatlamayan in the Huasteca of San Luis Potosí (DuSolier 1945) and Toluquilla in Querétaro (Marquina 1964: 240). In other instances, as westward at Xochicalco in the state of Morelos, the *tablero* is greatly reduced and functions as part of the cornice (see Molina and Kowalski, chapter 6, this volume). However, at El Tajín niches appear to never be totally suppressed, except possibly in the last brief phases of construction at the site when the cornice and *talud* disappear to be replaced by plain vertical walls. Even then, stairways may be adorned with niches (Buildings 19 and 23).

The variant forms of early niche construction, sometimes utilizing huge limestone flags, strongly recall the joining techniques of fine carpentry.

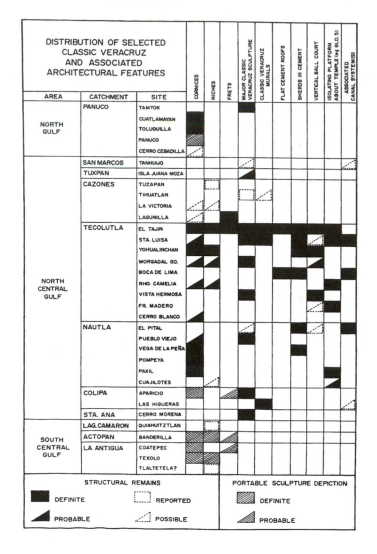

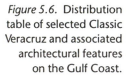

Figure 5.6. Distribution table of selected Classic Veracruz and associated architectural features on the Gulf Coast.

Regardless of the methodological origins of assembly, the first major structures with niches at the site are likely to date to the latter half of the Early Classic period (ca. A.D. 300–600). This corresponds to the approximate stylistic date of the huge corpus of sculpture from the sanctuary of the Temple of the Niches, which appears to celebrate the ritual prerogatives, and perhaps even apotheosis, of a singularly important ancestral ruler. At about the same time similar, albeit less carefully crafted (Palacios 1926), buildings covered in niches are built at Yohualinchan, a related site on a major contact route to the highlands via the Apulco branch of the Tecolutla River. Other structures at El Tajín, including the earliest portion of the North Ballcourt and the Great Xicalcoliuhqui may be of similar or slightly later date. This latter structure is actually a large, walled precinct capped with niches and in the form of a fret. It may herald the growing importance of new symbolism that would soon be utilized, even merged, with the niche format.

Figure 5.7. Ballgame palma from Banderilla depicting a (sacrificial?) ritual on an open platform with niches (drawing by Leopoldo Franco; sculpture in the Museo de Antropología, Xalapa).

Frets

The stepped fret at El Tajín eventually becomes nearly as common as the niche, and in some instances it was used as a surrogate. Clearly it had considerable importance in the later history of the site, a time when it was utilized in a multitude of forms. Unlike the niche, it is found frequently on palace walls, usually in vertical friezes. Here its varied repetitive designs may be made of stucco, sculpted upon stone armatures (Building of the Columns, Building A interior), or of finely cut stones set in a manner similar to that of the Puuc region of Yucatán (Building A exterior; figure 5.8). On temples (Building 5) and some administrative structures (Building C) it is recessed and linked so as to imitate a niche line. It also occurs in a similar manner on open platforms used for elite rituals as depicted on *palmas* from Texolo (figure 5.4) and Coatepec (Krickeberg 1933: grab. 9; Wilkerson 1990: 174). In some other cases, the deliberate illusion of niches is heightened by the extreme recessing of the frets and the addition of vertical dividing frames in the form of small

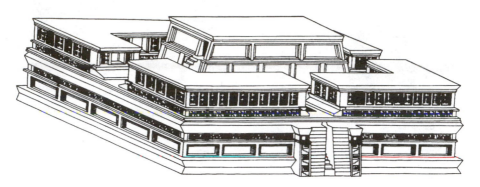

Figure 5.8. Hypothetical reconstructive rendering of Building A, El Tajín, by José García Payon (reproduced from Wilkerson 1987: 49).

columns (Building 12). Frets may also be used on basal walls (Building of the Columns, east exterior portico) or *taluds* (Building D). They were also painted on sanctuary walls and covered with Classic Veracruz scrolls (Building 11).

When used as niche substitutes, the frets tend to be arranged so that the stepped portions form vertical dividers, further enhancing the visual similarity to niche lines. When used on friezes, frets may be grouped in various multiple units, some even approximating a swastika (Building A interior). These more elaborate examples were often formed of polychrome stucco on interior walls or corridors. In general, the fret units appear to be freely combined and to have considerable versatility in their placement and architectural use. They also appear to coincide with an increased use in stucco decoration that also included stepped merlon forms (Buildings B and D) and other reticulated designs (Buildings D and A). Eventually much of this intricate decoration on interior palace walls and exterior structural surfaces and stairways was completely covered over in Tajín Chico, the portion of the city where it was most prevalent (for example: Buildings A, B, D, and J [recently relabeled as I]).

Frets are found also on balustrades such as that of the Pyramid of the Niches (figure 5.5). That same temple front is found reproduced, in a mode highly reminiscent of Maya Rio Bec architectural styling, as a low-relief stucco replica surrounding the corbeled entranceway of the palace Building A (figure 5.8). The large, stepped frets in stone of the balustrades of the Pyramid of the Niches, as well as the stepless fret format of the Great Xicalcoliuhqui, suggest that the symbol was already in use at the zenith of niche construction.

The stepped fret at El Tajín is likely to have connotations parallel to those of the niche, with its emphasis on divinity, sacredness, water, and rank. In documents such as the Lienzos de Tuxpan (Melgarejo 1970) and the *Relaciones Geográficas de Gueytlapan* (García Payón 1965), it is later used by indigenous artists in this same region in the decades immediately after the Spanish Conquest as a symbol for moving water. Its use at El Tajín is likely to be associated with both rain and wind. Rain-wind deities, or their surrogates, are often shown holding scrolled staffs or serpents in their hands in codices that may be from the Gulf Coast area (e.g., *Codex Laud*). These objects also appear in the deity depictions in the South Ballcourt and may have a meaning associated with that of the frets.

The frets may correspond to an increased emphasis on the wind god that extended throughout much of the coast at this time. This is not necessarily a simple variant of the "Quetzalcoatl complex" which came to be so important in Postclassic highland central Mexico, and which some have retrospectively generalized for the lowlands also. The origins here may ultimately pertain to the much earlier form of the wind deity that by 1000 B.C. was abundantly symbolized in this same region by the ehécatl-coxcatl ("wind jewel") glyph, a type of spiral stepped fret resembling a cut conch shell (Wilkerson 1972). In the sculptures of the South Ballcourt, the wind god is a personage second only to the rain god in significance (see figure 5.11). In fact, the wind god may well have been viewed at the time as a secondary or alternative manifestation of the rain god.

Regardless of the deity association, the use of the stepped fret at El Tajín again is likely to be an indicator of sacredness of the buildings that it adorns. It is most common on palaces and administrative structures used by the elite (see Sharp 1978). In such contexts it would also carry a strong connotation of the crucial relationship assumed to exist between the rulers and the powerful deities that control the often violent rains and winds of the Gulf Coast. After the niche, the stepped fret is one of the principal motifs of the city. At this time the limited evidence from other sites in the region suggests that its elaborate architectural use may be largely a phenomenon of the metropolitan center and its immediate satellites. This would be in keeping with the growing concentration of elite ritual activities there in the city as it grew in size, pan-regional importance, and established ritual and commercial interchange networks with distant centers.

Engineering Techniques

Many buildings at El Tajín display exceptional engineering skills. This is particularly apparent in Tajín Chico, where the use of concrete in a number of buildings is astonishingly sophisticated. Thick stucco and cement coverings had long been used at the site, not so much to bind masonry as to seal it and provide a base for paint. It would appear that as the large stone flags used frequently in earlier structures in the city became more scarce with time, there was a deliberate effort to use concrete in their stead. This change of medium made possible the creation of considerably larger rooms that greatly exceeded the small spaces characteristic of the earlier structures. It also led to design changes in the buildings, suggesting a deliberate and audacious experimentation with the new medium.

An excellent example of this is Building B, a two-story palace in the heart of the Tajín Chico acropolis (figure 5.9). The lowest story, elevated above a small plaza and accessible via a wide stairway, is an ample 9.75 by 7.25 meters. The story above is divided into two rooms, the larger of which was approximately 11 by 15 meters. This extensive space may have been used as some form of ritual meeting or council chamber, as a bench runs completely around it. Covering this room was a massive roof requiring nearly 350 cubic meters of concrete.

The great thickness of the roof slab, ranging up to about a meter, was necessitated by the lack of internal reinforcement of the concrete. Nevertheless, the bonding required for the successive layers of this massive amount of cement was achieved by placing jagged fragments of pottery in the upper portion of each poured cap. The bearing weight was also reduced by the use of ample amounts of pumice-stone nodules. The form apparently was attained by molding the roof shape with packed earth below and wood on the sides. The top of the huge roof was not completely flat but sloped for runoff.

This experimentation with concrete as a stone substitute created structural problems. The lack of internal support, today accomplished by steel rods, necessitated massive proportions of enormous weight, which in some cases resulted in dangerous sagging. This was remedied in Building B by increasing the size of the supporting pillars with thick coats of cement and rock, which in turn reduced the spaciousness of the rooms. In other structures this problem was reduced by not directly superimposing rooms, and instead using solid-fill support (Building A, figure 5.8) or by reducing one dimension of the span to be covered, creating a narrow gallerylike space (Building C).

There are other innovative structural uses of cement at El Tajín. Shell forms were employed in a few instances to reduce roof weights and increase the space being covered. There is a limited use of a shell form in Building C, a structure seemingly designed for official audiences. The largest example yet known is the entire east portico of the Building of the Columns. Here it appears that a massive shell rested on top of the thick, carved columns celebrating the rule of a man named 13 Rabbit (Wilkerson 1987: 51). Still other effective practices include coating fill and veneer masonry walls with an asphalt sealant (Building 5). There may also be some concrete roofs treated in the same manner with this natural and readily available impermeable substance.

In general, there were truly remarkable accomplishments in construction techniques and architectural design at El Tajín that set the city apart from its Mesoamerican contemporaries. These features, which are reminiscent of modern Western practices, undoubtedly were considered culturally symbolic at the time they were in use. Any ancient visitor would have been awed by the elaborate, multicolored buildings meant to exalt

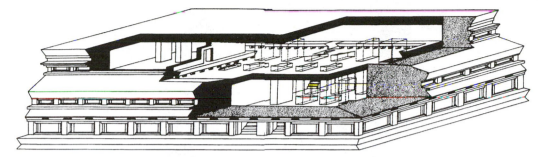

Figure 5.9. Interpretative rendering of Building B, El Tajín, by José García Payon (reproduced from Wilkerson 1987: 46–47).

the gods and rulers of the city. Based on the available archaeological evidence, the distribution of these attributes appears to be restricted to the environs of the metropolitan center, primarily in the nearby Tecolutla, Cazones, and Nautla drainages. El Tajín was an exceptionally creative expression of the apogee of Classic Veracruz architecture.

Ballgame Symbolism

Ballgame ritualism was extraordinarily significant at El Tajín. More than a dozen courts attest to a virtual obsession with the various forms of this ritual sport. Courts of differing dimensions and profiles are found throughout El Tajín proper, often in direct proximity to one another. These buildings constitute the dominant ritual structures of this important section of the metropolis and the true focal points of the entire city. A number of the courts have sculptures depicting deities and players in the various associated rites (Kampen 1972; Wilkerson 1980, 1984). Here we can observe the highly charged symbolism of architecture through the very eyes of the ballgame participants—thought to be both mortal and divine.

In the South Ballcourt there are a series of six large tablets carved with a series of sequential scenes that reflect a major version of the ballgame. These appear to represent consecutive ballgame rituals associated with the Venus and pulque cults (Wilkerson 1984, 1985, 1991). Beginning with the preparation for prisoner capture via warfare, the scenes with the human players as protagonists progress through hallucinatory contemplation and face-off in the court, to the sacrifice of a player who is to be a messenger to the gods. This latter scene (figure 5.10) is depicted in a court remarkably similar to the one where it was carved.

Two important subsequent scenes show the reaction of the gods to the ritual. The principal deities of these scenes, the rain and wind gods, are shown seated on the roof of a temple at the Mountain of Foam, a mythical place in the underworld associated with the origin of the ritual drink

Figure 5.10. The northeast panel of the South Ballcourt at El Tajín, showing a sacrificial scene in a ballcourt (redrawn by Leopoldo Franco from Kampen 1972, reproduced courtesy of the University of Florida Press).

pulque. The temple contains a chac mool-like deity and, like many of the stone and cement temples of El Tajín, is shown with a flat roof and merlons (figure 5.11). The rain god responds to the solicitation of the sacrificed ballplayer for the carefully guarded drink in the sanctuary, and in the last scene of the court replenishes the temple vat by autosacrifice.

The sequence of sculpted tablets interprets the ritual use of the court itself and presents its architectural features from the perspective of the inhabitants of El Tajín. The buildings in the mythical abode of the gods are in the same style and design as those of El Tajín. The ballgame rites in the formal courts of the city were associated with the afterlife and the underworld. In Tajín Chico such symbolism is found in stucco and masonry in elite residences or palaces. Some of these building may have spatial layouts directly reflecting cosmological designs (Sarro 1995: 161–165). The corbeled entrance stairway of Building A not only penetrates the stucco relief of a temple front but emerges in a stone corridor shaped like a miniature ballcourt (figure 5.8). Thus, even access to such privileged residential precincts was through entrances displaying deliberate symbolic architectural references to sacredness, death, and the core cosmological ritual of the city.

In the courts themselves, or attached to bordering buildings (such as Buildings 10 or 26), there are sometimes small structures which may have contained ritual vats very much like those shown in the sculptures. The one by the west end zone of the South Ballcourt was an impressive

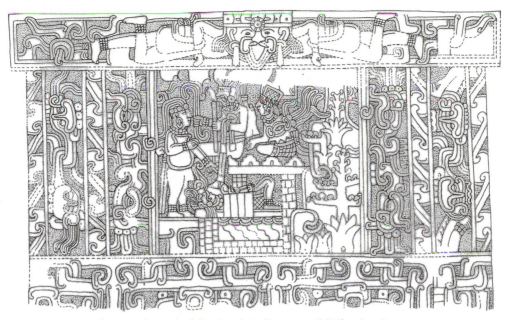

Figure 5.11. North-central panel of the South Ballcourt at El Tajín, showing a mythical scene of the pulque ritual set in and about a temple with a flat roof and merlons (redrawn by Leopoldo Franco from Kampen 1972, reproduced courtesy of the University of Florida Press).

megalithic structure, unfortunately only partially reconstructed at this time, with merlons that greatly resemble those in the ballcourt depictions. The city duplicated in its sacred structures the symbolism, design, and even the layout of the mythical world thought to lie just beyond death in the ballgame.

The many courts at El Tajín are likely to represent architectural monuments erected by a series of major rulers, each of whom felt compelled to construct one of these essential symbolic entranceways to immortality during his reign. These courts often form a part of a plaza complex of temples and administrative structures (such as the South Ballcourt and Buildings 14–15, 5, 15, and 3), or are adjacent to such structures (Buildings 34–35, 17–27, the Great Ballcourt) (figure 5.3). Such groupings are likely to have functioned as some sort of ritual-adminstrative-lineage unit. Still others, of smaller size, are concentrated in certain ritual precincts (such as within the Great Xicalcoliuhqui) or about major temple areas (Buildings 7–8, between 11 and the Pyramid of the Niches). Double (South Ballcourt and Building 14–15) and triple (the Great Xicalcoliuhqui) court arrangements, perhaps erected over time by closely related rulers of the same lineage, also occur and constitute ritual macroassemblages.

Not only is there an enormous concentration of formal ballcourts at El Tajín, when most Mesoamerican centers have only one or occasionally two, the courts occur abundantly throughout the Veracruz lowlands. In other contemporary sites with a high concentration of ballcourts, as at metropolitan Chichén Itzá (see Miller, chapter 15, this volume), the hinterland is often devoid of the structures. In the large region dominated by the culture of El Tajín the opposite is true. Most sites of moderate size have a court, and often more than one. Portable ballgame sculptures (yokes, *hachas*, *palmas*), stone representations of actual paraphernalia utilized in certain forms of the ritual, are found abundantly as mortuary offerings both within the sphere of El Tajín influence and well beyond (Proskouriakoff 1954; Wilkerson 1985, 1991).

Ballgame rites, and the courts themselves, lie at the heart of Classic Veracruz symbolism. If there is a single architectural monument that could represent the core of the worldview of the various cultures of the Gulf Coast since Olmec times, but particularly during the extended Classic Period, it is the ballcourt. While the ritual ballgame was essential to all the cultures of the area, the courts in the El Tajín region were the cultural focus par excellence. It is also probable that the associated ritual concepts and interwoven prerogatives of rulership, if not specific forms of the ballgame itself, influenced cultures at considerable distances beyond the Mesoamerican portions of the Gulf of Mexico and even in the Caribbean (Wilkerson 1984, 1985). Classic Veracruz was noninsular and likely the epicenter of this dynamic ritualism that surged out of Mesoamerica into other arenas of the Pre-Columbian world.

Agricultural Field Systems

Often overlooked in the treatment of Mesoamerican architecture are field systems for intensive agricultural production. These often colossal efforts to shape broad expanses of land are the largest earth movement achievements of New World antiquity. Although the examples in the El Tajín region took several forms, they all required considerable centralization of power to construct and maintain, and they constitute a forceful demonstration of the organizational ability of the polity that produced them. The field systems thought to be associated with El Tajín are exceptionally complex and large, with various configurations (Wilkerson 1983, 1990, 1994a). They are also suggestive of a pre-Aztec form of tribute state, where selected areas of high natural resource potential are required to produce far in excess of their local requirements for the nonadjacent metropolitan center.

The systems closest to El Tajín are those of the lower Tecolutla Valley in the vicinity of Santa Luisa, a major provincial site. Here a vast network of trunk, distribution, and feeder canals in various configurations covers the deltaic plain of the Tecolutla River. There are a series of systems, with the largest currently known approximately 6 square kilometers. Still other systems are found throughout the greater region. While the removal of water was the general goal of such endeavors, one of the distinctive features of this hydraulic architecture is that it appears to have adroitly maneuvered fresh water over rich soils between large bodies of salt and brackish water. These engineering projects appear to exceed in sophistication those of other regions in the southeastern lowlands of Mesoamerica.

Preliminary studies of the potential yields of the Santa Luisa system strongly suggest that it could routinely produce far more food than required by the substantially large, and archaeologically verifiable, population at the site. Its production was probably controlled and dictated by the metropolitan center. An initial ecological survey has also suggested that highly prized trade items, such as cacao and possibly cotton, were prime crops. At El Tajín one of the tablets of the important shrine of the Pyramid of the Niches shows a ceremony performed by an ancestral ruler on a structure that had been constructed directly in a cacao grove (figure 5.12). The development and control of such fields was vital to the rulership of El Tajín (Wilkerson 1983, 1990).

There is a considerable number of such field systems in lowland north-central Veracruz, the heartland of El Tajín culture (figures 5.1 and 5.6). Field systems also exist in the lower north Gulf and upper south-central Gulf areas, but in those regions they appear to lack the size and complexity of those in the greater El Tajín region. A review of the north-central Gulf locations and their temporal distribution, largely speculative outside of Santa Luisa, suggests that the oldest systems may be in the

Figure 5.12. Tablet from the sanctuary of the Pyramid of the Niches at El Tajín, depicting a ceremony on a platform in a cacao grove (redrawn by Leopoldo Franco from Kampen 1972, reproduced courtesy of the University of Florida Press).

deltaic areas of the Nautla and Tecolutla Rivers. These systems are likely to have been extended under the direct control of El Tajín at its apogee, but may have been initially constructed by an earlier metropolitan center known today as El Pital. The successful utilization of such forms of earthen field architecture in no small degree made possible the great concentration of wealth, religious fervor, and artistic and engineering talent at the metropolitan centers. It is fair to consider these gigantic constructions, impressive in scope and engineering skill, as the sustaining foundations of the Tajín state.

The Question of Origins

In spite of some two centuries of explorations, beginning in Veracruz with the discovery of El Tajín in 1785 (Ruíz 1785) and the formal archaeological expeditions initiated by Guillermo Dupaix in 1805 (Dupaix 1844), knowledge of the cultural chronologies of the central Gulf Coast is minimal given the magnitude of the ancient remains. Most archaeological endeavors have concentrated on the retrieval of sculptures and the reconstruction of buildings for tourism. Nevertheless, several aspects of the origins of Classic Veracruz art and architecture can be gauged and some hypotheses formulated.

In common with much Mesoamerican art (Coe 1965a), the Classic Veracruz art style has its roots in the late Olmec depictions of the Middle Formative period (ca. 600–300 B.C.) and the transitional Izapan style of the Late Formative (ca. 300 B.C.–A.D. 300). It then undergoes regional development during the Protoclassic (ca. A.D. 1–300) and Early Classic Periods (A.D. 300–600), although during the latter there is also a strong Teotihuacanoid influence, and perhaps presence, along portions of the Gulf Coast. A major geographical focus for these centuries appears to be near the juncture of the north-central and south-central areas. Here depictions and artifacts often combine stylistic attributes of both Teotihuacan and El Tajín. This has been provisionally labeled the Gulf Coast–Teotihuacan complex (Wilkerson 1993, 1994a). Apart from the omnipresent Classic Veracruz scrolls, it is characterized by a strong emphasis on ballgame symbolism and sacrificial or death motifs. This strong composite manifestation reflects not just major migrational events in the greater region but also strong local developments.

In terms of architecture, before this as-yet archaeologically untested complex, building platforms along the central coast were generally earth fill with burnt clay or mud coatings. Some of the more recent had thin concrete or stucco coatings. All tended to be of small or modest size. At Santa Luisa, currently with the longest known stratigraphic chronology in the El Tajín region, there is no evidence of stucco coatings until the Protoclassic and no buildings with cornices resembling those of El Tajín until the latter portion of the Early Classic.

During the Protoclassic in the north-central area, and very likely in the south-central also, there is a tremendous and rapid concentration of population at certain strategic points for food production, commerce, and political control. This in turn caused radical depopulation at many previously important centers (García Payón 1971; Wilkerson 1972, 1994a, b). Most interestingly, the early evidence for the focus of that demographic realignment is not at El Tajín, or in the same Tecolutla River Valley, but rather in the lower drainage of the Nautla. There, especially at the great site of El Pital, there is a considerable concentration of cultural remains, including many significant structures from the Late Formative, Protoclassic and Early Classic periods.

El Pital contains many of the largest structures, both in height and volume, known in the eastern Mexican lowlands (figure 5.13). These are generally earth-fill buildings consisting of a series of platforms in *talud*. They range in elevation to more than 30 meters and can be impressively huge. The most massive construction has a volume approximating 73,000 cubic meters, roughly 10 times that of the Pyramid of the Niches at El Tajín. The summits of most of the larger structures are thin rectangles that supported narrow perishable buildings. This is very unlike El Tajín, where the sophisticated management of cement permitted much larger masonry rooms on ample, nearly square, platform tops. Some of these summit constructions at El Pital had burnt clay walls; others appear to have employed a shell-derived lime stucco, perhaps for floors or certain basal *taluds* or lower walls. Like El Tajín, the cement sometimes had sherds and other aggregates to help bond it. The utilization here is probably the earliest major use of concrete on the Gulf Coast.

Although there are building complexes at El Pital that share large platforms, or low natural rises modified to appear as such, there are no defensive acropolis or hilltop groups as at El Tajín. There the Building of the Columns complex, Tajín Chico, the East Ridge, and the West Ridge are all defensive arrangments within a city itself situated within a steep-sided valley. El Pital, on the contrary, is almost totally laid out upon an exposed alluvial terrace amid numerous waterways. There also appears to be a 2 kilometer long causeway that joins the city with a satellite port area on an estuary. There are also avenues and a general grid that dictates the arrangement of structural complexes focused on plazas. El Pital is larger than El Tajín and mostly of earlier date, major portions apparently dating to the Late Formative (ca. 300 B.C.–A.D. 100) and the Protoclassic (ca. A.D. 100–300).

Nevertheless, there are similarities between the two cities. At El Pital there are some plaza building complexes, perhaps dating toward the end of the city's florescence in the Early Classic, which are comparable in size and layout to those of El Tajín. The ballgame ritual was also extremely important at this earlier city and is reflected in the many courts of various sizes and layouts. Additionally, artifacts carved in the Classic Veracruz style are found in and around both cities.

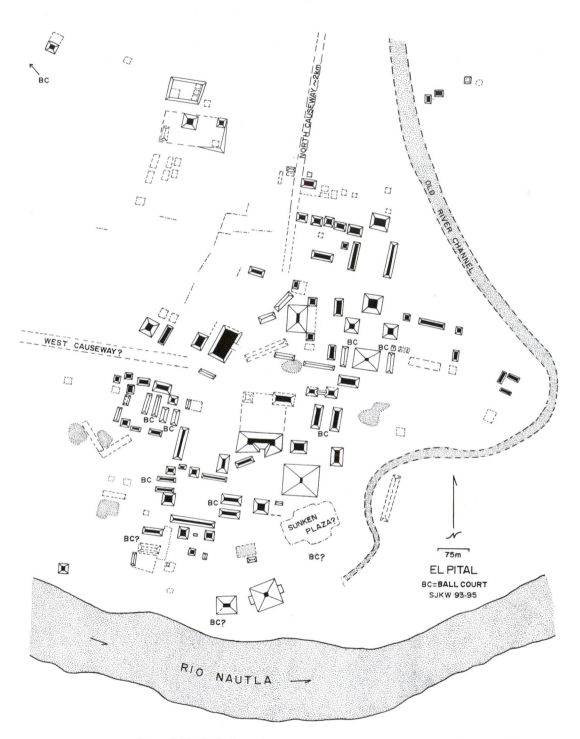

Figure 5.13. Preliminary interpretative map of the center of El Pital (modified from Wilkerson 1994a: figure 9).

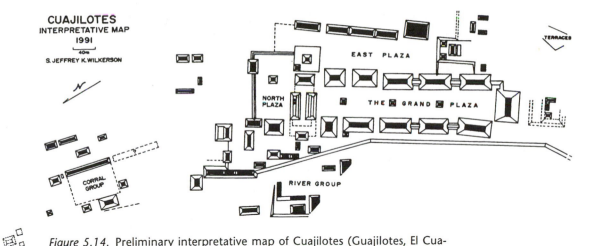

Figure 5.14. Preliminary interpretative map of Cuajilotes (Guajilotes, El Cuajilotes) (after Wilkerson 1993: figure 22).

The largely unexplored region about El Pital in the lower Nautla catchment has considerable architectural and other cultural remains that are suggestive of both Teotihuacan and later El Tajín (Wilkerson 1994a). *Talud-tablero* profiles similar to those of Teotihuacan (see Kowalski, chapter 4, this volume) have been reported from La Victoria (García Payon 1971: 527) and Cuajilotes (also known as Guajilotes and el Cuajilote; figures 5.4 and 5.14). Near El Pital are large agricultural irrigation systems (Wilkerson 1976, 1983, 1994a; Schmidt 1977) that appear to be contemporary with the city. The Nautla drainage was also the shortest route from the northern Gulf Coast to the major cities of central Mexico and is likely to have been an important corridor of cultural contact of great antiquity (Wilkerson 1972, 1993, 1994b).

Although it is far too early to be certain, this lowland region may well be the origin point of Classic Veracruz architecture and associated art in the north-central Gulf area. Although clearly the expression reached its zenith at El Tajín in the Late Classic and Epiclassic periods, it is likely that that great city absorbed much of its symbolism and art from a dynamic, nearby, and certainly powerful precursor—El Pital—that we are only now able to begin to evaluate and examine (Wilkerson 1997). The point when the early urban centers of the highlands began to interact with the resource-rich coastal lowlands has rarely been explored on the central Gulf Coast. It will have much to tell us about the beginnings of Classic Veracruz civilization and the regional nature of the "Teotihuacan Horizon."

The Impact of Classic Veracruz Architecture

The architecture of El Tajín is not confined to the north-central Gulf area. While the core region, stretching from Yohualinchan in the Sierra Madre

Oriental eastward to Santa Luisa near the Gulf, and from the lower Tuxpan (Pantepec) Valley south through the Nautla drainage and on to the vicinity of Las Higueras and Aparicio, is the crucible for most known examples, there are many manifestations elsewhere. Well northward in the Huasteca, at Cuatlamayan in distant San Luis Potosí, there are buildings with the characteristic cornices. Some shell gorgets from the Panuco area also appear to be depicting Tajín-like structures used in sacrificial rituals (Beyer 1934: plate 1; Wilkerson 1985: figure 16). At Cerro Cebadilla there are constructions reported to be reminiscent of El Tajín (Ochoa 1979: 83). Near the coast at Tanhuijo there are ballcourts with sculpture that may also be in the Classic Veracruz corpus, while from Isla Juana Moya there is a flagstone carved with a bifurcated depiction directly parallel to examples at El Tajín (Ochoa 1979: lams. 35a-b, 40). Southward, structures with niches and cornices, some on portable sculpture (Wilkerson 1990: 172–174; Arrellano and Beauregard 1981: plates 1, 2, 3, 7), are reported from various places from the Quiahuitztlan region through the Sierra de Chiconquiaco to Xalapa and on the ridges above the canyons in the environs of Jalcomulco. Even further to the southwest, on the uppermost reaches of the Rio Blanco in the Orizaba–Maltrata–Tacamaluca region, there is evidence for both this style of architecture and portable ballgame sculptures. Westward at the edge of the 2,400 meter high central plateau there are sites, such as San Juan Xiutetelco (García Payón 1950) and Napaltecutlan (Medellín 1953, 1960), which were seemingly dominated by Tajín culture and are awaiting further examination of both their stratigraphy and architecture.

The examples to the north are probably related to established trade activities near the mineral-rich flanks of the Sierra Madre and to the considerable impact of Tajín ballgame ritualism on the elites of the Huasteca (Wilkerson 1983, 1985). Such platforms with cornices, found at El Tajín in the vicinity of ballcourts, and frequently depicted as the locations for sacrificial rituals on *palmas*, may be indications of the aggressive spread of a particular form of ballgame ritualism. To the south the structures are frequently found at small or medium sized sites, many perched on elevated, defensible locations, such as Pompeya and Pueblo Viejo. Others, such as Paxil (García Payón 1947) and Vega de la Peña (Medellín 1950; Wilkerson 1993), are in more exposed stream bank locations and may have still older roots. These may be remnants of a migrational pathway that developed slowly during the middle portion of the Classic Period. The initial appearance of such structures likely represents the expansion of the area of control of El Tajín at the expense of older El Pital. Movement into this region probably accelerated as El Tajín and its immediate vicinity was pressed in turn by peoples on its northern and western flanks in later centuries. We will have to know more of these vestiges, particularly from the upper Nautla River region and southward, before we can fully comprehend the final phase of the culture of El Tajín and the extinction of Classic Veracruz architecture and art.

The western examples at higher elevations are likely to be part of the formal corridors of contact with the urbanized cultures of central Mexico. Yohualinchan, near an affluent of the upper Tecolutla River, may have been situated on a major route from El Tajín designed to avoid the area controlled by El Pital or later derived polities in the Nautla Valley. In a canyon of the upper Nautla River (also called the Bobos) are some important structures at sites likely to have once been dominated by either El Pital and El Tajín, or perhaps both in succession. One, Cuajilotes (Wilkerson 1993), is composed of a series of immense plazas, some of the largest known from the Gulf Coast. Although these elongated plazas almost certainly had commercial functions and are found at numerous sites in the region, the principal one at Cuajilotes is bordered by buildings rivaling and exceeding in volume many of those at El Tajín (figure 5.14). Most of these structures supported twin temples on their summits, a feature of only a few of the later temples at El Tajín. A similar structure is found at the satellite site of Vega de la Peña, which was later to become a major Aztec control center (Wilkerson 1993), and at a reoccupied suburb of El Pital.

These sites suggest several important points: (1) El Tajín, as well as perhaps other polities sharing essentially the same culture, utilized carefully selected control points on its frontiers; (2) large sites, seemingly derived from El Tajín culture, or heavily influenced by it, survived, and perhaps even thrived after the demise of that metropolitan center; and (3) the locations of these sites with their commercial and control features, as well as the growing use of twin temples, suggest a Gulf Coast origin of several attributes normally associated with the fifteenth-century Aztecs and their contemporaries.

Beyond the Central Gulf Coast

Relationships much farther afield should also be considered in appraising the Classic Veracruz expression (figure 5.15). In central Mexico, apart from early Teotihuacan contact (Wilkerson 1993, 1994a), there are a number of indications of Classic Veracruz influence. At Cholula in Puebla there is a plaza with carved altars and tablet backs (Garces et al. 1984: figures 2–6) sculpted in a variant of the same interlace style found at El Tajín. A northwestern portion of the Great Pyramid has a related platform profile with a square cornice (Gendrop 1984: 48). Southwestward in the Pacific watershed, at Xochicalco in Morelos, the Pyramid of the Plumed Serpents has a cornice and *tablero* profile similar to that of El Tajín (see Molina and Kowalski, chapter 6, this volume). The building also contains a carving of a cacao ceremony directly parallel to that of the Pyramid of the Niches at El Tajín. Southward, in the *Mixteca Baja* along the Oaxaca-Guerrero border, the Ñuiñe art style bears the imprint of Classic Veracruz influence (Paddock 1966: 176–200; Moser 1977). Well to the

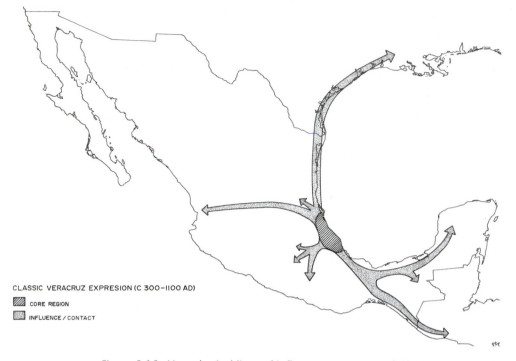

CLASSIC VERACRUZ EXPRESION (C 300–1100 AD)

▨ CORE REGION

▨ INFLUENCE / CONTACT

Figure 5.15. Hypothetical lines of influence or contact of Classic Veracruz art, architecture, and ballgame ritualism during the Classic and Epiclassic periods.

northwest, along the Pacific coast at Ixtlan del Río in Nayarit, there are temple platforms with cornices and *taluds* identical to many in the El Tajín region (Corona Nuñez 1953: figures 66–70).

East of the Isthmus of Tehuantepec, there was contact with the Puuc region, manifest at El Tajín in the finely cut stone and profile of Building A (figure 5.8). There also may be a sculptural relationship with sites such as Oxkintok in northwestern Yucatán. At Toniná in Chiapas, a Maya site with which El Tajín also shares some similarity of three-dimensional sculpture, there is an acropolis with stepped fret adornments reminiscent of Tajín Chico. Scattered over scores of sites from the Huasteca to central Mexico to the Maya realms as far south as Quelepa in El Salvador there are portable ballgame sculptures (*yokes, hachas, palmas*) that had their ultimate conceptual origin, and in many cases manufacture, in the central Gulf Coast. In the opposite direction, the symbolism of the El Tajín versions of the ballgame ritual appears well beyond the Mesoamerican frontiers in the art at numerous key Mississippian sites of the American Southeast (Wilkerson 1985).

Certainly these geographically diverse contacts were neither simultaneous nor of equal strength or duration. Nevertheless, it is clear that the Gulf Coast cultures of the Classic and Epiclassic periods, and especially that of El Tajín, had a major impact on their contemporaries. While it is impossible at this juncture to satisfactorily unravel the ebb and flow of the influence of the Classic Veracruz expression throughout broad regions of Mesoamerica and even past its borders, it can be affirmed that the Classic Veracruz florescence was both expansive and consequential. In this context, its architecture and art constituted a powerful and enduring statement of the dynamic symbolism of rulership, ritualism, and belief.

6

Public Buildings and Civic Spaces at Xochicalco, Morelos

Augusto Molina & Jeff Karl Kowalski

Since its discovery in 1770, Xochicalco, a pre-Hispanic city located approximately 60 kilometers south of Mexico City, has been the object of admiration and study by archaeologists and art historians (Litvak 1971). It has been characterized as "one of the most attractive and mysterious sites in central Mexico," (Hirth and Cyphers 1988: 151) as well as "one of the best examples of urban design in central Mexico during the centuries after Teotihuacán and before Tenochtitlán" (Hardoy 1964b: 99). The Pyramid of the Plumed Serpents, which stands on the uppermost part of the city, has been described as "one of the finest jewels of pre-Columbian architecture" (Heyden and Gendrop 1975: 230). The site has also been regarded by several scholars as an important center in the development of the cult of Quetzalcoatl, one of the most important deities of the Mesoamerican pantheon (e.g., Piña Chan 1977; Carrasco 1982).

Xochicalco was built on a hill, Cerro Xochicalco, that measures approximately 1,200 meters on its north–south axis by 700 meters east–west, and which rises about 130 meters above the surrounding valley floor (figures 6.1–6.3). The hill was completely modified artificially to create a series of large, level spaces on which the plazas and main architectural complexes were located and to make smaller terraces on which many residential units were built. The modifications to the natural topography were basically made by cutting large sections of bedrock and by the corresponding construction of large stone retaining walls, all of which gave the hill the appearance of a gigantic stepped pyramid of geological proportions.

Kenneth Hirth (1982, 1984) recently directed an extensive surface survey of Xochicalco which has increased our knowledge of the site considerably. Hirth considers that the site includes not only Cerro Xochicalco itself, but that it extends to incorporate other adjacent hills (see figure 6.4), and he estimates that at its maximum development Xochicalco

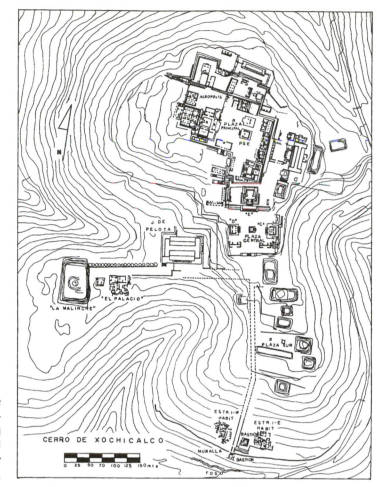

Figure 6.1. Map of the main hilltop at Xochi-calco, Morelos, showing location of the principal structures (map by Augusto Molina 1996).

Figure 6.2. Aerial photograph of recent excavation and reconstruction on the main hilltop at Xochicalco, Morelos, from the northeast (photograph by Antonio Berlanga Zubiaga, Dorset Servicios Fotográficos, Cuernavaca, Morelos).

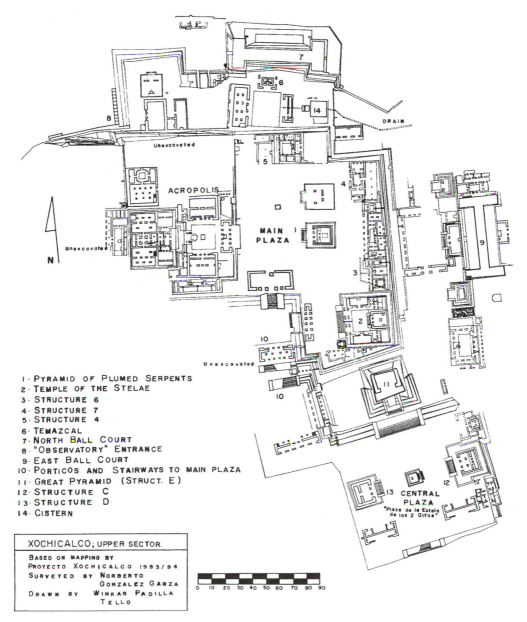

1 · PYRAMID OF PLUMED SERPENTS
2 · TEMPLE OF THE STELAE
3 · STRUCTURE 6
4 · STRUCTURE 7
5 · STRUCTURE 4
6 · TEMAZCAL
7 · NORTH BALL COURT
8 · "OBSERVATORY" ENTRANCE
9 · EAST BALL COURT
10 · PORTICOS AND STAIRWAYS TO MAIN PLAZA
11 · GREAT PYRAMID (STRUCT. E)
12 · STRUCTURE C
13 · STRUCTURE D
14 · CISTERN

XOCHICALCO; UPPER SECTOR.

BASED ON MAPPING BY
PROYECTO XOCHICALCO 1993/94
SURVEYED BY NORBERTO
GONZALEZ GARZA
DRAWN BY WINKAR PADILLA
TELLO

0 10 20 30 40 50 60 70 80 90

Figure 6.3. Plan of the upper zone of Cerro Xochicalco, showing the Central
Plaza (Plaza of the Stela of the Two Glyphs), the Ceremonial Plaza with the Pyramid of the Plumed Serpent and Structure A, the Acropolis containing probable
elite residential–administrative structures, and the North and East Ballcourts
(adapted from the 1994 plan by Norberto González Crespo).

covered approximately 4 square kilometers. Population density varied considerably, however, and of the total occupied area, only half contains visible remains of buildings. Cerro Xochicalco represents the most densely populated zone of the city, and it is mainly this area that is discussed in this chapter. No precise population estimate has been made, but the large percentage of area occuped by ceremonial and public spaces and structures exceeds both the needs of the city and the probable labor capacity of the resident population, suggesting that human labor and resources from the surrounding region were used to construct the center.

Chronology

There is evidence of human settlement in the vicinity of Xochicalco since the Middle Formative period (ca. 900–500 B.C.), but this consisted of small agricultural hamlets, located on the few tracts of productive agricultural land in the region, located mainly in Tlacoatzingo, one of the nearby hills which Hirth suggests forms part of greater Xochicalco. There is no evidence during this period of any ceremonial activities or constructions on the Xochicalco hill itself.

During the Classic period (ca. A.D. 200–650) there is evidence of a larger and denser occupation at Tlacoatzingo, including a small complex of religious architecture. There is also a small settlement at the base of Xochicalco hill, but still no remains of any religious or ceremonial architecture. We cannot be absolutely sure that some Classic period structures were not covered over or destroyed by the intense building activity of the next period. However, since most of the structures rest directly on bedrock and/or have no Classic ceramic or artifactual materials in their fill, most archaeologists consider that it was not until the Epiclassic period that Xochicalco acquired any significant population or political importance.

It was during the Epiclassic period (ca. A.D. 650–900) that the city developed rapidly into a great civic and ceremonial center and acquired is definitive form. Almost all the structures that are now visible belong to that period. The Epiclassic period, when Teotihuacan's influence and dominance began to wane in central Mexico, apparently was a time of poliltical instability and of large movements of peoples (Jiménez Moreno 1966; Diehl and Berlo 1989), and it is significant to note that it was during this time that some sites, like Xochicalco, Cacaxtla, Teotenango, and El Tajín grew in importance (see Wilkerson, chapter 5, this volume). It is also noteworthy that at Xochicalco, as at Cacaxtla, there is strong evidence of cultural contact with distant regions of Mesoamerica, leading to the creation of innovative and eclectic new art styles. In the case of Xochicalco, these cultural and artistic contacts included the Maya area, the Gulf Coast, the Valley of Oaxaca, and the Balsas River drainage. The stylistic and iconographic similarities between Xochicalco and other

Mesoamerican sites, some of which have been noted since the nineteenth century, have been studied by Jaime Litvak (1972), who analyzed their significance as evidence of cultural contact.

One of the possible evidences for outside connections is the South Ballcourt at Xochicalco. This court closely resembles the form of other ballcourts located in the Maya area (e.g., those at Cobá and Piedras Negras; Kubler 1984: 70). In this regard, the sculpted macaw head found in the rubble of the Xochicalco South Ballcourt is closely related conceptually to the macaw heads that served as markers in the Copan Main Ballcourt during several phases of its construction (Stromsvik 1952; Ramírez Vasquez et al. 1968: 77; Kowalski and Fash 1991; see Sharer et al., chapter 10, this volume).

The spatial arrangement of Structure A at Xochicalco is similar to that found in buildings IV and M at Monte Albán (see figure 6.3; see Marcus, chapter 3, this volume, figure 3.8). Since the nineteenth century, many authors have compared the seated figures sculptured on the Pyramid of the Plumed Serpents with figures from either small-scale or monumental Maya art. Other architectural features, such as the flaring cornice on the same pyramid, seem to be related to forms from distant regions, particularly to those of El Tajín (Kubler 1984: 68; see Wilkerson, chapter 5, this volume) and those of Monte Albán (Heyden and Gendrop 1975: 230; see Marcus, chapter 3, this volume). Litvak (1972) has also analyzed resemblances between numerical systems, glyphics, ceramics, and other features at Xochicalco and those of other regions of Mesoamerica as evidence of possible culture contact.

It is generally accepted that Xochicalco grew and prospered because of the political vacuum created by the decline of Teotihuacan. This conforms to the general pattern of the Epiclassic period, during which different peoples moved into central Mexico and newly emerging regional states flourished. Jaime Litvak (1970) has proposed that Xochicalco may also have actively participated in Teotihuacan's downfall by engaging in hostile actions, such as gaining control of trade routes with the Balsas River drainage.

Whether Xochicalco simply benefitted from or contributed to Teotihuacan's decline, the importance of the Morelos site was short lived. Toward A.D. 900 there was a notable decline in the size and density of population, and soon most of the city lay abandoned. By the time of the Spanish Conquest, Xochicalco was probably an "empty," site, though it continued to be venerated as an almost mythical pilgrimage center by the Mexica-Aztecs (see Umberger 1987).

Siting, Plan, and Principal Structures

The selection of the site for Xochicalco, on top of a large hill, is significant. Before the Epiclassic period, the preferred location for sites in central Mexico had been flat plains or valley floors. This hilltop location, which resembles the siting of Cacaxtla, Teotenango, and other Epiclassic sites, suggests the emergence of more militaristic societies, such as those documented for the Postclassic period in Mesoamerican archaeology (e.g., Tula, Hidalgo; see Kristan-Graham, chapter 7, this volume).

The military character of Xochicalco has been discussed by various archaeologists (e.g., Armillas 1951; Hirth 1989) and is demonstrated by the fact that a large section of the base of the hill is surrounded by ditches, moats, walls and other defensive works (figure 6.4). Hirth (1989) considers Xochicalco one of the first examples of military architecture in Mesoamerica.[1] Explicit militaristic iconography on the sculptured reliefs of the Pyramid of the Plumed Serpents, discussed in more detail later, seems to corroborate the view that the site's hilltop location served a practical defensive function.

The southern perimeter of the hill was protected by a deep moat cut into bedrock and by a stone rampart (figure 6.4). The moat was probably spanned by a wooden bridge that led to a stairway, which constituted the only ready access to the city on the south. The southern entry was controlled by two bastions that flanked it on both sides (figure 6.1). The buildings on top of the bastions were excavated in 1984–86 under the direction of Norberto González, who confirmed that they were not residential, but had administrative and defensive functions (González et al. 1995). There is clear evidence that at some point during the Epiclassic period the entrance was purposely narrowed to further restrict and control access to the site. One of the main pre-Hispanic roads in the Xochicalco region ends at this point, suggesting it was the principal entrance to the city (González and Garza n.d.; Hirth 1982).

Though undoubtedly situated for military purposes, the hilltop location of Xochicalco also expressed enduring concepts of the sacredness of certain landscape forms in Mesoamerican religious ideology. On a terrace on the northern slope is the entrance to an underground, artificially modified cave, earlier known locally as "Los Amates" and also called "The Observatory" because of a deep vertical shaft that connects a cave chamber with the outside. Apparently this viewing tube was used to observe the solar zenith passage (Aveni 1980: 43, 253, figure 85c). Richard Townsend (n.d.) has pointed out that caves traditionally were viewed as places of dynastic origin and that the use of the cave to observe zenith passage indicates a common Mesoamerican effort to link "ritual and the activities of society to the cycle of the seasons." He has suggested that Xochicalco's architecture formed part of a more comprehensive symbolic program in which the entire site was "a sacred mountain, a ritual landscape to which the symbols of government and local history were attached."

Starting at the southern entrance, a wide, paved causeway ascends the hill in a northerly direction (figures 6.1 and 6.2). The causeway follows the general slope of the terrain, but at certain intervals ramps were

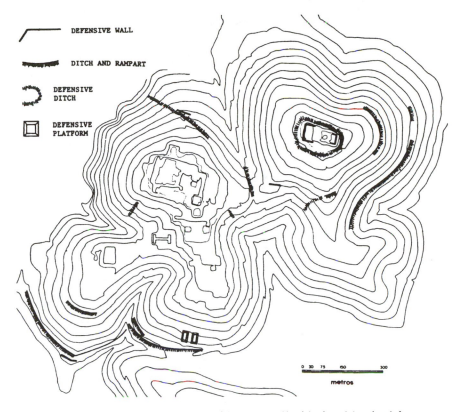

Figure 6.4. Distribution of defensive architecture at Xochicalco, Morelos (after Hirth 1989: figure 2).

constructed to make the inclination more regular. This causeway forms the main axis of the urban design and determined the orientation of all the main buildings in this section of the city. On both sides of the causeway, on the lower part of the hill, there are terraces with building compounds, each consisting of multiple patios surrounded by rooms. Based on ceramic remains, such as vessels for food prepraration and storage, as well as distinctive architectural features, González identifies these as residential compounds, probably occupied by extended family groups (González et al., 1995). Similar residential compounds also cover the lower slopes of Cerro Xochicalco and other adjoining hills and spread into the open plain at the north end of the city.

Leaving behind the residential terraces, the causeway ascends north- ward on a course that affords panoramic views of the valley to the west. Aligned along the eastern side are several large buildings, as yet unexcavated, and a large, level plaza measuring approximately 100 by 150 meters. At the center of this plaza is a low east–west oriented platform. Litvak (1971) refers to this plaza as "the Market." Whether this was its actual function cannot yet be confirmed, but it would have been an ideal location for public market activities.

Just to the north of this group of buildings the causeway intersects almost at right angles with another large avenue that descends toward the west. Along this east–west avenue, which forms another of the main axes of the urban design, are several of Xochicalco's most important buildings (figure 6.5). These include a multiroom structure with central patio known as the "Palace," one of the largest and most complex elite residential compound yet excavated in the city, and the South Ballcourt, one of the finest buildings of this type in central Mexico and one of the first in this region known to have used circular scoring rings. This ballcourt can be observed easily from several of the upper terraces, suggesting that games were viewed by groups of onlookers from above. Also along the east-west avenue, and set parallel to its axis, is a series of 20 circular platforms called the "Calendrical Altars," so named because it has been postulated that they marked the 20 day-names of the 260-day ritual almanac or *Tonalpohualli*.

A short distance to the north of its intersection with the east–west avenue, the main causeway reaches the "Central Plaza," a large, raised plaza that is limited on the east and west by Structures C and D, respectively (figures 6.3 and 6.6; Sáenz 1964b). These two buildings resemble each other and have temples on pyramidal platforms with steeply in-

Figure 6.5. View of the western spur of the Cerro Xochicalco, showing the arrangement of structures along an east–west avenue. The South Ballcourt and the columns of the "Calendrical Altars" building are visible in the middle distance. The "Palace" and a culminating platform mound are visible beyond (photograph by Augusto Molina).

clined walls which become vertical at the upper part, a variant of a *talud-tablero* or slope-and-panel architectural terrace profile typical at Xochicalco (Sáenz 1967: 10). To the north, Structure E, the largest pyramidal structure at the site, effectively and definitively closes the plaza and blocks the view of and passage to the uppermost part of the city. According to César Sáenz (1968: 186), who excavated the Central Plaza, the level surface was created by cutting horizontally through large sections of bedrock. One of the larger pieces of rock was then used to carve the "Stela of the Two Glyphs" that is set on a small altar platform in the center of the plaza.

Due to their very public and accessible position on a centrally located plaza at the end of the main axial thoroughfare of the city, these temples must have played an important part in public ritual and ceremonies involving a large portion of the population of the city and probably the surrounding region. Although the exact nature of these activities will never be known, some of their general cultic associations perhaps are suggested by the triadic arrangement of the principal pyramidal platforms. This may pertain in some way to the emphasis on a specialized "deity triad" identified on sculptured stelae found in association with Structure A in the Acropolis and Ceremonial Plaza (or Plaza Principal) area located on a higher level immediately to the north (see figures 6.3

Figure 6.6. View of the "Central Plaza" from the Acropolis on the north, showing Structure C facing the altar platform of the "Stela of the Two Glyphs." Probable residential building terraces appear in the distance (photograph by Augusto Molina).

and 6.11; Sáenz 1961, 1962). This must remain a hypothesis, however, because scholars have differed on the question of the relative historical versus ritualistic significance of these stelae. This debate is considered again later.

Until recently, no clear access had been found to the Ceremonial Plaza and the group of buildings known as the Acropolis, since, as has been noted, Structure E blocks the view and any direct approach to the upper-most levels of the site. Recent excavations (1993–94) by INAH archaeologists directed by González have revealed a series of monumental stairs that start on the western side of Structure E and ascend from the level of the Central Plaza to that of the Ceremonial Plaza (figure 6.3). At various intervals the stairway is interrupted by enclosed plazas and by colonnaded buildings or porticoes which probably served to control access to the upper levels of the city. In this case, it would seem that the upper part of the city was designated for the exclusive use of the higher echelons of the political hierarchy, incorporating the concept of a restricted acropolis. Such spatial concepts are more closely related to those evident at various Classic Maya centers rather than in the more open grid layout of the central Mexican city of Teotihuacan (cf. Hardoy 1964a, b; Kubler 1984).

The Acropolis, partially excavated in 1993–94, consists of a complex series of plazas and buildings around patios, apparently representing other residences for the elite and associated with buildings for civic and administrative activities (figures 6.2 and 6.3). Among the most interesting finds in the Acropolis are a collapsed and badly destroyed two-story building and a series of doorless rooms, probably granaries, that were entered through the roof.

A stairway descends from the uppermost part of the Acropolis to a large Ceremonial Plaza, which contains some of the most important buildings in the city. Among these buildings, and by far the best-known at Xochicalco, is the Pyramid of the Plumed Serpents (figures 6.7 and 6.8).[2] The finely proportioned *talud-tablero* and the beveled, flaring cornice on the lower platform give this structure a distinctive form. All the facades of this temple building are faced with andesite blocks sculpted in bold reliefs that originally bore polychrome paint. Interestingly, two different numerical systems are used in the inscriptions on these sculptures; one consists of bars and dots, generally associated with the Maya and Zapotec regions, and the other consists only of dots, more typical of highland central Mexico and the Mixtec region (see Berlo 1989). This, and other glyphic, iconographic, and stylistic aspects of these reliefs have been used to postulate influences from the Maya area, the Gulf Coast, and Oaxaca. The plumed serpent figural sculptures are now seen, as are the murals at Cacaxtla, as the result of communication among several regional states that were developing at this time in Mesoamerica (Litvak 1972; Nagao 1989).

The interpretation of the complex iconography of the reliefs is neither complete nor definitive, although several scholars have made substantial

Figure 6.7. General view of the Pyramid of the Plumed Serpents from the north-west (photograph by Augusto Molina).

Figure 6.8. View of the south facade of the sculptured lower terrace of the Pyramid of the Plumed Serpent, featuring relief sculptures of feathered snakes framing seated human figures. The local variant of the *talud-tablero* profile features a series of sculptured panels depicting seated figures along the tablero freize (photograph by Augusto Molina).

contributions to unlocking their meaning. The main motif on the basal *taludes* on the south, east, and north sides of the building consists of plumed serpents whose undulating bodies frame seated human figures (figure 6.8). The crosslegged position, hand positions, and sloping forehead profile of these figures have often been cited as evidence for Maya influence at Xochicalco (e.g., Seler 1960, 2: 158; Litvak 1970: 137; Kubler 1984: 72), although Nagao (1989: 94) notes that the pose of the Xochicalco figures is more rigid and less dynamic than that of comparable Maya figures. She also suggests that:

> Specific Maya symbols of the use of complexes revealing a knowledge of underlying organizational concepts are not evident in these Mayoid references at Xochicalco. Rather, Maya traits—architectural, stylistic, and iconographic—have been adapted to blend with the local visual system (Nagao 1989: 94).

Also framed by the bodies of the serpents are "Reptile's Eye" glyphs. Many authors have identified these serpents with the important Mesoamerican deity Quetzalcoatl, although it is clear that the image and cult of the feathered serpent meant something for the Epiclassic rulers of Xochicalco other than it did for the later Mexica-Aztecs, who conflated the attributes of the deity with those of the legendary priest-ruler Ce Acatl Topiltzín of Postclassic Tula, Hidalgo. Virginia Grady Smith (1988: 194) recently interpreted the Xochicalco feathered serpents as representing a "composite dragon associated with earth, water, fertility and blood . . . a tutelary deity and a symbol for authority." Townsend (n.d.: 5) has suggested that the principal source for the major icon on the Pyramid of the Plumed Serpents is Teotihuacan, where similar undulating feathered serpents adorn the facade of the Old Temple of Quetzalcoatl in the Ciudadela and also appear in various murals at the site (see Kowalski, chapter 4, this volume, figure 4.7). This connection has been stressed by Davíd Carrasco (1982: 131), who notes that:

> It is possible that in Xochicalco we have a significant identification among central shrine–royal priest–feathered serpent, a series of relations identified in Teotihuacan as well . . . just as Xochicalco made some claim as a "peripheral capital" to have woven together historical periods and cultural traditions, so Quetzalcoatl's image supports and weaves together the axis mundi of this hilltop place, uniting not only the ceremonial precinct but also the emblems and symbols of other urban traditions.

Serving as a connecting link among all of these recent interpretations is the intersection of religion and politics, with the notion that the feathered serpents function simultaneously as cosmological and dynastic-political symbols. The seated human figures represent rulers whose authority is confirmed by the image of Quetzalcoatl, their patron deity who indicates both their control over powerful natural forces and their legitimacy as heirs to the urban tradition of Teotihuacán.

The sculptures on the *tablero* of the platform show seated figures carrying knotted bags (figure 6.9). Although interpreted as generalized priest figures in the past, Hirth (1989) has convincingly reinterpreted these sculptures as warriors and/or tribute bearers associated with a series of conquered places identified by toponymic glyphs. The *tablero* is divided into a series of 30 rectangular panels, each of which contains a similar depiction of a seated figure, in front of each of whom appears a glyphic combination ordinarily consisting of a disembodied human mouth paired with (and apparently devouring) a quartered circle. Above this glyphic combination is a variable glyphic element. Because the seated figures have circular "goggles" over their eyes and trapeze-and-ray "year signs" in their headdresses, they have been interpreted has having a basically religious significance (e.g., Peñafiel 1890; Noguera 1946; Piña Chan 1977), and the "jaws and circle" glyph associated with them has been interpreted either as a reference to solar eclipse information (Noguera 1946; Angulo 1978: 24) or as a general reference to the passage of time (Peñafiel 1890; Abadino 1910). Hirth (1989: 73) takes issue with these interpretations, and instead proposes that "the tablero element cluster depicts the three-part association of warrior, conquest, and tribute." He

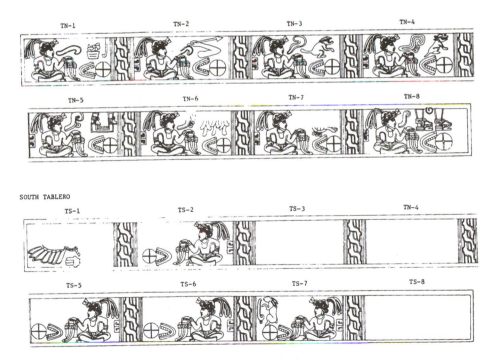

Figure 6.9. Sculptured frieze panels from the tablero of the Pyramid of the Plumed Serpent, Xochicalco, showing seated human figures holding bags and wearing storm god or Tlaloc attributes. They face glyphic motifs that have been interpreted as toponyms (place names), possibly recording places incorporated in the Xochicalco polity by conquest (after Peñafiel 1890: plate 190).

points out that the Tlaloc-related costume elements, such as the eye-rings and trapeze-and-ray "year sign" headdress, worn by these figures correspond to various examples of Tlaloc-related signs associated with warriors and sacrifice at Teotihuacan (Pasztory 1974: 15; C. Millon 1988) and at various other Epiclassic centers such as Cacaxtla, where warriors in the Battle Mural on Structure B display the "year sign" in their head-dresses and where Tlaloc elements appear in their belts and in front of their faces as masks (Foncerrada de Molina 1982; Baird 1989; cf. Berlo n.d.). Such Tlaloc-related iconography also has a clear association with warriors and either captive or personal sacrifice among the Classic Maya (Schele and Miller 1986: 177; Stone 1989). The "jaws and circle" combi-nation accompanying the figure is interpreted by Hirth (1989: 73) as meaning "I eat or consume [put] something precious [inside]," metaphor-ically referring to the taking of tribute. Although the non-repeating glyphic elements above the "jaws and circle" have been interpreted as calendrical signs, Hirth (1989: 73) accepts Leopoldo Batres's (1886) ear-lier suggestion that they represent "toponymic depictions of specific places." Janet Berlo (1989: 33, citing Smith 1983: 252) agrees with the general identification of the signs as designating place names, but sug-gests that the "jaws and circle" motif is "a pictorial (and perhaps pho-netic) locative indicator," pointing out that "In Mixtec writing, a profile jaw like the one used at Xochicalco represents the locative prefix "a-," meaning "at the place of." It is used particularly for place signs in the Nochixtlan Valley."

It is possible that some of these proposed toponyms, such as a human arm throwing a spear, correspond to known places in the vicinity of, and presumably under the political control of, Xochicalco (see figure 6.9). Hirth (1989: 74) suggests that this toponym could be translated either as Tlacochcalco (place of the house of spears) or as Miacatlan (abundant place of spears), and notes that the latter "may refer to the large Epiclas-sic site located on the hill overlooking the modern town of Miacatlan approximately 8 kilometers southwest of Cerro Xochicalco." Berlo (1989: 37–38, figure 19) has suggested that glyphic combinations on Xochicalco Stelae 1, 2, and 3, and on a stair block from a residential terrace may refer to the same nearby site (see figure 6.11). She notes:

> Litvak King (1972) has hypothesized that Miacatlan replaced Xochicalco as the dominant polity in this region after A.D. 900. It is logical to expect that, prior to this political upheaval, Miacatlan would be featured in Xochicalco's public narratives.

Following this line of reasoning, Hirth (1989: 75) suggests:

> The main purpose of the tablero sculpture on the Pyramid of the Plumed Serpent was to portray a list of the towns paying tribute to Xochicalco. Furthermore, the depiction of the seated figure in war-rior regalia was intended to convey the idea that the towns were conquered and/or the tribute can be credited to the actions of a

warrior group. The same symbolism was used to convey the idea of tribute in the Battle Mural at Cacaxtla, although in a somewhat different context. In Late Horizon religious cosmology warriors killed in battle were considered to be divine offerings to the gods. The blood of fallen warriors and sacrificial victims was perceived as a blood tribute needed to nourish the gods and maintain the stability of the universe.

Berlo (1989: 33), though differing in particulars, basically concurs with this interpretation and compares the wrap-around series of warrior figures and place names with the Mexica-Aztec Tizoc Stone, "on which glyphs of conquered territories are paired with images of rulers and deities." On the walls of the upper temple building, which was badly destroyed at the time of Batres's (1912) partial reconstruction of the edifice early in this century, are reliefs depicting 12 seated warriors, some accompanied by bound captives. The warriors are arrayed in battle costume and carry rectangular, fringed shields and darts (figure 6.10a). Such rectangular shields are a prominent part of the Teotihuacan-related Tlaloc-Venus warfare cult and associated costume that is featured on several Late Classic Maya monuments (see Stone 1989), as is the distinctive "balloon headdress" worn by several of the figures (figure 6.10b). According to Hirth (1989: 73), the walls of the temple also

> once contained many additional figures, judging from the loose carvings scattered around the base of the monument which could not be repositioned in the upper facade. Warrior figures also occupy prominent locations on the side of the stairway leading to the summit of the pyramid . . . There is no question that the Pyramid of the Plumed Serpent was one of the most spectacular and important temple structures at Xochicalco. The prevalence of warrior figures as the dominant theme indicates that they had both a prominent social and ceremonial role in the society and suggests

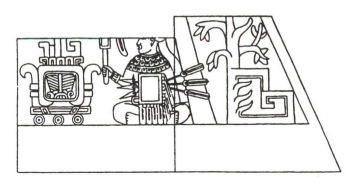

Figure 6.10a. Drawing of the sculptured panel on the sloping lower facade of upper temple of the Pyramid of the Plumed Serpent, showing a seated warrior with rectangular, fringed shield and spear cluster (after Peñafiel 1890).

Figure 6.10b. Seated warrior figure from sculptured panel on the upper temple of the Pyramid of the Plumed Serpent, wearing a turban like version of the "balloon headdress" related to Tlaloc-Venus conquest warfare (photograph by Jeff Kowalski).

that they were either intricately related to the maintenance of cult deities or involved in the ritual associated with this important temple.

According to Virginia Grady Smith (1988: 403,) the entire sculptural program of the Pyramid of the Plumed Serpents "established the power of Xochicalco's rulers and the validity of warfare as a social necessity and an economic institution." Nagao (1989) has contrasted the obvious fortifications and the more overt references to warfare and tribute evident at Xochicalco with the lesser prominence given to militaristic subjects in the art of Teotihuacan. She suggests that this new emphasis on bellicose iconography is related to the increased and more violent competition among Xochicalco and other Epiclassic successor states, each of which was attempting to consolidate their own regional political and economic power in the wake of Teotihuacan's decline. Thus, she argues that

> During the Epiclassic period, . . . armed figures, confrontation, conquest, and sacrifice are prominently displayed themes. Such aggressive imagery may have been both an exhortation and a warning, necessary under unstable political circumstances of decentralized authority. (Nagao 1989: 99)

Another important building in the Ceremonial Plaza is Structure A, apparently a temple compound erected on a large building platform (see

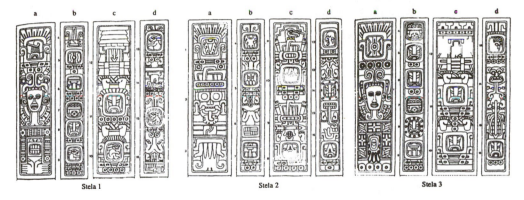

Figure 6.11. Stelae 1, 2, and 3, depicting three deities known as the Xochicalco stelae triad and named glyphically as "7 Reptile's Eye" (Stela 1), "7 Rain" (Stela 2), and "4 Motion" (Stela 3), found in Structure A at Xochicalco (after Sáenz 1961, plates 2-4; Berlo 1989: figure 15).

figure 6.3). Several authors have mentioned the similarity of this building with others at Monte Albán (e.g., Heyden and Gendrop 1975: 230). A wide stairway leads to a portico supported by pillars and then to a patio with flanking buildings on the north and south and a sanctuary on another smaller platform to the east. Here César Sáenz (1961) found three related stone stelae monuments (figure 6.11), strewn on the floor of the sanctuary, which has been named the "Temple of the Stelae." Sáenz (1964a) identified the deities on two of the stelae as Quetzalcoatl as the morning star, and a third as Tlaloc, the god of rain. Esther Pasztory (1973) more convincingly identified the three stelae as depicting a "deity triad" consisting of a sun god, who appears with the calendrical name 4 Motion on Stela 3, the sun god's wife, a fertility and moon goddess identified by the name 7 Reptile's Eye on Stela 1, and a Tlaloc-like earth deity named 7 Water on Stela 2. This triad is connected with architectural directional symbolism comprising groups of three buildings, such as the Cross Group at Palenque, or perhaps Xochicalco Structures C, D, and E mentioned above. Pasztory (1973) also interpreted the glyphic texts on the Xochicalco stela triad as basically mythological in character, associated with themes of sacrifice and agricultural fertility. This mythological interpretation has been questioned by both Virginia Grady Smith and Janet Berlo. Smith (1988: 349–351) views the stelae primarily as "records of events related to specific rulers" and as a "historical record of three militaristic rulers," although she accepts that there are some "cosmological and religious aspects" to the monuments' iconography. Berlo (1989: 34–37) also has interpreted the texts on the three stelae as basically historical in content and containing several identifiable place names in the Xochicalco region. It seems likely, then, that the texts on the monuments refer to historic events concerning rulership and the militaristic expansion of Xochicalco polity, but that such historical happenings were also validated by framing them in terms of a cosmic mythic paradigm.

The Ceremonial Plaza of Xochicalco is a fine example of Mesoamerican urban design. In some ways it resembles the mountaintop plaza layout at Monte Albán, but as Jorge Hardoy (1964a, b) has pointed out, in contrast to the enclosed view of Monte Albán, which is limited by the surrounding buildings, the architects of Xochicalco set the buildings back from the edges of the platforms to create "balconies" that afford views of lower sectors of the city and of the valley below. The Ceremonial Plaza is entered from the south through a porticoed building located at the top of the previously described monumental stairway. To the east and north the plaza is closed by a series of buildings with many rooms grouped around small patios, larger columned spaces, and porticos. The spatial arrangement of these structures suggests that they were residential compounds. The elevated location and controlled access to the Acropolis and the Ceremonial Plaza suggest that its use was largely limited to the Xochicalco elite, although officials from other sites in the region and other local inhabitants may have been admitted on special ocassions.

A series of terraces occupy the east and north flanks of Cerro Xochicalco. The recent excavations on these terraces revealed two ballcourts, both with I-shaped plans (figures 6.2 and 6.3). In the East Ballcourt, similar in design to the previously known South Ballcourt, one circular scoring ring was found in situ and is carved on both sides with representations of two macaws and a bat. No other ring was found. The rings of the North Ballcourt are undecorated and had fallen. They were found lying in the rubble at the center of the playing alley.

An elegant *temazcal* (steam or sweat bath) surrounded by a covered portico was found near the North Ballcourt (figure 6.3). It is one of the best preserved such structures yet found in Mesoamerica: the hearth and stones that were heated to produce the steam were found in their original location. The close proximity of these structures apparently confirms the association between the *temazcal* and the ballgame.

Other structures on these terraces include temple platforms, large colonnaded patios, a cistern, and a gallery-type building supported by columns. This section of the city is at approximately the same level as the Central Plaza on the south, but it is not as centrally located, nor as open and publicly accessible. Except for a very narrow stairway, no easy communication between this zone and the higher Ceremonial Plaza has yet been found. This zone probably represents an area functionally intermediate between the restricted Acropolis and the public areas below.

There is evidence that Xochicalco met a sudden and dramatic end. Many buildings in the upper part of the city were burned down, while groups of skeletons of mutilated individuals were found lying in heaps under the debris of such structures. Objects such as pottery, fragments of stone sculptures, and other sumptuary goods were thrown down the slopes and were found in heaps at the base of the retaining walls. Large and heavy sculptures were broken and the pieces were left scattered on the floors of rooms and patios. Several almost-life-size stone sculptures of seated felines were found in different places in the Ceremonial Plaza; all had been mutilated, their front legs and ears broken. In addition, in the houses at the lower levels of the city, many household goods, pottery, utensils, and so on, were left inside the rooms as if they were abandoned in haste. Norberto González (personal communication, 1995) interprets this as meaning that the city was razed by Xochicalco people living outside of the Cerro, or as a result of strife between conflicting factions of the elite.

Conclusions

There are some aspects of Xochicalco's urban design that are worth emphasizing in conclusion. The entire city plan does not give the impression of a slow, spontaneous and "organic" growth. Rather it appears that the site was planned according to preconceived criteria to simultaneously meet practical needs of communication and defense as well as to achieve desired aesthetic effects and convey a symbolic message. The chronology of the site indicates that this was achieved within a relatively short time.

The two main axes defined by the north–south and east–west causeways are important elements in the urban design. The orientation and location of civic and ceremonial buildings were determined by the causeways. The fact that they are partial axes, abruptly interrupted by a plaza or an intersection, as well as by the topography itself, created changing perspectives and complex spatial relationships. At the same time that the causeways served as elements of access and communication, they provided a sense of underlying and permanent order for the major buildings. This architectonic order surely confirmed in the mind of the viewer a sense of the greatness and power of the Xochicalco tribute state and of its rulers.

The military and defensive character of the site is evident in the existence of moats, ramparts, controlled access, and associated martial iconography from the Pyramid of the Plumed Serpents. This would seem to indicate that the Xochicalco state depended on force for its survival. As has been stated previously, the population of Xochicalco exceeded the carrying capacity of nearby agricultural land, and the city must have relied on produce from other parts of the region for its subsistence needs. Add to this Hirth and Cypher's (1988) interpretation of war, sacrifice and tribute as the main iconographic program of Xochicalco's sculpture, and the militaristic character of the site is quite evident, as is its role as a dominant regional political center. As noted, this emphasis on themes of sacrificial warfare reflects the political instability of various competing regional centers such as Xochicalco during the Epiclassic period and may have been calculated both to inspire zeal in local warriors and to serve as a propagandistic display of military might to would-be challengers. As recent excavations have demonstrated, however, the symbolism of power ultimately could not fend off the purposeful destruction and rapid abandonment of large parts of the city.

At Xochicalco the topography was modified so as to create well defined vertical divisions of the site which also function as social divisions. The lower terraces are occupied by smaller, less complex residential structures, undoubtedly the dwellings of people of lower social status. Higher up are more important temples, ballcourts, public buildings and ample civic spaces to which access is clear and well marked, and, although controlled, probably open to much of the population. Most of this part of the city is easily visible from several viewpoints. Also at this level is at least one large, complex residential compound, perhaps used by the officials of the cult associated with the South Ballcourt.

At the uppermost level is the "closed" Acropolis with residential and ceremonial buildings and spaces for the exclusive use of the elite. Access to this area was restricted, and the majority of the population was probably allowed entrance only on certain occasions.

It would seem that the urban design and public architecture of the city, as well as the iconographic themes of the sculptural program, was planned by the local elite, who were probably newcomers to the region and who could plausibly be described as a military theocracy, to symbolize their power and prestige and to convey this message to the population of Xochicalco and the surrounding region. The eclectic mixture of architectural forms, sculptural styles, and iconographic references evident at Xochicalco suggests that the site's parvenu rulership was attempting to forge a new architectural and artistic system. Scholars differ as to the character of this system. Townsend (n.d.: 8) has asserted that it represents an imperfect assemblage of forms borrowed from various well-established artistic and iconographic complexes of Classic period societies, speaking of "a new tradition still in the process of formation without yet achieving a fully-integrated synthesis of forms." By contrast, Nagao (1989: 97–100) has stressed the more positive, deliberate, and cosmopolitan nature of Xochicalco's architecture and art, observing:

> At Xochicalco the "best," that is, the most useful, elements from different areas were selected and melded with other nonlocal traits to form a distinctive style. By choosing traits from different visual systems, Xochicalco proclaimed the cosmopolitanism to communicate a public image of broad intellectual, commercial, and political horizons. Xochicalco's sophistication is further revealed in the highly structured and conceptual nature of its internal architectural organization and of its art style.

This latter view accords well with the evidence for Xochicalco's deliberate, planned architectural layout and individual building forms, discussed above, and acknowledges the manner in which the eclecticism evident in its architectural and sculptural styles is based not simply on a haphazard borrowing of "foreign" motifs, but represents a conscious decision to combine tradition and innovation. Xochicalco's rulers created an integrated ensemble of architecture well suited to the turbulent times of the Epiclassic period, in which they instituted iconographic programs that provided a foundation for the militaristic themes characteristic of later Posclassic Mesoamerican societies.

Notes

1. Although Xochicalco represents an early example of a deliberately fortified site in the Mexican highlands, evidence of defensive walls, accompanied by a moat, exists in the Maya region at Becan, Campeche; the walls are thought to date to the Late Preclassic period (Webster 1976).

2. See Litvak (1971) for a discussion of early accounts of this structure. Sáenz (1963) describes excavations carried out at the building.

7

The Architecture of
the Tula Body Politic

Cynthia Kristan-Graham

Le Corbusier's famous dictum, "Architecture or revolution," is a lucid reminder of the power of architecture to accommodate, placate, transform, and mediate loci of human populations—in short, to create a spatial, visual reality in which we live and think. Such fundamental properties of architecture are not limited to Le Corbusier's modern world, but are valid as well to other places and times, such as Mesoamerican antiquity.

A case in point is Tula, Hidalgo. Tula was an important center of economic and political authority in Early Postclassic central Mexico, A.D. 900–1200. It also was one of the largest repositories of Early Postclassic Mesoamerican art and architecture. Reliefs and free-standing sculpture enmeshed in an architectural matrix populate Tula with a variety of human figures, creatures, and symbols (figure 7.1).

Most attempts to analyze the Tula art tradition have proceeded from one of three paradigms: (1) that Tula was Tollan, the mythic home of the culture hero and deity Topiltzin Quetzalcoatl, (2) that the many images of arms and armor at Tula evidence a militaristic polity and art tradition, and (3) that the development of Tula is inextricably linked with the contemporaneous Maya site of Chichén Itzá, Yucatán, which shares with Tula traits of planning, architecture, and imagery.

These issues are integral to our understanding of Tula but have tended to frame the parameters of research too narrowly on mythic, militaristic, and Maya viewpoints that deny the full significance of Tula as the capital of a powerful polity. From this latter perspective, the Tula art tradition has a stratigraphy of meaning, including rulership, ethnicity, personal identity, ritual, and social formation. When the spatial, aesthetic, and narrative structure of Tula is read systematically, the site becomes a map of the body politic, representing the individuals and social groups that collectively constitute the polity.

Figure 7.1. Tula civic-ceremonial center (photograph by Mark Miller Graham).

It is within the context of emergent power that this reading may best be understood. Tula was one of a number of polities that competed to fill the void left by the decline of Teotihuacan in the kaleidoscopic central Mexican geography that followed the Classic period. In addition to central Mexicans, Tula's population included peoples from north and west Mexico and the lowlands (Healan et al. 1989: 241; Mastache and Cobean 1989: 55–56). Through consolidation of population and of resources such as arable land and obsidian, Tula rose to power in the ninth century. This era of Mesoamerican prehistory is defined in part by new highland–lowland political and economic alliances, trade routes, and eclectic art styles (Freidel 1986a). In this context, Tula became the center of an expansive site hierarchy, the hub of an economic network linking the Basin of Mexico with the far reaches of Mesoamerica, and one node in an emergent cartel of power that stretched to Chichén Itzá (Sanders et al. 1979:140–141). The polity thus required a variety of (elite) social groups —ruler, merchant and warrior—to develop and sustain its position of authority. The themes of emergent power and the body politic as prime referents of the Tula art tradition are evident in plan, architecture, and imagery.

Plan

The Tula civic-ceremonial center was the core of the polity and art tradition. The scale and dense concentration of art and architecture atop a high ridge project the civic-ceremonial center as the physical, symbolic, and ideational core of the polity (figure 7.2). On the east side of the plaza is Pyramid C, the tallest building at Tula; it is in a ruinous state and has undergone little exploration and restoration. A low unreconstructed range structure faces the southern rim of the plaza. The western portion is framed by Ballcourt 2. A cluster of restored buildings is on the north side of the plaza and includes Building 3, Vestibule 1, and Pyramid B.

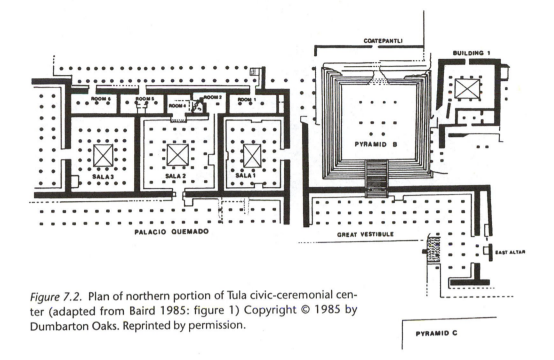

Figure 7.2. Plan of northern portion of Tula civic-ceremonial center (adapted from Baird 1985: figure 1) Copyright © 1985 by Dumbarton Oaks. Reprinted by permission.

These buildings no doubt served political and administrative needs, but the plan is also inscribed with a ritual pathway that directed traffic and provided settings for rites of power. This ritual circuit is visible north of the main plaza, where the best preserved buildings and imagery are found. The plan and decoration of Building 3, the Vestibule, and Pyramid B house choreograph and represent processions, offerings, funerals, and accessions of the body politic that form a three-dimensional tableau about the social formation of Tula.

Pyramid B

Pyramid B is the largest restored building at Tula, with five cornice-*talud-tablero* terraces and a central stairway on the south side leading to the plaza (figure 7.3). The rubble and mud core was encased in a thin stone facing, and much decoration remains in situ.

Reliefs on the north and east facades depict profile jaguars and coyotes in procession (see Kowalski, chapter 4, this volume). Tablero reliefs represent profile eagles and vultures eating human hearts alternating with recessed panels of composite frontal bird-serpent-jaguar creatures with human faces in their maws (Diehl 1983: figure 13). These mammals and birds are usually read as insignia of military orders, yet the binary sets of eagle/vulture and jaguar/coyote also may represent deliberate pairing of fauna selected for opposed behavioral traits, such as feeding.

Figure 7.3.
Pyramid B and adjacent buildings (photograph by Mark Miller Graham).

The composite creature, in contrast, has been identified as the Aztec deity Quetzalcoatl in his manifestation of Venus as the morning star. There is, however, little extant imagery to symbolically link the pyramid with any Venutian meaning (Ellen Baird, personal communication 1991).

On the summit of Pyramid B are the largest free-standing sculptures at Tula. Pieces of the monumental sculptures found behind the pyramid have been reassembled on the summit, where they apparently once supported a 4 meter high wooden roof. Although their present arrangement is speculative, they are the most overt symbols of the polity, clearly visible from several kilometers away and commanding a view of domestic sectors of the site, rural hinterlands, and trade routes.

Two columns that may have framed a temple doorway are in the form of inverted feathered serpents. They allude to Quetzalcoatl on a literal level, but they may also be symbols of the polity (Kubler 1982). Behind these columns is a row of four identical atlantids that have been variously identified as warriors, hunters, guards, and the Aztec deity Mixcoatl, father of Quetzalcoatl (Acosta 1961: 221; Nicholson 1971: 109; Graulich 1976; Kubler 1984: 83; Baird 1985: 109; Kristan-Graham 1989: 139–150) (figure 7.4). The martial gear—spearthrower, shield, and spears—has helped characterize such imagery as militaristic.

Finally, the four pillars forming a row behind the altlantids may be accession monuments. As the rollout drawing in figure 7.5 shows, weapons and a distinct individual are carved on each side to form an heraldic composition that wraps around each pillar. One figure wears the turquoise diadem or *xiuhuitzolli* of Aztec emperors. Others wear a headdress that conflates two traits of Late Classic Maya rulers from Palenque, the Drum-major headdess and stepped sidelocks (Kristan-Graham 1989: 123–129). The figures are framed at top and bottom by profile crocodilian heads commonly known by their Nahuatl name *cipactli*, a plausible reference to 1 Cipactli, a favored date for the coronation of Aztec emperors.

Figure 7.4. Atlantid from Pyramid B (adapted from Acosta 1961: figure 14; drawing by Cynthia Kristan-Graham).

Figure 7.5. Rollout drawing of a pillar from Pyramid B (adapted from Diehl 1983: figure 13; drawing by Dennis Campay).

On each of the two registers, two figures face each other across the pillar. Such opposed pairs are characteristic of accession monuments, notably the Aztec Dedication Stone (Klein 1990) and the tablet from the Temple of the Foliated Cross at Palenque.

Moreover, in a manner characteristic of representations of Mesoamerican notables, especially rulers and deities, name glyphs identify half of the figures: deer or dog, eagle, serpent, coyote, seated man or hunchback, and jaguar (Kristan-Graham 1989: 205–217). Two in particular, "Falling Eagle" (or Cuauhtemoc) and "Obsidian Serpent" (or Itzcoatl), are logographs of later Aztec rulers.

The Vestibule

South of Pyramid B is Vestibule 1, commonly called the Vestibule ("Great Vestibule" in figure 7.2), an L-shaped colonnaded hall and pyramid foyer. Vestibule 1 is lined with rubble and stone veneer benches whose battered bases are decorated with carved and painted reliefs. In situ bench friezes in the northwest corner and along the eastern wall show that two files of ornately dressed males appear to enter from the plaza, march around the room, and then meet at an altar and at the foot of the Pyramid B stairway (Diehl 1983: 64–65) (figure 7.6). The figures are not shown actually moving, but rather seem to appear in one frame of a continuous, ongoing narrative.

The frieze in the northwest corner represents 19 individuals who have been identified as *caciques* or local chiefs (Moedano 1947), but recent analysis indicates that these figures are more likely merchants (Kristan-Graham 1993). Items in the frieze such as staves, backpacks and a fan are common attributes of merchants throughout Mesoamerica (Thompson 1970: 137, 307; Morley et al. 1983: 434). There is, in addition, a remarkably close correlation between the bench imagery and descriptions of rituals performed by Aztec merchants, or pochteca, recorded in the *Florentine Codex*. *Pochteca* rituals most similar to the sculptural imagery of the Vestibule involve the beginning and ending of trading expeditions, the codification of the business relationship between the emperor and merchants, and the elevation of merchant status. Specific parallels include the carrying of red staves in the right hand and shields in the left and processions in colonnaded halls that conclude by placing offerings on altars and at the foot of a pyramid, precisely where the processions in Vestibule 1 meet (Sahagún 1950–1982, 9: 12–13, 22; Kristan-Graham 1993).

How might the striking parallels between merchant imagery at Tula and recorded *pochteca* behavior be explained? One answer may be the similar trajectories of early Tula and Aztec culture. During the Late Postclassic period, the Aztecs, as newcomers to the Valley of Mexico, from the same northern regions as some of Tula's early occupants, occupied Tula and intermarried with the remnants of its dynasty for cultural and

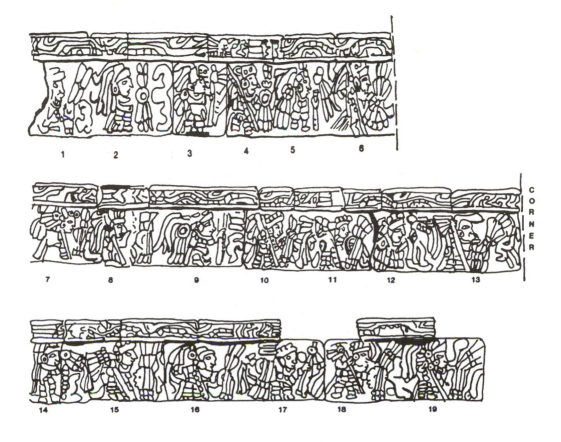

political legitimacy. The Aztecs conducted "treasure hunts" there (Sahagún 1950–1982, 10: 165), searching for artifacts that would form the symbolic building blocks of some of their own monuments, such as bench friezes. Given the close temporal, cultural, and geographic ties between Tula and the Aztecs, we might even ask whether some Aztec rituals were patterned after oral tradition, or even after imagery, from Tula. This would explain the close parallels between the Vestibule frieze and descriptions of *pochteca* rituals in the *Florentine Codex*.

Figure 7.6. Vestibule frieze (adapted from Moedano 1947: color-plate; Drawing by Dennis Campay).

Building 3

Building 3 is also known as the Palacio Quemado or Burnt Palace because a prehistoric fire turned the mud brick of the structure into adobe. It contains three large colonnaded halls facing the plaza and a row of smaller rooms in the rear. The large central room, Hall 2, opens onto the plaza. The bench lining the room perimeter is decorated with a carved and painted frieze that represents two files of males wearing luxury items, such as feather cloaks and jade, characteristic of nobles (figure 7.7). The figures appear to enter from Room 4 in the rear, march around the hall, and then meet at the doorway to the plaza, where presumably the procession metaphorically continues (Diehl 1983: 64).

Figure 7.7. Portion of frieze in Hall 2, Building 3 (adapted from de la Fuente et al., 1988: number 81; drawing by Cynthia Kristan-Graham).

Figure 7.8.top: Relief of prone figure in Hall 1, Building 3 (adapted from de la Fuente et al., 1988: number 108; drawing by Cynthia Kristan-Graham).

Figure 7.9. at right: Figure carved on a pillar from Pyramid B (drawing by Cynthia Kristan-Graham).

The adjacent Hall 1 has plain benches, but carved and painted panels found in the room debris likely once adorned the upper walls of the room (Acosta 1956: 91–112). On the basis of costume and regalia, key indicators of identity in Mesoamerican art, the panels seem to portray some of the rulers carved on the Pyramid B pillars. Prone poses and placement above benches and altars in a colonnaded hall next to a temple-pyramid recall descriptions of the rooms in which funerals for Aztec rulers and heroes took place in the Aztec capital Tenochtitlan (Duran 1964: 168– 177; Kristan-Graham 1989: 282–290) (figure 7.8). Therefore, the juxtaposition of similar figures in different architectural settings may memorialize rulers in both life and death (figure 7.9).

The Body Politic

Most of the extant imagery from the northern portion of the civic-ceremonial center portrays different visions of the elite polity: marching merchants and nobles, standing warriors and rulers, and fallen rulers and heroes. At Tula the human figure is the essential unit of representation, varied in appearance and location to illustrate the vital components of the body politic. The conceptual and visual equation between the human body and the body politic is a fundamental Mesoamerican principle. This rhetorical use of imagery may be traced as far back as Olmec art, accepting that carved altars and colossal heads are monuments of rulership. The typical Classic Maya dynastic and political monument, the carved stela, charts the history of the polity through royal biography and a portrait of the king. Likewise, in Aztec art the image of the emperor is all-pervasive and stands for his own person as well as for the Triple Alliance he oversaw.

The trope of the royal body doubling for that of the entire royal realm is not restricted to Mesoamerica. In a landmark analysis, Ernst Kantorowicz (1957) has outlined how this concept permeated Medieval European law and literature. Medieval English law recognized the dual body of the ruler, the mortal corporeal body of the king that was subject to taxes and death, and the immortal ruling political body of the king (Kantorowicz 1957: 7–24). Given this background, reading the Tula civic-ceremonial center is an act with far-reaching implications, for it not only brings Tula squarely into a basic Mesoamerican intellectual and visual tradition, but also makes the concept of the body politic understandable as a more universal phenomenon.

Narrative and Ritual at Tula

All of the aforementioned imagery from Tula is united by location and composition into a three-dimensional narrative that enmeshes the Tula civic-ceremonial center. While one reading centers on the body politic, one subtext of the overall content and composition stresses social and cultural cohesion. As figure 7.10 shows, in Building 3 a procession of nobles marches through Hall 2 and out to the plaza just as a file of merchants leaves the plaza, marches through the Vestibule, and is poised to place offerings at an altar and at the base of Pyramid B. Echoing the human processions, a symbolic menagerie winds around the pyramid face. Above on the pyramid summit stand monumental warriors and rulers that dominate the real and symbolic horizons of Tula. Meanwhile, in Hall 1 of Building 3, some of these same rulers appear as funerary images. The visual, spatial, and conceptual interlocking of these processions and rituals implies the harmonious interaction of the body politic and privileges group integration, a forceful paragon of social relations at an emergent center of power.

Another theme of these narrative episodes is power, especially the power of the polity and the power of ritual. The social groups illustrated represent the elite infrastructure of the Tula body politic. These groups are depicted at liminal moments such as death and accession, vulnerable times when transfer of power and change in status can reaffirm an

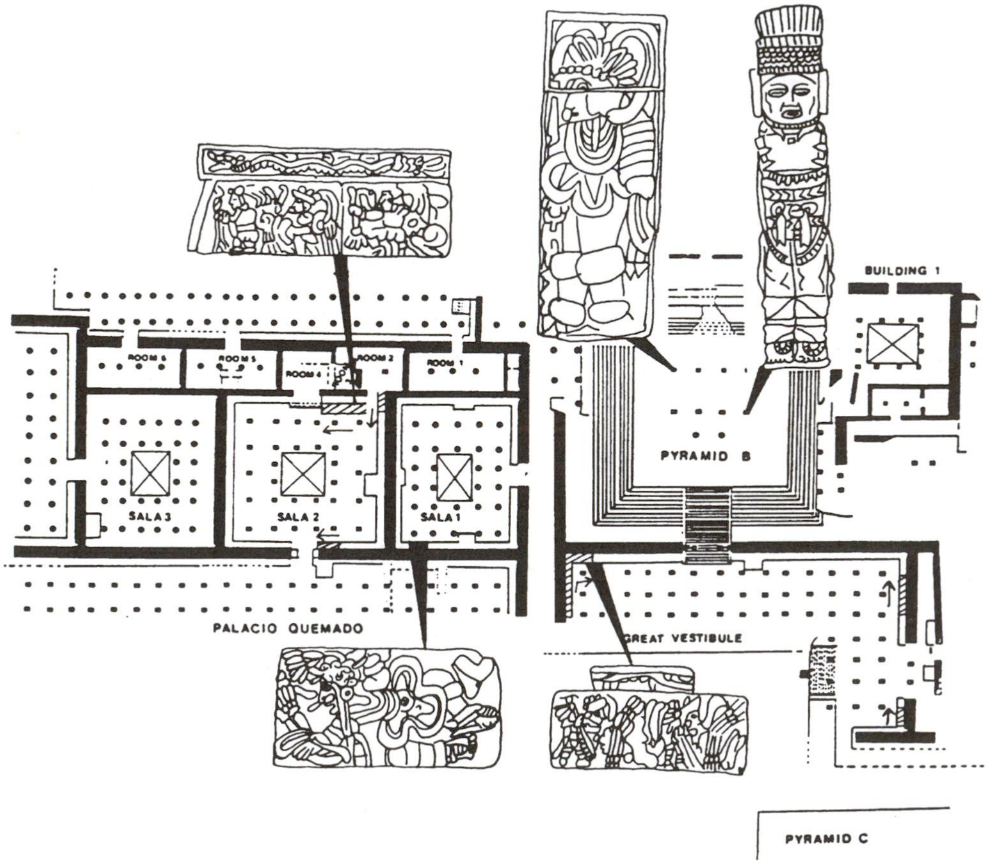

Figure 7.10. Plan of the northern portion of the Tula civic-ceremonial center with sculpture and arrows indicating processional routes (adapted from Baird 1985: figure 1. Drawings by Cynthia Kristan-Graham).

efficient bureaucracy and ideational system. Conversely, alterations in social, political, or religious institutions can be codified or sacralized at these same liminal moments. In this sense, the narrative program is a map of polity membership in which social relations and practices are embedded.

The distinctive manner in which rituals are portrayed reinforces the theme of solidarity. This is most evident in bench friezes, which typically are decorated with processional scenes. Elsewhere in Mesoamerica, processional compositions follow the same general format, with two files of figures converging on a central motif. In contrast, processional friezes at Tula turn corners and meet at doorways, but typically represent neither the beginning nor the finale of processions. However, since the axial and iconographic foci of the processions are keyed to open doorways, real actors could actually have been poised there to complete the processions and rituals portrayed, varying the finale for specific requisites, with the decorated benches serving alternately as stage, seat or altar (Kristan-Graham 1993). Bench friezes thus may have been more than mute, unreflexive backdrops; the actor(s) required to conclude the bench imagery ordered and was ordered by empirical reality and could literally act out the necessity of nobles or merchants to the ritual and to the polity.

The interactive nature of art and ritual applies to other narratives at Tula, highlighting groups and individuals vital to Tula's rise to power and sustained position as a major player in Mesoamerica. Besides choreographing movement and depicting rituals, the art-ritual matrix formed a network of power where social and political relations could be dramatized and reproduced. And even when these ritual spaces were not inhabited, the imagery continually echoed these rites of power. In this scenario, ritual and aesthetics may be viewed as active agents in the creation of power rather than mere reflections of preexistent conditions. The narrative program unfolds in time and space, becoming a three-dimensional text that at once tells (or shows) a story of ancient Tula and becomes the context for its own ritual reenactment. One value of narrativity is that events are projected as real whether or not they actually occurred (White 1981). Since the relationship between imagery and the material world is not necessarily straightforward, such imagery is not a secure indicator for historical reconstruction.

What, then, are the ramifications for the emphasis on the body politic in the Tula art tradition? The sculpture that dominates the civic-ceremonial center is not "hard" evidence that can ramify the existence of specific social groups or individuals there, however plausible or necessary the presence of rulers, nobles, warriors, and merchants may be at a major seat of economic and political authority. Instead, the narrative cycle may be more securely read as a tangible remnant of how the Tula polity told its own story and represented itself. In this scenario, the focus on the body politic represents the ideal of elite polity membership rather than actual membership proclaimed to Tula and the Mesoamerican world at large.

The Power of Architecture at Tula

The architecture of the civic-ceremonial center operates on a number of levels to reify the important position of Tula in Early Postclassic Mesoamerica. While the areal extent and architectural scale may seem paltry compared to other Mesoamerican centers, Tula nonetheless was one of the largest Early Postclassic sites in central Mexico. Its location pushed the limits of Mesoamerica to its northernmost margin, while its coherent narrative program helped to redefine Mesoamerican site symbolism and aesthetics.

The architectural vernacular there may be termed polyglot, for the referents include a variety of building types and decoration from disparate corners of Mesoamerica. The following is not a comprehensive inventory but rather a survey of pervasive traits that add to the composite flavor of architecture at Tula.

The memory of Teotihuacan resonates at Tula. Teotihuacanos formed part of the population, and the art and architecture echo that great Classic period power. Architectural traits at Tula likely based on Teotihuacan models include colonnaded halls and carved pillars from palace complexes; processional bench imagery modeled after decorated battered wall bases; terraced pyramids with a single stairway; and *talud-tablero* building profiles.

These same traits, along with innovative sculpture such as atlantids, also appear at Chichén Itzá, but geography and demographics deem Teotihuacan a more practical source of inspiration. Other Maya traits at Tula include carved stelae and royal regalia.

Central Mexican and Maya traits contribute to a hybrid architectural complex at Tula that forms a metaphorical mortar that binds together the composite population and complements the Postclassic highland–lowland character. Likewise, Tula's northern and western heritage is nearly invisible in the architectural program that is cloaked in easily recognizable Mesoamerican symbols. The architectural program thus helps to mediate the cultural makeup of the site as a paragon of cohesion for the real and ideal polity and was a formative force in the changing dialectics of self, polity, and power. The architectural vernacular therefore carries a heavy ideational burden: to place Tula firmly in the Mesoamerican world and express unity as a complement to the narrative program.

Finally, the civic-ceremonial center transforms the region into a social, cultural, and ritual space where art, architecture, and people coexist; but the architecture is more than a series of frames for pictures and vistas of the body politic. Rather, Tula is a three-dimensional arena that provides an ideal vision of polity heritage, membership, and power. The architectural complex and narrative cycle thus might be termed both actual and virtual (Krauss 1987: 171). The actual or physical presence of the buildings is complemented by the virtual, which is a construct of the viewer, who decided just how to read Tula. The actual building blocks of the site are the fundamental cues in reading and interpreting, but each viewer arranges the cues in unique ways, engendered by his or her own particular notions and experiences. Thus, meaning at Tula is not fixed stone, but suggested by the material and ideational constructs there. The site thus is as much a creation of ancient or modern readers of the text that is Tula as of its ancient builders.

Summary

Tula is an intricate web of architecture, imagery, and concepts, a world constructed of ideas as well as of mudbrick and stone. The civic-ceremonial center, in tandem with Tula's new role as an important political and economic center of authority, proclaimed the conquest of the northern frontier by transforming a region that before had been on the very fringes of Mesoamerica into a viable Mesoamerican capital with monumental art and architecture heralding its newfound status. The narrative program focuses on the body politic while the ritual interaction of these groups and individuals emphasizes solidarity and the sanctity of the polity and the architectural vernacular stresses an homogeneous heritage. The symbolic referents of the architectural matrix are a paragon for the ideal polity, a potent demonstration of innovative mores in the emerging Postclassic social order, especially highland–lowland alignments, economic vitality, and power invested in a collection of specialists rather than in one dominant individual. Moreover, this nexus helped to set a new pattern in which the rules of interaction are privileged over the rules of engagement, a sharp turn away from many preceding Classic themes. The narrative structure of Tula meanwhile fostered the ritual intermingling of imagery and real individuals, helping to form and mediate social relations vital to the polity and body politic. The radical shift at Tula from relative marginality to Mesoamericanization and from Classic to Postclassic aesthetics and content thereby indicate an emendation to Le Corbusier's dictum to suggest that, in a very real sense, architecture is revolution.

8

The Lintel Paintings of Mitla and the Function of the Mitla Palaces

John Martin Deland Pohl

The ruins of Mitla, or *Lyobaa* as it is known in Zapotec, lie 40 kilometers southeast of Oaxaca City. They have been a source of extraordinary fascination to Mexican, European, and American archaeologists since the early nineteenth century and remain a popular tourist attraction today. Despite its prominent reputation however, Mitla remains shrouded in considerable mystery. One of the problems with the site's interpretation has been that it was an architectural anomaly for its time, both in terms of its size and in complexity of construction (Robles et al. 1989; Robles and Moreira 1990). This has become increasingly evident through comparisons to the relatively small Zapotec Postclassic capital of Zaachila (Gallegos 1978; Blanton et al. 1982) and the Mixtec capital of Tilantongo (Byland and Pohl 1994). The results of these projects indicate that the highest ranking Postclassic Oaxacan administrative centers might better be described as great houses than as city-states.[1]

Archaeologists accustomed to correlating political importance with site size consequently have been frustrated by ethnohistorical accounts that describe Mitla as the location of a prominent funerary shrine, not as the center of political authority attributed to Zaachila and Tilantongo. Actually, the Spaniards never compared Mitla to any royal administrative capital, but rather to a Vatican of the Zapotec people where disputes between noblemen were arbitrated by an oracular priest, called the *Vuijatao* or "Great Seer" (Seler 1904a; Burgoa 1934a 26: 350–351; Acuña 1984: 263; Cordova 1987: 299v). The questions I address here concern how a unique form of narrative art at Mitla, the surviving Mixteca-Puebla style lintel paintings, may have been used to communicate the doctrine of national unity represented by this remarkable religious authority.

There are five major building compounds at Mitla with lesser known mounds and tombs in the neighboring community of Xaaga and in the hills to the west and east (figure 8.1a). The oldest of the Mitla palace

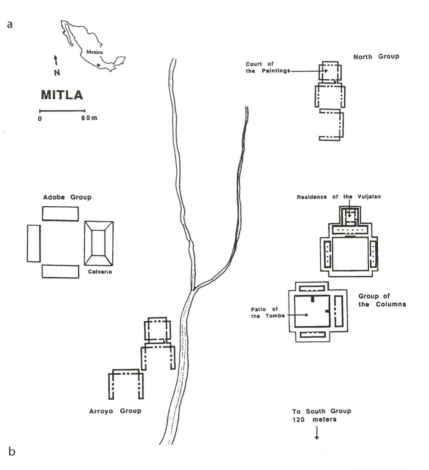

a

MITLA

0   60 m

Mexico

N

North Group

Court of
the Paintings

Adobe Group

Calvario

Residence of the Vuijatao

Group of
the Columns

Patio of
the Tombs

Arroyo Group

To South Group
120 meters

b

Figure 8.1. (a) Plan of the ruins of Mitla; (b) View of the Hall of the Columns in the Group of the Columns at Mitla. This structure is described as the residence of the prestigious oracular priest known as the *Vuijatao* (photograph by John Pohl).

complexes is the South Group, dating to the Monte Albán III or Classic period (Caso and Borbolla 1936; Marquina 1951: 371–389; Kubler 1975: 99–107; Flannery and Marcus 1983e: 295–296). The Adobe Group may also have been constructed during this period, but numerous hard, grey ceramic sherds in the rubble imply that the buildings enjoyed a florescence during the Postclassic period.

The other three constructions, the North Group, the Group of the Columns, and the Arroyo Group are all Monte Albán V Postclassic (A.D. 1000–1521) in date. Each of these palaces was designed in similar fashion, being conceived as quadrangular courts around which were constructed the habitations of a residential priesthood and visiting nobility. Both the exterior and interior walls were decorated with two or three levels of magnificent fretwork, called *guiyeii* in Zapotec, that have come to represent the hallmark of Mitla style (see figure 8.3). Although the Group of the Columns was left relatively intact throughout the Colonial period, the North Group was subsequently used for different purposes, including as a barn, by friars attending to the Church of San Pablo, while the Arroyo Group was eventually incorporated into a surrounding urban neighborhood.

Although a number of colonial historians have remarked on the site (Motolinia 1950: 197; Torquemada 1986: 312), our most valuable accounts concerning both the architectural plan and the ritual use of space are found in Alonso de Canseco's 1580 *Relación de Mitla* (Acuña 1984 2: 258–264) and Francisco de Burgoa's 1674 *Geográfica Descripción* (1934a: 26). These sources characterize the palaces as exclusive noble and priestly residences divided from the supporting urban population. Both historians describe the Group of the Columns by noting the location of cruciform tombs as well as the halls surrounding the quadrangle that served the kings who gathered at Mitla to discuss the affairs of government (figure 8.1b). The residence of the *Vuijatao*, the powerful oracular priest, was located in the northernmost court (Flannery and Marcus 1983e).

Burgoa (1934a 26: 123–125) described the subterranean tombs in the Group of the Columns as being dedicated to different social classes of priests, princes, and kings. Depending on the occasion, such as a feast or the funeral of a lord, the Vuijatao would emerge from his residence and descend into the Patio of the Tombs with a great retinue. Then after much preparation, he would fall into a trance and converse with idols in a low, unintelligible speech. Becoming possessed of the spirits of the gods, the oracle would continue to pray with "hideous grimaces and writhings, uttering inarticulate sounds that filled everyone present with fear and terror." When he emerged from his trance he would pronounce to the assembled kings in the patio what he had learned from the spirits of the dead.

Comparing the different accounts, it appears that the tomb beneath the north hall was reserved for the burial of the kings of Zaachila (Teozapotlan), noblemen whose portraits appear in the Mixtec Codex Zouche-Nuttall 33–35 (Gallegos 1978; Jansen 1982a; Paddock 1983) (figure 8.2). Zaachila was revered as the seat of the highest ranking lineage in the Valley of Oaxaca during the Postclassic (Acuña 1984 2: 158), a position probably attained when the founder of this dynasty, Lord 5 Flower, married a direct descendant of the great Mixtec Lord 8 Deer of Tilantongo sometime around A.D. 1280. The burial of the Zaachila kings beneath a patio in which the extended royal families met to arbitrate their disputes would have imbued the court with very special powers indeed.

Undoubtedly derived from textile designs, the masonry friezes have been the subject of considerable interest both for their method of manufacture and for the meaning of their various geometric forms (Holmes 1895–1897; Beyer 1924; Girard 1948; Kubler 1975; Hulsey 1977; Sharp 1978; Robles et al., 1989) (figure 8.3). Holmes described the fretwork as true mosaics achieved by carving small rectangles or squares of trachyte and fitting them into variations of eight basic patterns on a wet plaster foundation. He estimated that one room at Mitla contained more than 13,000 individual pieces of cut stone. Entire blocks of volcanic trachyte were carved in relief, but these were used principally in the construction

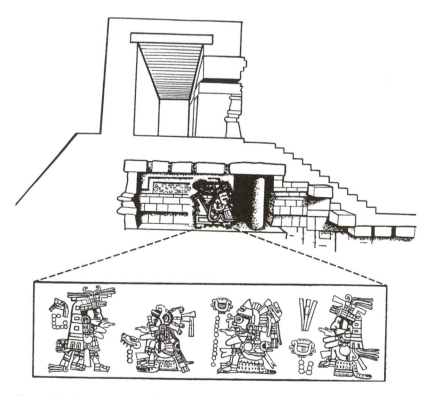

Figure 8.2. Canseco's *Relación de Mitla* and Burgoa's *Geográfica Descripción* both describe a tomb dedicated to the highest born Zapotec kings, the royal dynasty of Zaachila.

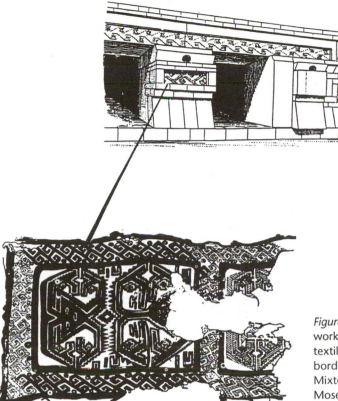

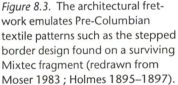

Figure 8.3. The architectural fret-work emulates Pre-Columbian textile patterns such as the stepped border design found on a surviving Mixtec fragment (redrawn from Moser 1983 ; Holmes 1895–1897).

of doorways and in the walls of subterranean tombs. Stacked in three-level arrangements, the exterior friezes of the Palace of the Columns are framed with protruding ornamental moldings abstracted from Caso's "jaws of the sky" motif, a bifurcated macaw head employed in earlier Zapotec artistic traditions (Caso 1928).

Holmes found that the some 150 panels were originally painted in varying shades of red and white. Friezes in these colors are specifically associated with temples dedicated to the culture hero 9 Wind "Quetzal-coatl" in the Mixtec Codex Zouche-Nuttall 15–21. A fragmentary narra-tive featuring this deity is found in the lintel paintings of the North Group. It may relate to the Toltec legend that Quetzalcoatl himself con-structed the Mitla palaces during his epic migration after the fall of Tula (Sahagún 1950–1982: 37). Although there are no Zapotec traditions specifically tying Quetzalcoatl to Mitla, there is a legend of a plumed ser-pent living in a well in the mountains to the east (Parsons 1936: 334).

The specific meaning of the different geometric designs has never been fully understood. A few design motifs are distinguished in local Zapotec terminology, but the names convey little more than formal descriptions (Stubblefield and Miller de Stubblefield 1991: 134). Stepped frets in general are associated with undulating serpents in Mesoamerican iconography, and naturalistic stone reliefs of serpents appear in similar panels on the earlier, Classic period buildings at Monte Albán. A comparison to lightning bolts has also been made, and both lightning and lightning serpents are powerful spirit forces in Mitla lore (Parsons 1936: 329–339). The terrace designs, on the other hand, can be compared to motifs employed by the Pueblo peoples of the American Southwest, where they are identified as rain clouds (Bunzel 1929). The intentional abstraction and consequent ambiguity in the fretwork therefore relates them to the most powerful spirit forces of agriculture and fertility in Mesoamerican thought (see Wilkerson, chapter 5, this volume).

Codex Magliabechiano 6 (Nuttall 1903) identifies a stepped fret motif on textiles as a *jicara* or drinking vessel (*xicalcoliuhqui* in Nahuatl). Remembering that Mixteca-Puebla polychrome ceramics feature the same design, the relationship between weaving and drinking may not be as fortuitous as it seems. Elsewhere I have proposed that textiles were produced and exchanged in an elite reciprocity economy that focused on palace feasting and drinking parties (Pohl 1994; see also Anawalt 1993). More fruitful approaches to interpreting the Mitla fretwork might come from studies of contemporary Mexican Indian weavers and embroiderers as well. For example, Walter Morris (1987: 109–112) found that the Tzotzil Maya women of neighboring Chiapas employ geometric designs in textiles as mnemonic devices for storytelling. When they are "stacked" on top of one another on a garment, they resemble the frieze arrangements at Mitla. That Pre-Columbian peoples used the same textile designs is confirmed through archaeological finds (see Moser 1983: 271; Pohl 1994).

Morris documented dozens of woven or embroidered representations related to primary spirit beings that are invoked in family and village stories deemed critical to social bonding. Although these must be checked with Oaxacan traditions to confirm standardization in meaning, a preliminary comparison indicates that designs resembling those identified in Tzotzil weaving as sun, star, scorpion's tail, flower, and snake path also are evident at Mitla. Significantly, Elsie Clews Parsons (1936) recorded stories featuring these same elements in connection with spirit beings residing in the mountains to the north and east of the Mitla palaces where rain, lightning, and thunder were thought to originate.

The Lintel Paintings

There are five surviving fragments of lintel paintings at Mitla. Four surround the main residential courtyard of the palace of the North Group, and the fifth is located in the Arroyo Group (Kubler 1975; Miller 1988). Despite their partial destruction due to both natural and human causes, enough of the critical information survives in the upper portions of the lintels to permit the identification of certain narrative themes that are

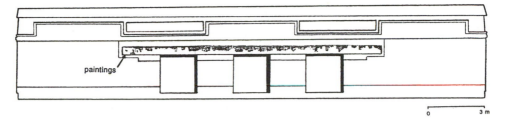

Figure 8.4. The north wall of the Church Group showing the location of the paintings in recessed panels over the doorways.

well documented in other sources including the Mixtec Codices, Pueblan maps, and religious stories from Central Mexico.[2] I have found three paintings of the North Group to be significant in terms of overall story content (figure 8.4). The fourth fragment depicts a procession of five unnamed deities on the south wall. I will defer a discussion of the painting of the Arroyo group to a future study.

West Wall: The Tolteca-Chichimeca Cosmogony

Eduard Seler (1904a, 1991) was the first scholar to comment on the Mitla paintings in any detail. He noted the appearance of the Central Mexican patriarch Mixcoatl-Camaxtli in the west panel (figure 8.4). Mixcoatl-Camaxtli was the culture hero of the Tolteca-Chichimeca, a confederation of peoples who claimed that their ancestors had been born from the seven caves of Chicomoztoc lying somewhere to the northwest of the Valley of Mexico. According to the Anales de Cuauhtitlan (Velázquez 1945: 3), Mixcoatl-Camaxtli and his four hundred brothers, called the Mimixcoa, were leading their people to a promised land when they were attacked by a hideous demon called Itzpapalotl, the Obsidian Butterfly. She devoured all but Mixcoatl, who had hidden himself. The hero later returned, killed the demon, and freed his brothers. Together they burned Itzpapalotl's body and rubbed her ashes on their faces. To the Mixtec, the Tolteca-Chichimeca became known as the *Sami Ñuu* or people with burnt faces. They appear on the wall paintings and in the Mixtec Codices with black "lone ranger"–style face masks (Pohl 1994).

Although badly damaged, perhaps intentionally, an image of Itzpapalotl being attacked by Mixcoatl appears in the paintings (figure 8.5a, see figure 8.5b-c for inconographic comparison). She is recognizable by the configuration of her hair featuring a crown with a large rosette, by her clawed jaguar skin feet, and by the obsidian knife border of her skirt (Spranz 1973: 88, 91). In another version of the story that appears in the Mitla narrative, a two-headed deer fell from heaven and was transformed into Itzpapalotl. Subsequently Itzpapalotl was burned and all that was left of her was a white sacrificial knife that Mixcoatl took away to worship as his god.

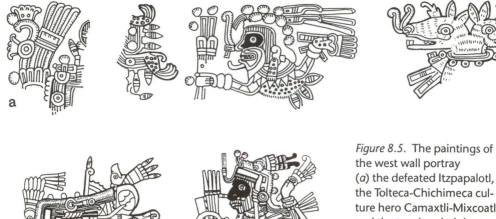

Figure 8.5. The paintings of the west wall portray (*a*) the defeated Itzpapalotl, the Tolteca-Chichimeca culture hero Camaxtli-Mixcoatl, and the two headed deer, (*b*) Itzpapalotl in *Codex Borgia 66* (figure reversed and rotated 45° for comparison), and (*c*) Camaxtli-Mixcoatl in *Codex Borgia 25*.

I have concluded, therefore, that the west wall depicts the creation legend particularly associated with the Tolteca-Chichimeca kingdoms of the Valley of Mexico, Tlaxcala, and Puebla, and, most notably for this discussion, in both Northern Oaxaca and the Mixteca Costa. According to the *Relación de Acatlan* (Acuña 1985), one of Mixcoatl's "sons" named Mixtecatl settled in Acatlan, where his people ruled lands extending from the Mixteca Baja to the coastal town of Tututepec, a mixed Chatino and Mixtec region. According to the relaciones from Guatulco and Pochutla, vassals of Tututepec, the people living throughout much of this coastal region claimed to be Chichimecs and worshipped Itzpapalotl as a goddess (Acuña 1984 1: 188, 193). A remarkable monolith discovered at Tututepec is probably a representation of Itzpapalotl. It is unusual in that it bears no likeness to any Mixtec or Zapotec sculptural tradition, but rather it resembles one of the colossal atlantid warriors of Tula, Hidalgo, the original Tolteca-Chichimeca capital (Piña Chan 1960: fot. 5 and 6).

Central Mexican and Pueblan sources also describe the peregrinations of a second group of Mixcoatl-Camaxtli's followers. These Tolteca-Chichimeca were led by another of Mixcoatl's sons named Xelhua (Motolinia 1950: 29; Torquemada 1986: 32; Pohl 1995). After the fall of Tula they migrated into the Tehuacan Valley of southern Puebla. According to the Anales de Cuauhtitlan, one of Xelhua's associates, named Atonal (Velázquez 1945: 15), then continued on to the *Mixteca Alta*, where he founded the kingdom of Coixtlahuaca in a mixed Chocho and Mixtec region (Velázquez 1945: 15). Atonal appears in the Mapa de

Cuauhtinchan II (Reyes 1977: 60) and in The Coixtlahuaca Lienzo de Tlapiltepec (Caso 1989: 95). It is these Tolteca-Chichimeca who appear in the Mixtec Codices allying themselves with the famous Lord 8 Deer of Tilantongo (Smith 1973: 72–75; Byland and Pohl 1994).

East Wall: The Mixtec Cosmogony

My examination of the east wall has led to the identification of a second cosmogony, this narrative being associated with the Mixtec centered around the Valley of Nochixtlan (figure 8.6a). According to Burgoa (1934a 25: 274), the first Mixtec kings were born from the trees that grew along the banks of rivers in the Valley of Apoala in the Mixteca Alta. This event is portrayed in a number of the Mixtec codices (Furst 1978a; Jansen 1982b). Codices Vindobonensis and Bodley identify the first couple as being specifically named Lord 1 Flower and Lady 13 Flower. On Codex Bodley 40, the couple emerge from the river qualified by a hand holding feathers as a place sign of Apoala (Caso 1960). Another place sign appears to the left consisting of a river qualified by the head of an exotic bird (figure 8.6b).

The same couple appear in Codex Vindobonensis 36 and 35. Here their parrotlike helmets are more clearly depicted. The symbols are unique to this couple in the codices in that the headdress partially covers the face over the eye (figure 8.6c). Examining the two principal figures on the Mitla painting of the east wall, we see that they also wear the same parrot headdresses and are posed as persons emerging from the earth in much the same way as in Codex Bodley. Although the numerals on the left-hand side have been destroyed, the combination of pose, headdress, and day-sign names positively mark this couple as Lady 13 Flower and Lord 1 Flower, the Mixtec progenitors of Apoala that appear in the codices. In addition, two place signs appear that also correlate with the Codex Bodley Scene. One is a river qualified by feathers and the other is a river upon which sit two exotic birds (see Miller 1988).

The Apoala cosmogony was particularly venerated by the powerful royal house of Yanhuitlan, lying in the northern end of the Valley of Nochixtlan in the Mixteca Alta, and Apoala itself was an important tributary of Yanhuitlan (Spores 1967: 167). By the late Postclassic, Yanhuitlan had confederated itself with the kingdom of Cuilapan, a community lying at the base of Monte Albán in the Valley of Oaxaca. According to the Relación de Teozapotlan (Zaachila), the Mixtec incursion into this traditionally more Zapotec territory came about when the sister-in-law of the king of Zaachila married a Yanhuitlan lord and Cuilapan was given to him as a gift. At that time the Yanhuitlan king brought a number of his Mixtec people to settle in the Valley of Oaxaca (Acuña 1984 2: 157). This event would explain how Friar Gregorio García (1981) happened to record the Mixtec Apoala creation story in Cuilapan.

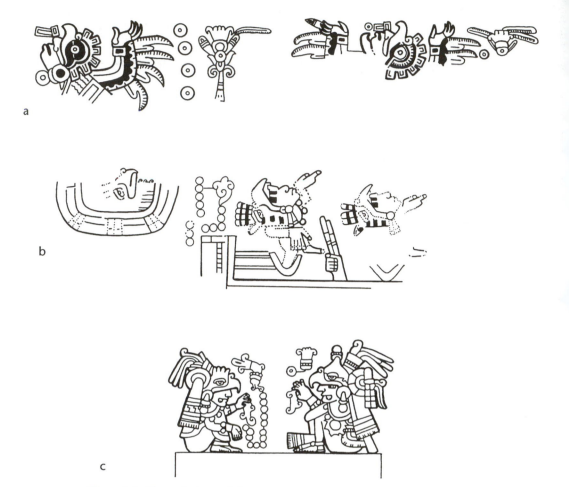

Figure 8.6. The paintings of the east wall portray (*a*) 4+ Flower and 1 Flower wearing exotic bird headdresses, (*b*) Lady 13 Flower and Lord 1 Flower emerging from the river of Apoala in Codex Bodley 40, and (*c*) Lady 13 Flower and Lord 1 Flower in Codex Vindobonensis 36.

North Wall: The Zapotec Cosmogony

Looking at the north wall, we likewise see symbols associated with cosmogonical precepts. The painting begins by giving the year-sign 1 Reed, which is associated with the beginning of time in the Mixtec codices (Furst 1978b). Following a series of events involving 9 Wind "Ehécatl-Quetzalcoatl," a scene appears in which place signs are carried on the backs of gods. One of these is called Hill of the Turkey, and it subsequently reappears paired with a second place sign representing Place of the Fruit Tree. Both of these signs contain palaces before which are seated two similar figures. They are both named by the day sign "flower" and wear the butterfly crowns associated with solar deities or members of the Xochipilli-Cinteotl complex of deities in the Central Mexican pantheon (Nicholson 1971: 416-417; Spranz 1973: 385).

The deity at Hill of the Turkey can be identified as the god 7 Flower in the Mixtec codices (figure 8.7a). On pages 33–31 of Codex Bodley, Lord 4 Wind visits three prominent oracular priests. The first is Lord 1 Death, the oracle of Achiutla. The second is Lady 9 Grass, the oracle of Chalcatongo, and the third is Lord 7 Flower, who is dressed like his Mitla counterpart and seated at Hill of the Turkey (figure 8.7b). Lord 4 Wind was a direct descendant of the Apoala progenitors portrayed on the east panel, and I have concluded given these special circumstances that 7 Flower must be one of the oracles of Mitla described by Burgoa. The Hill of the Turkey place sign appears only in the Codex Bodley scene and in the Mitla wall paintings.

The day name 7 Flower is in fact the name of the great creator god otherwise called Tonacatecuhtli in the Central Mexican pantheon. According to Codex Rios 1, he was known as the father of all the gods and lord of the 13th or highest heaven. Only those who had led the purest lives as great lords or children who had died before experiencing sin were pure enough to reside with him in his garden paradise after death. The description of this paradise matches the accounts of Mitla in which the deceased were thought to enjoy a bounteous life after death at a place which Burgoa (1934a 25: 64) compared to the Elysian Fields of Classical Roman and Greek mythology. As patron of the royal ancestors, it is not surprising that 7 Flower also appears in the Mixtec codices as the leader of the mushroom rituals by which the living would eat hallucinogens and thereby communicate with the dead (Furst 1978a: 204).

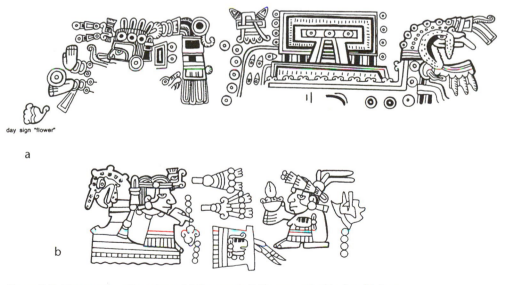

day sign "flower"

a

b

Figure 8.7. The north wall portrays (a) the oracle 7 Flower seated before his temple at Hill of the Turkey, (b) The oracle 7 Flower meeting with Lord 4 Wind, a descendant of 13 Flower and 1 Flower portrayed on the east wall. Lady 6 Monkey of Jaltepec was the mother of Lord 4 Wind.

I have been able to correlate Hill of the Turkey with a promontory located about 3.5 kilometers to the east of Mitla called El Guajolote in Spanish and *Guhdz Bedkol* in Zapotec (Briggs 1961: 103). The hill marks the border between Mitla and the town of Xaaga, a former dependency. Oscar Schmieder (1930), Elsie Clews Parsons (1936), and Charles Leslie (1960) all described the surrounding area as being the most sacred of natural features to the Mitla people, possibly because it is a source of the fresh springs that irrigate the Mitla Valley to the west. Pictographs have been identified in nearby rock shelters (Flannery and Marcus 1983e) and the land continues to be considered "bewitched" even today (figure 8.8).

Parsons (1936: 210, 220–221, 295–296, 340–342) documented legends of oracular spirit forces in the area. For example, it was here that a spirit named *Sus Giber* had a "ranch" where she fed the workmen who quarried the stone blocks for the construction of the Mitla palaces. Later she was transformed into a mass of rock upon the rising of the sun during the creation of the present epoch. *Sus Giber* is also venerated as the patroness of a nearby cave located a few hundred meters from the Hill of the Turkey. The cave is said to contain a market where people seek divine help in getting food, supplies, and money and where they go to pray for good fortune in long-distance trading ventures. The place sign for Hill of the Turkey illustrated in the lintel painting includes signs for mirrors set into the mountain (Seler 1904a: 318). Caves are referred to as "little mirrors" in stories told by the people of Mitla (Parsons 1936: 420).

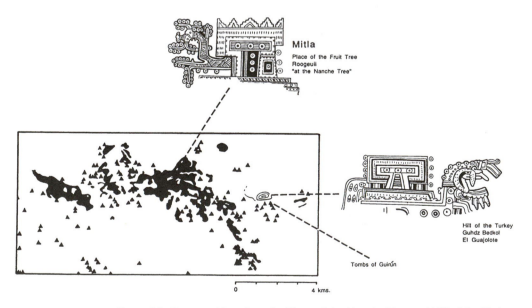

Figure 8.8. Proposed locations for Place of the Nanche Tree and Hill of the Turkey with regard to the Monte Alban V settlement distribution of the Mitla Valley (map adapted from Blanton et al. 1982).

On an adjacent slope to the east are the ruins and cruciform tombs of *Guirún* (*Guiaroo*) investigated by Marshall Saville (1909) at the turn of the century. The site resembles a natural stronghold, having a commanding view of the Mitla Valley. According to Burgoa (1934a 26: 242) such outlying burial shrines were dedicated to lesser ranking noblemen. For example, the nephew of the king of Zaachila was buried on a remote, lofty height so that he might rule over the four directions, east, west, north, and south, so that from these palaces where he had gone to sleep he could "guard the vassals and lands of his uncle."

The second figure associated with Place of the Fruit Tree is more problematical, as the place sign has not been identified in the Mixtec codices (figure 8.9). The Codex Rios 124, however, portrays a place sign for the Aztec conquest of Mitla that is represented by a fruit tree, while local legends persist in which the priests of Mitla maintained a bountiful orchard of fruit trees that was destroyed by the Aztecs. The orchard reputedly

a

day sign "flower"

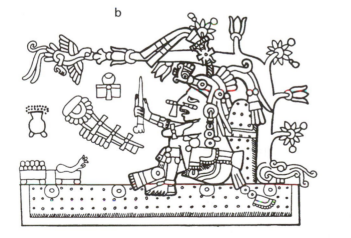

b

c

Figure 8.9. Another fragment of the north wall depicts (a) the oracle 13 Flower seated before a temple at Place of the Nanche Tree (note that he holds a cup of frothy pulque), and (b) the god Xochipilli-Cinteotl seated before a composite fruit tree in Codex Laud 16. (c) A nanche tree branch with berries.

included an abundance of nanches, guayabas, zapotes, and many other species (Martínez Gracida 1906: 677). Significantly, Codex Vaticanus A portrays a fruit tree with nanche berries as a symbol of the netherworld paradise of Tamoanchan, the Aztec equivalent to the 13th or highest heaven discussed earlier.

The name of the slope upon which the ruins of the Group of the Columns were built is *Roogeuii*, which is translated as "At the Nanche Tree" by many Mitla people, and these trees continue to grow in abundance all around the ruins today. The nanche tree is characterized by its clusters of small yellow or orange bitter fruits in a configuration that fits the place sign precisely. The nanche is also well known for its use in making a powerful liquor (Aguilera 1985: 126), probably the drink made from crushed fruits mixed with fermented pulque of maguey and consumed in great quantities by the noblemen and priests at Mitla in the course of their feasts and religious festivals (Burgoa 1934a 26: 125; Acuña 1984 2: 260). These potent alcoholic beverages were restricted to use among the upper class.

Employing an iconographic analysis of the deity's attributes, it is clear that he is *Bezelao* or 13 Flower, lord of the Zapotec netherworld and patron deity of Mitla according to the town's *relación* (Whitecotton 1982: 319, 325; Acuña 1984 2: 260). The day sign flower described earlier is associated with both the Mitla figure and *Bezelao*. A number of sources refer to *Bezelao* as the "prince of the devils," "supreme universal god," and the "god of hell" (Burgoa 1934a 26: 64–65; Acuña 1984 1: 89, 2: 91, 260; Cordova 1987: 141;). The "god of hell" or Lucifer was described in a 1635 report on Zapotec religious practices in the town of San Miguel Sola (Berlin 1988: 19). He holds the seventh place in a list of 13 gods that represent the 13 lords of the days in a Zapotec *tonalpohualli* (Caso 1971: 334–35; Marcus 1983b; Urcid 1991). His cognate in this calendrical system would be the deity known in Central Mexican nomenclature as Xochipilli-Cinteotl, a god whose attributes match those of the figure under discussion. These include not only the butterfly crown and red stripe around the eye, but also the trefoil red paint around the mouth.

Codex Fejervary-Mayer 9 shows a god with the attributes of Xochipilli Cinteotl as being patron of the rites enacted on the day 13 Flower, and Codex Laud 16 depicts him seated below a composite fruit tree which includes nanche berries in much the same way as the deity at Mitla (figure 8.8b). Although Cinteotl is more commonly considered a corn god, according to Codex Rios 30, he was also known as the patron of ritual drinking and inebriation along with his consort Mayahuel, the goddess of maguey and pulque. Mayahuel together with Cinteotl presided over the eighth *trecena* called 1 Grass in the 260-day ritual calendar (Caso 1971: 338). Significantly, the *Relación de Mitla* states that 13 Flower-*Bezelao* was worshipped along with his wife named *Quecuya* or Goddess 1 Grass (Whitecotton 1982: 319, 325; Acuña 1984 2: 260; Javier Urcid, personal communication).

This brief summary of my progress toward interpreting the architectural context of the Mitla lintel paintings is part of a larger project that addresses the nature of narrative art and oracular power at Mitla. A future study will include further analysis of the magnificent greca friezes, while there is still more to be examined in the paintings as well. For example, despite the thematic segmentation of the cosmogonies around the court, there appears to be a sequential reading order that begins in the southeast corner at the courtyard entrance and continues around the east, north, and west walls, ending with a procession of deities painted on the south wall.

Many other people, places, and things can be identified in the paintings, including the Mixtec culture hero, 9 Wind "Ehécatl-Quetzalcoatl," who appears prominently on the north wall, probably as the protagonist in the epic factional struggle known as the War of Heaven (Caso 1960; Rabin 1979; Byland and Pohl 1994). One god appears in two of the cosmogonies, 7 Flower, the lord of the royal paradise. He makes his first appearance on the east wall with the Mixtec dynastic founders, Lord 1 Flower and Lady 13 Flower. He then appears on the north wall as the oracle at Hill of the Turkey.

Royal Feasts

In writing about the exceptional aesthetic qualities of the Mitla palaces, George Kubler (1975) noted the striking individuality of each of the buildings, unusual by Mesoamerican standards in that they seem to have been constructed without any comprehensive plan of order. Kubler (1975: 99) felt that the isolated residences gave the effect of suburban villas, "jealous of their privacy, turning closed walls upon one another, walls which display wealth without inviting the spectator, without attempting to share a coherent space with neighboring edifices." These observations emphasize the effort invested in the creation of restricted space within the courtyards while maintaining massive, forbidding, even ominous exteriors.

The emphasis on privacy made the courts ideally suited to the feasting and drinking parties that characterized the aristocratic political life at Mitla (Burgoa 1934a 26: 123–125). Drinking to excess was the means by which petitioners communed with the ancestors whose advice was sought in the resolution of disputes or the arrangement of favorable alliances. According to a number of Oaxacan sources, the spirits spoke back through idols, mummies, or even the *Vuijatao* himself (Herrera 1945: 173; Acuña 1984 2: 48, 116, 238) while the ingestion of mushrooms allowed one to actually see the dead as ghostly shades (Acuña 1984 2: 172).[3]

Although the chaos induced through intoxication at political gatherings might seem counterproductive from a western point of view, it was and continues to be closely connected to most life-crisis rituals and the reverence for the dead not only at Mitla but throughout Oaxaca. The subject has been treated extensively in the anthropological literature (Parsons 1934; Leslie 1960; El Guindi 1986), while divination with hallucinogens, as well as the practice of going to Pre-Columbian tombs to discuss problems of property inheritance with the dead, continued at Mitla at least through the 1930s (Parsons 1936: 207, 312).

The different cosmogonies commemorated in the wall paintings would therefore have presented royal guests with religious allegories in keeping with the themes of factionalism and multinational decision making. The question is how might the artwork have been actually employed in these assemblies within the palaces? The Mitla paintings are unique in their manner of presentation, having been painted into recessed panels like precious works of art to set them off from the surrounding mass of architecture and greca friezes. In this way they can be compared to the Mixtec codices. Burgoa (1934b: 210) tells us that the codices were unfolded and hung on the palace walls, where they were consulted by the kings during their assemblies. The theater of statecraft would then be enacted as noble poets used the codices like storyboards to recite royal genealogies. The Mitla paintings may not have been simply "read" therefore but actually performed (Byland and Pohl 1994).

The performance of historical and religious stories was an integral part of Postclassic Mexican royal feasts and religious gatherings. Festivities often included a kind of literary symposium in which kings and priests alike donned costumes and enacted specific roles, dancing and singing their parts to musical accompaniment (León Portilla 1969; Ekdahl Ravicz 1970: 1–25). The Mixtecs of Cuilapan for example annually reenacted a drama of Oaxacan factionalism that climaxed with the mock hanging of a Zapotec prince of Zaachila played by a costumed performer (Burgoa 1934a 25: 396). Herrera (1945: 170) states that Mixtec lords even wore garments with pictures of the "history of their gods," thereby emulating the wall paintings and codices from which they recited, while drinking from polychrome pottery vessels decorated with the same historical narratives.

Feasting was not only an essential part of alliance-building but also an elite economic exchange (Brumfiel 1987; Pohl 1994). We know that the production of art in many ancient Mexican societies was supervised, if not actually executed, by the aristocratic class, thereby creating specialized forms of wealth that were restricted to consumption by persons of noble birth. These goods were not exchanged through the common marketplace, but rather through competitive gift-giving at feasts and royal fairs (Burgoa 1934a 25: 352).

Polychrome drinking vessels were not only props for the drama of ancestor rituals, but were used to promote political alliances as prized gifts that were later interred with their owners. Other commodities including precious stones and metals, exotic feathers, cacao, and woven capes functioned like currency in the buying and selling of prestige and political power.

These exchanges were patronized by the ancestors themselves. Burgoa (1934a 26: 124) described Mitla penitents as seeking the royal paradise where they believed their ancestors were holding a great "fair" or market. The tradition of these fairs continues in the contemporary belief in spirits that hold periodic markets in the cave adjacent to the Hill of the Turkey and in the Calvario of the Adobe Group ruins (Parsons 1936: 210, 221, 322, 402). We know that the god of this royal paradise, 7 Flower, was the patron of elite art production. He appears in Codex Zouche-Nuttall 76b as a personified gold pectoral or wearing the headdress of a macaw, the animal bred for its feathers—which were exchanged on the northern Mexican frontier for Anasazi (Ancient Pueblo) turquoise (Hargrove 1970; Harbottle and Weigand 1992). Sahagún (1950–1982, book 4: 7) described the day 7 Flower as being dedicated to artisans, weavers, and the painters of codices, exquisite polychrome vessels, or even wall paintings (Furst 1978a: 241–242).

The significance of the Mitla murals therefore lies in the nature of their narrative content and their particular placement within the architectural setting. The Tolteca-Chichimeca, Mixtec, and Zapotec lords of Oaxaca who met in these courts all claimed a form of divine status through descent from the three groups of ancestors who are portrayed in the murals. These ancestors were miraculously created from environmental phenomena: caves, trees, and the heavens. Ancestor worship therefore became not only a primary religious concern but also a means of determining class rank, paramountcy, and titles to elite domains.[4]

Claims of descent from the different ancestral groups also defined elite forms of ethnicity that cross-cut variance in local language and customs (figure 8.10). Nevertheless, Oaxacan noblemen engaged in multiple marriages between social groups in order to expand economic and political opportunities. This practice, however, also produced offspring who commonly disputed titles of inheritance and became embroiled in wars of succession that dissipated national cohesion. In the interests of unity, the kings submitted to the authority of oracular priests like the *Vuijatao* of Mitla.

The oracular manifestation of political power was founded on the physical control of the highest ranking royal dead, the most prominent of whom were grouped at Mitla and used as reliquary symbols of genealogical reckoning so important to arguing claims of descent and control of the land. The depiction of cosmogonies around a palace courtyard that relate the origins of the three most powerful Postclassic Oaxacan social groups metaphorically points to forms of social unity supervised by the Mitla oracle that have received little attention in studies of comparable ancient Mexican political systems to date.

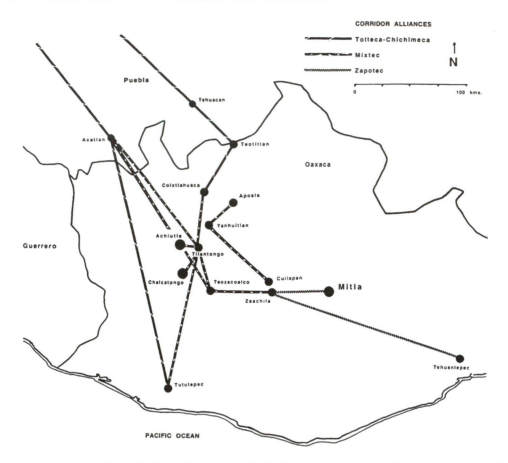

Figure 8.10. During the Postclassic, Oaxaca was dominated by confederations of city-states that allied themselves through intermarriage and defined their allegiances on the basis of descent from different groups of deified ancestors portrayed in the codices, on polychrome feasting vessels, and on wall paintings like those at Mitla. The Codex Zouche-Nuttall obverse portrays the Zaachila dynasty as part of an alliance system constructed between roughly A.D. 1150 and 1300 that ultimately linked the royal houses of Tilantongo, Teozacoalco, and Zaachila. By the time of the Spanish conquest, a rivalry had broken out between Yanhuitlan and Tilantongo in the Valley of Nochixtlan, while Cuilapan and Zaachila were engaged in a state of open conflict in the Valley of Oaxaca.

Conclusions

Mitla was the residence of one of three powerful oracles in Oaxaca. The other two were located at Chalcatongo and Achiutla in the Mixteca Alta, and these can be identified in the Mixtec codices. Chalcatongo is represented as Place of the Skull, where the oracular priestess 9 Grass conferred rulership on Lady 6 Monkey of Jaltepec (Jansen 1982b) and Achiutla is Hill of the Sun, where the oracle 1 Death was instrumental in placing 8 Deer on the throne of Tilantongo (Byland and Pohl 1994). The evidence from the Mixtec codices indicates that the oracles described by Burgoa were the deity impersonators of an archetypal death goddess and a sun god. This suggests that 13 Flower and 7 Flower in the Mitla paintings of the north wall may in fact be portrayals of the *Vuijatao* themselves.[5]

The codical appearances of oracles not only as great priests, but also as arbitrators in dynastic disputes between Lord 8 Deer, Lady 6 Monkey, and Lord 4 wind are confirmed in Burgoa's references to the powers with which Oaxacan oracles were invested. For instance, the oracle of Achiutla was said to have had superior authority over the Mixtec kings in deciding matters of peace and war. Burgoa (1934a 25: 319; Pohl 1994) even refers to temple armies that the priests could use to enforce their decisions. The *Vuijatao* at Mitla was likewise said to have had superior authority over the Zapotec kings in many affairs of state (Burgoa 1934a 26: 125).

The great funerary cave of Chalcatongo was where the royal house of Tilantongo, the descendants of 8 Deer, were mummified and enshrined in much the same way the Zapotec lords of Zaachila were placed in the tomb at Mitla (Burgoa 1934a 25: 372, 338–340; 26: 121). Elsewhere I have argued that the patroness of this cave, the oracle 9 Grass, served as an important political functionary at Chalcatongo (Pohl 1994). By presiding over the mummified dead, she was empowered to control the ancestor cult to which all of the Mixtec kings subscribed (figure 8.11).

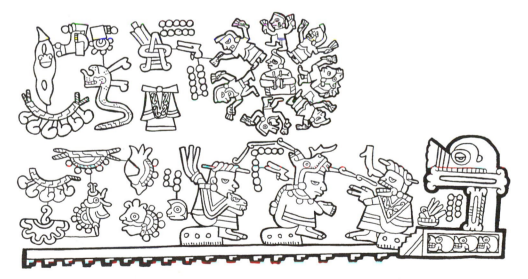

Figure 8.11. Codex Selden 6–7 depicts an encounter between the oracle 9 Grass of Chalcatongo and Lady 6 Monkey with her future husband 11 Wind. The couple seek the oracle's assistance in formulating a marriage between their two kingdoms. Note the impressive exchange of precious gold and silver jewels to the left. A few years later the couple dance in a circle with the gods 9 Grass, 9 Wind, 1 Eagle, 1 Grass, and possibly 7 Flower.

In conclusion, the oracles of Oaxaca were not rulers in their own right, but rather they were empowered to ajudicate those aspects of the social order that entailed problems of divine inheritance and the well being of extended royal kinship structures as a whole. This view is consistent with Spanish references to the oracles not as kings, but as late renaissance archbishops, or as in the case of Mitla, a "pope."

The size and complexity of Mitla therefore reflects its position as a kind of national courthouse and not its authority as a political center dominating any significant portion of the Oaxaca region. The portrayal of the three Oaxacan cosmogonies further demonstrates that the site did not subscribe to any one of the several competing alliance corridors that defined Tolteca-Chichimeca, Mixtec, and Zapotec factionalism, but rather the oracle's palaces and courts represented a sacred space in which all were united and recognized as equals. Today Mitla serves as one of the most important pilgrimage shrines in Oaxaca. During the feast of Todos Santos, for example, Mixtec-, Zapotec-, and Chatino-speaking people, inheritors to the traditions of the cosmogonies in the lintel paintings, continue to journey to what is still addressed as "Mitla, the middle of the world."

Acknowledgments   Research and writing for this article was supported by fellowships from Dumbarton Oaks, Trustees of Harvard University, and the Center for Advanced Study, National Gallery of Art. I acknowledge the help of my colleagues and members of the Mitla community with whom I discussed my interpretation of the Mitla lintel paintings. Special thanks go to Ernesto González Licón, director of the Centro Regional del Instituto Nacional de Antropología e Historia, Oaxaca, Oaxaca. Centro Regional Archaeologist Nelly Robles García identified the location of El Guajolote and gave me a tour of the area. Confirmation that this location was also called Guhdz Bedkol was provided by Emiliano Saabedra M., INAH guardian at the Mitla ruins. I am also indebted to Patricio Aragón Martínez, Roberto Zárata Morán, Elizabeth Boone, Javier Urcid, Marcus Winter, Frank Lipp, and Bruce E. Byland.

Notes

1. Although the Classic period had been characterized by the rise of large urban centers like Yucuñudahui in the Mixteca Alta and Monte Albán in the Valley of Oaxaca, the subsequent Postclassic period saw the break up of centralized authority followed by a tremendous regional variety of settlement systems. While city-states like Cuilapan and Mitla were indeed flourishing as prominent economic and/or religious centers, the ethnohistorical sources suggest that much of the political decision-making was carried out by a widely dispersed elite living on isolated private estates as well (see Blanton et al. 1982; Kowalewski 1983; Winter 1989 for discussion).

2. The principal means for identifying individuals in Mixteca-Puebla style art is through an analysis of the headdress that indicates personal naming and through the birth date calendar sign. This is the information preserved in the upper registers of the Mitla paintings. The techniques of analysis I am employing to interpret the fragments have been used successively by codex scholars in the past (see Troike 1980). Facsimiles of Mixtec and central Mexican codices, published by the Fondo de Cultura Económica and the Sociedad Mexicana de Antropología, México were consulted in researching this paper. Facsimile editions have also been published by the Akademische Druck- und Verlagsanstalt, Graz, Austria.

3. Drunkeness during religious festivals is mentioned in numerous Oaxacan relaciones (Acuña 1984, 1:150, 157, 256, 270, 331, 335; 2: 79, 172, 260).

4. Joyce Marcus (1983b) has discussed Zapotec religion and ancestor cults in detail.

5. Burgoa (1934a 26: 350) suggests that there may have been more than one *Vuijatao* at Mitla. Perhaps he is referring to priests who held power in the outlying shrines as well.

9

The Templo Mayor
of Tenochtitlan

Cosmic Center of the Aztec Universe

Eduardo Matos Moctezuma

Sacred Time and Sacred Space

We are able to affirm that the various peoples of the earth, throughout history and in all circumstances, have had concepts of sacred time and space. Students of comparative religion coincide in pointing out, in general terms, the characteristics which define this specialized time and space, which do not refer to simple chronological or historical time nor to a uniform space, but rather refer to the zone of the sacred.

In addition, it is recognized that sacred facts are expressed in many diverse aspects, including myths, rituals, symbols, venerated objects, sacred places, persons, animals, plants, and so forth. That is to say that human beings are confronted by a broad range of phenomena which, in certain circumstances, they have considered to be sacred. As well, the "sacred" is established as an opposition to the "profane," which is to say that the sacred is related to religious life, while the profane is connected with secular life. The sacred can be present in (and manifested by) time and space when these two categories acquire the essential religious character of the sacred.

Conceived of in this way, sacred time transcends "history" and is the time of eternity. This sense of eternal time is recoverable and can be apprehended by means of ritual actions. Mircea Eliade (1959, 1973), in his book *Lo sagrado y lo profano* (The Sacred and the Profane), tells us how this sense of sacred time can be effected in such rituals. He writes:

> religious man lives in two kinds of time, of which the more important, sacred time, appears under the paradoxical aspect of a circular time, reversible and recoverable, a sort of eternal mythical present that is periodically reintegrated by means of rites. This attitude in regard to time suffices to distinguish religious from non-religious man; the former refuses to live solely in what, in modern

terms, is called the historical present; he attempts to regain a sacred time that, from one point of view, can be homologized to eternity (Eliade 1959: 70).

Eliade has outlined several of the important defining characteristics of sacred space. Thus, the sacred place is never simply chosen by human beings, but rather is "discovered" by them. Such space is discovered by means of certain "signals" or "signs," which generally feature the presence or involvement of an animal in some fashion. Upon having encountered the special place, it will be delimited with reference to ordinary or profane space, thus marking a fundamental existential difference between one and the other (Eliade 1959: chpt. 1, 1979). All of the above characteristics are manifested clearly in the central ceremonial precinct of the Aztecs, and most concretely in their principal edifice, the Templo Mayor (Great Temple) of Tenochtitlan. In this chapter, I will describe formal and ideological aspects of this structure in a more deliberate fashion. However, it is necessary to note that such sacred elements were not evident only in Aztec architecture, but that there are important architectural examples in central Mexico that demonstrate the presence of related concepts of sacred space among peoples who preceded and were ancestral to the "People of the Sun."[1]

Antecedents

It is important to observe that one of the best-known architectural elements of the ceremonial precinct of Tenochtitlan, which separated the sacred space of the precinct from the profane space surrounding it, was the barrier the chroniclers called the Coatepantli, or the Wall of Serpents. Various conquest-period historians refer to this wall in their descriptions of the architectural characteristics of the ceremonial precinct of Tenochtitlan (e.g., Fray Bernardino de Sahagún (1950–1982, 2: Appendix; Fray Diego Durán 1971). In his description of the Templo Mayor, Durán (1971: 76) describes the ritual precinct of Huitzilopochtli's temple: "Its own private courtyard was surrounded by a great wall, built of large carved stones in the manner of serpents joined to one another. . . . These stones . . . formed the wall of the Temple of Huitzilopochtli. This wall was called Coatepantli, Snake Wall."

Archaeologically, sections of the actual Aztec precinct walls of this type have been encountered in the area behind (east of) the Templo Mayor and in the northeast corner of the ceremonial precinct of Tlatelolco. However, other antecedents for such walls exist. They are found at Teotihuacan, Tula, and Tenayuca.

It appears that the most ancient evidence now known for an architectural element that served primarily to surround and delimit the sacred space of a pyramid temple occurs at Teotihuacan, where it occurs as the enormous U-shapted platform that frames three sides of the great Pyramid of the Sun (see Kowalski, chapter 4, this volume). This platform effectively surrounds the temple on its north, south, and east sides (figure 9.1). On the south side of the Pyramid of the Sun, part of this platform has been excavated, and there we can see that it is a great sloping wall constructed of stone and still partly covered by plaster. On its upper part, particularly where the platform begins at its western extreme, a series of habitations have been discovered. At the eastern end, before it turns north, the southern platform was trenched by Don Leopoldo Batres at the beginning of the twentieth century to create an opening for a train that could be used to carry away the debris from the excavations he carried out in the Pyramid of the Sun (Batres 1906, 1913). Neither the eastern nor the northern side of this boundary platform have been excavated. I am interested in initiating a series of excavations in this platform with the objective of defining its architectural character, its chronological position, and its symbolism.

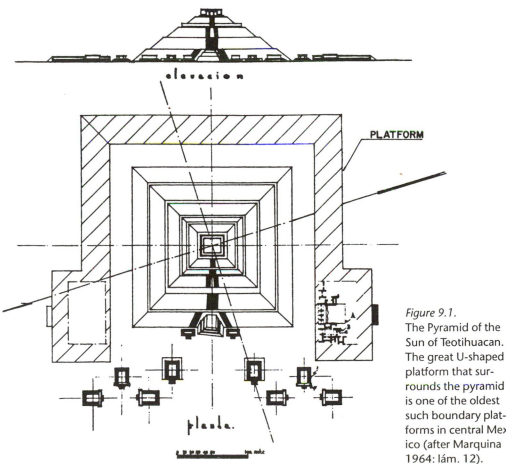

Figure 9.1.
The Pyramid of the Sun of Teotihuacan. The great U-shaped platform that surrounds the pyramid is one of the oldest such boundary platforms in central Mexico (after Marquina 1964: lám. 12).

In the past, several investigators have attempted to interpret the function of this platform, the first being Don Ramón Almaraz (1865). Almaraz viewed the platform as a kind of defensive wall or trench. At a later date, Batres (1913) thought that it could be considered some type of buttress wall, built to insure the stability of the larger pyramid. Rémy Bastien (1947) saw three possible functions for the platform: mechanical, aesthetic, and/or military.

Because of the particularities of its location and form, this platform probably served to delimit and separate a sacred space (that of the Pyramid of the Sun) from the surrounding spaces. It is well known that the Pyramid of the Sun stands over a place marked by the presence of a subterranean spring (or artificial watercourse) which runs through a cave originally discovered by Don Jorge Acosta in the 1970s. It is easy to imagine the significance that this natural feature had for an agricultural people like those of Teotihuacan, so it is not surprising that a religious symbolism was associated with this cave, which was viewed as a sacred source of water (and probably associated with sacred origins and creation mythology as well; see Kowalski, chapter 4, this volume), and that the enormous edifice constructed above this place was considered equally sacred.

Another architectural complex with similar characteristics regarding the definition of sacred space is the Ciudadela. At present, we know that this great enclosed plaza constituted the existential center of the city of Teotihuacan, with the north–south avenue the Street of the Dead passing in front of it and the east and west avenues departing from it, giving the city plan an appearance similar to the layout that Tenochtitlan acquired centuries later as part of a deliberate repetition of all of the symbolic charge of the earlier city.

Two important architectural features can be defined: the delimitation of a particular edifice, as in the case of the Pyramid of the Sun; as well as the delimitation of an open space, such as the plaza of the Ciudadela, which constituted the central space of the city. Both types of boundary can also be observed in the architecture of settlements that developed in central Mexico after the fall of Teotihuacan.

We turn now to the evidence which has been encountered at Tula, Hidalgo (Matos 1976a, b; Diehl 1983). It has been revealed that the principal plaza of this site is surrounded by several imposing structures, one of which, Pyramid B, is known as the Tlahuizcalpantecuhtli Pyramid, or Pyramid of the Atlantean Warriors (see Kristan-Graham, chapter 7, this volume). This temple is also framed by a boundary wall, which has been termed a Coatepantli (Serpent Wall) (figure 9.2). It consists of a wall, subdivided into a sloping basal zone (*talud*), and a vertical upper zone subdivided into three horizontal framed panels (*tableros*). The central panel of the upper zone is a sculptured frieze featuring partly skeletal and partly fleshed figures associated with rattlesnakes. Above these figures is a panel of stepped or terraced designs (*greca*) crowned by a series of

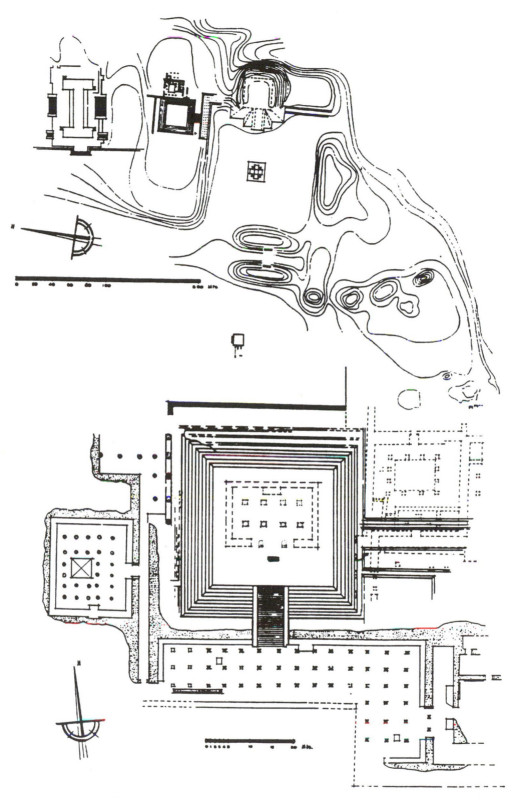

Figure 9.2. Pyramid B at Tula, Hidalgo, showing the Coatepantli or "serpent wall" that frames the pyramid base on its north and northwest sides (after Marquina 1964: lám. 45).

merlons (*almenas*) in the form of shells. The best preserved section of the Coatepantli wall is behind Pyramid B, although there are remnants indicating that the wall turned south and also flanked the west side of the pyramid-temple. Here again we are in the presence of a restricted plaza of a sacred character, as well as an edifice which, because of its importance, was surrounded by a protective wall separating it from external, secular space.

At Tenayuca (Palacios 1935; Marquina 1964: 164–180; Kubler 1984: 88–90), an Aztec period site dating to the Late Postclassic (A.D. 1200–1521) the principal pyramid-temple is surrounded by a series of serpents on three of its sides, leaving the principal facade free (figure 9.3). This spatial treatment, calculated to define a sacred precinct for the edifice, is similar to that at the Pyramid of the Sun at Teotihuacan as well as at Pyramid B at Tula, with the major difference being that the Tenayuca and Teotihuacan buildings face the west, while the Tula structure faces the south.

The Aztec city of Tlatelolco was in important center of commerce which rose to power concurrently with the Mexica-Aztec capital of

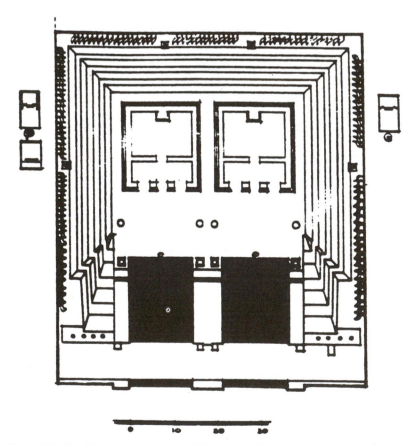

Figure 9.3. The Tenayuca twin pyramid, showing the rows of serpent sculptures that demarcate the sacred precinct (after Marquina 1964: lám. 51).

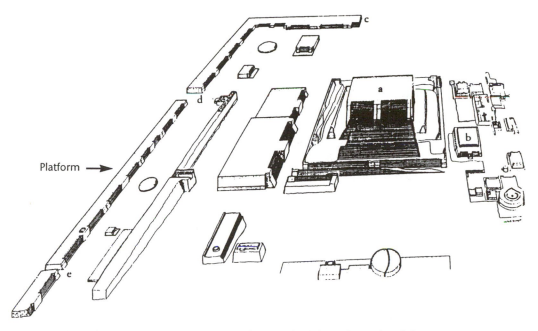

Figure 9.4. The temple precinct of Tlatelolco. At the left (indicated as "Platform") can be seen a section of the great Coatepaneli or platform that separated sacred space of the ritual precinct from profane space of the city.

Tenochtitlan and was located on the northern section of the same island as the latter city. Tlatelolco retained its independence until 1473, when it was conquered by the Mexica-Aztec emperor Axayácatl (Davies 1980: 128–134). Excavation has revealed that the central temple precinct at Tlatelolco was enclosed by a specialized wall that corresponds to the Coatepantli or Serpent Wall described for Tenochtitlan (figure 9.4). In this chapter, however, I concentrate on the ceremonial precinct of Tenochtitlan and present several pertinent sources of historical information regarding the foundation of the city before discussing the Templo Mayor and all its symbolic content, comparing this later example with information furnished from study of the history of religions and with related examples of architecture from Mesoamerican antiquity.

Foundation of Tenochtitlan

The foundation of any city is an occasion that typically is accompanied by a series of symbolic acts and associated with symbolic aspects that are independent of the actual causes that motivated the settlement. Thus, in many instances a city has been settled due to diverse economic, political, social, and related motives, and these are later cloaked in mythological explanations to legitimize the foundation. This is clearly the case with the Mexica-Aztec city of Tenochtitlan.

In effect, we know that after lengthy peregrinations, the Mexica-Aztecs finally settled in the middle of Lake Texcoco on lands that belonged to the Tepanec *señorio* of Azcapotzalco. This occurred in the year "2 House," probably corresponding to A.D. 1325. It is clear that rulers of Azcapotzalco, who exercised political power and control over other lakeside towns, were going to permit the Mexica-Aztecs to settle permanently on several islands, with the expectation that they would be tributaries of Tezozomoc, the Tepanec ruler. Thus the Mexica-Aztecs were the economic and political subjects of Azcapotzalco. In this situation the Mexica-Aztecs converted the historical situation into a myth, with the result that their arrival at their island settlement was attributed to the guidance of the solar deity Huitzilopochtli, who indicated to the Mexica-Aztecs the place where they must establish themselves. This spot was marked by certain important symbols, such as the apparition of an eagle on a nopal cactus growing out of a stone (figure 9.5). It is interesting to note that the eagle represents Huitzilopochtli in his solar aspect. It is necessary to emphasize that in their desire to legitimize the act of foundation, the Mexica-Aztecs returned to several ancient Toltec myths, as in the case of their description of white serpents, fish, frogs, and plants which were in a spring with two streams. We note that these same elements were present in the sacred city of Cholula, where the Toltec arrived according to the description provided in the *Historia Tolteca-Chichimeca*.[2] In fact, the Mexica-Aztecs relate that they "encountered" these ancient symbols on the first day and that on the following day they witnessed their own individualized vision. Durán (1964: 28–29) describes the events as follows:

> The first thing they beheld was a juniper tree, all white and very beautiful, and the spring came forth from the foot of this tree. The second thing they saw was a group of willows around the spring, all white, without a single green leaf. The reeds there were white, also, and so were the rushes surrounding the water. White frogs and fish came out of the water. There were water snakes, too, shiny and white. The spring flowed out from between two large rocks, the water so clear and limpid that it was pleasing to behold.

Durán's account tells us that after seeing these symbols the Mexica-Aztecs returned to their houses to continue the search for their own particular symbols on the following day. This literary device separates one type of symbol from the other, while establishing a parallel between them. On the following day the search began and then the Mexica-Aztecs encountered the promised signal:

> Thus they returned to the clear, transparent spring they had seen the day before. Now the water rushed out in two streams, one red like blood, the other so blue and thick that it filled the people with awe. Having seen these mysterious things the Aztecs continued to seek the omen of the eagle. Wandering from one place to another,

Figure 9.5. The foundation of Tenochtitlan, as depicted in the *Codex Tovar.*

they soon discovered the prickly pear cactus. On it stood the eagle with his wings stretched out toward the rays of the sun, basking in their warmth and the freshness of the morning. In his talons he held a bird with very fine feathers, precious and shining (Durán 1964: 31).

In another study I examined the mythological aspects of this foundation tale, and how they served to relate the Mexica-Aztecs not only to the gods, but also to give them added legitimacy by associating them with the Toltecs, who were considered the paragons of greatness by all the Aztec peoples (Matos 1986, 1988).[3]

At any rate, once they had "encountered" their sacred place, this location was then converted into a fundamental center, and the construction of the city was begun according to the vision that Mexica-Aztecs had of the organization of the cosmos. In doing so, they represent a particular example of a general procedure that has been described by Eliade (1958: 374):

The founding of a new town repeats the creation of the world; once the spot has been confirmed by ritual, a square or circular enclosure is put round it with four gates corresponding to the four points of the compass. . . . Towns are divided into four in imitation of the Cosmos, in other words, they are a copy of the Universe.

The ceremonial precinct of Tenochtitlan clearly adheres to this cosmological model. We see that once the symbols indicating the sacredness of the island location in Lake Texcoco had been encountered, then the god Huitzilopochtli ordered that the sacred space be separated from profane space and that the Mexica-Aztecs settle themselves in four principal barrios:

> That night after the Aztecs had finished their god's temple, when an extensive part of the lake had been filled in and the foundations for their houses made, Huitzilopochtli spoke to his priests. "Tell the Aztec people that the principal men, each with his relatives and friends and allies, should divide the city into four main wards. The center of the city will be the house you have constructed for my resting place (Durán 1964: 32).

Pertaining to this description, we have a pictorial representation from the Codex Mendoza (figure 9.6), in which we can clearly observe the symbol of the eagle perched atop the nopal cactus, which signifies the sacred center where the temple of Huitzilopochtli was erected, the Templo Mayor which served as the lodging of the solar divinity. From the temple emerge four streams of water that divide the city into four quarters. In this manner sacred as well as profane spaces were established. The first of these was converted into the center of their cosmovision and was delimited by a platform or walled precinct approximately 500 meters per side, with four gateways from which four causeways oriented to conform to the world directions. Thus, the Tepeyac (present-day Villa de Guadalupe) causeway ran toward the north, that of Iztapalapa toward the south, that of Tlacopan (Tacuba) toward the west, and a causeway of smaller dimensions extended to the east and the lake, which served as an aquatic transportation route. We can observe this layout in the sixteenth-century plans of the city of Tenochtitlan that have been preserved, such as the plan attributed to Hernán Cortés (figure 9.7). At the convergence of these "world quarters," in the center of the ceremonial precinct was located the Templo Mayor of Tenochtitlan.

The Templo Mayor as a Fundamental Center

Once the center expressed in the form of the sacred space or ceremonial precinct, which according to Sahagún (1950–1982) contained some 78 separate edifices or ritual locations including the Templo Mayor, was established, it is clear that the latter pyramid-temple constituted the center of centers.[4] This indicated by its central location in Sahagún's (1905) simplified plan of the ceremonial precinct of Tenochtitlan (figure 9.8), and is confirmed by the descriptions of numerous sixteenth-century chroniclers. By means of the Templo Mayor it was possible to ascend to the celestial levels or to descend into the underworld, it was the point at

Figure 9.6. The foundation of Tenochtitlan, as depicted on frontispiece of the Codex Mendoza (ca. 1525).

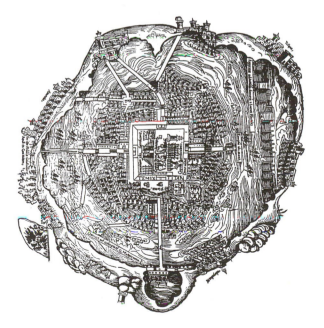

Figure 9.7. A view of the island city of Tenochtitlan, traditionally attributed to Hernán Cortés. Four principal avenues emerge from the central ceremonial precinct and lead to causeways to the north (*top*), west (*left*), and south (*bottom*), and to a canoe port on the east (*right*). The Templo Mayor is incorrectly shown on the west side of the precinct with its twin stairways facing east. Note the small face of the sun between the twin temples of the Templo Mayor. This plan first appeared in the Atlas by Bendetto Bordone, edited in Venice in 1528.

Figure 9.8. The ceremonial precinct of Tenochtitlan, according to the description of Fray Bernardino de Sahagún in a manuscript from the second half of the sixteenth century. At the center is the Templo Mayor, with its two stairways stained by the blood of human sacrifices, and the two sanctuaries of Tlaloc (left) and Huitzilopochtli (right) at its summit. Below it appear the skull rack platform (tzompantli), the great ballcourt (Teotlachco), and a platform associated with gladiatorial sacrifice, as well as other temples and priestly structures (after Sahagún (1905), *Primeros Memoriales del Códice Matritense*, f. 16. Patrimonio de la Real Casa, Palacio Real, Madrid).

which these cosmic levels were united. From the Templo Mayor the four quarters of the universe and the cardinal points were partitioned. In its architectural form was expressed the concept of duality, and the mass of its basal platform subdivided into terraces incorporated the concept of different levels of ascent.

The two temples or god-houses on its summit, along with the twin stairways that led to them (i.e., each half of the edifice) symbolically represented a sacred mountain and incorporated an important myth. The Templo Mayor was, ultimately, the most sacred place of the Mexica-Aztecs. In the book *Vida y muerte en el Templo Mayor* (*Life and Death in the Templo Mayor*; Matos 1982, 1995) I have described it in this fashion:

> The Templo Mayor was thus converted into the fundamental center where all the sacred power was found and all the levels intersected. We believe, however, that it not only occupied that privileged place but that the very form and characteristics of its architecture represented all of the Mexica cosmogonic concepts (Matos 1995: 61)

Let us examine this edifice in light of what Eliade has told us about the principal temples in other ancient societies. He observed three characteristic features in such sacred buildings:

(1) The Sacred Mountain—where heaven and earth meet—is at the center of the world; (2) Every temple or palace—and, by extension, every sacred city or royal residence—is a sacred mountain, thus becoming a Center; (3) As an *axis mundi*, the sacred city or temple is regarded as the meeting point of heaven, earth, and hell (Eliade 1965: 12).

In referring to the architectonic characteristics of temples, Eliade says:

All these sacred constructions symbolically represent the whole universe: the floors or terraces are identified with the "heavens" or cosmic levels. In one sense, each one reproduces the cosmic mountain, that is, it is considered to have been built in the "center of the world". . . because they are situated in the center of the cosmos, the temples or sacred city always constitute the point where the three cosmic regions meet (Eliade 1979: 334, 337).

What are the architectural features that are particular to the principal Mexica-Aztec temple? Until fairly recently we knew of its appearance and principal features primarily from colonial period descriptions and illustrations (e.g., figure 9.8), augmented by several minor excavations. Sahagún (1969, 1: 232) described the Templo Mayor as follows:

This temple was divided at the top so that it appeared to be two, and it had two shrines or altars at the summit, each one with its spire. And at the top of each of these had its insignia or special emblems. In one of these shrines, the principal one, was the statue of Huitzilopochtli . . . . In the other, there was an image of the god Tlaloc. Before each one of these [images] there was a round stone like a chopping block, called *techcatl*, upon which they killed those who were sacrificed in honor of that god. And from these [sacrificial] stones to the base of the Temple flowed a stream of blood from those [victims] who were slain on them. And it was the same in all the other temples. These towers [temples] faced west. The stairways were narrow and straight, from the base of the summit, on all these temples, all alike, and one ascended [the stairways, to reach the top].

Fortunately, archaeological investigations carried out during the Proyecto Templo Mayor between 1978 and 1982 now permit us to know more precisely the characteristics of this edifice (figure 9.9). These excavations revealed that the Templo Mayor, like many other Mesoamerican pyramid-temples, was rebuilt and enlarged several times during its period of use. Some seven principal construction stages, beginning with the building of the small, impermanent sanctuary built by the Aztecs in 1325 to the final early sixteenth-century enlargement of the temple which existed when the Spaniards arrived in Tenochtitlan, have been documented.[5] Although the temple underwent dramatic enlargment in size during this period and featured various unique sculptures, burials, caches, etc., associated with particular construction stages, it neverthe-

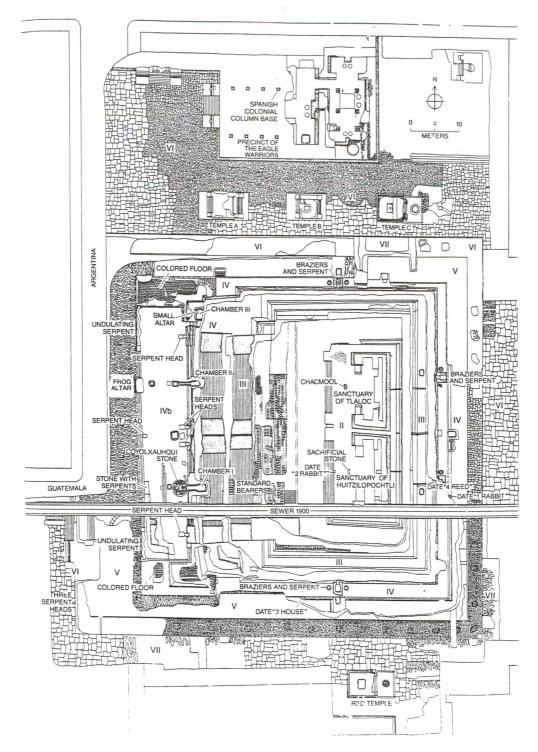

Figure 9.9. Plan of the excavated remains of the Templo Mayor, showing the principal features of construction stages II–VI. Note the location of the Coyolxauhqui Stone at the base of the stairway of the stage IVb Huitzilopochtli Temple.

less conserved certain basic architectural features, most of which possess a symbolic meaning. The architectural similarities between the Construction Stage IV temple, built between ca. A.D. 1454 and 1469 during the reign of the Tlatoani (emperor) Motecuhzoma I, and its successors were particularly pronounced. It was from this time onward, as a result of imperial expansions begun during Motecuhzoma's reign, that the Templo Mayor increased in size dramatically.

As Sahagún noted, in all versions the temple's principal facade was oriented toward the west, keyed to the movement of the sun, which is described by Motolinía (1971) as rising directly between the twin temples on the solar equinoxes (Aveni and Gibbs 1976; Aveni, Calnek, and Hartung 1988; see figure 9.7).[6] Later versions of the Templo Mayor rested on a basal platform which has a single stairway also facing west. The lower platform of the Construction Stage IV temple I have identified as representing the terrestrial level. In it the greatest number of offerings dedicated to the deities who occupied the temple have been discovered, and, in addition, it supports sculptured representations of serpents as symbols of the earth as well as sculptures of frogs connected with the cult of the earth and rain deity, Tlaloc. From this lower platform rose the main pyamidal platform composed of four superimposed terraces, which we interpret as symbolizing the four celestial levels. On the main facade were two stairways that led to the summit, the place where the *adoratorios* or god-houses were located. These were dedicated to the god of water (Tlaloc) and the god of war (Huitzilopochtli), as a clear expression of the most urgent necessities of a people, such as Mexica-Aztecs, whose survival was based both on agriculture and conquest warfare.[7] The best preserved examples of the twin temples pertain to Construction Stage II, which predates 1428 and is associated with a sculptured panel bearing the year-bearer date "2 Rabbit," most likely corresponding to the year 1390. These structures feature the placement of a "Toltec" style Chacmool sculpture in the doorway of the Tlaloc temple, and, located at the entrance to Huitzilopochtli's shrine (figure 9.10), the specialized black volcanic stone block (*techcatl*) associated with sacrificial heart extraction.

As mentioned previously, each side of the pyramid-temple symbolized a sacred mountain. The north side associated with the water god Tlaloc represents the Tonacatepetl or the "Mountain of Sustenance," the place where, according to a myth recorded in the *Leyenda de los Soles* (Legend of the Suns), were guarded the maize grains stolen by Quetzalcoatl to provide the food for humanity (*Códice Chimalpopoca* 1975: 121). Johanna Broda (1987a, b) has analyzed the content of the caches associated with the northern or Tlaloc side of the Templo Mayor as an expression of this mythic cosmovision, suggesting that the large numbers of aquatic creatures deposited in such offerings were used to create the idea of the pyramid as the "fertile mountain" (see López Luján 1994). In addition, it seems likely that the Tlaloc temple is related to various shrines and sanctuaries dedicated to the rain god and located in the mountains

Figure 9.10. Polychrome painted stone "Chacmool" sculpture, located at the entrance to Tlaloc's construction stage II shrine. Such figures have been interpreted as divine messengers, carrying to the gods sacrificial offerings placed in the receptacles they hold on their abdomens.

surrounding the Basin of Mexico, the most important of which was the sacred enclosure perched on Mount Tlaloc to the east in Puebla (Broda 1987a: 73–74; Matos 1988: 142). In this regard, the large number of child sacrifices found in Offering 48, located at the northwest corner on the Tlaloc side of the Templo Mayor, is closely related to similar child sacrifices offered to Tlaloc at his mountain shrines.[8]

The south side of the Templo Mayor, associated with Huitzilopochtli, corresponds to the Coatepetl or the "Mountain of the Serpent," the mythical place where the god of war did battle against his sister, Coyolxauhqui, and his brothers, the stars of the southern sky (León-Portilla 1978; Paso y Troncoso 1981). Led by their sister Coyolxauhqui, they sought to slay their mother, the earth goddess Coatlicue, who had miraculously become pregnant with none other than the war god Huitzilopochtli. But the young war god emerged fully armed, cutting his sister to pieces with his weapon, the turquoise serpent dart thrower (xiuhcoatl), and routing his brothers.[9]

The importance of this identification was underscored by the discovery of the remarkable Coyolxauhqui Stone in 1978, the event which set in motion the Proyecto Templo Mayor (figure 9.11). The Coyolxauhqui Stone is a monumental (3.25 meter diameter) circular volcanic stone disk featuring a low-relief sculpture of the dismembered and beheaded goddess Coyolxauhqui (Garcia Cook and Arana 1978). This sculpture was located at the foot of the stairway of the Huitzilopochtli temple of Construction Stage IVb, suggesting that it was the place where the bodies of sacrificial victims came to rest after their sacrifice at the temple platform's summit. This suggests that each victim was offered up not only as "food" for Huitzilopochtli, but also as a surrogate for the original sacrificial victims (Coyolxauhqui and the Centzon Huitznaua) in the cosmogonic myth of Huitzilopochtli's birth (see Matos 1981: 51–52; Broda 1987a: 77–78; Carrasco 1987: 134–135).[10]

One of the most important instances of this mythic performance took place during the 20-day "month" of Panquetzaliztli, when a great feast celebrating Huitzilopochtil occurred. During Panquetzaliztli, priests carried an amaranth dough image of Huitzilopochtli to the top of the Templo Mayor, where offerings were made to the deity. A wooden image of Paynal ("the runner"), a transfiguration of Huitzilopochtli, was carried down from the temple by the chief priest, who took it to the Divine Ball-

Figure 9.11. The monumental stone disk (approximately 3.25 meters in diameter) bearing the sculptured relief image of Coyolxauhqui after her dismemberment by her brother, the solar god Huitzilopochtli. This stone sculpture was found in 1978 at the foot of the stage IVb temple stairway, and led to the Great Temple Project (Proyecto Templo Mayor) between 1978 and 1982.

court (Teotlachco), where captives were sacrificed, as in a version of the Huitzilopochtli–Coyolxauhqui myth described by Hernando Alvarado Tezozomoc (1944: 11–14) and Diego Durán (1964: 21). After making a circuit of different wards of the city, the Paynal image was returned to the summit of Huitzilopochtli's temple, after which there were further feasts, dances, music, food offerings, and human sacrifices in his honor (Sahagún 1950–1982, 2: 27–28, 175–176). This ritualistic aspect of the Templo Mayor is very important, because it transformed the edifice from a lifeless symbol into a place of public theater and spectacle at which the populace could see the fundamental Mexica-Aztec myths of cosmic creation reenacted and "brought to life." Such ritual action provided a powerful mechanism for explaining Mexica-Aztec conquests and justifying the inequalities in Aztec society.

In addition to the more specific mythic connotations connected with the cult of Huitzilopochtli, it is important to add that the general platform (representing the terrestrial level), which supported the pyramid–temple, and the two halves of the pyramid–temple proper associated with the cults of the water and war gods, was the place where those individuals passed who died of natural causes and who were destined to journey to Mictlán. Because it was the point where the cosmic levels were united, it is logical that the Templo Mayor provided access to the land of the dead, the underworld. The deceased were destined to undertake a journey of four years, passing through various dangers and torments before finally arriving at Mictlán, the place where they encountered Mictlantecuhtli and Mictecacihuatl (the god and goddess of death) and in which were deposited the bones of those who died of natural causes. Regarding the passage to Mictlán, it must be emphasized that in book 3 of the *Florentine Codex* Sahagún tells us that one of the first challenges that the deceased had to undergo was passing through two mountains that clashed together. These two mountains were the Tonacatepetl and the Coatepetl, precisely those represented by the Templo Mayor of Tenochtitlan.

The deities created the different celestial, terrestial, and underworld levels of the Aztec cosmos. An Aztec creation myth in the "Historia de los mexicanos por sus pinturas" (1973; Matos 1995: 19) records this transcendental event:

> They [the gods Quetzalcoatl and Huitzilopochtli, working as agents of Tonacatecuhtli and the four Tezcatlipocas] then made Mitlitlatteclet (Mictlantecuhtli) and Michitecaciglat (Mictecacihuatl), husband and wife. They were the gods of hell, . . . They they created the heavens beyond the thirteenth, and they created water, and in it they created a big fish called cipoa cuacli (Cipactli), which was like an alligator, and from that fish they made the earth, . . .

The earth, frequently personified as the Cipactli monster, also was known as Cemanahuac ("the place surrounded by water"), symbolized by a disk of earth completely surrounded by and floating on water. Although they used the term to describe the earth in a general sense, the Mexica-Aztecs also referred to their capital city specifically as Cemanahuac. In this manner the Templo Mayor, located at the hub of the island city of Tenochtitlan (see figure 9.6), was considered the fundamental center of the universe and an expression of its vital order. By claiming to be situated at a cosmic center, the Mexica-Aztecs could project the message that they were a divinely chosen people.

Conclusions

From the preceding discussion, we are able to explain how a work of architecture such as the Templo Mayor was converted into a living symbol, which incorporated in every one of its parts a wealth of ancestral meanings. Among some of these meanings are those known to us by way of the myths important to the society that erected the Templo Mayor to embody its unique cosmovision in which the political, religious, social, economic, and other aspects of life were united. The Templo Mayor, while representing the ideology of its ruling class in particular, expressed religious themes that were of enormous importance to maintaining the order of Aztec society in general. Thus, the field of the sacred played a determining role for this people who, with their creative power, discovered how to capture the numinous power of the universe and to transform it into the physical form of their city and their principal temple, creating a sacred space where the originary time of the gods was converted into terraces, walls, and sculptures of stone.

Notes

1. For an introduction to the religious and cosmological beliefs of the Mexica-Aztecs, see Caso (1958), who terms them the "People of the Sun."

2. When the Toltecs reached the end of their migration at Tlachiualte-pec, the great artificial mountain or pyramid at Cholula, they found, "the place of dark waters, where the quetzal bird stands, where the bed of water stretches out, where the white quail awakens . . . where the eagle feeds . . . where blue water flows . . . where white reeds grow . . . where white rushes grow . . . where white willows stand" (*Historia Tolteca-Chichimeca* 1979: 79, plate VIII).

3. For a general discussion of the importance of the Toltecs as the founders of civilization and the source of legitimate political power for the later Aztecs, see León-Portilla (1980). For a discussion of the Mexica-Aztec's efforts to incorporate Toltec symbols in the Templo Mayor, see Matos and López Luján (1993).

4. Descriptions of the Templo Mayor and its ritual precinct appear in the works of various native authors and Spanish chroniclers. Among the most comprehensive are those of Fray Bernardino de Sahagún (1956, 1950–1982) and Fray Diego Durán (1964, 1967, 1971). For an overview of

accounts and previous interpretations of the Templo Mayor, see Marquina (1960), Matos (1986, 1988), and Boone (1987).

5. See Matos (1988: chpt. 3) for a summary of these construction stages. Henry Nicholson (1987) provides a summary of scholarly debate regarding the precise dating of each construction stage or substage.

6. According to the sixteenth-century friar Motolinía (Toribio de Benavente), the Mexica-Aztec festival of Tlacaxipehualiztli ("flaying of men") took place "when the sun stood in the middle of Uichilobos [Huitzilopochtli, i.e., the Templo Mayor] which was at the equinox."

7. In a number of articles and books, several of which are cited in the bibliography, I have endeavored to demonstrate how the economic basis of Mexica-Aztec society played a role in determining and was reflected in certain aspects of their religious–ideological belief system. This intersection is given a particularly powerful and visible expression in the Templo Mayor.

8. Offering 48 was discovered within a small altar at the northwest corner of the Stage IVb pyramid. It contained at least 42 skulls and associated bones of children, along with masks and painted funerary urns filled with seashells. It was located above another offering, known as Chamber 3, which was also dedicated to Tlaloc. See Matos (1987: 33, 42, 45). Offering 48 is one of more than 100 such offerings that the Mexica-Aztecs placed in and around the Templo Mayor. Many of these offerings include objects from conquered provinces, probably brought to Tenochtitlan as tribute payments, and perhaps serving to symbolically bind the peripheral zones of the empire to its religious–political center. For further discussion of these offerings, their cultural and geographical associations, and their symbolism see Matos (1987, 1988) and Broda (1987a, b), Carrasco (1987), and López Luján (1994).

9. Huitzilopochtli's defeat of his sister and brothers is described as follows by Sahagún (1969, 1: 272–273):

> He was arrayed in his war dress, his shield of eagle feathers, his darts, his blue dart thrower, which is called the xiuatlatl, the turquoise dart-thrower. He painted his face with diagonal stripes, with the color called "child's paint" [offal]. On his head he placed fine feathers, he put on his ear ornaments. And one of his feet, the left one, was thin; he wore a sandal covered with feathers, and both legs and both arms were painted blue. And he who was called Tochancalqui set fire to the serpent made of resinous wood called the xiuhcoatl, at Huitzilopochtli's command. With this [Huitzilopochtli] attacked Coyolxauhqui, he cut off her head, which was left abandoned on the slopes of Coatepetl. The body of Coyolxauhqui went rolling down as it fell, dismembered, in different places fell her hands, her legs, her body. Then Huitzilopochtli rose up, he pursued the four hundred Southerners, he harrassed them, he put them to flight from the summit of Coatepetl, the mountain of the serpent.

10. That there was a continuity in the identification of Huitzilopochtli's pyramid-temple with Coatepec is demonstrated by the fact that Coyolxauhqui images also occur in a number of other building stages of the Templo Mayor. Another relief sculpture of the goddess was located directly beneath the Coyolxauhqui Stone on the Stage IVa platform. In addition, a stone fragment representing part of a face of this goddess was

discovered during excavations and may pertain to a later construction stage. Finally, the impressive, in-the-round diorite head of Coyolxauhqui, now in the National Museum of Anthropology in Mexico City, is known to have come from the vicinity of the Templo Mayor, and Nicholson and Quiñones Keber (1983: 49–50) have argued that "this monumental sculpture, representing Coyolxauhqui's decapitated head, was positioned on the top platform or on one of the stages of the Templo Mayor to commemorate this mythic incident."

10

Continuities and Contrasts in Early Classic Architecture of Central Copan

Robert J. Sharer, William L. Fash, David W. Sedat,
Loa P. Traxler, & Richard Williamson

In this chapter we review some of the results of recent and ongoing archaeological research at Copan, Honduras, bearing on the nature and evolution of Classic Maya architecture. Of particular concern are the continuities and variations in architecture as seen in the Early Classic levels under the Copan Acropolis (figure 10.1). Specifically we address the question of continuity of form and function in successions of superimposed buildings. One corollary to this is the presence of adobe architecture in the earliest Classic levels beneath the Acropolis. These adobe constructions appear both as antecedents and contemporaries of masonry constructions that are more typically associated with lowland Maya architecture.

The beginnings of Early Classic architecture beneath the Copan Acropolis actually comprise three separate foci of development. The Acropolis proper is known as the "Mini-Acropolis of the South" (or MAS) for most of the Early Classic era (see figure 10.2). It began as a cluster of monumental buildings constructed on a low, plastered platform situated on the higher ground about 100 meters west of the Río Copán. From its beginning MAS comprised the major ceremonial, residential, and funerary structures associated with Copan's historically known kings. Today this earliest monumental complex sits directly beneath Structure 10L-16 and the heart of the Acropolis in its final (Late Classic) form. To the east, closer to the west bank of the Río Copán, there were a series of earlier nonmonumental earthen and cobble constructions that probably supported perishable residences. Today these remains are beneath the base of the corte of the Río Copán along the eastern flank of the Acropolis. About the time of the establishment of the earliest Acropolis platform to the west, larger earth and cobble constructions were built in the northern part of this riverine settlement. These soon developed into a series of elite residential structures known as the Northeast Courtyard Group, probably the first palaces of the royal lineage. During its several stages of development and expansion, the Northeast Courtyard Group was first displaced, and then eventually buried, by the expanding MAS complex. Once established, MAS rapidly expanded in all directions, first joining and then burying the eastern courtyard groups to the northeast, to form the core of the Early Classic Acropolis (and eventually developing into the Copan Acropolis visible today). To the north of these two complexes, another ceremonial group composed of a sequence of temples and ballcourts began to develop at about the same time. Now buried beneath Structure 10L-26 and the famous Late Classic ballcourt, this third component of the evolving Acropolis developed adjacent to a group of low Early Classic platforms located beneath the Ballcourt and Monument Plazas (Cheek 1983) and served as a focus for the veneration of Copan's royal dynasty.

The pace of construction that produced these three architectural foci and merged them into a single complex was exceedingly rapid. At present we date the beginnings of monumental construction beneath the Acropolis at ca. A.D. 400. By ca. A.D. 450 these three centers of architectural development became connected by common floors and platforms. Soon thereafter (by ca. A.D. 500) all three had become essentially integrated into a single, elevated architectural mass that came to define the Copan Acropolis. Thus the interval of time we concentrate on in this chapter—the time it took for the Copan Acropolis to coalesce into a single monumental elevated complex—was no more than 150 years.

Research Methodology

Our understanding of the development of Maya monumental architecture is severely limited by a problem familiar to most Maya archaeologists; the visible remains of Maya buildings are often merely the latest versions of a whole series of constructions, one built on top of the other. To document the underlying earlier buildings, archaeologists must normally use destructive trenching or clearing excavations. Such excavations are not only increasingly difficult to justify ethically, but are often extremely expensive.

Tunnel Excavations at Copan

The Copan Acropolis Archaeological Project (or PAAC in its Spanish acronym) has solved the excavation problem through a concerted program of architectural tunneling within the Acropolis. The Acropolis is the site core during Copan's Classic period (ca. A.D. 300–900) development (figure 10.1), containing the palaces, temples, and administrative buildings used by Copan's ruling elite, together with their tombs and funerary shrines. Like most ancient Maya monumental construction, the Copan Acropolis is the result of a long-term accumulation of superimposed

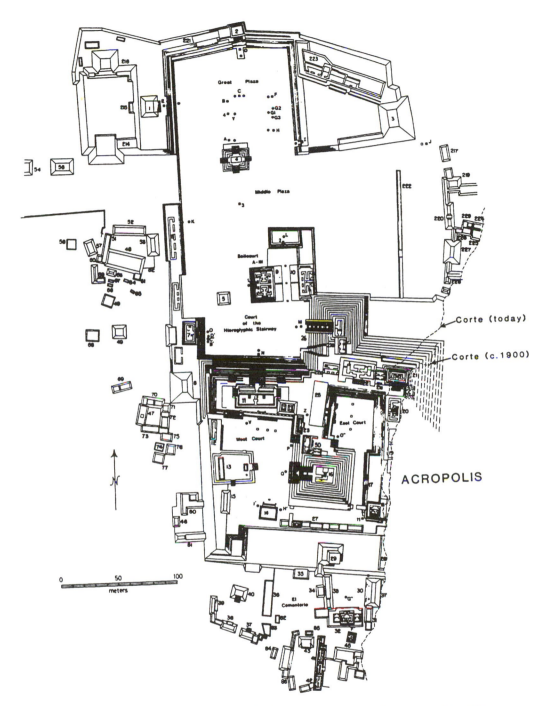

Figure 10.1. Map of the final phase Copan Acropolis (ca. A. D. 600–820).

constructions (platforms and the superstructure or buildings they support). Most individual structures within this accumulation comprise a series of renovations that were carried out over their span of use. When they became obsolete, these buildings were usually partially demolished so that the debris from roofs and upper walls could be used to fill their rooms and support new overlying construction (these fills, together with the original hearting of building platforms, are composed of mixtures of wet-laid mud and rock, and prove to be extremely stable). Occasionally, especially important buildings were buried more or less intact. This pattern of use, renovation, demolition, and burial has produced a stratified sequence of construction with remnants sufficiently complete to reveal and record architectural plans and partial building elevation data (including decorative elements). The result is an excellent record of the entire sequence of construction and evidence of use (such as caches, burials, architectural motifs, and inscriptions).

The PAAC tunnels follow and expose the buried remnants of architecture without destroying later superimposed construction. Because far less material has to be removed to create tunnels than to trench from above, the cost in time and money is far lower than conventional excavations. Thus, tunneling into Copan's Acropolis offers an essentially nondestructive and cost-effective opportunity for fully documenting and understanding the development of this example of Classic Maya monumental architecture.

The first tunnels at Copan were excavated by the Carnegie Institution of Washington during their research at the site in the 1930s. Tunnels were dug into the pyramidal substructures of Structures 10L-11, 10L-16, and 10L-26. These tunnels each had their point of departure just to the right of the central staircase of their respective buildings and were dug

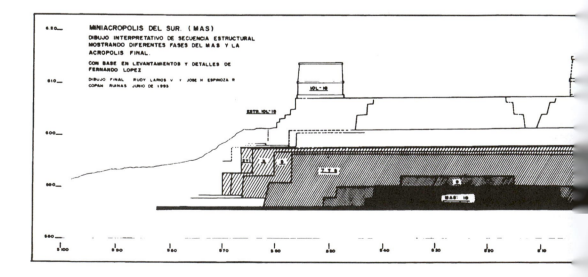

parallel to the central axis of the stairs in search of buried earlier structures. Of the three, the most extensively excavated was Structure 11, where an early hieroglyphic text was found on the threshold of a buried structure. In Structure 26, the terrace of an Early Classic substructure with a partially preserved stucco mask was discovered and reported by Stromsvik (1952). Stromsvik linked this early terrace to the construction epoch of Ballcourt I, based on its stratigraphic position and the floor it shared with the earliest Copan court. Subsequently, Charles Cheek (1983) tied these features from the Main Ballcourt, Structure 26, and Structure 11 into the overall architectural sequence for the Great Plaza area that he constructed as part of the investigations of the first phase of the Copan Archaeological Project.

In 1986, William Fash reinitiated tunneling into the substructure of 10L-26 as part of the Hieroglyphic Stairway Project. The goal of these investigations was to see how this locus had been used over the course of the Classic Period prior to the final phase monument dedicated by the 15th ruler. The magnificent hieroglyphic stairs and temple text of Structure 10L-26 1st were known to contain abundant historical material, and the conservation, documentation, reconstruction, and analysis of this final-phase material were the central goals of the project. The tunnel investigations were designed to "test" the dynastic history inscribed on the final version of the structure by documenting the archaeological and behavioral context of pictorial sculpture and associated hieroglyphic inscriptions (Fash 1988; 1991; Fash et al. 1992). Richard Williamson (1993) began working with Fash on the tunnels beneath Structure 26 in 1989 and continued to do so through the summer of 1994. Fash and Williamson also did some investigations of the earlier versions of the ballcourt buried beneath both Structure 10L-26 and the eastern building

Figure 10.2. Interpretive section view of the Mini-Acropolis of the South (MAS), showing different phases and the profile of the final Acropolis (final drawing by Rudy Larios V. and José H. Espinoza R.).

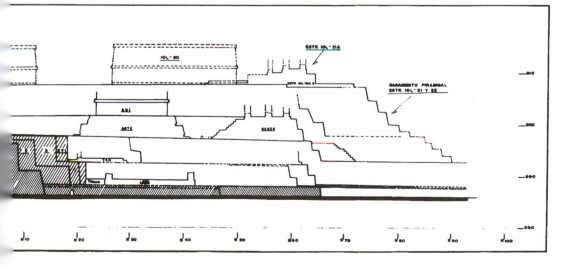

of Ballcourt III (Structure 10L-10). Williamson will be developing some of the findings at these loci in his dissertation regarding the origins of complex society in Copan.

Once Fash began the larger endeavor known as the Copan Acropolis Archaeological Project in 1988, with Rudy Larios as co-director in charge of architectural restoration, the work expanded far beyond Structure 10L-26 and the ballcourt. In 1989 Robert Sharer began the Early Copan Acropolis Program (ECAP), designed to tackle the massive task of documenting and investigating the archaeological features exposed in the Copan Acropolis Cut and excavating transverse tunnels into the Acropolis from its face. Ricardo Agurcia also joined the Acropolis Project (PAAC) in 1989 as the co-director in charge of the investigations of Structure 10L-16. Agurcia proceeded to excavate parts of the final phase structure, and continued some initial extensions of the Carnegie tunnels that Fash had begun in 1988. Agurcia's extensive tunnels into the substructure of 10L-16 have uncovered a long sequence of constructions at this central locus, the most notable of which is the magnificent Rosalila Structure (Agurcia and W. Fash 1991). The investigations of Structures 10L-26, the ballcourt, and Structure 10L-16 will form an integral part of the monographs that will eventually be produced based on the ECAP research.

In conjunction with the programs defining the architectural sequence of Structures 10L-16 and 10L-26, ECAP (with Sharer as director and David Sedat as field director) is responsible for the documentation of the eastern half of the Acropolis in the area between Structures 10L-16 and 10L-26 (figure 10.1). The full sequence of architecture beneath the Acropolis is uniquely accessible due to the famous cross-section ("corte") along its eastern edge, exposed by erosion from the Río Copán. This exposure reveals a complex sequence of stratified construction, along with evidence of related activities, over its extent (over 200 meters north–south, up to 45 meters high). The first corte tunnels were excavated under the direction of George Guillemin in 1978, during the initial phase of the current work at Copan, the *Proyecto Arqueológico Copan I*. After one season of work, during which some 100 meters of tunnels were opened, the corte project was suspended following Guillemin's death. After a hiatus of 11 years, ECAP renewed the corte tunneling excavations in 1989. By tunneling within each of the major construction levels sectioned by the corte, the goal of ECAP research is to trace the full developmental history of the Acropolis as seen in its architecture and residues of associated activities (figure 10.2). By 1996, after its eighth season of work, ECAP and its collateral programs beneath Structures 10L-16 and 10L-26 had excavated more than 3 kilometers of tunnels. As of 1996 the tunnel excavations were esentially completed, although architectural recording and consolidation is planned to continue for several more seasons.

The overall objective of all PAAC tunneling programs is to document the architectural development beneath the Copan Acropolis and relate this to the sequence of events recorded in the historical texts at the site

Table 10.1 Provisional Correlation of Copan Acropolis Architecture and Historical Dynastic Sequence

| Time Span (A.D.) | Architectural Units | | | Ruler |
| | South Acropolis | North Acropolis | | |
		Courts	Other	Succession and Name
763–822	*Str. 10L-18* * (Yax Pac tomb and shrine?) Str. 10L-16	**Str. 10L-21A**	*Str. 10L-11* *	16 (Yax Pac)
749–763		**Str 10L-21**	Str. 10L-26-1st*	15 (Smoke Shell)
738–749		Str. 10L-22A		14 (Smoke Monkey)
695–738		*Str. 10L-22* *	Ballcourt III Str. 10L-26-2nd Ballcourt IIB	13 (18 Rabbit)
628–695		**Begin Court I** (East Court)	Str. Esmeralda Scribe's tomb (Butz Chan?)	12 (Smoke Imix)
578–628		**Filling Court II**		11 (Butz Chan)
553–578	Str. Rosalila (A.D. 571)*	**Latest Court II bldgs**[a] **(Ante rededicated A.D. 573)**	Str. Chorcha Ballcourt IIA	10 (Moon Jaguar)
ca. 544–553		**Sub Jaguar Tomb Middle Court II bldgs**[a]		8, 9 (names unknown)
ca. 504–544	(Begin elite occupation of Cemetery Group*)	**Str. Ante/Ani (AD 542)*** **Earliest Court II bldgs**[a] **Str. Zopilote**		7 (Waterlily Jaguar)
ca. 480–504	**MAS 1 and 2 MAS 3**	**Courts III A and B**[a]	Str. Mascaron?	5, 6 (names unknown)
ca. 460–489	**MAS 4 MAS 5**	**Courts IV A-C**[a]	Papagayo* (rededicated A.D. 485?)	4 (Cu Ix)
ca. 440–460	**MAS 8–6**			3 (name unknown)
(Margarita cancelled)			Papagayo (Stela 63)	
ca. 435–440	**Margarita modified Margarita and tomb tomb*** (A.D. 437) **Str. Maravilla**		Mot Mot Altar Str. Mot Mot/ Ballcourt I (9.0.0.0.0 celebrated)	2 ("Kinich Holpop")
ca. 420–435	**Witik (Margarita)**	Court V	Str. Yax?	
ca. 250–420	**Yune (Yeh-Nal) Chinchilla (Oregano)**	Papo Floor	"Pre-dynastic"	1 (Yax K'uk Mo')

Notes: All architecture except that shown in italics excavated by PAAC; architecture excavated by ECAP (PAAC) shown in boldface; Architectural chronology and placement within specific reigns based on stratigraphic positions and associations with hieroglyphic texts (indicated by *); Sources for dynastic sequence: Stuart (1992); *Copan Notes* (Linda Schele, editor).

(Fash and Sharer 1991). Present evidence indicates that construction beneath the Acropolis dates from the Terminal Preclassic/Early Classic through the Late Classic periods (ca. A.D. 100–800). This time interval corresponds to both the dynastic period of Copan, based on Classic-era texts that record a sequence of 16 rulers (ca. A.D. 426–821) and the later portion of the predynastic period (ca. A.D. 100–426). Temporal control for the sequence of architecture is founded on stratigraphy, supplemented by radiocarbon assessments, obsidian hydration dates, associations with ceramics and other artifacts, and dateable Maya texts. More specifically, the earliest levels beneath the Acropolis are dated to the predynastic period (ca. A.D. 100–420), based mainly on associated radiocarbon dates and ceramics (Bijac pottery, ca. A.D. 100–400, and the beginnings of Acbi pottery, ca. A.D. 400–450). The remaining constructions are correlated to the dynastic period (ca. A.D. 420–820), based on radiocarbon dates, a series of calendric inscriptions, and ceramics (the bulk of Acbi pottery, ca. A.D. 450–650, and Coner pottery, ca. A.D. 650–850). But we expect that these conclusions will be further modified as our research continues, so both the dating and historical associations of the Acropolis architectural sequence should be considered provisional. For the time being, however, we can summarize this information in table 10.1, a preliminary and much simplified correlation of the known architectural sequence with the historically recorded rulers of Classic period Copan. (It should be noted that this historical sequence is far from complete or resolved; see Fash and Stuart 1991, Stuart 1992.)

Computer-assisted Mapping of Architecture

Recording the three-dimensional forms of buildings and the spatial relations between them within such a vast extent of tunnels has necessitated the adoption of a new approach to architectural mapping. Because our goal is to understand the evolution of the architectural organization, precise spatial recording in both horizontal layout and vertical relation is critical. The extensive and yet disconnected tunnel exposures of architecture in the Acropolis create problems for traditional surveying methods.

By following buried architecture with tunnels, there are numerous turns which severely limit lines of sight and require more survey stations than in any surface excavation. Also, since most architecture is exposed from the side rather than from above, the "plan" view of any structure is a composite of vertical surfaces which may be seen from several different tunnels. To handle the task of large-scale architectural mapping and data management, in 1991 a program conducted by Loa Traxler began using a computer-assisted mapping package based on an integrated electronic total station and computer assisted drafting (CAD) environment.

The spatial data are collected by the electronic total station, which consists of a digital one-second theodolite and an infrared-emitting electronic distance measurer. Both components are controlled by a central microprocessor that performs the trigonometry usually done in the surveyor's notebook. Through data collection and communication software developed at the University of Pennsylvania's Museum Applied Science Center for Archaeology, the total station sends the survey data to a handheld data recorder that transforms these data into north and east coordinates and elevations for the entire Acropolis area. The resulting data files are then transferred to a portable Macintosh computer and the CAD environment, where two-dimensional plans or maps and three-dimensional renderings are created.

Early Classic Nonceremonial Architecture

We begin our discussion with a summary of the known developmental sequence for the Northeast Courtyard Group, typified by low, substructural platforms and multiroomed (and often multi-doorwayed) superstructures. This form of architecture is most often associated with "nonceremonial" (residential, administrative, and storage) functions in Maya archaeological contexts. The architectural sequence is divided into a somewhat arbitrary sequence of six major construction episodes as seen in the stratigraphy of the corte exposure along the eastern side of the Acropolis. These are known as Division 6 (earliest) through Division 1 (latest—the surface architecture visible today). These corte-based subdivisions work reasonably well for the construction episodes in the northeastern quadrant of the Acropolis. They are less reliable in ordering the monumental constructions that comprise the MAS and Structure 26 sequences, although temporal equivalents can usually be determined by architectural linkages.

Division 6 (ca. A.D. 250–400)

The earliest known architecture constructed along the west bank of the Río Copán (the area that was to grow into the Copan Acropolis) consisted of cobble-faced earthen platforms, similar to a Bijac-period (A.D. 100–400) platform discovered in Group 9N-8 (Fash 1991). The initial evidence for cobble platforms beneath the Acropolis came from the 1988–1989 test pits along the Corte supervised by Murillo (1989). These low, cobble-faced platforms, some of which were associated with subfloor burials, were probably used to support residences built of perishable materials. Murillo provisionally dated these to the Preclassic era, but ECAP's more recent excavations and reassessments of the cultural debris (sherds, obsidian fragments, carbon, shells, etc.) found in the lowest stratigraphic levels alng the river support a late Bijac date (Terminal Preclassic/Early Classic).

The earliest known cobble platforms are associated with natural ground surfaces or discontinuous floors sealed beneath the lowest earth and *cascajo* surfacing known as Chinchilla Floor (average elevation 585.35 meters), apparently representing the initial artificial leveling or terrace construction along the west bank of the Río Copán. In our deepest probes beneath the Northwest Courtyard Group, cultural debris begins 0.75 meters below Chinchilla Floor and is continuous thereafter. Known only from a few deep probes, our information about this Division 6 settlement is extremely limited.

Division 5 (ca. A.D. 400–460)

The Chinchilla surface is associated with the first monumental cobble constructions, including an apparent cobble and earth boundary wall that ran north–south parallel to the river course. Only a portion of this wall escaped destruction by erosion or later building activity; this section is preserved beneath one of the large earthen platforms that formed part of the first stage of the Northeast Courtyard Group. Contemporary with Chinchilla Floor, the first stage of MAS was constructed on the slightly higher group to the west (see below). These events roughly correspond to the beginnings of Acbi pottery (ca. A.D. 400) in the Copan ceramic sequence.

The Chinchilla surface was buried by an apparent filling operation that raised the west bank occupational surface by a little over a meter. This produced a more formalized terrace with a well-defined surface, composed of gravel and crushed rock and known as Papo Floor (average elevation 586.45 meters). These levels collectively define Division 5 in the northeast section of the Acropolis, and are marked by a diverse assemblage of architecture that used river cobbles, earth and adobe, and cut-stone masonry. Of course, earth and adobe construction are often closely associated with highland Maya architectural traditions, as at the sites of Kaminaljuyú (Shook and Kidder 1952), Chalchuapa (Sharer 1978), and the Salama Valley (Sharer and Sedat 1987), whereas masonry architecture is closely associated with the traditions of lowland Maya architecture (Pollock 1965). It may be that these different construction methods at Copan have their origins in these different traditions of the highlands and lowlands. Regardless of their origins, at Copan these different materials were used to construct both substructural platforms and superstructures or buildings, sometimes separately but at other times in combination.

Because of more extensive excavation, the architecture associated with Papo floor is better documented than its predecessors, and includes the first-defined Northeast Courtyard Group constructed of earthen platforms, each with a (later demolished) earthen superstructure built on Papo floor in the northern sector of the corte. These constructions form courtyard groups, designated 5A–5C (figure 10.3), probably used for residential and perhaps administrative purposes, tentatively dated to the reigns of Copan's first two kings. The substructure on the eastern side of

Court 5B had two terraces, the lower western substructure was single ter-raced. The summit of the northern single-terraced substructure was reached by an outset south-facing stairway. Both terrace and building surfaces were covered with an earth-based red paint.

A second courtyard group, Court 5C, apparently existed immediately west of Court 5B. This western court is less well defined in our tunnels thus far, but was bounded on the north by a sequence of low adobe plat-forms ("Tartan") and on the east by Court 5B.

Poor preservation makes it difficult to determine the details of the earthen buildings that once stood on the summits of these Division 5 platforms. But at least one—the building on the western platform of Court 5B—had a tamped earth surface covered with a series of very thin plaster floors. This summit building had thin interior partitions indi-cated by interruptions in its plaster floor, forming interior corners and lipping up to presumed vanished walls. Evidence for the type of roofing used on these buildings comes from remnants of burned wooden sup-ports and possible thatching, found associated with the low adobe plat-form on the north side of Court 5C.

Thicker and more durable floors appear to have been used outside of these adobe buildings to pave open courts or plazas during Division 5, as can be seen with Papo Floor, which provided the original plaza surface of Court 5B. The plaza surface of Court 5C appears to have been unpaved, but was later covered by a plaster floor during Division 4 times. True plaster floors, including the addition of subfloor ballast of crushed rock, developed rapidly within Division 5 times and began to be used both inside and outside of buildings.

Division 4 (ca. A.D. 460–500)

This stage of the Acropolis was associated with the complete filling of the Court 5B plaza. This was accomplished by the incorporation of Court 5B within a new monumental masonry platform, known as Caimito, that was constructed against the northeast corner of MAS, marking the formal union of these two previously separated architectural complexes. Caim-ito platform extended some 40 meters north–south, but its east–west dimension remains unknown since eastern limits have been destroyed by the Río Copán. Its plastered floor surface abutted the doorways of the superstructures on the eastern and northern platforms of Court 5B, so that for a time these buildings continued to be used. However, the lower western adobe platform was completely buried by Caimito, and its super-structure was totally demolished. To the west, at the same time Caimito platform was constructed, a new plaster plaza floor refurbished the older Court 5C, which continued to be used into Division 4 times.

After an undetermined interval within Division 4 times, the remnant adobe buildings of Court 4B were in turn demolished and replaced by new masonry constructions. These consisted of two low substructure

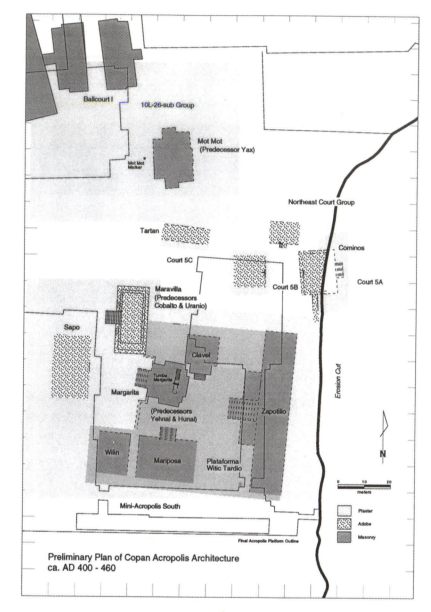

Figure 10.3.
Computer
Map of Courts
5A–C (ca. A.D.
400–460).

platforms built on Caimito platform (averaging about 1 meter in height) surmounted by multi-doorwayed, multiroomed buildings on their summits (figure 10.4). Later, two more masonry buildings were added to Court 4B, forming its west and south sides. During its use, the back wall of the southern building abutted the northern terrace of MAS. Although the upper zones of these courtyard buildings were anciently demolished, enough evidence survives to infer elite residential and possibly administrative functions from the arrangement, size, number of rooms, and other details. Judging from the great quantities of painted and modeled stucco

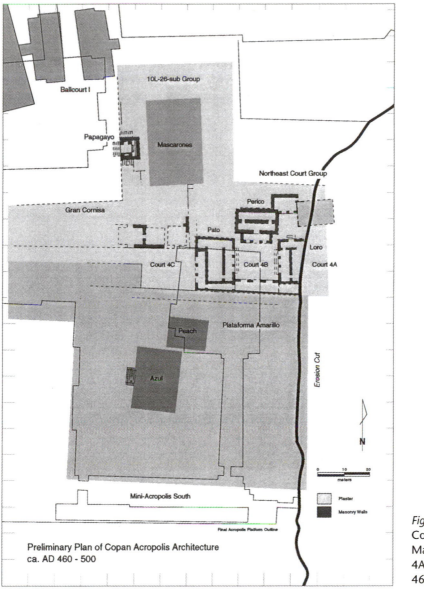

Preliminary Plan of Copan Acropolis Architecture
ca. AD 460 - 500

Figure 10.4.
Computer
Map of Courts
4A–C (ca. A.D.
460–500).

in the demolition layers of these structures, their upper zones were once
adorned with elaborate masks and other decorations. In the case of the
eastern building, the interior medial wall was decorated by two columns
of glyphs rendered in orange and red, largely destroyed when the building was demolished.

    To the west of Court 4B, sometime later during Division 4 times,
the old Court 5C was also filled in and covered with a new plaster floor,
bringing it up to the level of Caimito platform and forming Court 4C (figure 10.4). This new floor is also associated with Papagayo structure (see

below), marking the first formal union of the courtyard complex with the sequence of buildings to its north, under Structure 10L-26. A low masonry platform supporting a very large, multiroomed masonry building was then constructed on the north side of Court 5C (its southern and western limits were defined by the high terraces of MAS). To the east of Court 4B, a corresponding Court 4A was constructed, although it was later destroyed by the Río Copán. In its final form, therefore, this northern residential complex formed an arrangement around three east–west aligned courtyards, Courts 4A–C (figure 10.4), bounded on the south by progressively larger and higher monumental platforms of the early Acropolis. Overall, the evidence points to this entire northern courtyard complex being the palaces of some of Copan's Early Classic rulers and/or their immediate kin, approximately corresponding to the reigns of Rulers 3 and 4 (table 10.1).

Division 3 (ca. A.D. 500–540)

At about A.D. 500 the northern palaces of Courts 4A–C were demolished and buried under a massive new expansion of the growing Acropolis to the south. This Acropolis expansion extended the original elevated ceremonial complex some 40 meters farther north. To the north of this expanded Acropolis, a new platform provided the foundation for a new courtyard complex of multiroomed, multi-doorwayed buildings (figure 10.5). These seem to have been the residential and administrative structures that replaced the earlier and now buried buildings of Courts 5A–C and 4A–C, except that the new complex has only two preserved, east–west aligned groups (Court 3A and B). Although there is no evidence linking this extensive renovation with a specific ruler, what we know about its timing from the stratigraphic record indicates it occurred about the time of Rulers 5 and 6 (table 10.1).

Overall, if viewed from the Río Copán during Division 3 times, the expanded Acropolis would have formed a tri-level, north–south profile against the sky. The highest portion of the Acropolis remained on the south, the summit of MAS rising in two monumental terraces, surmounted by the elaborate temples and palaces of Copan's rulers. There was a broad mid-level area north of the highest platform (beneath which were buried the courts of Divisions 5 and 4) that was to be the setting for a series of new buildings. Later destruction has removed almost all traces of their construction. And farthest to the north was the lowest complex, composed of two east–west aligned courtyard groups, known as Court 3A and B. The latter complex essentially replaced and continued the functions of the earlier residential complexes (Court 5A–C and Court 4A–C).

Division 2 (ca. A.D. 540–650)

The new northern court complex was destined to be short lived, for it was soon engulfed by an even larger northward expansion that was the

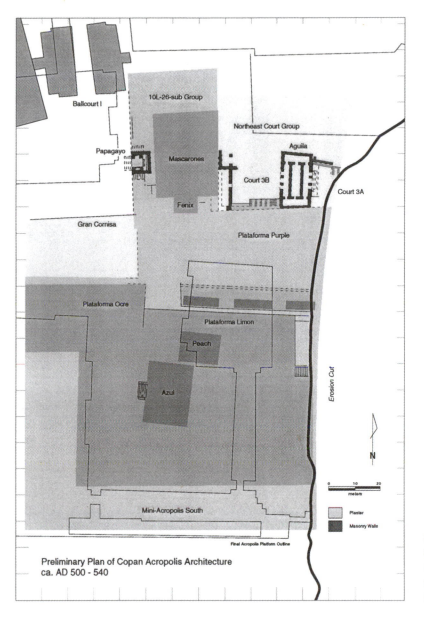

Preliminary Plan of Copan Acropolis Architecture
ca. AD 500 - 540

Figure 10.5.
Computer Map
of Courts 3A
and B (ca. A.D.
500–540).

first to define the Acropolis as it remains today. This renovation resulted
in the reversal of the fundamental architectural pattern of the entire
Acropolis. For with this final northward expansion of MAS, there was no
space for another northern courtyard complex. It seems likely that the
displaced courtyard complex was relocated elsewhere at Copan. The best
candidate may be to the south of the Acropolis, where excavations
directed by E. Wyllys Andrews V (in press; Andrews V and Fash 1992)
point to a surge of new buildings at the beginning of the Late Classic, in
what had formerly been a small group, that converted and expanded this
into a new elite residential and administrative complex. In any case,

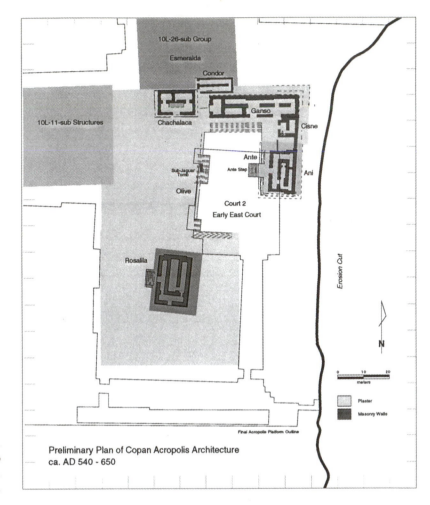

Figure 10.6.
Computer Map
of Court 2 (ca.
A.D. 540–650).

Preliminary Plan of Copan Acropolis Architecture
ca. AD 540 - 650

from this time onward, the core of Copan was composed of a southern elite palace group flanked on the north by an Acropolis, a 180° reversal of the original pattern followed during the first century of architectural growth.

The newly expanded Acropolis now covered an area in its north–south axis equivalent to its final stage. This new architectural complex was apparently planned and begun during the reign of the seventh ruler, Waterlily Jaguar (table 10.1). The sequence of buildings belonging to this span is long and complex, involving many renovations, additions, and superimposed constructions, and probably extended through the reign of the 11th ruler, Butz Chan, about the time the Late Classic (Division 1) version of the Acropolis seems to have begun (table 10.1).

An important component of Division 2, the penultimate major Acropolis renovation, was a new court in its northeast quadrant, directly over the earliest courtyard groups (those of Divisions 5 and 4), known as Court 2 (figure 10.6). Over its span of use, Court 2 developed into a series of masonry and vaulted buildings erected around a central courtyard—a smaller version of its Division 1 form known as the East Court. Court 2 was defined on the west by a terraced platform with an outset staircase, known as Olive, later covered by the Jaguar stairway; on the north by a broad stairway leading to several important buildings; and on the east by an elaborately decorated platform and building. This eastern building is known as "Ante," a two-terraced, west-facing substructure, elaborately decorated with stucco masks representing macaws, once brightly painted in red, green, and other colors. Ante platform supported a multiroomed building named "Ani," also decorated by elaborate stucco masks and other motifs (figure 10.7). Ante is situated beneath and some 10 meters west of its probable successor, the now-destroyed Structure 10L-20 constructed in Division 1 times.

But Court 2 represents a functional change from that of its underlying predecessors. Ante's location was apparently consecrated by a cache symbolizing the three layers of Maya cosmos (the sky, the earth, and the

Figure 10.7. General view of the Division 2 Ante/Ani structure, located beneath the massive stairway on the east side of the East Court, visible on the right (photograph by Barbara Fash, with permission).

watery underworld) embodied by three layers of jade artifacts, shells, pigments, and bird bones arranged inside a large stone vessel, sealed with a stone lid. Ante was then constructed directly over this cache (no caches of any kind are yet known from any of the buildings around the courts of Divisions 5–3).

Ante was the first known building in the newly constructed Court 2. A carved hieroglyphic text (Morales, Miller, and Schele 1990) on the west-facing stairway of the Ante platform begins with a Maya Long Count date corresponding to A.D. 542 and a reference to the seventh ruler, Waterlily Jaguar. This date appears to place the initiation of both Ante and Divison 2 at ca. A.D. 540, during the reign of Waterlily Jaguar. The Ante text closes with a second date, possibly corresponding to A.D. 573, and the name of the 10th ruler, Moon Jaguar, both seemingly in reference to a rededication of the Ante stairway.

An intact masonry-tomb chamber sealed by eight large stone beams was discovered under the Olive stairway, on the west side of the Division 2 court. It contained the skeletal remains of a male, covered with carved shell and jade adornments. On the floor beneath the slab were pottery vessels and other offerings. The tomb vessels have been assigned a date of ca. A.D. 550 based on their form and typological affiliation (René Viel, personal communication, 1992). The most secure carbon sample, taken from within one of the tomb vessels, provides a somewhat later date with a two-sigma range of A.D. 595–860. The architectural stratigraphy indicates the tomb dates later than the construction of Ante platform (with its date of A.D. 542). The evidence points to the tomb being that of Ruler 7, mentioned first on the Ante step, or either Ruler 8 or 9, both little-known kings with short reigns between ca. A.D. 544 and 553. But Ruler 10, Moon Jaguar, in power at the time of the apparent date of the rededication of the Ante stairway A.D. 573), cannot be discounted.

During the span of use of Court 2, a variety of buildings were constructed and renovated on its northern and western perimeters. On the north side of this court, several of the immediate antecedents of well-known Division 1 East Court buildings, Structures 10L-21, 21A, 22, and 22A, were constructed (figure 10.1). Particularly noteworthy are several predecessors of Sructure 10L-22, dedicated by the 13th ruler, 18 Rabbit (Waxaklahun U'bah K'awil), decorated like their Division 1 successor with carved and stuccoed corner masks. All of these Division 2 buildings continued to be used for a time after Court 2 was filled in and covered by new plaster floors before finally being terminated and replaced by the buildings of Division 1. The filling of the Court 2 clearly signaled the beginning of the last major renovation of the eastern Acropolis, corresponding to the beginning of the Late Classic period. We currently date the filling in of Court 2 to the reign of ruler 11, Butz Chan (A.D. 578–628). The span of construction of the new Division 1 buildings which followed, comprising the Acropolis East Court visible today, is dated to the reigns of the last five rulers of Copan (A.D. 695–822; table 10.1).

Continuities in the Architecture of
the Early Classic Acropolis

We now turn to the origins and development of the Acropolis proper, known in its Early Classic developmental history as MAS. From the beginning, the individual structures of MAS were supported by a successive series of plaster-surfaced platforms, drained by well-designed subfloor conduits constructed of either cobbles (in its earliest stages) or masonry (in its later stages). Three major platforms, each with three or more substages, have been defined for the era corresponding to Divisions 5–3 (ca. A.D. 400–540), before the final Early Classic expansion of Division 2 (ca. A.D. 540–650) created an Acropolis with essentially the same mass as in its Late Classic (Division 1) manifestation. (The numbered MAS stages in table 10.1 generally correspond to these platform stages, although this numbered sequence is no longer used.) Because the architectural history of MAS is far more complex than either of the other two foci of Early Classic construction in the core of Copan, we have been selective in extracting two contrasting examples to illustrate important continuities of architectural development within the MAS sequence.

Adobe Architecture in the Early Classic Acropolis
(ca. A.D. 420–500)

The first MAS platform dates to ca. A.D. 420–440 (within Division 5 times). It was only about 1 meter high, had a plaster floor that covered an area of about 5,000 square meters (or some 70 meters on each side), and seems to have been bounded by low parapet walls. This initial MAS platform supported a group of four substructures, two of earth and two of masonry. The earthen platforms (with presumed or documented adobe summit buildings) were undoubtedly related to the architectural traditions of the southeastern Maya area and Maya highlands that extend back into the Preclassic era. We have already seen examples of this type of construction in the nonceremonial adobe platforms of the Division 5 court complex.

On the north side of this first MAS platform, there was the first of a sequence of three superimposed adobe substructural platforms (figure 10.3). The first of these earthen constructions (named "Uranio") is little known, yet for almost a century, while the other buildings of MAS were progressively engulfed by the expanding Acropolis, Uranio and its successors remained outside of the ever larger and higher Acropolis platforms that encroached on it southern and eastern flanks. Uranio was encapsulated by a later, two-terraced earthen substructure, "Cobalto." After an undetermined period of use, Cobalto was terminated by a ritual that left a large offering of burned jade (with hundred of fragments of jade and large quantities of burned wood, perhaps from its superstructure). It was then buried by a larger earthen substructure, Maravilla, which was modified and kept active for a longer period than its predecessors. Although its southern and eastern terraces were progressively incorporated into the expanding MAS platforms, the base of Maravilla's western staircase remained at the level of the base of the Aropolis. Maravilla was not terminated and buried until ca. A.D. 500.

Maravilla was painted with a reddish earthen paint and rose in three high narrow terraces to a height of at least 5 meters, measuring 20 meters north–south and 10 meters east–west. Remnants of a red-painted, adobe superstructure have been found on the platform summit, initially reached by narrow inset adobe steps. Both superstructure and terraces were protected from the elements by a roof supported by four massive timber uprights, one at the base of each platform corner. Later, an outset, west-facing staircase was constructed of adobe in its upper extent, connecting to masonry steps in its lower extent outside of the roof dripline.

There were several other adobe constructions associated with this Early Classic complex. Some were built entirely of adobe or were hybrid adobe/masonry constructions. One of these, known as "Concepción," was located on the eastern side of MAS, while another, named "Sapo," defines the western limit of the first MAS platform. Concepción has a masonry lower terrace and an adobe upper terrace (its superstructure has yet to be revealed).

Adobe architecture was on the wane by the end of Division 5 times, but a few adobe structures are known to have survived into Division 4 (ca. A.D. 460–500). These include the presumed temple building on the summit of Maravilla, together with the apparent residential buildings on the summits of the adobe courtyard complex to the north, already discussed. In both cases, however, by Division 4 times the original substructures had been encroached and covered by later masonry construction so that access to these relic adobe buildings was directly from elevated, plastered plaza surfaces. The importance of the adobe building on the summit of Maravilla was such that it survived for a considerable length of time while the surrounding and far more durable masonry architecture of MAS was being refurbished and rebuilt on a near-continuous basis.

Masonry Architecture in the Early Classic Acropolis (ca. A.D. 400–600)

The earliest examples of masonry construction appear together with the adobe buildings of Division 5 and rapidly develop throughout the remainder of the history of the Acropolis (Divisions 4–1). The initial examples of masonry appear in the earliest levels of the MAS complex and used a range of natural-shaped, rough-cut stones aligned to form low platform or terrace walls, open drains, and possibly some superstructures (most having been demolished before later construction). These early masonry terrace and platform surfaces were coated with lime-based plaster and painted red and other colors.

Perhaps the longest sequence of masonry platforms, each decorated by elaborate plaster-modeled and painted masks and motifs, lies at the heart of MAS and at the core of the entire Acropolis. The culmination of this sequence is Structure 10L-16, the highest temple of the Copan Acropolis, constructed by the last known dynastic ruler, Yax Pac. Directly beneath lie a series of masonry structures (figure 10.8).

The initial building in the center of the first Acropolis platform, Hunal, was built of masonry (figures 10.3 and 10.8). Its substructure was decorated by a red-painted, talud-tablero facade. (Its northern and eastern sides have survived; the remainder was demolished when its successor was constructed.) The style and proportions of Hunal's *talud-tablero* facade are similar to those found on Early Classic structures in Tikal's "Lost World" group (see Kowalski, chapter 4, this volume). Hunal's stairway faced north and gave access to a central doorway in its summit building, which had at least two rooms: one on the north and one on the south (all but totally demolished by the Maya). One surviving basal "curtain holder" indicates that the doorway between these two rooms could be screened for privacy. Hunal's demolition debris includes fragmentary wall blocks decorated by remnants of multicolored frescos, indicating that its interior walls were once brilliantly decorated by murals. Based on its stratigraphic position, Hunal is tentatively dated to ca. A.D. 420–430.

Before Hunal's termination, a vaulted tomb chamber was introduced beneath the eastern half of its northern room. An individual was interred in this chamber, supine with head to the south. Afterward Hunal was terminated and encapsulated by a new substructural platform named Yehnal (figures 10.3 and 10.8). Yehnal's staircase faces west, establishing a new orientation for this locus that was followed for almost 400 years by its successors, including the final temple in the sequence, Structure 10L-16. The staircase and its summit building were also all but demolished when Yehnal was terminated. Based on its stratigraphic position, Yehnal is tentatively dated at ca. A.D. 430–440.

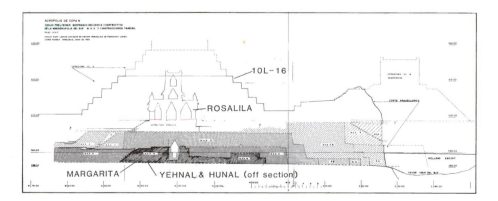

Figure 10.8. East–west section drawing of Structure I0L-16 with Rosalila and Margarita Structures (drawing by Rudy Larios).

The unweathered surface of Yehnal and its single coat of painted plaster indicate that it was used for a relatively short period. Perhaps a decade or so after its construction, Yehnal was superseded by a larger platform named Margarita (figures 10.3 and 10.8). This platform was also decorated by two large stucco-relief panels on either side of its west-facing staircase. The preservation of these panels is extraordinary and includes both modeled deity figures and hieroglyphs. But the central element (fully exposed on the south side of the staircase only) is a full-figure emblem representing Yax K'uk' Mo' represented by two intertwined birds (a quetzal or *k'uk'* on the left, and a macaw or *mo'* on the right), each with crest composed of a yax sign. Margarita's position in the Acropolis sequence provides a tentative date of ca. A.D. 440–450 (table 10.1).

Within Margarita platform was constructed a vaulted tomb chamber, originally reached by a staircase that led from the floor of its superstructure (much like the later and larger Temple of the Inscriptions at Palenque). Within this burial chamber are the remains of an individual upon a dais constructed of a single stone slab. After a relatively short period of use, the building of the summit of Margarita was demolished and replaced by a vaulted upper offering chamber directly above the tomb chamber. This upper chamber included a feature unique among all known Maya tombs: the southern end wall of the passageway incorporated a well-preserved stone monument with a carved hieroglyphic inscription. Several features of the text are unusual or even unique, but thus far only a tentative reading of its date can be made (equivalent to 9.0.2.0.0 or A.D. 437). The initial phrase of the text mentions the Copan Ahau, Ruler 2 ("Mat Head"), apparently associated with a "death place." The final portion of the text gives the titles and name of the dynastic founder, Yax K'uk' Mo'. At first it was assumed that this tomb contained one of the early rulers depicted on Altar Q, but analysis of the skeletal remains indicates that the occupant was a woman, perhaps the wife of the founder. Further excavation revealed that the Hunal platform contained a tomb that has tentatively been identified as that of Yax K'uk Mo' (Stuart 1997: 82-90).

Regardless of the identity of the female occupant, it is clear that the Margarita tomb was reentered on one or more occasions after the deceased woman was placed in it. These later entries were made possible by the construction of a vaulted passageway leading to the original tomb staircase from a new and larger temple located to the north. (Unfortunately, the entrance to this new access was destroyed by subsequent construction.) Reentry is evidenced by the resettling of several pottery vessels in the upper offering chamber and by red pigment (cinnabar) scattered on both the bones of the interment and on fallen debris within the burial chamber.

Sometime around A.D. 465 this passageway to the Margarita tomb was sealed by the north-facing terrace of a new and larger MAS platform. This stage was soon followed by several later and even larger MAS platforms, equivalent to Divisions 4–3 (ca. A.D. 460–540). Although much more needs to be learned about the buildings pertaining to these stages, we know that in Division 2 times (ca. A.D. 540–650), when the Acropolis had expanded almost to its present extent on all sides (figure 10.6), a truly extraordinary building was erected directly over Margarita and its tomb chamber (by this time buried some 10 meters below; figure 10.6 and 10.8). This building, named Rosalila, has been revealed in extensive tunnels directed by Ricardo Agurcia Fasquelle (see Fash 1991: 100).

A carved text on the staircase of the platform supporting Rosalila indicates it was sponsored by the 10th ruler, Moon Jaguar. This would place its construction within Division 2 times, flanking the southwest quadrant of Court 2, discussed previously. Rosalila's location and the motifs preserved on its elaborately decorated facade suggest it was a shrine dedicated to the founder, Yax K'uk' Mo'. Rosalila was such an important building that it had an unusually long span of use, extending well into Division 1 times, long after Court 2 had been superceded by the East Court still visible today. When the time came for Rosalila to be terminated, it was carefully preserved intact, its rooms laboriously filled in (unlike all other terminated Copan buildings) before being covered and sealed by Structure 10L-16 (figure 10.8).

Continuities in the Early Classic Ballcourts and Dynastic Temple

The earliest known architecture in the area occupied by Structure 10L-26 is known as "Yax" Structure and is dated to Division 5 (figures 10.1 and 10.3). Yax, like Hunal substructure to the south, begins a notable sequence of superimposed architecture that spans Copan's dynastic period. In this case the sequence culminates in Structure 10L-26 1st and its famed Hieroglyphic Stairway, which was completed during the reign of the 15th ruler, Smoke Shell, but was in use until the end of dynastic rule. Yax was built of masonry with a west-facing stairway on the western side of the building that was mostly destroyed by subsequent constructions. Although all of the superstructure and most of the substructure walls were destroyed during the construction of its successor building, a U-shaped stucco adornment survives on the central axis on the east side of the substructure. Also, enough of its plan survives in the form of the basal course of masonry or lip scars in the plaster floor to map its original dimensions and layout. The substructure was built on a thin plaster floor and was served by a slightly more extensive apron known as Yax floor. The apron floors suggest that Yax was built and in use at about the same time as Tartan and MAS stages 10-6, since all of these were served by similar plaster aprons.

Yax was succeeded by a slightly larger substructure, "Motmot" (figure 10.3), that maintained the western stairway and the overall layout of the

Yax plan, but enlarged it slightly to the east. Motmot's facade was also decorated with modeled stucco designs in the form of four sky-band motifs (two each on the east and west sides), and a central panel on the east side bearing the face of G1 with a bird atop his headdress. This central eastern panel probably represents an elaboration of the themes originally expressed in modeled stucco on the analogous spot on the east side of Yax Structure. In front of the western stairway on its central axis was a floor marker that contains an extensive hieroglyphic text and portraits of the first two rulers of the site (figure 10.9). The text cites both K'inich Yax K'uk' Mo', the founder of the dynasty, and his successor, known as "Mat Head." The founder is named in association with the Period Ending date 9.0.0.0.0 8 Ahau 14 (sic) Ceh; the second ruler is mentioned in connection with the dedication of the floor marker itself, apparently some seven years after the completion of the Baktun. The imagery shows the two figures seated facing each other and the central column of glyphs that separate them, within the confines of a quatrefoil sign. The headdresses worn by the figures are identifiable as the name glyphs of their wearers, K'inich Yax K'uk' Mo' on the left (glyphs A6–7), and K'inich "Mat Head" on the right (glyph B6).

Beneath the Motmot floor marker was a cylindrical tomb containing a complete skeleton of an adult female in his early 40s, accompanied by 11 ceramic vessels, numerous partial mammalian and bird skeletons, 3 severed human heads, and much jewelry and ritual paraphernalia. The cylindrical form of the Motmot tomb is certifiably unique in Copan (where more than 500 graves have been excavated), but in fact quite common in the Merchant's Barrio and La Ventilla barrios at Teotihuacan. The subsequent depictions of K'inich Yax K'uk' Mo' with goggles over his eyes (symbolic of some sort of Teotihuacan connection) have led Fash and co-workers to posit that this tomb evinces an intimate knowledge of Teotihuacan burial and other ritual practices. The 9.0.0.0.0 date, the rededication of the Motmot tomb, and the placement of the floor marker were events recalled several times in later texts both at this locus and elsewhere in the kingdom. The repeated citation of these events and the curation of the temple that succeeded Motmot at this locus lead us to conclude that Motmot was established as a dynastic shrine or temple in honor of the first ruler and his founding of a ritual center at this locus.

Motmot's floor extends farther in all directions than did that of Yax and can be unequivocally tied to the construction of the original ballcourt, labeled IA by Stromsvik (1952). Excavations inside the lowermost western terrace wall of Structure 10L-26 1st and beneath Structure 10L-10 1st revealed portions of the stucco decorations that embellished this first ballcourt. Two full-figure royal macaws were placed on the back wall of the western substructure of Ballcourt IA. Based on principles of symmetry, presumably two such macaws also graced the back wall of the eastern substructure as well. The inclined benches of both structures were topped with three macaw heads, all facing the playing alley. These

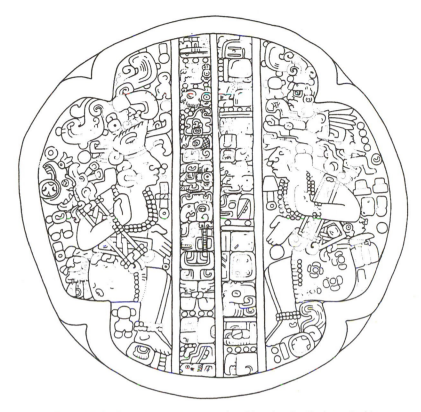

Figure 10.9. The Motmot floor marker (drawing by Barbara Fash).

formats and motifs were to be repeated in all the subsequent versions of the Copan ballcourt and constitute clear evidence of continuity through time. The only difference that occurs is that by the time the 13th ruler, 18 Rabbit, built the final court (labeled III by Stromsvik), he had the full-figure macaws carved in stone on all four of the facades of the superstructures, quadrupling the number of depictions in the process. Obviously, the sun symbolism associated with the macaws (Kowalski and Fash 1991) was an integral part of the ballgame and its associated cosmology and ritual from the time of the founding of the Copan dynasty.

It is noteworthy that the Motmot floor marker cites a "4 macaw" at the end of the text. This glyph may refer to the four full-figure macaws on the substructures of the original ballcourt, which, as we have seen, was built at the same time as Motmot and the dedication of the marker. The marker also cites "4 sky" (glyph A11), which may be a reference to the four sky-bands on Motmot Structure itself. Thus, the Copanecs seem to have been in the practice of naming their structures in associated monuments, from the inception of dynastic rule at the site. Perhaps this particular name for the ballcourt refers to its association with the solar macaw and his celestial domain.

Motmot Structure was subsequently buried and its superstructure virtually destroyed completely when the next building complex went up at this locus. Consisting of a frontal temple called "Papagayo" Structure on the west (figure 10.10) and a larger and more elevated pyramid-temple called "Mascarones" Structure directly east of it (figure 10.4), this much larger complex still retained the overall substructure floor plan of its predecessors, Motmot and Yax. Integral to the construction of Papagayo was the erection of Stela 63 (Fash 1991: 81, figure 37), placed in the rear chamber of the building on its central axis. Like the Motmot floor marker, this text cites the 9.0.0.0.0 Period Ending date in association with the name of K'inich Yax K'uk' Mo', but was in fact dedicated by his successor Mat Head. The dedication date is unspecified, but this inscription gives the important information that the second ruler claims to have been the son of the founder. At a somewhat later date, the fourth ruler (Cu Ix) placed in front of Stela 63 a hieroglyphic step that cites him as the protagonist of the text. At the same time he laid down a second floor inside the temple that lipped up to the bottom of the inscribed step. In back of Papagayo, Mascarones Structure underwent a number of modifications over the years, but for the final version we can document a stucco sky band on the north side of the stairway. Again, given principles of symmetry as well as the precedent of Motmot Structure's four sky-bands, it seems reasonable to conclude that Mascarones Structure also had four sky bands, two flanking the stairway on the west side and two on the back side of the substructure.

Although the dynastic shrine that was Papagayo Structure was deemed so sacred that it was left open for more than 200 years, the Mascarones pyramid-temple was subsequently covered over with a structure known as "Chorcha" at the time that Ballcourt II was built. The substructure of Chorcha was apparently not embellished by modeled plaster, and the superstructure sported eight pairs of large masonry columns that supported a perishable roof. This superstructure was similar in form to that of Ballcourt I; we do not yet know what kind of superstructure was built on Ballcourt II. Inside of Chorcha was a royal tomb (Agurcia and Fash 1989) which we believe to be that of the 11th ruler, Butz Chan. The tomb was then immediately covered over by the construction of the much larger structure known as "Esmeralda" (figure 10.6), which we believe was built by the 12th dynast, Smoke Imix-God K. This building also lacked exterior, sculptured adornment, but it did have a two-roomed "temple"-type superstructure on top of its pyramidal substructure. Esmeralda was subsequently modified by the addition of a massive stairway on the east side, later covered by the construction of Structure 10L-26 2nd, and finally by 10L-26 1st. The 13th ruler, 18 Rabbit, was responsible for modifying Ballcourt II by placing a new floor and set of playing-alley floor markers. Subsequently this same king covered over Ballcourt II with Ballcourt III, in the process changing its orientation and shifting its placement northward (Stromsvik 1952) due to the exigencies of his new design for Structure 10L-26 2nd and the Acropolis as a whole.

Figure 10.10. Photograph of the stucco sculpture on the back (east) side of Papagayo Structure, showing a crocodilian figure (photograph by Barbara Fash.

Thus, there were a number of important continuities in the structures occupying the locus of the dynastic temple of Structure 10L-26 and the ballcourt. The imagery of the ballcourt was established during the construction of the original version of the court and was maintained (with structural modifications and quadruplication) over the course of the ensuing three centuries. For the dynastic temple of 10L-26, the floor plan of the earliest temple was maintained through two subsequent constructions. The dynastic information recorded on the inscription associated with the second temple was replicated on a stela in the third version; this third version was considered so sacred that—unlike any other building known in the Acropolis at Copan—it was curated for more than two centuries, even as newer and larger pyramid-temples arose behind it. The hieroglyphic stair placed inside this third temple was later replicated on an unprecedented scale in the Hieroglyphic Stairway that graced the final version of Structure 10L-26, begun by Ruler 13 and completed by the Ruler 15 in A.D. 751. Here again, the contrasts are more in the form of structural changes (having to do with enlargement of the edifice) and greater quantities and elaboration of sculpture than with changes in function or meaning of the monuments. The ballcourt and the dynastic temple of Structure 10L-26 seem to have maintained the same uses, significance, and place of reverence over the entire span of dynastic rule at Copan.

Summary and Conclusions

The original three architectural foci of the Acropolis were established by the founder of the Copan dynasty and his successor: (1) a southern royal center destined to become the Acropolis proper, (2) a Northeastern Courtyard Group, destined first to be pushed farther north, then canceled and transferred elsewhere by the rapidly expanding central mass of the Acropolis, and (3) a northern temple/ballcourt group that eventually became physically linked to the Acropolis itself. The massive Acropolis to the south supported ceremonial buildings, flanked on the north by courtyard arrangements of low platforms supporting multiroomed "residential" buildings, and the ballcourt-dynastic temple complex to the north. It is postulated that the Early Classic Acropolis (MAS) was the preserve of the rulers of Copan and their immediate kin—the palaces, courts, and temples used by the top echelon of the Copan state. The courtyard groups were probably occupied by elite with close kin and client ties to the ruling lineage—the palaces, administrative, and storage buildings used by the second echelon of the Copan kingdom. The northern ballcourt/temple complex was the ceremonial interface between the public assembly and ritual areas in the Great Plaza farther north and the nonpublic, elite area to the south.

This architectural template undoubtedly had meanings for its creators manifest in Maya cosmology; that is, the southern Acropolis (and its adjacent Northeastern Courtyard Group) was probably associated with the earthly realm of Copan's rulers, while the northern temple and ballcourt was probably associated with the otherworld of royal ancestors (Sharer et al. 1992.; cf. Ashmore 1989, 1992).

Over a span of little more than a century after the founding, 11 definable stages of MAS were constructed—roughly 1 per decade. From the original nucleus of MAS buildings covering an area of about 3,000 square meters (ca. A.D. 420–430), an Acropolis covering an estimated minimum of 22,500 square meters was achieved by A.D. 540. This represents an area 7.5 times greater than the original complex and is almost as great an area as maintained in its final Division 1 stage. The great amount and extremely rapid pace of construction over this span seems to reflect the presence of a statelike system of organization and authority. The Division 2 Acropolis (ca. A.D. 540) was apparently planned and begun during the reign of the seventh ruler, Waterlily Jaguar, who perhaps should now be recognized as one of Copan's great builders (Sharer, et al. 1992). The form of the Division 2 Acropolis changed one component of the original three-group pattern established by the founder. The old northeast location of the adjacent courtyard complex was terminated and may have been transferred to a new location south of the Acropolis corresponding to the final-phase Group 10L-2 (Andrews V and Fash 1992; Andrews V in press). The long and complex sequence of buildings of Division 2 probably extended through the reign of Ruler 11, Butz Chan. The Acropolis had essentially reached its maximum extent by the end of the early Classic (and the end of the reign of Butz Chan). The reign of his successor, Smoke Imix God K, marks the beginnings of the final version of the Acropolis, corresponding to Division 1 and the well-known building complexes of the late Classic period (Miller 1986; W. Fash 1991; B. Fash 1992; Freidel, Schele, and Parker 1993;).

11

The Path of Life

Toward a Functional Analysis
of Ancient Maya Architecture

David Freidel & Charles Suhler

Pre-Columbian Maya architecture is a legacy to the world, declaring the aesthetic sophistication that master builders can achieve with simple tools and good organization. But as archaeologists, we are not content to witness, document, and admire this legacy. We study ancient Maya buildings to know why they were made and what functions they served for the people who made them. These functions are, in many cases, neither obvious nor familiar. Their investigation is an open-ended process of discovery, one requiring us to abandon what we think we already know about the relationships between form and function and to learn from what the Maya did and continue to do. Fortunately, we do not have to proceed in ignorance. There are many Maya sources providing insight into the subject, including painted and carved pictures of buildings being used, Classic period (ca. A.D. 200–900) glyphic texts describing what buildings were made for, eyewitness accounts of how buildings were used in the period of the European encounter (sixteenth century), and detailed documentation of how and why the Maya people today, descendants of the master builders and their crews, make buildings. What we intend to do here is offer one object lesson in this process of discovering the functions of Maya architecture.

We have been working at the ruined city of Yaxuná, next to the modern village of the same name, for six summer field seasons. Yaxuná is in the northern lowlands, about 20 kilometers south of the famous site of Chichén Itzá. We still do not know the full extent of the old community, but we have mapped more than 640 mounds, large and small, within an area of 1.75 square kilometers (figure 11.1). In 1990, as part of an examination of the settlement patterns of the site, Charles Suhler began excavation on a rather small (3 meter high) mound near one of the major acropolis groups in the ceremonial center (Suhler 1992) (figure 11.2). Judging from the surface contours, he thought Structure 6E-120 might be an elite

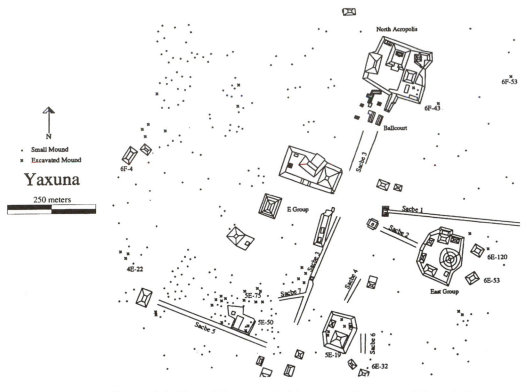

Figure 11.1. Map of the central civic-ceremonial sector of Yaxuná, Yucatan, showing the overall distribution of major structures and *sacbes*.

residence platform dating to the Terminal Classic period (ca. A.D. 750–1000)—one of the major periods of occupation at Yaxuná. The postholes he encountered while clearing the summit encouraged him to think he might have the remains of a perishable superstructure of pole and thatch, but then his Maya workmen from Yaxuná village exposed beige, plastered walls that extended down from the summit into the heart of the mound.

When David Freidel came on site soon after, Suhler knew he had Late Preclassic (300 B.C.–A.D. 200) ceramics associated with the building, and that whatever the postholes were, this did not appear to be a Terminal Classic perishable residence. While the workmen patiently stripped back the summit surface to expose a pattern of plastered walls defining corridors over it, all descending into the mound, Suhler and Freidel tried to make sense of the situation. By digging from the known down into the unknown, excavating within areas defined by the plastered walls, they began to see an unfamiliar pattern (figure 11.3). The building did not fit into either of two standard categories in Maya architecture of this scale: it was neither an ordinary solid platform suitable for supporting a superstructure of perishable materials, nor was it a ground-level masonry

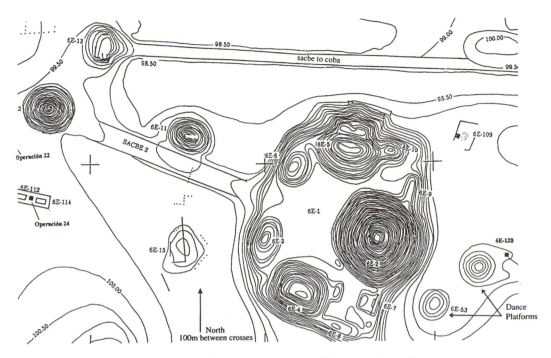

Figure 11.2. Map of Group 6E, Yaxuná, showing location of "dance platforms" (Structures 6E-120 and 6E-53) discussed in this chapter.

superstructure. To be sure, the outside of the building was designed as a modest stepped platform, but the inside was a labyrinth of subsurface corridors linking doorways piercing the basal terrace of the pyramid to a sanctum chamber buried within its center (figure 11.3). Even more bizarre, there was a stairway leading out of one of the corridors to what could only have been a horizontal trapdoor in the summit of the platform.

Structure 6E-120 immediately challenged us to think about Maya-building function in new ways. The main point of the design was evidently to enter into what would normally be a solid platform or pyramid. Beyond this peculiar violation of expectation, the usual means of getting up and down such a platform, an outer stairway, was here replaced by an internal stairway and the trapdoor on the summit. Obviously, what mattered to the master builders who put up 6E-120 was that people were to move through the platform as they went up and down it. What might be taken for a prosaic act, going up and down a stairway to get from the bottom to the top of a platform, was here explicitly designed as an elaborate journey. It was this journey that we had to understand and explain. To this end, we needed to marshal an array of information on how the Maya used platforms and got up, down, into and out of them.

We found one spectacular example of a hidden chamber in a performance platform from an early Spanish observation described in English by Michael Coe (1989: 161–162):

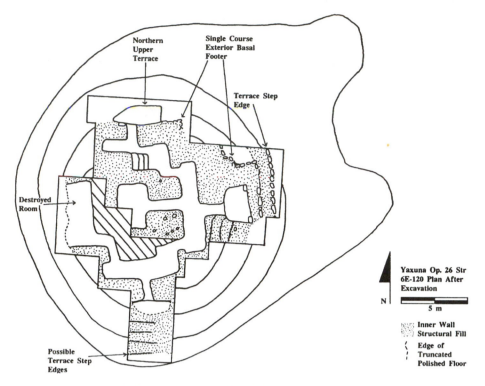

Figure 11.3. Plan of Structure 6E-120, Yaxuná, showing the mazelike quatrefoil-form subterranean passageway.

Similar dramatic performances almost surely took place in the great cities of the Classic Maya, and persisted in the highlands following the Spanish conquest. One such display is documented for the Q'eqchi' [K'ekchi'] Maya [Estrada Monroy 1979: 168–174] and was tied into an assertion of suzerainty by a local Maya dynast, a "cacique of all caciques," named *Ah Pop'o Batz'* (Lord Howler-monkey). This was held under the auspices of the Dominican friars of Verapaz on Sunday, June 24th, 1543, to celebrate and affirm the foundation of a new town, San Juan Chamelco, and to consolidate the power of the native ruler. Lord Howler-monkey was seated upon a dais covered with monkey skin, while two warriors draped a quetzal-feather cape over his shoulder. After he had been duly baptized, and a Christian mass sung, the Q'eqchi' drama began, to the sound of shell trumpets, turtle carapace, and other instruments. This was the Dance of *Hunahpu* and *Xbalanke*, the Hero Twins, and their defeat of the Lords of the Underworld, *Xibalba*.

The performance opened with the appearance of two youths in the plaza, wearing tight-fitting garments and great black masks with horns. They proceeded to a platform covered with clean mats and adorned with artificial trees; a small brush pile covered a hidden exit. After conversing with two nahuales named Xul Ul and Pakan . . . they came into the presence of other masked beings—the dread Lords of Xibalba. The Xibalbans tried to kill the Hero Twins, but they evaded the dangers and emerged unscathed to the discomfiture of their enemies.

The youths then began to dance before the Underworld lords, the dance becoming progressively more violent and frenzied; little by little the lords became fascinated, until they also were caught up in it. *Hunahpu* and *Xbalanke* appeared to fly above bonfires set around the periphery of the dance ground. Suddenly, unsuspected by the Xibalbans, they lit a multitude of incensarios, and in the midst of dense smoke they set fire to the grove of trees and to the mats. Everything turned into a great conflagration. Facing one another, with extended arms, *Hunahpu* and *Xbalanke* hurled themselves into the fire, which consumed the trapped Xibalbans as well. The smoke from the copal obscured all that was taking place in the bonfire, and even those "in the know" were frightened by the cries of the dying lords. When the smoke cleared, only ashes remained.

Then, on the ground, a compartment opened up, from which issued an emissary cloaked in a feather cape: in one hand he carried an incensario, while with the other he indicated the open chamber. As drums, shell trumpets, and the like sounded, the Hero Twins appeared from the compartment, covered with beautiful feather capes, wearing on their brows ornaments appropriate to great lords. Their former masks had been replaced with those of two handsome youths. The Twins proudly greeted the populace, which acclaimed them for their victory over the fearsome Xibalbans.

The story of the Hero Twins and their father, Hun Hunahpu, or Hun-Nal-Ye in the Classic period, was central to Pre-Columbian Maya religion (Freidel, Schele, and Parker 1993). Essentially, it is a story about the triumph of the human gods over death and the gods of death through the ability of human beings to experience not only death but also birth. For the ancient Maya, and for many of their descendants today, souls could be recycled through death and back into life. In the K'iche' drama just described (and as detailed in the *Popol Vuh*, their Book of Council, see Tedlock 1985), the lords of the spirit world are defeated not because the twins are immortal, but because they are able to return to life after being sacrificed or killed. The special correspondence between the design of the K'iche' platform and the one that we had excavated at Yaxuná led us to formulate an initial hypothesis of function based on analogy. Because of the formal similarities, perhaps the Yaxuná platform, like the K'iche' one, was used to perform a journey into death and back into life, a journey represented in the K'iche' case by going down into the platform while its summit shack of poles and mats burns and then ascending unscathed, literally rising from the ashes.

To be useful, a hypothesis has to lead to new possibilities of observation, analysis, and interpretation. The idea that this platform might have served as a place of ritual death and resurrection led us to look at other aspects of its design from this vantage. One of the things about the design that intrigued us was the way the corridors undulated around the sanctum chamber. While this undulation had no practical value as far as we could discern, it did give the corridors an overall horizontal pattern that looks much like a quatrefoil symbol. A similar quatrefoil represented a crack in a great cosmic turtle's back, a turtle floating in the heavens, out of which the Maya First Father, Hun Nal-Ye, was reborn to reorder the world after his sacrifice (figure 11.4). Hun-Nal-Ye was helped in this rebirth by his Hero Twin sons in Classic period imagery and mythology. The name of this quatrefoil in Classical Mayan glyphs was *Ol*, which can mean the heart of a place, but in modern Yucatec there is also a related word, *Hol*, which means portal or doorway. So here the horizontal pattern inside the platform signified a place where the Hero Twins facilitated the resurrection of their father.[1]

One problem we faced with this platform was that it was evidently unique in its specific design. That is, no other archaeologists had ever reported buildings that looked quite like it. It lost this distinction, however, during the following field season, when Suhler excavated Structure 6E-53, a nearby mound of similar size, and found that it was nearly identical to 6E-120 (Suhler 1993) (figure 11.5). So now we had two of these platforms with subsurface corridors, trapdoors, and sanctums, right next to each other, and both dated to the Late Preclassic period. This was grounds to identify this platform design as a type, albeit as a special one. But we were not content to think that the people of Yaxuná had dreamed up a special kind of platform at the dawn of Maya civilization, particularly in light of the prospects that the K'iche' were using similar platforms in the sixteenth century on the other side of Maya country.

We started looking for Pre-Columbian Maya buildings that might have had designs and functions related those of the Yaxuná platforms. The closest anology we came up with is a magnificent Late Classic temple perched high above the trees at the site of Copan in Honduras. Tatiana Proskouriakoff (1946) drew a magnificent restoration perspective of Temple 11 at Copan, a major Late Classic period structure. We think it fits the essential design we were looking at in a period in between the Yaxuná dance platforms and the K'iche' one. Temple 11 (Structure 10L-11) is perched on top of the acropolis of Copan in the southeastern zone of the lowland Maya country (figure 11.6; see Sharer et al., chapter 10, this volume for a discussion of early architecture at the Copan Acropolis). It is designed as a solid platform pierced by north–south and east–west oriented corridors which open onto doorways on each side of the rectangular building. From what we have preserved on our two Late Preclassic platforms at Yaxuná, these also had doorways on the four sides leading into the corridors. Where the corridors meet at the center of Temple 11, there is a throne bench with an elaborate decoration in carved masonry. Flanking the throne-bench on both sides, there are stairways leading up to trapdoor entrances. Not enough of Temple 11 was preserved at the

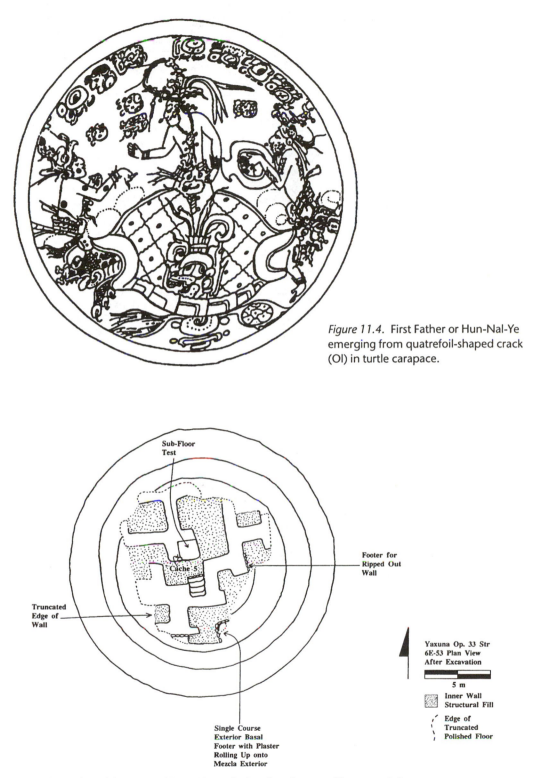

Figure 11.4. First Father or Hun-Nal-Ye emerging from quatrefoil-shaped crack (Ol) in turtle carapace.

Sub-Floor Test

Footer for Ripped Out Wall

Truncated Edge of Wall

Cache 5

Yaxuna Op. 33 Str 6E-53 Plan View After Excavation

5 m

Inner Wall Structural Fill

Edge of Truncated Polished Floor

Single Course Exterior Basal Footer with Plaster Rolling Up onto Mezcla Exterior

Figure 11.5. Plan of Structure 6E-53, Yaxuná, showing the mazelike quatrefoil-form subterranean passageway.

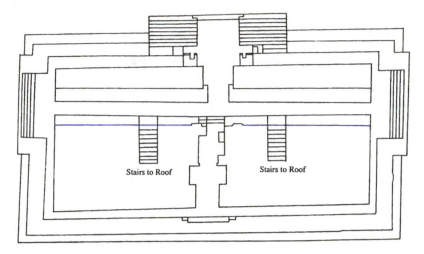

Figure 11.6. Plan and elevation of Temple 11 (Structure 10L-11) at Copán, Honduras, showing the cruciform room arrangement. A stairway led to the upper level, probably to permit the ruler to ascend into the realm of the sky, symbolized by a great Cosmic Monster in the upper facade sculpture (after Baudez 1994: figure 1).

time of initial professional inspection to be certain that the roof area above the platform was open rather than a second story of masonry or wood, but Proskouriakoff regarded it as an open summit and it is certainly a reasonable possibility.

Temple 11 illustrates the other two major sources of information on the function of Maya buildings which we outlined at the beginning: symbolic decoration and glyphic texts. Thanks to intensive work by specialists in Mayan glyphs who have been working at Copan recently, we know quite a bit about what the Maya thought this building was made for (see Schele and Freidel 1990: 322; Fash 1991: 168 for brief summaries). Inscriptions carved on stone panels set into the entranceways of the building mention the accession of king Yax-Pac, the last great king of Copan, on July 2, A.D. 763. The inscriptions suggest that the building was dedicated on September 26, A.D. 776 and that it was one of the first major construction projects of this king.

The proper name of the building in glyphic Mayan includes the phrase "*pat chan*," which means "underside of the sky" or "constructed sky." These allusions to the sky are commensurate with the sculpture that adorned the outside of the building. Great statues of Pawahtunob, old gods of the four quarters, held up a massive serpent that flowed across the top of the front or north side of the temple. We think this serpent represents the Cosmic Monster, the ecliptic path of the sun, and the major constellations (Freidel, Schele, and Parker 1993). The design of the building was thus such that when the king went from inside the corridors up through the trapdoors to the summit, he symbolically entered into the sky.

The symbolism inside the building is equally telling. The throne-bench at the crossing place of the corridors is framed by a mosaic sculpture of the maw of the White Bone Dragon. This image represents the deadly doorway between the world of the gods and ancestors and the world of the living. As Linda Schele showed in her brilliant analysis of the celestial imagery of the Classic Maya (Freidel, Schele, and Parker 1993: 87), the maw of the White Bone Dragon also represented the Milky Way when it rimmed the southern sky, the sky lying down upon the horizon before it rose again in triumph as the Stood-Up-Sky Milky Way in one of its two north–south positions. Her complete argument is quite complex, and must be consulted for further supporting evidence. Suffice it to say that there is powerful evidence to show that the image surrounding the throne-bench inside Temple 11 represented the place of the lying down sky, of the black place of oblivion out of which First Father was resurrected as a soul at the beginning of the Maya creation. This throne or bench sanctuary area inside Temple 11 at Copan was further decorated along its base with 20 seated figures, 16 of which were the kings of the Copan dynasty. These ancestors were depicted coming out of the portal of death to witness and to accompany Yax-Pac as he sat in this place of death before ascending into the sky as First Father had before him.

In our view, Temple 11 at Copan strengthens the hypothesis that the design we are investigating, subsurface corridors with sanctuary spaces, and trapdoor stairways, functioned to allow impersonators of the gods to perform the journey out of the place of death in the earth up into the place of rebirth in the sky. Temple 11 elaborates that hypothesis by implicating the design in the rituals of accession of kings. For although Temple 11 was built after Yax-Pac's accession to the throne of Copan, its texts mention this event, and the array of his royal ancestors on the throne bench in the building also shows the transfer of authority to this king. This very important role for the building also makes sense of its location, for Temple 11 covers an earlier structure that David Stuart discovered was called a holy Copan house of the founder of the royal dynasty, Yax-K'uk-Mo' (see Schele and Freidel 1990: chpt. 8, for discussion).

Another Late Classic building, House E of the Palace at Palenque, shows relationships to this general design (figure 11.7). Palenque is on the far western side of the Maya lowlands, as Copan is on the far southeastern side. Nevertheless, these communities not only shared general ideas of royal government, they also had royal marriage ties late in their history (Schele and Miller 1986). House E of the Palace at Palenque was the coronation throne room for the later dynasty of that site (Kubler 1969; Robertson 1985). The front room of this building contained a wall panel displaying the accession of the great king Pakal II in the presence of his mother, the monarch Zak-K'uk. House E contains a trap-door stairway that leads down into a subterranean labyrinth of corridors and rooms inside the platform supporting the Palace. This is a design element shared with the platforms we have been discussing. Additionally, the

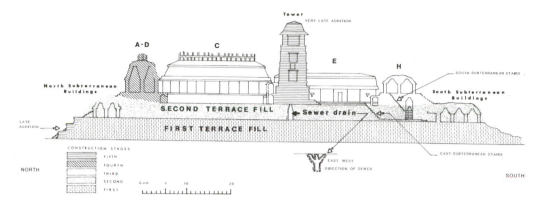

Cosmic Monster appears as a design over the one of the doorways of House E, identifying it with the sky as in the case of the facade of Temple 11 at Copan. Intriguingly, out in front of House E, a late king of the community raised a remarkable free-standing masonry tower. We think this tower is a more permanent version of a wooden scaffold of a kind used by kings to metaphorically enter into the sky in the course of major ritual events, including their accessions to power (Taube 1988a). If we are correct in this supposition, then the House E complex included a scaffold, an important element of the design found in the sixteenth century K'iché example and implied by postholes in Structure 6E-120 at Yaxuná, which perhaps sustained a scaffolding of poles and other materials.

Unfortunately, wooden scaffolds have not been preserved in the archaeological record of the Maya area. Nevertheless, there are other depictions of these perishable buildings. At the site of Piedras Negras on the Usumacinta River, there is a series of carved stone stelae depicting kings acceding to power seated inside niches on top of scaffolds that they have climbed into using ladders (Proskouriakoff 1960; see Taube 1988a, 1994 for discussion of these scaffolds and their function in accession rituals). The Piedras Negras scaffolds are decorated with cosmological symbols: Cosmic Monsters decorated with sky bands along their bodies frame the seated kings; headless caiman effigies lie at their feet. There is reason to regard these as images of kings entering into the sky.

Indeed, there are special features of Classic Maya temple architecture, called *cresterias* or roof combs (see Griffin 1978), that we think might also be masonry monuments to wooden scaffolds used by kings to enter the sky. At Palenque, Merle Greene Robertson's reconstruction of the roof comb composition on the Temple of the Sun (Griffin 1978: figure 19) shows a lord seated inside a scaffold of masonry decorated with the Maya "sky-band," as in the royal niche figures on stelae at Piedras Negras (figure 11.8). Bearing in mind that this is a reconstruction based on fragmentary evidence, it still shows remarkable potential for understanding the architecture it graces. A further parallel between these two compositions is the presence of a magical bird's head directly over the head of the lord on top of the skyband. This bird is Itzam-Yeh, the Magic-Giver bird, an important mythical being in Maya cosmology (Freidel, Schele, and Parker 1993: 231; Taube 1994: 673). Below the seated lord is a monster head with a cleft in its forehead, the image of *witz* (Stuart 1987), or mountain. This cleft in the head of the mountain is a profile of the quatre-foil *Ol*, or portal place, in the back of the celestial turtle we discussed earlier. It is clear compositionally that the lord, presumably king Chan-Bahlum, the patron of the temple, has come out of the mountain-turtle and up into the sky-scaffold.

The concept of creating or picturing a path from the earth to the sky is an old and widespread architectural composition among the Classic Maya. There is a wonderful example in modeled and painted stucco on the roof of a spectacularly well-preserved Early Classic period palace recently discovered at the site of Bahlum-Ku in southern Campeche. There, the seated lord is not just coming out of a clefted mountain head, but his several images are literally being burped out of squatting creatures sitting in the clefts of *witz* monsters. One of these creatures is clearly a frog. The up-facing head of a frog is the Mayan glyph for "to be born" and that is what we think this Early Classic image at Bahlum-Ku intends to convey: the birth of the lord in the sky.

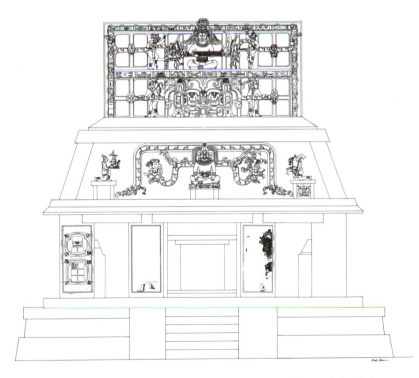

Figure 11.8. View of the Temple of the Sun at Palenque, Chiapas (after Roberston 1991: figure 74).

At the Temple of the Sun at Palenque, the seated lord is flanked by four dancing divinities. Spirit companions are sometimes portrayed with Maya kings, climbing on their regalia or floating around them (Schele 1985). The heads of four other divinities decorate the crossbeams of the scaffold, riding on snakes' bodies or functioning as their heads as they undulate along the beams. Disembodied heads decorate other examples of scaffolds in Classic Maya art, but they are evidently human sacrificial victims rather than gods. The most spectacular architectural expression of this theme is found at Toniná on an elaborate modeled stucco frieze decorating one of the massive terraces of that mountain center. The stucco frieze depicts a scaffold on which individuals are being sacrificed (see Stuart and Stuart 1993: 98 for a picture of this facade). A great dancing skeletal figure is named on the frieze as a holy lord of Pia, a historical polity northeast of Toniná. The skeletal figure carries a freshly severed human head in one hand. We will return to this relationship between scaffolds used to display seated monarchs and those used to display sacrificial victims.

The register of the decoration applied directly to the roof of the Temple of the Sun depicts a lord seated on a throne framed by the White Bone Dragon as a double-headed serpent. This throne is compositionally directly underneath the clefted mountain, that is to say, in the position of being inside it. The notion that this scene represents the inside of the mountain is supported by the presence of a second double-headed framing snake, within the frame formed by the White Bone Snake. This inner snake has as its heads two supernaturals. The heads of these same supernaturals float on the Panel of the Sun on the back wall of the sanctuary inside the Temple of the Sun. Schele suggests that these heads represent supernatural localities (Freidel, Schele, and Parker 1993: figures 4:28, 6:11, 7:13) and at least in one other case one of them is associated with the White Bone Dragon. One of the glyphic names given the sanctuaries inside of the Temples of the Cross Group, including the Temple of the Sun, is *pib-nail* "underground house." The other reason for positing that the seated lord on the roof is represented inside of that "underground house" or alternatively *kunil*, "magic/throne house," is the presence of two kneeling lords flanking the throne and displaying two deity effigies, of the Flint-Shield and of K'awil. These same deities are displayed by king Chan-Bahlum and his father, Pakal the Great, on the Panel of the Sun inside the sanctuary.

In sum, we think that the imagery of the roof shows the scene inside the mountain, that is, inside the "underground house" with one important substitution. On the Panel of the Sun, the throne holds the impaled severed head of a jaguar, representing sacrifice in war, while the roof image shows a seated lord, presumably the king himself. This substitution is consistent with the convergence of sacrifice and "seating" in other locations, including scaffolds. The association of this seated lord with the White Bone Dragon inside the mountain parallels the imagery inside

Temple 11 at Copan as described above. The White Bone Dragon maw is a major portal between this world and the Otherworld of the gods and ancestors. Concomitantly, we think that the roof comb depicts the sky scaffold into which the king climbs after being in the mountain, inside the ground, showing his ability to experience rebirth as First Father did in the sky (see Freidel, Schele, and Parker 1993: chap. 2).

The Temple of the Cross, the central of the three buildings raised by king Chan-Bahlum at Palenque, has no decoration left on its roof comb. Nevertheless, its interior sections are preserved and still carry smooth plastered surfaces. One can walk inside the roof comb, and Schele observed (Griffin 1978: 145; Schele personal communication 1994) that there are still stone outset braces for a wooden ladder that led from the roof surface to an opening in the top of the roof comb. Although Griffin supposed that this was designed for maintenance of the roof comb, we think that it allowed the roof comb to actually function as a scaffold to be ascended by the king , just as the kings of Piedras Negras ascended their ladders into their niche thrones.

There is a throne at the site of Toniná in Chiapas which strongly resembles the Piedras Negras scaffold seat. Dating to the Late Classic period and part of the discoveries made by Mexican archaeologists carrying out conservation at the site, this throne is in a dramatically roofed niche containing a raised dais. This niche is reached by a narrow stairway that spans a corbeled arch. The stair, which resembles a medieval flying buttress, is remarkably close to replicating in stone the effect of the wooden ladder in front of the throne-niche. In 1993, on a tour of Toniná, Schele (personal communication 1993) explained to Freidel that the stuccoed figures behind the throne represented a giant Venus glyph in front of the two Peccaries—representing the constellation Gemini. This throne place was surely meant to be up in the sky. But right behind the throne is an entrance into a labyrinth of subterranean corbel-roofed corridors inside one of the massive terraces built against the side of Toniná's mountain. In this case, the underground place is situated right behind the sky place.

So far, we have compared several Late Classic examples of Maya art and architecture, combined with glyphic inscriptions, showing that Late Classic Maya lords practiced ritual journeys from underworld places to sky places. What we are contemplating here is not some simple and constant building design, some readily recognizable "temple" or "palace," but rather an array of examples all intended to facilitate a common performance strategy and to create an architectural path for a journey from the underworld to the sky. We think that Maya master masons were aware of the differences between small buildings with constricted interior spaces and big buildings with ample interior spaces—archaeologists' "temples" and "palaces"—but they could conflate such buildings functionally by calling them the same name: *witz* or mountain (Stuart 1987; Freidel 1992b). They did not have a simple one-to-one correlation between named categories of buildings and forms. Public buildings served many functions at the same time. While they facilitated activities, they also symbolized powerful ideas or mythical events (Freidel and Schele 1988). What we are working to define here is a category of "path places" that encompasses a variety of formal designs. These are related by their symbolic intentions and by their physical expression of a vertical path leading from an underground or interior sanctuary to above ground, to a roof area, and, ideally, to a scaffold in the air.

In 1993, as we thought through the implications of the "dance platforms" discovered in 1991 and 1992, we found ourselves excavating a related architectural design. Structure 6F-3 is the largest pyramid of a triadic group of buildings that anchor the northern acropolis at Yaxuná (Suhler and Freidel 1994) (figure 11.9). We had seen a depression in the summit that ran parallel to the southern edge, and we thought it might be a tomb. As it turned out, it was a subterranean corridor, with a collapsed corbeled roof, inside the pyramid. Upon excavation in 1993, this corridor opened up to the south, along the centerline of the pyramid, into a subsurface chamber. This chamber, in turn, had a doorway into another corridor that ran east–west. This final corridor ran underneath a stairway that rose to the raised plaza area on top of the pyramid. Here was an amazing and complex design in a place where one might have expected to find a simple stairway leading to the summit of the building (figure 11.10).

Superficially, Structure 6F-3 could not be more different from the little dance platforms at Yaxuná, Structures 6F-53 and 6F-120. Structure 6F-3 is a massive pyramid, the largest in the northern part of the site and the apical feature of the north–south axis of Yaxuná's civic-religious plan during its Early Classic heyday. Nevertheless, our 1993 excavations revealed that the centerline design of this pyramid looked a lot like the dance platforms: an underground sanctuary and labyrinthine corridors. What the design lacked was the trapdoor access to the summit, but then we had not completely excavated the design by the end of the field season. In 1994, we found that the western part of the corridor inside the body of the pyramid had a tall ledge on the western end, turned a corner to the north, and stepped up onto the summit. The soffit spring-stones of the corbel-vaulted roof ended just east of the ledge and were replaced by straight vertical walls. Although access to this labyrinth must have required a short ladder, it was indeed a trapdoor entrance from the upper plaza down into the labyrinth. So all of the vital design criteria for our path place type are also met by Structure 6F-3 in its main Early Classic phase.

If Early Classic Structure 6F-3 at Yaxuná in the northern lowlands functioned like the Late Classic examples from the southern lowlands we discussed previously, then we would expect to find other evidence that it was associated with royalty and, at best, with accession rituals. Unlike the southern lowland Maya, however, the northerners wrote few public glyphic inscriptions on their monuments before the Terminal Classic period. Yaxuná is no exception to this rule. We have found one fragment

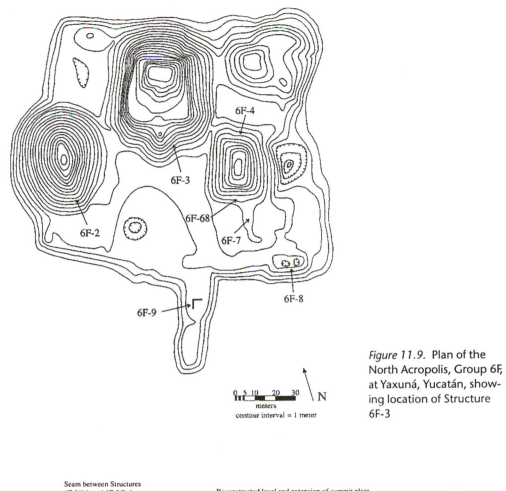

Figure 11.9. Plan of the North Acropolis, Group 6F, at Yaxuná, Yucatán, showing location of Structure 6F-3

6F-4

6F-3

6F-2

6F-68

6F-7

6F-8

6F-9

0 5 10 20   30
meters
contour interval = 1 meter

N

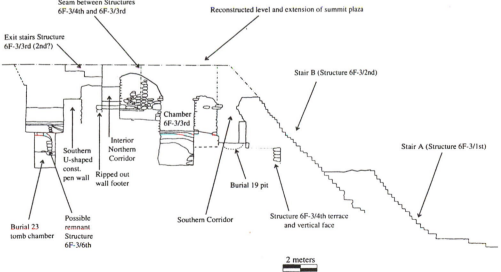

Seam between Structures
6F-3/4th and 6F-3/3rd

Reconstructed level and extension of summit plaza

Exit stairs Structure
6F-3/3rd (2nd?)

Stair B (Structure 6F-3/2nd)

Stair A (Structure 6F-3/1st)

Chamber
6F-3/3rd

Interior
Northern
Corridor

Southern
U-shaped
const.
pen wall

Ripped out
wall footer

Burial 19 pit

Burial 23
tomb chamber

Possible
remnant
Structure
6F-3/6th

Southern Corridor

Structure 6F-3/4th terrace
and vertical face

2 meters

Figure 11.10. North–south cross-section through Structure 6F-3 at Yaxuná, Yucatán.

of a carved monumental text and that is in a Terminal Classic setting. Nevertheless, we have found ways of extrapolating from the richer southern lowland record on royalty into northern lowland contexts at Yaxuná, and they do confirm the use of Structure 6F-3 by Early Classic kings.

In 1993, while exploring the eastern arm of the corridor inside Structure 6F-3, Suhler discovered an internal masonry wall north of it, descending to a lower plastered plaza level of an earlier version of the pyramid. This internal mason's wall was of rough blocks laid without any grout in the shape of a U, with the open end on the east (figure 11.11). The plastered floor of the earlier version of the pyramid within this large U-shaped pen had been cut through in antiquity and then refilled with packed marl and rubble. Above the level of this floor, laborers had filled the pen with loose rubble and earth and then completed the pyramid phase that included the labyrinth. Upon excavation, the hole in the floor turned out to be directly over the antechamber of a vaulted tomb directly to the west. The stratigraphy showed that this tomb had been originally sealed under the plaster floor of the earlier pyramid and then reopened and resealed by the person who built the later pyramid covering it.

The elaborate nature of these activities was clearly warranted by the contents of the tomb: a single male individual in his fifties with rich mortuary furniture. In the marl and rubble blocking the antechamber Suhler found a small, polished greenstone head, pierced for suspension. This head has a trefoil headdress associated with the "Jester God," now deciphered in Classical Mayan as *Sak-Hunal*, "White Eternity, White Oneness." It is the royal insignia par excellence. We know that individuals who were high elite but not kings might also wear this jewel under some circumstances, particularly when they were *Sahal*, a Late Classic aristocratic status in the Usumacinta river drainage. Nevertheless, it is also certain that the crowning of Maya kings regularly involved the placement of this jewel, or the white headband it represented, on the forehead of the king.

We found more evidence that the man in this tomb, Burial 23 at Yaxuná, was a king as excavation by forensic anthropologist Sharon Bennett proceeded to reveal the artifacts and contexts. In the southwestern corner of the tomb, she found yet another *Sak-Hunal* jewel near the head of the man. The man had been laid out on a bed of white earth sprinkled with sea shells on the western end, head to the west. Ritualists had placed a rough stone under his head, a second stone by his groin, and a third stone at his feet. For the Classic Maya, and for their descendants, the Milky Way is the White Path. In the hypothesis proposed by Schele in *Maya Cosmos* (Freidel, Schele, and Parker 1993: chpt. 2) the First Three-Stone-Place was a triangle of stars representing the hearth of heaven. The central star of this triangle was also the central star in the three stars that line up to make the belt of Orion, in our reckoning, or the great turtle in Maya cosmology. Recall that the Maya First Father was born out of a crack in the celestial turtle, the *Ol*, the portal place (figure 11.4). We think that the white bed of marl in this tomb represents the Milky Way and that the

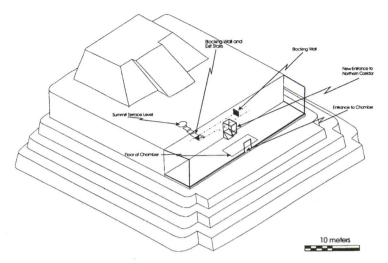

10 meters

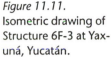

Figure 11.11.
Isometric drawing of
Structure 6F-3 at Yax-
uná, Yucatán.

three stones represent the Three-Stone-Place and the Turtle. A confirmation that the people of Yaxuná thought this way in the fourth century is
found in the intense fire which a later lord built on the central stone
when he broke through the plaza floor and reentered this tomb to carry
out more rituals there.

The occupant of this tomb also wore large and elaborate ear-flares of
carved orange/red spondylus shell. These are insignia of two gods, First
Father and Chaak. First Father we have already discussed; the Classic
period Chaak gods were guardians of the celestial portal and also responsible for cracking open the turtle shell with their lightning axes to release
First Father at rebirth. So this individual was laid out on the White Path,
next to the Three-Stone-Place, wearing the insignia of the god born there.
His body was tightly bound, presumably in a shroud, and the cloth was
decorated with jade and shell sequins. His hands were directly over his
loins, clutching three large jade beads. We think these were strung on the
strap of a bundle, for directly below his hands was a concentration of
jewels in shell and stone that were probably inside the bundlebag. These
included a profile greenstone head wearing the white headband of lord-
ship, another expression of the royal status. There were two small full-
figured dancers dubbed "Charlie Chaplins" in Maya archaeology. In
southern lowland monumental imagery, these are companions on the
sky-snakes, back-racks, and celestial scaffolds accompanying kings.
Finally, the bundle contained the face of a young lord with his hair cut
into sweeping scrolls on the sides and a square patch in the middle. The
sweeping forward of the hair in a scroll is diagnostic of the ancestral hero
twins in Classic iconography. Scrolls can represent clouds in Maya and
even earlier Olmec art (Houston and Stuart 1990; Stone 1996; Reilly
1996; Taube 1996) and recently Karl Taube (personal communication,
1993) has made the case that such head scrolls as found on the Yaxuná
carving represent the rain gods, the Chaaks. Finally, the image wears a

grand handlebar moustache, a fashion of some Maya kings of this part of the Early Classic period. In the last analysis, this is what Schele and Jeffrey Miller (1983) called an *Ahaw* Pectoral, another insignia of kings and other high elite.

We think this shell visage represents the deceased as he imagined himself reborn in the sky after his journey into the underworld. In addition to the Three-Stone-Place patterns, we have one other piece of relevant evidence. Up against the northwestern wall of the tomb, the ritualists had placed a turtle shell. For the Classic Maya, the turtle constellation descended into the northwestern horizon as a prelude to the rising of the Stood-Up-Sky, world tree, form of the Milky Way. The setting of the turtle marked the sacrificial death of First Father in the underworld; the rising of the Stood-Up-Sky north–south oriented form of the Milky Way was associated with the act of entering the sky or entering the white path by First Father and subsequent Maya kings. So not only do we propose that the occupant of this tomb was a king, but we also think that he was arranged in the midst of his final performance on the path that led from down inside the world up into the sky above it.

Thus, an earlier version of Structure-6F-3 was the resting place for a Maya king, a man placed right on the centerline of the structure in a resurrection pose. How does this relate to the later building with its centerline path plan? We cannot be absolutely certain of how the connection worked at this phase of research because we have not finished excavating the corridors of the labyrinth. Nevertheless, there is surely a direct relationship between the earlier building and its patron and the later building and its patron. We can say this because the person who commissioned the creation of the new building phase also built the U-shaped enclosure over the plaza floor sealing the antechamber of the tomb. During the course of the construction of this new pyramid, when the labyrinthine corridors were raised to about half their final height, ritualists broke through the floor of the antechamber area and reentered the tomb. There they lit a fire inside a ceramic container on the central stone of the three stones. They also piled freshly quarried stones into sloping heaps on both sides of the body, careful not to disturb it or the 13 vessels in the tomb. In this way, with the same stones they were using to create the new great mountain over the old one, they made a miniature clefted mountain inside the tomb with the dead king in its center.

They took some things from the tomb in this ritual. We found one polished *Sak-Hunal* greenstone jewel in the antechamber debris in 1993, and another *Sak-Hunal* jewel was discovered on the back dirt pile in 1994. Evidently this had been missed in the screening of excavated dirt in the previous season. So actually there were three royal jewels, and this is how the Maya preferred to depict the royal crown from Preclassic times onward (Freidel 1990; Freidel and Suhler n.d.). Ritualists had taken two of the jewels from inside the tomb and cast them into the construction fill of the antechamber area and above it as they resealed the tomb area. We think that they did this to tie the king in the tomb into the new pyramid that they were building over it. We tend to think of construction as an activity that is distinct from the uses of buildings when they are completed. For the Maya, the construction process was itself ritualized and continuous with the uses of the completed structure (Freidel and Schele 1989; see Sharer et al., chapter 10, this volume).

In the case of this pyramid, the man who built the new, grander version of the structure literally went into an underground house, the tomb of a predecessor, by means of a great horizontal U-shaped cleft in the mountain. Then he came out of that underworld and went up onto the surface of the new mountain by means of his uncompleted labyrinthine corridors. He finished his building with a permanent subsurface labyrinth, a doorway into the front centerline face of the pyramidal mountain, and probably with the trapdoor access to the raised plaza above. Recall that king Yax-Pac in Temple 11 at Copan displayed his ancestors on his sanctuary throne inside the death portal of the White Bone Dragon. At the center of the panel depicting these kings and other ancestors, the founder of the Copan dynasty, Yax K'uk-Mo', is shown displaying a scepter to Yax-Pac. Inside the sanctuaries of the Cross Group at Palenque, Chan-Bahlum depicted himself in communion with his dead father, wrapped in his shroud. They both display unwrapped bundles containing powerful images of the gods, including the *Sak-Hunal*. We think that the Yaxuná patron of the labyrinth in Structure 6F-3 was performing just such rites, only with a real body and with real insignia.

The next patron of Structure 6F-3 modified this path plan by adding a sanctuary room on the centerline in front of the original doorway into the labyrinth. This new subsurface sanctuary echoes the sanctuaries in the Late Preclassic dance platforms at Yaxuná. The new front of the centerline replicated the massive terrace design of the original labyrinth doorway, a clear declaration that the doorway led not into a freestanding stone superstructure, but directly into the interior of the pyramid-mountain. Intriguingly, the doorway from the new sanctuary into the old labyrinthine corridors was not at floor level, but set 1.2 meters above it. Moreover, the old doorway was severely narrowed into a niche just large enough for a person to stand or sit in. We think that is precisely what was intended: a niche set above floor level, suitable for entry by means of a short ladder. That is the design displayed on the Piedras Negras accession stelae. Recall that the stone version of this stairway-niche design at Toniná has the doorway into the labyrinth inside the terrace right behind it. We have only design evidence so far, but it suggests that Structure 6F-3 was used by a succession of kings during the Early Classic period for rituals of journeying along the path from the underworld to the upper world.

The general meaning and sacredness of this design must have survived the time of great kings at Yaxuná. Much later, during the Terminal Classic period, this old and abandoned pyramid was refurbished by new lords. They made a new subsurface corridor in front of the sanctuary

door, cut back the terraces on each side of the sanctuary so that it was literally an underground house, and placed a stairway over the centerline.
What they did with this design we cannot say with certainty, although
kings at Uxmal in the nearby Puuc region designed the Temple of the
Magician in the Terminal Classic period, and so they evidently understood the basic message of the path plan (see Kowalski and Dunning,
chapter 12, this volume). Later still, enemies destroyed the centerline
sanctuary and corridors in Structure 6F-3 at Yaxuná with elaborate sacrificial rituals, including the killing of a sacrificial victim as they brought
down the corbeled roofs.

We have reviewed several examples of the path plan design dating
from the Late Preclassic period, the Early Classic period, the Late Classic
period and the Conquest period. This suggests that we are dealing with a
very old and enduring function for public architecture in the lowlands.
We might be accused, were we to expand our discussion here, of seeing
path plans everywhere. Actually, the sample of documented literal
"underground" houses or labyrinths giving access to above surface areas
that might have supported perishable or masonry scaffolds is not that
large. The problem is that there are some clear metaphorical facsimiles of
the literal plan in such buildings as the Cross Group temples at Palenque.
When dealing with such symbolic variations on the theme, we run into
the problem that there are other equally valid ways of conceiving the
function of such places. For example, Stephen Houston (1996) recently
proposed that the sanctuaries in the Cross Group at Palenque were symbolic sweatbaths, another "underground house" reading. Karl Taube
(1994: 661) makes a cogent case for identifying the coronation room of
the Palace at Palenque as a metaphorical birthing hut. The magic bird
above the sky band inside that building carries a rope in his mouth similar to the rope slung over a roof beam and clung to by birthing Maya
women. Sweatbaths are places for curing people, preparing them for rituals or carrying them out, or helping women recover from giving birth.
Birth enclosures, small dark sanctums, are still made inside some Maya
houses today to prevent exposure to evil winds (Grace Bascope personal
communication, 1994). Birth is an integral feature of our own understanding of the path plan journey from the sanctuary into the scaffold,
the pivotal act of resurrection by First Father. We believe that the Maya
understood and cultivated multiple symbolic meanings and functions
for public buildings and that this quality reinforced the transcendent
power of such places. So the path plan might be a literal design for a
building, and under such circumstances the journey from death back
into life was probably the major ritual there. But it could also be a symbolic aspect of a building not literally designed for it, alluding to that
journey while other performances of a different kind were enacted.

The Maya path plan, in our view, was primarily incorporated in public buildings to celebrate the accession of kings. The journey of First
Father into the world of the dead, his sacrifice, and his resurrection in

the middle of the sky was enacted in such buildings by the holy lords who followed him. If we are right in this functional hypothesis, then the little dance platforms we found.at Yaxuná should be such accession facilities. So far, we have no direct evidence for royal use of these two platforms, although they do conform in many respects to a pattern of "throne-seats" (Schele n.d.) and scaffolds that is emerging in Maya research. As Schele shows (Freidel, Schele, and Parker 1993), the First Three-Stone-Place where First Father was reborn in the sky was composed of three "throne-seats"(*kunob* in Maya). The glyph for the Three-Stone-Place is made with a cluster of three round stones. At Copan, William Fash has discovered a remarkable round bas-relief carved marker deep inside Structure 10L-26 (see Stuart and Stuart 1993: 37; Sharer et al., chapter 10, figure 10.9, this volume). This marker, framed in the quatrefoil *Ol* or portal place symbol, shows the founder of the Copan dynasty and his first successor. One passage in the glyphic text makes reference to the "smoking" of a *kun* or throne-seat (Schele n.d.). The Maya word for smoke, *butz*, also means spirit and likely here refers to the consecration and ensouling of this stone. If so, then this stone is itself the throne-seat mentioned in the text. On top of this stone, Fash discovered a burnt offering, in the midst of which were three large round stones laid in a triangle. Thus a quatrefoil *Ol* is associated with the founder of a royal dynasty depicted on a throne-seat such as characterized the birth place of First Father with three real stones on top of it.

Structure 6E-53 at Yaxuná, the second dance platform we excavated there, had an undulating quatrefoil pattern of corridors around the sanctuary. Our test excavation through the floor of the sanctuary revealed an offering of a large Late Preclassic red bucket with a plate lid. Inside this bucket was a single large, round stone smoothly pecked from local limestone. Underneath this round stone ritualists had placed a greenstone axehead nestled into a greenstone mirror. The axe is associated with the god *K'awil* and also with the god Chaak—the Chaaks used axes to open the turtle in some images of the resurrection of First Father. The mirror is associated with the *Sak-Hunal*, the White Eternity, and also with *Tzuk*, a glyph meaning partition and having to do with the centering and ordering of the world (Freidel, Schele, and Parker 1993: 140). We propose that this offering marks the structure as a *kun*, a throne-seat, and as an effigy of one of the first three throne-seats marking the place where First Father was reborn.

Recall that the other dance platform, Structure 6F-120, had evidence of postholes suitable for scaffolding on its summit. Remember also that the sanctuaries inside the Cross Group temples at Palenque are called *kunul*, magic houses, throne-seat houses; and that there are masonry scaffolds on the roofs of these same temples. The main text of the Temple of the Cross pertains to the consecration and dedication of the world as the house of First Father, the Raised-Up-Sky Place, the eightfold partition place. We suspect that there is a significant cosmological relationship between throne-seats, scaffolds, and First Father. There is an important image on Classic Maya painted vases called the Holmul Dancer, after the site of Holmul in Guatemala (see Reents-Budet 1994, for a review of this imagery). This composition depicts the resurrected First Father dancing in his finery. Typically, the god wears an elaborate backrack that, as Schele (n.d.) describes it, has a celestial band arching across the top, the magic bird, Itzam-Yeh, perched on this band marking it as a "conjuring house" or *kunul*, and usually a *witz* or mountain (pyramid) personified mask at the base. One of these Holmul Dancer vases (Kerr 3400) has a text referring to one of the dancers that reads *Wak-Chan-Nal Ch'akte'tan kun Kan Ahaw*. Schele (n.d.) deciphers this text as "Six-Sky Maize *chakte* in the seat of the snake lord" (king of Calakmul, a great southern lowland kingdom). However, Nikolai Grube and Werner Nahm (1994) have suggested the reading of scaffold for *ch'akte'* and Schele (personal communication, 1994) accepts this reading. Moreover, *Wakah-Chan-Nal*, a very close statement to that given on the vase, is deciphered elsewhere by Schele (Freidel, Schele, and Parker 1993: 71, figure 2:8) as Raised-Up-Sky Place, one of the names of the world when First Father ordered it as his house at the beginning of this creation. It is the place First Father set in order when he entered the sky and was reborn in the Three-Stone Place. So we would gloss this text as "Raised-Up-Sky Place scaffold in the throne-seat of the snake lord (the king of Calakmul)." For us, this image represents the king of Calakmul dancing as First Father at the place of his throne and scaffold.

As social scientists working with material evidence of architecture, how can we confirm such hypothesized functions at Yaxuná? We think we can make predictions on the basis of such ideas and then carry out research to test them in the field. In the case of the dance platforms, we offer the following observations and predictions. First, the reason we could document the two dance platforms is that they were carefully and ritually destroyed, then completely abandoned for the rest of the occupation at Yaxuná—more than 1,000 years. The corridors and sanctuaries were packed with the debris from the summit and upper levels of the stepped platforms. Before bringing down the roofs, enigmatic niches and holes in the corridors were packed with debris and sealed with plaster plugs.

We postulate that these dance platforms were ritually terminated because their patron was deceased. At first, we thought perhaps the patron was buried inside one of these two platforms. But thorough excavation revealed no evidence for a penetration through the floors or walls for the insertion of a tomb or cyst burial. With analysis, however, we could see that these two platforms could not conform to our understanding of Maya cosmology or spatial pattern by themselves. The dominant Late Preclassic ceremonial pattern is the triadic arrangement of pyramids (see Freidel, Schele, and Parker 1993: 140, 433). Moreover, that is the dominant pattern at Yaxuná. Cosmologically, the triad is the primordial pattern of the Three-Stone-Place, the place of First Father's birth. We have already found one of the "stones" in one of the sanctuaries, Structure 6F-53. As we carry out stabilization and consolidation in Structure 6F-120, we predict that we will find a duplicate offering with another round stone in it under the floor of the sanctuary.

But if these dance platforms are as we identify them, throne-stone-scaffold places, we think that there might well be three of them rather than the two we can see on our topographic map. The pattern of the three-stone-places in architecture is a triangle. To complete a more or less equilateral triangle with the existing dance platforms, there ought to be a third one on the western side—underneath the main pyramid of the eastern acropolis at Yaxuná. That great pyramid forms another triad with two pyramids to its west on the raised surface of the acropolis. We postulate that this pyramid was built to bury the remains of the patron of the dance platforms, remains that are in the sanctuary, the "throne-stone" place, of a third and western dance platform which was ritually destroyed at the same time as the other two dance platforms that we have investigated. We further predict that when we excavate into the back side of the pyramid and discover this third dance platform, the person buried in the sanctuary will have among his mortuary furniture insignia jewels of the kingship. We might not find what we predict, and while that would not disconfirm the overall functions we ascribe to the dance platforms, it would tell us we were wrong in some important particulars—notions of symmetry in civic planning at Yaxuná, for instance. But we correctly predicted the highly improbable feature of the trapdoor entrance out of the labyrinth on Structure 6F-3 onto the raised plaza of that pyramid. Working from the Maya perspective, a third dance platform would be consistent with what they think about such matters. One cannot prove the validity of ideas this way, but it does show reasonable connections between interpretations and evidence.

Maya architecture ranks among the finest in the Pre-Columbian world, some would say in the world as such. More than a simple gauge of organized social energy, it is a rich resource for insight into how this ancient society thought about the human and natural cycles. We have argued that some Maya buildings were designed not simply as static monuments to the power of their human patrons, but as places for the performance of transcendent events linking those rulers both to their both human followers and their supernatural patrons. We have a long way to go on the Maya path of life, but we are striving to follow where it leads.

Note

1. A more complete discussion of the mythological concepts and figures discussed above, and their associated artistic imagery and iconography, appears in chapter 2 of Freidel, Schele, and Parker (1993).

12

The Architecture of Uxmal

*The Symbolics of Statemaking at
a Puuc Maya Regional Capital*

Jeff Karl Kowalski & Nicholas P. Dunning

The site of Uxmal, located in the hilly region south of the Puuc range in northwestern Yucatán, is generally considered one of the major centers of the ancient Maya (figure 12.1). Based on the imposing size and the architectural sophistication of its major edifices as well as the prominent role it plays in the native historical accounts contained in the Books of Chilam Balam of Chumayel, Mani, and Tizimin, Sylvanus G. Morley (1946: table VII) included Uxmal in his class 1 ranking of Maya sites. More recently, Uxmal was classed as a rank 1 site in the evaluation of Adams and Jones (1981) and also in the survey of northern Maya sites in the *Atlas arqueológico del estado de Yucatán* (Garza Tarazona and Kurjack 1980).

In this chapter we outline some more recent evidence indicating that Uxmal was the dominant site in the eastern Puuc district during the late Terminal Classic period and that it became the capital of a regional state which coalesced during the late ninth and early tenth centuries. Two sources of evidence are adduced in support of this interpretation. First we examine several key examples of Uxmal's architecture, architectural sculpture, and dynastic monuments to discover what types of messages concerning the site's ideological and political significance the elite encoded therein. Then we present a summary of evidence regarding Uxmal's position in a settlement hierarchy in the eastern Puuc district. These combined emic and etic perspectives provide us with two mutually supportive, though not identical, sources of evidence indicating Uxmal's regional political importance.

Uxmal and the Puuc Region

It has been known for some time that Uxmal, like many other Puuc centers such as Kabah, Sayil, and Chacmultún, had its greatest floruit during

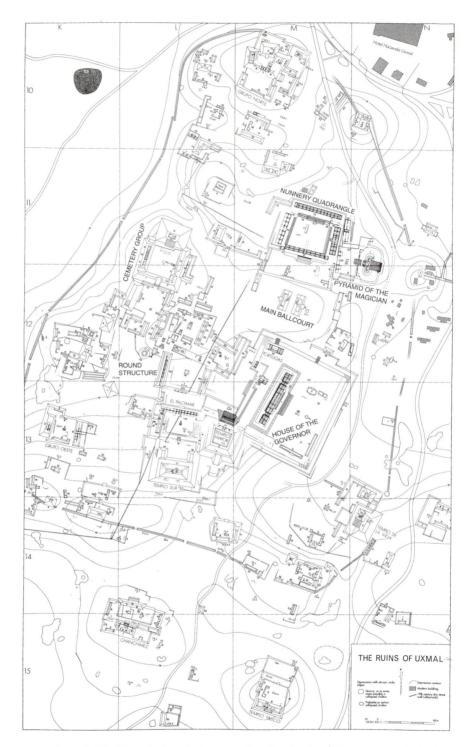

Figure 12.1. Map of Uxmal, showing the distribution of structures within the walled central civic-ceremonial zone (adapted from Graham 1992).

the Terminal Classic period, between approximately A.D. 770 and 950 (Andrews V 1979; Ball 1979a; Pollock 1980; Andrews V and Sabloff 1986; Kowalski 1987). Furthermore, Uxmal seems to have had a particularly pronounced episode of building during the reign of a late ruler known as "Lord Chac," whose name glyph appears on the hieroglyphic rings of the Main Ballcourt (Ballcourt 1) in connection with a probable date corresponding to A.D. 905.[1] This ruler's name also appears on a painted capstone in the Nunnery Quadrangle plausibly dated to A.D. 907 (Thompson 1973: 61–62; Kowalski 1987: 34–35, 72). The House of the Governor, similar to the Nunnery Quadrangle in concept, architectural style, and specific elements of architectural sculpture, has also been dated to around A.D. 890–910. On the roughly contemporary late Terminal Classic Stela 14 (figure 12.2), "Lord Chac" stands on a double-headed jaguar throne closely related to the actual bicephalic jaguar seat on a low platform in front of the House of the Governor.

An examination of Uxmal's architecture and associated architectural sculpture supports the idea that Uxmal exerted some sort of regional

Figure 12.2. Uxmal Stela 14, showing "Lord Chac" standing on a two-headed jaguar throne and accompanied by a warrior resembling "Toltec" or Itzá figures at Chichén Itzá (after Graham 1992).

political dominance during the Terminal Classic period. One building critical to this interpretation is the House of the Governor (figure 12.3). The House of the Governor rests on a primary platform some 25–40 feet (7.4–11.8 meters) high and 540 feet (160 meters) long by 450 feet (133 meters) wide, one of the largest such basal platforms constructed in northern Yucatán (the platform of the Kinich K'akmo pyramid at Izamal is comparable; Barrera Rubio 1991). It has been estimated that approximately 1,200 laborers would have needed to work 40 days a year for some 33 years to complete the edifice (Kowalski 1987: 93; cf. Erasmus 1965). Although such computations are subject to some adjustments, it is clear that the person who commissioned the building was able to call on large pool of laborers from Uxmal and its immediate surroundings. The upper facade of the 328-foot (97 meter) long range of the House of the Governor itself is blanketed by a complex, interpenetrating array of architectural sculpture executed in a "stone mosaic" technique typical of Puuc architecture (Foncerrada 1965; Sharp 1978; Kowalski 1987). These sculptures include a "lattice" pattern background which duplicates the strand-over-strand structure of a woven mat, a well-known symbol of rulership (Robicsek 1975), and bold step-fret designs which were a symbol shared by elites in Oaxaca, the Gulf Coast, and the northern Maya at this time (Sharp 1978; see Wilkerson, chapter 5, this volume). In addition, dozens of long-snouted reptilian mask panels believed to represent

Figure 12.3. The House of the Governor at Uxmal, with a two-headed jaguar throne visible in the foreground (photograph by Jeff Kowalski).

the Yucatec rain god, Chaak, adorn the House of the Governor. On the eastern front of the building, human figural sculptures of different sizes and "ranks" culminate in the depiction of dominant individual, presumably "Lord Chac" himself, above the central doorway (figure 12.4). He is portrayed as a cosmic ruler surrounded by two-headed serpents with "sky-band" bodies. The imposing size of the House of the Governor, as well as the depiction of "Lord Chac" at the center of a series of ranked figures, implies that Uxmal's ruler intended to convey the message that he stood at the apex of both an intrasite and regional political hierarchy. Other specific symbols, such as a bicephalic jaguar throne in front of the House of the Governor, also seem to have been intended to indicate and reinforce the primacy of Uxmal's ruler. Because its parallel-vaulted, multiroomed, range-type plan seems like a much expanded version of typical, smaller masonry houses in the Puuc region (Ruppert and Smith 1957; Barrera Rubio 1981), the House of the Governor has been interpreted as a combined royal residence and adminstrative center constructed during the reign of and occupied by "Lord Chac" (Kowalski 1987).[2]

In addition to the House of the Governor, the Nunnery Quadrangle was the other most imposing architectural group constructed during the reign of "Lord Chac" (figure 12.5). In the Nunnery Quadrangle "Lord Chac" and his architect seem to have made a conscious effort to embody

Figure 12.4. Central figural sculpture of the House of the Governor, depicting the ruler "Lord Chac" seated against a "cosmic" backdrop of bicephalic serpents with "sky-band" bodies (photograph by Jeff Kowalski).

Figure 12.5. General view of the Nunnery Quadrangle from the south, showing the Main Ballcourt in the foreground (photograph by Jeff Kowalski).

key elements of essential Maya cosmological concepts in the plan and sculpture to convey the idea that Uxmal had become the primary religious center and political capital of the eastern Puuc region. In particular, it appears that the quadrangular layout and approximate correspondence of the principal buildings to the cardinal points represents an effort to replicate the well-documented quadripartite horizontal organization of the Maya cosmos, with east and west associated with the rising and setting sun and north and south corresponding to the upperworld and underworld.[3]

This interpretation is necessarily hypothetical, but there is significant evidence to support it in the form of relative heights of building platforms, doorway counts, and specific elements of architectural sculpture. First, regarding the correlation of buildings to the upperworld, middleworld, and underworld, it is noteworthy that the North Structure occupies the highest platform in the complex, the South Structure rests on the lowest, and the East and West Structures are supported on platforms of equal, intermediate height. The North Structure, located in the presumed Upperworld position, also has 13 exterior doorways, conforming to the number of celestial layers in Maya cosmology (Roys 1967: 99; Thompson 1970: 280). Small huts surmounted by two-headed serpents are visible above several of its doors. Bicephalic reptilian creatures, depicted in forms such as the Cosmic or Celestial Monster (Thompson 1970; Carlson and Landis 1985: 117–120, 129; Schele and Miller 1986: 45) or the Ceremonial Bar (Spinden 1913: 49–50; W. Taylor 1941; Kubler 1984: 248), have well-documented upperworld associations and relate to the homophony between the words for serpent and sky in Yucatec and Chol Maya (Houston 1984: 791).

The West Structure, corresponding to a postulated middleworld position corresponding to the point of the sun's descent into the underworld, has seven doorways, perhaps associated with Maya concepts regarding a seven-layered earth (Thompson 1960: 276; Roys 1967: 101; Kubler 1977). The earth-related aspect of the West Structure seems confirmed by the appearance of the aged male turtle-man earth deity, God N, above the central doorway (figure 12.6a), and as several smaller versions elsewhere on the facade. God N, or Pawahtun, is the Maya "world sustainer," an earth- and sky-bearer corresponding to the Mam, an earth-dwelling mountain deity of the Kekchi and Pokomchi, and to the Tzotzil Maya Vasak Men,

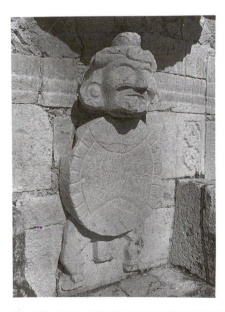

Figure 12.6. (*a*) (*at left*) Sculpture of God N turtle-man figure above the central doorway of the West Structure of the Nunnery Quadrangle (photograph by Jeff Kowalski).

Figure 12.6. (*b*) (*below*) Drawing of Tikal Altar 4 (after Jones and Satterthwaite 1982: fig. 58).

the gods who stand at the four corners of and hold up the earth (Coe 1973: 14–15; Vogt 1976: 15–16; Schele and Miller 1986: 4, 61; Taube 1989: 355). God N is associated with the entrance to the underworld on Tikal Altar 4 (Jones and Satterthwaite 1982: 79, figure 58), depicting four old turtle-men contained in cavelike mouths of mountain/earth *kawak/witz* monsters (Taylor 1979; Tate 1982; Spero 1987; Stuart 1987: 17–25) (figure 12.6b). God N could be referred to as a Bakab as well as a Pawahtun (Taube 1988b). It is the Bakab'ob, whom Landa describes as closely related to the Chaaks and the Pawahtuns, who are associated with the great flood which preceded the present formation of the present world (Tozzer 1941), and with the subsequent reestablishment of quadripartite order through the raising of the Trees of Abundance at the quadrants of the world.

The South Structure has nine openings (eight doors and central portal vault) on its north and south sides, perhaps correlating with the concept of the nine-layered underworld (Thompson 1960: 208–210; Aveni and Hartung 1986: 34). Above the doorways are miniature Maya huts crowned with reptilian masks and sprouting vegetation scrolls (Ruz Lhuillier 1959: 21; Kubler 1984: 270; Barrera Rubio 1987: 90) (figure 12.7a). These images recall the maize plant rising from the earth reptilian with kan cross forehead on the Tablet of the Foliated Cross at Palenque (Maudslay 1889–1902, 4: plate 81), and a related depiction of a leafy maize god emerging from a cleft *kawak/witz* monster head on the sculptured pillars of the Lower Temple of the Jaguars at Chichén Itzá (Taube 1985: 175) (figure 12.7b). In a similar image, the maize god and two other God K figures are portrayed emerging from cleft turtle carapaces on a sculptured cylindrical stone from Uxmal (Pollock 1980: 271, figure 468). Various related scenes occur on Late Classic polychrome or "Codex Style" vases (Robicsek and Hales 1981: figure 59; Taube 1985: 175, figure 6a). Taube (1985: 175) suggests that the young maize god rising from the turtle carapace is also a variant of Hun Hunahpu, the "first father" of the Hero Twins in the *Popol Vuh*, and a solar-maize deity who is resurrected annually in the underworld. The maize-sprouting masks of the South Structure of the Nunnery Quadrangle seem to pertain to this mythic complex, thus referring to the regeneration of the maize/sun god within the earth.

The Main Ballcourt (Ballcourt 1) at Uxmal occupies a centralized position, located between the primary platforms of the Nunnery Quadrangle and the House of the Governor (see figures 12.1 and 12.5). Although the dating of Ballcourt 1 has been disputed (cf. Morley 1920: 514–515; Blom 1934; Ruz Lhuillier 1958; Bricker and Bricker 1996), present evidence indicates that it was constructed during the Terminal Classic period. As noted, Kelley (1982: 15) suggests that the date on the east ring of the court corresponds to 10.3.15.16.14 2 *Ix* 17 (written 16) *Pop* (A.D. 905). The fact that the Uxmal ruler, "Lord Chac," is referred to on both rings (Kelley 1982: 16; Kowalski 1987: 68–74) provides strong support for the early tenth century date.

Figure 12.7. (a) (at left)
Miniature hut surmounted by a reptilian mask and sprouting vegetation, located above the doorways of the South Structure of the Nunnery Quadrangle (photograph by Jeff Kowalski).

Figure 12.7. (b) (top)
Maize god emerging from a cleft kawak/witz reptilian head-turtle carapace, upper panel of piers in the Lower Temple of the Jaguars, Chichén Itzá (after Seler 1960, 5: abb. 192).

The central axis of the Main Ballcourt's playing alley is aligned so that it forms part of an integrated architectural assemblage, uniting it in the north with the vaulted entrance through the South Structure of the Nunnery Quadrangle and with a stairway leading up to the House of the Turtles in the south (Ruz Lhuillier 1958: 639; Hartung 1971: 52–53; G. Andrews 1975: 287–289; Barrera Rubio 1988: 38). The relationship between the Main Ballcourt and the Nunnery Quadrangle is particularly emphatic, suggesting that the court was situated so that its meanings would complement those of the quadrangle. In general, Mesoamerican ballcourts have strong associations with the underworld and with mythic cycles involving the death and resurrection of deities connected with astronomical bodies such as the sun, Venus, and the moon, and with corresponding seasonal agricultural cycles (Krickeberg 1966; Pasztory 1972; Cohodas 1975; Gillespie 1991; Kowalski 1993). Classic Maya ballplayers sometimes impersonated the Classic versions of the Hero Twins, Hunahpu and Xbalanque, mentioned in the *Popol Vuh*. The central marker of Ballcourt A-IIb at Copan, Honduras, portrays a figure glyphically named Hun Ahau (Hunahpu) confronting an underworld deity within a quatrefoil frame symbolizing the opening to the underworld (Baudez 1984; Schele and Miller 1986: 251–253; Kowalski and Fash 1991). Solar macaw sculptures and maize cobs and leafy vegetation formed part of the architectural sculpture, indicating that one of the purposes of the game was to magically sustain astronomical/agricultural cycles. According to Ruz Lhuillier (1958: 638) "a sculptured stone of small size which apparently symbolized a cob of maize" probably formed part of the facade of the east building of Uxmal Ballcourt 1. Presumably, the maize refers to the agricultural fertility associations for the game at Uxmal.

It is probable that the architect of the Nunnery Quadrangle located the primary platform and aligned the South Structure to take advantage of and incorporate into a more comprehensive planning scheme the already extant Pyramid of the Magician, located to the east (figure 12.8). The Pyramid of the Magician was constructed in several phases. The earliest of these was the Lower West Building, a range-type structure forming the east side of a small quadrangular courtyard that also includes the House of the Birds on the west. Following the construction of two temples now encased by the substructure of the later pyramid, a western temple featuring a Puuc replica of the Chenes-style dragon mouth entrance was built as the fourth stage. The stacked masks flanking the stairway, as well as the gaping reptilian doorway, identify the fourth-stage pyramid-temple as an artificial mountain or *witz*, with a cavelike portal to the earth's interior at its summit. Flanking the doorway of the temple are sky-bands containing symbols of the sun, Venus, and other celestial bodies (Carlson and Landis 1985). The entrance to this temple is visible above and to the east of the East Structure of the Nunnery Quadrangle from the center of

Figure 12.8. The Pyramid of the Magician as seen from the north facade of the South Structure of the Nunnery Quadrangle (photograph by Jeff Kowalski).

the courtyard, but, more notably, it lies directly on axis with a line extended from the north facade of the South Structure, and a viewer looking along this sightline sees the cave-dragon mouth entrance framed by the corners of the East and South Structure (figure 12.8). The placement seems to form a critical transition from the underworld position of the South Structure to the middle world location of the East Structure. In this respect, a human ruler emerging from the dragon maw would be likened to Venus or the sun rising out of the monstrous earth gullet.[4]

It has been known for some time that the House of the Governor at Uxmal has an orientation that is skewed relative to many of the other major structures at Uxmal, so that an alignment perpendicular to its central doorway, then over the Picote column and the small platform supporting the two-headed jaguar throne in front of the building, points to a small mound on the horizon: a pyramidal platform at the site of Cehtzuc (formerly identified as the site of Nohpat; Aveni 1975: 184–185, table 5; Sprajc 1990; Bricker and Bricker 1996). This alignment (118° 05') marks the azimuth of Venus rise at its most southerly declination around A.D. 750 (118° 03'). Interestingly, this same azimuth is also delineated by a line passing from the dragon mouth entrance of the Pyramid of the Magician, across the East and West ranges of the Nunnery Quadrangle, and over the Stela Platform (Dunning 1992: 148). Recently, Dunning has observed that if this line is extended it passes out through the gap in the Puuc hill ridge to the northwest, which he interprets as the "mouth of the celestial serpent and earth monster as manifest in the landscape." In addition, he has suggested that:

> The Uxmal-Nohpat-Kabah sacbe system may have further manifested this geomantic alignment, by recreating the celestial serpent on the terrestrial landscape. A Maya ruler emerging from the Adivino mask temple would have embodied the power of Venus as lord of the Underworld and companion of the Sun, and the spirits of his divine ancestors through this synergized union of ritual, architecture, and landscape. (Dunning 1992: 148)

According to the cosmological model we are proposing, the East Structure of the Nunnery Quadrangle is associated with the middleworld and the direction of the emergence of the sun from the underworld. The iconographic evidence is not as clearcut in this instance, but it is probably significant that the edifice has five doorways, a number related to the earth's surface, associated with the quadripartite division of horizontal space centered on a world axis. It also is possible that the distinctive, reticulated owl sculptures located at the center of the tiered serpent bar arrangements above the doorways pertain to a Teotihuacan-related cult of war and sacrifice connected with Venus and the emergence of the Sun from the underworld (cover illustration). Classic Maya art often features owls coupled with other prominent Teotihuacan-derived costume elements and iconographic motifs in contexts associated with warfare and captive or personal sacrifice (Stone 1989; Schele and Freidel 1990: 156–164, 443–444, n. 45; Taube 1992). Taube (1992: 2, 37) has related the reticulated appearance of the Uxmal owls to the appearance of the "war serpent" creatures which alternate with feathered serpent heads on the Old Temple of Quetzalcoatl at Teotihuacan (see Kowalski, chapter 4, this volume), and which also occur as a basic component of the Teotihuacan warrior complex in Classic Maya art. He suggests that such Teotihuacan iconographic elements may have been connected with a cult of sacred warfare associated with "cosmogonic acts of creation," particularly the creation of the sun at Teotihuacan. Thus, the Uxmal owl sculptures could pertain to a martial complex connected with the birth (and cyclical rebirth) of the sun and Venus. In addition, the East Structure's "owl-and-weapons" symbol might also be an iconographic reference to the ethno-historically documented "founder" of Uxmal, Ah Kuy Tok Tutul Xiu ("he of the owl flint Tutul Xiu"?).[5]

The approximate center of the Nunnery Quadrangle was marked by an upright, cylindrical stone column (see figure 12.8). This monument recalls the large stone column worshiped as the *Yaxcheel Cab* ("Green Tree of Abundance" or "First Tree of the World") by the Itzá at their Island capital of Tayasal, as well as recalling the *akantun*, the stelalike stone pillars erected at the four entrances to a Yucatec Maya town. According to Roys (1967: 171), each of these was considered a directional tree, and "probably had its mythological counterpart at one of the four cardinal points." It is probable that the Nunnery Quadrangle's column was similarly conceived of as the gigantic ceiba tree that formed the central axis of the

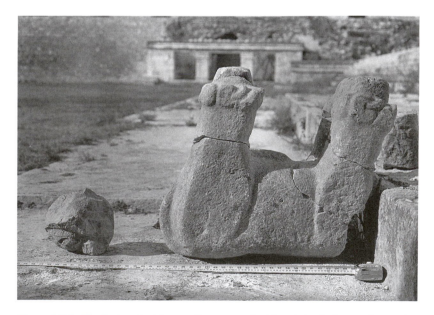

Figure 12.9. Single-headed jaguar throne, probably originally located near the center of the Nunnery Quadrangle (photograph by Jeff Kowalski).

cosmos. A single-headed jaguar throne was originally discovered on a low platform near the remains of the stone column just described (Ruz Lhuillier 1955: 50; 1959: 14; Kowalski 1990) (figure 12.9). Juxtaposing the jaguar throne and the columnar "world tree" apparently reflects a long-lived Maya tradition that equated the king and the *Yaxcheel Cab* (Schele and Miller 1986: 109), associating the ruler with primordial acts of world creation (Freidel, Schele, and Parker 1993: 66–68).

This analysis of the Nunnery Quadrangle indicates that a human ruler occupying the central jaguar throne formed the focal point of an architectural assemblage whose quadripartite plan, doorway counts, structural platform levels, and aspects of whose architectural sculpture seem to embody traditional Maya cosmological concepts. Many of the other architectural sculpture motifs of the Nunnery Quadrangle, although not as clearly integrated into this scheme, can also be interpreted as symbols of rulership and political authority. For example, both the North and West Structures display various warrior and captive figures, suggesting that Uxmal's elite boasted of their victories in battle on the facades of buildings, just as southern Maya rulers did on their stelae, lintels, and mural paintings (Marcus 1978). The roofline of the North Structure is broken by crenellations formed of stacks of long-snouted rain god masks surmounted by goggle-eyed masks depicting the Teotihuacan Storm God (often referred to by his Postclassic Nahuatl name of Tlaloc). The presence of Storm God images has been interpreted as a "non-Classic" cultural influence at Uxmal (Foncerrada 1965), but the Teotihuacan Storm God appears frequently in Late Classic Maya art, normally in contexts associated with warfare, captive sacrifice, and personal bloodletting (Stone 1989; Schele and Freidel 1990). Because the Storm God retained associations with the Classic period metropolis of Teotihuacan, these masks also lent legitimacy and prestige to Uxmal's rulers (Pasztory 1988b; Stone 1989)

Finally, the West Structure of the Nunnery Quadrangle features two gigantic, intertwined feathered serpent sculptures across its facade. These are normally associated with the cult of the central Mexican deity Quetzalcoatl, known in the northern Maya area as K'ukulkan. Knowledge of this foreign religious cult may have been introduced to Yucatán by the Itzá, the Maya group(s) from the southwestern Gulf Coast region (Thompson 1970; Kowalski 1989) or the Peten lakes region of northern Guatemala (Schele, Grube, and Boot 1997), who established a capital at Chichén Itzá during the ninth century. Quetzalcoatl-K'ukulkan is known to have been associated with the planet Venus, and the small visage emerging from the serpent's mouth on the West Structure is apparently an impersonator of the rain god Chaak, whose close counterpart, GI, has ties to Venus in Classic Maya inscriptions (Taube 1992: 138). Large, feathered serpent sculptures also adorned the platform walls of the Main Ballcourt at Uxmal. Its meanings at Uxmal perhaps parallel those at the Great Ballcourt at Chichén Itzá, where it also probably served as a manifestation of Venus (Milbrath 1988; Kowalski 1993). Although presented in different formats, connections among the sun, Venus, the underworld, agricultural fertility, and human sacrifice are evident in the architecture and art of both Chichén Itzá and Uxmal. In addition to its cosmological importance, the antiquity of the feathered serpent and its assocation with Teotihuacan caused it to be displayed as a symbol of divinely sanctioned political authority at many Epiclassic and Postclassic Mesoamerican elite centers and capital cities (e.g., Xochicalco, Cacaxtla, Chichén Itzá, Tula, Tenochtitlan; Carrasco 1982, Freidel 1986: 426)).

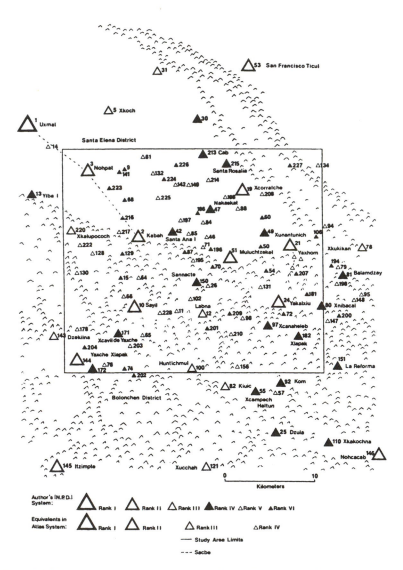

Figure 12.10. Map of the eastern or "Santa Elena" Puuc region, indicating comparative hierarchical ranks of various centers (after Dunning and Kowalski 1994: figure 3).

The themes of cosmic rulership that permeate the major structures at Uxmal imply that the site was a significant political center in the Eastern Puuc district. The nature of this role can be examined and further clarified using evidence from a recent settlement survey of the northeastern "Santa Elena District" Puuc region conducted by Dunning (1992, 1994) (figure 12.10). Dunning determined the approximate areal extent of settlements, and inventoried and mapped their settlement features. Eastern Puuc sites were ranked hierarchically based on the following factors: (1) the areal extent of the sites (which is assumed to correlate with site population); (2) the estimated volume of architecture in the site cores; and (3) the presence or absence of significant political–ideological features such as stelae, glyphic inscriptions, ballcourts, and large pyramid-temples. For each site, rank-order values were assigned to each of these values, which were then combined to determine the overall ranking of the site.

Significantly, Dunning's data indicate that Uxmal is the only Rank 1 site in the Eastern Puuc region (although Uxmal itself lies just outside of the geographic boundaries of the Santa Elena District survey zone), reconfirming Garza Tarazona and Kurjack's (1980) earlier site hierarchy in the *Atlas arqueológico del estado de Yucatán*. Uxmal covers an estimated settlement area of about 10–12 square kilometers and its civic-ceremonial core features a highly ordered assemblage of monumental architecture occupying the most massive supporting platforms in the northeastern Puuc region. As noted, the dimensions and volume of the primary platform supporting the House of the Governor surpass those of almost any other edifice in northern Yucatán, comparable only to structures such as the massive Kinich K'akmo platform at Izamal (Barrera Rubio 1991). Uxmal is also connected to two large Rank 2 sites, Nohpat and Kabah, by an artificial roadway or *sacbe* with several smaller sites clustered along its route (Kurjack, Garza, and Lucas 1979: 40; Carrasco V. 1993). In general, such intersite *sacbe* systems have been interpreted as indicating the presence of multicity polities in northern Yucatan. We have suggested that although Kabah and Nohpat originally may have been autonomous centers, Uxmal seems to have gained some sort of regional dominance and became *primus inter pares* in this *sacbe* system during the late ninth and early tenth century (Dunning and Kowalski 1994).

Andrews and Robles Castellanos (1985; Robles Castellanos and Andrews 1986) have suggested that two large-scale territorial states, with capital cities at Chichén Itzá and Cobá, arose in northern Yucatán during the Terminal Classic period. The combined evidence from architectural iconography and settlement pattern studies outlined in this chapter suggests that during the later ninth and early tenth century, Uxmal briefly became the capital of another regional state incorporating several other Santa Elena District Puuc centers. The more traditional "Classic Maya" aspects of the architecture, sculptural iconography, and dynastic inscriptions of Uxmal and other Eastern Puuc centers such as Kabah and Sayil suggest that these originally may have been politically independent kingdoms, but that at some point during the ninth century, probably as a response to the growth of centralized power at Chichén Itzá, some of the Puuc cities (e.g., Kabah, Nohpat, Uxmal) confederated in a regional state centered at Uxmal (Freidel 1992a; Dunning and Kowalski 1994).

The Chichén Itzá, Cobá, and Puuc polities (and possibly others, such as that centered at Ek Balam; Ringle, Bey, and Peraza 1991) apparently thrived concurrently and competed politically and militarily during the Terminal Classic period. Apparently, however, Chichén Itzá eventually gained the upper hand and the Puuc centers, including Uxmal, succumbed between about A.D. 925–975.[6] Although it has seemed reasonable to suppose that Chichén Itzá was vying with various cities in the Eastern Puuc region for access to and control over agricultural land and trade routes (Andrews V and Sabloff 1986: 450; Kowalski 1987: 237–239; Dunning 1992), the relationship between the elite of Uxmal and that of Chichén Itzá seems to have been a complex one. There is some important evidence Uxmal may have established close political ties and a more cooperative relationship with Chichén Itzá during the late ninth and early tenth century. Such ties are indicated by references to Chichén Itzá personages (particularly a Chichén Itzá noblewoman known as Lady Kayam K'uk) in Uxmal inscriptions (Kelley 1982; Kowalski 1986), by the presence of feathered serpent sculptures on prominent Uxmal buildings, by iconographic details on some examples of architectural sculpture or stelae, and by the parallel use of distinctive round temples.

A round structure was discovered at Uxmal in 1988 and was excavated in 1992 (figure 12.11).[7] Excavation revealed that this structure consisted of a round basal platform some 18 meters in diameter, faced with well-squared masonry, and surmounted by a single-room circular structure some 10 meters in diameter. The upper building had a masonry lower wall, but the upper walls apparently were of wattle and daub and supported a conical pole-and-thatch roof. Based on ethnohistoric sources and the discovery of an Ehécatl-like sculpture elsewhere at Uxmal, it is likely that this structure served as a temple dedicated to Ehécatl, the wind-god manifestation of Quetzalcoatl (Pollock 1936). Round buildings, probably temples to the same deity, and thought to represent Itzá influence in the Maya area, were also constructed at Chichén Itzá (e.g., the Caracol, the Casa Redonda; Ruppert 1935, 1952), Seibal (Structure C-79; Smith 1982), and Nohmul (Structure 9; Chase and Chase 1982) during the Terminal Classic-Early Postclassic period. The masonry style of the Uxmal Round Structure and associated Cehpech ceramics are consistent with a probable late ninth or early tenth century date for its construcion and use. It may represent an attempt to emulate the roughly contemporary Caracol structure at Chichén Itzá.

Even more specific similarities between Uxmal and Chichén Itzá are evident on Uxmal Stela 14, which shows the ruler "Lord Chac" accompanied by a secondary warrior figure who wears a "Toltec" sandal type common at Chichén Itzá and a distinctive necklace worn by several figures on a sculptured column from Structure 6E1 at that site (Proskouri-akoff 1950, 1970). The Uxmal warrior also carries an *atlatl* spearthrower and circular shield decorated with crescent-shaped motifs identical to those on shields adorning the frieze of the Upper Temple of the Jaguars at Chichén Itzá (Marquina 1964: lam. 267). In addition, the lower panel of Uxmal Stela 13 (Graham 1992: 4.105), a "panel-style" monument, fea-tures a figure wearing a "back mirror" and holding a circular shield like those worn and carried by "Toltec" or Itzá warriors at Chichén Itzá. He approaches a seated, higher-ranking figure on the right. Some of the less specific similarities between the two sites could be interpreted as evi-dence that Uxmal's elite were ethnically related to the rulers of Chichén Itzá (cf. Schele and Freidel 1990: 348–349), as well as indicating that they were absorbing many of the same "non-Classic" influences and cult practices visible at the latter site. The more specific parallels between the warrior on Uxmal Stelae 14 and 13, and various "Toltec-Maya" or Itzá figures at Chichén Itzá, however, could reflect some more formal military–political alliance that existed between the elites of the two cities, perhaps with "Lord Chac" and the allied rulers of Kabah and Nohpat using Chichén Itzá warriors to solidify their power in the Puuc region during the late ninth and early tenth century.

Figure 12.11. (a) The Round Structure (Structure 52) at Uxmal, one year after excavation and consolidation in 1992 (photograph by Jeff Kowalski).

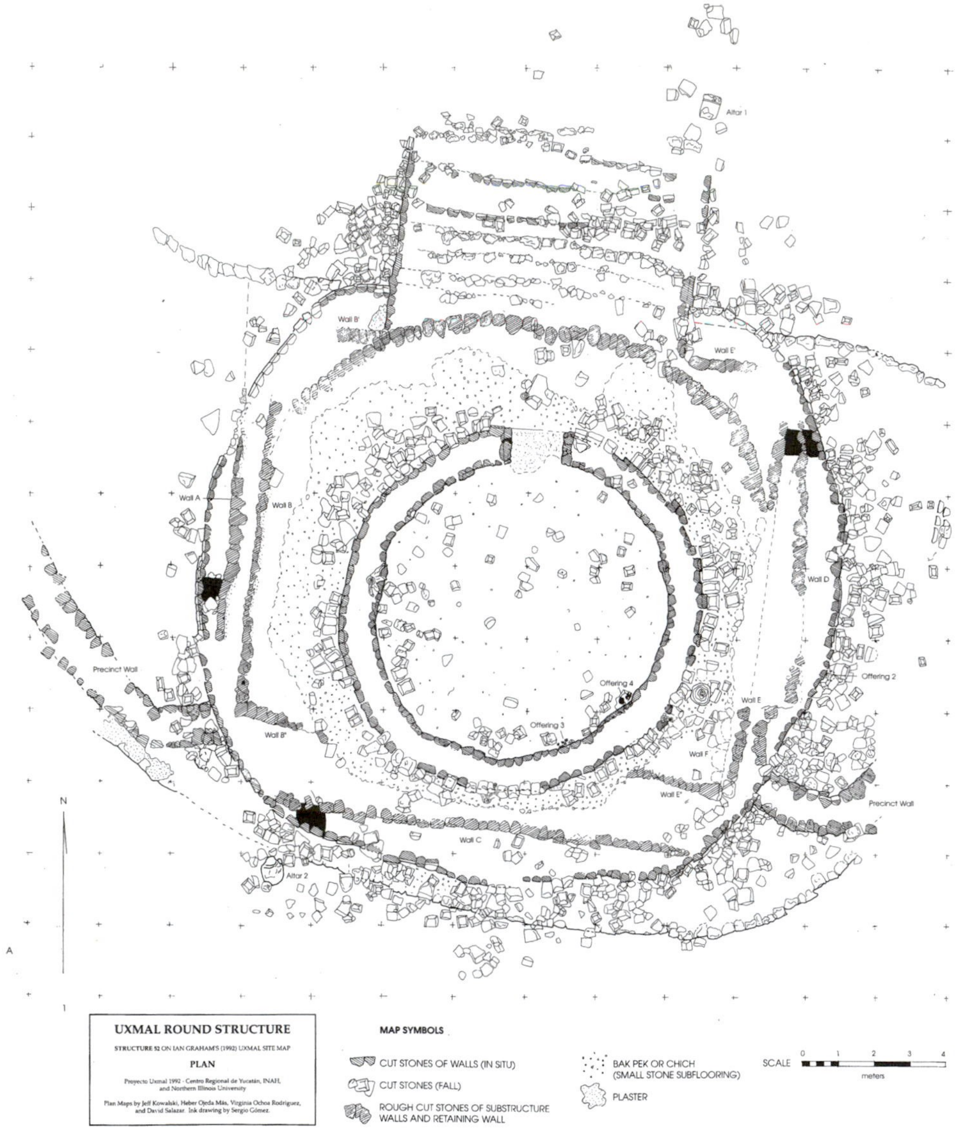
Altar 1
Wall B'
Wall E'
Wall A
Wall B
Wall D
Precinct Wall
Offering 4
Offering 2
Wall E
Offering 3
Wall B"
Wall F
Wall E"
Precinct Wall
N
Wall C
Altar 2
A
UXMAL ROUND STRUCTURE
STRUCTURE 52 ON IAN GRAHAM'S (1992) UXMAL SITE MAP
PLAN
Proyecto Uxmal 1992 - Centro Regional de Yucatán, INAH, and Northern Illinois University
Plan Maps by Jeff Kowalski, Heber Ojeda Más, Virginia Ochoa Rodriguez, and David Salazar. Ink drawing by Sergio Gómez.
MAP SYMBOLS
CUT STONES OF WALLS (IN SITU)
CUT STONES (FALL)
ROUGH CUT STONES OF SUBSTRUCTURE WALLS AND RETAINING WALL
BAK PEK OR CHICH (SMALL STONE SUBFLOORING)
PLASTER
SCALE
0 1 2 3 4
meters

Figure 12.11. (*b*) The plan of the Round Structure (Structure 52) at Uxmal.

This alliance, whatever its exact nature, apparently did not survive the tenth century. In addition to the fact that there is no evidence for significant large-scale construction at Uxmal following the major edifices built during the reign of "Lord Chac," the recent excavation of the Uxmal Round Structure revealed three separate offerings of paired Tohil Plumbate vessels located in layers of masonry debris, indicating that the vessels were deposited some time after the Round Structure had begun to collapse or was deliberately dismantled. This suggests that the dynastic organization responsible for maintaining such masonry buildings no longer controlled the site, but that new occupants who still had access to Tohil Plumbate, a valuable long-distance tradeware probably imported through Chichén Itzá, still occupied Uxmal.

Conclusions

Our analysis of architectural iconography, combined with evidence from settlement survey of the Eastern Puuc region, suggests that Uxmal became the capital of a regional state there during the Terminal Classic period. Between about A.D. 850 and 925 Uxmal's links with Chichén Itzá, perhaps involving some sort of military and political alliance between the two sites, permitted Uxmal to attain a temporary supremacy in the Puuc region. This was coupled with a peak in population and settlement growth in the Puuc region and was given visible expression in the form of a building campaign that dramatically altered Uxmal's civic-ceremonial center with the erection of the largest structures at the site, such as the House of the Governor, the Main Ballcourt, and the Nunnery Quadrangle.

Apparently, elite activities at most Puuc centers ended during the early tenth century. The cessation of monumental architectural construction and maintenance at Uxmal shortly after 10.4.0.0.0 (A.D. 909) may have been the result of the breakup of the short-lived Uxmal–Chichén Itzá alliance and the subsequent conquest of Uxmal and other Puuc cities by Chichén Itzá. Such a conquest was probably made possible by a combination of Chichén Itzá's military might and by its different form of conciliar government (*multepal*).[8] It has been suggested that Uxmal can appropriately be described as a "regal-ritual city" typical of the Classic Maya, whereas Chichén Itzá may have represented an "administrative city" serving as the capital of a more aggressive and hegemonic tributary state.[9] Uxmal may have been vulnerable to Chichén Itzá's warriors after the death of its charismatic ruler, "Lord Chac," and it and other Puuc centers may have been experiencing internal political stress due to an increasingly precarious balance between local population and food production (Dunning 1992; Dunning and Kowalski 1994). For a brief period during the late ninth and early tenth century, the ruler "Lord Chac" was able to consolidate the several of the Eastern Puuc centers into a regional state with Uxmal as its capital, a political paramountcy that was both given visible form and reinforced ideologically by the construction of buildings such as the House of the Governor, the Main Ballcourt, and the Nunnery Quadrangle. But even as such structures proclaimed Uxmal's cosmic charter of rulership, the Itzá rulers of Chichén Itzá were developing alternate forms of government and warfare and new forms of architecture to sanction these changes (see Andrea Stone, chapter 13, this volume). Ultimately, Chichén Itzá's innovations proved more viable, and it probably outlasted the demise of Uxmal and the Puuc centers to become the eastern capital of the Early Postclassic Mesoamerican "world system"(Kepecs, Feinman, and Boucher 1994) for another 100–200 years.

Acknowledgments   Jeff Kowalski's work at the Nunnery Quadrangle in 1988 and 1989 was made possible by a J. Paul Getty Postdoctoral Fellowship and a sabbatical leave funded by Northern Illinois University. Additional support for studies of the Nunnery Quadrangle and the Uxmal Round Structure have been provided by the Center for Latino and Latin American Studies at NIU. Kowalski's and Alfredo Barrera Rubio's excavations of the Uxmal Round Structure were were undertaken with the permission of the Consejo de Arqueología del Instituto Nacional de Antropología e Historia (INAH) and with the gracious cooperation of the Centro Regional de Yucatán del INAH in Merida. Excavations were sponsored by the Committee for Research and Exploration of the National Geographic Society (grant 4456-91) and were also facilitated by a research scholarship from the Council of International Exchange of Scholars of the Fulbright Scholars Program. Nicholas Dunning's regional settlement-pattern survey was undertaken with the aid of funding provided by the University of Minnesota Graduate School and the Organization of American States and was made possible through the cooperation of the Centro Regional de Yucatán del INAH. Collaborative research was also undertaken with the Sayil Project, initially under the direction of Jeremy Sabloff and Gair Tourtellot and subsequently under Michael Smyth and Christopher Dore, and with the Xkipché Project, under the direction of Hanns J. Prem. The authors thank E. Wyllys Andrews V, Joseph Ball, and David Freidel, who provided many helpful critical comments regarding the interpretations put forward in papers provided the basis for this chapter.

Notes

1. The name of this ruler was coined by Kowalski (1987). The name of the rain god, Chaak, apparently was adopted as a royal name or title by this ruler, who also is named as a *k'ul ahaw* (*ahau*), "sacred or divine lord" in the inscription on Uxmal Altar 10 (Grube 1994). When referring to the rain god, the spelling chaak, based on the orthography of the *Diccionario Maya Cordemex* (Barrera Vásquez 1980) will be used through-

out this paper. However, in order to remain consistent with previous references, the spelling of the Uxmal ruler's name as "Lord Chac," based on the spelling of the rain god's name in Landa's Relación (Tozzer 1941), and used in several previous publications by Kowalski (e.g., 1987; 1994), is retained in this article.

2. Recently, B. Fash et al. (1992: 438) have suggested that the House of the Governor may have served as a *popol nah*, a community house where lineage heads/residential "ward" leaders met in conference to conduct community business and in connection with which dances were learned and performed. This is a plausible interpretation, although the "mat symbol," which seems to be more specifically to identify Structure 10L-22A at Copán, Honduras as such a "mat house," is more ubiquitous at Uxmal, leaving other major structures, such as the Nunnery Quadrangle, as possible candidates for a *popol nah*.

3. Basic discussion of cosmological and cosmographical concepts of the Maya appears in Anders (1963: 68–76) and Thompson (1934, 1970: 194–196). Coggins (1980, 1983b) and Ashmore (1989) discuss architectural embodiments of such concepts. Additional discussion of cosmographical urban design in Puuc sites can be found in Aveni and Hartung (1986) and Dunning (1992). Evidence for the correspondence between north and the upperworld, and south and the underworld, is found in Gossen (1974), Brotherston and Ades (1975), Brotherston (1976), Coggins (1980, 1988), Bricker (1983, 1988), Sosa (1986), Closs (1988), and Ashmore (1989). See Kowalski (1994a) for an earlier discussion.

4. Providing support for this interpretation is the presence of goggle-eyed Storm Gods or "Tlalocs" with trapeze-and-ray headdresses on sculptured panels that adorned the Lower West Building, as well as several sculptured serpent heads containing human figures/deities in their maws, that originally adorned the Lower West Building (Seler 1917; Sáenz 1969: figure 1, fot. 9–10; Maldonado Cárdenas and Repetto Tio 1991). Several of the deity heads resemble GI' and GI of the Palenque Triad, both of whom have Venus associations and who have been identified as Classic period counterparts of Hun Hunahpu ("First Father") and Hunahpu, respectively (see Lounsbury 1985; Schele and Miller 1986).

5. Weldon Lamb (1980) suggested that the count of the lattice X's in the tiered-bar arrangements on the East Structure of the Nunnery Quadrangle corresponded to the 584-day synodic period of Venus and noted the appearance of Venus signs on the long-snouted masks on the building. Kowalski (1987) originally resisted this interpretation because the lattice X's were concealed beneath plaster and formed a unified "mat weave" pattern. However, Lamb's original interpretation should be reconsidered in light of present evidence. An argument identifying the owl-and-weapons sculpture as the emblem of the founder of Uxmal, Ah Kuy Tok Tutul Xiu, mentioned in the books of Chilam Balam (Barrera Vasquez and Morley 1949: 33), appears the paper "Seats of Power and Cycles of Creation: Continuities and Changes in Political Iconography and Political Organization at Dzibilchaltun, Uxmal, Chichén Itzá, and Mayapan," co-authored by Jeff Kowalski, Rhonda Silverstein, and Mya Follansbee. This paper was presented at the 49th International Congress of Americanists Meetings in Quito, Ecuador, July 7-11, 1997 and has been submitted for publication in *Estudios de Cultura Maya*.

6. Dunning and Kowalski (1994) have argued that the elite administration at Uxmal had disintegrated by this time, although there is evidence for a continuing, though sparser late occupation. Other scholars,

such as Gendrop (1983), G. Andrews (1986), and Barrera Rubio (1991) have proposed that Uxmal continued to thrive as an important center until the late tenth or early eleventh century. Excavations since 1992, directed by José Huchim Herrera in the area between the Nunnery Quadrangle and Ballcourt 1 have revealed late, unvaulted, residential buildings constructed with re-used Puuc stone sculptural elements and clearly postdating the major elite occupation of the site (Huchim, personal communication, 1997).

7. The Uxmal Round Structure was discovered by Ian Graham in 1988 during the mapping of the site center and appears on his Uxmal map (1992) as Structure 52. Jeff Kowalski and Alfredo Barrera Rubio codirected excavations of the structure in 1992 (Barrera Rubio and Kowalski 1994). A preliminary discussion of the Uxmal Round Structure appears in the proceedings of the 1993 Palenque Round Table Conference (Kowalski et al. 1996).

8. Discussion of evidence for a conciliar form of government known as *multepal* ("joint or crowd rule") at Chichén Itzá appears in Schele and Freidel (1990), Marcus (1993: 117), Grube (1994), and Krochock (1988).

9. Joseph Ball (1994: 391–392) suggests that Uxmal conforms to the expected attributes of the regal-ritual city as defined by Richard Fox (1977: 41):

> The term regal-ritual cities signifies the essential quality of these settlements. Their primary urban role is ideological. This cultural role emerges from the prestige and status of the state ruler or the cohesive power of state religion. All cities have this ideological cultural role in varying degrees. What makes the regal-ritual urban type distinctive is that its existence depends almost entirely on ideological functions. Such regal-ritual cities are particularly associated with the type of political system known as the "segmentary state" (Southall 1956: 260; 1988), the "galactic polity" (Tambiah 1976, 1977), or the "theater state" (Geertz 1980).

Various Mayanists have argued that such political organization characterized Classic Maya polities (Ball and Taschek 1991; Demarest 1992; Houston 1993). The segmentary state model seems consonant with much of what is known of the settlement pattern in the Santa Elena Puuc district, and about the relationship between Uxmal and other Puuc centers. The "duplication of administrative structures at provincial sites" (Houston 1993: 142) predicted seems attested in the Puuc region. As Dunning (1992, 1994) points out, many third- or fourth-rank Puuc communities share features of basic spatial organization and have overlapping ideological attributes such as pyramid-temples, range-type masonry "palaces," and hieroglyphic stelae and altars pertaining to the dynastic monument cult. Uxmal's position in the Puuc region also seems consonant with the "galactic polity" model of political organization, originally devised by Tambiah (1976, 1977) to describe Southeast Asian polities.

Houston (1993: 143) observes that such "galactic polities" typically display "extreme fluidity of polity boundaries, principally as a result of diminished or augmented power at a capital" dependent on the success or failure of charismatic rulers in consolidating power through alliances, suppressing hereditary rights of provincial rulers, maintaining a sense of their ritual sanctity, and in warfare or taking captives. As we have noted, the emergence of a political confederation dominated by Uxmal was apparently a late and short-lived episode. Although the evidence is open to some variant interpretations, this consolidation seems to be associated with the reign of a particularly successful ruler, "Lord Chac," who maintained strong contacts and perhaps concluded an alliance with the Itza rulers of Chichén Itzá. The personal, charismatic authority of "Lord Chac," with its basis in cyclical, theatrical ritual, was sanctified by the manifold religious and cosmological references in buildings such as the House of the Governor, the Main Ballcourt, and the Nunnery Quadrangle. We would add the caution, however, that while much of the data from Uxmal and the Puuc region seems consistent with the segmentary state model, recent interpretations of the Mul-Chic murals by Rachel Walters and Kowalski (1995) suggest that the warfare and captive sacrifice depicted therein may have been associated with the process of regional state formation in the Santa Elena Puuc district, and may have involved the taking of territory and tribute rather than simply representing ritualistic validation of the king's battle prowess (cf. Freidel 1986b).

13

Architectural Innovation in the Temple of the Warriors at Chichén Itzá

Andrea Stone

It is now widely acknowledged that the great Early Postclassic Maya city of Chichén Itzá was a very different kind of political entity from the Classic Maya cities that preceded it. Where an essentially monarchical government had characterized Maya urban life during the Classic period, that is, a *single* member of a royal lineage inherited the right to rule from his predecessor (usually, we believe, his father), Chichén Itzá appears to have embraced some form of *shared* governance.[1] This idea must frame our understanding of the urban landscape at Chichén Itzá, which, as no other pre-Hispanic Maya city, exhibits pervasive architectural and iconographic innovations. This chapter takes the position that the decentralization of Chichén Itzá's political institutions motivated the development of its innovative architectural style.[2] It addresses this issue by examining one of the most important buildings in the history of Mesoamerican architecture, the Temple of the Warriors.

The Temple of the Warriors

The Temple of the Warriors is a massive, 80-foot (about 24 meters) high temple resting on a terraced platform, flanked by colonnades on the south and west (figures 13.1 and 13.2). Set in the architectural heart of Chichén Itzá, it lies on the eastern side of the Gran Nivelación (Great Terrace) that supports the site's best known "Toltec"-style buildings, including the Castillo and the Great Ballcourt. Abutting the Temple of the Warriors on the west is the 150-foot (45 meters) long Northwest Colonnade with which it forms a unit, herein called the Temple of the Warriors Complex (Kristan-Graham 1988). In its pristine state this complex boasted colorful reliefs, full-round sculptures, and murals,[3] though it is most distinguished by the more than 300 three-quarter-lifesize human

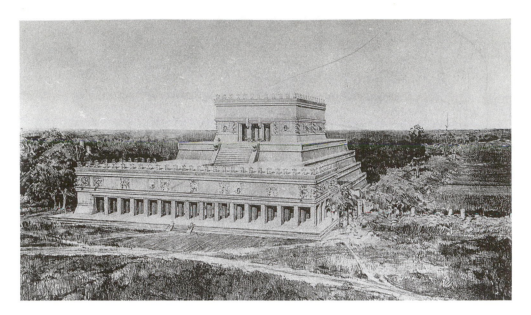

Figure 13.1. Architectural restoration of the Temple of the Warriors and the Northwest Colonnade by Kenneth G. Conant (after E. Morris 1931b: plate 27).

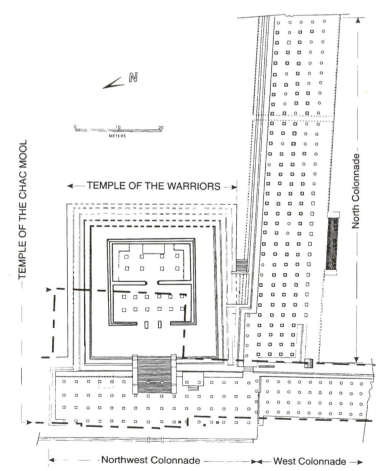

Figure 13.2.
Plan of the Temple of the Warriors Complex showing location of the Temple of the Chac Mool and its associated colonnade in heavy dashed line (modified from Marquina 1964: lam. 268).

figures, carved onto 81 square columns that supported the roofs of both the temple and fronting gallery. Unfortunately, since ancient times these roofs and their respective vaults have collapsed. The Temple of the Warriors is also noteworthy in that its principal staircase rises from the center of the Northwest Colonnade, blocking access to the temple from open plaza space (figure 13.1). This kind of plan has no precedent in Classic Maya architecture.

The Temple of the Warriors Complex overlies and was modeled after the Temple of the Chac Mool (figure 13.2). Parts of this earlier temple were reused in the Temple of the Warriors,[4] but mainly it served as construction fill. Flanking these structures, though not contemporaneous with them, are the North Colonnade and West Colonnade.[5]

The Number Four as a Modular Design Unit

A sense of highly structured planning pervades the Temple of the Warriors Complex; this is particularly evident in the use of fourfold design elements. For instance, both the Temple of the Warriors and the Temple of the Chac Mool have four-stage terraced platforms.[6] Figural compositions of attached sculpture are also frequently fourfold, as seen, for example, in the square columns with their four main figures; but the columns themselves are also grouped in units of four or a multiple. Each chamber of the Temple of the Chac Mool contains a single row of four columns. Similarly, the Temple of the Warriors has two rows of four columns in the rear chamber; however, the front chamber has two rows of six columns. This asymmetry appears to result from the unusual vault system. The front half of the temple originally had three vaults parallel with the front wall, measuring 61 feet (18 m) in length (Morris 1931a: 169). Running perpendicular to them were five shorter vaults (around 29 feet in length) in the inner chamber. This arrangement of vaults is unique in Maya architecture, as far as I am aware. In any case, the lengthier front chamber vaults must have required the use of more supporting columns: hence the disparity. Nevertheless, the superstructure vaults, totaling eight, are in harmony with a fourfold plan, just as the Northwest Colonnade had four north–south vaults.

The Northwest Colonnade is based on a plan of four rows of 16 columns (figure 13.2). Some thematically related carved columns also occur in groups of four, such as the captive figures with bound wrists which appear in two rows of four columns at the foot of the staircase.[7] Sculptures in the frieze of the Northwest Colonnade, such as the "statuette panel," and "bird mask," (Morris 1931b: figure 4) are each represented by four examples.

Figural groups on decorated daises are also fourfold. The processional scene carved on the Northwest Colonnade dais includes two groups of 16 figures.[8] Sixteen echoes the number of columns in one row of the Northwest Colonnade. The Temple of the Chac Mool had a pair of painted, L-shaped benches against the back wall, which flanked a throne supported by atlantids (figure 13.3). Unfortunately, both benches were shattered in antiquity, but the decoration, reconstructed from fragments of painted stone, does show that each bench portrayed groups of thematically related figures, some of which occur in units of four.

We might ask if the use of four, or a multiple, in the planning of the Temple of the Warriors Complex simply represents an aesthetic choice. After all, the number four is well suited to compositional symmetry in rectangular-plan buildings. Or does the number four, in light of its significance in Mesoamerican religion, have other, ritual implications? Certainly, there is evidence that some of the images in the Temple of the Warriors Complex approximate real activities associated with particular areas of the building (Kristan-Graham 1988). For instance, the representation of an assembly of seated figures on the Temple of the Chac Mool benches is indicative of the close relationship between images and some architectural features (figure 13.3). Hence, these fourfold compositions, particularly as they define figure groups, could also reflect aspects of ritual performed in the Temple of the Warriors Complex.

The opposing groups of figures on the Temple of the Chac Mool benches isolate the primary types of actors represented in the Temple of the Warriors Complex (figure 13.3). Painted on the north bench is a series of typical Chichén warriors, wearing back mirrors and furry knee and ankle bands, and carrying darts in their left hands and atlatl spearthrowers in their right. They sit on stone jaguar thrones resembling real ones found in the Lower Temple of the Jaguar and the inner Castillo and also depicted in reliefs in the interior of the Lower Temple of the Jaguar and the North Ballcourt Temple (Wren 1989: figure 9). On the south bench, a group of eight figures sits opposite the warriors; three wear long skirts and five portray a kind of figure carrying a staff. These figures have long been recognized as "priests" or "god impersonators" in contrast to the ubiquitous armed warrior (Charlot 1931). But much more can be said about their identities.

Chaak Impersonators

Earl Morris (1931a: 186) likened the staff-bearing figure to an impersonator of God B of the codices, widely recognized today as Chaak, the rain and lightning god. This identification was also proposed later by Jeff Kowalski (1987: figure 162) and Karl Taube (1988b: figure 4e). Taube (1988b: 60–61) provides a summary of the attributes of Chaak, many of which occur on the bench figure: the wide-brimmed, fringed hat, here with additional zoomorphic heads, a long-snouted zoomorphic face mask often composed of mosaic plaques, and serpent imagery, symbolic of lightning. Serpents usually form Chaak's staff. In depictions on carved

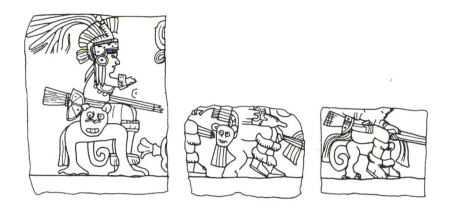

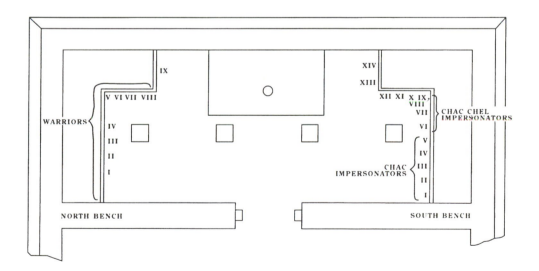

Figure 13.3. Temple of the Chac Mool bench figures (after Schele and Freidel 1990: figure 9.19) and plan (after A. Morris 1931: figure 271).

columns, Chaak sometimes holds a wavy serpent staff, perhaps the most obvious representation of lightning (figure 13.4a). At other times, as on the Chac Mool bench (figure 13.3b), the serpent occurs in the form of the serpent-footed God K Manikin Scepter. Here, too, serpents exude from Chaak's mouth, as noted by Taube. These figures also hold a round shield and sit on a jaguar-skin cushion as a sign of their lordly status. As proposed by Morris, the Chaak figures appear to be deity impersonators donning the rain god's regalia; this is further suggested by their associated name glyphs, indicating that they have a personal identity.

These Chaak impersonators recall colonial accounts of priestlike representatives of the fourfold Chaaks, gods of rain and lighting and the agricultural fields, associated with the world directions. Taking the name of the rain god, they were called Chaaks (*chaak-o'ob*). Landa (Tozzer 1941: 103) describes them as four "old and honorable men" who were chosen to "aid the priest in the ceremonies on the day of the festival." The Chaak priests at Chichén Itzá seem more like actual impersonators of the rain god than the Chaak priests of Landa's day, who by this time did not dress in a masquerade.[9] But in both cases the office was held by an aged individual, as the Chaak priests at Chichén Itzá are usually shown as elderly.

Chaak priests occur with marked frequency in the Temple of the Warriors Complex: on carved columns in the Northwest Colonnade (figure 13.4a), the Temple of the Warriors (figure 13.4b), and the Temple of the Chac Mool (figure 13.4c), as well as on the processional scenes of the Northwest and North Colonnades' carved daises (figure 13.4d). On each carved dais, there are exactly four of these Chaak priests, corresponding to the number stated by Landa (though obviously the Temple of the Chac Mool painted bench, with its five Chaak priests (figure 13.3), does not conform to this pattern). The Chaak impersonators have a fairly restricted spatial distribution in the art of Chichén Itzá, being found mainly in these related structures.[10]

Chac Chel Impersonators

The companions of the Chaak priests on the Temple of the Chac Mool painted bench are also representatives of a deity (figure 13.3b). They wear long skirts covered with disks, a broad collar composed of disks, and a broad-brimmed, fringed hat similar to that worn by Chaak, but lacking additional zoomorphic heads. Only one figure is depicted as old, though this type of figure, like most of the priestly figures in Chichén reliefs, is usually shown as elderly. Each of the long-skirted figures carries a square shield and holds a bowl of offerings, in contrast to the Chaak priests' round shield and Manikin Scepter; but they sit on the same kind of cushion covered with jaguar skin.

This long-skirted figure occurs widely in the art of Chichén Itzá. However, except in one possible instance (see note 10), it is only in the Tem-

a

b

Figure 13.4. Chaak impersonators: from (*a*) the Northwest Colonnade, Column 48N (redrawn from Charlot 1931: plate 113); (*b*) the Temple of the Warriors, Column 11E (redrawn from Charlot 1931: plate 51); (*c*) the Temple of the Chac Mool, Column 6E (redrawn from Charlot 1931: plate 37); and (*d*) the carved dais of the Northwest Colonnade (redrawn from (Charlot 1931: plates 126 and 128).

c

d

ple of the Warriors Complex and the Temple of the Chac Mool that the long-skirted figure is associated with Chaak priests. Indeed, they appear together frequently here; sometimes in conjunction with other elderly priestlike figures, such as the God N performers in the Temple of the Chac Mool (Column 5E and N, Column 6N and W) and Northwest Colonnade (Column 4N, W, and S and 8E). One distinction between them, though, is that the long-skirted figure is not found on the carved daises of the Northwest and North Colonnades.

Unlike the Chaak impersonator, the long-skirted figure in appears various architectural contexts at Chichén Itzá. Apart from the Warriors and Chac Mool superstructures (figures 13.5a,b and 13.6f) and the Northwest Colonnade (figures 13.6d,e), this entity also occurs in the Temple of the Big Tables (Structure 2D7; figure 13.5c), the Temple of the Little Tables (Structure 3D8), the Upper Temple of the Jaguars (figure13.5d), the Lower Temple of the Jaguars (figure 13.6c), the South Ballcourt Temple (figure

Figure 13.5. Chac Chel and her impersonators from (a) the Temple of the Warriors, Column 12S (redrawn from Charlot 1931: plate 52); (b) the Temple of the Chac Mool, Column 4S (redrawn from Charlot 1931: plate 35); (c) the Temple of the Big Tables (from photograph by Andrea Stone); (d) the Upper Temple of the Jaguars (redrawn from Miller 1977: figure 2); (e) the South Ballcourt Temple (from photograph by Andrea Stone); and (f) the North Ballcourt Temple (redrawn from Tozzer 1957: figure 679).

13.5e), and the North Ballcourt Temple (figure 13.5f). In many of these cases the long-skirted figure has a close association with Bakab/ Pawahtun depictions or acts like a Bakab in assuming an atlantean pose.

Chichén Itzá's long-skirted figure seems to be related to the cult of an aged goddess who is best known from the codices (figures 13.6a,b). Here she often has bestial attributes, like distended lips and clawed fingers and toes, as well as a pervasive association with death symbolism. In one case her eyeball is extruded, and death attributes usually crowd her costume. She frequently wears human bones as a waistband or crossed bones on her skirt. Another important attribute is a serpent coiled on top of her head. She also wears symbols of weaving in her hair, such as a yarn-wrapped spindle or a yarn formed into a figure eight (Stone n.d.).

The name of the codical goddess has the rather straightforward phonetic reading of *chac chel* (Kelley 1976: figure 22). Because of the *chel* "rainbow" component of her name and other iconographic attributes, it has been suggested that this old goddess is the Postclassic version of Ix Chel, known from early contact Yucatán (Knorozov 1967: 56; Kelley 1976: 69; Taube 1988b: 119). The strongest argument that the codical goddess, called Chac Chel, is related to the long-skirted figure at Chichén Itzá can be made by examining one carved square column in the Lower Temple of the Jaguars (figure 13.6c). Each side (only two of which are shown here) bears one version of a Chac Chel-like figure. On the south and east sides she has sagging breasts, indicative of an aged female. Her costume is rife with death imagery. On the south side her skirt bears

d

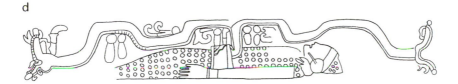

e

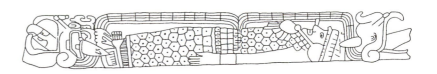

f

Figure 13.5 (continued)

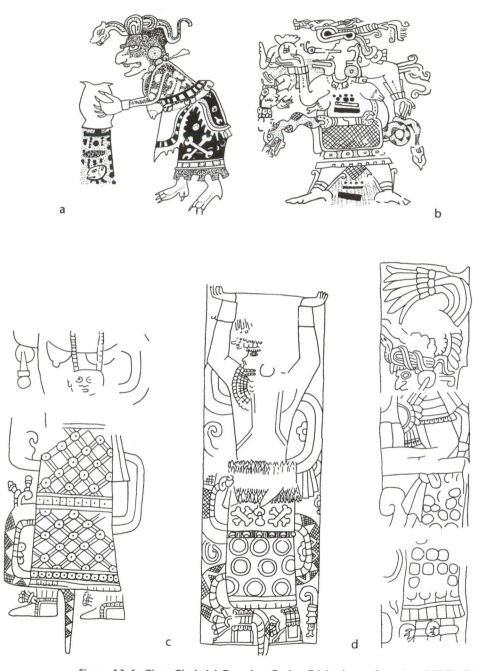

Figure 13.6. Chac Chel. (a) Dresden Codex 74 (redrawn from Lee 1985); (b) Madrid Codex 32 (redrawn from Lee 1985); (c) Lower Temple of the Jaguars piers (left, from photograph by Andrea Stone; right, redrawn from Tozzer 1957: figure 196); (d) Temple of the Warriors, Column 12W (redrawn after Charlot 1931: pl. 52); (e) Temple of the Warriors, Column 12N (redrawn from Charlot 1931: plate 52); (f) Temple of the Chac Mool, Column 4N (redrawn from Charlot 1931: plate 35); (g) Tulum, Structure 5, Mural 1 (redrawn from Miller 1982: plate 28).

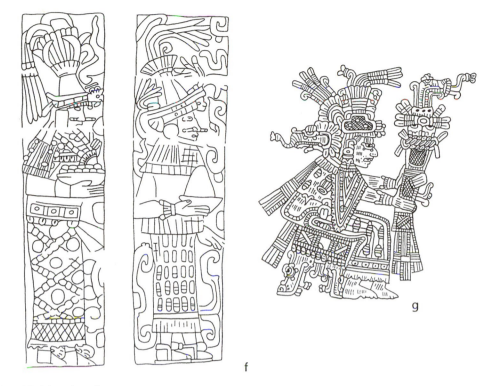

Figure 13.6 (continued)

crossed bones and a death collar. Skeletal imagery is also seen on the north side, where the figure has a skull head and crossed bones depicted on her costume. The long skirt of this figure is also covered with disks, which provides a bridge to the disk-skirted figure under discussion. On the east and west sides of the column the figures wear net skirts, which seems to be an alternative form of the goddess's costume, one with roots in the Classic period.[11]

Apart from this carved column, however, other versions of the long-skirted figure at Chichén Itzá show no sign of being biological females.[12] One must conclude therefore that male figures are garbed in the manner of this goddess of creation and fertility, known in the codices as Chac Chel. While a long skirt in and of itself might not be convincing evidence that the male figures are related to the codical Chac Chel, more particular traits do connect them. Most striking is the fact that Column 12W in the Temple of the Warriors superstructure shows one of these long-skirted male figures wearing a coiled serpent headdress (figure 13.6d), a trait common to Chac Chel as well as the young codical goddess, often called the Moon Goddess.[13] In light of this, it is interesting that the long-skirted figure depicted on Column 39S of the Northwest Colonnade stands in front of a large lunar glyph.

Another figure on Column 12 wears a disk skirt with a net pattern (figure 13.6e; see also Column 60 of the Northwest Colonnade). The alternation between disk and net skirt costumes further links these figures with the carved column from the Lower Temple of the Jaguars, which clearly portrays Chac Chel (figure 13.6c). Moreover, one version of the skirt, worn by a column figure in the Temple of the Chac Mool (figure 13.6f) and by one of the Chac Mool bench figures (figure 13.3), bears lozenge-shaped ornaments segmented by horizontal lines, which resembles a jewel-flower motif. It recalls the skirt of an old goddess in Mural 1, Structure 5 at Tulum (figure 13.6g).

Another image supporting the proposal that male priests impersonated Chac Chel and that they are depicted as such in the Temple of the Warriors comes from a relief in the North Ballcourt Temple (figure 13.7). Here we see four figures wearing long skirts covered by crossed-bones, a hallmark of the codical Chac Chel (figure 13.6a), as well as her Classic antecedent.[14] The skirts are also decorated with large disks, suggesting that the disk form of the skirt is simply one variant of the type with death symbols. Because of the condition of the carving, however, it is ambiguous whether the figures portray biological females. In any case, four priestlike figures who appear to be impersonators of Chac Chel can be identified.

The thematic contexts of the disk-skirted figure are also in keeping with what we know about the codical Chac Chel. As stated earlier, in the Temple of the Warriors Complex the disk-skirted figure is associated with Chaak priests, both in terms of placement within figure groups and in shared attributes, such as the fringed, wide-brimmed hat (figure 13.3) and the serpent staff (figure 13.5b). Likewise, in the codices Chac Chel frequently occurs in the company of Chaak, God B (Taube 1988b: 120), and on Dresden 38a she is named as his wife. The disk-skirted figure also acts like a Bakab or is actually paired with Bakabs. This may have to do

Figure 13.7. North Ballcourt Temple, South Arch (after Wren 1989: figure 8b).

with Chac Chel's function as an ancestral creator goddess who supports the world in the manner of a Bakab, Pawahtun, or Mam. As suggested by Coggins (1984: 160), the disk-skirted figure in the supine pose (e.g., figures 13.5d,f) may allude to a Mother Earth-like being representing the earth's surface. Indeed, Chac Chel seems to have been, among other things, an earth and fertility goddess, in many ways foreshadowing the Coatlicue goddess complex of the Aztecs.[15] Further study of Chichén Itzá's disk-skirted figure is needed before we can firmly grasp her complex role at the site.

In the Temple of the Warriors, the Chac Chel priests typically carry a bowl, the contents of which seem to vary. Some bowls hold round objects with sticklike protrusions (figure 13.8a), while others contain a pile of small, circular objects (figure 13.8b). Bowls carrying small balls of material at Chichén Itzá sometimes have smoke scrolls rising from them, suggestive of burning copal incense (figure 13.8c). Other bowls hold one large pile of material (figure 13.8d) or several oblong or rounded objects (figure 13.8e). Certain conical offerings shown in the *Madrid Codex* (figure 13.8f), which can be identified as steamed maize dough offerings or *wa* (Love 1989), resemble the offerings shown on the Chac Mool bench (figure 13.8g). The fact that they are colored yellow is also suggestive of

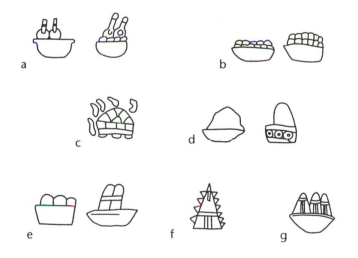

Figure 13.8. Comparison of objects carried in bowls by Chac Chel impersonators: (*a*) balls with sticks, Northwest Colonnade, Columns 39S and 60N (redrawn from Charlot 1931: plates 105 and 122); (*b*) balls, Temple of the Warriors, Column 12E and 12N (redrawn from Charlot 1931: plate 52); (*c*) balls with smoke (redrawn from Tozzer 1957: figure 674); (*d*) large cone, Temple of the Chac Mool, Column 4N and Northwest Colonnade, Column 59N (redrawn from Charlot 1931: plates 35, 121); (*e*) multiple ovoids, Northwest Colonnade, Column 59S and Temple of the Warriors, Column 12S (redrawn from Charlot 1931: plates 121, 52); (*f*) Madrid Codex 98a (redrawn from Lee 1985); (*g*) Temple of the Chac Mool bench figure (redrawn from A. Morris 1931: plate 133).

maize. What can be said with certainty is that the Chac Chel priests were charged with the task of presenting these bowl offerings in rituals associated with the Temple of the Warriors.

The positioning of the Chaak priests and Chac Chel priests in the Temple of the Warriors Complex bears further comment. Charlot (1931: 270) and Kristan-Graham (1988) noted that priestly figures mainly occupy the south end of the Northwest Colonnade, but they did not point out the pervasive nature of this pattern. More precisely, in the Northwest Colonnade, Chac Chel impersonators occupy all sides of Columns 59 and 60 at the very southern end of the gallery, and on Column 39S (figure 13.9). This parallels the Temple of the Warriors superstructure, where the Chac Chel priests occupy all four sides of Column 12 at the south end of the front chamber. Similarly, in the carved bench of the Temple of the Chac Mool, the Chac Chel and Chaak priests occupy the south side. In the

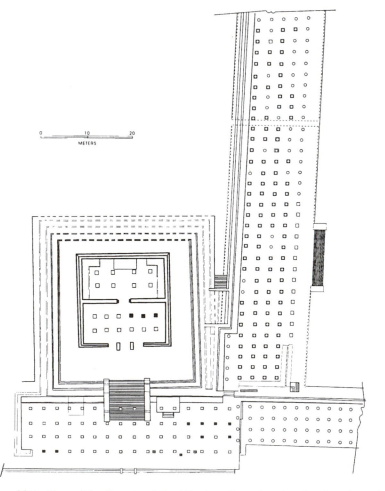

Figure 13.9. Plan of the Temple of the Warriors Complex showing location of priests (modified after Marquina 1964: lam. 268).

carved columns most of the Chaak priests occur on the south side, as in the Northwest Colonnade (Columns 48, 51, 52, and 56) and in the Temple of the Warriors superstructure (Columns 10 and 11). However, in the Northwest Colonnade, Chaak priests can be found on Columns 4 and 8 as well, on the extreme north side. One might generalize by saying that in the Northwest Colonnade the priestly figures tend to be found at the perimeter. This may mean that they followed processionals or tended to stay at the perimeter of ritual performances. Placement of priests at the edges or corners of compositions probably reflects the actual spatial arrangement of ritual participants.[16]

Architectural and Iconographic Innovation

With its hundreds of warriors and priestlike deity impersonators, the Temple of the Warriors Complex signals a new role for religious architecture in a Maya city. No longer serving the cult of a single lionized ruler, Chichén Itzá's art and architecture place new emphasis on the religious *institutions* which formed the cohesive thread in a fragmented political climate. The interest in priestly functionaries in Temple of the Warriors iconography is far beyond anything seen in Classic Maya art. Likewise, in the Classic, only the ruler was portrayed as a Chaak impersonator, but in the Temple of the Warriors Complex, state priests were memorialized in this role. The Chac Chel priests are another class of functionaries given new iconographic emphasis. They appear to represent the revival or, perhaps, reinvention, of a female cult of a kind relegated to an obscure position during the Classic period, a time when female symbolism centered almost exclusively on the ruler's kinship, mainly maternal, ties (Stone n.d.).

In other ways the Temple of the Warriors Complex can be seen as an adaptation to a new sociopolitical context for Maya art and architecture. First of all we find here one of the largest continuous enclosed precincts of any pyramid-temple complex in the Maya area. Lincoln (1990: 594), for one, has noted the exceptionally large area of the Temple of the Warriors superstructure when compared with other pyramid-temples, such as the Castillo. Certainly the flanking colonnades add to this one of the largest sheltered spaces known from any Maya site. One can only surmise that the augmentation of enclosed space arose from the size of participant parties. The decorated column was ingeniously used in this quest to incorporate into public ritual performance numerous individuals holding different offices as well as having different kinship affiliations. First, with the spacious colonnade, large groups (as opposed to a select few) could act *en masse* within a sanctified architectural precinct. Second, by decorating the column, members of the participant groups could be memorialized in large-scale portraits that recorded their distinct attributes and affiliations. Finally, the embedding of the temple's staircase in a semienclosed gallery (figure 13.1) served to validate the status of the group congregated in front of the temple.

I would further suggest that the Temple of the Warriors Complex served as common ground for the disparate factions that made up Chichén Itzá's political landscape. As early as 1970, Proskouriakoff (1970: 466) observed that political power at Chichén Itzá was divided among several factions, although her observation was grounded in a hypothetical Toltec presence. It is more likely, however, that these factions were lineage-based enclaves. Evidence of this has been emerging in studies of Chichén Itzá's hieroglyphic texts and iconography. For instance, Grube and Stuart (1987: 8, 10) have identified the *Cocom* patronym in several texts at the site, and Ringle (1990) has tentatively proposed readings for the *Copol*, *Kauil*, and *Hau* patronyms. Kristan-Graham (1988) notes possible readings of Yucatecan patronyms, including the *Xiu*, *Cocom*, and *Chel*, in pictographs and iconography associated with many warrior figures. Given this and other ethnohistoric evidence of lineage rivalries, it seems reasonable to suggest that political factions divided along lineage affiliation vied for and perhaps shared power at Chichén Itzá. Lincoln (1990) proposes that the *Xiu* and *Cocom* were the primary rival lineages involved in joint rule, but this matter has not yet been resolved.

If this scenario proves correct, then we can expect to find that specialized structures at Chichén Itzá were associated with the activities of distinct lineages[17] and served as their council houses, perhaps in the manner of the K'iche' (Quiché) *nim ha* or "big house" (Carmack 1981). The *nim ha* is a building type found at Late Postclassic K'iché sites such as Utatlán. It is composed typically of a gallery open at one end, supported by piers, and accessed by a forecourt, with both gallery and forecourt elevated on a platform (Carmack 1981: figure 9.10). Against the back wall of the gallery was a bench, where Carmack suggests members of the lineage sat in council. In terms of their accessibility to viewing, attenuated plan, and rear bench, the *nim ha* recalls Chichén Itzá's gallery–patio structures (Ruppert 1950). In addition, both gallery–patio structures and *nim ha* are repetitive architectural forms at their respective sites. There may have been as many as 24 *nim ha* at Utatlán, corresponding to the number of lineages noted by the chronicler Ximénez (Carmack 1981: 288), while Ruppert identified 11 gallery–patio structures at Chichén Itzá. Based on the above correspondences, then, I would propose that gallery–patio structures served as the chambers for a lineage council, akin to the K'iché *nim ha*.

Chichén Itzá's recurrent gallery-patio-temple complexes found in outlying areas seem to replicate on a modest scale major constructions located in the site center, such as the Temple of the Warriors, the Mercado, and their associated colonnades. One such outlying complex on the Platform Ho' Che is discussed by Lincoln (1990: chpt. 6, pp. 407–408) who states that the principal temple "imitates not the Castillo, but the secondary ranking temple of the Gran Nivelación, the Temple of the Warriors." This resonance between recurrent secondary architectural complexes in outlying areas and buildings of far grander proportions located in the site center suggests that the latter not only provided a model for the former, but also served to unify the multiplicity of complexes in the outskirts. Therefore, it is not surprising that *sacbe-o'ob* connect these outlying complexes with the large constructions in the heart of the city (Lincoln 1990: 578). I would argue that the Temple of the Warriors was such a vehicle of group cohesion, an architectural setting wherein lineage-based factions dispersed throughout the site could unite in a central place for major public ceremonies. Conflict was resolved by these cooperative undertakings, if only temporarily.

The Temple of the Warriors and the Pacum Chac

Given the pervasive military iconography of the Temple of the Warriors Complex—the prolific number of warriors and the eight captive columns, as well as the fragmentary mural showing an apparent conquest of a village—the ceremonies held there clearly had martial overtones. It has been suggested that the rites concerned the celebration of a successful battle (Kristan-Graham 1988). But it is also possible that military rites timed by the calendar were performed there.

Landa (Tozzer 1941: 164–166) describes one such military ceremony held in the month of *Pax* called *Pacum Chac* which "concerned matters of war, and obtaining victory over their enemies." This celebration brought together military representatives from a wide area as, according to Landa, "lords and priests of the lesser villages joined those of the more important towns." The *Nacom*, one of the two war chiefs, was honored during *Pacum Chac*. He was carried (on a litter?) to the temple of *Cit Chac Coh*, where copal was burned to him "as to an idol" in Landa's words. Later warriors joined in a dance "with long martial steps" called *holcan okot* or "dance of the warriors." The Chaaks, the fourfold group of elderly priests mentioned earlier, also participated in the festivities. They probably performed the *tup' k'ak* (extinguish fire) ceremony noted by Landa, as this was one of their typical charges. They also sacrificed the heart of a dog and broke a large jar filled with drink.[18] Following the big public gathering in the temple, the *Nacom* was escorted to his house, and festivities continued in the residence of some principal lord where priests distributed great quantities of incense.

The festival of *Pacum Chac* provides a model to consider the iconography of the Temple of the Warriors Complex. The participation of the Chaaks can be compared with the many depictions of Chaak impersonators. The distribution of incense recalls some of the bowl offerings carried by the Chac Chel priests. The idea that warriors' dances like the *holcan okot* were performed in the Temple of the Warriors Complex is also tenable. Indeed, a fragmentary mural found above the Northwest Colonnade carved dais shows eight warriors who could be dancing (figure 13.10). It is also interesting that Milbrath (1988) notes that the orientation of the Temple of the Warriors falls within 2° of the solar zenith passage sunset on May 25th. During Landa's time, May 25th fell during the month of Pax when the *Pacum Chac* was held.

While rites associated with the Temple of the Warriors Complex were martial in character, I propose that they also concerned agricultural fertility and world creation. The emphasis placed on Chaak and Chac Chel impersonators provides supportive evidence for this idea. But Chaak is also alluded to on the exterior of the Temple of the Warriors superstructure. A band of sculpture encircling the medial portion of the facade includes stacked long-nosed masks at the corners of the building in typical Puuc fashion, as well as flanking the doorway and in the middle of the wall. The long-nosed masks are generally accepted as abbreviated representations of Chaak (Kowalski 1987: 93)[19] Their rather distinctive use here, in a part of Chichén Itzá where these masks are otherwise absent as architectural decoration, may say something about the function of this building complex.

Figure 13.10. Mural above the Northwest Colonnade dais (redrawn from A. Morris 1931b: plate 166).

The way the Temple of the Warriors Complex integrates Puuc style elements, notably the Chaak masks in the superstructure, with hybridized central Mexican-Maya style architecture and sculpture is another of its innovative features (figure 13.1). The platform uses a modified version of *talud-tablero* construction found at Teotihuacan, though with comparatively smaller *tableros*, as noted by Marquina (1964: 869; see Kowalski, chapter 4, this volume). The idea of decorating the roof perimeter with repetitive, geometric elements (*almenas*) also derives from Teotihuacan architecture. I speculate that the striking juxtaposition of these two styles derives from the new way that military and agricultural rites were integrated and performed in the Temple of the Warriors Complex. A comparison can be made with the Aztec Templo Mayor, where military and agrarian cults were also linked in a context of creation mythology (see Matos Moctezuma, chapter 9, this volume). However, this building employs a different strategy—the twin temple, one dedicated to the god of war and one to the god of rain and agriculture. In linking these two aspects of religious ideology and ritual practice, the Temple of the Warriors Complex is a harbinger of the Templo Mayor, as it is in other ways, including the latter's flanking colonnaded halls with carved processional daises (Klein 1987).

In conclusion, the iconography and spatial organization of the Temple of the Warriors Complex provides a kind of mini-laboratory to explore the sociopolitical dynamics of Chichén Itzá. The innovations evident throughout these buildings can be understood as an adaptation to a new Postclassic world order in which omnipotent kings no longer held sway, but rather where various factions and institutions negotiated power. In the Temple of the Warriors, new solutions to the creation of architectural space and ornamentation could serve new forms of religious activity and political organization.

Notes

1. Lincoln (1990) proposes a model of shared governance by two rival lineages, the *Xiu* and the *Cocom*. Schele and Freidel (1990: 360–361) have suggested a form of joint rule (*multepal*) by a group of brothers. Also see Krochock (1991) for hieroglyphic evidence of conciliar political organization at Chichén Itzá.

2. This chapter does not consider the wholesale importation of a foreign art style from Tula, Hidalgo as the best explanation of the origin of Chichén Itzá's eclectic Mexican-Maya style of art and architecture, commonly referred to as "Toltec." Rather, it works on the assumption of the internal development of this art style, which borrowed from non-Maya cultures and fused these borrowings with indigenous art traditions and religious concepts.

3. See Morris, Charlot, and Morris (1931) for illustrations of all works of art mentioned in the text but not illustrated.

4. Ann Morris (E. Morris 1931a: 143) discovered that the atlantean throne in the Temple of the Warriors originally came from the Temple of the Chac Mool.

5. In terms of building sequence, E. Morris (1931a: 202–204) proposes that the West Colonnade was built first, and then a portion of it was torn down to make way for the Temple of the Chac Mool. Upon the partly demolished remains of this structure, the Temple of the Warriors Complex was built, and finally, flanking its south side, the North Colonnade was constructed.

6. However, E. Morris (1931b: 38–39) suggests that only three stages were originally planned for the Temple of the Warriors and that a fourth stage was added later.

7. These are Columns 26, 29, 33, and 37 and Columns 25, 28, 32 (except 32W), and 36.

8. It is interesting that the carved daises from the North Colonnade and the Mercado diverge from the multiple of four in consistent ways. In both cases this occurs in the right-hand group on the front side of the dais, where the North Colonnade has seven figures and the Mercado has five. On these daises all other processional groups occur in multiples of four.

9. A Chaak impersonator, known as the *kunku-chaak*, described by Redfield and Villa Rojas (1934: 142) in a modern *ch'a-chaak* ceremony, carries a "lightning axe" in the form of a wooden machete and a gourd from which the *chaak-o'ob* pour rain down on the agricultural fields.

10. The sculpted circular stone found at the Caracol seems to portray Chaak impersonators in addition to one long-skirted figure (Ruppert 1935: figure 169). In addition, Taube (1988b: 61) identifies one figure found in the Lower Temple of the Jaguars interior reliefs, with a snake in his mouth and wide headdress (Maudslay 1889–1902, 3: plate 48), as Chaak.

11. I have argued elsewhere (Stone n.d.) that the royal women on Classic monuments dressed in the codified "female costume" with a net skirt, *xoc*-fish, and shell waist ornament, and so on, allude to the *Chac Chel* complex. Hence, it is not surprising to find the Classic net form of her costume at Chichén Itzá.

12. Seler (1902–23: 204, 209, 213–214) identified long-skirted figures in the Temple of the Big Tables, Temple of the Little Tables, and the North Ballcourt Temple as female divinities. Tozzer (1957: 110) also mentioned the location of certain female depictions at Chichén Itzá. Charlot (1931: 281, figure 187) identified the figure on the Temple of the Warriors Column 16E as an old woman. She has a sagging breast and thus does appear to be female, but she lacks a disk-covered or netted skirt; so her relationship to Chac Chel is ambiguous. Interestingly, Charlot compared an element of her headdress with a headdress motif found on a depiction of Chac Chel in the *Madrid Codex*. In the codices this ovoid headdress element represents a yarn-wrapped spindle (Stone n.d). Whether this identification holds true for the Column 16E figure is not entirely clear owing to the sketchy nature of Charlot's illustration.

13. Admittedly, two warrior figures, on Column 1E from the Temple of the Warriors and Column 57E from the Northwest Colonnade, also have a coiled serpent headdress. This casts some doubt on the idea that the coiled serpent headdress at Chichén Itzá necesssarily refers to Chac Chel.

14. Taube (1988b: 120, fig. 40b) pointed out that a Late Classic polychrome vase depicting an elderly goddess with crossed bones on her skirt probably represents a Late Classic version of Chac Chel, designated as Goddess O in the Schellhas classification.

15. It is quite possible that the Chac Chel figure of Chichén Itzá is a predecessor of the Central Mexican earth monster, often represented in a hocker position. It is true, however, that one version of the supine, long-skirted figure with a tree growing out of the stomach occurs on a relief at Tula (de la Fuente et al. 1988: figure 113). The costume, however, is decorated with square plaques. Rather, it is the Maya version of the goddess that exhibits the pervasive death symbols associated with this figure in Aztec art.

16. A deliberate north–south opposition in the Temple of the Warriors superstructure is also suggested by the fact that the north and south dados of the front chamber were painted, respectively, black and red (E. Morris 1931b: 20).

17. George Kubler (1982: 108, 110) suggested that various structures with serpent-column doorways, such as the Temple of the Warriors, may have been used as "Council Houses" associated with different city wards. His interpretation, based on the presence of tablelike raised seats or daises supported by atlantean figures within such structures, differs somewhat from that presented in this chapter, in which gallery–patio type structures are considered more likely parallels for the K'iché Maya *nim ha* council house. It is possible that both types of spaces may have served as spaces for elite meetings and official audiences, as is suggested by the multifigure paintings on the benches in the Temple of the Chac Mool and the multifigure processional scene on the Mercado sculptured dais. Ringle (1990: 240) has also suggested that the Akab Dzib, a more traditional "palace" type building, was a lineage house for the Cocom.

18. Note that a water jar is tied to the back of an elderly figure depicted on the Temple of the Chac Mool painted bench (A. Morris 1931: plate 137).

19. Freidel, Schele, and Parker (1993) have proposed an alternative identification of these masks as Itzam Yeh, the Classic Maya counterpart of the "false sun," Wukub Kakix ("Seven Macaw") of the *Popol Vuh* (Tedlock 1985). An identification as either Chaak or Itzam Yeh would be consistent with the general themes of world creation and the establishment of cycles of agricultural fertility proposed here.

14

Structure 16, Tulum, Quintana Roo

*Iconography and Function of a
Late Postclassic Maya Building*

Merideth Paxton

The "village so large that Seville could not look larger or better," flourishing in 1518 as Juan de Grijalva sailed along the east coast of the Yucatán peninsula, has long been associated with Tulum, Quintana Roo.[1] John L. Stephens, the distinguished explorer, made this identification during his 1842 visit to the ruin[2] and also provided the first published account of its architecture. Stephens described impressive stone buildings surrounded by a massive wall, with additional remains outside this area.[3] Like most investigators, Stephens was drawn to the richly ornamented structures inside the wall. The ornament he encountered there included relief sculpture, made primarily of stucco, and wall painting; the most completely decorated of the buildings was Structure 16, the Temple of the Frescoes (Lothrop 1924: plate 20b; Miller 1982: figures 72–73; also see figures 14.1 and 14.2 of this discussion). This chapter offers a new interpretation of one of the primary Structure 16 paintings, suggesting that it is associated with rainmaking, and examines the function of the building in the Maya society of the immediate preconquest period.

General Description

The importance of Structure 16 is suggested in part by the amount of artistic effort directed toward the enhancement of the basic structure and by the attention the building commands through the addition of a second story. The temple is the result of four main construction phases (figure 14.3a), beginning with a single room. This was followed by a second structure which created gallerylike spaces around the small initial building. During the third phase, the room that makes the second story was built directly above the earliest construction. As the load-bearing walls did not provide adequate support for this enlargement, reinforcement was required in a minor fourth modification (Lothrop 1924: 92).

CARIBBEAN SEA

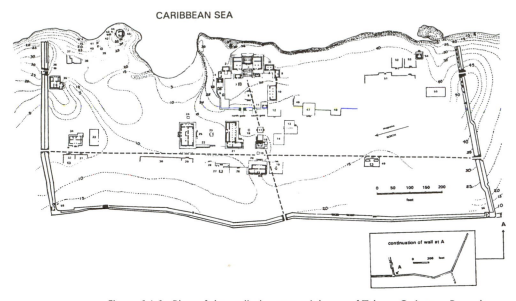

Figure 14.1. Plan of the walled ceremonial area of Tulum, Quintana Roo, show-ing structures arranged along a north–south axis with a proposed quadripartite division (based on Lothrop 1924: plate 25).

The ideology reflected by Structure 16 is conveyed through the com-plex program of painting and sculpture referred to above. The forms on the exterior of the Temple of the Frescoes are primarily on the western facade (figure 14.3b), consisting of high-relief stucco figures placed in niches, other motifs modeled in lower relief, and some remains of painted designs (Lothrop 1924: plates 2 b,d; 3 b,d, figures 74, 24; Miller 1982: plates 30–33). The iconography and composition of the Structure 16 decoration is generally unified, with several depictions appearing on the interior and exterior of the building, in both painted and sculpted media. The best-preserved architectural decoration is in the interior space created by the construction of the latest building.

Virtually the only remaining interior painting[4] is found on the walls that were once the northern, western, and southern facades of the earliest structure. It is, nevertheless, evident that this painting dates from late in the architectural history of Structure 16, because it overlaps one wall of the second phase construction (Paxton 1986: pl. 238) and incorporates a fourth phase reinforcing pillar. The compositions seem to form discrete but related units. These compositions are always arranged in horizontal bands, which are, as Kubler (1984: 320) has observed, reminiscent of manuscript painting. Because so many of the elaborately costumed fig-ures between the bands are oriented toward the scene painted on the western side of the northwest corner (Miller 1982: plate 37),[5] it appears that this section is especially significant.

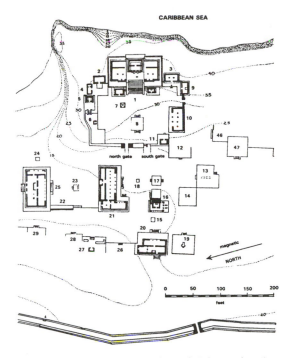

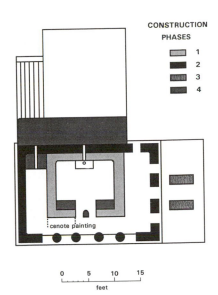

Figure 14.2. Detail of the plan of Tulum, showing Structure 16 (The Temple of the Frescoes) and the immediate vicinity (based on Lothrop 1924: plate 25).

Figure 14.3a. Construction phases of Structure 16 (The Temple of the Frescoes) (based on Lothrop 1924: figure 70).

Figure 14.3b. View of the west facade of Structure 16 (The Temple of the Frescoes).

Rainmaking and Agriculture

The scene on the north end of the west wall of the earliest building of the Temple of the Frescoes (figure 14.4) covers all the space below the two moldings and continues into the area between them. In the lower section, horizontal bands of figures are framed along the sides by massive saurian upper jaws and, across the bottom, by an aquatic band and a continuation of the jaws. In the following discussion I argue that this saurian motif is a cenote and that the plant forms which also figure prominently in the painting are food crops typically found in the field with corn. While it is not currently possible to cite any single motif in the painting

Figure 14.4. Structure 16, painting on north end of of earliest building (based on Lothrop 1924: plate 7; see also Paxton 1982: photos 4 and 5; Paxton 1986: plates 177–179, 181–183, 184–196). The background color of the painting is black. Grey areas of this figure indicate blue color (approximated by Pantone 324u and 325u [Pantone, Inc. 1977]) in the original mural.

on the north end of the west wall as definitive proof, I further argue that the best overall explanation for the assembly of forms is that the fresco evokes a ritual conducted to obtain rain for agriculture. The placement of the cenote painting in Structure 16 may be related to the projection of the Maya cosmological system, in which cenotes are associated with the center direction, on the planning of the largest walled precinct of Tulum.

The Cenote

The interpretation of the saurian jaws and aquatic band as a cross-sectional view of a cenote, or sinkhole, is supported by several elements in the design. The space between the water level and the top edges of the snouts resembles the distance from ground level to water at the well-known Sacred Cenote at Chichén Itzá (Piña Chán 1970: fot. 8, plan 2) and at other cenotes in the peninsula, such as the Xelhá cenote near Tulum.[6] The shape of this framing device, with inward curving termination of the rim, is the same as one of the four basic cenote forms identified in the geology of the peninsula (Pearse, Creaser, and Hall 1936: 6). Other artistic representations of cenotes that have been identified, as in the *Codex Dresden* (*Codex Dresdensis* 1975: 36c, center; J. E. S Thompson 1972: 104) and a painted capstone from the Temple of the Owls at Chichén Itzá (Gómez-Pompa, Flores, and Fernández 1990: 253), also have this inward curving termination.

Additional support for the idea that the body of water in the Tulum Structure 16 painting is a cenote comes from broader preconquest Mesoamerican iconographic conventions, encountered in non-Maya manuscript painting and other sources (cf. Gay 1972: figure 11), in which cave entrances are depicted as saurian mouths. For instance, one of the symbols in the Codex Borgia, where such a mouth can be seen, has been identified as Oztotl, the cave in the mountain (*Codex Borgia* 1976: 2, bottom center; Seler 1980, 3: 2). The *Codex Borgia* also shows the entry of a sacrificial victim into the underworld, with the corpse passing through the mouth of a saurian creature (1976: 42, center left). An illustration of the underworld entrance incorporating only the jaws of the serpentine earth monster in the *Codex Laud* (1966: 21, upper right). Because of the physical resemblance of cenotes to caves and the location of some cenotes inside them, this conceptual similarity to the Tulum creature appears to be significant. That the pre-Hispanic Maya also recognized the analogy is indicated by the nearly equivalent ritual functions of caves and cenotes (Thompson 1975; Pohl 1983: 86; Bassie-Sweet 1991: 77–82).[7]

The location of Tulum on the literal edge of the eastern coastline of the Yucatán peninsula necessitates consideration of the possibility that the body of water depicted in the Structure 16 painting could be the ocean. The animals which swim in the band at the bottom of the painting are stylized to the extent that it is not possible to establish their identities in nature, so a fresh or salt water habitat cannot be discerned. The bulbous form at the lower right could be a bewhiskered catfish commonly encountered in cenotes (Hubbs 1936: 183, plate 1), or it could be an ocean dwelling sting ray. Moreover, it is possible that there was overlap of oceans and cenotes in preconquest Maya thought, as J. E. S. Thompson's studies of the moon goddess, Ix Chel, suggest. Although the moon goddess resides in cenotes, one of her titles is Lady of the Sea (Thompson 1976: 244–245). Modern Maya belief also holds that cenotes are linked with the ocean (Redfield and Villa Rojas 1934: 165). However, the body of water in the Tulum Structure 16 painting surely must be a cenote, not only because of the overall shape of the motif, but also because of the plants in the scene. These are food crops, and salt water obviously could not have substituted directly for fresh water in support of agriculture.

Agricultural Motifs

One of the major visual themes of the north painting is corn and vegetation. In the upper register, for example, ritual offerings of corn are made by the ornately costumed figure at the left end. These offerings are also shown, near the center, in a large urn, and are placed in the mouths of the adjacent serpents. Ceremonial grinding of corn is performed in this band of the composition by a figure kneeling at an elaborately decorated metate. Below, the main scene of the painting shows similar corn offerings, corn headdress elements, and a possible digging stick for planting. Additionally, it includes two plant forms that can be associated with *milpa* (Yucatec *kol*)[8] agriculture.

Beans

As botanical surveys have noted (Steggerda 1943; Barrera Marín, Barrera Vázquez, and López Franco 1976: 30), cultivation in the typical modern Maya *milpa* is not limited to a single food. The first of the crops that I propose to identify in the Structure 16 painting as a companion to the corn in preconquest fields is a common bean, possibly *Ib* (*Phaseolus lunatus* L., or lima bean), but more likely the now standard *Xkolibuul* (*Phaseolus vulgaris* L., the black bean usually associated with contemporary Latin American cuisine; Barrera Marín, Barrera Vázquez, and López Franco 1976: 268–269; Standley 1930: 300–301). This follows from the *Relación de las cosas de Yucatán* (ca.1566) of Diego de Landa (Tozzer 1941: 195), where it is recorded that "there are two kinds of small beans, some black and others of different colors."[9] The bean motif in the Tulum painting has previously been identified by O. F. Cook as cacao (Lothrop 1924: 58).[10] However, these painted beans are not similar to cacao pods recently discovered growing in the state of Yucatán (Gómez-Pompa, Flores, and Fernández 1990: figure 2). Nor do they follow the artistic convention for cacao known from the hieroglyphically labeled illustration on page 70a (left) of *Codex Madrid* (Lee 1985) 11 and the painted capstone from the Temple of the Owls at Chichén Itzá (Gómez-Pompa, Flores, and Fernández 1990: figure 5). Rather, the Tulum pod and leaf motifs correspond much more closely with those of *Phaseolus vulgaris* L. (see figure 14.5); both the painted and naturally occurring forms of the plant are vines. Further indication of the importance of beans in the painting can be observed in a detail from the left side of the middle register of the section beneath the lower molding (see figure 14.5a-3). Here, there is a figure draped with a vine that bears bean leaves and whose feet are depicted as beans.

Squash

The second companion plant of the corn represented in the Structure 16 painting is best seen at the upper right side of the middle register (figure 14.6a-2). This has previously been identified by Cook (Lothrop 1924: 58) as *Dorstenia contrarerva* L., a medicinal herb (Steggerda 1943: 205; see also Bolles 1974). However, this opinion does not consider the presence in the painting of numerous circular shapes that appear to be squash or

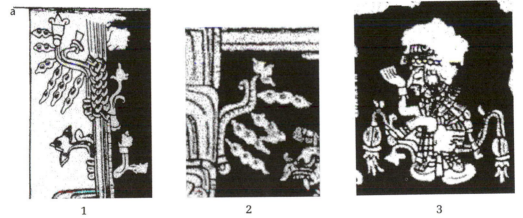

1   2   3

Figure 14.5. Structure 16, bean motifs: (*a*) painted details(1–3) based on figure 14.3 of chapter 14, (*b*) *Phaseolus vulgaris* (photograph by Merideth Paxton).

Figure 14.6. Structure 16, squash motifs: (*a*) painted details based on figure 14.3 of chapter 14, (*b*) *Cucurbita moschata* (photographs by Merideth Paxton).

pumpkin fruit with withered blossoms attached. Alicia Bárcena Ibarra, who was in 1981 the director of the Mérida, Yucatán office of the Instituto Nacional de Investigaciones sobre Recursos Bióticos, has suggested (personal communication, 1981) that the motif previously regarded as *Dorstenia contrarerva* L. could as easily be interpreted as a squash blossom, viewed from the back. While I would not claim to have found the only possible model for the Tulum painted motif, I have grown a squash that demonstrates the general plausibility of such a correlation (see figure 14.6b). The Magdalena Big Cheese (*Cucurbita moschata*), one of the oldest cultivated squashes in the Americas, produces large, ribbed, flattened-pumpkin-shaped fruit (Native Seeds/Search 1991: 23). The circular forms in the painting could easily correspond with the immature fruit of this plant, and the serpent bodies to which the various elements are attached seem to imply the serpentine tendrils of the Magdalena Big Cheese squash vines. Direct depiction of the vines is found with the figure at the left side of the middle register, along with the previously mentioned bean vines (figure 14.6a-1). In the modern *milpa* either bean or squash seed are often planted in the same holes as the corn, so that the cornstalks support the vines (Redfield and Villa Rojas 1934: 46; Villa Rojas 1945: 56–57). If this was also common agricultural practice during the preconquest era, the close association of beans and squash with corn and with each other that is seen in the Tulum painting would have been routine.

Further support for this identification of the bean, squash, and corn motifs in the Structure 16 painting comes from colonial period accounts of religious rituals. Landa's *Relación* mentions (Tozzer 1941: 158) that during the month of *Xul*, for instance, offerings were made of "food cooked without salt or pepper and of drinks made of their beans and the seeds of squashes." One of the New Year ceremonies, also detailed in Landa's *Relación* (Tozzer 1941: 141–142), records the presentation of "a heart . . . of bread and another kind of bread with the seeds of squash."[12] The Chilam Balam of Chumayel (Roys 1973: 99; Tozzer 1941: 142) describes the offering of "hearts of small squash-seeds, large squash seeds (*ca*), and beans."

Ethnographic Descriptions of Agricultural Ritual

The prominence in the Tulum Structure 16 painting of offerings, maize, bean, and squash iconography and the cenote suggests that this could be a portrayal of an actual ceremony conducted to obtain rain. However, the quality of the soil at the archaeological site of Tulum is so poor (Vargas, Santillán, and Vilalta 1986: 67) that the first consideration must be whether farming could have been practiced in the immediate vicinity to an extent sufficient to indicate probable preconquest interest in such ritual.[13] In fact, it is clear that agriculture must have been significant in the Tulum area. Lothrop (1924: 63) made reference to inland *milpas* of the modern Maya settlement near the ruin, and around 1947 Heyden (1967: 240–241) collected information concerning idol worship by milperos there.[14] Additionally, in 1975, Martínez Guzmán and Folan (n.d.: 11) conducted reconnaisance work outside the Tulum wall (mostly toward the south and west) that established "the presence of several ancient property walls, metates and manos." Thus, it is plausible to search for descriptions of rites comparable to the Structure 16 scene. Indeed, several observances emerge as subjects possibly referred to in the painting.

The Ch'a chaak *Ritual*

The most important modern agricultural ceremony is also the one in which cenotes figure most prominently. This is the *ch'a chaak* ("bring-rain," or "summoning the Chaaks") ritual, practiced widely in the

Yucatán peninsula and northern Belize as a remedy for drought (Gann 1917; E. H. Thompson 1932: 53–64; Redfield and Villa Rojas 1934: 138–143; J. E. S. Thompson 1976: 260–262; Rejón García 1981: 31–40; Cardeña Vázquez 1982; Taube 1989b; Bricker 1991). Details of the rites vary according to the locations where they are performed, but one of the standard features is the offering of beverages and special breads made from the crops customarily grown (maize, beans, squash). These offerings are presented on altars constructed to reflect the shapes of the fields, as well as general Maya perceptions of the universe in which they live. The *ch'a chaak* ceremony also includes the prayers of the h-men directing the activity, and the simulation of a rainstorm by his assistants. While similar food offerings and altars may be used in other agricultural ceremonies as well, the mimetic storm is found only in the *ch'a chaak* ritual. Redfield and Villa Rojas (1934: 115) observed that at Chan Kom the Chaaks, who sometimes water *milpas* by pouring water over the land from gourds, are thought to replenish their supplies from cenotes. This belief evidently reflects the importance of cenotes as the primary source of fresh water in the Yucatán peninsula, where surface rivers and lakes are scarce (Wilson 1980: 17–18; Folan, Kintz, and Fletcher 1983: 33).[15] Further information on the function of cenotes in the *ch'a chaak* ceremony comes from Telchaquillo, where the residents conduct the ritual at the edge of the easternmost cenote (because the home of the Chaaks is in the eastern sky) within the wall of the ruin of Mayapan, and the h-men reportedly throws part of the offerings into the cenote (Thompson 1976: 261).

The most important rainmaking ritual of Yucatán during the late pre-Hispanic period, a likely counterpart to the modern *ch'a chaak*, was the famous human sacrificial rite conducted at the Sacred Cenote of Chichén Itzá. As reported in Diego de Landa's *Relación de las cosas de Yucatán* (Tozzer 1941: 54), extreme drought and famine occurring after the departure of the Spaniards from the peninsula in 1535 prompted members of the Xiu lineage to request safe passage through the territory of enemy Cocom lords so that they could sacrifice slaves at this well. The *Relación* of Tomas López Medel, who was in Yucatán around 1552, adds that the victims could be thrown alive into the cenote to communicate requests for rain to the gods who resided there (Tozzer 1941: 180–181, 223).

The Tup k'ak' Ritual

Landa's *Relación* (Tozzer 1941: 162-164) informs us of two other rainmaking rituals that appear related to the modern *ch'a chaak*. Conducted during the 20-day calendrical interval of *Mac* in the 365-day solar year, these are a rite referred to as the *tup k'ak'* ("to put out or kill the fire"), and a second, unnamed rite. During the *tup k'ak'*, offerings of sacrificial hearts from creatures of the field were burned in a specially kindled fire, which is symbolic of the burning milpa being cleared for planting, drought, or perhaps ultimately of both. Then the fire was put out by pitchers of water poured by four persons representing the Chaaks. The latter aspect of the ceremony provides a link to the modern *ch'a chaak*, as well as to a scene from the pre-Hispanic *Codex Madrid*. Thompson (1976: 261) reports that in the current practice of the *ch'a chaak* of Telchaquillo, four impersonators of the Chaaks, each of whom has a (rain) gourd and a lightning machete, stand at the directionally oriented corners of the altar. In the Chan Kom *ch'a chaak*, the corners of the altar are occupied by young boys who imitate the croaking of frogs summoning rain. As Thompson (1976: 258) commented, this corresponds with the directionally placed frogs disgorging rain on page 31a of *Codex Madrid*. During the second ceremony described by Landa for *Mac*, offerings of incense and food were made, and an altarlike construction was anointed with mud from a cenote. The stated purpose of the two events (Tozzer 1941: 163) was "to obtain a good year of rains for their grains." Hence, it seems that, like the *ch'a chaak*, the *tup k'ak'* was conducted to bring rain, but that it was performed at regular intervals rather than only in time of drought.[16]

The U Hanli Col *Ritual*

A third religious observance in which cenotes have special significance is the *u hanli col* ("dinner of the *milpa*") as it is performed at Chan Kom (Redfield and Villa Rojas 1934: 134–137). This ritual is owed to the Chaaks and other deities every four years at the time when the maize grown on newly cleared land is ripening; the prudent farmer sponsors special offerings and prayers of gratitude according to this schedule to maintain his prosperity and health. The importance of cenotes in the *u hanli col* is the key component of the primary prayer. In this part of the ritual, names of modern villages, ancient ruins (Cobá, Chichén Itzá, and Oxkinkiuic), small family farm residences, and cenotes are invoked. According to Redfield and Villa Rojas, the unifying concept underlying the selection of the cited places is that they all have cenotes. While these authors concluded that the significance of the cenotes is in the deities residing there (Chaaks and [*balams*?]), and not in the cenotes per se, it appears that the motivation for addressing the Chaaks is probably their function as rainmakers. Indeed, Redfield and Villa Rojas (1934: 138) also remarked that "the ritual forms used in the *ch'a chaak* conform to the pattern represented by the u hanli col, . . . cast on a larger scale."

The Okotbatam *Ritual*

The Villa Rojas (1945: 113–115) study of the X-Cacal subtribe of Maya residing in east central Quintana Roo recorded a fourth agricultural ritual in which cenotes have prominence.[17] This is the *okotbatam* ("petition"), the main ceremony observed in Tusik in 1935, which seems to substitute for the more commonly celebrated *ch'a chaak* while combining aspects of this ceremony and the *u hanli col*. Although the principal purpose of the offerings and prayers associated with this event is to ensure adequate rainfall while the corn is in a critical stage of growth, the *okotbatam* is performed annually even when rain has been abundant.[18] During time of drought, all of the villages of the subtribe seek relief by cooperatively staging a larger scale *okotbatam* in the shrine village of X-Cacal. As in the *u hanli col* ceremony, one of the prayers of the *okotbatam* invokes deities (guardians of the bush where the *milpas* are located), who are called according to the various cenotes where they reside.

Interpretation

The review of information on rituals pertaining to agriculture, rainmaking, and cenotes during the pre-Hispanic through modern periods has thus far established that the strongest association of cenotes is with rainmaking for agriculture. Hence, the most obvious explanation for the combination of the cenote with maize, bean, and squash motifs in the Tulum Structure 16 painting is that some pre-Hispanic ceremony for rain to support regular agriculture or relieve drought is represented. The descriptions of the twentieth century ceremonies show that performances for relief of drought are elaborations of the more routine rainmaking practices. Although it is not certain, there is reason to think that the pre-Hispanic versions of the *tup k'ak'* and *ch'a chaak* rituals may also be parallel in this way. The basic form of the *tup k'ak'* (or the unnamed event that followed) might have been enhanced through human sacrifice during time of drought. This interpretation is suggested by the lack of reference to such sacrifice in the descriptions in Landa's *Relación* (Tozzer 1941: 151–166) of the *tup k'ak'*, as well as in his descriptions of all other cyclical rituals of the 365-day solar year.[19] Rather, when rationalization is provided, the deliberate ceremomial killing of humans is always associated in the colonial documents with response to a crisis. Besides drought (de la Garza et al. 1983, 2: 323), the circumstances under which such sacrifices were made in Yucatán include attempts to save the life of an ailing cacique and to save the inhabitants of a settlement from a storm (Tozzer 1941: 44, 115). If this comparison of early colonial and modern ritual is valid, one might surmise from the absence of human sacrifice in the Tulum Structure 16 painting that it probably presents a pre-Hispanic equivalent of some cyclical event like the *tup k'ak'*.

The Tulum Architectural Context of the Cenote Painting

The Temple of the Frescoes appears to have functioned within an important but secondary level of the Late Postclassic architectural hierarchy at Tulum. The building is outside the wall that partitioned the most imposing construction at the site, Structure 1 (the Castillo), and its associated structures. Yet, it is centrally located in the overall plan of the larger walled area of the settlement, a fact that may be significant in terms of the function of this temple as a cultural symbol.

Adjacent Structures

In addition to the effort directed toward artistic decoration and the imposing nature of its overall form, the importance of Structure 16 is also signaled by its prominent siting at the approximate midpoint of the north–south avenue identified by Lothrop (1924: 67) as the main street of Tulum, where the street widens to about 40 feet (11.8 meters). It is likely that the structure was used in conjunction with at least one nearby construction toward the east that is in what I regard as a large plaza. A platform mound where early visitors to Tulum reported finding stelae abuts the east side of the temple (Lothrop 1924: 95–96), and a few feet farther east (in a direct line) is Structure 17, a square platform 4 feet (1.2 meters) high and 17 feet (5 meters) on a side. Concerning the platforms, Lothrop (1924: 96) remarked that "the correspondence of these two is so exact that they evidently belonged together." Structure 17 is located at the north–south center of the proposed plaza, which is framed on one end by Structure 21 and on the other end by Structures 13 and 14 (see figure 14.1). Along the east, the space is defined by one line of the wall which controls access to the Inner Inclosure [sic], where Structure 1 and its related buildings are found. It has not been demonstrated that Structure 17 was not the base for a building made of perishable materials. However, the placement of the structure in the approximate center of the open area parallels that of Structure 8 of the Inner Inclosure, a platform evidently used to elevate the persons presiding over public rituals. It seems plausible that Structure 17 could have had a similar function. The widening of the street to the west of Structure 16 and the ready availability of the plaza space to its east suggest an architectural unit that could have conveniently accommodated groups of people normally residing outside the main wall, gathered there for ceremonies (see note 3). Structure 16 and its east plaza resemble the architectural setting described in Landa's *Relación* (Tozzer 1941: 162–164) in connection with his account of the *tup k'ak'* and the second, unnamed, ritual:

> They hunted for all the animals and creatures of the field . . . and they came together with them in the court of the temple in which the Chacs and the priest took their places seated in the corners, as they were wont to do . . . each having a pitcher of water . . . . They placed in the middle a great faggot of dry sticks tied together . . . and first burning some of their incense in the brazier they set fire to the sticks, and while they were burning, they took out a great many of the hearts of the animals and birds and threw them into the fire to burn . . . . When all the hearts were consumed, the Chacs extin-

guished the fire with the pitchers of water. They did this, so as by means of it and of the following festival, to obtain a good year of rains for their grains. Then they celebrated the festival...the people and the priest and officials assembled in the court of the temple where they had erected a heap of stones with its steps, and all very clean and ornamented with green foliage. The priest gave incense prepared beforehand for the host, who burned it, and so they say the evil spirit fled away. This done . . . they annointed the first step of the heap of stones with mud from the well, and the other steps with a blue paste, and they scattered smoke from the incense many times, and invoked the Chacs and Itzamna with their prayers, and devotions, and made their offerings. This finished they comforted themselves, eating and drinking what had been offered, very confident of the good year, as a result of their services and invocations.

Perhaps the cenote painting inside Structure 16 commemorates a public ritual, like the *tup k'ak'* (or the related rite), which was actually performed in the Structure 17 plaza.

While the Temple of the Frescoes and the adjoining space to the east could easily have accommodated an agricultural ceremony for rainmaking, this is certainly not the only appropriate site for such activity within Tulum. Of course, the plaza of the Inner Inclosure could have been used in this way. It also seems that Structure 35, at the northeast end of the largest walled part of the settlement, would have been a reasonable choice for the ritual because it is built above a cenote and linked to it by a shaft (Sanders 1960: 180). In fact, the archaeological record of ceramic deposition shows little differentiation of activity within the walled area of Tulum. Sherds from censer wares have been found with most buildings (Sanders 1960: 187, table 2), indicating that religious observances were common.[20] Thus, a question is raised concerning whether there could have been a specific reason for the selection of Structure 16 as the site of the cenote painting.

Structure 16 and the Ideal Model of the Universe

The Temple of the Frescoes is, as mentioned earlier, located almost exactly at the center of the largest area enclosed by the main wall of Tulum. It is at the approximate midpoint of Lothrop's main street, identified as the westerly connection between openings in the northern and southern extensions toward the sea of the longest wall. It is also about midway between the west entrance in the main Tulum wall and Structure 1, at the eastern edge of the site. The placement of the Structure 16 cenote painting may derive from the broader concept of centrality in the pre-Hispanic Maya cosmological system, which has been reconstructed from such colonial sources as Landa's *Relación* and the *Chilam Balam of Chumayel* (Thompson 1934). This system was a projection of the movement of the sun onto the surface of the earth, after a rotation of the plane that contained it from vertical to horizontal. The rising position was associated with east, the highest position with north, the setting position with west, and the lowest underworld position with south (Kelley 1977: 56; Coggins 1980; Bricker 1983; Kowalski 1994a; see Kowalski and Dunning, chapter 12, this volume). The quadripartite scheme also included a fifth, or center, direction, and color symbolism for each of the divisions.

It is not surprising that this directional system has been recognized in the planning of Maya sites of both preconquest and modern eras. For example, the twentieth century residents of Chan Kom consider their village[21] to be square with four directionally oriented "corners," which are entrances marked by wooden crosses and protected by buried caches of pre-Hispanic lithic fragments. The center direction at Chan Kom is the cenote, also at one time marked by a cross. In describing this feature, Redfield and Villa Rojas (1934: 114) commented that the marking of a cenote with a cross to denote the concept of center was practiced "in most villages." Thus, it is clear (Redfield 1941: 119) that cenotes can substitute for the more widely recognized center marker, the *yaxcheel cab*, or ceiba tree. Thought to have originated at the time of creation, this tree is one of the most important symbols of Maya religion, as it is the source of ancestral lineage and a symbol of abundance, and serves as a path from the earth to the celestial level of the universe (Thompson 1971: 71).[22]

It is possible to interpret the plan of the walled area of Tulum as an expression of the quadripartite cosmological model. In addition to the placement of the cenote painting at the center of the site, some locations may correspond to the four directional entrances of Chan Kom. The Castillo, and perhaps its architectural group, could correlate with the east position, not a formally constructed entrance because of the location of the structure literally on the coastline of the peninsula. The other three entrances could be at the west ends of the north and south legs of the perimeter wall and in the approximate center of the west wall. The north–south axis would then be Lothrop's main street. It seems likely that a second axis could have followed a line running approximately from the entrance in the west wall to the Castillo. This interpretation is a slight variation of that proposed by G. Andrews (1977: 428). Andrews has pointed out that, although there is no indication of a street leading from the western entrance toward the interior of Tulum, the axis of the wall opening focuses directly on this building. However, his interpretation of the site plan is that the space immediately north of Structure 16, extending from the main street eastward along Structure 21 to the west wall of the Inner Inclosure, formed a secondary plaza with two entrances to the main plaza (Lothrop's Inner Inclosure). Andrews regards this secondary plaza as the focus of the north-south street, which would seem to imply that it forms an axis perpendicular to the main street. Because the southern entrance to the Inner Inclosure is the wider of the two (Lothrop 1924: 89–90), and is almost on the line from the west gate to the Castillo (figures 14.1 and 14.2), my opinion is that this line of view is a more likely second axis and that the plaza west of the Inner Inclosure included Structure 17 and the space demarcated by all of the surrounding structures.

The placement of Structure 19, with one side obstructing the line from the west gate to the Castillo, apparently contradicts the axis system proposed above. Little is known about the structure, and it is, of course, possible that it is a late interjection to the Tulum plan. However, there are two other entrances, at the eastern ends of the north and south sections of the wall enclosing the largest precinct, which cannot be interpreted according to the quadripartite world view. Perhaps this is because the plan does not follow such a system of organization. On the other hand, the resolution of these discrepancies may be that the quadripartite division was a theoretical ideal, subject to considerable variation in actual interpretation. Such is clearly the case in the Chan Kom example (also see Freidel and Sabloff 1984: 158). The village cenote is indeed centrally located in the main plaza. However, instead of the four entrances oriented according to the cardinal directions that the residents describe, there are seven entrances to Chan Kom. None of the four entrances designated by the villagers as having religious significance has the expected alignment according to the compass (Redfield and Villa Rojas 1934: 113–114). Despite the burial of the caches of lithic offerings, the official Chan Kom entrances would probably not be clearly recognizable archaeologically because of their lack of directional correlation. The question of whether special offerings were buried at some of the Tulum entrances has not, so far as I am aware, been investigated. The quadripartite division of the walled precinct remains unproved. It is, nevertheless, a reasonable conjecture that would explain the placement of the cenote painting in Structure 16.

Conclusions

The painted scene on the western wall of the northwest corner of the inner building of the Temple of the Frescoes (Structure 16) at Tulum, Quintana Roo has been interpreted as the evocation of rainmaking ritual which could have actually been conducted in the plaza immediately to the east of the temple. The scene appears to be a commemoration of a religious rite because offerings are prominent in the painting, as they have been in these Maya ceremonies for at least as long as Western descriptions have been recorded. The subject of the ritual is communicated through several motifs identified in the present study. The saurian mouth which frames the scene is a cenote; another important visual theme is crops grown in the pre-Hispanic *milpa* (corn, beans, squash). The presence of the cenote in the mural may also be related to the placement of the work in the particular building where it resides, as cenotes can designate the center direction according to the Maya perception of the universe. Because Structure 16 is centrally located in the largest walled precinct at Tulum, it seems that this directional system may have been imposed on the planning of the area.

Acknowledgments   Support for this research was provided in part by a Fulbright fellowship. I wish to express appreciation to Prof. Angel García Cook and Lic. Javier Oropeza y Segura of the national office of the Mexican Instituto Nacional de Antropología e Historia and to Arqlgo. Norberto González, of the Mérida, Yucatán office of the institution for permission to study and photograph the Tulum paintings. Joann M. Andrews of Mérida graciously allowed me to reproduce the early photos of the Structure 16 paintings that Samuel K. Lothrop made and saved in an album, now in her library at Quinta MARI. Daniel W. Jones, Jr., Photo Archivist at the Peabody Museum of Archaeology and Ethnology, Harvard University, aided my search for other early Lothrop photos in the collection of the museum. Some ideas presented here were initially developed for a session of an annual meeting of the American Society for ·Ethnohistory organized by Betty Ann Brown (Paxton 1981). Further development was encouraged by my participation in the session chaired by Jeff Kowalski at the 1991 annual meeting of the Society of Architectural Historians.

Notes

1. This description was recorded by Juan Díaz, a clergyman accompanying Juan de Grijalva (Wagner 1969: 72). Lothrop (1924: 11) notes that the preconquest name for Tulum was Zama.

2. This opinion was based on Diaz's location of the ruin in terms of a geographic feature which Stephens (1963, 2: 278) recognized as the modern Bay of Ascension. Although Wagner (1969: 190) was not in complete agreement with Stephens on this point, he did accept the general connection of the Díaz description with Tulum.

3. Subsequent archaeological investigation has shown that some of the features outside the wall are house mounds (Barrera Rubio 1977: 27–32; Vargas, Santillán, and Vilalta 1986: 65–69; Velázquez Valdez 1976: 59–60); an early European description of Tulum in the *Littera Mandata* estimated the size of this population to be about 4,000 hearths (Wagner 1969: 190). Reconnaisance of the area between Tulum and Tancah by Tomás Gallareta (Benavides and Andrews 1979: 50) indicates that the two sites may represent a single settlement population.

4. According to Stephens's (1963, 2: 276) account, the walls on both sides of the corridor were at one time covered with paintings, as were the walls on the interior of the earliest structure.

5. Plate 37 in Miller (1982) provides an excellent overview of the assembly of the component paintings on the north facade and the north end of the west facade of the first construction and on the west side of the fourth-phase reinforcing pillar. Nevertheless, a minor ambiguity is raised by the inclusion (at the right side) of a narrow section of the scene from

the south end of the west facade of the first construction. The segment suggests that the south scene, or at least the device that frames it, is an almost mirror image of the scene at the north end of the wall. The plaster on the south end is extensively damaged, and the mural is only faintly visible. However, the photographs of the painting that I made under varying light conditions during 1980 and 1981 do not show the framing device, and I do not recall having seen it. Nor does the Lothrop (1924: plate 7) illustration of this end of the wall show the motif. The main scene on the south end does not repeat that of the north end (Paxton 1986: plate 214).

6. There is a cenote inside the Tulum wall, beneath Structure 35. Further discussion follows in this chapter in the section "The Tulum Architectural Context of the Cenote Painting."

7. There are no preconquest Maya images that unequivocally show the dead entering the underworld through caves or cenotes, although such a scene is probably depicted on page 66a (right) of *Codex Madrid* (see Los Códices Mayas 1985; Lee 1985). The eyes of the person in this illustration are open, but the text above includes the glyph collocation (15.736:140 in the Thompson [1962] system) that Bricker (1986: 13,101) has read as *ah-cam-al* (dead person). There is also documentation of early colonial acceptance of this belief; Barrera Vásquez et al. (1980: 889) cite the Motul dictionary listings of *ts'onot* meaning abyss, as well as cenote, and *tu ts'onotil mitnal* meaning infernal abyss. Also see Tozzer (1941: 132). In addition, the underworld maw that encompasses the dead king Pakal on the sarcophagus lid from the Temple of the Inscriptions at Palenque resembles the monster maw-cenote depiction in the Tulum mural (Robertson 1983: plates 98–99).

8. The spelling conventions for Yucatec words in this chapter generally follow the Cordemex dictionary (Barrera Vásquez et al. 1980). However, the words used by earlier authors have not been standardized.

9. For a description of the various beans which may be grown in the twentieth-century *milpa*, see Pérez Toro (1977: 188).

10. Another possibility suggested in the Lothrop study is *hymenia*, which I have been unable to find in standard references on the plants of Yucatán. Although *Hymenaea Courbaril* L. is registered (Standley 1930: 289), this is clearly not what is shown in the Tulum painting.

11. The reading of the *ca-ca-w(a)* collocation (T25:25:130) is discussed by Lounsbury (1973: 138).

12. The Tozzer edition of the *Relación* translates the last part of this phrase as "bread with the seeds of gourds"(Tozzer 1941: 142). The Spanish text (Landa ca.1566: 29v) is "pepitas de calabaças," which I would translate as "squash seeds."

13. The 1579 *Relación de Zama* (de la Garza 1983, 2: 147–148) is ambivalent on this point. On one hand, it states that "los naturales darse mas a la pesquería que no a labrar tierras de pan, y de esta causa les falta siempre pan [the natives are more inclined to fishing than farming and therefore they always lack bread]." On the other hand, it records that "En el tiempo de su gentilidad . . . comían el grano del maíz y pescado que ahora comen [During the period of their heathendom . . . they ate the corn and fish that they now eat]." Corn is among the tribute items listed in this *Relación*.

14. The modern village is located three leagues (9 miles) west of the Tulum archaeological site (Heyden 1967: 237). According to the Secretaria de Programación y Presupuesto (1982), the maximum distance from

the ocean to arable land in the Tulum vicinity is about 5 kilometers (3.1 miles).

15. Cenotes also receive emphasis in the Chan Kom *ch'a chaak* ceremony through the requirement that the food offerings be prepared using *suhuy haa'* ("uncontaminated, or virgin water"). The water for the ritual breads for all other ceremonies is drawn from the regular village cenote before dawn, when it is thought to be too early in the day for contamination to have been created by women arriving to collect household water. *Suhuy haa'* must, however, be obtained from a sacred cenote in a remote location (Redfield and Villa Rojas 1934: 139).

16. Villa Rojas (1945: 116–117) has reported on the modern *tup k'ak'* of east central Quintana Roo. As in the *tup k'ak'* of Landa's description, the modern ceremony is paired with a second agricultural rite dedicated to the Chaaks and other agricultural gods (an expression of gratitude, the *u hanli col*). If these ceremonies do indeed correspond to the Landa events held during *Mac*, some elements must have been lost over time. The quenching of evil heat left in the *milpa* after its burning is done with a maize beverage, not water, and there is no reference to a cenote in the second rite.

17. This modern population is not descended from the pre-Hispanic residents of Tulum. According to information from Nancy Farriss (Benavides and Andrews 1979: 59), the Tulum occupants were resettled in Boloná (Xcan) and Chemax in 1688.

18. This is in order that the gods do not feel cheated and send retribution.

19. However, a human sacrifice scene involving Gods B and K is part of the almanac on page 3a (center) of *Codex Dresden* (Thompson 1972).

20. The scarcity of censer fragments in Sanders' Trenches 11, 48, 49, and 50 is in accordance with his suggestion that the area between Structures 25 and 33 might have been a market.

21. For further discussion of directionally oriented planning, see Coe (1965c), Coggins (1980, 1983), Freidel and Sabloff (1984), and Kowalski (1994a).

22. Barrera Vásquez (1970: 72) has observed the apparent form of the ceiba tree in the stalagtites and stalagmites at the center of the chambers of the cave of Balankanche, where rainmaking ceremonies were conducted.

15

The Skull Rack in Mesoamerica

Virginia E. Miller

Of the many indigenous Mexica customs encountered by the Spanish conquerors, none fascinated and appalled them as much as the practice of human sacrifice. In addition to offering vivid descriptions of the act of sacrifice itself, often performed at the summit of pyramid-temples, six-teenth-century chroniclers also mention a type of structure that was closely linked with sacrificial rites. The *tzompantli*, a Nahuatl word translated as "skull rack,"[1] was a low stone platform on which were displayed the skulls of vanquished enemies, pierced and strung vertically or horizontally on wooden beams (figure 15.1).

Because most documented skull racks occurred within the sacred precinct of Tenochtitlan and because of the long-standing reputation of the Mexica-Aztecs as the most "bloodthirsty" of all Mesoamericans, it has long been assumed that the *tzompantli* is a Postclassic, central Mexican invention. The presence of a large and elaborate skull rack at Chichén Itzá, for example, continues to be attributed to the influence of Toltec invaders. Recent thinking about Chichén Itzá, however, has begun to reshape our understanding of that site and its history (see Stone, chapter 13, this volume). While some scholars still support the idea of a Toltec invasion of Yucatán, others have posited a different sort of relationship between Tula and Chichén Itzá.[2]

Given that the Maya are now recognized as having practiced both captive and personal blood sacrifice, it is difficult to believe that it was the aggressive Toltecs who introduced the idea of a structure for the display of skulls to the "peace-loving" Maya. Indeed, many motifs represented at Chichén Itzá that were once thought to be evidence of foreign intrusions have their origins in Classic Maya iconography. Architectural features like the skull rack may have indigenous roots as well. As will be demonstrated, the origins of skull display and its corollary, the skull rack, are

Figure 15.1. The Great Temple and the tzompantli at Tenochtitlan (after Durán 1967, 1: plate 4).

still unclear, but appear to lie well outside the area with which the structure is most closely associated, highland central Mexico.

Mexica Tzompantlis

The conquistadors had every reason to react with horror to the practice of decapitation and skull display: both accounts of the conquest and recent excavations show graphically that they, and even their horses, suffered the same fate as the vanquished natives (Martínez Vargas 1993; Barber 1994). In any case, rather detailed, if not always accurate, written and visual records of Mexica skull racks can be found in colonial chronicles.

According to Sahagún's informants, there were at least six skull racks within the sacred precinct of Tenochtitlan (Sahagún 1950–1982, 2: appendix). The location of these structures remains problematical because only one or two of them have been accounted for archaeologically. In any case, it is not certain that all of the 78 ritual components described by Sahagún were actually placed within the sacred precinct: some may have been scattered throughout the city (Seler 1904b: 770). For example, an illustration of what may be a skull rack in the ward of Tetzicuauhtitlan appears in Diego Muñoz Camargo's account of the Tlaxcalan contribution to the Spanish siege of Tenochtitlan (Hassig 1988: figure 32).

Sahagún's (1974) reconstruction drawing of the precinct from his *Primeros Memoriales* places the Great Skull Rack between the Great Temple and a *cuauhxicalli*, a recipient for hearts (see figure 9.8, this volume). The 1524 plan of Tenochtitlan that accompanied Cortés's second letter shows two *tzompantlis*, one in front of the Templo Mayor and the other on its north side (figure 15.2). De Bry's fanciful engraving combines the pyramid and the *tzompantli*, probably at least in part because they were so closely connected in the European mind as sites of human sacrifice (Boone 1987: figure 6).

The confusion regarding the number and placement of the skull racks is reflected in Ignacio Marquina's various reconstructions and plans of the sacred precinct. He tended to rearrange structures within it, slightly realigning the principal *tzompantli*, setting it southwest of the Templo Mayor, and removing the one he had earlier placed in the northeast corner of the sacred precinct that had been derived from the Cortés map (Boone 1987: 52, figures 32, 35). During the recent excavations at

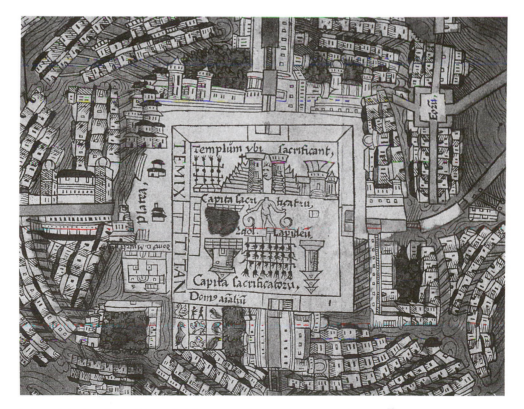

Figure 15.2. Detail of Hernan Cortés's map of Tenochtitlan, Nuremburg 1524. Woodcut on paper (photograph courtesy of Newberry Library, Chicago).

Figure 15.3. Structure B, Templo Mayor Precinct, Tenochtitlan (photograph courtesy of Richard F. Townsend).

Tenochtitlan, however, it was this latter structure that came to light, but immediately adjacent to the Templo Mayor just as the Cortés map had indicated. Structure B, as it is known, most likely dates to the reign of Ahuitzotl (1486–1502), who rededicated the Templo Mayor with an unprecedented number of sacrifices over a four-day period (Townsend 1987b: 383). This platform has a stairway on the west and is decorated on the three remaining sides with 240 stuccoed stone skulls (Matos 1987b: 197) (figure 15.3). However, since no human skulls were discovered within this structure, it may only symbolically have represented the larger functional skull rack with its real skulls (Heyden and Villaseñor 1984: 31).[3] The placement of this structure on the north side of the pyramid may have been meant to reflect the Mexica cosmos, with the land of the dead on the north: no such platform is present on the south side (Matos 1987b: 197).

In 1900, Batres (1902) excavated three platforms carved with skulls and crossbones north of the cathedral. Interred within one altar were two year bundle stones, suggesting the ritual burial of a 52-year-cycle. As will be seen, platforms with similar reliefs are found throughout the Maya area, perhaps anticipating this one.

What may have been the Great Skull Rack, aligned along Guatemala street opposite the Templo Mayor, was uncovered during excavations near the Metropolitan Cathedral from 1968 to 1976 (Cabrera Castro 1979:

plano 8; Gussinyer 1979: 70, fot. 13) (figure 15.4). Almost 60 meters long, it had staircases at each end. To date, however, little has been published on it.

Durán (1971: 79) provides a detailed description of the principal skull rack of Tenochtitlan as it looked when the skulls were in place, strung along thin rods between poles set in rows, about 6 feet apart (figure 15.1). According to López de Gómara's Spanish informants, 136,000 skulls were found displayed on the *tzompantli*, excluding those forming two towers at either end of the structure (López de Gómara 1964: 167). No complete bodies were found during excavations at the Templo Mayor, only the skulls of beheaded victims, perhaps a reference to the beheading of the goddess Coyolxauhqui, whose myth and image figure prominently here (Matos 1984: 161; see Matos, chapter 9, this volume).

More than 100 severed and perforated skulls were found when the Plaza de las Tres Culturas at Tlatelolco was excavated in the 1960s (Durán 1971: 79, note 8; Sánchez Saldaña 1972). Furthermore, a painted frieze of skulls and crossbones was also found on an altar that may have functioned as a skull rack. A similar one occurs at Tenayuca, suggesting that the skull-and-crossbones motif was widespread at this time (Villagra 1971: 152–155, figures 29, 33).

Painted images of actual skull racks occur, of course, in post-conquest codices (figure 15.1).[4] But there are earlier images as well. A Postclassic (probably Toltec) rock painting at Ixtapantongo in the state of Mexico depicts a decapitated woman next to a tree hung with skulls and banners (Villagra 1971: figure 27). Because the word *pantli* means "flag" as well as "wall" it seems likely that the image is meant to be read as a *tzom-*

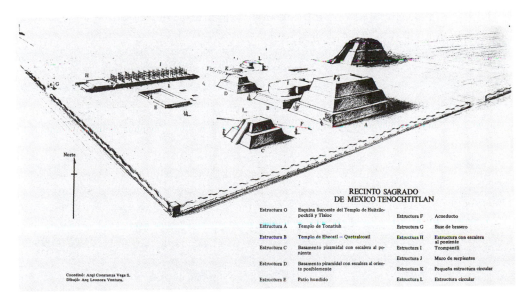

Figure 15.4. Reconstruction of ritual precinct, Tenochtitlan (after Vega Sosa 1979: op. 50).

pantli.[5] A more elaborate skull rack is illustrated on page 19 of the *Codex Borgia* (1976). Here, the deity Tlahuizcalpantecuhtli kneels on a platform marked by Tlaltecuhtli at the base, with pierced skulls strung on a horizontal pole behind him. Behind the figure a vertical wooden rack merges into flowering branches, each marked with a banner similar to the ones on the Ixtapantongo painting.[6]

These images of skulls in trees recall the fate of Hun Hunahpu, whose decapitated head was placed in the fork of a calabash tree, causing it to bear fruit .[7] Bones or skeletonization are symbols of regeneration among many cultures, including the Maya (cf. Furst 1982), and in the *Popol Vuh* myth the skull impregnates a young woman of Xibalba who gives birth to the Hero Twins. These late visual and written references to skull display may indicate an ancient custom of using trees for hanging skulls, then building wooden racks, and finally creating permanent stone structures. As will be demonstrated, evidence for wooden racks has indeed been found.

Skull Caches and Skull Display during the Formative and Classic Periods in Mesoamerica

Although Late Postclassic Mesoamerican cultures provide the most vivid and complete record of what might be termed a skull cult, decapitation is recorded in the art and archaeology of Mesoamerica beginning in the Formative Period (Moser 1973). During the Classic period, caches of skulls buried individually or in groups occur with some frequency over a widespread area. The well-known skull from Kaminaljuyú is among a small number of intricately incised skulls unearthed in the Maya area during the Early Classic (cf. Robicsek 1991). Two worked human crania, one carved to represent a face, were uncovered at Xochicalco (Hirth 1989: 76). At the beginning of the Late Classic, at the site of Saltillo in Tehuantepec, 10 adult male skulls were deposited in a large funerary urn and buried over the crushed skull of a child (Zeitlin 1993: 126).

The earliest recorded evidence of Mesoamerican skull display, as opposed to caches or burials, also occurs in Oaxaca, at La Coyotera during the Protoclassic (figure 15.5). At this site between the Tehuacan and Oaxaca valleys, 61 human skulls aligned more or less in rows had fallen from a collapsed wooden skull rack in front of the most important pyramid of the Late and Terminal Formative Lomas phase (ca. 200 B.C.–A.D. 200) (Spencer 1982: 236–239). The presence of this structure has been interpreted as evidence of the political expansion into the Cuicatec-speaking area by the Zapotec with the resultant destruction of the previously autonomous site (Redmond and Spencer 1983: 120). If so, the invaders took strong measures to ensure control or quash rebellion: the skulls were of individuals of both sexes and all ages, so entire families may have died.

Figure 15.5. Artist's reconstruction of the skull rack at Loma de La Coyotera (after Spencer 1982: figure 5.12).

The next documented examples of skull display occur at the distant sites of Cerro del Huistle, Jalisco, and Alta Vista, Zacatecas, both belonging to the northern Chalchihuites culture. The former, located on an isolated and desolate meseta in the Sierra del Nayar, was occupied from approximately A.D. 1 to 900, when it was destroyed by fire. During its final phase (ca. A.D. 500–900), broad ceremonial plazas were constructed and around them was erected a series of wooden skull racks, one of which probably held about 60 perforated skulls (Hers 1989: 89). On the floor of an adobe structure were found the remains of other skulls, without perforations, that may have somehow been displayed on its facade or hung from the wooden columns of its portico (Hers 1989: 93). As a frontier site between the nomadic tribes of the north and the sedentary peoples farther south, Cerro del Huistle must have experienced considerable conflict.[8]

Alta Vista was apparently exploited by Teotihuacan both as a mining center and workshop for processing turquoise imported from New Mexico (Diehl 1983: 153).[9] A shrine containing a headless burial accompanied by eight skulls may date from this period (A.D. 400–750) of close contact with Teotihuacan and indeed may even have been dedicated by Teotihuacanos (Holien and Pickering 1978; J. Kelley 1990: 12). At a later date, in at least two locations at the site, a number of skulls pierced to be suspended vertically by ropes from a beam or rack, along with femurs, were found where they had fallen (E. Kelley 1978; Pickering 1985: 303). The Temple of the Skulls, in use around the mid-eighth century to perhaps the mid-ninth century, supported one of these groups. Another set apparently fell from a burnt porch beam in an entryway of a palacelike structure built ca. A.D. 830–835 (J. Kelley 1990: 13). The osteological evidence indicates that a relatively small number of individuals, largely males of warrior age, were sacrificed sequentially, rather than in massive numbers at one time (Pickering 1985: 317).

Surprisingly, there is no evidence at Teotihuacan itself for a skull rack. Although skull imagery is rare in the art of Teotihuacan, decapitated skulls have been uncovered from time to time at the site.[10] Despite this evidence, it has been suggested that head-taking, a trophy head cult, and even cannibalism may have been adopted by Mesoamerican frontier centers such as Alta Vista from their Sierra Madre Occidental neighbors and then diffused into central Mesoamerica during the Postclassic period (E. Kelley 1978).[11] As will be seen, however, the Maya were already practicing both decapitation and skull display around the same time as the inhabitants of Alta Vista.

Skull racks do not appear in the Gulf Coast area until the Postclassic. During the Late Classic, however, skulls served as burial offerings or were occasionally buried singly (Wilkerson 1984: 114). At the shrine of El Zapotal, noted for its remarkable large-scale clay representation of an enthroned death god, a 3-meter high stack of 80 skulls was discovered buried in a pit within a burial mound (Torres Guzmán 1972).

The Classic Maya: Skull Caches and Skull Motifs

Unlike Teotihuacan, Classic Maya art is replete with skull imagery, particularly in painted ceramics. On stelae, warriors wear what appear to be trophy heads around their necks. A head lies on the steps among the prisoners depicted on the wall of Room 2 at Bonampak. And a recently uncovered stucco wall at Toniná displays a macabre underworld scene involving sprawling prisoners and a dancing skeleton grasping the hair of a severed head (Stuart and Stuart 1993: 98–99). In general, however, the Maya did not feature skull imagery in their architectural decoration until the Terminal Classic.

Although securely identified *tzompantlis* from Classic Maya cities have not been uncovered, interred severed heads have been excavated throughout the Maya area.[12] Mass skull deposits are especially common during the Terminal Classic, when several sites appear to have suffered a violent end, as at Colhá, Belize, where 28 human skulls were found in a pit (R. E. W. Adams cited in Wren and Schmidt 1991: 210).

At Dos Pilas, Guatemala, 16 skulls were buried in various deposits within a complex and an adjacent plaza north of the central plaza

(Wright 1990; Inomata et al. 1992). This complex's function apparently changed from residential to mortuary in the mid-eighth century. At least three skulls were of young men who, unlike others found in the same complex, share the same type of head deformation and encrusted teeth. Furthermore, the heads appear to have been buried immediately after being severed from the body. These features led the excavator to speculate that these young men were sacrificed captives, perhaps surrogate ballplayers (Wright 1990: 30). Although not immediately adjacent to the ballcourt, the complex is less than 100 meters to the northwest of it (Wright 1990: figure 2.1). Alternatively, the heads might have been those of warriors deposited during the siege of Dos Pilas: the cache is only a few meters from a defensive wall where other archaeological evidence demonstrates that a battle took place (Arthur Demarest, personal communication, February 1994).

At Copan, a small three-room vaulted annex (Structure 10L-230) to the temple of the Hieroglyphic Stairway pyramid (Structure 10L-26) was once decorated with reliefs of fleshless human long bones and skulls. While no bodies were found, a broken eccentric flint on the floor of the central chamber hints at a possible sacrificial function (Fash 1991: 149). Dated to the mid-eighth century, this structure may be the earliest in Mesoamerica to display the skull-and-bone motif that becomes so prominent in the Postclassic. Echoing the war and death themes of both Structure 10L-26 and 10L-230, the later Structure 10L-16's facade was decorated with tenoned stone skulls (Fash 1991: 169).

At Seibal, a four-sided platform close to one end of the ballcourt, Structure A-13, was found to contain the remains of 11 males, possible sacrificial victims. Although not a skull rack, the platform may have served as a place to sacrifice and inter victims in association with the ballgame (Smith 1982: 240). It dates to approximately A.D. 930, which dovetails nicely with the probable "foreign" occupation of Chichén Itzá, presumably by Itzá relatives of Seibal's inhabitants (see Kowalski 1989).

Low platforms decorated with reliefs of skulls and other related motifs occur at Uxmal and Nohpat, as well as on the basal molding of a structure at Dzibilchaltún (Andrews IV 1965: figure 17b). At Uxmal four low platforms are found in the so-called Cemetery Group west of the Nunnery Quadrangle. On each, carved blocks of frontal skulls in low relief alternate with crossbones and another motif, possibly the "death eye" motif common in Maya art (figure 15.6). The skulls still wear cloth earplugs, a trait of captives and others who have let blood, and their hair is still in place. Durán's account of the *tzompantli* at Tenochtitlán mentions that skulls were displayed without the flesh but with the hair intact.

The reliefs of the possible *tzompantli* of Nohpat, illustrated by Catherwood (Stephens 1963, l: figure 21), closely resemble those of nearby Uxmal. Frontal skulls alternate with crossed bones, although the skull stones drawn by Catherwood have subsequently disappeared (Dunning

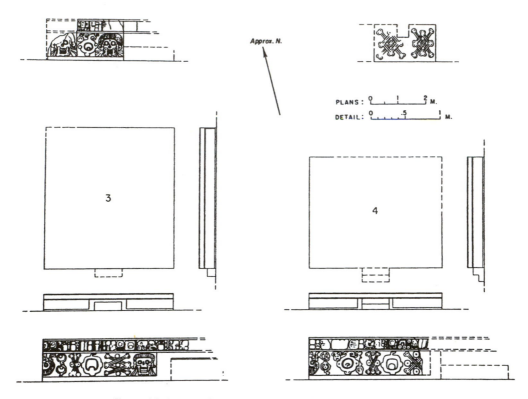

Figure 15.6. Uxmal, Cemetery Group, Sculptured Platforms 3 and 4 (after Pollock 1980: figure 408).

1987: 99). The platform was topped by five sculptures, four of which were apparently feline figures with heads broken at the neck, and a single stone column. Dunning (n.d.) suggests that the five monoliths once marked the four directions and the center, thus recreating the Maya cosmos on the surface of the small platform.[13] This much-destroyed platform lies just south of the ballcourt, marks the northern end of a sacbe from Kabah, and is close to the end of another one from Uxmal. The platform's prominent position and the accompanying relief and three-dimensional sculptures suggest that it served an important ceremonial function, whether or not skulls were ever placed on it.

Three-dimensional or high relief frontal stone skulls also decorated other types of structures in the northern Maya lowlands, including the Great Pyramid at Uxmal (Gallenkamp and Johnson 1985: figure 127) and a palace-type structure at Nacuché (Hermann 1993: figure 133).

The Tzompantli at Chichén Itzá

The largest, most complete, and most elaborate *tzompantli* is at Chichén Itzá (figure 15.7a). Located just to the east of the Great Ballcourt, it is oriented 17° east of north. In plan it is in the shape of a T, with a staircase located in the center of the east side.[14] The head of the T is decorated with low reliefs of carved profile skulls shown pierced vertically and strung on poles (figure 15.7b). The walls of the body of the T are covered with alternating rows of warriors and eagles oriented toward the staircase and framed by moldings of undulating serpents (figure 15.8). The total number of skulls would have been around 2,400, with 20 warriors, 16 eagles, and about 50 serpents (Tozzer 1957: 131).

Eduard Seler was the first to write about the *tzompantli*, which he called Mausoleum II, illustrating his work with photographs taken by

Figure 15.7. Views of the tzompantli at Chichén Itzá: (a) general view; (b) detail of skull reliefs (photographs by Virginia Miller).

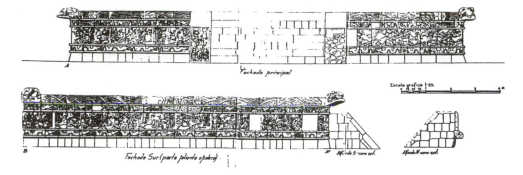

Figure 15.8. Drawing of main and south facades of the *tzompantli* at Chichén Itz á (after Salazar 1952: figures a, b).

Maler (Seler 1915: 361–365, plates 39, 41). It was explored and partially reconstructed in 1927 by José Erosa Peniche, who also assembled many of its scattered carved reliefs. In 1951 Jorge Acosta and Ponciano Salazar undertook its excavation and restoration (Salazar 1952; Acosta 1954). Two burials were found within the structure, each consisting of a human skull and offerings of jade, shell beads, and mosaic pyrite plaques (Salazar 1952: 39). In addition, a chacmool sculpture similar in style to that found in the Platform of the Eagles by Augustus LePlongeon was uncovered from the transverse axis of the *tzompantli*. Two other chacmools had been found within the structure by earlier excavators (Ruppert 1952: appendix V). Finally, fragments of a carved ballcourt ring, now reconstructed in the small museum at the entrance to the site, were also found near the chacmool.

Significantly, perhaps, a headless chacmool was also excavated in the small altar next to the *tzompantli* at Tula, a four-stairway structure comparable to the two platforms at Chichén Itzá (Diehl 1983: 150; Zambrano 1985: 35–36, figures 28–29). If Mary Ellen Miller's (1985) hypothesis that chacmools represent captives is correct, they may have served as surrogate victims for the dedication of platforms and other structures at Tula and Chichén Itzá.[15]

Although Salazar drew all the reliefs on the *tzompantli* (figure 15.8), Seler's drawings are more detailed (figure 15.9). He notes that not only the balustrade figures have skeletal legs (figure 15.9c) but some of the processional figures have them as well (figure 15.9b). He thought they represented the souls of dead warriors (Seler 1915: 364). The costume, headdress, and weapons of these warriors are similar to others at the site, but there are other elements, like skeletal legs, that set them apart. The balustrade figures, for example, seem to have pointed flint blades attached to their feet. While other figures at the site are surrounded by a single large serpent, here each warrior has a series of smaller snakes seemingly growing out of his body and even wrapping around his ankles.

Figure 15.9. Details of reliefs on the *tzompantli* at Chichén Itzá: (*a*) warrior; (*b*) warrior with skeletal legs; (c) legs of balustrade figure (after Seler 1915: figures 237–239).

Perhaps these figures are members of the serpent "faction" at Chichén Itzá, led by K'ukulcan, represented in other reliefs and paintings, notably in the Upper and Lower Temples of the Jaguars. If so, the followers of "Sun Disk"—perhaps K'akupacal—the other war captain, are absent here, unless the flamelike scrolls around them are meant as references to him.[16]

Although the reliefs can be divided into two groups, each converging on the single stairway, the groups are identical and do not appear to be confronting one another. They have some of the features that have been identified as "Toltec," such as round back shields, *atlatl* spearthrowers, and fur wristlets. But efforts in the past to distinguish between Toltec victors and Maya losers in reliefs and paintings at the site have not been convincing. The "non-Classic" facial features, accoutrements, and costume of the many figures represented here have been documented elsewhere in the Maya area (cf. Kowalski 1989; Kurjack et al. 1991).

Although warrior figures are ubiquitous at Chichén Itzá, skeletal ones are rare, with the exception of a few wearing skull masks. One scene comparable to the skull series of painted skeletal figures, also with alternating eagles (and other creatures), is from the exterior basal zone of the north side of the Temple of the Warriors (Morris, Charlot, and Morris

1931: figures 288, 289). Like the *tzompantli* figures, they grasp heads by the hair.[17] The well-known reliefs of the Great Ballcourt also feature ballplayer/warriors carrying decapitated heads, a theme duplicated at the roughly contemporaneous Red House ballcourt (Structure 3C10) and ballcourt 3D4 (Ruppert 1952: figures 124b,c, 129c,d). The tzompantli figures may also be ballplayers, as they wear the padded armband seen on the ballcourt figures. Whether warriors or ballplayers, here they also serve as executioners.

The eagles on the *tzompantli* panels, in much larger scale than the human figures, are the familiar birds holding human hearts in their claws that also occur on the tableros of Temple of the Warriors and on the Platform of the Eagles. The undulating serpents framing the figures above and below have parallels in the bench figures of the Mercado and elsewhere at the site.

Given the increasing evidence that the Great Ballcourt dates from the Terminal Classic (e.g., Leyenaar and Parsons 1988: 81–83; Kowalski 1989: 175n. 4; Wren and Schmidt 1991: 209), it would seem likely that the *tzompantli*, closely connected with decapitation rituals, was constructed around the same time, but certainly not earlier. [18]

The large number of ballcourts at Chichén Itzá indicates that other skull racks might also be present. Certainly caches of skulls are known from other structures at Chichén Itzá, including one of at least 14 near the threshold of the Caracol (Ruppert 1935: 120–123). Lincoln (1990.: 404–405) suggests that such a structure exists next to a small ballcourt (5D5) included in his recent survey of a platform complex at the site. In addition to this small mound (5D26) parallel to the ballcourt, he notes two others (5D22 and 5D23) nearby that may be the equivalent in function and placement to the Platforms of the Eagles and Venus situated near the Great Ballcourt on the main plaza. It seems likely, then, that although the number of skull racks at Chichén Itzá does not approach those reported for Tenochtitlan, more than one was in operation at the earlier site.

Postclassic Tzompantlis, Skull Deposits, and Skull Imagery

The possible skull racks, representations of skulls in art, and the presence of a colonnaded hall at Alta Vista have been cited as prototypes for the same features at Tula (Diehl 1983: 50). The Proyecto Tula excavated a largely destroyed, T-shaped *tzompantli* base littered with human skull fragments at the east edge of Ballcourt II (Diehl l983: 66, figure 12). Matos (1976a: 14), who excavated the site, believes it to be a Mexica addition. The ballcourt itself, however, was covered over with a Mexica steam bath and homes (Zambrano 1985: 35). It would be strange to find a ballcourt and nearby skull rack built at different times, and whether Mexica or

Toltec, the two structures must have functioned together for at least a short time.[19]

At El Corral, near Tula, a small altar flanking the pyramid's stairs on the north side is decorated with a lower *talud* of reclining figures, a central *tablero* of crossbones and "speaking" skulls, and an upper tablero of warriors in procession (Acosta 1974) (figure 15.10). Two burials were found within it. While there is no direct evidence to suggest that this altar functioned as a *tzompantli*, its iconography, its position on the north side of the pyramid, and the presence of burials suggest a strong association with death in general and human sacrifice in particular.[20] The altar also recalls the carved daises placed on either side of the stairway of the Temple of the Warriors at Chichén Itzá, which also feature processions of warriors (Morris, Charlot, and Morris 1931, 2: plates 124–129; see Stone, chapter 13, this volume).

There is some archeological evidence for the existence of true *tzompantlis* in highland Guatemala during the Postclassic. At Chalchitan a platform exists with indentations in its walls that may once have held plastered human skulls (Smith 1955: 14, figures 6, 53). If so, they may have been removed when the structure was covered over by later construction. Such skulls, some encased in balls of stucco, have been found elsewhere in the highlands: in one case the skull was still attached to a ledge on the exterior of a platform.[21] This practice may anticipate the towers of human skulls reported at Tenochtitlan. At Iximché, 48 skulls

Figure 15.10. Restored altar to north of staircase of the pyramid of El Corral, Tula (after Acosta 1974: figure 7).

were found in one area, most in individual pits in the plaza floor. They were apparently ritual offerings, accompanied by obsidian blades (Guillemin 1967: 33).

A miniature temple at Cholula containing the burials of a man and a woman was excavated near the top of the Great Pyramid (Noguera 1937; Marquina 1951: 124). Again, although the structure was not strictly a *tzompantli*, its *tableros* were decorated with three frontal skulls made of stuccoed clay. Decapitated heads were also ritually interred at Cholula (López et al. 1970).

As noted previously, during the Late Classic in Veracruz, skulls were neither displayed on skull racks nor discarded, but served as burial offerings or were occasionally buried singly (Wilkerson 1984: 114). However, Postclassic *tzompantlis* or *tzompantli*-like structures are known from the Gulf Coast region, most notably at Cempoala, where clay skulls painted with white lime appear on the walls of two different structures, the Templo de las Caritas and the recently excavated portico building of the Edificio el Pimiento. Six skulls were also found within a pedestal in front of this latter structure, possibly interred after being displayed there (Brueggemann 1992: 58). More skull racks are documented in *lienzos* from this area (Wilkerson 1984: 104).

Decapitation, Tzompantlis, and Ballcourts

Like the *tzompantli* at Chichén Itzá, the principal skull rack of Tenochtitlan was adjacent to the ballcourt, as yet unexcavated.[22] This was apparently a traditional act of settlement: during their migration toward Tenochtitlan, the Mexica established themselves at Coatepec by building a ballcourt and *tzompantli* (Tezozomoc 1975: 32). The connection between the ballgame and human sacrifice, especially decapitation, is well documented throughout Mesoamerica (Gillespie 1991). The Codices *Nuttall*, *Borbonicus*, and *Magliabecchiano*, for example, depict skulls within ballcourts. The reliefs on the walls of ballcourts at El Tajín document scenes of sacrifice as well (see Wilkerson, chapter 5, this volume).

Among the Maya, ballgame images sometimes include the conflation of the ball and a sacrificial victim (Miller and Houston 1987), as on the Yaxchilan Structure 33 steps (Graham 1982: steps VII, VIII). The ball may contain a human head or skull, as exemplified by the Chichén Itzá ballcourt reliefs and the so-called Great Ball Court Stone (Schele and Freidel 1990: figure 9.24; Wren and Schmidt 1991: figure 9.2). Hieroglyphic texts suggest that important captives met their deaths as part of a ballgame: Bird Jaguar of Yaxchilan's famous captive Jeweled Skull, as well as Dos Pilas captive Paw Jaguar of Seibal both apparently died this way (Schele and Miller 1986: 249–250). Indeed, an "axe" event cited in the texts accompanying the Yaxchilan ballplaying scenes probably refers to the act of decapitation (Schele and Freidel 1990: 293). Copan's ruler 18 Rabbit

(Waxaklahun Ubah K'awil) apparently met the same fate, possibly also in ballgame sacrifice, at the hands of Cauac Sky of Quirigua (Schele and Freidel 1990: 487n. 28, 488n. 34).

The *Popol Vuh* provides ample evidence that the Maya saw the ballgame not simply as a sport but as a life-or-death battle. The Lords of the Underworld even try to deceive the Hero Twins into playing with a skull rather than with a rubber ball. Ballgames involving mythical and human protagonists or humans disguised as supernaturals are also featured in Maya art (see Schele and Miller 1986; Kowalski and Fash 1991).

While ballcourts were originally considered to be a Late Classic innovation in Maya architecture, Early Classic courts are now known from Palenque, Tikal, and Copan (see Sharer et al., chapter 10, this volume), and even earlier ones occur at Cerros, Colhá, and Pacbitún during the Late Preclassic (Scarborough et al. 1982: n. 5, 23; Scarborough 1991: 132; Healy 1992). Evidence for human sacrifice, of course, occurs at least as early as the Olmec. A Middle Preclassic grave at Copan included a decapitated skeleton and two children's skulls (Fash 1991: 701). Sacrificial decapitation may also have been practiced at Cuello by the Late Middle Preclassic (Robin and Hammond 1991: 210). Given the antiquity of both the ballgame and decapitation, then, it would be surprising if the display of trophy heads were not a part of Maya ritual long before the construction of the elaborate *tzompantli* and the Great Ballcourt at Chichén Itzá.

The proximity of possible *tzompantlis* or cached skulls to ballcourts has already been noted at Dos Pilas, Seibal, Nohpat, and Tula. In the Guatemalan highlands, small platforms in line with the long axis of the playing court are present at a number of sites, providing a possible setting for the display of captives, for sacrifice, or for presentation or burial of trophy heads (Smith 1955; 1982: 240).

In the northern Maya lowlands, representations of the ballgame and its aftermath far outnumber actual ballcourts. According to Kurjack, Maldonado, and Robertson, only 25 ballcourts are known from 12 northern sites, 13 of which are found at Chichén Itzá (Kurjack et al. 1991), although Dunning's (1992: 121n. 5) survey of the Puuc region suggests that others are present. Those that have been excavated appear to be of Late or Terminal Classic or Early Postclassic date, with none known from the Late Postclassic (Kurjack et al. 1991). While the ballgame may have been popular among the Mexica at the time of the conquest, it apparently had lost its importance among the lowland Maya, the loss perhaps signaling a general cultural reorientation.

Conclusions

The building of an elaborate *tzompantli* in the central plaza of Chichén Itzá may reflect a shift from individual sacrifice during the Late Classic to mass, state-sponsored executions that reached their peak during the Late Postclassic at Tenochtitlan (cf. Demarest 1984). Indeed, many features once thought to have originated in the central Mexican highlands are now known to have existed simultaneously at Tula and Chichén Itzá. Furthermore, it could be argued that rather than borrowing from earlier central Mexican sources, the Maya may at times have anticipated Aztec practices and iconography (cf. Lincoln 1990.; Wren and Schmidt 1991; M. Miller 1993).

Despite early descriptions of the Great Skull Rack at Tenochtitlan, it has yet to be thoroughly documented archaeologically. As we have seen, the structure to the north of the Templo Mayor may not have been a skull rack at all. The supposed prototype for both the Chichén and Tenochtitlan skull racks, that of Tula, was apparently undecorated and in any case is hopelessly deteriorated. The Chichén *tzompantli* is certainly no later than that of Tula and could prove to be earlier, given the redating of much of Chichén Itzá to the Terminal Classic, rather than the Postclassic. Finally, the lack of either a ballcourt or a skull rack at Teotihuacan and the presence of what seem to be proto-*tzompantlis* in the Maya area and elsewhere give weight to the thesis that the concept of skull display on a specially designed platform originated outside central Mexico.

In an earlier paper (V. Miller 1988) I hypothesized that the carved benches with reliefs depicting processions of warriors that are so typical of Chichén Itzá were normally found in private or semiprivate areas where autosacrifice took place. On the other hand, most representations of captives, sacrifice, decapitated heads, and skeletal figures occur in public areas. This dichotomy was probably not accidental: elite autosacrifice did not have to be witnessed by crowds, but captive display and sacrifice would serve well to not only intimidate enemies but to keep the local populace in check, particularly in times of unrest (cf. Lincoln 1990: 196–197). Undoubtedly the grisly sight of fresh human skulls stacked on top of the *tzompantli*, right in the center of the main plaza, helped quell any thought of rebellion or even dissent. At times when the skull rack may have been empty, the reliefs of surrogate skulls and marching executioners below must have served as an intimidating reminder of the power of the state.

It has been demonstrated that although *tzompantlis* and related platforms are prominent features at Tenochtitlan and elsewhere during the Postclassic, they are by no means exclusively a late innovation nor a strictly central Mexican one. While the origins of the skull rack remain obscure, both human sacrifice by decapitation and ballcourts have deep roots in the Maya area. Skull racks, on the other hand, have rather shallow roots in central Mexico, despite their widespread presence there in the Late Postclassic. It is possible that the large and elaborate platform at Chichén Itzá is one of the first true tzompantlis, based on earlier and simpler models that are architecturally insignificant or undecorated—and therefore unidentified. As we have seen, earlier at La Coyotera and the

Chalchihuites sites, skulls were displayed on simple wooden racks or simply hung from beams. In any case, the excavated skull altars at Tenochtitlan certainly have more in common with the skull rack of Chichén Itzá than with the rather unimpressive platform of Tula. Undoubtedly, other skull racks remain to be uncovered and will help reveal the cultural and geographical origin of the Mesoamerican *tzompantli*, the "Wall of Skulls."

Notes

1. One of the Nahuatl terms for "skull" is *tzontecomatl* (literally, "scalp pot") (Frances Karttunen, personal communication, July 1993).

2. See Diehl (1983, 1993) for discussion and summaries of the arguments regarding Chichén Itzá's relationship with Tula.

3. An offering of musical instruments, a Tlaloc effigy vessel, and jaguar remains were found within the structure (Matos 1988: figure 58)

4. See also Sahagún's *Primeros Memoriales* (1974), figure 2, which depicts a skull rack and the *Codex Mendoza* plan of Tenochtitlan (1938: plate 2). I thank Ellen T. Baird for pointing out these examples, as well as helping me with Nahuatl terms.

5. Flags are sometimes used to represent the Nahuatl locative *pan*, however (Frances Karttunen, personal communication, July 1993).

6. I thank Karl Taube (personal communication, July 1993) for calling my attention to both the rock painting and the image in the *Codex Borgia*.

7. In Nahuatl, the words for pot (*tecomatl*), part of the word for skull, and calabash (*atecomatl*) are obviously related (Frances Karttunen, personal communication, July 1993). Even contemporary Maya note the resemblance between gourds and heads (Andres Xiloj, cited in Dennis Tedlock's 1985 translation of the *Popol Vuh*, p. 329).

8. Marie-Arete Hers (1989) devotes a lengthy chapter to the skull racks at Cerro del Huistle and elsewhere. See also the article by Fauconnier (1992) which summarizes some of the work completed at the site by the Belgian Archaeological Mission to Mexico.

9. I appreciate Robert Pickering's help in tracking down sources on Alta Vista.

10. A cached Gulf-Coast type stone yoke with a human trophy skull was found at Tepantitla, for example (Leyenaar and Parsons 1988: 35). Serrano Sánchez (1993) outlines the archaeologically documented cases of cached skulls at the site. Real and imitation human upper jaws were made into necklaces worn by sacrificial victims at the Temple of Quetzalcoatl as well (Cabrera Castro 1993; see additional references in Kowalski, chapter 4, this volume).

11. A construction of human and animal bones at Casas Grandes has also been mentioned as a possible analogue to the skull-and-bone racks at Alta Vista (Pickering 1985: 303).

12. Welsh (1988) documents burials and deposits of skulls throughout the Maya lowlands, noting that some might reflect ancestor worship rather than evidence of sacrifice. It is important to realize that not all skulls were taken from unwilling victims. Landa (Tozzer 1941: 131) reported that after death the heads of Cocom lords were cleaned of their flesh, then cut in half, and the missing flesh replaced with modeled bitumen to reconstruct the original features. A painted and plastered human

skull was recovered from the Cenote at Chichén Itzá, but whether it was the head of a sacrificial victim or a revered ancestor can no longer be determined (Coggins and Shane 1984: figure 199).

13. I thank Nicholas Dunning for sharing information about Nohpat and for sending recent photographs of the remains of the carved platform. He was also responsible for informing me of the skull deposit at Dos Pilas.

14. The head of the T measures 55.10 meters by 12.02 meters, while the rest of the structure measures 12.70 meters east–west and 16.30 meters north–south. The staircase is 6.45 meters wide. The head of the T is 1.8 meters high. The addition of the serpent cornices makes the body of the platform 25 centimeters higher than the head of the T.

15. Coggins (1987) believes that the chacmool and pyrite mirrors, normally found together wherever they have been excavated at the site, were part of a New Fire ceremony introduced from central Mexico to mark the completion of a period of time.

16. See Lincoln (1990: 77ff) for the identification of the figure dubbed "Captain Sun Disk" by Arthur Miller (1977) as the Itzá war leader, K'akupacal.

17. Fragments of the collapsed arch of the North Temple of the Great Ballcourt include skeletal figures. These scenes have been interpreted as representing the death rites of an elite individual (Wren and Schmidt 1991: 215).

18. Cohodas (1978: 180, Chart III) dates the *tzompantli* to Style V, the last phase of his Chichén Itzá chronology, dating from A.D. 900–1000, but thinks the Great Ballcourt is earlier (A.D. 630–900). Coggins (1987: 476) dates the *tzompantli* to a "Toltec" period, after A.D. 1000. Kurjack et al. (1991: 154, 157) do not discuss the *tzompantli*, but seem to date the Great Ballcourt to the Early Postclassic, prior to the construction of Uxmal's ballcourt.

19. Hers (1989: 114n. 27) argues that the presence of Mexica ceramics points to the persistence into Late Postclassic times of the structure's use rather than to a strictly Mexica occupation.

20. Cynthia Kristan-Graham (1989: 291), however, believes that the reliefs represent fallen Tula leaders.

21. A skull used as a support for a crudely modeled stucco human face was recently reported in a private collection in Guatemala (Robicsek 1991: 67–68).

22. Data on Mexica ballcourts are scanty. Ballgame elements such as rings have been found in Mexico City (Baños Ramos 1990), and a possible ballcourt has been excavated in the Ciudadela area (Martos López and Pulido Méndez 1989).

Bibliography

Abadino, Francisco. 1910. Xochicalco–Chico-moztoc–Culhuacan. In *Dos monografías arqueológicas*: 13–25. México.

Abrams, Eliot M. 1994. *How the Maya Built Their World: Energetics and Ancient Architecture*. University of Texas Press, Austin.

Ackerman, J. 1984. *Palladio*. Penguin Books, New York.

Acosta, Jorge R. 1954. Exploraciones arqueológicas efectuadas en Chichén Itzá, Yucatán, 1951. *Anales del Instituto Nacional de Antropología e Historia* 6: 27–40.

———1956. Resumen de los informes de las exploraciones en Tula, Hgo. durante las VI, VII y VIII temporadas 1946–1950. *Anales del Instituto Nacional de Antropología e Historia* 8: 37–115.

———1961. La indumentaria de los cariatides de Tula. In *Homenaje a Pablo Martínez del Rio*, pp. 221–229. Instituto Nacional de Antopología e Historia, México, D.F.

———1964. *El Palacio de Quetzalpapalotl*. Memorias del Instituto Nacional de Antropología e Historia. México, D.F.

———1965. Preclassic and Classic Architecture of Oaxaca. In *Handbook of Middle American Indians*, vol. 3, Robert Wauchope (general editor) and Gordon R. Willey (volume editor), pp. 814–836. University of Texas Press, Austin.

———1974. La piramide de El Corral de Tula, Hgo. In *Proyecto Tula*, 1a parte, Eduardo Matos M. coordinador, pp. 27–50. Colección Científica 15. Instituto Nacional de Antropología e Historia, México, D.F.

———n.d. Exploraciones en Monte Negro, Oaxaca. Manuscript in the archives of the Instituto Nacional de Antropología e Historia. México, D.F.

Acosta, José de. 1962. *Historia natural y moral de las Indias* (2nd ed.), edited by E. O'Gorman. Fondo de Cultura Económica, México, D.F.

Acuña, René. 1984. *Relaciones Geográficas del Siglo XVI: Antequera*, vols. 1 and 2. Universidad Nacional Autónoma de México, México, D.F.

———1985. *Relaciones Geográficas del Siglo XVI: Tlaxcala*, vol. 2. Universidad Nacional Autónoma de Mexico, Mexico, D.F.

Adams, Richard E. W. 1991. *Prehistoric Mesoamerica* (2nd ed.). University of Oklahoma Press, Norman.

Adams, Richard E. W., and R. C. Jones. 1981. Spatial Patterns and Regional Growth among Classic Maya Cities. *American Antiquity* 46: 301–322.

Aguilera, Carmen. 1985. *Flora y Fauna Mexicana: Mitología y Tradiciones*. Editorial Everest, Leon, Spain.

Agurcia Fasquelle, Ricardo, and William L. Fash. 1989. A Royal Maya Tomb Discovered. *National Geographic* 176 (4): 480–487.

———1991. Maya Artistry Unearthed. *National Geographic* 180 (3): 94–105.

Alberti, Leon Battista. 1986. *The Ten Books of Architecture*. Dover Publications, New York.

Alcorn, Janis B. 1984. *Huastec Ethnobotany*. University of Texas Press, Austin.

Almaraz, Ramón. 1865. Apuntes sobre las Pirámides de San Juan Teotihuacan. In *Memoria de los Trabajos Efectuados por la Comisión Científica de Pachuca en el Año* 1864, pp. 349–358. J. M. Andrade and F. Escalante, Ciudad de México.

Anales de Cuauhtitlan. 1973. In Codice Chimalpopoca: Anales de Cuauhtitlan y Leyenda de los Soles (2nd ed.), translated by Primo Feliciana Velasquez, pp. 3–68. Instituto de Investigaciones Historicas, Universidad Nacional Autónoma de México, México, D.F.

Anawalt, Patricia. 1993. Rabbits, Pulque, and Drunkeness: A Study of Ambivalence in Aztec Society. In *Current Topics in Aztec Studies: Essays in Honor of Dr. H. B. Nicholson*, edited by Alana Cordy-Collins and Douglas Sharon, pp. 17–38. San Diego Museum Paper 30. San Diego Museum of Man, San Diego, California.

Anders, Ferdinand. 1963. *Das Pantheon der Maya.* Akademische Druck- und Verlagsanstalt, Graz, Austria.

Andrews, Anthony P., and Fernando Robles Castellanos. 1985. Chichen Itza and Coba: An Itza-Maya Standoff in Early Postclassic Yucatan. In *The Lowland Maya Postclassic*, edited by Arlen F. Chase and Prudence M. Rice, pp. 62–72. University of Texas Press, Austin.

Andrews, E. Wyllys, IV. 1965. Archaeology and Prehistory in the Northern Maya Lowlands: an Introduction. In *Handbook of Middle American Indians* 3, edited by Gordon R. Willey, pp. 288–330. University of Texas Press, Austin.

Andrews, E. Wyllys, IV and E. Wyllys Andrews V. 1980. *Excavations at Dzibil-chaltun, Yucatan, Mexico.* Middle American Research Institute Publication 48. Tulane University, New Orleans, Louisiana.

Andrews, E. Wyllys, V. 1979. Some Comments on Puuc Architecture of the Northern Yucatan Peninsula. In *The Puuc: New Perspectives*, edited by Lawrence Mills, pp. 1–17. Scholarly Studies in the Liberal Arts no. 1. Central College, Pella, Iowa.

———1981. Dzibilchaltun. In *Handbook of Middle American Indians*, Supplement 1, Archaeology, edited by Victoria R. Bricker and Jeremy A. Sabloff, pp. 313–341. University of Texas Press, Austin.

———n.d. Group 10L-2, Residence of the Last Copan kings. In *The Rise and Fall of the Classic Maya Kingdom of Copan*, edited by William L. Fash and E. Wyllys Andrews V. To be published by the School of American Research.

Andrews, E. Wyllys, V, and Barbara W. Fash. 1992. Continuity and Change in a Royal Maya Residential Complex at Copán. *Ancient Mesoamerica* 3 (2): 130–147.

Andrews, E. Wyllys, V, and Jeremy A. Sabloff. 1986. Classic to Post-classic: A Summary Discussion. In *Late Lowland Maya Civilization: Classic to Postclassic*, edited by Jeremy A Sabloff and E. Wyllys Andrews V, pp. 433–456. University of New Mexico Press, Albuquerque.

Andrews, George F. 1975. *Maya Cities: Placemaking and Urbanization.* University of Oklahoma Press, Norman.

———1977. *Maya Cities: Placemaking and Urbanization* (2nd printing). University of Oklahoma Press, Norman.

———1986. *Los Estilos Arquitectónicos del Puuc: Una Nueva Apreciación.* Instituto Nacional de Antropología e Historia, México, D.F.

Angulo Villaseñor, Jorge. 1978. *El museo de Cuahtetelco: Guía Oficial.* Instituto Nacional de Antropología e Historia, México, D.F.

Arana, Raul, and César Quijada. 1984. Teticpac el Viejo, un sitio con talud-tablero en Guerrero. In *Cuadernos de Arquitectura Mesoamericana* 2, pp. 57–59. Universidad Nacional Autónoma de México, México, D.F.

Arellanos, Ramón, and Lourdes Beauregard. 1981. Dos Palmas Totonacas. *La Palabra y el Hombre*, nos. 38–39, Nueva Época, Abril–Septiembre, pp. 144–160.

Armillas, Pedro. 1945. Los Dioses de Teotihuacan. *Anales del Instituto Etnologia Americana*, vol. 6: 35–61. Universidad Nacional Cuyu, Mendoza, Argentina.

———1947. La Serpiente Emplumada, Quetzalcoatl y Tlaloc. *Cuadernos Mesoamericanos* 31 (1): 161–178.

———1951. Mesoamerican Fortifications. *Antiquity* 25 (8): 77–86.

Ashmore, Wendy. 1989. Construction and Cosmology: Politics and Ideology in Lowland Maya Settlement Patterns. In *Word and Image in Maya Culture: Explorations in Language, Writing, and Representation*, edited by William F. Hanks and Don Rice, pp. 272–286. University of Utah Press, Salt Lake City.

———1992. Deciphering Maya Architectural Plans. In *New Theories on the Ancient*

Maya, edited by Elin C. Danien and Robert J. Sharer, pp. 173–184. The University Museum, University of Pennsylvania, Philadelphia.

Aveni, Anthony F. 1975. Possible Astronomical Orientations in Ancient Mesoamerica. In *Archaeoastronomy in PreColumbian America*, edited by Anthony F. Aveni, pp. 163–190. University of Texas Press, Austin.

———1980. *Skywatchers of Ancient Mexico*. University of Texas Press, Austin.

Aveni, Anthony F., Edward E. Calnek, and Horst Hartung. 1988. Myth, Environment, and the Orientation of the Templo Mayor of Tenochtitlan. *American Antiquity* 53 (2): 287–309.

Aveni, Anthony F., and Sharon L. Gibbs. 1976. On the orientation of pre-Columbian buildings in Central Mexico. *American Antiquity* 41 (4): 510–517.

Aveni, Anthony F., and Horst Hartung. 1986. *Maya City Planning and the Calendar*. Transactions of the American Philosophical Society 76 (7). Philadelphia.

Aveni, Anthony F, Horst Hartung, and Beth Buckingham. 1978. The Pecked Cross Symbol in Ancient America. *Science* 202 (4365): 267–279.

Baird, Ellen T. 1981. The Toltecs as 'Inheritors' of the Teotihuacan Tradition. Paper presented at the 1981 Society for American Archaeology Meeting, San Diego, California.

———1985. Naturalistic and Symbolic Color at Tula, Hidalgo. In *Painted Architecture and Polychrome Monumental Sculpture in Mesoamerica*, edited by Elizabeth H. Boone, pp. 115–144. Dumbarton Oaks Research Library and Collections, Washington, D.C.

———1989. Stars and War at Cacaxtla. In *Mesoamerica after the Decline of Teotihuacan A.D. 700–900*, edited by Richard A. Diehl and Janet C. Berlo, pp. 105–122. Dumbarton Oaks Research Library and Collections, Washington, D.C.

Ball, Joseph A. 1979a. Ceramics, Culture History, and the Puuc. In *The Puuc: New Perspectives*, edited by Lawrence Mills, pp. 18–35. Scholarly Studies in the Liberal Arts no. 1. Central College, Pella, Iowa.

———1979b. Southeastern Campeche and the Mexican Plateau: Early Classic Contact Situations. *Actes du XLII Congres International des Américainistes* (Paris 1976), pp. 271–280. Paris.

———1994. Northern Maya Archaeology: Some Observations on an Emerging Paradigm. In *Hidden among the Hills: Maya Archaeology of the Northwest Yucatan Peninsula*, edited by Hanns J. Prem, 389–396. Acta Mesoamericana 7. Verlag Von Flemming, Möckmühl, Germany.

Ball, Joseph W., and Jennifer T. Taschek. 1991. Late Classic Lowland Maya Political Organization and Central-Place Analysis. *Ancient Mesoamerica* 2: 149–165.

Baños Ramos, Eneida. 1990. Elementos de Juegos de Pelota Mexicas en la Ciudad de México, D.F. *Mexicon* 12 (4): 73–75.

Barber, Marta. 1994. Conquistadors and the Mexica. *Institute of Maya Studies Newsletter* 23 (2).

Barrera Marín, Alfredo, Alfredo Barrera Vázquez, and Rosa María López Franco. 1976. *Nomenclatura Etno-botánica Maya: una Interpretación Taxonómica*. Instituto Nacional de Antropología e Historia. Coleccíon Científica, no. 36. México, D.F.

Barrera Rubio, Alfredo. 1977. Exploraciones Arqueológicas en Tulum, Quintana Roo. *Boletín de la Escuela de Ciencias Antropológicas de la Universidad de Yucatán*, no. 24: 23–63.

———1981. Patrón de asentamiento en al area de Uxmal, Yucatán, Mexico. *In Memoria del Congreso Interno* 1979, pp. 71–82. Centro Regional del Sureste, Instituto Nacional de Antropología e Historia, México, D.F.

———1987. *Guia Oficial: Uxmal*. Instituto Nacional de Antropología e Historia, México, D.F.

———1991. La gran plataforma del palacio del gobernador de Uxmal. *Cuadernos de Arquitectura Mesoamericana* 12: 41–56.

Barrera Rubio, Alfredo, Tomás Gallareta Negrón, Carlos Pérez Alvarez, Lourdes Toscano Hernández, and José G. Huchim Herrera. 1988. Restauración e investigación arqueológica en Uxmal (1986–1987). *Mexicon* 10 (2): 37–40.

Barrera Rubio, Alfredo, and Jeff Karl Kowalski. 1994. Una estructura circular en Uxmal, Yucatan. Paper presented at the Segundo Congreso Internacional de Mayistas, Mérida, Yucatán, México, August 20–4, 1994.

Barrera Vásquez, Alfredo. 1970. The Ceremony of *Tsikul T'an Ti' Yuntsiloob* at Balankanche. In *Balankanche, Throne of the Tiger Priest*, by E. Wyllys Andrews IV, pp. 72–78. Middle American Research Institute, Publication 32. Tulane University, New Orleans, Louisiana.

Barrera Vásquez, Alfredo (director), Juan Ramón Bastarrachea Manzano and William Brito Sansores (editors), and Refugio Vermont Salas, David Dzul Góngora and Domingo Zool Poot (collaborators). 1980. *Diccionario Maya Cordemex: Maya Español, Español-Maya*. Editions Cordemex, Mérida, Yucatán, México.

Barrera Vásquez, Alfredo, and Sylvanus G. Morley. 1949. *The Maya Chronicles*. Contributions to American Archaeology and History, 10, no. 48. Carnegie Institution of Washington, Publication 585. Washington, D.C.

Bassie-Sweet, Karen. 1991. *From the Mouth of the Dark Cave: Commemorative Sculpture of the Late Classic Maya*. University of Oklahoma Press, Norman.

Bastien, Auguste Rémy. 1947. La pirámide del sol en Teotihuacan. Thesis, Escuela Nacional de Antropología e Historia, Mexico, D.F.

Batres, Leopoldo. 1886. Les ruines de Xochicalco au Mexique. *La nature* 14:308– 310.

———1902. *Archaeological Explorations in Escalerillas Street, City of Mexico: Year 1890*. J. Aguilar Vera and Company, Mexico City.

———1906. *Teotihuacan*. Fidencio S. Soría, México, D.F.

———1913. Discubrimientos y consolidación de los monumentos arqueológicos de Teotihuacan. In *Proceedings of the 18th International Congress of Americanists*, pp. 188–193. London.

Baudez, Claude. 1984. Le roi, la balle, et le mais: Image du jeu de balle Maya. *Journal de la Société des Américanistes*, n.s., 62: 139–154. Paris.

———1994. *Maya Sculpture of Copán: The Iconography*. University of Oklahoma Press, Norman.

Bell, Betty. 1971. Archaeology of Nayarit, Jalisco, and Colima. *Handbook of Middle American Indians* 11, part 2, edited by Gordon Ekholm and Ignacio Bernal, pp. 694–753. University of Texas Press, Austin.

Benavides C., Antonio, and Anthony P. Andrews. 1979. Ecab: Poblado y Provincia del Siglo XVI en Yucatán. *Cuadernos de los Centros Regionales, Centro Re-gional del Sureste*. Instituto Nacional de Antropología e Historia, México, D.F.

Benson, Elizabeth P. 1971. *An Olmec Figure at Dumbarton Oaks*. Studies in Pre-Columbian Art and Archaeology, no. 8. Dumbarton Oaks Research Library and Collections, Washington, D.C.

Benson, Elizabeth (editor). 1981. *Mesoamerican Sites and World-views*. Dumbarton Oaks Research Library and Collections, Washington, D.C.

Berlin, Heinrich. 1988. Las Antiguas Creencias en San Miguel Sola, Oaxaca, Mexico. In *Idolatría y Superstición entre Los Indios de Oaxaca: Textos de Heinrich Berlin, Gonzalo de Basalobre and Diego de Hevia y Valdés* (2nd ed). Ediciones Toledo, México, D.F.

———1976. The Teotihuacan Trapeze-and-Ray Sign: A Study of the Diffusion of Symbols. M.A. Thesis, Department of the History of Art, Yale University.

———1984. *Teotihuacan Art Abroad: A Study of Metropolitan Style and Provincial Transformation in Incensario Workshops*, 2 vols. BAR International Series 199. British Archaeological Reports, Oxford.

———1985. *The Art of Pre-Hispanic Mesoamerica: An Annotated Bibliography*. Reference Publications in Art History. G.K. Hall and Co., Boston.

———1989. Early Writing in Central Mexico: In Tlilli, In Tlapalli before A.D. 1000. In *Mesoamerica after the Decline of Teotihuacan A.D. 700–900*, edited by Richard A. Diehl and Janet C. Berlo, pp. 19–47. Dumbarton Oaks Research Library and Collections, Washington, D.C.

———1991. Beyond Bricolage: Women and Aesthetic Strategies in Latin American Textiles. In *Textile Traditions of Mesoamerica and the Andes: An Anthology*, edited by M. B. Schevill, J. C. Berlo, and E. B. Dwyer, pp. 437–439. Garland Publishing Co., New York.

———1992. Icons and Ideologies at Teotihuacan: The Great Goddess Reconsidered. In *Art, Ideology, and the City of Teotihuacan*, edited by Janet C. Berlo, pp. 129–168. Dumbarton Oaks Research Library and Collections, Washington, D.C.

Bernal, Ignacio. 1963. *Teotihuacan: Descubrimientos, reconstrucciones*. Instituto Nacional de Antropología e Historia, Mexico, D.F.

———1965a. Archaeological Synthesis of Oaxaca. In *Handbook of Middle American Indians*, vol. 3, Robert Wauchope (general editor) and Gordon R. Willey (volume editor), pp. 788–813. University of Texas Press, Austin.

———1965b. Architecture in Oaxaca after the End of Monte Albán. In *Handbook of Middle American Indians*, vol. 3, Robert Wauchope (general editor) and Gordon R. Willey (volume editor), pp. 837–848. University of Texas Press, Austin.

———1969. *The Olmec World*, translated by Doris Heyden and Fernando Horcasitas. University of California Press, Berkeley and Los Angeles.

Bernal, Ignacio, and Arturo Oliveros. 1988. *Exploraciones arqueológicas en Dainzu.* Colección Científica, Serie Arqueología, Instituto Nacional de Antropología e Historia, México, D.F.

Berrin, Katherine (editor). 1988. *Feathered Serpents and Flowering Trees: Reconstructing the Murals of Teotihuacan.* Fine Arts Museums of San Francisco, San Francisco.

Beyer, Herman. 1924. El Origen, Desarollo y Significado de la Greca Escalonada. *El Mexico Antiguo*, vol. 2, pp. 1–13.

———1934. *Shell Ornament Sets from the Huasteca, Mexico.* Middle American Research Institute, Publication 5, pp. 153–215. Tulane University, New Orleans, Louisiana.

Blanton, Richard E. 1978. *Monte Albán: Settlement Patterns at the Ancient Zapotec Capital.* Academic Press, New York.

Blanton, Richard E., Stephen A. Kowa-lewski, Gary Feinman, and Jill Appel. 1982. Monte Alban's Hinterland, Part 1: Prehispanic Settlement Patterns of the Central and Southern Parts of the Valley of Oaxaca, Mexico. In *Prehistory and Human Ecology of the Valley of Oaxaca*, vol. 7, edited by Kent V. Flannery and Richard A. Blanton. Memoirs of the University of Michigan, no. 15. Museum of Anthropology, Ann Arbor, Michigan.

Blanton, Richard E., Stephen A. Kowalewski, Gary M. Feinman, and Laura M. Finsten. 1993. *Ancient Mesoamerica: A Comparison of Change in Three Regions* (2nd ed.). New Studies in Archaeology. Cambridge University Press, Cambridge.

Blom, Frans. 1934. Short Summary of Recent Explorations in the Ruins of Uxmal, Yucatan. In *Proceedings of the 24th International Congress of Americanists*, pp. 55–59. Hamburg, Germany.

Boehm de Lameiras, Brigitte, and Phil C. Weigand (editors). 1992. *Origen y Desar-rollo de la Civilización en el Occidente de México.* Colegío de Michoacán, Zamora, Mexico.

Bolles, John H. 1974. Notes on a Floral Form Represented in Maya Art and Its Iconographic Implications. In *Primera Mesa Redonda de Palenque*, part 1, edited by Merle Greene Robertson, pp. 121–127. The Robert Louis Stevenson School, Pebble Beach, California.

Boone, Elizabeth H. 1985. The Color of Mesoamerican Architecture and Sculpture. In *Painted Architecture and Polychrome Monumental Sculpture in Mesoamerica*, edited by Elizabeth H. Boone, pp. 173–186. Dumbarton Oaks Research Library and Collections, Washington, D.C.

———1987. Templo Mayor Research, 1521–1978. In *The Aztec Templo Mayor*, edited by Elizabeth H. Boone, pp. 5–69. Dumbarton Oaks Research Library and Collections, Washington, D.C.

Bordone, Benedetto. 1528. Libro di Benedetto Bordone. Nel quale si ragiona di tutta l'isole del mondo con li lor nomi antichi y moderni. Venice.

Bourdieu, Pierre. 1977. *Outline of a Theory of Practice*, translated by R. Nice. Cambridge University Press, Cambridge.

Bricker, Harvey M., and Victoria R. Bricker. 1996. Astronomical References in the Throne Inscriptions of the Palace of the Governor at Uxmal. *Cambridge Archaeological Journal* 6 (2): 191–229.

Bricker, Victoria R. 1983. Directional Glyphs in Maya Inscriptions and Codices. *American Antiquity* 48: 347–353.

———1986. *A Grammar of Mayan Hieroglyphs.* Middle American Research Institute, Publication 56. Tulane University, New Orleans, Louisiana.

———1988. A Phonetic Glyph for Zenith: Reply to Closs. *American Antiquity* 53: 394–400.

———1991. Faunal Offerings in the Dresden Codex. In *Sixth Palenque Round Table, 1986*, Merle Greene Robertson, general editor, and Virginia M. Fields, volume editor, pp. 285–292. University of Oklahoma Press, Norman.

Briggs, Elinor. 1961. *Mitla Zapotec Grammar.* Instituto Linguistico de Verano y Centro de Investigaciones Antropológicas de México, México, D.F.

Broda, Johanna. 1983. Ciclos Agricolas en el Culto: Un Problema de la Correlación del

Calendario Mexica. In *Calendars in Meso-america and Peru: Native American Computations of Time*, edited by Anthony F. Aveni and Gordon Brotherston, pp. 145–165. BAR International Series 174. British Archaeological Reports, Oxford.

——1987a. Templo Mayor as Ritual Space. In Broda, Johanna, David Carrasco, and Eduardo Matos Moctezuma, *The Great Temple of Tenochtitlan: Center and Periphery in the Aztec World*, pp. 61–123. University of California Press, Berkeley.

——1987b. The Provenience of the Offerings: Tribute and "Cosmovision." In *The Aztec Templo Mayor*, edited by Elizabeth H. Boone, pp. 211–256. Dumbarton Oaks Research Library and Collections, Washington, D.C.

Brotherston, Gordon. 1976. Mesoamerican Description of Space II: Signs of Direction. *Ibero-Amerikanisches* Archiv (N.F.) 2: 39–62.

Brotherston, Gordon, and Dawn Ades. 1975. Mesoamerican Description of Space I: Myths; Stars and Maps; and Architecture. *Ibero-Amerikanisches* Archiv (N.F.) 1: 279–305.

Brown, Kenneth. 1977a. The Valley of Guatemala: A Highland Port of Trade. In *Teotihuacan and Kaminaljuyu: A Study in Prehistoric Culture Contact*, edited by William T. Sanders and Joseph Michels, pp. 205–236. Pennsylvania State University Press, University Park.

——1977b. Toward a systematic explanation of culture change within the Middle Classic Period of the Valley of Guatemala. In *Teotihuacan and Kaminaljuyu: A Study in Prehistoric Culture Contact*, edited by William T. Sanders and Joseph Michels, pp. 411–440. Pennsylvania State University Press, University Park

Brueggemann, Juergen. 1992. *Guia Oficial: Cempoala*. Gobierno del Estado de Veracruz/INAH-Salvat, México, D.F.

Brumfiel, Elizabeth M. 1987. Elite and Utilitarian Crafts in the Aztec State. In *Specialization, Exchange, and Complex Societies*, edited by Elizabeth M. Brumfiel and Timothy K. Earle, pp. 102–118. Cambridge University Press, New York.

Bunzel, Ruth L. 1929. *The Pueblo Potter: A Study of Creative Imagination in Primitive Art*. Columbia University Press, New York.

Burgoa, Francisco de. 1934a [1674, bks. I-II]. *Geográfica Descripción*. Publicaciones del Archivo General de la Nación,vols. 25 and 26. Talleres Gráficos de la Nación, México, D.F.

——1934b. *Palestra Historial*, vol. XXIV. Publicaciones del Archivo General de la Nación, México, D.F.

Byland, Bruce E., and John M. D. Pohl. 1994. *In the Realm of 8 Deer: The Archaeology of the Mixtec Codices*. University of Oklahoma Press, Norman.

Cabrera Castro, Rubén. 1979. Restos arquitectónicos del recinto sagrado en excavaciones del métro y de la recimentación de la catédral y sagrario. In *El recinto sagrado de Mexico-Tenochtitlán. Excavaciones 1968–69 y 1975–76*, Costanza Vega Sosa (coordinador), pp. 55–66. Instituto Nacional de Antropología e Historia, México, D.F.

——1990. El proyecto templo de Quetzalcoatl y la practica a gran escala del sacrificio humano. In *La época clásica: Nuevos hallazgos, nuevas ideas*, edited by Amalia Cardós Mendez, pp. 123–146. Instituto Nacional de Antropología e Historia, Museo Nacional de Antropología, México, D.F.

——1993. Human Sacrifice at the Temple of the Feathered Serpent. In *Teotihuacan: Art from the City of the Gods*, edited by Kathleen Berrin and Esther Pasztory, pp. 100–107. The Fine Arts Museums of San Francisco, in association with Thames and Hudson, New York.

Cabrera Castro, Rubén, Ignacio Rodriguez, and Noel Morelos (editors).

——1982a. *Teotihuacan 80–82: Primeros Resultaldos*. Instituto Nacional de Antropología e Historia, México, D.F.

——1982b. *Memoria del Proyecto Arqueológico Teotihuacan 80–82*. Colección Científica 132. Instituto Nacional de Antropología e Historia, México, D.F.

Cabrera Castro, Rubén, and Saburo Sugiyama. 1982. La reexploración y restauración del Templo Viejo de Quetzalcóatl. In *Memoria del Proyecto Arqueológico Teotihuacán 80–82*, edited by Rubén Cabrera Castro, et. al., pp. 163–183. Instituto Nacional de Antropología e Historia, México, D.F.

Cabrera Castro, Rubén, Saburo Sugiyama, and George L. Cowgill. 1991. The Templo de Quetzalcoatl Project at Teotihuacan: A Preliminary Report. *Ancient Mesoamerica* 2: 77–92.

Cabrero Garcia, María Teresa. 1989. *Civilización en el Norte de México: Arqueología de la cañada del Río Bolanos* (Zacatecas y Jalisco). Serie Antropológicas 103. Instituto de Investigaciones Antropológicas, Universidad Nacional Autónoma de México, México, D.F.

Cardeña Vázquez, Indalecio. 1982. Los Hijos del Maíz (Don Goyo). *Boletín de la Escuela de Ciencias Antropológicos de la Universidad de Yucatán* no. 57: 3–26.

Carlson, John B., and Linda C. Landis. 1985. Bands, Bicephalic Dragons, and Other Beasts: The Skyband in Maya Art and Iconography. In *Fourth Palenque Round Table*, 1980, edited by Elizabeth P. Benson, pp. 115–140. Pre-Columbian Art Research Institute, San Francisco.

Carmack, Robert M. 1981. *The Quiché Mayas of Utatlán: The Evolution of a Highland Guatemala Kingdom*. University of Oklahoma Press, Norman.

Carot, Patricia. 1992. La Cerámica Protoclásica del Sitio de Loma Alta, Municipio de Zacapú, Michoacán: Nuevos Datos. In *Origen y Desarrollo de la Civilización en el Occidente de México*, edited by B. Boehm de Lameiras and Phil C. Weigand, pp. 69–101, Colegío de Michoacán, Zamora, Mexico.

Carrasco, David. 1982. *Quetzalcoatl and the Irony of Empire: Myths and Prophecies in the Aztec Tradition*. University of Chicago Press, Chicago.

———1987. Myth, Cosmic Terror, and the Templo Mayor. In *The Great Temple of Tenochtitlan: Center and Periphery in the Aztec World*, edited by Johanna Broda, Davíd Carrasco, and Eduardo Matos Moctezuma, pp. 124–162. University of California Press, Berkeley and Los Angeles.

———1990. *Religions of Mesoamerica*. Harper and Row, San Francisco.

Carrasco Vargas, Ramón. 1993. Formación sociopolítica en el Puuc: el sacbé Uxmal–Nohpat–Kabah. In *Perspectivas Antropológicas en el Mundo Maya*, edited by M. J. Iglesias Ponce de León and F. Ligorred P., pp. 199–212. Sociedad Española de Estudios Mayas.

Caso, Alfonso. 1927. *El Teocalli de la Guerra Sagrada*. Publicaciones de la Secretaria de Educación Pública, Monografias del Museo Nacional de Arquelogía, Historia, y Ethnografía, Talleres Gráficas de la Nación, México, D.F.

———1928. *Las estelas zapotecas*. Secretaría de Educación Pública, Mexico.

———1958. *The Aztecs: People of the Sun*, translated by Lowell Dunham. University of Oklahoma Press, Norman.

———1960. *Interpretation of the Codex Bodley 2858*. Sociedad Mexicana de Antropología, México, D.F.

———1965a. Lapidary Work, Goldwork, and Copperwork from Oaxaca. In *Handbook of Middle American Indians*, vol. 3, Robert Wauchope (general editor) and Gordon R. Willey (volume editor), pp. 896–930. University of Texas Press, Austin.

———1965b. Sculpture and Mural Painting of Oaxaca. In *Handbook of Middle American Indians*, vol. 3, Robert Wauchope (general editor) and Gordon R. Willey (volume editor), pp. 849–870. University of Texas Press, Austin.

———1965c. Zapotec Writing and Calendar. In *Handbook of Middle American Indians*, vol. 3, Robert Wauchope (general editor) and Gordon R. Willey (volume editor), pp. 931–947. University of Texas Press, Austin.

———1969. *El Tesoro de Monte Albán*. Memorias del Instituto Nacional de Antropología e Historia, no. 3. México, D.F.

———1971. Calendrical Systems of Central Mexico. In *Handbook of Middle American Indians*, vol. 10, edited by Gordon Ekholm and Ignacio Bernal, pp. 333–348. University of Texas Press, Austin.

———1989. Los lienzos mixtecos de Ihuitlán y Antonio de León. In *Alfonso Caso: de arqueologia a la antropología*. Instituto de Investigaciones Antropologicas UNAM. Etnologia Serie Antropológicas 102, pp. 75–103. Universidad Nacional Autónoma de México, México, D.F.

Caso, Alfonso and Ignacio Bernal. 1952. *Urnas de Oaxaca*. Memorias del Instituto Nacional de Antropología e Historia, no. 2. México D.F.

———1965. Ceramics of Oaxaca. In *Handbook of Middle American Indians*, vol. 3, Robert Wauchope (general editor) and Gordon R. Willey (volume editor), pp. 871–895. University of Texas Press, Austin.

Caso, Alfonso, Ignacio Bernal, and Jorge R. Acosta. 1967. *La cerámica de Monte Albán*. Memorias del Instituto Nacional de Antropología e Historia, no. 13. México D.F.

Caso, Alfonso, and D.F. Rubín de la Borbolla. 1936. *Exploraciones en Mitla 1934–1935*.

Publicación no. 21. Instituto Panamericano de Geografía e Historia, México, D.F.

Charlot, Jean. 1931. Bas-Reliefs from the Temple of the Warriors Cluster. In *The Temple of the Warriors at Chichen Itza, Yucatan*, 2 vols. by Morris, Earl H., Jean Charlot, and Ann Axtell Morris, pp. 229-346 of vol. 1 and pp. 28-129 of vol. 2. Carnegie Institution of Washington Publication 406. Washington, D.C.

Chase, Diane Z., and Arlen F. Chase. 1982. Yucatecan Influence in Terminal Classic Belize. *American Antiquity* 47: 596–609.

———1992. *Mesoamerican Elites: An Archeological Assessment*. University of Oklahoma Press, Norman.

Cheek, Charles D. 1977a. Excavations at the Palangana and the Acropolis, Kaminaljuyu. In *Teotihuacan and Kaminaljuyu: A Study in Prehistoric Culture Contact*, edited by William T. Sanders and Joseph Michels, pp. 1–204. Pennsylvania State University Press, University Park.

———1977b. Teotihuacan Influence at Kaminaljuyu. In *Teotihuacan and Kaminaljuyu: A Study in Prehistoric Culture Contact*, edited by William T. Sanders and Joseph Michels, pp. 441–452. Pennsylvania State University Press, University Park.

———1983. Excavaciones en la Plaza Principal. *Introducción a la Arqueología de Copán, Honduras, Tomo II*, pp. 191–290. Instituto Hondureño de Antropología e Historia, Tegucigalpa, Honduras.

Chippindale Christopher. 1986. Archaeology, Design Theory, and the Reconstruction of Prehistoric Design Systems. *Environment and Planning B: Planning and Design* 13, pp. 445–485.

Clark, John E. 1986. From mountains to molehills: A critical review of Teotihuacan's obsidian industry. In *Research in economic anthropology*, supplement 2, edited by Barry Isaac, pp. 23–74. JAI Press, Greenwich, Connecticut.

Clavijero, Francisco, Javier. 1807. *The History of Mexico. Collected from Spanish and Mexican Historians, from Manuscripts and ancient paintings of the Indians . . . . By Abbé Francesco Saverio Clavigero*. Translated from the original Italian by Charles Cullen, 2nd. ed. J. Johnson, London.

Closs, Michael P. 1988. A Phonetic Version of the Maya Glyph for North. *American Antiquity* 53: 386–393.

Codex Borgia (facsimiles). 1976. Cod. Borg.

Messicano 1, Biblioteca Apostolica Vaticana. *Codices Selecti: Phototypice Impressi*, vol. 58 (Karl A. Nowotny, commentator). Akademische Druck- und Verlagsanstalt, Graz, Austria.

Codex Dresden (facsimiles). 1975. Codex Dresdensis. Mscr. Dresd. R 310, Säch- sische Landesbibliothek Dresden. *Codices Selecti: Phototypice Impressi*, vol. 54. Akademische Druck- und Verlagsanstalt, Graz, Austria.

Codex Laud (facsimile). 1966. Codex Laud. Ms. Laud Misc. 678, Bodleian Library Oxford. *Codices Selecti: Phototypice Impressi*, vol. 11. Akademische Druck- und Verlagsanstalt, Graz, Austria.

Codex Mendoza (facsimile). 1938. Codex Mendoza, 3 Vols., edited and translated by James Cooper-Clark. Waterlow and Sons, London.

Códice Chimalpopoca. 1975. Anales de Cauahtitlan y Leyenda de los Soles, translated from the Nahuatl by Primo Feliciano Velázquez (2nd ed.). Instituto de Investigaciones Históricas, Universidad Nacional Autónoma de México, México, D.F.

Los Códices Mayas (facsimiles of the Dresden, Grolier, Madrid, and Paris Codices). 1985. Universidad Autónoma de Chiapas, Tuxtla Gutiérrez, Chiapas.

Coe, Michael D. 1956. The funerary temple among the Classic Maya. *Southwestern Journal of Anthropology* 12: 387–394.

———1965a. The Olmec Style and Its Distribution. In *Handbook of Middle American Indians*, vol. 3, edited by Robert Wauchope and Gordon R. Willey, pp. 739–775. University of Texas Press, Austin.

———1965b. Archaeological Synthesis of Southern Veracruz and Tabasco. In *Handbook of Middle American Indians*, vol 3, edited by Robert Wauchope and Gordon R. Willey, pp. 679–715. University of Texas Press, Austin.

———1965c. A Model of Ancient Community Structure in the Maya Lowlands. *Southwestern Journal of Anthropology* 21 (2): 97–114.

———1973. The Maya Scribe and his World. The Grolier Club, New York.

———1977. Olmec and Maya: A Study in Relationships. In *The Origins of Maya Civilization*, edited by Richard E. W. Adams, pp. 183–195. School of American Research, University of New Mexico Press, Albuquerque.

————1981. Religion and the Rise of Meso-american States. In *The Transition to State-hood in the New World*, edited by Grant D. Jones and Robert R. Kautz, pp. 157–171. New Directions in Archaeology. Cambridge University Press, Cambridge.

————1984. *Mexico* (3rd ed.). Thames and Hudson, New York.

————1987. *The Maya* (4th ed.). Thames and Hudson, New York.

————1989. The Hero Twins: Myth and Image. In *The Maya Vase Book: A Corpus of Roll-out Photographs of Maya Vases*, vol. 1, by Justin Kerr, pp. 161–184. Kerr and Associates, New York.

Coe, William R. 1967. *Tikal: A Handbook of the Ancient Maya Ruins*. The University Museum, University of Pennsylvania, Philadelphia.

————1972. Cultural Contact between the Lowland Maya and Teotihuacan as Seen from Tikal, Guatemala. In *Teotihuacan, XI Mesa Redonda*, 1966, pp. 157–271. Sociedad Mexicana de Antropología, México, D.F.

Coggins, Clemency C. 1975. *Painting and Drawing Styles at Tikal: An Historical and Iconographic Reconstruction*. Ph.D. Dissertation, Department of Art History, Harvard University. University Microfilms, Ann Arbor, Michigan.

————1980. The Shape of Time: Some Political Implications of a Four-Part Figure. *American Antiquity* 45: 727–739.

————1983a. An Instrument of Expansion: Monte Alban, Teotihuacan, and Tikal. In *Highland-Lowland Interaction in Meso-america: Interdisciplinary Approaches*, edited by Arthur G. Miller, pp. 49–68. Dumbarton Oaks Research Library and Collections, Washington, D.C.

————1983b. *The Stucco Decoration and Architectural Assemblage of Structure 1-sub, Dzibilchaltun, Yucatan, Mexico*. Middle American Research Institute, Publication 49. Tulane University, New Orleans, Louisiana.

————1984. Murals in the Upper Temple of the Jaguars, Chichen Itza. In *Cenote of Sacri-fice: Maya Treasures from the Sacred Well at Chichen Itza*, edited by Clemency C. Coggins and Orrin C. Shane III, pp. 157–166. University of Texas Press, Austin.

————1987. New Fire at Chichen Itza. In *Memorias del Primer Coloquio Interna-cional de Mayistas, 5–10 Agosto, 1985*, pp.

427–484. Universidad Nacional Autónoma de México, México, D.F.

————1988. Reply to Closs: A Phonetic Version of the Maya Glyph for North. *American Antiquity* 53: 401.

————1993. The Age of Teotihuacan and Its Misson Abroad. In *Teotihuacan: Art from the City of the Gods*, edited by Kathleen Berrin and Esther Pasztory, pp. 140–155. The Fine Arts Museums of San Francisco, in association with Thames and Hudson Publishers, New York.

Coggins, Clemency C., and Orrin Shane III. 1984. *Cenote of Sacrifice: Maya Treasures from the Sacred Well at Chichen Itza*. University of Texas Press, Austin.

Cohen, Abner. 1974. *Two-Dimensional Man: An Essay on the Anthropology of Power and Symbolism in Complex Society*. University of California Press, Berkeley.

Cohodas, Marvin. 1975. The Symbolism and Ritual Function of the Middle Classic Ball Game in Mesoamerican. *American Indian Quarterly* 2 (2): 99–130.

————1978. *The Great Ball Court at Chichen Itza, Yucatan, Mexico*. Garland Publishing Co., New York.

Conrad, Geoffrey W., and Arthur A. Demarest. 1984. *Religion and Empire: The Dynamics of Aztec and Inca Expansionism*. New Studies in Archaeology. Cambridge University Press, Cambridge.

Cordova, Juan de. 1987. *Vocabulario en Lengua Zapoteca* (facsimile edition of the original 1578 edition). Ediciones Toledo, México, D.F.

Corona Núñez, José. 1953. Relaciones Arque-ológicos entre las Huastecas y los regiones al poniente. In *Huastecos, Totonacos, y sus Vecinos*, pp. 479–484. Sociedad Mexicana de Antropología, México, D.F.

Cortés, Hernando. 1977. Hernando Cortés. *His Five Letters of Relation to the Emperor Charles V*, 2 vols., edited by Francis Augustus MacNutt. Rio Grande Press, Glorieta, New Mexico.

Cowgill, George L. 1979. Teotihuacan, Internal Militaristic Competition, and the Fall of the Classic Maya. In *Maya Archaeology and Ethnohistory*, edited by Norman Hammond and Gordon R. Willey, pp. 51–62. University of Texas Press, Austin.

————1983. Rulership and the Ciudadela: Political Inferences from Teotihuacan Architecture. In *Civilization in the Americas*, edited by Richard Leventhal and Alan

J. Kolata, pp. 313–343. University of New Mexico Press, Albuquerque.

———1992. Social Differentiation at Teotihuacan. In *Mesoamerican Elites: an Archaeological Assessment*, edited by Diane Z. Chase and Arlen F. Chase, pp. 206–220. University of Oklahoma Press, Norman.

Cowgill, George L., Jeffrey H. Altschul, and Rebecca S. Sload. 1984. Spatial Analysis of Teotihuacan: A Mesoamerican Metro-polis. In *Intrasite Spatial Analysis in Archaeology*, edited by H. Hietala, pp. 154–195. Cambridge University Press, Cambridge.

Cyphers Guillén, Ann. 1994. San Lorenzo Tenochtitlan. In *Los olmecas en Mesoamérica*, edited by John Clark, pp. 43–68. Citibank/México, México, D.F.

Dahlin, Bruce. 1976. *An Anthropologist looks at the Pyramids: A Late Classic Revitalization Movement at Tikal, Guatemala*. Ph.D. Dissertation, Department of Anthropology, Temple University. University Microfilms, Ann Arbor, Michigan.

Dalgrén de Jordan, Barbara. 1954. *La Mixteca: su Cultura e Historia Pre-hispánica*. Colección de Cultura Mexicana, núm. 1. México, D.F.

Davies, Nigel B. 1975. Tula, Reality, Myth, and Symbol. In *Sociedad Mexicana de Antropología, XIII Mesa Redonda*, pp. 59–72. México, D.F.

———1977. *The Toltecs: Until the Fall of Tula*. University of Oklahoma Press, Norman.

———1980. *The Aztecs: A History*. University of Oklahoma Press, Norman. [Originally published by Macmillan London Ltd., 1973.]

———1982. *The Ancient Kingdoms of Mexico*. Allen Lane, Penguin Books, London.

———1984. The Aztec Concept of History: Teotihuacan and Tula. In *The Native Sources and the History of the Valley of Mexico*, edited by Jacqueline de Durand-Forest, pp. 207–214. BAR International Series 204. British Archaeological Reports, Oxford.

Delgado Pang, Hildegard. 1992. *Pre-Columbian Art: Investigations and Insights*. University of Oklahoma Press, Norman.

Demarest, Arthur A. 1984. Overview: Sacrifice in Evolutionary Perspective. In *Ritual Human Sacrifice in Mesoamerica*, organized by Elizabeth P. Benson, and edited by Elizabeth H. Boone, pp. 227–243. Dumbarton Oaks Research Library and Collections, Washington, D.C.

———1992. Ideology in Ancient Maya Cultural Evolution: The Dynamics of Galactic Politics. In *Ideology and Pre-Columbian Civilizations*, edited by Arthur A. Demarest and Geoffrey Conrad, pp. 135–158. School of American Research Press, Santa Fe, New Mexico.

Demarest, Arthur A., and Geoffrey W. Conrad (editors). 1992. *Ideology in Pre-Columbian Civilizations*. School of American Research Press, Santa Fe.

Demarest, Arthur A., and Antonia E. Foias. 1993. Mesoamerican Horizons and the Cultural Transformations of Maya Civilization. In *Latin American Horizons,* edited by Don S. Rice, pp. 147–192. Dumbarton Oaks Research Library and Collections, Washington, D.C.

Diehl, Richard A. 1983. *Tula: The Toltec Capital of Ancient Mexico*. Thames and Hudson Publishers, New York.

———1989. A Shadow of Its Former Self: Teotihuacan during the Coyotlatelco Period. In *Mesoamerica after the Decline of Teotihuacan A.D. 700–900*, edited by Richard A. Diehl and Janet C. Berlo, pp. 9–18. Dumbarton Oaks Research Library and Collections, Washington, D.C.

———1993. The Toltec Horizon in Meso-america: New Perspectives on an Old Issue. In *Latin American Horizons*, edited by Don S. Rice, pp. 263–294. Dumbarton Oaks Research Library and Collections, Washington, D.C.

Diehl, Richard A., and Janet C. Berlo (editors). 1989. *Mesoamerica after the Decline of Teotihuacan A.D. 700–900*. Dumbarton Oaks Research Library and Collections, Washington, D.C.

Dirks, Nicholas B., Geoff Eley, and Sherry B. Ortner. 1994. Introduction. In *Culture/Power/History: A Reader in Contemporary Social Theory*, edited by Nicholas B. Dirks, Geoff Eley, and Sherry B. Ortner, pp. 3–45. Princeton University Press, Princeton.

Dow, James W. 1967. Astronomical Orientations at Teotihuacan: A Case Study in Astroarchaeology. *American Antiquity* 32: 326–334.

Drennan, Robert D. 1976. *Fábrica San José and Middle Formative Society in the Valley of Oaxaca*. Prehistory and Human Ecology of the Valley of Oaxaca, vol. 4. Memoirs of the Museum of Anthropology, no. 8, University of Michigan. Ann Arbor.

———1983. Ritual and Ceremonial Development at the Early Village Level. In *The Cloud People: Divergent Evolution of the*

Zapotec and Mixtec Civilizations, edited by Kent V. Flannery and Joyce Marcus, pp. 46–50. Academic Press, Orlando, Florida.

Drucker, R. David. 1974. *Renovating a Reconstruction: The Ciudadela at Teotihuacan, Mexico: Construction Sequence, Layout, and Possible Uses of the Structure.* Ph.D. Dissertation, Department of Anthropology, University of Rochester. University Microfilms, Ann Arbor, Michigan.

———1977. A Solar Orientation Framework for Teotihuacan. In *XV Mesa Redonda* 2, pp. 69–375. Sociedad Mexicana de Antropología, México, D.F.

Drucker, Philip. 1952. *La Venta, Tabasco: A Study of Olmec Ceramics and Art.* Smithsonian Institution, Bureau of American Ethnology Bulletin 153. U. S. Government Printing Office, Washington, D.C.

———1981 On the Nature of the Olmec Polity. In *The Olmec and Their Neighbors: Essays in Memory of Matthew W. Stirling*, edited by Elizabeth P. Benson, pp. 29–47. Dumbarton Oaks Research Library and Collections, Washington, D.C.

Drucker, Philip, Robert F. Heizer, and Robert J. Squier. 1959. *Excavations At La Venta, Tabasco, 1955.* Smithsonian Institution, Bureau of American Ethnology Bulletin 170. U. S. Government Printing Office, Washington, D.C.

Dunning, Nicholas P. 1987. Monuments in Yucatan and Campeche. *Mexicon* 9 (5): 99.

———1992. *Lords of the Hills: Ancient Maya Settlement in the Puuc Region*, Yucatan, Mexico. Prehistory Press, Madison, Wisconsin.

———1994. Puuc Ecology and Settlement Patterns. In *Hidden among the Hills: Maya Archaeology of the Northwest Yucatan Peninsula*, edited by Hanns J. Prem, pp. 1–43. Verlag Von Flemming, Möckmühl, Germany.

———n.d. Report on a Tzompantli Platform and Associated Sculpture at Nohpat, Yucatan. Manuscript.

Dunning, Nicholas P., and Jeff K. Kowalski. 1994. Lords of the Hills: Classic Maya settlement patterns and political iconography in the Puuc region, Mexico. *Ancient Mesoamerica* 5: 63–95.

Dupaix, Guillermo. 1844. *Antiquités Mexicaines, Relation des Trois Expeditions du Colonel Dupaix, ordonnées en 1805*, 1806 et 1807. Paris.

Durán, Fray Diego. 1964. *The Aztecs, The History of the Indies of New Spain*, translated by Doris Heyden and Fernando Horcasitas. Orion Press, New York.

———1967. *Historia de las Indias de Nueva Espana e Islas de la Tierra Firme*, 2 vols., edited by Angel Maria Garibay K. Editorial Porrua, México, D.F.

———1971. *Book of the Gods and Rites and the Ancient Calendar*, translated and edited by Fernando Horcasitas and Doris Heyden. University of Oklahoma Press, Norman.

DuSolier, Wilfrido. 1945. Estudio Arquitectónico de los Edificios Huaxtecas. In *Anales del Instituto Nacional de Antropología e Historia*, Tomo I, 1939–1940, pp. 121–146. México, D.F.

Easby, Elizabeth K. and John F. Scott. 1970. *Before Cortés: Sculpture of Middle America.* New York Graphic Society, Metropolitan Museum of Art, New York.

Ekdahl Ravicz, Marilyn. 1970. *Early Colonial Religious Drama in Mexico: From Tzompantli to Golgotha.* Catholic University of America Press, Washington, D.C.

El Guindi, Fadwa. 1986. *The Myth of Ritual: A Native's Ethnography of Zapotec Life-Crisis Rituals.* Abel Hernández Jímenez (collaborator). University of Arizona Press, Tucson.

Eliade, Mircea. 1954. *The Myth of the Eternal Return, or, Cosmos and History*, translated by Willard R. Trask. Bollingen Series XLVI. Princeton University Press, Princeton, New Jersey.

———1958. *Patterns in Comparative Religion.* Sheed and Ward, New York.

———1959. *The Sacred and the Profane: The Nature of Religion.* Harcourt, Brace, and World, New York.

———1965. *The Myth of the Eternal Return*, translated by Willard R. Trask. University of Chicago Press, Chicago.

———1973. *Lo Sagrado y Lo Profano.* Editorial Guadarrama, Madrid.

———1979. *Tratado de historia de las Religiones.* Editorial Era, Mexico, D.F.

Erasmus, Charles J. 1965. Monument Building: Some Field Experiments. *Southwestern Journal of Anthropology* 21 (4): 277–301.

Espíndola, Nicolás. 1580 [1905]. *Relación de Chichicapa y su Partido. Geografiá y Estadística*, edited by Francisco del Paso y Troncoso, vol. 4, pp. 115–143. Papeles de Nueva España: Segunda Serie, Madrid.

Estrada Monroy, Augustín. 1979. *El mundo k'ekchi' de la Vera-Paz.* Editorial del Ejército, Guatemala.

Evans, Susan T., and Janet Catherine Berlo.

1992. Teotihuacan: An Introduction. *In Art, Ideology, and the City of Teotihuacan,* edited by Janet Catherine Berlo, pp. 1–26. Dumbarton Oaks Research Library and Collections, Washington, D.C.

Fash, Barbara W. 1992. Late Classic Architectural Sculpture Themes in Copán. *Ancient Mesoamerica* 3 (2):89–104.

Fash, Barbara W., William L. Fash, Sheree Lane, Rudy Larios, Linda Schele, Jeffrey Stomper, and David Stuart. 1992. Investigations of a Classic Maya Council House at Copan, Honduras. *Journal of Field Archaeology* 19 (4):419–442.

Fash, William L. 1988. A New Look at Maya Statecraft from Copán, Honduras. *Antiquity* 62: 157–169, 234.

———1991. *Scribes, Warriors, and Kings: The City of Copan and the Ancient Maya.* Thames and Hudson, New York.

Fash, William L., and Robert J. Sharer. 1991. Sociopolitical Developments and Methodological Issues at Copán, Honduras: A Conjunctive Perspective. *Latin American Antiquity* 2 (2):166–187.

Fash, William L., and David Stuart. 1991. Dynastic History and Cultural Evolution at Copán, Honduras. In *Classic Maya Political History: Hieroglyphic and Archaeological Evidence,* edited by T. Patrick Culbert, pp. 147–179. Cambridge University Press, Cambridge.

Fash, William L., Richard V. Williamson, Carlos Rudy Larios, and Joel Palka. 1992. The Hieroglyphic Stairway and Its Ancestors: Investigations of Copán Structure 10L-26. *Ancient Mesoamerica* 3 (2): 105–116.

Fauconnier, Françoise. 1992. Projet: Sierra del Nayar. Résultats des travaux menés par la mission archéologique belge au Mexique. *Mexicon* 14 (2): 24–30.

Fewkes, Jesse Walter. 1907. *Certain Antiquities of Eastern Mexico.* Twenty-First Annual Report of the Bureau of American Ethnology, pp. 221–296. Washington, D.C.

Fields, Virginia. 1990. The Iconographic Heritage of the Maya Jester God. In *Sixth Palenque Round Table, 1986,* edited by Merle G. Robertson and Virginia Fields, pp. 167–174. University of Oklahoma Press, Norman.

Flannery, Kent V. 1968. The Olmec and the Valley of Oaxaca: A Model for Inter-Regional Interaction in Formative Times. In *Dumbarton Oaks Conference on the Olmec,* edited by Elizabeth P. Benson, pp.

79–117. Dumbarton Oaks Research Library and Collections, Washington, D.C.

———1972. The Cultural Evolution of Civilizations. *Annual Review of Ecology and Systematics* 3: 399–426.

———1983. Monte Negro: A Reinterpretation. In *The Cloud People: Divergent Evolution of the Zapotec and Mixtec Civilizations,* edited by Kent V. Flannery and Joyce Marcus, pp. 99–102. Academic Press, Orlando, Florida.

Flannery, Kent (editor). 1976. *The Early Mesoamerican Village.* Academic Press, New York.

Flannery, Kent V., and Joyce Marcus. 1976a. Evolution of the Public Building in Formative Oaxaca. In *Cultural Change and Continuity: Essays in Honor of James Bennett Griffin,* edited by Charles Cleland, pp. 205–221. Academic Press, New York.

———1976b. Formative Oaxaca and the Zapotec Cosmos. *American Scientist* 64 (4): 374–383.

———1983a. The Growth of Site Hierarchies in the Valley of Oaxaca: Part I. In *The Cloud People: Divergent Evolution of the Zapotec and Mixtec Civilizations,* edited by Kent V. Flannery and Joyce Marcus, pp. 53–64. Academic Press, Orlando, Florida.

———1983b. The Rosario Phase and the Origins of Monte Albán I. In *The Cloud People: Divergent Evolution of the Zapotec and Mixtec Civilizations,* edited by Kent V. Flannery and Joyce Marcus, pp. 74–77. Academic Press, Orlando, Florida.

———1983c. San José Mogote in Monte Alban II: A Secondary Administrative Center. In *The Cloud People: Divergent Evolution of the Zapotec and Mixtec Civilizations,* edited by Kent V. Flannery and Joyce Marcus, pp. 111–113. Academic Press, Orlando, Florida.

———1983d. Monte Alban and Teotihuacan. Editor's Introduction. In *The Cloud People: Divergent Evolution of the Zapotec and Mixtec Civilizations,* edited by Kent V. Flannery and Joyce Marcus, pp. 161–166. Academic Press, Orlando, Florida.

———1983e. Urban Mitla and Its Rural Hinterland. In *The Cloud People: Divergent evolution of the Zapotec and Mixtec Civilizations,* edited by Kent V. Flannery and Joyce Marcus, pp. 295–300. Academic Press, Orlando, Florida.

Flannery, Kent V. and Joyce Marcus (editors). 1983. *The Cloud People: Divergent Evolu-*

tion of the Zapotec and Mixtec Civilizations. Academic Press, Orlando, Florida.

Flannery, Kent V., Joyce Marcus, and Stephen A. Kowalewski. 1981. The Preceramic and Formative in the Valley of Oaxaca. In *Handbook of Middle American Indians*, Supplement 1: Archaeology, Victoria R. Bricker (general editor) and Jeremy A. Sabloff (volume editor), pp. 49–93. University of Texas Press, Austin.

Folan, William J., Ellen R. Kintz, and Laraine A. Fletcher. 1983. Coba. *A Classic Maya Metropolis.* Academic Press, New York.

Foncerrada de Molina, Marta. 1965. *La escultura arquitectónica de Uxmal.* Universidad Nacional Autónoma de México, México, D.F.

————1982. Signos glificos relacionados con Tlaloc en los murales de la batalla en Cacaxtla. *Anales del Instituto de Investigaciones Estéticas* 50 (1): 23–34. México, D.F.

Foucault, Michel. 1980. *Power/Knowlege: Selected Interviews and Other Writings, 1972–1977,* edited and translated by Colin Gordon. Pantheon Publishers, New York.

Fox, John W. 1987. *Maya Postclassic State Formation: Segmentary Lineage Migration in Advancing Frontiers.* Cambridge University Press, Cambridge.

Fox, Richard. 1977. *Urban Anthropology.* Prentice Hall, Englewood Cliffs, New Jersey.

Freidel, David A. 1986a. Terminal Classic Lowland Maya: Successes, Failures, and Aftermaths. In *Late Lowland Maya Civilization: Classic to Postclassic,* edited by Jeremy A. Sabloff and E. Wyllys Andrews V., pp. 409–432. University of New Mexico Press, Albuquerque.

————1986b. Maya Warfare: An Example of Peer Polity Interaction. In *Peer Polity Interaction and the Development of Sociopolitical Complexity,* edited by Colin Renfrew and John Cherry, pp. 93–108. Cambridge University Press, Cambridge.

————1990. The Jester God: The Beginning and End of a Maya Royal Symbol. In *Vision and Revision in Maya Studies,* edited by Flora S. Clancy and Peter D. Harrison, pp 67–78. University of New Mexico Press, Albuquerque.

————1992a. Children of the First Father's Skull: Terminal Classic Warfare in the Northern Maya Lowlands and the Transformation of Kingship and Elite Hierarchies. In *Mesoamerican Elites: An Archaeological Assessment,* edited by Diane Z. Chase and Arlen F. Chase, pp. 99–117. University of Oklahoma Press, Norman.

————1992b. The Trees of Life: Ahaw as Idea and Artifact in Classic Maya Lowland Civilization. In *Ideology in Pre-Columbian Civilizations,* edited by Arthur A. Demarest and Geoffrey W. Conrad, pp. 115–133. Society for American Research Press, Santa Fe, New Mexico.

Freidel, David A., and Jeremy A. Sabloff. 1984. *Cozumel: Late Maya Settlement Patterns.* Academic Press, Orlando, Florida.

Freidel, David A., and Linda Schele. 1988. Symbol and Power: A History of the Lowland Maya Cosmogram. In *Maya Iconography,* edited by Elizabeth P. Benson and Gillett G. Griffin, pp. 44–93. Princeton University Press, Princeton, New Jersey.

————1989. Dead Kings and Living Mountains: Dedication and Termination Rituals of the Lowland Maya. In *Word and Image in Maya Culture,* edited by William Hanks and Don S. Rice, pp. 233–243. University of Utah Press, Salt Lake City.

Freidel, David A., Linda Schele, and Joy Parker. 1993. *Maya Cosmos: Three Thousand Years on the Shaman's Path.* William Morrow and Company, New York.

Freidel, David A. and Charles K. Suhler. n.d. The Crown of Creation, The Development of the Maya Royal Diadems in the Late Prelassic and Early Classic Periods. Paper in a volume of symposium proceedings edited by Nikolai Grube, University of Bonn, Germany.

de la Fuente, Beatríz, Silvia Trejo and Nelly Gutiérrez Solána. 1988. *Escultura en piedra de Tula.* Instituto de Investigaciones Estéticas, Universidad Nacional Autónoma de México, México, D.F.

Furst, Jill Leslie. 1978a. *Codex Vindobonensis Mexicanus 1: A Commentary.* State University of New York Institute for Mesoamerican Studies, Publication no. 4. Albany.

————1978b. The Year 1 Reed, Day 1 Alligator: A Mixtec Metaphor. *Journal of Latin American Lore* 4 (1): 93–128.

————1982. Skeletonization in Mixtec Art: A Re-evaluation. In *The Art and Iconography of Late Post-Classic Central Mexico,* organized by Elizabeth P. Benson and edited by Elizabeth Hill Boone, pp. 207–226. Dumbarton Oaks Research Library and Collections, Washington, D.C.

Furst, Peter D. 1968. The Olmec Were-Jaguar in

the Light of Ethnographic Reality. In *Dumbarton Oaks Conference on the Olmec*, edited by Elizabeth P. Benson, pp. 143–178. Dumbarton Oaks Research Library and Collections, Washington, D.C.

————1973. West Mexican Art: Secular or Sacred? In *The Iconography of Middle American Sculpture*, pp. 98–133. The Metropolitan Museum of Art, New York.

Gallegos Ruiz, Roberto. 1978. *El Señor 9 Flor en Zaachila*. Universidad Nacional Autónoma de México, México, D.F.

Gallenkamp, Charles and Regina E. Johnson (editors). 1985. *Maya: Treasures of an Ancient Civilization*. Harry N. Abrams, New York.

Galvan, Javier. 1984. *Las Tumbas de Tiro del Valle de Atemajac*, Jalisco, 2 vols. Centro Regional de Jalisco, Guadalajara.

Gamio, Manuel. 1922. *La Población del Valle de Teotihuacan*. Dirección de Talleres Gráficas, Secretaria de Educación Pública, Mexico City.

Gann, Thomas. 1917. The *Chachac*, or Rain Ceremony, as Practised by the Maya of Southern Yucatan and Northern British Honduras. In *Proceedings of the Nineteenth International Congress of Americanists*, Washington, D.C., 1915, pp. 409–418. Washington, D. C.

Garcés F., Fernando, José Mendiolea O., Guadalupe Sepeda M., and Patricia Fournier G. 1984. La Restuaración Arqueológica en México. *Cuadernos de Arquitectura Mesoamericana* 3, pp. 11–18. Universidad Nacional Autónoma de México, México, D.F.

Garcia, Gregorio. 1981. *Origen de los Indios del Nuevo Mundo* (preliminary study by Franklin Pease). Fondo de Cultura Economica, México, D.F.

García Cook, Angel. 1981. The Historical Importance of Tlaxcala in the Cultural Development of the Central Highlands. In *Handbook of Middle American Indians*, Supplement 1, Archaeology, Jeremy A. Sabloff (general editor) and Victoria R. Bricker (volume editor), pp. 244–276. University of Texas Press, Austin.

————1984. Dos elementos arquitectónicos "tempranos" en Tlalancaleca, Puebla. *Cuadernos de Arquitectura Mesoamericana* 2, pp. 29–32. Universidad Nacional Autónoma de México, México, D.F.

García Cook, Angel, and Raúl M. Arana A. 1978. *Rescate arqueológico del Monolito de Coyolxauhqui*. Instituto Nacional de Antropología e Historia, Secretaria de Educación Pública, México, D.F.

García Payon, José. 1947. Exploraciones arqueológicas en el Totonacapan Meridional (Region de Misantla). *Anales del Instituto Nacional de Antropología e Historia*, vol. 2, pp. 73–111. México, D. F.

————1950. Exploraciones en Xiuhtetelco, Puebla. *Uni-Ver.* II, Núm. 22, pp. 397–426, 155–164. Xalapa, Veracuz.

————1965. *Descripción del pueblo de Gueytlalpan, por Juan de Carrion*. Universidad Veracruzana, Xalapa.

————1971. Archaeology of Central Veracruz. In *Handbook of Middle American Indians*, vol. 11, pp. 505–542. University of Texas Press, Austin.

de la Garza, Mercedes, Ana Luisa Izquierdo, Ma. del Carmen León, and Tolita Figueroa. 1983. *Relaciones Histórico-Geográficas de la Gobernación de Yucatán*, 2 vols. Universidad Nacional Autónoma de México, México, D.F.

Garza Tarazona de González, Sylvía, and Edward B. Kurjack. 1980. *Atlas arqueológico del estado de Yucatán*. Instituto Nacional de Antropología e Historia, México, D.F.

Gay, Carlo. 1972. *Chalcacingo*. International Scholarly Book Services, Inc., Portland, Oregon.

Geertz, Clifford. 1973. *The Interpretation of Cultures*. Basic Books, Inc., New York.

————1980. *Negara: The Theater State in Nineteenth-Century Bali*. Princeton University Press, Princeton.

Gendrop, Paul. 1983. *Los estilos Rio Bec, Chenes y Puuc en la arquitectura Maya*. Universidad Nacional Autónoma de México, México, D.F.

————1984. El tablero-talud y otras perfiles arquitectónicos en Meso-america. *Cuadernos de Arquitectura Mesoamericana* 2, pp. 48–49. Universidad Nacional Autónoma de México, México, D.F.

Giddens, Wendy Louise. 1995. Talud-Tablero Architecture as a Symbol of Mesoamerican Affiliation and Power. Master's Thesis, Department of Anthropology, University of California, Los Angeles.

Gillespie, Susan D. 1989. *The Aztec Kings: The Construction of Rulership in Mexica History*. University of Arizona Press, Tucson.

————1991. Ballgames and Boundaries. In *The Mesoamerican Ballgame*, edited by Vernon

L. Scarborough and David R. Wilcox, pp. 317–345. University of Arizona Press, Tucson.

Girard, Rafael. 1948. Génesis y función de la greca escalonada. *Cuadernos Americanos Año* VII, 40 (4): 141–151. México, D.F.

Gómez-Pompa, Arturo, José Salvador Flores, and Mario Aliphat Fernández. 1990. The Sacred Cacao Groves of the Maya. *Latin American Antiquity* 1: 247–257.

González Crespo, Norberto, and Silvia Garza Tarazona. n.d. Comunicaciones y accessos de Xochicalco. Manuscript.

González Crespo, Norberto, Silvia Garza Tarazona, Hortensia de Vega Nova, Pablo Mayer Guala, and Giselle Canto Aguilar. 1995. Archaeological Investigations in Xochicalco, Morelos, 1984–1986. *Ancient Mesoamerica* 6: 223-236.

González Lauck, Rebecca. 1988. Proyecto arqueológico La Venta. In *Arqueologia*, Vol. 4, edited by Alba G. Mastache, pp. 121–165. Instituto National de Antropología e Historia, México, D.F.

———1994. La antigua ciudad olmeca en La Venta, Tabasco. In *Los Olmecas en Mesoamerica*, edited by John E. Clark, pp. 93–112. Citibank/Mexico, México, D.F.

Gossen, Gary H. 1974. *Chamulas in the World of the Sun: Time and Space in a Maya Oral Tradition*. Harvard University Press, Cambridge, Massachussetts.

———1986. Mesoamerican Ideas as a Foundation for Regional Synthesis. In *Symbol and Meaning Beyond the Closed Community: Essays in Mesoamerican Ideas, Studies on Culture and Society*, vol. 1, edited by Gary H. Gossen, pp. 1–8. Institute for Mesoamerican Studies, State University of New York at Albany, Albany.

Graham, Ian. 1982. *Corpus of Maya Hieroglyphic Inscriptions 3 (3) Yaxchilan*. Peabody Museum of Archaeology and Ethnology, Harvard University, Cambridge, Massachussetts.

———1992. *Corpus of Maya Hieroglyphic Inscriptions, 4 (2), Uxmal*. Peabody Museum of Archaeology and Ethnology, Harvard University, Cambridge, Massachussetts.

Graulich, Michel. 1976. Las peregrinaciones Aztecas y el ciclo de Mixcoatl. *Estudios de Cultura Nahuatl* 11: 311–354.

Griffin, Gillett G. 1978. Cresterias of Palenque. In *Tercera Mesa Redonda de Palenque*, vol. IV, edited by Merle Greene Robertson, pp. 139–146. Pre-Columbian Art Research Institute and Herald Printers, Monterey, California.

Grove, David. 1973. Olmec Altars and Myths. *Archaeology* 26 (2): 128–135.

———1981. Olmec Monuments: Mutilation as a Clue to Meaning. In *The Olmec and Their Neighbors: Essays in Memory of Matthew W. Stirling*, edited by Elizabeth P. Benson, pp. 49–68. Dumbarton Oaks Research Library and Collections, Washington, D.C.

———1989. Olmec: What's in a Name? In *Regional Perspectives on the Olmec*, edited by Robert J. Sharer and David C. Grove, pp. 8–14. Cambridge University Press, Cambridge.

———1995. Monumental Art and Preclassic Sacred Landscapes. Paper presented at the Maya Weekend, the University Museum, University of Pennsylvania, Philadelphia, April 8, 1995.

———1996. Chalcatzingo's Monuments, Mounds, and Sacred Landscape. Paper presented in a reviewed session on "Architecture and Ritual Space as Sacred Landscape" at the 61st Annual Meeting of the Society for American Archaeology, New Orleans, Louisiana, April 11, 1996.

Grube, Nikolai. 1994. Hieroglyphic Sources for the History of Northwest Yucatan. In *Hidden among the Hills: Maya Archaeology of the Northwest Yucatan Peninsula*, edited by Hanns J. Prem, pp. 316–358. Verlag Von Flemming, Möcksmühl, Germany.

Grube, Nikolai, and Werner Nahm. 1994. A Census of Xibalba: A Complete Inventory of Way Characters on Maya Ceramics. In *The Maya Vase Book*, vol. 4. A Corpus of Roll-out Photographs by Justin Kerr, pp. 686–715. Kerr Associates, New York.

Grube, Nikolai, and David Stuart. 1987. *Observations on T110 as the Syllable* ko. Research Reports on Ancient Maya Writing 8. Center for Maya Research, Washington, D.C.

Guidoni, Enrico. 1975. *Primitive Architecture*. Harry N. Abrams, Inc., New York.

Guillemin, Jorge. 1967. The Ancient Cakchiquel Capital of Iximché. *Expedition* 9 (2): 22–35.

Gussinyer, Jordi. 1970. Un adoratorio azteca decorado con pintura. *Boletín del Instituto Nacional de Antropología e Historia* 40: 30–35.

———1979. La arquitectura prehispánica en los alrededores de la catédral. In *El recinto sagrado de Mexico-Tenochtitlán. Excava-*

ciones 1968–69 y 1975–76, Costanza Vega Sosa (coordinador), pp. 67–74. Instituto Nacional de Antropología e Historia, México, D.F.

Guthrie, Jill (editor). 1995. *The Olmec World: Ritual and Rulership.* The Art Museum, Princeton University, Princeton, New Jersey.

Harbottle, Garman and Phil C. Weigand. 1992. Turquoise in Pre-Columbian America. *Scientific American* 266 (2): 78–85.

Hardoy, Jorge. 1964a. *Ciudades Precolombinas.* Ediciones Infinito, Buenos Aires.

———1964b. *Pre-Columbian Cities.* Walker and Company, New York.

Hargrove, Lyndon C. 1970. *Mexican Macaws: Comparative Osteology.* University of Arizona Anthropology Papers no. 20. University of Arizona Press, Tucson.

Hassig, Ross. 1988. *Aztec Warfare: Imperial Expansion and Political Control.* University of Oklahoma Press, Norman.

Hartung, Horst. 1970. Notes on the Oaxaca Tablero. *Boletín de Estudios Oaxaqueños* 27: 2–8. Mexico City College, México, D.F.

———1971. *Die Zeremonialzentren der Maya.* Akademische Druck- und Verlagsanstalt, Graz, Austria.

Haviland, William A. 1991. *Anthropology* (6th ed.). Holt, Rinehart, and Winston, Philadelphia.

Healan, Dan M., Robert H. Cobean, and Richard A. Diehl. 1989. Synthesis and Conclusions. In *Tula of the Toltecs*, edited by Dan M. Healan, pp. 239–251. University of Iowa Press, Iowa City.

Healy, Paul F. 1992. The Ancient Maya Ballcourt at Pacbitun. *Ancient Mesoamerica* 3 (2): 229–239.

Heizer, Robert F., John A. Graham, and Lewis K. Napton. 1968. The 1968 Investigations at La Venta. In *Papers on Mesoamerican Archaeology, no. 5. Contributions of the University of California Archaeological Research Facility*, July 1968. Department of Anthropology, University of California, Berkeley.

Helmuth, Nicholas M. 1987. *The Surface of the Underwaterworld: Iconography of the Gods of Early Classic Maya Art in Peten, Guatemala.* Foundation for Latin American Anthropological Research, Culver City, California.

Herrera, Antonio de. 1945. *Historia General de los Hechos de los Castellanos, en las Islas, y Tierra-Firme de el Mar Oceano*, vol. 4. Editorial Guarania, Buenos Aires.

Herrmann, Andreas. 1993. *Auf den Spuren der Maya.* Eine Fotodokumentation von Teobert Maler. Akademische Druck- und Verlags-anstalt, Graz, Austria.

Hers, Marie-Areti. 1989. *Los toltecas en tierras chichimecas.* Universidad Nacional Autónoma de México, México, D.F.

Heyden, Doris. 1967. Birth of a Deity: the Talking Cross of Tulum. *Tlalocan* 5 (3): 235–242.

———1973. Un Chicomoztoc en Teotihuacan? La cueva bajo la Piramide del Sol. *Boletín del Instituto Nacional de Antropología e Historia*, época II, núm. 6, pp. 3–18.

———1975. An Interpretation of the Cave underneath the Pyramid of the Sun in Teotihuacan, Mexico. *American Antiquity* 40: 131–147.

———1981. Caves, Gods, and Myths: World View and Planning at Teotihuacan. In *Mesoamerican Sites and World Views*, edited by Elizabeth P. Benson, pp. 1–35. Dumbarton Oaks Research Library and Collections, Washington, D.C.

Heyden, Doris, and Paul Gendrop. 1975. *Pre-Columbian Architecture of Meso-america.* Harry N. Abrams Publishers, New York.

Heyden, Doris and Luis Francisco Villaseñor. 1984. *The Great Temple and the Aztec Gods.* Minutiae Mexicana, México, D.F.

Hirth, Kenneth. 1982. Transportation Architecture at Xochicalco, Morelos, Mexico. *Current Anthropology* 23 (3): 322–324.

———1984. Xochicalco: Urban Growth and State Formation in Central Mexico. *Science* 225: 579–586.

———1989. Militarism and Social Organization at Xochicalco, Morelos. In *Mesoamerica after the Decline of Teotihuacan A.D. 700–900*, edited by Richard A. Diehl and Janet C. Berlo, pp. 69–82. Dumbarton Oaks Research Library and Collections, Washington, D.C.

Hirth, Kenneth, and Ann Cyphers Guillen. 1988. *Tiempo y Asentamiento en Xochicalco.* Instituto de Investigaciones Antropológicas, Universidad Nacional Autónoma de México, México, D.F.

Historia de los mexicanos por sus pinturas. 1973. *Historia de los mexicanos por sus pinturas.* In Teogonia e historia de los mexicanos: Tres opusculos del siglo XVI, edited by Angel Maria Garibay K., pp. 23–66. Editorial Porrua, México, D.F.

Historia Tolteca-Chichimeca. 1979. *Historia Tolteca-Chichimeca.* Antigua Librería Robredo, Porrúa, México, D.F.

Holien, Thomas. 1977. Mesoamerican Pseudo-Cloisonné and Other Decorative Invest-ments. Ph.D. Dissertation, Department of Anthropology, Southern Illinois University, Carbondale.

Holien, Thomas and Robert B. Pickering. 1978. Analogues in Classic Period Chalchihuites Culture to Late Mesoamerican Ceremonialism. In *Middle Classic Mesoamerica: A.D. 400–700*, edited by Esther Pasztory, pp. 148–157. Columbia University Press, New York.

Holmes, William H. 1895–1897. *Archaeological Studies among the Ancient Cities of Mexico.* Field Columbian Museum, Chicago.

Houston, Stephen D. 1984. An Example of Homophony in Maya Script. *American Antiquity* 49: 790–805.

——1993. *Hieroglyphs and History at Dos Pilas: Dynastic Politics of the Classic Maya.* University of Texas Press, Austin

——1996. Symbolic Sweatbaths of the Maya: Architectural Meaning in the Cross Group at Palenque, Mexico. Latin *American Antiquity* 7 (2): 132–151.

Houston, Stephen D., and David Stuart. 1990. T632 as Muyal, "Cloud." Central Tennessean Notes in Maya Epigraphy. Note circulated by the authors.

Hubbs, Carl L. 1936. Fishes of the Yucatan Peninsula. In *The Cenotes of Yucatan: A Zoological and Hydrographic Survey*, by A. S. Pearse, Edwin P. Creaser, and F. G. Hall, pp. 157–287, and 15 plates. Carnegie Institution of Washington, Publication 457. Washington, D.C.

Hulsey, Shirley S. Goldenberg. 1977. A Visual Analysis and Catalog of the Architectural Frieze Patterns on the Superterrestrial Structures at Mitla, Oaxaca, Mexico. Master's Thesis in Fine Arts, California State University, Long Beach. University Microfilms no. 13-10265, Ann Arbor, Michigan.

Inomata, Takeshi, Joel Palka, Maria Teresa Robles, Stacey Symonds, and Lori E. Wright. 1992. Excavaciones en Grupos Residenciales de Dos Pilas. In *IV Simposio de Argueología Guatemalteca, Museo Nacional de Arqueología y Etnología*, Julio de 1990, pp. 141–142. Ministerio de Cultura y Deportes/Instituto de Antropología e Historia/Asociación Tikal, Guatemala.

Ixtlilxochitl, Fernando de Alva. 1952. *Obras Historicas*, 2 vols. Editorial Nacional, México, D.F.

Jansen, Marteen E.R.G.N. 1982a. Viaje al Otro Mundo: La Tumba 1 de Zaachila. In *Los Indigenas de México en la Época Prehispánica y en la Actualidad*, edited by M.E.R.G.N. Jansen and Th. J.J. Leyenaar. Rutgers BV, Leiden.

——1982b. *Huisi Tacu: Estudio Interpretivo de un Libro Mixteco Antiguo: Codex Vindobonensis Mexicanus I.* CEDLA, Incidentale Publicates 24, vols. 1 and 2. Amsterdam.

Jaramillo, Ricardo. 1984. Patrón de Asentamiento en el Valle de Valparaiso, Zacatecas. Tésis, Escuela Nacional de Antropología e Historia, México, D.F.

Jarquín Pacheco, Ana Maria, and Martínez Vargas, Enrique. 1982. Exploración en el lado este de la Ciudadela (Estructuras 1G, 1R, 1Q, y 1P). In *Memoria del Proyecto Arqueologico Teotihuacan 80-82*, edited by R. Cabrera, I. Rodriguez, and N. Morelos, pp. 19–47. Instituto Nacional de Antropología e Historia, México, D.F.

Jiménez Moreno, Wigberto. 1941. Tula y los Toltecas según las fuentes históricas. *Revista Mexicana de Estudios Antropológicos* 5: 79–83.

——1966. Mesoamerica before the Toltecs. In *Ancient Oaxaca,* edited by John Paddock, pp. 1–82. Stanford University Press, Palo Alto, California.

Jones, Christopher, and Linton Satterthwaite. 1982. *The Monuments and Inscriptions of Tikal: The Carved Monuments.* University Museum Monograph no. 44, Tikal Report no. 33, part A. The University Museum, University of Pennsylvania, Philadelphia.

Jones, Lindsay. 1995. *Twin City Tales: A Hermeneutical Reassessment of Tula and Chichén Itzá.* Unversity Press of Colorado, Niwot.

Joralemon, Peter David. 1971. *A Study of Olmec Iconography. Studies in Pre-Columbian Art and Archaeology* 7. Dumbarton Oaks, Washington, D.C.

——1976. The Olmec Dragon: A Study in Pre-Columbian Iconography. In *Origins of Religious Art and Iconography in Pre-Classic Mesoamerica*, edited by H. B. Nicholson, pp. 27–71. University of California at Los Angeles, Latin American Center Publications, Los Angeles.

Kampen, Michael E. 1972. *The Sculptures of El Tajín, Veracruz*, Mexico. University of Florida Press, Gainesville.

Kan, Michael, Clement Meighan, and H. B. Nicholson. 1989. *Sculpture of Ancient*

West Mexico: Nayarit, Jalisco, Colima. University of New Mexico Press, Albuquerque.

Kantorowicz, Ernst A. 1957. *The King's Two Bodies: A Study in Medieval Political Theology*. Princeton University Press, Princeton, New Jersey.

Kelley, David Humiston. 1976. *Deciphering the Maya Script*. University of Texas Press, Austin.

———1977. *Deciphering the Maya Script* (2nd printing). University of Texas Press, Austin.

———1982. Notes on Puuc Inscriptions and History. In *The Puuc: New Perspectives*, edited by Lawrence Mills. Scholarly Studies in the Liberal Arts no. 1, Supplement. Central College, Pella, Iowa.

Kelley, Ellen. 1978. The Temple of the Skulls at Alta Vista, Chalchihuites. In *Across the Chichimec Sea: Papers in Honor of J. Charles Kelley*, edited by Ellen Kelley and B. C. Hedrick, pp. 102–126. Southern Illinois University Press, Carbondale.

Kelley, John Charles. 1974. Speculations on the Culture History of Northwestern Mesoamerica. In *The Archaeology of West Mexico*, edited by Betty Bell, pp. 19–39. West Mexican Society for Advanced Studies, Ajijic.

———1990. The Classic Epoch in the Chalchihuites Culture of the State of Zacatecas. In *La época clásica: Nuevos hallazgos y nuevas ideas*, edited by Amalia Cardós de Mendez, pp. 11–14. Instituto Nacional de Antropología e Historia, México, D.F.

Kepecs, Susan, Gary Feinman, and Sylviane Boucher. 1994. Chichen Itza and its Hinterland: A World-Systems Perspective. *Ancient Mesoamerica* 5: 141–158.

Kidder, Alfred V., Jesse D. Jennings, and Edwin M. Shook. 1946. *Excavations at Kaminaljuyu, Guatemala*. Carnegie Institution of Washington, Publication 561. Washington, D.C.

Kirchoff, Paul. 1943. Mesoamérica, sus límites geográficos, composición étnica, y caracteres culturales. *Acta Americana* 1: 92–107.

———1952. Mesoamerica: Its Geographical Limits, Ethnic Composition, and Cultural Character. In *Heritage of Conquest*, edited by Sol Tax, pp. 17–30. University of Chicago Press, Chicago.

Klein, Cecelia. 1986. Masking Empire: The Material Effects of Masks in Aztec History. *Art History* 9 (2): 135–167.

———1987. The Ideology of Auto-sacrifice at the Templo Mayor. In *The Aztec Templo Mayor*, edited by Elizabeth H. Boone, pp. 293–370. Dumbarton Oaks Research Library and Collections, Washington, D.C.

———1990. To Bleed Forever: The Function of Stone-Carved Images of Aztec Royal Bloodletting Rites. In *World Art: Themes of Unity in Diversity*, edited by Irving Lavin, pp. 439–444. Acts of the 17th International Congress of the History of Art.

Knorozov, Yuri. 1967. *The Writing of the Maya Indians*. Russian Translation Series 4. Peabody Museum of Archaeology and Ethnology, Harvard University, Cambridge, Massachussetts.

Kostof, Spiro. 1985. *A History of Architecture: Settings and Rituals*. Oxford University Press, Oxford.

Kowalewski, Stephen A. 1983. Monte Alban Settlement Patterns in the Valley of Oaxaca. In *The Cloud People: Divergent Evolution of the Zapotec and Mixtec Civilizations*, edited by Kent V. Flannery and Joyce Marcus, pp. 348–351. Academic Press, Orlando, Florida.

Kowalewski, Stephen A., Gary M. Feinman, Laura Finsten, Richard E. Blanton, and Linda Nicholas. 1989. *Monte Albán's Hinterland, Part II: Prehispanic Settlement Patterns in Tlacolula, Etla, and Ocotlán, the Valley of Oaxaca, Mexico*. Memoirs of the Museum of Anthropology, no. 23, University of Michigan. Ann Arbor.

Kowalski, Jeff K. 1986. Some Comments on Uxmal Inscriptions. *Mexicon* 8: 93–95.

———1987. *The House of the Governor, a Maya Palace at Uxmal, Yucatan*, Mexico. University of Oklahoma Press, Norman.

———1989. Who am I among the Itza? Links between Northern Yucatan and the Western Maya Lowlands and Highlands. In *Mesoamerican after the Decline of Teotihuacan A.D. 700–900*, edited by Richard A. Diehl and Janet C. Berlo, pp. 173–186. Dumbarton Oaks Research Library and Collections, Washington, D.C.

———1990. A Preliminary Report on the 1988 Field Season at the Nunnery Quadrangle, Uxmal, Yucatan, Mexico. *Mexicon* 12: 27–33.

———1993. Astral Deities and Agricultural Fertility: Fundamental Themes in Mesoamerican Ballgame Symbolism at Copan, Chichen Itza, and Tenochtitlan. In *The Symbolism in the Plastic and Pictorical*

Representations of Ancient Mesoamerica, edited by Jacqueline de Durand-Forest and Marc Eisinger, pp. 49–71. Holos Verlag, Bonn, Germany.

———1994a. The Puuc as seen from Uxmal. In *Hidden among the Hills: Maya Archaeology of the Northwest Yucatan Peninsula*, edited by Hanns J. Prem, pp. 93–120. Verlag Von Flemming, Möcksmühl, Germany.

———1994b. Uxmal como un ciudad "real-ritual." Paper presented at the Primero Seminario de la Mesa Redonda de Palenque, Palenque, Chiapas, Mexico, September 29–October 1, 1994.

Kowalski, Jeff K., Alfredo Barrera Rubio, Heber Ojeda Más, and José Huchim Herrera. 1996. Archaeological Excavations of a Round Temple at Uxmal: Summary Discussion and Implications for Northern Maya Culture History. In *Eighth Palenque Round Table, 1993,* Merle Greene Robertson, general editor, Martha J. Macri and Jan McHargue, volume editors, pp. 281–296. The Pre-Columbian Art Research Institute, San Francisco.

Kowalski, Jeff K., and William L. Fash. 1991. Symbolism of the Maya Ball Game at Copán: Synthesis and New Aspects. In *Sixth Palenque Round Table, 1986*, Merle Greene Robertson, general editor, Virginia M. Fields, volume editor pp. 59–67. University of Oklahoma Press, Norman.

Krauss, Rosalind. 1987. Death of a Her-meneutic Phantom: Materialization of the Sign in the Work of Peter Eisenman. In *House of Cards*, pp. 166–186. Oxford University Press, Oxford.

Krickeberg, Walter. 1933. *Die Totonaken*. Baessler-Archiv, Band VII, Band IX. Berlin.

———1966. El Juego de Pelota mesoamericano y su simbolismo religioso. *Traducciones Mesoamericanistas* 1, pp. 191– 313. Sociedad Mexicana de Antropología, México, D.F.

Kristan-Graham, Cynthia B. 1988. Identification of Lineage in the Art of Chichén Itzá. Paper presented at the 53rd Annual Meeting of the Society for American Archaeology, Phoenix, Arizona.

———1989. *Art, Rulership and the Mesoamerican Body Politic at Tula and Chichen Itza*. Ph.D dissertation, University of California at Los Angeles, Department of Art History.

———1993. The Business of Narrative at Tula: an Analysis of the Vestibule Frieze, Trade, and Ritual. *Latin American Antiquity* 4 (1): 3–21.

Krochock, Ruth. 1991. Dedication Ceremonies at Chichén Itzá: The Glyphic Evidence. In *Sixth Palenque Round Table, 1986*, Merle Green Robertson, general editor, Viginia Fields, volume editor, pp. 43–58. University of Oklahoma Press, Norman.

———1988. The Hieroglyphic Inscriptions and Iconography of the Temple of the Four Lintels and Related Monuments, Chichen Itza, Yucatan, Mexico. Master's Thesis, Department of Anthropology, University of Texas, Austin.

Kubler, George. 1967. *The Iconography of the Art of Teotihuacan*. Studies in Pre-Columbian Art and Archaeology 4. Dumbarton Oaks Research Library and Collection, Washington, D.C.

———1969. *Studies in Classic Maya Iconography*. Memoirs of the Connecticut Academy of Arts and Sciences, no. 15. New Haven, Connecticut.

———1973. Iconographic aspects of architectural profiles at Teotihuacan and in Mesoamerica. In *The Iconography of Middle American Sculpture*, pp. 24–39. The Metropolitan Museum of Art, New York.

———1975. *The Art and Architecture of Ancient America: The Mexican, Maya, and Andean Peoples* (2nd ed.). The Pelican History of Art. Penguin Books, Harmondsworth, Middlesex, England.

———1977. *Aspects of Classic Maya Rulership on Two Inscribed Vessels*. Studies in Pre-Columbian Art and Archaeology 18. Dumbarton Oaks Research Library and Collections, Washington, D.C.

———1982. Serpent and Atlantean Columns: Symbols of Maya-Toltec Polity. *Journal of the Society of Architectural Historians* 41 (2): 93–115.

———1984. *The Art and Architecture of Ancient America: The Mexican, Maya, and Andean Peoples* (3rd ed.). The Pelican History of Art. Penguin Books, Harmondsworth, Middlesex, England.

———1985. Renascence and Disjunction in the Art of Mesoamerican Antiquity. In *Studies in Ancient American and European Art: The Collected Essays of George Kubler*, edited by Thomas F. Reese, pp. 351–359. Yale University Press, New Haven, Connecticut.

Kurath, Gertrude P. 1967. Drama, Dance, and Music. In *Handbook of Middle American*

Indians 6, edited by Manning Nash, pp. 158–190. University of Texas Press, Austin.

Kurath, Gertrude P., and Samuel Marti. 1964. *Dances of Ana-huac: The Choreography and Music of Precortesian Dances*. Viking Fund Publication in Anthropology no. 38. Aldine Publishing Company, Chicago

Kurjack, Edward B., Sylvia Garza Tarazona, and Jerry Lucas. 1979. Archaeological Settlement Patterns and Modern Geography in the Hill Region of Yucatan. In *The Puuc: New Perspectives, Papers Presented at the Puuc Symposium, Central College, May 1977*, edited by Lawrence Mills, pp. 35–45. Pella, Iowa.

——1981. Pre-Columbian Community Form and Distribution in the Northern Maya Area. In *Lowland Maya Settlement Patterns*, edited by Wendy Ashmore, pp. 287–309. University of New Mexico Press, Albuquerque.

Kurjack, Edward B., Rubén Maldonado C., and Merle Greene Robertson. 1991. Ballcourts of the Northern Maya Lowlands. In *The Mesoamerican Ballgame*, edited by Vernon L. Scarborough and David R. Wilcox, pp. 145–160. The University of Arizona Press, Tucson.

Lamb, Weldon. 1980. The Sun, Moon and Venus at Uxmal. *American Antiquity* 45: 79–86.

Landa, Diego de. ca. 1566. *Relación de las Cosas de Yucatán*. Photographic copy of manuscript, in Special Collections, University of New Mexico General Library, Albuquerque.

——1941. *Landa's Relación de las Cosas de Yucatan, a Translation*. Edited with notes by Alfred M. Tozzer. Papers of the Peabody Museum of American Archaeology and Ethnology, Harvard University, vol. 18. Cambridge, Massachusetts.

LaPorte, Juan Pedro. 1985. El "Talud-Tablero" en Tikal, Peten: Nuevos Datos. Paper presented at the Primer Coloquio Internacional de Mayistas, Instituto de Investigaciones Antropológicas y Centro de Estudios Mayas, Universidad Nacional Autónoma de México, México, D.F.

LaPorte, Juan Pedro, and Vilma Fialko C. 1990. New Perspectives on Old Problems: Dynastic References for the Early Classic at Tikal. In *Vision and Revision in Maya Studies*, edited by Flora S. Clancy and Peter D. Harrison, pp. 33–66. University of New Mexico Press, Albuquerque.

Lee, Thomas A. Jr. 1985. Introduction and Bibliography. In *Los Códices Mayas*. Universidad Autónoma de Chiapas, Tuxtla Gutiérrez, Chiapas.

Leon-Portilla, Miguel. 1963. *Aztec Thought and Culture: A Study of the Ancient Nahuatl Mind*. University of Oklahoma Press, Norman.

——1969. *Pre-Columbian Literatures of Mexico*. University of Oklahoma Press, Norman.

——1978. *El Templo Mayor de Tenochtitlan, su espacio y tiempos sagrados*. Instituto Nacional de Antropología e Historia, México, D.F.

——1980. *Toltecayotl, aspectos de la cultura náhuatl*. Fondo de Cultura Económica, México, D.F.

Leslie, Charles M. 1960. *Now We Are Civilized: A Study of the World View of the Zapotec Indians of Mitla, Oaxaca*. Wayne State University Press, Detroit, Michigan.

Leyenaar, Ted J. J., and Lee A. Parsons. 1988. *Ulama: The Ballgame of the Mayas and Aztecs*. Spruyt, Van Mantgem, and De Does Bv, Leiden, The Netherlands.

Lincoln, Charles. 1990. *Ethnicity and Social Organization at Chichen Itza. Yucatan, Mexico*. Doctoral dissertation, Department of Anthropology, Harvard University, 1990. UMI Dissertation Information Service, Ann Arbor, Michigan.

Litvak King, Jaime. 1970. Xochicalco en la caida del Clásico: Una Hipotesis. *Anales de Antropología* 8: 131–144.

——1971. Investigaciones en el Valle de Xochicalco, 1569–1970. *Anales de Antropología* 8: 101–124.

——1972. Las relaciones externas de Xochicalco. *Anales de Antropología* 9: 243–276. Universidad Nacional Autónoma de México, México, D. F.

——1985. *Ancient Mexico: An Overview*. University of New Mexico Press, Albuquerque.

Lombardo de Ruiz, Sonia, et al. 1986. *Cacaxtla: El Lugar donde Muere la Lluvia en la Tierra*. Instituto Nacional de Antropología e Historia, México, D.F.

López A., Sergio, Zaid Lagunas R., and Carlos Serrano S. 1970. Sección de antropología fisica. In *Proyecto Cholula, Ignacio Marquina* (coordinador), pp. 143–152. Instituto Nacional de Antropología e Historia Serie Investigaciones 19, México, D.F.

López Austin, Alfredo, Leonardo López Lujan,

and Saburo Sugiyama. 1991. The Temple of Quetzalcoatl at Teotihuacan: Its Possible Ideological Significance. *Ancient Mesoamerica* 2: 93–105.

López de Gómara, Francisco. 1964. *Cortés. The Life of the Conqueror, by His Secretary*, translated and edited by Lesley Byrd Simpson. University of California Press, Berkeley.

López Luján, Leonardo. 1994. *The Offerings of the Templo Mayor of Tenochtitlan*. University of Colorado Press, Boulder.

Lothrop, S. K. 1924. *Tulum: An Archaeological Study of the East Coast of Yucatan*. Carnegie Institution of Washington, Publication 335. Washington, D.C.

Lounsbury, Floyd G. 1973. On the Derivation and Reading of the 'Ben-Ich' Prefix. In *Mesoamerican Writing Systems*, edited by Elizabeth P. Benson, pp. 99–144. Dumbarton Oaks Research Library and Collections, Washington, D.C.

———1985. The Identities of the Mythological Figures in the "Cross Group" of Inscriptions at Palenque. In *Fourth Palenque Round Table, 1980*, vol. 6, edited by Elizabeth P. Benson, pp. 45–58. Pre-Columbian Art Research Institute, San Francisco.

Love, Bruce. 1989. Yucatec Sacred Breads through Time. In *Word and Image in Maya Culture: Explorations in Language, Writing, and Representation*, edited by William Hanks and Don Rice, pp. 336–350. University of Utah Press, Salt Lake City.

MacNeish, Richard S. 1964. Ancient Mesoamerican Civilization. *Science* 143: 531–537.

Maldonado Cárdenas, Ruben, and Beatríz Repetto Tio. 1991. Tlalocs at Uxmal. In *Sixth Palenque Round Table 1986*, Merle Greene Robertson, general editor, Virginia M. Fields, volume editor, pp. 97–101. University of Oklahoma Press, Norman.

Manzanilla, Linda. 1990. Sector Noroeste de Teotihuacan: Estudio de un conjunto residencial y rastreo de tuneles y cuevas. In *La época clásica: Nuevos hallazgos, nuevas ideas*, edited by Amalia Cardos de Mendez, pp. 81–88. Museo Nacional de Antropología, Instituto Nacional de Antropología e Historia, Mexico, D.F.

———1993. Daily Life in the Teotihuacan Apartment Compounds. In *Teotihuacan: Art from the City of the Gods*, edited by Kathleen Berrin and Esther Pasztory, pp. 90–99. The Fine Arts Museums of San Francisco, in conjunction with Thames and Hudson, New York.

Manzanilla, Linda, Luis Barba, René Chavez, Jorge Arzate, and Leticia Flores. 1989. El inframundo de Teotihuacan: Geofísica y arqueología. *Ciencia y Desarrollo* 15 (85): 21–35.

Marcus, Joyce. 1974. The Iconography of Power Among the Classic Maya. *World Archaeology* 6 (1): 83–94.

———1976a. The Iconography of Militarism at Monte Albán and Neighboring Sites in the Valley of Oaxaca. In *Origins of Religious Art and Iconography in Preclassic Mesoamerica*, edited by Henry B. Nicholson, pp. 123–139. Latin American Studies Series no. 31. UCLA Latin American Center, Los Angeles.

———1976b. The Origins of Mesoamerican Writing. *Annual Review of Anthropology* 5: 35–67.

———1976c. The Size of the Early Meso-american Village. In *The Early Meso-american Village*, edited by Kent V. Flannery, pp. 79–90. Academic Press, New York.

———1978. Archaeology and Religion: A Comparison of the Zapotec and Maya. *World Archaeology* 10 (2): 172–191.

———1980. Zapotec Writing. *Scientific American* 242: 50–64.

———1983a. Teotihuacan Visitors on Monte Alban Monuments and Murals. In *The Cloud People: Divergent Evolution of the Zapotec and Mixtec Civilizations*, edited by Kent V. Flannery and Joyce Marcus, pp. 175–181. Academic Press, Orlando, Florida.

———1983b. Zapotec Religion. In *The Cloud People: Divergent Evolution of the Zapotec and Mixtec Civilizations*, edited by Kent V. Flannery and Joyce Marcus, pp. 345–351. Academic Press, Orlando, Florida.

———1989. Zapotec Chiefdoms and the Nature of Formative Religions. In *Regional Perspectives on the Olmec*, edited by Robert J. Sharer and David C. Grove, pp. 148–197. Cambridge University Press, Cambridge.

———1993. Ancient Maya Political Organization. In *Lowland Maya Civilization in the Eighth Century A.D.*, edited by Jeremy A. Sabloff and John S. Henderson, pp. 111–183. Dumbarton Oaks Research Library and Collections, Washington, D.C.

Marcus, Joyce and Kent V. Flannery. 1994. Ancient Zapotec Ritual and Religion: An

Application of the Direct Historical Approach. In *The Ancient Mind*, edited by Colin Renfrew and Ezra Zubrow, pp. 55–74. Cambridge University Press, Cambridge.

———1996. *Zapotec Civilization: How Urban Society Evolved in Mexico's Oaxaca Valley.* Thames and Hudson, London.

Marquina, Ignacio. 1951. *Arquitectura Prehispánica.* Instituto Nacional de Antropología e Historia, México, D.F.

———1960. *El Templo Mayor de México.* Instituto Nacional de Antro-pología e Historia, México, D.F.

———1964. *Arquitectura Prehispánica* (2nd ed.). Memorias 1, Instituto Nacional de Antropología e Historia, México, D.F.

Martínez Gracida, Manuel. 1906. Historia de la fundación de Mitla. Tomo II. Manuscript preserved in the Biblioteca Genaro V. Vasquez, Casa de Cultura, Oaxaca.

Martínez Guzmán, Maria de Lourde, and William J. Folan. n.d. Tulum. Quintana Roo: Recent Discoveries.

Martínez Vargas, Enrique. 1993. Trascendental hallazgo en Zultepec. *Arqueología Mexicana* 1 (4): 62–64.

Martos López, Luis Alberto, and Salvador Pulido Méndez. 1989. Un juego de pelota en la ciudad de México. *Arqueologia* (2a. época) Enero-Junio: 81–88.

Mastache, Alba Guadalupe, and Robert H. Cobean. 1989. The Coyotlatelco Culture and the Origins of the Toltec State. In *Mesoamerica after the Decline of Teotihuacan A.D. 700–900*, edited by Richard A. Diehl and Janet Catherine Berlo, pp. 49–67. Dumbarton Oaks Research Library and Collections, Washington, D.C.

Matos Moctezuma, Eduardo. 1965. El adoratorio decorado de las calles de Argen-tina. *Anales del Instituto Nacional de Antropología e Historia* no. 17: 127–138.

———1976a. *Tula.* Ediciones Orto, México, D.F.

———1976b. *Proyecto Tula, segunda parte.* Coleccion Cientifica 33. Instituto Nacio-nal de Antropologia e Historia, México, D.F.

———1981a. *Una Visita al Templo Mayor de Tenochtitlan.* Instituto Nacional de Antropología e Historia, México, D.F.

———1981b. Los hallazgos de la arqueología. In *El Templo Mayor*, edited by López Portillo, José, Miguel León Portilla, and Eduardo Matos Moctezuma, pp. 106–181. Beatrice Trueblood, Mexico, D.F.

———1982. *El Templo Mayor: Excavaciones y Estudios.* Instituto Nacional de Antropología e Historia, México, D.F.

———1984. The Templo Mayor of Tenochtitlan: Economics and Ideology. In *Ritual Human Sacrifice in Mesoamerica*, organized by Elizabeth P. Benson, and edited by Elizabeth H. Boone, pp. 133–164. Dumbarton Oaks Research Library and Collections, Washington, D.C.

———1986. *Los dioses que se negaron a morir . . . , Arqueología y crónicas del Templo Mayor.* Secretaria de Educación Pública, México, D.F.

———1987a. The Templo Mayor of Tenochtitlan: History and Interpretation. In *The Great Temple of Tenochtitlan: Center and Periphery in the Aztec World*, edited by David Carrasco, pp. 15–60. University of California Press, Berkeley.

———1987b. Symbolism of the Templo Mayor. In *The Aztec Templo Mayor*, edited by Elizabeth H. Boone, pp. 185–209. Dumbarton Oaks Research Library and Collections, Washington, D.C.

———1988. *The Great Temple of the Aztecs, Treasures of Tenochtitlan*, translated by Doris Heyden. Thames and Hudson, New York.

———1995. *Life and Death in the Templo Mayor*, translated by Bernard R. Ortiz de Montellano and Thelma Ortiz de Montellana. The University Press of Colorado, Niwot, Colorado.

Matos Moctezuma, Eduardo, and Leonardo López Luján. 1993. Teotihuacan and its Mexica Legacy. In *Teotihuacan: Art from the City of the Gods*, edited by Kathleen Berrin and Esther Pasztory, pp. 156–165. The Fine Arts Museums of San Francisco, in conjunction with Thames and Hudson, New York.

Maudslay, Alfred P. 1889–1902. *Archaeology*, 4 vols. Biologia Centrali-Americana. R. H. Porter and Dulau, London.

McAnany, Patricia A. 1995. *Living with the Ancestors: Kinship and Kingship in Ancient Maya Society.* University of Texas Press, Austin.

McClung de Tapia, Emily, and Evelyn Childs Rattray (editors). 1987. *Teotihuacan: Nuevos datos, nuevas síntesis, nuevos problmas.* Instituto de Investigaciones Antropológicas, Serie Antropológica 72. Universidad Nacional Autónmoma de México, México, D.F.

Medellin Zenil, Alfonso. 1950. Informe de la visita a Vega de la Peña, Veracruz. Unpublished report, Archivo Técnico, Instituto Nacional de Antropología e Historia, México, D.F.

———1953. Informe de los trabajos de 1953. Report, Archivo Técnico, Instituto Nacional de Antropología e Historia, México, D.F.

———1960. *Ceramicas del Totonacapan*. Universidad Veracruzana, Xalapa.

Melgarejo Vivanco, José Luis. 1970. *Los Lienzos de Tuxpan*. Editorial La Estampa Mexicana, México, D.F.

Michelet, Dominique, et al. 1989. El Proyecto del C.E.M.C.A. en Michoacan. Etapa I: un Balance. *Trace*, no.16, pp. 70–87. Mexico, D.F.

Milbrath, Susan.1988. Astronomical Images and Orientations in the Architecture of Chichen Itza. In *New Directions in American Archaeoastronomy*, edited by Anthony Aveni, pp. 57–79. BAR International Series 454. British Archaeological Reports, Oxford.

Miller, Arthur G. 1973. *The Mural Painting of Teotihuacan*. Dumbarton Oaks Re-search Library and Collections, Washington, D.C.

———1977. 'Captains of the Itza': Unpublished Mural Evidence from Chichen Itza. In *Social Process in Maya Prehistory*, edited by Norman Hammond, pp. 197–225. Academic Press, New York.

———1982. *On the Edge of the Sea: Mural Painting at Tancah-Tulum, Quintana Roo, Mexico*. Dumbarton Oaks Research Library and Collections, Washington, D.C.

———1988. Pre-Hispanic Mural Painting in the Valley of Oaxaca, Mexico. *National Geographic Research* 4 (2): 233–258.

Miller, Mary Ellen. 1985. A re-examination of the Mesoamerican Chacmool. *Art Bulletin* 67: 1–17.

———1986. *The Art of Mesoamerica: Olmec to Aztec*. Thames and Hudson, New York.

———1993. On the Eve of the Collapse: Maya Art of the Eighth Century. In *Lowland Maya Civilization in the Eighth Century*, edited by Jeremy A. Sabloff and John S. Henderson, pp. 355–413. Dumbarton Oaks Re-search Library and Collections, Washington, D.C.

Miller, Mary E., and Stephen D. Houston. 1987. The Classic Maya Ballgame and its Architectural Setting. *RES: Anthropology and Aesthetics* 14: 46–65.

Miller, Virginia E. 1988. Processional Banquettes at Chichén Itzá. Paper presented at the annual meeting of the Society for American Archaeology, Phoenix, April 1988.

Millon, Clara H. 1973. Painting, Writing, and Polity in Teotihuacan, Mexico. *American Antiquity* 38: 294–314.

———1988. A Reexamination of the Teotihuacan Tassel Headdress Insignia. In *Feathered Serpents and Flowering Trees: Reconstructing the Murals of Teotihuacan*, edited by Kathleen Berrin, pp. 114–134. The Fine Arts Museums of San Francisco, San Francisco.

Millon, René. 1970. Teotihuacán: Completion of Map of Giant Ancient City in the Valley of Mexico. *Science* 170: 1077–1082.

———1973. *Urbanization at Teotihuacan: The Teotihuacan Map*, vol. 1, part 1, text. University of Texas Press, Austin.

———1976. Social Relations in Ancient Teotihuacan. In *The Valley of Mexico*, edited by Eric R. Wolf, pp. 205–248. University of New Mexico Press, Albuquerque.

———1981. Teotihuacan: City, State, and Civilization. In *Handbook of Middle American Indians*, Supplement 1, Archaeology, edited by Victoria R. Bricker and Jeremy A. Sabloff, pp. 198–243. University of Texas Press, Austin.

———1988a. The Last Years of Teotihuacan Dominance. In *The Collapse of Ancient States and Civilizations*, edited by Norman Yoffee and George L. Cowgill, pp. 102–164. University of Arizona Press, Tucson.

———1988b. Where Do They All Come From? The Provenance of the Wagner Murals from Teotihuacan. In *Feathered Serpents and Flowering Trees: Reconstructing the Murals of Teotihuacan*, edited by Kathleen Berrin, pp. 78–113. The Fine Arts Museums of San Francisco, San Francisco.

———1992. Teotihuacan Studies: From 1950 to 1990 and Beyond. In *Art, Ideology, and the City of Teotihuacan*, edited by Janet C. Berlo, pp. 339–429. Dumbarton Oaks Research Library and Collections, Washington, D.C.

———1993. The Place Where Time Began: An Archaeologist's Interpretation of What Happened in Teotihuacan History. In *Teotihuacan: Art from the City of the Gods*, edited by Kathleen Berrin and Esther Pasztory, pp. 16–3. The Fine Arts Museums of San Francisco, in association with Thames and Hudson Publishers, New York.

Millon, René, R. Bruce Drewitt, and George L. Cowgill. 1973. *Urbanization at Teotihuacan, The Teotihuacan Map*, part 2; Maps. University of Texas Press, Austin.

Moedano Koer, Hugo. 1947. El friso de los caciques. *Anales del Instituto Nacional de Antropología e Historia* 2: 113–136.

Moholy-Nagy, S. 1957. *Native Genius in Anonymous Architecture*. Horizon Press, New York.

Morales, Alfonso, Julie Miller, and Linda Schele. 1990. The Dedication Stair of "Ante" Structure. Copan Note 76. Copan Acropolis Archaeological Project and the Instituto Hondureño de Anthropología, Honduras.

Morley, Sylvanus G. 1920. *The Inscriptions at Copán*. Carnegie Institution of Washington Publication 219. Washington, D.C.

———1946. *The Ancient Maya*. Stanford University Press, Palo Alto, California.

Morley, Sylvanus G., George W. Brainerd, and Robert J. Sharer. 1983. *The Ancient Maya* (4th ed.). Stanford University Press, Stanford, California.

Morris, Ann Axtell. 1931. Murals from the Temple of the Warriors and Adjacent Structures. In *The Temple of the Warriors at Chichen Itza, Yucatan*, by Morris, Earl H., Jean Charlot, and Ann Axtell Morris, vol. 1, pp. 347–485, vol. 2, plates 130–170. Carnegie Institution of Washington Publication 406. Washington, D.C.

Morris, Earl H. 1931a. *The Temple of the Warriors: The Adventure of Exploring and Restoring a Masterpiece of Native American Architecture in the Ruined Maya City of Chichen Itza*. C. Scribner's Sons, New York.

———1931b. Description of the Temple of the Warriors and Edifices Related Thereto. In *The Temple of the Warriors at Chichen Itza, Yucatan*, by Morris, Earl H., Jean Charlot, and Ann Axtell Morris, vol. 1, pp. 13–227, vol. 2., plates 1–27. Carnegie Institution of Washington Publication 406. Washington, D.C.

Morris, Earl H., Jean Charlot, and Ann Axtell Morris. 1931. *The Temple of the Warriors at Chichen Itza, Yucatan*, 2 vols. Carnegie Institution of Washington Publication 406. Washington, D.C.

Morris, Walter F. Jr. 1987. *Living Maya*. Harry N. Abrams, Inc., Publishers, New York.

Moser, Christopher L. 1973. *Human Decapitation in Ancient Mesoamerica*. Studies in Pre-Columbian Art and Archaeology no. 11. Dumbarton Oaks Research Libary and Collections, Washington, D.C.

———1977. *Ñuiñe Writing and Iconography of the Mixteca Baja*. Publications in Anthropology no. 19. Vanderbilt University, Nashville, Tennessee.

———1983. A Postclassic Burial Cave in the Southern Cañada. In *The Cloud People: Divergent Evolution of the Zapotec and Mixtec Civilizations*, edited by Kent V. Flannery and Joyce Marcus, pp. 270–72. Academic Press, New York.

Motolinia [Toribio de Benavente]. 1950. *Motolinia's History of the Indians of New Spain*. Translated and Edited by Elizabeth Andros Foster. Bancroft Library, Berkeley.

———1971. *Memoriales o Libro de las cosas de Nueva España y de los naturales de ella*, edited by E. O'Gorman. Universidad Nacional Autónoma de México, México, D.F.

Mukarovsky, Jan. 1978. On the Problem of Function in Architecture. In *Structure, Sign and Function: Selected Writings of Jan Mukarovsky*, edited by J. Burbank and P. Steiner. Yale University Press, New Haven.

Murillo, Saúl. 1989. Investigaciones del corte arqueológico, Ruinas de Copan. Report on file, Instituto Hondureño de Antropología e Historia, Copan, Honduras.

Nabokov, Peter, and Robert Easton. 1989. *Native American Architecture*. Oxford University Press, Oxford and New York.

Nagao, Debra. 1989. Public Proclamation in the Art of Cacaxtla and Xochicalco. In *Mesoamerica after the Decline of Teotihuacan A.D. 700–900*, edited by Richard A. Diehl and Janet C. Berlo, pp. 83–104. Dumbarton Oaks Research Library and Collections, Washington, D.C.

Native Seeds/Search. 1991. Seedlisting. Native Seeds/SEARCH, Tucson, Arizona.

Neal, Lynn, and Phil Weigand. 1990. The Salt Procurement Industry of the Atoyac Basin, Jalisco. Paper presented at the 1990 Meeting of the American Anthropological Association, New Orleans, Louisiana.

Nicholson, Henry B. 1957. Topiltzin Quetzalcoatl of Tollan: A Problem in Mesoamerican Ethnohistory. Ph.D. Dissertation, Department of Anthropology, Harvard University, Cambridge, Massachussetts.

———1971a. Major Sculpture in Pre-Hispanic Central Mexico. In *Handbook of Middle American Indians*, vol. 10, edited by Gordon F. Ekholm and Ignacio Bernal, pp. 92–134. University of Texas Press, Austin.

———1971b. Religion in pre-Hispanic Mexico.

In *Handbook of Middle American Indians*, vol. 10, edited by Gordon F. Ekholm and Ignacio Bernal, pp. 395–446. University of Texas Press, Austin.

———1979. Ehecatl Quetzalcoatl vs. Topiltzin Quetzalcoatl of Tollan: A Problem in Mesoamerican Religion and History. *Actes du XLIIe Congres International des Américanistes*, vol. 6: 35–47. Paris.

———1987. Symposium on the Aztec Templo Mayor: Discussion. In *The Aztec Templo Mayor*, edited by Elizabeth H. Boone, pp. 463–484. Dumbarton Oaks Research Library and Collections, Washington, D.C.

———1990. Late Pre-Hispanic Central Mexican ("Aztec") Sacred Architecture: The "Pyramid Temple." In *Circumpacifica: Festschrift für Thomas S. Barthel*, edited by Bruno Illius and Matthias Laubscher, pp. 303–324. Peter Lang, Frankfurt.

Nicholson, Henry B., with Eloise Quiñones Keber. 1983. *Art of Aztec Mexico: Treasures of Tenochtitlan*. National Gallery of Art, Washington, D.C.

Noguera, Eduardo. 1937. *El altar de los cranios esculpidos de Cholula*. Talleres gráficas de la nación, México, D.F.

———1946. Cultura de Xochicalco. In *Mexico prehispánico: Antología de Esta Semana, This Week, 1935–1946* (Jorge Vivo, editor), pp. 185–193. Editorial Emma Hurtado, México, D.F.

———1965. *La Cerámica Arqueológica de Mesoamérica*. Instituto de Investigaciones Historicas, Universidad Nacional Autónoma de México, México, D.F.

Norberg-Schulz, Christian. 1988. *Architecture: Meaning and Place: Selected Essays*. Electa/Rizzoli, New York.

Nuttall, Zelia. 1903. *The Book of the Life of the Ancient Mexicans (Codex Magliabecchi XIII, 11, 3)*. University of California Press, Berkeley.

1926. Official Reports on the Towns of Tequizistlan, Tepechpan, Acolman, and San Juan Teotihuacan Sent by Francisco de Castaneda to His Majesty, Philip II, and the Council of the Indies, in 1580. *Papers of the Peabody Museum of American Archaeology and Ethnology* 11, no. 2. Harvard University, Cambridge, Massachussetts.

Ochoa, Lorenzo. 1979. *Historia Prehispánica de la Huasteca*. Serie Antro-pológica 26. Instituto de Investigaciones Antropológicas, Universidad Nacional Autónoma de México, México, D.F.

Oliveros, Arturo. 1974. Nuevas Exploraciones en El Opeño, Michoacán. In *The Archaeology of West Mexico*, edited by Betty Bell, pp. 182–201. West Mexican Society for Advanced Studies, Ajijic.

———1989. Las Tumbas mas Antiguas de Michoacán. *Historia General de Michoacan*, vol. 1, cap. 1, pp. 123–234. Gobierno del Estado de Michoacán, Morelia.

Paddock, John. 1983. *Lord 5 Flower's Family: Rulers of Zaachila and Cuilapan*. Vanderbilt University Publications in Anthropology no. 29. Nashville, Tennessee.

Paddock, John (editor). 1966. *Ancient Oaxaca: Discoveries in Mexican Archeology and History*. Stanford University Press, Stanford, California.

Palacios, Enrique Juan. 1926. *Yohualinchan y El Tajín*. Monumentos arqueológicos en Cuetzalan descubiertos por la Dirección de Arqueología, México. México, D.F.

———1935. *Tenayuca, Estudio Arqueológico de la Pirámide*. Departmento de Monumentos, Secretaria de Educación Pública, México.

Palladio, Andrea. 1965. *The Four Books of Architecture*. Dover Publications, New York.

Panofsky, Erwin. 1960. *Renaissance and Renascences in Western Art*. Almquist and Wicksell, Stockholm.

Pantone, Inc. 1977. *Pantone Matching System* (16th ed.). Pantone, Inc., Moonachie, New Jersey.

Parsons, Elsie Clews. 1936. *Mitla, Town of Souls*. University of Chicago Press, Chicago.

Parsons, Lee A. 1969. *Bilbao, Guatemala: An Archaeological Study of the Pacific Coast Cotzumalhuapan Region*. Publications in Anthropology 12. Milwaukee Public Museum, Milwaukee, Wisconsin.

Paso y Troncoso, Francisco del. 1981. Descripción, historia y exposición del Códice Borbónico. In *Códice Borbónico*. Siglo XXI Editores, México, D.F. Originally published in 1898 as Descripción, historia y exposición del códice pictórico de los antiguos Navas que se conserva en la Biblioteca de la Cámara de Diputados de Paris. Tipografía de Salvador Landi, Florence.

Pasztory, Esther. 1972. The Historical and Religious Significance of the Middle Classic Ball Game. In *Religión in Mesoamérica*, edited by Jaime Litvak King and Noemi Castillo Tejero, pp. 441–455. Sociedad Mexicana de Antropología, XII Mesa Redonda. México, D.F.

————1973. The Xochicalco Stelae and a Middle Classic Deity Triad in Mesoamerica. In *Actas del XXIII Congreso Internacional de Historia del Arte*, pp. 185–215. Granada.

————1974. *The Iconography of the Teotihuacan Tlaloc*. Studies in Pre-Columbian Art and Archaeology 15. Dumbarton Oaks Research Library and Collections, Washington, D.C.

————1976. *The Murals of Tepantitla, Teotihuacan*. Garland Publishers, New York.

————1978. Artistic Traditions of the Middle Classic Period. In *Middle Classic Mesoamerica: A.D. 400–700*, edited by Esther Pasztory, pp. 108–142. Columbia University Press, New York.

————1983. *Aztec Art*. Harry N. Abrams, Inc., New York.

————1984. The Function of Art in Mesoamerica. *Archaeology* 37 (1):18–25.

————1988a. A Reinterpretation of Teotihuacan and Its Mural Painting Tradition. In *Feathered Serpents and Flowering Trees: Reconstructing the Murals of Teotihuacan*, edited by Kathleen Berrin, pp. 45–77. The Fine Arts Museums of San Francisco, San Francisco.

————1988b. The Aztec Tlaloc: God of Antiquity. In *Smoke and Mist: Meso-american Studies in Memory of Thelma D. Sullivan*, edited by Kathryn Josserand and Karen Dakin, pp. 289–327. BAR International Series 402. British Archaeological Reports, Oxford.

————1990. El poder militar como realidad y rétorica en Teotihuacan. In *La época clásica: Nuevos hallazgos, nuevas ideas*, edited by Amalia Cardós Mendez, pp. 181–204. Instituto Nacional de Antropología e Historia, Museo Nacional de Antropología, México, D.F.

————1991. Still Invisible: The Problem of the Aesthetics of Abstraction for Pre-Columbian Art and its Implications for Other Cultures. *RES: Anthropology and Aesthetics* 19/20: 105–136.

————1992. Abstraction and the Rise of a Utopian State at Teotihuacan. In *Art, Ideology, and the City of Teotihuacan*, edited by Janet Catherine Berlo, pp. 281–320. Dumbarton Oaks Research Library and Collections, Washington, D.C.

Pasztory, Esther (editor). 1978 *Middle Classic Mesoamerica: A.D. 400–700* (editor). Columbia University Press.

Paxton, Merideth. 1981. A Fresco from Structure 16, Tulum, Quintana Roo: Additional Comments. Paper presented at the annual meeting of the American Society for Ethnohistory, October 29–November 1, 1981, Colorado Springs, Colorado.

————1982. Los Frescoes de Tulum, Quintana Roo: Algunas Fotos de Samuel K. Lothrop. *Boletín de le Escuela de Ciencias Antropológicas de la Universidad de Yucatán*, no. 53: 50–53.

————1986. *Codex Dresden: Stylistic and Iconographic Analysis of a Maya Manuscript*. Ph.D. dissertation, University of New Mexico. University Microfilms, Ann Arbor, Michigan.

Pearse, A. S., Edwin P. Creaser, and F. G. Hall. 1936. *The Cenotes of Yucatan: a Zoological and Hydrographic Survey*. Carnegie Institution of Washington, Publication 457. Washington, D.C.

Penafiel, Antonio. 1890. *Monumentos del arte mexicana antiguo*. A. Ascher, Berlin.

Pendergast, David M. 1971. Evidence of early Teotihuacan-Lowland Maya contact at Altun Ha. *American Antiquity* 36: 455–459.

Pérez Toro, Augusto. 1977. La Agricultura Milpera de los Mayas de Yucatán. In *Enciclopedia Yucatanense*, 6, pp. 173–204 (2nd ed.). Integrated by Luís H. Hoyos Villanueva, Rodolfo Ruz Menendes, Renan Irigoyen Rosado, and Humberto Lara y Lara. Gobierno de Yucatán, México, D.F. [Originally published 1944–47].

Pickering, Robert B. 1985. Human Osteological Remains from Alta Vista, Zacatecas: An Analysis of the Isolated Bone. In *The Archaeology of West and Northwest Mexico*, edited by Michael S. Foster and Phil C. Weigand, pp. 289–326. Westview Press, Boulder, Colorado.

Piña Chan, Román. 1960. Algunos sitios arqueológicos de Oaxaca y Guerrero. *Revista Mexicana de Estudios Antro-pológicos* 16: 65–76.

————1970. Informe preliminar de la reciente exploración del Cenote Sagrado de Chichén Itzá. Instituto Nacional de Antropología y Historia, Investigaciones, no. 24. México, D.F.

————1975. *Teotenango: El antiguo lugar de la muralla*, 2 vols. Dirección de Turismo, Gobierno del Estado de México, México, D.F.

————1977. *Quetzalcoatl, Serpiente Emplumada*. Fondo de Cultura Económica, México, D.F.

Pohl, John M.D. 1994. *The Politics of Symbol-*

ism in the Mixtec Codices. Vanderbilt University Publications in Anthropology. Vanderbilt University, Nashville, Tennessee.

Pohl, John M.D., and Bruce E. Byland. 1990. Mixtec Landscape Perception and Archaeological Settlement Patterns. *Ancient Mesoamerica* 1 (1): 113–131.

Pohl, Mary. 1983. Maya Ritual Faunas: Vertebrate Remains from Burials, Caches, Caves and Cenotes in the Maya Lowlands. In *Civilization in the Ancient Americas: Essays in Honor of Gordon R. Willey,* edited by Richard M. Leventhal and Alan L. Kolata, pp. 55–103. University of New Mexico Press, Albuquerque, and Peabody Museum of Archaeology and Ethnology, Harvard University, Cambridge, Massachusetts.

Pollock, H. E. D. 1936 *Round Structures of Aboriginal Middle America.* Carnegie Institution of Washington, Publication 471. Carnegie Institution of Washington, Washington, D.C.

———1965. Architecture of the Maya Lowlands. In *Handbook of Middle American Indians,* vol. 2, edited by Robert Wauchope and Gordon R. Willey, pp. 378–440. University of Texas Press, Austin.

———1980. *The Puuc: An Architectural Survey of the Hill Country of Yucatan and Northern Campeche, Mexico.* Memoirs of the Peabody Museum of Archaeology and Ethnology 19. Harvard University, Cambridge, Massachussetts.

Porter Weaver, Muriel. 1981. *The Aztecs, Maya, and Their Predecessors: Archaeology of Mesoamerica* (2nd ed.). Academic Press, New York.

———1993. *The Aztecs, Maya, and Their Predecessors: Archaeology of Mesoamerica* (3rd ed.). Academic Press, New York.

Preziosi, Donald. 1979. *The Semiotics of the Built Environment: An Introduction to Architectonic Analysis.* Indiana University Press, Bloomington.

———1989. *Rethinking Art History: Meditations on a Coy Science.* Yale University Press, New Haven, Connecticut.

Proskouriakoff, Tatiana. 1946. *An Album of Maya Architecture.* Carnegie Institution of Washington Publication 558. Washington, D.C. [Reprinted by the University of Oklahoma Press, Norman, 1963.]

———1950. *A Study of Classic Maya Sculpture.* Carnegie Institution of Washington, Publication 593. Washington, D.C.

———1954. *Varieties of Central Veracruz Sculpture.* Contributions to American Anthropology and History, pp. 61–121. Carnegie Institution of Washington, Publication 606. Washington, D.C.

———1960. Historical Implications of a Pattern of Dates at Piedras Negras, Guatemala. *American Antiquity* 25: 454–475.

———1970. On Two Inscriptions at Chichen Itza. In *Monographs and Papers in Maya Archaeology,* edited by William R. Bullard, pp. 439–467. Papers of the Peabody Museum of Archaeology and Ethnography 61. Harvard University, Cambridge, Massachussetts.

———1971. Classic Art of Central Veracruz. In *Handbook of Middle American Indians* 11, edited by Gordon F. Ekholm and Ignacio Bernal, pp. 558–572. University of Texas Press, Austin.

Rabin, Emily. 1979. The War of Heaven in Codices Zouche-Nuttall and Bodley: A Preliminary Study. In *Actes du XLII Congres Internacional des Americanistes, Paris* 7: pp. 171–182. Paris.

Ramírez Vásquez, Pedro, Luis Aveleyra, Ramon Piña Chan, Demetrio Sodi, Ricardo de Robina, and Alfonso Caso. 1968. *The National Museum of Anthropology, Mexico: Art, Architecture, Archaeology, Anthropology.* Harry N. Abrams, Inc., New York.

Rapaport, Amos. 1969. *House Form and Culture.* Foundations of Cultural Geography Series, Prentice Hall, Inc., Englewood Cliffs, New Jersey.

Rappaport, Roy A. 1971. The Sacred in Human Evolution. *Annual Review of Ecology and Systematics* 2: 23–44.

Redfield, Robert. 1941. *The Folk Culture of Yucatan.* University of Chicago Press, Chicago.

Redfield, Robert and Alfonso Villa Rojas. 1934. *Chan Kom, a Maya Village.* Carnegie Institution of Washington, Publication 448. Washington, D.C.

Redmond, Elsa M., and Charles S. Spencer. 1983. The Cuicatlán Cañada and the Period II Frontier of the Zapotec State. In *The Cloud People: Divergent Evolution of the Zapotec and Mixtec Civilizations,* edited by Kent V. Flannery and Joyce Marcus, pp. 117–120. Academic Press, Orlando, Florida.

Reents-Budet, Dorie. 1994. *Painting the Maya Universe: Royal Ceramics of the Classical Period.* Duke University Press, Durham, North Carolina.

Reilly, F. Kent, III. 1991. Olmec Iconographic Influences on the Symbols of Maya Rulership: An Examination of Possible Sources. In *Sixth Palenque Round Table, 1986*, Merle Greene Robertson, general editor, and Virginia Fields, volume editor, pp. 151–166. University of Oklahoma Press, Norman.

——1994a. *Visions to Another World: Art, Shamanism, and Political Power in Middle Formative Mesoamerica*. Ph.D. Dissertation, University of Texas, Austin. University Microfilms, Ann Arbor, Michigan.

——1994b. Enclosed Ritual Spaces and the Watery Underworld in Formative Period Architecture: New Observations on the Function of La Venta Complex A. In *Seventh Palenque Round Table, 1989*, edited by Merle Green Robertson and Virginia M. Fields, pp. 125–135. The Pre-Columbian Art Research Institute, San Francisco.

——1995. Art, Ritual, and Rulership in the Olmec World. In *The Olmec World: Ritual and Rulership*, edited by Jill Guthrie, pp. 27–46. The Art Museum, Princeton University, Princeton, New Jersey.

——1996. The Lazy-S: A Formative Period Iconographic Loan to Maya Hieroglyphic Writing. In *Eighth Palenque Round Table, 1993*, Merle Greene Robertson, general editor, Martha J. Macri and Jan McHargue, volume editors, pp. 413–424. The Pre-Columbian Art Research Institute, San Francisco.

Rejón García, Manuel (Marcos de Chimay). 1981. *Supersticiones y Leyendas Mayas*. Reprinted by José Díaz-Bolio, Mérida, Yucatán. [Originally published 1905, La Revista de Mérida, Mérida.]

Reyes Garcia, Luis. 1977. *Cuauhtinchan del Siglo XII al XVI. Formación y Dessarrollo Historico de un Señorío Prehispánico*. Franz Steiner, Wiesbaden, Germany.

Ribera Grijalba, Victor. 1984. Tepepulco. *Cuadernos de Arquitectura Mesoamericana* 2: 41–46.

Ringle, William. 1990. Who Was in Ninth Century Chichén Itzá. *Ancient Mesoamerica* 1 (2): 233–243.

Ringle, William M., George J. Bey, and Carlos Péraza. 1991. An Itzá Empire in Northern Yucatan? A Neighboring View. Paper presented at the 47th International Congress of Americanists, New Orleans, Louisiana.

Robertson, Donald. 1963. *Pre-Columbian Architecture*. George Braziller, New York.

Robertson, Merle Greene. 1983. *The Sculpture of Palenque, volume I. The Temple of the Inscriptions*. Princeton University Press, Princeton, New Jersey.

——1985. T*he Sculpture of Palenque, volume II. The Early Buildings of the Palace and the Wall Painting*. Princeton University Press, Princeton, New Jersey.

——1991. *The Sculpture of Palenque, volume IV. The Cross Group, the North Group, the Olvidado, and Other Pieces*. Princeton University Press, Princeton, New Jersey.

Robicsek, Francis. 1975. *A Study in Maya Art and History: The Mat Symbol*. The Museum of the American Indian, Heye Foundation, New York.

——1991. Three Decorated Skulls found in the Maya Area. *Mexicon* 13 (4): 65–69.

Robicsek, Francis, and Donald Hales. 1981. *The Maya Book of the Dead: The Ceramic Codex*. University of Virginia Art Museum, Charlottesville.

Robin, Cynthia, and Norman Hammond. 1991. Ritual and Ideology. In *Cuello: An Early Maya Community in Belize*, edited by Norman Hammond, pp. 204–234. Cambridge University Press, Cambridge.

Robles Castellanos, Fernando, and Anthony P. Andrews. 1986. A Review and Synthesis of Recent Postclassic Archaeology in Northern Yucatan. In *Late Lowland Maya Civilization: Classic to Postclassic*, edited by Jeremy Sabloff and E. Wyllys Andrews V, pp. 53–98. University of New Mexico Press, Albuquerque.

Robles García, Nelly, Alfredo Moreira Quirós, Rogelio González Medina and Victor Jiménez Muñoz. 1989. *Mitla*. Editorial Tule, México, D.F.

Robles García, Nelly, and Alfredo Moreira Quirós. 1990. *Proyecto Mitla: restauración de la zona arqueológica en su contexto urbano*. Instituto Nacional de Antropología e Historia, México, D.F.

Roosevelt, Anna C. 1991. *Moundbuilders of the Amazon: Geophysical Archaeology on Marajo Island, Brazil*. Academic Press, New York.

Roys, Ralph L. 1967. *The Chilam Balam of Chumayel*. University of Okla- homa Press, Norman. [Originally published 1933, Carnegie Institution of Washington, Washington, D.C.]

——1973. *The Book of Chilam Balam of Chumayel* (2nd printing of 2nd ed.). University of Oklahoma Press, Norman.

Rudofsky, B. 1964. *Architecture without Architects*. Exhibition Catalogue, Museum of Modern Art, New York.

Ruíz, Diego. 1785. Papantla. *Gazeta de México*, Martes 12 de Julio, México.

Ruppert, Karl. 1935. *The Caracol at Chichen Itza, Yucatan, Mexico.* Carnegie Institution of Washington, Publication 454. Washington, D.C.

———1950. Gallery-patio Type Structures at Chichen Itza. In *For the Dean: Essays in Anthropology in Honor of Byron Cummings*, pp. 249–258. Hohokam Museum Association and the Southwest Monuments Association, Tuscon, Arizona and Santa Fe, New Mexico.

———1952. *Chichen Itza: Architectural Notes and Plans.* Carnegie Institution Washington, Publication 593. Washington, D.C.

Ruppert, Karl, and Augustus L. Smith. 1957. *House Types in the Environs of Mayapan and at Uxmal, Kabah, Sayil, Chichen Itza, and Chaccob.* Carnegie Institution of Washington Current Reports, no. 39. Cambridge, Massachussetts.

Rust, William F., III. 1992. New Ceremonial and Settlement Evidence at La Venta, and Its Relation to Preclassic Maya Culture. In *New Theories on the Ancient Maya*, edited by Elin C. Danien and Robert J. Sharer, pp. 123–130. The University Museum, University of Pennsylvania, Philadelphia.

Ruz Lhuillier, Alberto. 1958. El juego de pelota. *Miscellanea Paul Rivet, Octogenario Dictata.* México, D.F.

———1959. *Guía oficial de Uxmal.* Instituto Nacional de Antropología e Historia, México, D.F.

Sáenz, César. 1961. Tres estelas en Xochicalco. *Revista Mexicana de Estudios Antropológicos* 17: 39–66.

———1962. Xochicalco, Temporada 1960. *Informes* 11. Instituto Na-cional de Antropología e Historia, México, D.F.

———1963. Exploraciones en la Piramide de las Serpientes Emplu-madas, Xochicalco, Morelos. *Revista Mexicana de Estudios Antropológicos* 19: 7–25.

———1964a. Las Estelas de Xochicalco. *Actas del XIV Congreso Internacional de Americanistas* 2 : 69–86.

———1964b. Ultimos descubrimientos en Xochicalco. *Informes* 12. Instituto Nacional de Antropología e Historia, México, D.F.

———1967. Nuevas exploraciones y hallazgos en Xochicalco, Morelos. *Informes* 13. Instituto Nacional de Antropología e Historia, México, D. F.

———1968. Cuatro piedras con inscripciones en Xochicalco, México. *Anales de Antropología* 5: 181–192.

———1969. Exploraciones y restauraciones en Uxmal, Yucatán. *Boletín del Instituto Nacional de Antropología e Historia* 36 (junio): 5–13.

Sahagún, Bernardino de. 1905. *Historia General de las Cosas de la Nueva España por Fr. de Sahagún.* Edición Parcial en Facsimile de los Codices Matritenses en Lengua Mexicana que se Custodian en las Bibliotecas del Palacio Real y de la Real Academia de Historia, vol. 6. Francisco del Paso y Troncoso, editor. Hauser y Menet, Madrid.

———1950–1982. *Florentine Codex: General History of the Things of New Spain*, 12 books in 13 volumes, translated from the Nahuatl and edited by Arthur J. O. Anderson and Charles E. Dibble, Monographs of the School of American Research, no. 40. School of American Research and the University of Utah Press, Santa Fe, New Mexico.

———1969. *Historia General de las Cosas de Nueva España*, 4 vols. (2nd ed.), edited by Angel María Garibay K. Editorial Porrúa, México, D.F.

———1974. *Primeros Memoriales,* translated with commentary by Wigberto Jiménez Moreno. Colección Científica 16, Instituto Nacional de Antropología e Historia, México, D.F.

Salazar O., Ponciano. 1952. El tzompantli de Chichén Itzá, Yucatán. *Tlatoani* 1: 36– 41.

Sanchez, Sergio, and Emma Marmolejo. 1990. Algunas Apreciaciones sobre el Clásico en el Bajío Central, Guanajuato. In *La época clásica: Nuevos hallazgos, nuevas ideas*, edited by Amalia Cardos Méndez, pp. 267–278. Museo Nacional de Antropología/INAH, México, D.F.

Sánchez Saldaña, Patricia. 1972. El tzompantli de Tlatelolco. In *Religion en Mesoamerica, XII Mesa Redonda de la Sociedad Mexicana de Antropología*, edited by Jaime Litvak King and Noemi Castillo Tejero, pp. 387–392. México, D.F.

Sanders, William T. 1960. *Prehistoric Ceramics and Settlement Patterns in Quintana Roo, Mexico.* Carnegie Institution of Washington. Contributions to American Anthropology and History no. 60. Washington, D.C.

———1977. Ethnographic Analogy and the Teotihuacan Horizon Style. In *Teotihuacan and Kaminaljuyu: A Study in Prehistoric Culture Contact*, edited by William T. Sanders and Joseph Michels, pp. 397–410. Pennsylvania State University Press, University Park.

———1981. Ecological Adaptation in the

Basin of Mexico: 23,000 B.C. to the Present. In *Handbook of Middle American Indians*, Supplement 1, edited by Victoria R. Bricker and Jeremy A. Sabloff, pp. 147–197. University of Texas Press, Austin.

Sanders, William T., Jeffrey R. Parsons, and Robert S. Santley. 1979. *The Basin of Mexico: Ecological Processes in the Evolution of a Civilization*. Academic Press, New York.

Sanders, William T., and Robert S. Santley. 1983. A Tale of Three Cities: Energetics and Urbanization in Pre-Hispanic Central Mexico. In *Prehistoric Settlement Patterns: Essays in Honor of Gordon R. Willey*, edited by Evon Z. Vogt and Richard M. Leventhal, pp. 243–291. University of New Mexico Press, Albuquerque.

Sanders, William T., and Barbara Price. 1968. *Mesoamerica: The Evolution of a Civilization*. Random House, New York.

Sanders, William T., and David L. Webster. 1988. The Mesoamerican Urban Tradition. *American Anthropologist* 90 (3): 521–546.

Santley, Robert S. 1983. Obsidian Trade and Teotihuacan Influence in Mesoamerica. In *Highland-Lowland Interaction in Mesoamerica: Interdisciplinary Approaches*, edited by Arthur G. Miller, pp. 69–124. Dumbarton Oaks Research Library and Collections, Washington, D.C.

Sarro, Patricia Joan. 1991. The Role of Architectural Sculpture in Ritual Space at Teotihuacan, Mexico. *Ancient Mesoamerica* 2: 249–262.

———1995. The Architectural Meaning of Tajín Chico, The Acropolis at El Tajín, Mexico. Ph. D. Dissertation, Columbia University. University Microfilms, Ann Arbor, Michigan.

Saussure, Ferdinand de. 1959. *Course in General Linguistics*, edited by Charles Bally, Albert Sechehay, and Albert Riedlinger, translated by Wade Baskin. Philosophical Library, New York.

Saville, Marshall Howard. 1909. *The Cruciform Structures Near Mitla*. Bulletin of the American Museum of Natural History 8, pp. 201–218.

Scarborough, Vernon. 1991. Courting in the Southern Maya Lowlands: A Study in Pre-Hispanic Ballgame Architecture. In *The Mesoamerican Ballgame*, edited by Vernon L. Scarborough and David R. Wilcox, pp. 129–144. The University of Arizona Press, Tucson.

Scarborough, Vernon, Beverly Mitchum, Sorraya Carr, and David Freidel. 1982. Two Late Preclassic Ballcourts at the Lowland Maya Center of Cerros, Northern Belize. *Journal of Field Archaeology* 9: 21–34.

Schele, Linda. 1974. Observations of the Cross Motif at Palenque. In *Primera Mesa Redonda de Palenque, Part I*, edited by Merle Green Robertson, pp. 41–61. Robert Louis Stevenson School, Pebble Beach, California.

———1985. The Hauberg Stela: Bloodletting and the Mythos of Classic Maya Rulership. *Fifth Palenque Round Table, 1983*, vol. VII, Merle Greene Robertson, general editor, and Virginia M. Fields, volume editor, pp. 135–151. Pre-Columbian Art Research Institute, San Francisco.

———1992. The Founders of Lineages at Copán and other Sites. *Ancient Mesoamerica* 3 (1): 130–139.

———n.d. Seats of Power at Copán. A paper prepared for a symposium at the School of American Research, Albuquerque, New Mexico, September 1995.

Schele, Linda, and David Freidel. 1990. *A Forest of Kings: The Untold Story of the Ancient Maya*. William Morrow and Company, New York.

Schele, Linda, and Nikolai Grube. 1990. The Glyph for Plaza or Court. *Copan Note 86*. Copan Acropolis Archaeological Project and the Instituto Hondureño de Anthropología, Honduras.

Schele, Linda, Nikolai Grube, and Erik Boot. 1997. Some Suggestions on the K'atun Prophecies in the Books of Chilam Balam in Light of Classic-period History (preliminary version). Texas Notes, Center of the History and Art of Ancient American Culture (CHAAAC), Department of Art, University of Texas at Austin. Unpublished.

Schele, Linda, and Jeffrey H. Miller. 1983. *The Mirror, the Rabbit, and the Bundle: Accession Expressions from the Classic Maya Inscriptions*. Studies in Pre-Columbian Art and Archaeology no. 25. Dumbarton Oaks Research Library and Collections, Washington, D.C.

Schele, Linda, and Mary Ellen Miller. 1986. *The Blood of Kings: Dynasty and Ritual in Maya Art*. George Braziller, Inc., New York, in association with the Kimbell Art Museum, Fort Worth.

Schmeider, Oscar. 1930. *The Settlements of the Tzapotec and Mije Indians*. University of

California Publications in Geography, vol. 4. University of California Press, Berkeley.

Schmidt, Peter J. 1977. Un sistema de cultivo intensivo en la Cuenca del Rio Nautla. *Boletín del Instituto Nacional de Antropología e Historia*, época III, no. 20, pp. 50–60. México, D.F.

Schondube B., Otto, and J. J. Galvan V. 1978. Salvage Archaeology at El Grillo-Tabachines, Zapopan, Jalisco, Mexico. In *Across the Chichimec Sea: Papers in honor of J. Charles Kelley*, edited by C. L. Riley and B. C. Hedrick, pp. 144–164. Southern Illinois University Press, Carbondale.

Scott, Stuart. 1985. Core versus Marginal Mesoamerica: A Coastal West Mexican Perspective. In *The Archaeology of West and Northwest Mesoamerica*, edited by M. Foster and P. Weigand, pp. 181–191. Westview Press, Boulder, Colorado.

———1992. The Prehispanic Cultures of the Northwest Mexican Coast. In *Cultural Dynamics of Precolumbian West and Northwest Mesoamerica*, edited by M. Foster and S. Gorenstein. Center for Indigenous Studies in the Americas, Phoenix, Arizona.

Secretaria de Programación y Presupuesto, Dirección General de Geografía del Territorio Nacional, Estados Unidos Méxicanos. 1982. *Uso Potencial: Agricultura* (map, Merida sheet). México, D. F.

Séjourné, Laurette. 1959. *Un palacio en la ciudad de los dioses: Exploraciones en Teotihuacán, 1955–58*. Instituto Nacional de Antropología e Historia, México, D.F.

———1966. *Arquitectura y Pintura en Teotihuacan*. Siglo Veintiuno Editores, México, D.F.

Seler, Eduard. 1904a. Wall Paintings of Mitla. In *Mexican and Central American Antiquities, Calendar Systems and History*. Smithsonian Institution Bureau of Ethnology Bulletin 28, pp. 243–324. Washington, D.C.

———1904b. Die Ausgrabungen am Orte des Haupttempels in Mexico. *Gesammelte Abhandlungen zür Amerikanischen Sprach- und Alterthumskunde*, 2: 767–904. [2nd ed., Akademische Druck- und Verlagsanstalt, Graz, Austria, 1960–61.]

———1915. Die Ruinen von Chich'en Itza in Yucatan. *Gesammelte Abhandlungen zür Amerikanischen Sprach- und Alterthumskunde* 5: 197–388. [2nd ed., Akademische Druck- und Verlagsanstalt, Graz, Austria, 1960-61.]

———1902–1923 Die Ruinen von Chichen Itza in Yucatan. *Gesammelte Abhandlungen zur Amerikanischen Sprach- und Alterthumskunde* 5: 151–239. Berlin.

———1917. Die Ruinen von Uxmal. *Abhandlungen der Königlich Preussischen Akademie für Wissenschaften, Philosophisch-Historis-che Klasse* 2. Berlin.

———1960. Die Ruinen von Xochicalco. *Gesammelte Abhandlungen zür Amerikanischen Sprach- und Alter-thumskunde* 2: 123–167. Akade-mische Druck- und Verlagsanstalt, Graz.

———1980. *Comentarios al Códice Borgia*. 3 vols. (reprint of 1963 Spanish translation, by Mariana Frenk). Fondo de Cultura Económica, México. [Originally published 1904–09 as Eine Altmexi-kanische Bilderschrift der Bibliothek der Congregatio de Propaganda Fide. Berlin.]

———1991. Archaeological Results of My First Trip to Mexico. In *Collected Works in Mesoamerican Linguistics and Archaeology*. English translations of German papers from Gesammelte Abhandlungen zür Amerikanischen Sprach- und Alterthumskunde made under the supervision of Charles P. Bowditch with slight emendations to Volumes IV and V by J. Eric S. Thompson. Edited by J. Eric S. Thompson and Francis B. Richardson. General Editor Frank Comparato. 2nd ed., vol. II. Labyrinthos, Culver City, California.

Serrano Sánchez, Carlos. 1993. Funerary Practices and Human Sacrifice in Teotihuacan Burials. In *Teotihuacan: Art from the City of the Gods*, edited by Kathleen Berrin and Esther Pasztory, pp. 108–115. Thames and Hudson, New York.

Sharer, Robert J. (general editor). 1978. *The Prehistory of Chalchuapa, El Salvador* (3 vols.). Museum Monographs, The University Museum. University of Pennsylvania Press, Philadelphia.

Sharer, Robert J., and David W. Sedat. 1987. *Archaeological Investigations in the Northern Maya Highlands, Guatemala: Interaction and the Development of Maya Civilization*. University Museum Monograph 59. The University Museum. University of Pennsylvania Press, Philadelphia.

Sharer, Robert J., Julia C. Miller, and Loa P. Traxler. 1992. Evolution of Classic Period Architecture in the Eastern Acropolis, Copán: A Progress Report. *Ancient Mesoamerica* 3 (1): 145–160.

Sharp, Rosemary. 1978. Architecture as Interelite Communication in Preconquest Oaxaca, Veracruz, and Yucatan. In *Middle Classic Meso-america: A.D. 400–700*, edited by Esther Pasztory, pp. 158–171. Columbia University Press, New York.

Shook, Edwin W., and A. V. Kidder. 1952. *Mound E-III-3, Kaminaljuyu, Guatemala*. Carnegie Institution of Washington, Publication 596, Contribution no. 53. Washington, D.C.

Siller, Juan Antonio. 1984. Presencia de elementos arquitectónicos Teotihuacanos en occidente: Tingambato, Michoacan. *Cuadernos de Arquitectura Mesoamericana* 2: 60–65.

Smith, Augustus L. 1955. *Archaeological Reconnaissance in Central Guatemala*. Carnegie Institution of Washington, Publication 608. Washington D.C.

———1982. Major Architecture and Caches. In *Excavations at Seibal, Department of Peten, Guatemala, No. 1*, edited by Gordon R. Willey. Memoirs of the Peabody Museum of Archaeology and Ethnology, no. 15, Harvard University. Cambridge, Mass.

Smith, Mary Elizabeth. 1973. *Picture Writing from Ancient Southern Mexico: Mixtec Place Signs and Maps*. University of Oklahoma Press, Norman.

———1983. Codex Selden: A Manuscript from the Valley of Nochixtlan? In *The Cloud People*, edited by Kent Flannery and Joyce Marcus, pp. 248–255. Academic Press, Orlando, Florida.

Smith, Virginia Grady. 1988. *The Iconography of Power at Xochicalco, Morelos*. Ph.D. Dissertation, Department of Anthropology, University of Kentucky, Lexington. University Microfilms, Ann Arbor, Michigan

Sodi M., Demetrio. 1962. Consideraciones sobre el origen de la Toltecayotl. *Estudios de Cultura Nahuatl* 3: 55–74, 85–106.

Sosa, John M. 1986. Maya Concepts of Astronomical Order. In *Symbol and Meaning Beyond the Closed Community: Essays in Mesoamerican Ideas*, edited by Gary H. Gossen, pp. 185–196. Studies on Culture and Society No. 1. Institute for Mesoamerican Studies, State University of New York, Albany.

Soto de Arechavaleta, Dolores. 1982. Análisis de la Tecnología de Producción del Taller de Obsidiana de Guachimontón, Teuchitlán, Jalisco. Tésis Professional, Escuela Nacional de Antropología e Historia, México, D.F.

Southall, Aidan W. 1956. *Alur Society: A Study in Processes and Types of Domination*. Heffer, Cambridge.

———1988. The Segmentary State in Africa and Asia. *Comparative Studies in Society and History* 30: 52–82.

Spence, Michael W. 1981. Obsidian Production and the State in Teotihuacan. *American Antiquity* 46: 769–788.

———1987. The Scale and Structure of Obsidian Production in Teotihuacan. In *Teotihuacan: Nuevos datos, nuevas síntesis, nuevos problemas*, edited by Emily McClung de Tapia and Evelyn Childs Rattray, pp. 429–450. Instituto de Investigaciones Antropológicas, Serie Antropológica 72. Universidad Nacional Autónoma de México, México, D.F.

———1992. Tlailotlacan, a Zapotec Enclave in Teotihuacan. In *Art, Ideology, and the City of Teotihuacan*, edited by Janet C. Berlo, pp. 59–88. Dumbarton Oaks Research Library and Collections, Washington, D.C.

Spence, Michael, Phil Weigand, and Dolores Soto de Arechavaleta. 1980. Obsidian Exchange in West Mexico. In *Rutas de intercambio en Mesoamerica y el norte de México*, pp. 357–361. XVI Mesa Redonda de la Sociedad Mexicana de Antropología. Sociedad Mexicana de Antropología, Mexico, D.F.

Spencer, Charles S. 1982. *The Cuicatlán Cañada and Monte Albán: A Study of Primary State Formation*. Academic Press, New York.

Spero, Joanne M. 1987. Lightning Men and Water Serpents: A Comparison of Maya and Mixe-Zoquean Beliefs. Unpublished Master's Thesis, Department of Anthropology, University of Texas, Austin.

Spinden, Herbert J. 1913. *A Study of Maya Art: Its Subject Matter and Historical Development*. Memoirs of the Peabody Museum of American Archaeology and Ethnology no. 6. Harvard University, Cambridge, Massachussetts.

Spores, Ronald. 1967. *The Mixtec Kings and Their People*. University of Oklahoma Press, Norman.

Sprajc, Ivan. 1990. Cehtzuc: a new Maya site in the Puuc region. *Mexicon* 12: 62-63.

Spranz, Bodo. 1973. *Los Dioses en los Codices Mexicanos de Grupo Borgia*. Fondo de la Cultura Económica, México, D.F.

Standley, Paul C. 1930. *Flora of Yucatan.* Field Museum of Natural History, Botanical Series, vol. 3, no. 3. Chicago.

Steggerda, Morris. 1943. *Some Ethnological Data Concerning One Hundred Yucatan Plants.* Smithsonian Institution, Bureau of American Ethnology Bulletin 136 (Anthropological Papers no. 29). Washington. D.C.

Stephens, John L. 1963. *Incidents of Travel in Yucatan.* 2 vols. Reprinted by Dover Publications, New York. [Originally printed 1843 Harper & Brothers, New York.]

Stiny, G. 1976, Two Exercises in Formal Composition. *Environment and Planning B*, 3: 187–210.

Stirling, Matthew W. 1941. Expedition Unearths Buried Masterpieces of Carved Jade. *The National Geographic Magazine* 80 (3): 277–302.

———1945. *Stone Monuments of Southern Mexico.* Smithsonian Institution, Bureau of American Ethnology Bulletin 138. Washington, D.C.

Stirling, Matthew W., and Marion Stirling. 1942. Finding Jewels of Jade in a Mexican Swamp. *The National Geographic Magazine* 82 (5): 635–661.

Stone, Andrea. 1989. Disconnection, Foreign Insignia, and Political Expansion: Teotihuacan and the Warrior Stelae of Piedras Negras. In *Mesoamerica after the Decline of Teotihuacan A.D. 700–900*, edited by Richard A. Diehl and Janet C. Berlo, pp. 153–172. Dumbarton Oaks Research Library and Collections, Washington, D.C.

———1992. From Ritual in the Landscape to Capture in the Urban Center: The Recreation of Ritual Environments in Mesoamerica. *Journal of Ritual Studies* 6 (1): 109–132.

———1996. The Cleveland Plaque: Cloudy Places of the Maya Realm. In *Eighth Palenque Round Table, 1993*, Merle Greene Robertson, general editor, Martha J. Macri and Jan McHargue, volume editors, pp. 403–412. The Pre-Columbian Art Research Institute, San Francisco.

———n.d. The Two Faces of Eve: The Grandmother and the Unfaithful Wife as a Paradigm in Maya Art. Manuscript.

Storey, Rebecca. 1985. An Estimate of Mortality in a Pre-Columbian Urban Population. *American Anthropologist* 87 (3): 519–535.

———1992. *Life and Death in the Ancient City of Teotihuacan: a Modern Paleodemographic Synthesis.* University of Alabama Press, Tuscaloosa.

Stresser-Pean, Guy. 1991. Primera campaña de excavación en Tamtok, cerca de Tamuín, Huasteca. In *Arqueología de San Luis Potosí*, edited by Patricio Dávila Cabrera y Diana Zaragoza Ocaña, pp. 15–30. Instituto Nacional de Antropología e Historia, México, D.F.

Stromsvik, Gustav. 1952. The Ball Courts at Copán, with notes on Courts at La Unión, Quiriguá, San Pedro Pinula, and Asunción Mita. In *Contributions to American Anthropology and History* 11 (55), pp. 185–222. Carnegie Institution of Washington, Publication 596. Washington, D.C.

Stuart, David. 1987. *Ten Phonetic Syllables.* Research Reports on Ancient Maya Writing 14. Center for Maya Research, Washington, D.C.

———1988. Blood Symbolism in Maya Iconography. In *Maya Iconography*, edited by Elizabeth P. Benson and Gillet G. Griffin, pp. 175–221. Princeton University Press, Princeton, New Jersey.

———1992. Hieroglyphs and Archaeology at Copán. *Ancient Mesoamerica* 3 (1): 169–184.

Stuart, Gene S., and George E. Stuart. 1993. *Lost Kingdoms of the Maya.* National Geographic Society, Washington, D.C.

George E. Stuart. 1997. The Royal Crypts of Copán. *National Geographic* 192 (6): 68–93.

Stubblefield, Morris and Carol Miller de Stubblefield. 1991. *Diccionario de Mitla, Oaxaca.* Instituto Linguistico de Verano, México, D.F.

Sugiyama, Saburo. 1989a. Burials dedicated to the Old Temple of Quetzalcoatl at Teotihuacan, Mexico. *American Antiquity* 54: 85–106.

———1989b. Iconographic Interpretation of the Temple of Quetzalcoatl at Teotihuacan. *Mexicon* 11 (4): 68–74.

———1992. Rulership, Warfare, and Human Sacrifice at the Ciudadela: An Iconographic Study of Feathered Serpent Representations. In *Art, Ideology, and the City of Teotihuacan*, edited by Janet C. Berlo, pp. 205–230. Dumbarton Oaks Research Library and Collections, Washington, D.C.

Suhler, Charles. 1992. Operation 26, Structure 6E-120. In *The Selz Foundation Yaxuna Project, Final Report of the 1991 Field Season*, pp. 76–82. Southern Methodist University Department of Anthropology, Dallas, Texas.

———1993. Op.33: Structure 6E-53. In *The Selz Foundation Yaxuna Project, Final Report of the 1992 Field Season*, pp. 35–40. Southern Methodist University, Department of Anthropology, Dallas, Texas.

Suhler, Charles, and David Freidel. 1994. Section 2, Excavations in the Structure 6F-3 Locality. In *The Selz Foundation Yaxuna Project, Final Report of the 1993 Field Season*, pp. 18–37. Southern Methodist University, Department of Anthropology, Dallas, Texas.

Tambiah, Stanley J. 1976. *World Conqueror and World Renouncer: A Study of Buddhism and Polity in Thailand against a Historical Background*. Cambridge Studies in Social Anthropology no. 15. Cambridge University Press, Cambridge.

———1977. The Galactic Polity: The Structure of Traditional Kingdoms in Southeast Asia. *Annals of the New York Academy of Sciences* 293: 69–97.

Tate, Carolyn. 1982. The Maya Cauac Monster's Formal Development and Dynastic Contexts. In *Pre-Columbian Art History: Selected Readings*, edited by Alana Cordy-Collins, pp. 33–54. Peek Publications, Palo Alto, California.

Taube, Karl A. 1985. The Classic Maya Maize God: A Reappraisal. In *Fifth Palenque Round Table, 1983*, edited by Merle Greene Roberston and Virginia M. Fields, pp. 171–182. Pre-Columbian Art Research Institute, San Francisco.

———1986. The Teotihuacan Cave of Origin: The Iconography and Architecture of Emergence Mythology in Mesoamerica and the American Southwest. *RES: Anthropology and Aesthetics* 12: 51–82.

———1988a. A Study of Classic Maya Scaffold Sacrifice. In *Maya Iconography*, edited by Elizabeth Benson and Gillett Griffin, pp. 331–351. Princeton University Press, Princeton, New Jersey.

———1988b. *The Ancient Yucatec New Year Festival: The Liminal Period in Maya Ritual and Cosmology*. Ph.D. Dissertation, Department of Anthropology, Yale University, New Haven, Connecticut.

———1989a. Ritual Humor in Classic Maya Religion. In *Word and Image in Maya Culture*, edited by William F. Hanks and Don S. Rice, pp. 351–382. University of Utah Press, Salt Lake City.

———1989b. The Maize Tamale in Classic Maya Diet, Epigraphy, and Art. *American Antiquity* 54: 31–51.

———1992a. The Temple of Quetzalcoatl and the Cult of Sacred War at Teotihuacan. *RES: Anthropology and Aesthetics* 21: 53–87.

———1992b. The Iconography of Mirrors at Classic Teotihuacan. In *Art, Ideology, and the City of Teotihuacan*, edited by Janet C. Berlo, pp. 169–204. Dumbarton Oaks Research Library and Collections, Washington, D.C.

———1992c. *The Major Gods of Ancient Yucatan*. Studies in Pre-Columbian Art and Archaeology 32. Dumbarton Oaks Research Library and Collections, Washington, D.C.

———1994. The Birth Vase: Natal Imagery in Ancient Maya Myth and Ritual. In *The Maya Vase Book*, vol. 4, by Justin Kerr, pp. 652–685. Kerr Associates, New York.

———1995. The Olmec Maize God: The Face of Corn in Formative Mesoamerica. Paper presented at the Thitrteenth Annual Maya Weekend, University of Pennsylvania Museum, Philadelphia, April 8–9, 1995.

———1996. The Rainmakers: The Olmec and Their Contribution to Mesoamerican Belief and Ritual. In *The Olmec World: Ritual and Rulership*, pp.83–104. Exhibition Catalogue, The Art Museum, Princeton University. Princeton, New Jersey.

Taylor, Dicey. 1979. The Cauac Monster. In *Tercera Mesa Redonda de Palenque*, vol. 4, edited by Merle Greene Robertson and Donald Jeffers, pp. 79–89. Pre-Columbian Art Research Institute, Monterey, California.

Taylor, R. E., and C. W. Meighan (editors). 1978. *Chronologies in New World Archaeology*. Academic Press, New York.

Taylor, Walter. 1941. The Ceremonial Bar and Associated Features in Maya Ornamental Art. *American Antiquity* 7: 41–63.

Tedlock, Dennis. 1985. *Popol Vuh: The De-initive Edition of the Mayan Book of the Dawn of Life and the Glories of God and Kings*. Simon and Schuster, New York.

Tezozomoc, D. Hernando Alvarado. 1944. *Crónica Mexicana escrita hacia el año de 1598*, edited by Manual Orozco y Berra. Editorial Leyenda, México, D.F.

———1975. *Crónica Mexicayotl*. Universidad Nacional Autónoma de México, México, D.F.

Thompson, Edward Herbert. 1932. *People*

of the Serpent: Life and Adventure Among the Mayas. Houghton Mifflin Company, Boston.

Thompson, J. Eric S. 1934. *Sky Bearers, Colors and Directions in Maya and Mexican Religion*. Carnegie Institution of Washington. Contributions to American Archaeology no. 10. Washington, D.C.

———1960. *Maya Hieroglyphic Writing: an Introduction* (2nd ed.). University of Oklahoma Press, Norman. [Originally published 1950, Carnegie Institution of Washington, Washington, D.C.]

———1962. *A Catalog of Maya Hieroglyphs*. University of Oklahoma Press, Norman.

———1970. *Maya History and Religion*. University of Oklahoma Press, Norman.

———1971. *Maya Hieroglyphic Writing: an Introduction* (3rd ed.). University of Oklahoma Press, Norman.

———1972. *A Commentary on the Dresden Codex, a Maya Hieroglyphic Book*. Memoirs of the American Philosophical Society, vol. 93. Philadelphia.

———1973. The Painted Capstone at Sacnicte, Yucatan, and two others at Uxmal. *Indiana* 1: 59–63.

———1975. Introduction. In *The Hill-Caves of Yucatan*, by Henry C. Mercer, pp. vii–xliv. Reprinted by University of Oklahoma Press, Norman. [Originally published 1896, J. B. Lippincott Company, Philadelphia.]

———1976. *Maya History and Religion* (3rd printing). University of Oklahoma Press, Norman. [Originally published 1970.]

Tobriner, Stephen. 1972. The Fertile Mountain: An Investigation of Cerro Gordo's Importance to the Town Plan and Iconography of Teotihuacan. In *Teotihuacan, XI Mesa Redonda, 1966*, pp. 103–115. Sociedad Mexicana de Antropología, México, D.F.

Torres Guzmán, Manuel. 1972. Hallazgos en El Zapotal, Veracruz. *Boletín del Instituto Nacional de Antropología e Historia*, época II, no 2: 3–8.

Torquemada, Juan de. 1986. *Monarquia Indiana* (6th ed.), vol. I. Introduction by Miguel León Portilla. Editorial Porrua, México, D.F.

Totten, George O. 1926. *Maya Architecture*. The Maya Press, Washington, D.C.

Tourtellot, Gair, Jeremy A. Sabloff, and Kelli Carmean. 1992. "Will the Real Elites Please Stand Up?": An Archaeological Assessment of Maya Elite Behavior in the Terminal Classic Period. In *Mesoamerican Elitesz: An Archaeological Assessment*, edited by Diane Z. Chase and Arlen F. Chase, pp. 80–98. University of Oklahoma Press, Norman.

Townsend, Richard F. 1979. *State and Cosmos in the Art of Tenochtitlan*. Studies in Pre-Columbian Art and Archaeology, no. 20. Dumbarton Oaks Research Li-brary and Collections, Washington, D.C.

———1983. Xochicalco: Deciphering an Ancient Capital of Highland Mexico. Paper presented at the 1983 Annual Meeting of the College Art Association, February 16-18, Philadelphia, Pennsylvania.

———1987. Coronation at Tenochtitlan. In *The Aztec Templo Mayor*, edited by Elizabeth H. Boone, pp. 371–410. Dumbarton Oaks Research Library and Collections, Washington, D.C.

Townsend, Richard F. (editor). 1992. *The Ancient Americas: Art from Sacred Landscapes*. The Art Institute of Chicago, Chicago.

Tozzer, Alfred M., translator and annotator. 1941. *Landa's Relación de las Cosas de Yucatan, a Translation*. Papers of the Peabody Museum of American Archaeology and Ethnology, vol. 18. Cambridge, Massachussetts. (See Diego de Landa).

———1957. *Chichen Itza and its Cenote of Sacrifice*. Memoirs of the Peabody Museum of Archaeology and Ethnology, vols. 11 and 12. Harvard University, Cambridge, Massachussetts

Troike, Nancy. 1980. The Identification of Individuals in the Codex Colombino-Becker. *Tlalocan* 8: 397–418.

Turner, Victor. 1969. *The Ritual Process*. Aldine Publishers, Chicago.

Tzonis, A., and L. Lefaivre. 1987. *Classical Architecture: The Poetics of Order*. M.I.T. Press, Cambridge.

Umberger, Emily. 1987. Antiques, Revivals, and References to the Past in Aztec Art. *RES: Anthropology and Aesthetics* 13: 62–105.

Urcid, Javier. 1991. *Zapotec Hieroglyphic Writing*. Ph.D. dissertation, Department of Anthropology, Yale University, New Haven, Connecticut.

Valenzuela, Juan. 1945. Las exploraciones effectuadas en los Tuxtlas, Veracruz. *Anales del Museo Nacional de Arqueología, Historia, y Etnología* 3: 83–107.

Van Gennep, Arnold. 1960. *The Rites of Passage*, translated by Monika B. Vizedom and Gabrielle L. Caffee. University of Chicago Press, Chicago.

Vargas P., Ernesto, Patricia Santillán S., and Marta Vilalta C. 1986. Apuntes para el Análisis del Patrón de Asentamiento en Tulum. *Estudios de Cultura Maya* 16: 55–84.

Vega Sosa, Costanza (coordinator). 1979. *El recinto sagrado de Mexico-Tenochtitlán. Excavaciones 1968–69 y 1975–76*. Instituto Nacional de Antropología e Historia, México, D.F.

Velázquez, Primo Feliciano. 1945. *Codice Chimalpopoca: Anales de Cuauhtitlan y Leyenda de los Soles*. Imprenta Universitaria, México, D.F.

Velázquez Valadez, Ricardo. 1976. Informe de las Exploraciones Arqueológicas y Trabajos de Mantenimiento en la Zona de Tulum, Quintana Roo, 1975. In *Cuadernos de los Centros. Centro Regional del Sureste*, no. 27: 19–93. Instituto Nacional de Antropología e Historia, México, D.F.

Villa Rojas, Alfonso. 1945. *The Maya of East Central Quintana Roo*. Carnegie Institution of Washington, Publication 559. Washington, D.C.

Villagra, Agustin. 1971. Mural Painting in Central Mexico. In *Handbook of Middle American Indians* 10, part 1, edited by G. Ekholm and I. Bernal, pp. 135–156. University of Texas Press, Austin.

Vogt, Evon Z. 1976. *Tortillas for the Gods: A Symbolic Analysis of Zinacanteco Rituals*. Harvard University Press, Cambridge, Massachussetts.

von Winning, Hasso, and Olga Hammer. 1972. *Anecdotal Sculpture of Ancient West Mexico*. Ethnic Arts Publication, Los Angeles County Museum, Los Angeles.

von Winning, Hasso, and Alfred Stendahl. 1968. *Pre-Columbian Art of Mexico and Central America*. Harry N. Abrams Publishers, New York.

Wagner, Henry R. 1969. Introduction and notes. In *The Discovery of New Spain in 1518 by Juan de Grijalva: a translation of the original texts*. Reprinted by Kraus Reprint Co., New York. [Originally published 1942 by The Cortés Society, Pasadena, California.]

Wallrath, Matthew. 1966. The Calle de los Muertos Complex: A Possible Macrocomplex of Structures near the Center of Teotihuacan. In *Teotihuacan, Onceava Mesa Redonda* 1. Sociedad Mexicana de Antropología e Historia, México, D.F.

Walters, Rachel, and Jeff K. Kowalski. 1995. The Mul-Chic Murals and State Formation in the Eastern Puuc Region. Paper presented at the 1995 Annual Meeting of the Society for American Archaeology, Minneapolis, Minnesota, May 3–8, 1995.

Washburn, Dorothy K. 1983. Toward a theory of structural style in art. In *Structure and Cognition in Art*, edited by Dorothy K. Washburn, pp. 1–7. Cambridge University Press, Cambridge.

Webster, David. 1976. Lowland Maya Fortifications. *Proceedings of the American Philosophical Society* 120: 361–371.

———1993. The Study of Maya Warfare: What it Tells Us about the Maya and What it Tells Us about Maya Archaeology. In *Lowland Maya Civilization in the Eighth Century A.D.*, edited by Jeremy A. Sabloff and John S. Henderson, pp. 415–444. Dumbarton Oaks Research Library and Collections, Washington, D.C.

Wedel, Waldo R. 1952. Structural Investigations in 1943. In *La Venta, Tabasco, A Study of Olmec Ceramics and Art*, by Philip Drucker. Smithsonian Institution, Bureau of American Ethnology Bulletin 153. U.S. Government Printing Office, Washington, D.C.

Weigand, Phil C. 1977. The Formative-Classic and Classic-Postclassic Transitions in the Teuchitlán-Etzatlan Zone of Jalisco. In *Los procesos de cambio en Mesoamerica y áreas circunvecinos*, vol. 1, pp. 412–423. XV Mesa Redonda de la Sociedad Mexicana de Antropologia. Sociedad Mexicana de Antropología, México City and Universidad de Guanajuato, Guanajuato.

———1982. Mining and Mineral Trade in Prehispanic Zacatecas. In *Mining and Mining Techniques in Ancient Mesoamerica*, edited by P. Weigand and G. Gwynne, pp. 87–134. Anthropology (special issue), vol. 6 (31, 32),

———1985a. Evidence for Complex Societies During the Western Mesoamerican Classic Period. In *The Archaeology of West and Northwest Mesoamerica*, edited by M. Foster and P. Weigand, pp. 47–91. Westview Press, Boulder, Colorado.

———1985b. Considerations on the Archaeology and Ethnohistory of the Mexicaneros, Tequales, Coras, Huicholes, and Caxcanes of Nayarit, Jalisco, and Zacatecas. In *Contributions to the Archaeology and Ethno-*

history of Greater Mesoamerica, edited by William Folan, pp. 126–187. Southern Illinois University Press, Carbondale.

———1991. The Western Mesoamerican Tlachco: a Two Thousand Year Perspective. In The Mesoamerican Ballgame, edited by Vernon Scarborough and David Wilcox, pp. 73–86. University of Arizona Press, Tucson.

———1992a. Central Mexico's Influences in Jalisco and Nayarit during the Classic Period. In Resources, Power, and Interregional Interaction, edited by Edward Schortman and Patricia Urban, pp. 221–232. Plenum Press, New York.

———1992b. Ehécatl: Primer Dios Supremo del Occidente? In Origen y Desarrollo de la Civilización en el Occidente de México, edited by B. Boehm and P. Weigand, pp. 205–237. Colegio de Michoacán, Zamora, Mexico.

———1992c. Los Códices Prehispánicos de Teuchitlán, Jalisco. El Occidente en la Cultura, núm. 352: 1–3. Guadalajara, Mexico.

———1992d. Ensayos Sobre el Gran Nayar: entre Coras, Huicholes, y Tepehuanes. Instituto Nacional Indigenista/C.E.M.C.A./Colegio de Michoacán, Zamora, Mexico.

———1993a. Evolución de una Civilización Prehispánica: Arqueología de Jalisco, Nayarit, y Zacatecas. Colegio de Michoacán, Zamora, Mexico.

———1993b. Large-Scale Hydraulic Works in Prehistoric Western Mesoamerica. In Economic Aspects of Water Management in the Prehispanic New World, edited by Vernon L. Scarborough and Barry L. Isaac, pp. 223–262. Research in Economic Anthropology, Supplement no. 7. JAI Press, Greenwich, Connecticut.

Weigand, Phil C., and Michael Spence. 1982. The Obsidian Mining Complex at La Joya, Jalisco. In Mining and Mining Techniques in Ancient Mesoamerica, Anthropology (special issue) 6 (1, 2), edited by P. Weigand and G. Gwynne, pp. 175-188.

Wells, Camille. (editor). 1987. Perspectives in Vernacular Architecture, vol. 1. University of Missouri Press, Columbia.

Welsh, W. B. M. 1988. An analysis of Classic Lowland Maya Burials. BAR International Series 409. British Archaeological Reports, Oxford.

Whalen, Michael E. 1981. Excavations at Santo Domingo Tomaltepec: Evolution of a Formative Community in the Valley of Oax-

aca, Mexico. Prehistory and Human Ecology of the Valley of Oaxaca, vol. 6, edited by Kent V. Flannery. Memoirs of the Museum of Anthropology, University of Michigan, 12. Ann Arbor.

Wheatley, Paul. 1971. The Pivot of the Four Quarters: A Preliminary Enquiry into the Origins and Character of the Ancient Chinese City. Aldine Publishing Company, Chicago.

White, Hayden. 1981. The Value of Narrativity in the Representation of Reality. In On Narrativity, edited by W. J. T. Mitchell, pp. 1–23. University of Chicago Press, Chicago.

Whitecotton, Joseph W. 1982. Zapotec Pictorials and Zapotec Naming: Towards an Ethnohistory of Ancient Oaxaca. In Native American Ethnohistory, edited by Joseph W. Whitecotton and Judith Bradley Whitecotton, pp. 285–336. Papers in Anthropology, vol. 23, no. 2, University of Oklahoma, Norman,

Wilkerson, S. Jeffrey K. 1972. Ethnogenesis of the Huastecs and Totonacs: Early Cultures of North-Central Veracruz at Santa Luisa, Mexico. University Microfilms, Ann Arbor, Michigan.

———1974a. Sub-Culture Areas of Eastern Mesoamerica. In Primera Mesa Redonda de Palenque, part II, pp. 89–102. Robert Louis Stevenson School, Pebble Beach, California.

———1974b. Report on the 1974 Season of the Florida State Museum–National Geographic Society Cultural Ecology Project in Mexico. University of Florida, Gainesville.

———1975. Report on the 1975 Season of the Florida State Museum–National Geographic Society Cultural Ecology Project in Mexico. University of Florida, Gainesville.

———1976. Report on the 1976 Season of the Florida State Museum–National Geographic Society Cultural Ecology Project in Mexico. University of Florida, Gainesville.

———1978. Report on the 1977–78 Season of the Florida State Museum–National Geographic Society Cultural Ecology Project in Mexico. University of Florida, Gainesville.

———1980. Man's Eighty Centuries in Veracruz. National Geographic Magazine 158 (2): 202–231.

———1983. So Green and Like a Garden: Intensive Agriculture in Ancient Veracruz. In Drained Field Agriculture in Central and South America, edited by J. P. Darch, pp.

55–90, BAR International Series 189. British Archaeological Reports, Oxford.

———1984. In Search of the Mountain of Foam: Human Sacrifice in Eastern Mesoamerica. In *Ritual Human Sacrifice in Mesoamerica*, edited by Elizabeth H. Boone, pp. 101–132. Dumbarton Oaks Research Library and Collections, Washington, D.C.

———1985. *Sacrifice at Dusty Court: Evolution and Diffusion of the Ritual Ball Game of Northeastern Mesoamerica*. Institute for Cultural Ecology of the Tropics, Tampa, Florida.

———1986. Interpretative Map of the Archaeological Site of El Tajín.

———1987. *El Tajín. A Guide for Visitors*. Government of Veracruz, México.

———1988. Cultural Time and Space in Ancient Veracruz. In *Ceremonial Sculpture of Ancient Veracruz*, edited by Marilyn M. Goldstein, pp. 6–17. Hillwood Art Gallery, Long Island University, New York.

———1990. El Tajín: Great Center of the Northeast. In *Mexico: Splendors of Thirty Centuries*, edited by Kathleen Howard, pp. 155–181. The Metropolitan Museum of Art, New York

———1991. And They Were Sacrificed: The Ritual Ballgame of Northeastern Mesoamerica Through Time and Space. In *The Mesoamerican Ballgame*, edited by Vernon L. Scarborough and David R. Wilcox, pp. 45–72. University of Arizona Press, Tucson.

———1993. Escalante's Entrada: The Lost Aztec Garrison of the Mar del Norte in New Spain. *National Geographic Research and Exploration* 9 (1): 12–31.

———1994a. The Garden City of El Pital: The Genesis of Classic Civilization in Eastern Mesoamerica. *National Geographic Research and Exploration* 10 (1): 56–71.

———1994b. Nahua Presence on the Mesoamerican Gulf Coast. In *Chipping Away on Earth: Studies in Prehispanic and Colonial Mexico*, edited by Eloise Quiñones Keber, pp. 177–186. Labyrinthos Press, Lancaster, California.

———1994c. *El Pital y Los Asentamientos Prehispánicos de la Cuenca Inferior del Río Nautla*. Informe al Instituto Nacional de Anthropología e Historia, México.

———1994d. *Catalogo Provisional #1 de Zonas Arqueológicas en la Cuenca Inferior del Río Nautla*. Informe al Instituto Nacional de Anthropología e Historia, México.

———1997. El Tajín und der Höhepunkt der Klassischen Veracruz-kultur. In *Mexiko: Präkolumbische Kulturen am Golf von Mexiko*, pp. 61–76. Museum Rietberg Zürich, Zürich.

Willey, Gordon R., and Philip Phillips. 1958. *Method and Theory in American Archaeology*. University of Chicago Press, Chicago.

Williamson, Richard V. n.d. Investigations of Structure 10L-26, Copán. Paper presented at the Katun Mesa Redonda, Palenque, Chiapas, Mexico, June 1993.

Wilson, Eugene M. 1980. Physical Geography of the Yucatan Peninsula. In *Yucatan, A World Apart*, edited by Edward H. Mosley and Edward D. Terry, pp. 5–40. University of Alabama Press, University, Alabama.

Wilson, Lee Anne. 1993. Shelter as Symbol: Uses and Meanings of Architectural Space. In *Arts of Africa, Oceania, and Native America: Selected Readings*, edited by Janet Catherine Berlo and Lee Anne Wilson, pp. 271–274. Prentice Hall, Englewood Cliffs, New Jersey:

Winter, Marcus. 1989. *Oaxaca: The Archaeological Record*. Minutiae Mexicana, México, D.F.

Wobst, Martin. 1977. Stylistic Behavior and Information Exchange. In *Papers for the Director: Research Essays in Honor of James B. Griffin*, edited by C. E. Cleland, pp. 317–342. Anthropological Papers no. 61. Museum of Anthropology, University of Michigan, Ann Arbor.

Wren, Linnea H. 1989. Composition and Content in Maya Sculpture: A Study of Ballgame Scenes at Chichén Itzá, Yuc-atán, México. In *Ethnographic Encounters in Southern Mesoamerica: Essays in Honor of Evon Zartman Vogt, Jr.*, edited by Victoria R. Bricker and Gary H. Gossen, pp. 287– 301. Institute for Meso-american Studies, State University of New York, Albany.

Wren, Linnea, and Peter J. Schmidt. 1991. Elite Interaction during the Terminal Classic Period: New Evidence from Chichen Itza. In *Classic Maya Political History: Hieroglyphic and Archaeological Evidence*, edited by T. Patrick Culbert, pp. 199–225. School of American Research and Cambridge University Press, Cambridge, Massachussetts.

Wright, Lori. 1990. Operación DP1: Sondeos en el Grupo L4-3. Proyecto Arqueológico Regional Petexbatun. Informe Preliminar Num. 2, Segunda Temporada, 1990, edited by Arthur A. Demarest and Stephen D. Houston, pp. 13–30.

Zambrano, José Antonio. 1985. *La zona arque-ológica de Tula*. Editorial del Magisterio "Benito Juarez," México, D.F.

Zeitlin, Judith Frances. 1993. The Politics of Classic-Period Ritual Interaction: Icon-og-raphy of the Ballgame Cult in Coastal Oaxaca. *Ancient Mesoamerica* 4 (1): 121–140.

Index